The Destruction of Aboriginal Society

C. D. Rowley was Professor of Political Studies, University of Papua and New Guinea from 1968 to 1974, and Director of the Social Science Research Council of Australia's Aborigines Project from 1964 to 1967. He was formerly Principal of the Australian School of Pacific Administration, which from the mid-1950s has trained field officers for work with the Aborigines in the Northern Territory, and has studied the politics of cross-cultural situations and plural societies as they relate to Indian and Eskimo administration in the United States and Canada.

In 1974, he was appointed Executive Director of the Academy of Social Sciences in Australia. From 1975 until 1980 he was Chairman of the Aboriginal Land Fund Commission. He resigned from the Academy in 1979, and was Visiting Fellow at the Australian National University for the next three years. He is currently visiting Fellow at the Australian Institute of Aboriginal Studies.

This book is the first volume of a trilogy. The others are *Outcasts in White Australia* and *The Remote Aborigines*, both published in 1971. The trilogy won the Research Medal of the Royal Society of Victoria for 1972, and brought him a rare D. Litt. by examination from the University of Sydney.

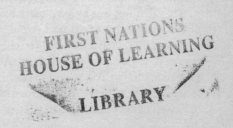

Other books by C. D. Rowley

The Australians in German New Guinea (1958)
The Lotus and the Dynamo (1960)
The New Guinea Villager (1965)
The Politics of Educational Planning in Developing Countries (1971)
Outcasts in White Australia (1971)
The Remote Aborigines (1971)
A Matter of Justice (1978)

THE DESTRUCTION OF ABORIGINAL SOCIETY

C. D. Rowley

PENGUIN BOOKS

Penguin Books Australia Ltd,
487 Maroondah Highway, P.O. Box 257
Ringwood, Victoria, 3134, Australia
Penguin Books Ltd,
Harmondsworth, Middlesex, England
Penguin Books,
40 West 23rd Street, New York, N.Y. 10010, U.S.A.
Penguin Books Canada Limited,
2801 John Street, Markham, Ontario, Canada
Penguin Books (N.Z.) Ltd,
182-190 Wairau Road, Auckland 10, New Zealand

First published by Australian National University Press 1970
Published by Penguin Books 1972
Reprinted 1974, 1978, 1980, 1983 (with Note to Preface), 1986
Copyright © Social Science Research Council of Australia

Typeset in Monotype Bembo
Made and printed in Hong Kong by LP Printing Ltd

All rights reserved. Except under the conditions described in the
Copyright Act 1968 and subsequent amendments, no part of this publication
may be reproduced, stored in a retrieval system, or transmitted in any
form or by any means, electronic, mechanical, photocopying, recording,
or otherwise, without the prior permission of the copyright owner.
Except in the United States of America, this book is sold subject to
the condition that it shall not, by way of trade or otherwise, be lent,
re-sold, hired out, or otherwise circulated without the publisher's
prior consent in any form of binding or cover other than that in which
it is published and without a similar condition including this condition
being imposed on the subsequent purchaser.

CIP

Rowley, Charles Dunford, 1906-1985
The destruction of Aboriginal society

(Aboriginal policy and practice; vol. 1).
Index
First published, Canberra: Australian National
University Press, 1970.
Bibliography
ISBN 0 14 021452 6

[1.] Aborigines, Australian – Treatment. 2. Aborigines,
Australian – Government relations. I. Title. (Series).

305.8'9915

PREFACE

The Aborigines Project of the Social Sciences Research Council of Australia (1964-7) was the first independently financed and controlled survey of Aborigines throughout Australia. By that time it was becoming clearer that their situation posed basic political and moral questions. The governments responsible were maintaining administrative structures and making pronouncements which illustrated the long-standing concentration on tuition and on authoritarian management and administration. If these had not proved very effective in the period from first settlement, even greater effort along the lines which offered no threat to the old inter-racial adjustment seemed called for; and so did greater expenditure, for the country could afford a more tender conscience in government—expenditure on training schemes, bigger and better settlements and the like, with the eventual, and distant, goal of assimilation.

Aboriginal affairs had been neglected by social scientists other than anthropologists, and the result was a dearth of ideas in such fields as economics and politics. Bureaucratic inertia, and the political inertia arising from the strength of old prejudices, made it seem at the beginning of the 1960s that systems of Aboriginal administration completely discredited among the Aboriginal people would be continued indefinitely.

The Council was mainly interested in the social and economic situation of persons of Aboriginal descent in the closely settled areas, but such a part could be explained only in relation to the whole Aboriginal question. This survey should, I believed, be as comprehensive as possible, offering a coherent view of past and present policies and practices, since there were no Australia-wide studies which could offer background on the situations which would have to be considered by policy makers if the project was to be something more than an academic effort. I have to thank the Council, and the trustees of the Myer Foundation, for having accepted this view.

By 1964-7 economic and other changes were weakening the foundations of the caste relationship of black to white within Australia;

and there was a new questioning of the White Australia myth. This was the merest trend, but the time seemed right for a comprehensive report—to the nation, to governments, and especially to the Aboriginal people. Though the last were beginning to be heard in new places, above all they needed to know how things got the way they are.

Our resources did not allow for a large fulltime staff, but elsewhere research was either projected or in progress, and so we were able to assist the work of some scholars and university departments. The results of this assisted work are either published in this series or are available in the files of the Project. There was a great deal which should have been done for which we had neither funds nor research workers—for instance, an expert economic survey of the Aboriginal community or urban surveys of the Aboriginal communities in Darwin or Townsville. Had suitable workers been available and known to us at the time, our priorities could have been different. But once such a Project, with limited funds no matter how generous, has been set up, every week spent in waiting for the ideal situation and the better plan of action involves a diminution of what is to be financially possible. We had to do our best, with the certain knowledge that this syndrome in Australian society would inevitably attract more and more attention from social scientists and that it was bound to become a major political issue. There was one obvious gap in current information, to the elimination of which a high priority was given. This was in the metropolitan areas. The exception was Melbourne, which had just been the locale of Dr Diane Barwick's fine study.

Field work by Project staff was in two main areas. The first was the situation of mainly part-Aboriginal families in the closely settled areas. This was my own direct responsibility. My research colleague, J.P.M. Long, took over responsibility for the study of Aboriginal stations and settlements. Though many of these have been 'opened up' since the Project years, the situation as described in his work will remain for a long time significant in explaining the attitudes of the Aboriginal people.

The three volumes on Aboriginal Policy and Practice were written in draft during the period 1964-7, plus a few months early in 1968 after the period of the Project had expired. They were then checked and revised during the following two years from Papua and New Guinea; distance thus made it necessary to adhere to 1967 as the 'cut-off' year.

This first volume, on The Destruction of Aboriginal Society, is an attempt to assemble on continental scale the facts of frontier clash and its aftermath, from the first days of settlement in each colony until the period of reconsideration and expedited changes which followed World War II.

PREFACE

The second volume examines the emergence of the part-Aboriginal communities of the closely settled areas, and the special policies of goverments applied to their situation. A detailed description of some typical situations as they were in the 1960s follows, supported by statistical data collected during the Project and by the work published by anthropologists and others. There are some recommendations for action by governments and by Aborigines, without whose more confident initiative there can be little change in what is basically a political issue. The third volume examines the situation of Aborigines in what I call the 'colonial' areas of Australia—the settlements, illustrating the effects of frustrated urbanisation, the effects of land policies, of mining developments and of labour policies. Recommendations are made for these situations also.

Hundreds of people helped to make possible these volumes and the whole series. I thank them all—all those who helped me personally, or who contributed personally to the Project, or whose writings on Aboriginal affairs did so. I owe deep gratitude to the Social Science Research Council and to the Trustees of the Myer Foundation and the Sidney Myer Trust. These organisations placed their own reputations in my keeping, in a sense; and to a degree which enslaves the recipient. In this connection I remember especially Professors R.S. Parker, W.D. Borrie, and Herbert Burton, of the Council; and Miss Meriel Wilmot, Secretary of the Myer Foundation. The Principal of the School of Public Health and Tropical Medicine, University of Sydney, Sir Edward Ford, gave the Project a home for two years. I owe a particular debt to Professor R.H. Black, for encouragement when it all seemed impossible, and for criticism when it all seemed to be getting somewhere. Mr Ray Hill, of the Commonwealth Trading Bank, established us as a viable business enterprise. Mrs Fancy Lawrence made a most complicated index work. Dr Godfrey Scott introduced me to the principles of quantification of social data; and Dr Peter Moodie learned and applied the techniques of computer programming. Mr Herbert Simms, widely known among the Aboriginal people, proved especially effective in the collection of accurate data from them, and in a way which enhanced later co-operation. Irene, my wife, transformed dozens of motel rooms into offices, took notes and typed them, and kept the coffee flowing to informants—all as her own contribution. I owe a great deal to Professor A.P. Elkin for the generosity with which he offered information from his lifetime of experience, as well as for his writings. Professor W.E.H. Stanner made me aware of something of the profundity of the Aboriginal view of existence and offered most valuable criticism of volumes II and III.

viii PREFACE

There were others whose help at some time or other in those four years was decisive. Among them were people of Aboriginal descent, often our hosts; many of whom have entrusted us with their confidences. One hopes that the results of our work will play some small part in opening up their way to equality and justice.

C.D. ROWLEY

Note to Preface, 1983

Since this book was first published in 1970, we have learned much more about the enormous span of time over which Aboriginal communities lived in Australia; it is likely that finds will be made indicating human occupation back beyond five hundred centuries. In this context, the catastrophe of colonisation and subsequent repression appears as sudden as it was violent. Other research on the size of that destruction in terms of human lives suggests that the number of people living in Australia in 1788 could have been round ten times greater than the 300,000 to 350,000 that was the informed guess half a century ago.

These are things which many Australians do not want to know, but they have to be taken into account if the black and white communities are to approach reconciliation. The wealth of historical material now being published, the establishment of Aboriginal Studies in universities and colleges, the *Journal of Aboriginal History* – these and many other indicators show how the climate of informed opinion has changed.

Despite such changes, this book apparently remains useful. Recommendations for changed policies (in the other two volumes of the trilogy) were directed against what were, in retrospect, very obvious injustices. It is sobering to reflect that they were not so clear at the time. It is even more sobering to have to acknowledge that partial implementation of the recommendations has aroused such opposition. I made further comments on policies and practices in *A Matter of Justice* (1978).

C. D. Rowley, 1983

CONTENTS

	Preface	*v*
I	**THE FAILURE OF COLONIAL ADMINISTRATION**	
1	History and Aboriginal Affairs	*1*
2	Some Results of Colonial Administration	*10*
3	Eastern Frontiers: New South Wales	*27*
4	The frontier in Western Australia from 1829	*64*
5	The Colony that Was to be Different	*74*
6	Christian Subjects of the Crown: Civilisation by Tuition	*86*
7	Race Relations—a Closer Look	*108*
8	The Failure of Colonial Administration: Retrospect	*125*
II	**THE DESTRUCTION OF ABORIGINAL SOCIETY**	
9	The Frontiers after 1856	*145*
10	The Queensland Frontier, 1859–1897	*157*
11	The Extension of Settlement in Western Australia	*187*
12	The South Australian Frontier, 1860–1911	*201*
13	The Commonwealth Enters the Field of Aboriginal Administration	*222*
14	Missions and Extensive Reserves	*246*
15	Expert Advice on Northern Territory Problems	*255*

| 16 | Reactions to Spectacular Injustice | 288 |
| 17 | The Commonwealth Looks for an Aboriginal Policy, 1934–1948 | 305 |

APPENDIXES

A	Who is an Aboriginal? The Answer in 1967	341
B	The Aboriginal Population	365
	References	399
	Index	407

TABLES

1	Estimated Aboriginal population, 1961 and 1964	*367*
2	Distribution of Aboriginal population in 'Colonial Australia' and in the more closely settled areas by States (30 June 1961)	*376*
3	Southern and Eastern areas ('Settled Australia')	*376*
4	Populations of the Capital Cities excluding Canberra and Hobart	*380*
5	Aborigines—Urban and Rural (excluding Tasmania)	*381*
6	Part-Aborigines—Urban and Rural	*381*
7	Aborigines—Urban and Rural	*382*
8	Some Estimates of the Number and Distribution of Aborigines in the States and Territories of Australia, 1788 to 1966	*384*
9	Population Age Structure—Part-Aboriginal, Aboriginal, and Australian, 1961	*392*
10	A Projection of Population Growth Among Mixed-Blood Aborigines in Australia, 1961 to 1981	*394*
11	A Projection of Population Growth Among Full-Blood Aborigines in Australia, 1961 to 1981	*395*

MAPS

	Distribution of Aboriginal population (Census, 1961)	*xiv–xv*
1	Aboriginal population density, New South Wales	*369*
2	Aboriginal population density, Victoria	*370*
3	Aboriginal population density, Queensland	*371*
4	Aboriginal population density, Western Australia	*372*
5	Aboriginal population density, South Australia	*373*
6	Aboriginal population density, Northern Territory	*374*
7	Land-use map, showing 'colonial' and 'settled' Australia	*377*

FIGURES

1	Age distribution of mixed-blood Aborigines by single years of age: 1961 Census	*385*
2	Age distribution of full-blood Aborigines by single years of age: 1961 Census	*386*
3	N.S.W.: Part-Aborigines in rural and non-metropolitan urban areas, 1965	*387*
4	Eyre Peninsula: Part-Aborigines in rural and non-metropolitan urban areas, 1965	*388*
5	Aborigines in New South Wales, 1958–63	*389*
6	Whites in rural New South Wales, 1961	*390*
7	Indians in the United States of America, 1960	*391*
8	Maori, 1961	*392*

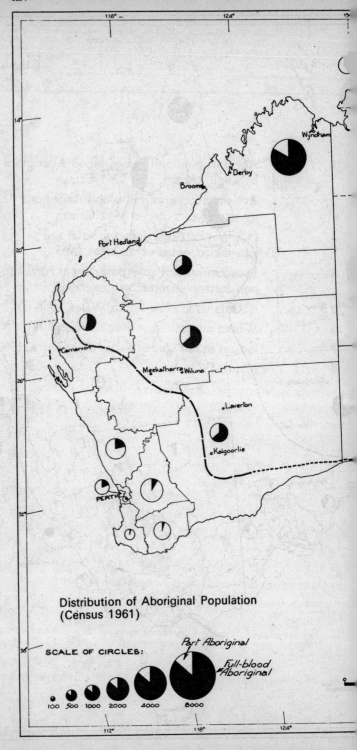

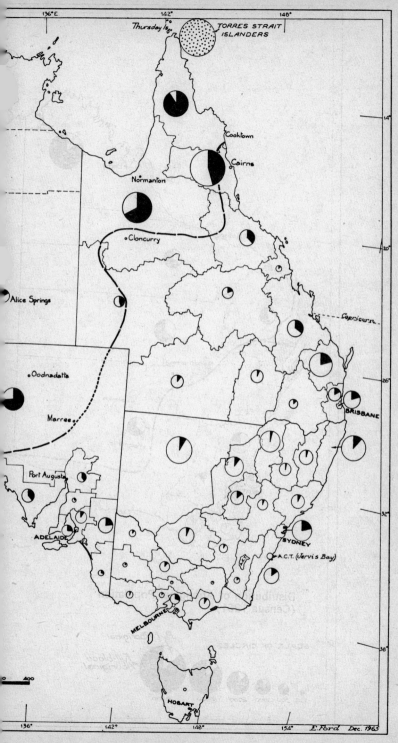

THE FAILURE OF
COLONIAL ADMINISTRATION

I

1

HISTORY AND ABORIGINAL AFFAIRS

Part of the Australian case for restricted migration is that Australia may thus be kept free from inter-racial tensions. The assumption is curious, but typical in its disregard of relations of the Aborigines with the nation at large.[1] When this volume was commenced, there were laws which restrained Aboriginal movements, controlled their places of residence, and placed other restraints on their civil rights. In Queensland, even marriage of an Aboriginal required special permission. Some were legally confined to institutions. Many were excluded from the protection of award wages. There were special limitations on social service benefits. These exclusions and restraints applied only to those who legally enjoyed Aboriginal status, which was defined in terms of degrees of Aboriginal descent. This often meant that (in the absence of genealogies) they applied to those who looked like Aborigines. For those of Aboriginal descent who had been 'passing' for generations, appearance, not achievement, opened the way to equality.

Certain special features of Aboriginal behaviour were generally attributed to racial (latterly cultural) causes. But the pattern of behaviour in the presence of non-Aborigines, and especially of officials, which had appeared to frustrate official policies, could be explained, with equal

---

[1] Where the term 'Aborigines' is used without qualification, it refers to all those who either identify or are forced, by law, social, or economic circumstances, to identify as members of a group which has the status, social, economic, or legal, of an Aboriginal group. It thus includes persons of Aboriginal descent who have not 'passed'; for instance, it includes Aborigines and part-Aborigines in the Northern Territory, who are no longer subject to special legislation except in the matter of wages for the 'full-bloods'—an administrative term for which I apologise.

credibility at least, as normal reactions by members of any minority with a comparable history and subjected to these special restrictions; and as the only forms of resistance possible. They have been paralleled in colonial societies, among the American Indians and Negroes, and among the Maoris.

An almost unique feature of the situation was the long-established administrative habit of confining Aborigines in managed institutions, not for having committed offences or being mentally deficient, but because they belonged to a particular racial minority. To match such a tradition of management, one may look to institutions used to confine enemy aliens in wartime. The progress of the Aboriginal from tribesman to inmate has been a special feature of colonial administration and of white settlement in Australia. Some of the reasons have been humane, but institutions have also been a method of settling or deferring political and moral issues such as those related to rights arising from prior occupation of the land.

These issues had been raised in the first confrontation of the races in each Australian colony, but had not been the subjects of inter-racial negotiation and settlement, even of formal settlement imposed under duress. Enduring resistance may be explained by the fact that the continued separateness of the races and Aboriginal living conditions raised the same basic issues in each generation. It could be expressed only through non-co-operation with authority, affront to middle class *mores*, withdrawal, or small-scale acts of defiance (usually in country towns or Aboriginal institutions).

Australian historians have tended to play down the continuing effects of white settlement on Aboriginal life and have generally consigned the moral and political issues to the past. But in the last decade a renewal of interest in these issues has led to much debate on the earlier policies of British colonial administration.

Perhaps this new interest partly explains why governments have only recently had to face criticism both of their Aboriginal policies and of the assumptions underlying them. A basic assumption has been that the Aboriginal, as an individual, has special need for treatment which the government can provide, so that he may 'advance' into the white community. There was also the hope that this 'problem' group of people would somehow disappear, possibly by 'dying out'. More recently there has been a reversion to the hopes, expressed in the first official policies, for disappearance in another way, by 'assimilation'.

This goal has not been clearly defined. It has obviously implied equality —in housing, health, and education facilities, in civil rights, and in employment. But no precise goals, eventual or interim, have been set. Nor have

HISTORY AND ABORIGINAL AFFAIRS

governments been prepared to require the community at large, and vested interests in the *status quo*, to concede racial equality. (South Australia, with its anti-discrimination law, is the exception.) It is still a common official assumption that equality, in a monolithic 'white' community, comes when the minority is merged in the majority, a process still often conceived, even by those responsible for Aboriginal administration, as disappearance of Aboriginal physical characteristics through miscegenation. The emphasis until now (for there are encouraging signs of harder thinking and in most states practice has become more realistic than policy) has been on the *training* of the Aboriginal.

The policy itself, and the arguments advanced to justify it, are interesting anachronisms, as a cursory examination of the history of Amerindian and Maori affairs will show. The Meriam Report of 1928 indicated clearly enough the disastrous consequences for Indian society of several decades of intensive 'social engineering' to promote assimilation.[2] In Australia, the implied deferment of equality masks the lack of a real will to meet the costs of change. I refer here not only to financial costs for governments, although it is clear enough from the financial priorities given in most states to expenditure on Aboriginal welfare that there is little real determination to incur them. But insistence on equality of opportunity involves real pressure on local governments to allocate land for re-housing in country towns and the brushing aside of fears about property values and Aboriginal misconduct. It may involve priority for Aborigines over others, to redress imbalances so as to provide the minimal opportunity for amelioration and social mobility, with the accompanying financial and political risks involved, for instance, in a higher priority in the long queues awaiting houses. It involves overcoming trade union opposition to adult training schemes in industry, at least for the benefit of the Aboriginal. It involves practical planning for a series of short-term objectives, to provide for members of Aboriginal groups the material facilities, or at least the reasonable chance of acquiring them, without which the Aboriginal cannot hope to move out of his inferior status.

'Social engineers' seldom if ever produce the social changes they predict; the interactions of social life are far too complex. Governments can provide the things without which desired changes cannot occur, and they can, within the law, repress actions which diminish human dignity and bar the way to freer association among all members of the nation. They can also use the generally accepted sanctions to compel Aborigines

---

[2] Lewis Meriam and Associates, *The Problem of Indian Administration*.

THE FAILURE OF COLONIAL ADMINISTRATION

to meet their legal obligations as citizens. But, in the main, the emphasis in administrative practice has remained on 'keeping them up to it'—on tuition before equality. This is not basically the fault of the departments of government concerned with Aboriginal affairs, for in the light of what equality will cost, tuition is cheaper than material requirements in any annual budget. That the promise of reward, of admission to the full exercise of membership of the white community, should be regarded as a patent stimulus of Aboriginal effort indicates how easily we can ignore the history of a problem.

For lack of historical background, the Aboriginal community is treated as a more or less static society. Contrariness and apathy are explained in terms of tenacious adherence to Aboriginal cultural norms; or, in practice, and more often, especially by the more authoritarian officials, as due to stupidity. Most officers are well meaning and conscientious, and they work in a tradition very like that of the conscientious colonial official in his day. But the Aboriginal group is outside European society; and because there are no Aboriginal institutions or village headmen, the official tends to deal with individuals, to become the accepted (but often detested) father figure who is brought into personal disputes and family squabbles and is forever dealing with recalcitrant brawlers, neglected children, deserted wives, jobless men.

The same pattern is to be found in the records of four or five decades ago, and it is repeating itself now throughout the whole of this continent: it is a history of intensive interference and paternal control. The Aboriginal can do little more than play out his role in relation to this administrative tradition. To breach this cycle requires some knowledge of how it developed. In each succeeding generation, *ad hoc* policies, with low priorities, have been justified by the view that the reason lies in Aboriginal society and personality; that Aborigines have always been like this; and that only great effort over long periods will 'change them'. In fact Aboriginal society has been kept in continual tension by what appeared to Aborigines arbitrary and pointless interference with their lives; and as Lagassé wrote of the Metis in Canada 'no single generation has yet had the patience to wait for the Indian to adjust'.[3]

Since Australian governments adopted the 'assimilation' policy, emphasis has remained on promoting changes among the Aborigines. Though increasingly aware that colour prejudice against the Aborigines is basic in the syndrome, governments still devote administrative efforts

[3]Jean H. Lagassé, 'Community Development in Manitoba', *Human Organization*, vol. 20, no. 4, Winter 1961-2, p. 234.

HISTORY AND ABORIGINAL AFFAIRS

to making Aborigines 'acceptable', to achieve which, paternal control is still widely used. Moreover, the officials responsible are generally poorly paid and most of them are intellectually unprepared for what would be the most difficult of all teaching assignments, even if the schoolmasterly approach had any chance of success. Only now is the question beginning to be asked: Is not the conduct of the Aboriginal group basically common to all human groups under stress? If this is true, as seems likely, it is essential to seek the causes of that stress in Aboriginal beliefs, and the long history that has produced them, as well as in the Aboriginal caste status.

If it is *not* true, then Aborigines exhibit all the symptoms of protest just because they are Aborigines, with special inherited cultural characteristics (like the alleged in-born fondness for strong liquor), and the situation is one we just have to live with. This belief is precisely what racial prejudice is based on: and the past expenditure on Aboriginal affairs indicates how widespread it has been.

Historical studies of the role played by the Aboriginal since contact with white settlers are sparse. Not only is the historical dimension of Aboriginal affairs dimly seen, except perhaps for the state of Western Australia, but the Aboriginal part in Australian history as a whole remains to be defined. In the broad scope of Australian historical studies he appears as an almost completely passive figure. Yet it is difficult to believe that long association and the most intimate personal relationships in frontier areas have failed to influence the style of Australian life, especially, perhaps, in attitudes to leadership and to formal institutions. Even conflict along the frontiers must have had deeper implications for succeeding generations than the hunting down of kangaroos and emus and other fauna regarded as pests.

Australian historians have paid little attention to the Aboriginal groups' resistance to white settlement. We are not yet in any position to assess the full significance of what appears, from the records, as somewhat sporadic and periodic. Yet there is, in my own view and from a detailed examination of evidence in one region (see ch. 7), enough to describe it in some regions as a series of deliberate, if limited, guerilla skirmishes. (Aboriginal society lacked the type of organisation which makes possible a campaign of warfare.) This is hard to recognise because, with the proclamation of sovereignty over all lands in a colony and the consequent definition of such lands as Crown lands, the resistance of the dwellers thereon to officials of the Crown such as the police (including the Native Police) cannot appear in the official reports as frontier war. If not rebellion, it becomes criminal activity of some convenient kind—for both white and black.

THE FAILURE OF COLONIAL ADMINISTRATION

The real problem for the colonial government then became one of keeping the peace between two kinds of British subjects—the whites and the blacks.

This was typical of a frontier situation which got out of hand. There were two possibilities where Europeans were extending a 'frontier'. One was that settlers be allowed only in areas where the government was already in control—the 'restricted area' policy which was developed in the 1920s in Australian New Guinea. This proved impossible in Australia once the demand for fine wool called the squatters out beyond the 'limits of location', with the result that government authority lagged behind the frontier of contact and there was no possibility of controlling the process of dispossession. When the representatives of government do get to a frontier area, the habit of frontier violence, and of control by the threat of violence, is firmly established. Even if the government tries to enforce the law (as Governor Gipps had in New South Wales), the representatives of the law tend to accept settler *mores*. Acts of violence may be kept 'administratively clean' by their absenting themselves on such occasions.

It is not so surprising that the obliteration of the tribes from the most valuable land areas should be bowdlerised in the school history books, though this has quite serious implications. The power of government to deal with a social problem depends largely on the electorate's understanding what that problem is; and what it is cannot be stated without some indication of how it arose. In the absence of clear light shed upon the past, racial prejudice is free to make its own interpretations. And by far the great majority of us interpret history, to suit our prejudices, from the stories we remember from the school history book.

White Australian attitudes have been partly based on the belief that Aborigines were an inferior race 'fading away' in the face of western culture. This attitude has been more decisive for inter-racial avoidance and tension than the Aboriginal folk memory of harsh treatment. Continuing bitterness is the legacy of generations of rejection. Nor have the recent opportunities for schooling helped very much, since the implications of Aboriginal inferiority remain in the school syllabuses. In his recent sharing in educational opportunity, the Aboriginal will have found that the classroom lesson largely confirms the often very hard lesson of the common playground: that he is a member of a group which must be led into more effective imitation of the whites; that his ancestors, cut off from the Europeans for so long, started a long way behind, but may come at last into the dominant and superior group. One result of such education, then, is to confirm the lesson of living and growing up in Aboriginal

HISTORY AND ABORIGINAL AFFAIRS

society, of the differences coinciding with differences of racial origin, or even of skin coloration. He can accept the predominant view and either sink into apathy or battle for 'assimilation'; or he can turn in upon the group, and by his actions and unresponsive attitudes confirm impressions of a closed cycle of ignorance, poverty, ill-health, and petty delinquency which are symptomatic, as Lagassé has said, of more complex problems.[4] Their full complexity cannot be stated without some reference to their origins.

In particular the makers of policy in Aboriginal affairs cannot afford to ignore the possibility that a lack of historical studies of the interaction of the two racial groups has helped bowdlerise the role of settlers and governments. No real allowance has been made for the extreme violence of the treatment of the Aboriginal; for the facts are easily enough established that homicide, rape, and cruelty have been commonplace over wide areas and long periods. Cultural deprivation has been as complete as possible over most of the continent; and it is still lightly weighed in the face of possible economic development of Aboriginal reserves. Economic dispossession has been complete—so complete that in the dry centre of the continent possibly more people died from the direct and indirect effects of starvation than from infection by the newly introduced diseases or the use of the gun. It is surely relevant that in some places these things have been so recent that people, Aboriginal and others, who remember them, are still alive. There are still persons living who could kill an Aboriginal with impunity if not legality when they were young; and Aboriginal tribesmen who remember such incidents.

On the one side, among those who have studied or who have remembered the past, there is an interesting mental block. P.M.C. Hasluck, a very sound historian and a pioneer of historical studies of race relations in this area, found it necessary to apologise, in the late 1930s, for his restrained and accurate illustrations of what could happen as a result of settler attitudes. Dealing with the so-called 'battle' of Pinjarra, and one of the punitive expeditions in the north-west, he wrote that his descriptions were

not for sensationalism, nor with any wish to give them undue prominence in the story of violence, but because these two events among many reveal in high colours an element in the attitude we are studying. The fact with which we are concerned is not the incidents themselves but that public opinion appeared to accept both as necessary and even praiseworthy.[5]

[4] Ibid.
[5] *Black Australians: A survey of native policy in Western Australia 1829-1897*, pp. 185-6.

His remark raises two interesting points in the context of the mid-sixties. Organisations now pressing for reforms in Aboriginal policy and practice repeatedly refer to former ill-treatment of the Aborigines, but their criticisms are usually unspecific and generalised. The impact of their arguments is diminished by the lack of a common fund of historical knowledge. Too often, the arguments themselves, for want of precise information, lack hitting power and conviction; often the remedies, advanced in vague and general terms, show little appreciation of the considerable historical and other differences between situations in different regions of Australia, or of changed circumstances, which render earlier ideas for compensation obsolete. If Hasluck were writing now he might not feel the same need to prepare his reader. In lieu of the widespread but inexplicit breast-beating among the champions of the Aboriginal (whose own occasional voice is beginning to be heard, mainly as an echo of this advocacy), his book, long and undeservedly buried in libraries, would provide a fund of precise and explicit information.

The second point is that the mental block has by no means disappeared. It seems partly to result from a majority sentiment that raking up the misdeeds of the past serves no good purpose. What is done is done and should now be forgotten. A few young historians are beginning to work in the field of Aboriginal affairs, but it is mainly the anthropologists, in their attempts to explain how things got the way they are, who have been forced to write history.

The most important attempt at an overall assessment of changing race relations since the first contacts is that of A.P. Elkin in 1951.[6] Made without the advantages of comprehensive historical studies other than Hasluck's work, this seminal study has tended to mould a good deal of anthropological and official thinking, especially the concept of 'intelligent parasitism' as a term to describe the beaten Aboriginal's adaptation to the settler. It is interesting that what was correctly an abstraction from the known facts of race relations should have become so widely known, while the facts themselves, which need only time to elucidate, remain so vague; and that Hasluck's quietly telling study should have failed to get out of the first edition. There are still historians who regard Aboriginal affairs as not very important in the development of the Australian nation; even in some university departments, some who think there is something vaguely disreputable about such studies. The mental block may well be reinforced by official caution. We have inherited quite a grim history, as so many

[6] 'Reaction and Interaction: A food gathering people and European settlement in Australia', *American Anthropologist*, vol. 53, no. 2, 1951.

HISTORY AND ABORIGINAL AFFAIRS

other nations have; and for many reasons we must learn to apply to the facts of our own past and to current attitudes the same sociological principles which it is so much easier for us to apply to situations elsewhere.

Politicians and administrators sometimes assume that the people for whose welfare they plan are reacting to their current plans; that a recent re-orientation of policy, such as has been proclaimed in Australia, operates in some kind of historical vacuum. Careful delineation of the origins of the problem itself may seem, then, a pointless academic exercise. Lagassé, a student of human relations and social change among the Metis of Manitoba, dealt effectively with this atttitude of the 'practical' man. The Metis, he said, faced a 'galaxy of problems'. Among these were inadequate housing, unemployment, poor educational standards, and ill health.

These, however, are but symptoms of more complex causes. Concern over the genesis of social and cultural problems could be regarded as purely academic were it not that rehabilitative programs are based on the concepts of policy makers concerning the origins and causes of these problems. Too frequently in the past, for lack of more adequate information, it became necessary to deal with symptoms and attempt to prevent them from causing too much damage before the real cause of trouble could be identified.[7]

No adequate assessment of the Aboriginal predicament can be made so long as the historical dimension is lacking; it is the absence of information on background which has made it easy for intelligent persons in each successive generation to accept the stereotype of an incompetent group.

[7] 'Community Development in Manitoba', p. 233.

SOME RESULTS OF
COLONIAL ADMINISTRATION

Colonial practice in the 'colonies of settlement' in Australia is in instructive contrast with the two areas, north America and New Zealand, where the current situations are frequently compared with the Australian. In north America and in New Zealand the invaders met indigenous people with concepts of warfare, and with organisation for it, which could not be ignored. Furthermore, the first settlements in north America were made in a period when the technology of Europe, especially in the strange conditions, gave the settlers less advantage, while the European nations' competition for the support of the tribes was one factor which aided the Indians by putting guns and ammunition into their hands. In addition, the European political philosopher could idealise the social and political organisation of the Iroquois—even though the settler on the spot did not necessarily share his view.

Possibly two factors in European culture have made western imperialism profoundly different from any known before. One is the intense proselytising zeal which Christendom has shared with Islam and followers of other Middle East 'religions of the Book'. The disruption of Christendom, in the Reformation and the religious wars in Europe, had not weakened that value of the culture which was 'the belief in its own superiority and the conviction that native cultures were moral evils which should be destroyed'.[1] The categorical imperative of the missionary allowed for little compromise; and the colonial administrators, at best, tended to see themselves as extending the boundaries of the Kingdom of God as well as the power of the nation state. This quite fundamental

[1] Lagassé, 'Community Development in Manitoba', p. 234.

SOME RESULTS OF COLONIAL ADMINISTRATION

intolerance, by discounting the native systems of belief, paved the way for more debased ideologies of colonialism, such as the popularised pseudo-Darwinism of the late nineteenth century, with the doctrines of the 'survival of the fittest' and the 'white man's burden'.

The other profound element in European culture (by the mid-twentieth century it has thrown every static and traditional culture in the world into chaos) was intense concern with *change* in the material circumstances of life. Curiosity, freed from dogma, had produced the technology which made the first exploitation of the New World possible. Overwhelming advantages in technology brought corresponding temptation to the conquerors and settlers, succumbing to which was facilitated by the Europeans' conviction of superiority, by the assumptions that the Christian settler was a civilising force and that economic exploitation was the basis for civilisation. In the north American story, the promise of great riches from the new technology of the industrial and agrarian revolutions swept aside the traditional restraints of colonial administration. Over the centuries the initial respect gave way to dispossession—'This land is my land'—and the frontier tradition that the only good Indian was the dead Indian. This 'schism' in the western 'soul' had been plain enough in the contrast of brutal conquest with devoted proselytisation in central and south America. Perhaps the contrast, from that point onward, between colonial Europeans' words and deeds explains failure of European colonialism to win over those who have either stubbornly retained their own cultures or have preferred some vestiges of them, even in deprived and bastardised sub-cultures of protest.

In the initial north American experience, the rights of the Indian 'nations' had been established, if somewhat tenuously, in European law. The tradition of recognising as war the means by which land was taken, and that of making treaties with each tribe or group of tribes to end it, did establish in most of north America rights to the occupation and use of part of the tribal lands. Thus European legality recognised that prior occupation gave certain rights to certain defined groups of Indians, great numbers of whom retained limited property rights together with some semblance of tribal organisation. Their modern descendants have sometimes been lucky: what centuries ago seemed useless may prove very valuable today; in the last couple of decades a very rich United States has been able to afford a somewhat tender conscience, paying retrospective compensation, in some cases, for dishonoured or broken treaties, or treaties long lost and now rediscovered.[2]

[2] In 1959 Dr A.G. Langone of the Library of Congress told me of the searches he and his team of scholars had made for treaties of the Spanish and French governments with Indian tribes now within the United States.

THE FAILURE OF COLONIAL ADMINISTRATION

No Aboriginal 'tribes' of the Amerindian type existed in Australia; no treaties concerning land were ever signed or rights recognised. Had they been, and if the concept of freehold tribal land rights had included the first claim to minerals, the great expansion of mining in northern Australia now under way (see Distribution of Population Map) would have brought very great wealth indeed into the pockets of the tribal remnants.

The situation of the Aboriginal appears to be more uniformly depressed than that of other indigenous minorities overwhelmed by British colonisation. The predicament of the Amerindian in the United States and Canada encompasses a far greater range of situations. In the United States there are rural Indian communities with problems and poverty comparable with those of Aboriginal communities, but there are others far better off, especially economically. In some there are very wealthy people—for instance those who hold freehold title to lands with stands of valuable timber, or those whose Indian title has been accepted as giving rights to oil found there.[3] But it would be difficult to find one wealthy Australian Aboriginal or well-to-do member of a group which is identified as Aboriginal.

In United States cities there is a much larger group of non- whites into which the Indian can merge. There is also the philosophy of the melting pot, a moral stance quite different from the ethnocentric attitudes implied in 'assimilation' in Australia. Where prejudice is strongest, it is the Negro who must bear the brunt of it. The Aboriginal situation resembles that of the American Negro in one very important respect. Although the Aboriginal is indigenous, with the same moral claim (for what that is worth), that the Amerindian has to property rights arising from the fact of prior occupation, there is no more legal recognition of a *prior* claim to the wealth of his country than there is for the descendants of Negro slaves brought to America. He has the same right as any other citizen to buy and own land and property, as government sources frequently assert;[4] so, of course, has the American Negro, and often he has done so and become a man of property, even though he still identifies and is identified as a Negro. There *may* be many wealthy persons of Aboriginal descent in Australia; but it would be difficult to find any who are known or consider themselves to be members of an Aboriginal community.

The Aboriginal minority, then, is far less socially and economically

[3] Since 1938 Indians in the U.S.A. have had mineral and timber rights on Indian lands, following a decision of the Supreme Court (United States *v.* Shoshone Tribe, 304 U.S. 113).
[4] For a good example of this kind of argument, see the Annual Report of the Director of Native Affairs, Queensland, of 30 June 1965, p. 3: Q.P.P., 1965.

SOME RESULTS OF COLONIAL ADMINISTRATION

diverse than is the American Negro or the Amerindian minority. One reason has been the long period of institutionalisation of Aboriginal communities. The Negro, once freed from slavery, was not incarcerated in an institution. Indians who also were shut away from the white community on their reserves did receive title to property. The Aborigines did not. The Aboriginal communities are thus rather comparable with those Indians of the United States who lost their tribal lands; they inherited the worst of both worlds, that of the Amerindian and that of the American Negro. For a long time, as with the Indian, the Aboriginal's proper place was considered to be within a reserve and away from the dominant social group; but this reserve was never conceded to be part compensation. As happened with the poorest Indian groups, Aborigines obtained no property from legal settlements. The Aboriginal, as legally defined, remained suspended like a migrant in white society, like the Negro; and so long as he remained recognisably Aboriginal (again like the Negro) he faced social rejection. Only now, within the last few years, has the process of re-establishing his legal equality begun (for at the time of first settlement he had the full legal status of a British subject).

If we compare his situation with that of the Indian in Canada, a basic difference is once again evident: it springs from the existence of treaties with Indian nations and the recognised rights to Indian lands. These rights, as in the United States, were established or recognised for hunting and gathering communities as well as for those where some agriculture was practised, a fact which somewhat blurs the argument that the Aboriginal failed to secure similar consideration because he was a nomad without agriculture.

Perhaps it is significant here that the settlement of Australia occurred during a later period, when the Industrial Revolution was in full swing, with Britain the heart of it. Britishers, from the first discovery that Australian grass could be very profitably turned into fine wool, consistently brushed aside in practice Aboriginal 'rights' where there was money to be made, at the same time condemning the fecklessness of the 'native' who became a poverty-stricken hanger-on on what had been his own lands. All Australian settlements attracted people with the same industrially determined moral standards, and all within a relatively brief span of time. Since Aboriginal society also was basically homogeneous, it is not surprising that similar social, economic, and geographic ingredients produced similar results in each colony.

By contrast, New Zealand and perhaps the British colonies in Africa south of the Sahara, as well as the events that occurred when the Australian frontier was extended into Papua, show an entirely different pattern of settlement when settlers of the same type as in Australia came up against a very different kind of society—stubborn in resistance, capable of organised warfare in defence of interests, and organised in settled villages.

Catastrophe among settled villagers is a more obvious reproach to administrative consciences than among nomads; the devastation of a village by disease or maltreatment can be easily recognised, and is more easily dealt with or prevented. Villagers on their own land have a clear claim to consideration from the conquerors. Moreover, being gardeners with a long tradition, they form an economic asset of first importance as sources of labour and suppliers of food. Being settled, they are also a potential market for industrial goods, at first at the trade-store level of trade. By and large it was in the interests of the colonists to work for an increasing and healthy 'native' population, especially where the plantation system developed or large public works were required to open country for industrial types of land use. In the Pacific and in Africa, labour was an asset of prime economic importance to be brought from the villages: by its application local resources could be most cheaply developed. The village, as the source of labour, had to be preserved.

The Aboriginal, having taught the newcomers how to live in the bush, tended to remain available as required for other station tasks and for tracking and exploration: here he remained the master, as he still is where the economic need remains. But his labour was not recognised by the settlers as important enough to have him treated as an economic asset, especially as inter-racial strife increased.

Not being a villager, he had no clearly recognisable claim to a particular area of land; his more subtle relationship with his country was either ignored or not understood. He lacked the organisation which could have enabled effective warfare in defence of his interests. He did not have the multi-purposed leadership offered by the system of tribal chiefdoms; and his society was marked by the absence of hierarchical organisation. Thus he had neither the obvious prior right to a certain area, which might have influenced governments, nor the organisation to defend any part of his traditional hunting and gathering area.

This situation was to have special legal consequences. By the principles of common law, annexed land vested in the Crown, and any variations had to be specifically enacted or otherwise provided for. They could be made as a result of subsequent treaty. In the American colonies, treaties were made with many Indian tribes; and the fashion remained in use after the War of Independence. Had the Amerindians lacked the organisation for war, there may well have been no Indian treaties.

SOME RESULTS OF COLONIAL ADMINISTRATION

Over four decades before the Papuan proviso safeguarding native lands, the Treaty of Waitangi (1840) had guaranteed to the New Zealand tribes 'full and undisturbed possession of their lands' and had established the usual safeguard that only the government could purchase land from the villagers. Whatever happened later, the Maoris had established a claim in the statutory law from 1840. The next three decades attest that they also possessed the organisation to fight effectively in defence of that claim. The Treaty of Waitangi resulted because in New Zealand the settlers found themselves opposing a developed tribal and village organisation of subsistence gardeners. In the state of war that developed, warrior bands with a recognisable pattern of leadership fought pitched battles for the possession of particular land areas. Maori resistance made the establishment of peace by treaty essential for the settlers.

The Australian nomads' resistance was far less effective. There was never an official and consistent recognition of a war of conquest; and there were no treaties. Nothing was achieved by Aboriginal defenders to force the British government to vary by statute the common law assumption that all lands annexed to the Crown are Crown lands. There was thus no need for treaties providing the basis for 'native' title. The only check effected by Aboriginal resistance was to the consciences of a few settlers and officials, and to occasional enterprises when the first settler was forced to go elsewhere. At the same time, and very early in the history of the frontier, the Australian grasslands were proved a major resource for the industrial technology of England. The sale of the first few bales of fine Merino wool from Sydney made more inevitable a rapid dispossession of the Aboriginal through wide areas of the colony, a brushing aside of the feeble gestures by governors and the British government at traditional colonial administration, and a relegation of Aboriginal resistance from the status of defence of tribal lands to that of wasteful depredation of the wealth of the colony. The Maori was respected as a warrior; the Aboriginal was despised as a rural pest.

One of the interesting and obvious differences in stories of the American and of Australian frontiers is that the first is full of the names of the tribes and of great tribal federations, from the Six Nations of the Iroquois westwards. The Australian story contains very few such references, because there were no 'tribes' in the form of effective political or military units. Aboriginal social organisation was so strange to Europeans that government and mission tended to assume that there was none worth the study. Even had there been, the common law assumption, unvaried by treaty or statute, that all lands annexed remained Crown lands made the identification of 'native' claims to the lands unnecessary. In 1836 a court in New South

Wales decided that, because of their small numbers and lack of political organisation, the Aborigines could not be regarded as living as members of 'free and independent tribes' with claims to the land areas they occupied.[5]

By that time, of course, the question of rights based on prior occupation had already been settled in practice. Nomadism also made it easy to assume that one area of land was as good for the Aboriginal as another. Such a situation was uniquely favourable for colonisation of the most rapacious type: that which takes all land and only the *land*—i.e. on which even the labour of the Aboriginal was unwanted so long as other labour was available. Since no Aboriginal group had ever been recognised legally as owning any part of the continent which Aborigines have occupied for at least eighteen millenia, nothing like negotiation *had* to occur before settlement; where it did, it resulted from an individual negotiator's unusual perception, not from the requirements of the law.

This tradition may never have been established, had circumstances forced the first settlers, as they did in most colonies of settlement, to see the indigenous people as a major resource. The most unskilled labour is an essential commodity where no other labour is available. It has to be trained and husbanded, and the native' labour given opportunities to reproduce; otherwise there are no labourers for the next generation. Anything less is to mine the labour resource recklessly, to the detriment of future economic development.

When the wool industry began to flourish in New South Wales, slavery was becoming outmoded as a source of labour for the British colonies; it was about to be replaced by the indenture system, which quite carefully applied the principles of good animal husbandry to the labour force. The Aboriginal never had either the value or the protections of the slave or the advantage of veterinary principles well established in law governing 'migrant labour'. He was to establish his value, especially in the frontier lands, in the cattle industry; but although there were, later, more or less vague gestures towards an indenture system, this labour asset was to be recklessly squandered. It is significant in this context that only in the parts of the continent designated 'colonial Australia' (see endpapers) and where it proved impossible to get other labour has the Aboriginal *community* survived; and that a very substantial proportion of the 'full-bloods' are established in camps on pastoral properties which in some cases may be located in what was their own 'country'.

[5] Burton J. in Rex v. Jack Congo Murrell (1836), 1 Legge (N.S.W.) 72. I am indebted for the reference to P. Biskup, Native Administration and Welfare in Western Australia 1897-1954 (M.A. thesis, University of Western Australia, 1965).

SOME RESULTS OF COLONIAL ADMINISTRATION

The beginning of the pattern, though by no means the complete explanation of the attitudes which allowed it to happen, are to be found in the conditions of the early settlement in the east. The first settlements were established with a high proportion of labour, convict and other. So long as there were convict workers, and enough of them, there was less need to adjust to the Aboriginal as a worker. Nor was the Aboriginal without his pride, and his concept of the poor 'croppies' may well have conditioned his attitude to the kind of work they did. In South Australia and Western Australia the settler groups, in accordance with the prevalent Wakefieldian theory, included the labouring classes and lower orders.

In the economics of colonial development the Aboriginal seemed, to those who did not have some special urge or reason to consider his position, to have no economic value; having no economic value, he had no 'value of his own'.[6]

The cultures were hopelessly at variance. Settlement almost always developed into an unacknowledged conquest. The early phases of sporadic guerilla resistance (generally regarded and often dealt with as 'treachery') or the Aborigines' attempts to use the new situation for their own purposes were generally followed by their complete subjection to the settler. Attitudes established early in the eastern frontier lands spread and took root in the south and west as overlanders with stock, land seekers, miners and the like moved from one frontier to the others. The self-interest of settlers in areas where Aboriginal labour had to be used, and the attraction of material goods and station life generally to the tribes, led to the minimal adjustment of black labour to white management which was the basis of the cattle industry and, in the first part of the century and in many areas afterwards, of the sheep industry also.

Far less attention was given to the development of labour incentives than has characterised most colonies. Force and the threat of force are the most primitive of incentives management can use, and the least productive of efficiency; but the situation often tended to freeze at this level. The pastoral enterprise operated as a 'closed' economic venture, with little cash: so that at best its use as an incentive was limited. Some excellent relationships of station management to Aboriginal worker developed, with deep personal loyalties involved, but the economic development of the pastoral industry was to make almost an anachronism of the Aboriginal worker:

---

[6] J.H.P. Murray applied this phrase to the Papuan, in a minute of 13 January 1913, to his Director of Mines. The Papuan, he said, should not be considered merely as an asset, but as having a 'value of his own'.

THE FAILURE OF COLONIAL ADMINISTRATION

isolated on the fringe of the cash economy, he had to learn to be content with a diet of flour, sugar, tea, and beef (often offal) for so long that a set tradition of minimal output was established to match the poor level of incentive. He inherited the position of the assigned servant; only the free worker profited from better conditions.

The greatest potential economic asset in a conquered people is willingness to work hard, and usually the big firms supported the governments in their efforts to preserve this asset. The governments, for humanitarian and economic reasons, enacted restrictive laws to preserve the wellbeing of 'native' workers at a minimum level. Where efficient production has been one of its objectives, careful regulation of feeding, limits on punishments for breaches of labour discipline, careful regulation of the length of the term of employment—all these and other steps are necessary to preserve the worker himself, to ensure that there will be a subsequent generation of workers adequate for economic policies, and to develop an eagerness to work, if possible for cash, since cash opens up new ranges of demand and therefore produces new incentives to earn more. For the last purpose there will be careful fixing of minimum wages and steps taken to see that these are paid in cash as far as possible and that trade stores are accessible, both to develop the cash incentive and to ensure that the worker has an element of choice in what he gets for his work. Far-sighted employers plan for these facilities and support minimum conditions of employment; the poor employer benefits no one.

Simply to enumerate the requirements for reasonable management of the 'native labour' asset is to indicate how ineffectual Australian governments were when judged by these basic criteria of colonial administration. Only Queensland made a serious attempt of this kind: and it is significant that pastoral wages for controlled Aborigines have been higher there than in Western Australia or the Northern Territory, or in the north of South Australia where similar frontier conditions apply.

In spite of the best intentions expressed by the British government towards its Aboriginal subjects, very few of the governors could make more than a token gesture, even against the massacre of great numbers of them. Gipps, a man of conscience who knew what colonial principles were, was pressing hopelessly against the whole trend of events. In what passed for colonial administration in New South Wales, for instance, the Lands Commissioners with their Border Police presided over, managed to be absent from, or ineffectively opposed the settlers' methods of dealing with the Aboriginal depredator. When the states became self-governing they simply continued practices so scandalous as eventually to provide one of

SOME RESULTS OF COLONIAL ADMINISTRATION

the reasons for the hesitation of the British government to annex eastern New Guinea in the late 1870s and early 1880s.

It would be anachronistic to apply to the first period of Australian settlement the principles of colonial administration which were to take shape mainly in the colonisation of Africa and in relation to societies of village gardeners. There, all three interests concerned—government, missions, and business—stood to gain from the conservation of the village as a stable social unit, as the basis for revenue, for salvation in mission communities, and for permanent labour supply. Attempts were made to apply to Aboriginal nomads the principles of village administration; but to stabilise the nomad was to institutionalise him. His technology of survival could not maintain him in the limits of a small reserve. That groups died out so quickly and consistently indicated that stability often meant malnutrition and physical infections due to lack of static hygiene: for nomads, hygiene consisted of moving away from one's waste. The hygiene of static living had to be learned.

The attitudes of the first Australian governments were in a long tradition which illustrates both basic ethnocentricity and the best of intentions. One assumption was that 'natives' in colonies would learn by precept and example to live in equality with the lower orders of the colonial society, with all the protections of the law. Powers vested in the Crown enabled the governors to act as the trustees of 'native' rights, actual and potential. From time to time, in the first years of settlement, instructions from the Secretary of State for Colonies reminded the governors of this duty, which extended in the line of tradition back to the time of Charles II.[7] Instructions to Phillip had been in the tradition: he was to establish intercourse with the natives; 'our subjects' were to live in amity with them, and be punished for destroying them or for 'unnecessary interruption' of their occupations; the 'enforcement of due observance of religion' was enjoined upon the Governor. In all, the tradition could be interpreted as an injunction to Christianise the heathen.[8] Governor Darling was to 'promote Religion and Education among the Native Inhabitants' while protecting their persons and the 'free enjoyment of their possessions'[9]—somewhat difficult while at the same time establishing the settlers on their land. This royal command to protect Aboriginal British subjects follows an earlier instruction from Bathurst to Darling

[7] For a useful brief summary of this tradition, see Hasluck, *Black Australians*, pp. 44 *et seq.* Hasluck makes the point that although Stirling in 1829 had no such special instructions, he warned the settlers that the Aborigines had the full rights and protection of British subjects.

[8] *H.R.A.* (1), vol. I, pp. 13-14.

[9] Ibid, vol. XII, p. 125.

respecting the manner, in which the Native Inhabitants are to be treated when making hostile incursions for the purpose of Plunder . . . when such disturbances cannot be prevented or allayed by less vigorous measures . . . to oppose force by force, and . . . repel such Aggressions in the same manner, as if they proceeded from the subjects of any accredited State.[10]

This instruction was tantamount to recognition of a condition of warfare, the Aboriginal British subjects being regarded for the purpose of operations as though they were subjects of a hostile 'nation'. The practical situation was that settlement implied dispossession; this in turn made attack and counter-attack inevitable. The only way in which Phillip could have avoided 'unnecessary interruption' of Aboriginal pursuits, or his successors have safeguarded the 'free enjoyment' of Aboriginal possessions, was to pack up the whole enterprise and return to England.

The Select Committee on Aborigines, which reported to the House of Commons in June 1837, was set up to examine the means of protecting civil rights and of imparting civilisation and Christianity—near-synonyms to the ethnocentric Britons of the time. The Committee was mainly concerned with Africa, but for the Australian colonies it recommended missionaries for the natives, protectors for their defence, reservation of hunting lands, schooling for the young, and special codes of law to protect the Aboriginal until he learned to live within the framework of British law.[11] This report revealed genuine concern for the wellbeing of the people being colonised—a concern that assumes that European colonisation is inevitable, beneficial in the long run, and a duty. Its implications are clear: the 'native' must be protected; and to be protected he must be the subject of special legislation—i.e. his special separate status defined in the law. Thus began a process of cause and effect, since protective legislation is inevitably discriminatory in effect. Moreover, the categories of protected persons are often most easily defined in racial terms. The very attempt to protect the 'native' British subject in such rights as are to be left to him involves a separate status in law, which places him at the discretion and the mercy of the protecting agencies. Traditionally, emphasis has been on control and tuition as the prelude to eventual full citizenship. Thus while the goal of 'assimilation' expressed the best intentions, the special laws introduced to bring it about through tuition and control inevitably set the 'native' apart in a special category of wardship: the greater the effort towards assimilation, the more rigidly defined the differences in status become.

[10] Ibid., vol. XII, p. 21, 14 July 1825.
[11] *P.P.* (House of Commons), 1837, no. 425—Select Committee on Aborigines (British Settlements). Report, evidence and appendix.

SOME RESULTS OF COLONIAL ADMINISTRATION

The separate status of the Aboriginal developed gradually in the law from quite early times. A significant early example was his exclusion from the right to be a witness before the courts, even in his own defence. Even more important was the cultural gulf which separated him from the processes of the law, which operates on the general assumption that all citizens know what it is and how it works. He nevertheless continued to enjoy, theoretically, most rights of the subject, while his land and property were taken, his person often destroyed, and the basic needs for his life ignored. Thus, until the middle of the century, in spite of efforts to educate him and to protect his person, he was being destroyed by *laissez-faire*. The most effective efforts at protection could be applied only to social remnants and involved multi-purpose institutions. The Aboriginal and the part-Aboriginal (who because of his associations, or because of legal definitions, shared his fate) tended more and more to become prisoners, contained through special protective laws.

Today much of what was being thought and said about the situation before 1850 is part of our folk-lore, and it is the basis of many political decisions. Thus a historical diagnosis of the situation—time and space will not permit a complete account—is of primary importance.

Colonisation has posed two kinds of question for colonial administrators. One is, how (given that intruders are determined to take control of the land and the people) the frontier should be extended. It is a very difficult question indeed, and in practice has been generally left to those who are willing to take risks for gain or for souls or for some other purpose. The other question is what role the conquered people are to play in the situation produced by conquest. Obviously the questions are closely related: what happens on the frontier as the intruder extends his power will affect attitudes of either party to the other and establish the basic property relationships which will determine other relations between the races for a long time to come.

The first settlements in eastern Australia, in Western Australia, and in South Australia raised both kinds of question; and it was some time before frontiers had moved so far from the various seats of government that it was possible to separate the problem of conquest from that of indigenous participation. When this separation happened, the Aboriginal fringe-dweller or institutionalised community member could become the object of special policies of assistance, even while governments, sometimes the same governments, were involved, at least by the actions of the police and others, in group reprisals, even extermination, farther out.

In the first period of settlement the cross-cultural confusion was further

THE FAILURE OF COLONIAL ADMINISTRATION

confounded by the fact that frontier-type conquest, and what may be called the residual problems after pacification, were not only posed at the same time and in places at least very close together but the cultures involved proved so mutually uncongenial and repulsive (except that the artefacts and foodstuffs of the whites strongly attracted Aborigines) that the autonomy of the conquered indigenous social order was completely shattered. Violence flowed from contact first with whites who were criminal outcastes from their own society, and then with land seekers for whom Aboriginal resistance, such as it was, appeared as a barrier to considerable riches. In colonial frontiers in the Pacific, Asia, and Africa, the Europeans had overrun but not destroyed the village social unit, which was allowed to maintain its own identity and internal cohesion or was stubbornly and strongly enough established to resist. Its autonomy could only have been shattered by its destruction (which was generally not in the interests of the conquerors), or by the establishment of a village-based foreign bureaucracy, which never happened because it was not worth while economically—for the reason Wittfogel has called the 'law of diminishing administrative returns'.[12]

But the Aborigines were not villagers. They had no recognisable claim as evidenced by tilled areas and no fixed centre for resistance such as, culturally at least, the villages were. The material bases of Aboriginal culture were easily destroyed as the rest of the natural environment was turned to new uses. It is inextricably rooted to topography, flora, and fauna, all of which were wrecked by farming and stock, new grasses, fences, etc. Aboriginal autonomy was shattered perhaps as much by the attraction of new things as by interference with physical movement and the flora and fauna. It is true enough no doubt that in the first days (as Elkin has pointed out) the Aboriginal saw industrial goods as the products of the white man's dreaming and without much curiosity; but there is also much evidence of the crowding in to the new centres of settlement, of the avid demand for tea, flour, sugar, beef, and especially liquor.

There were economic and other reasons for this. Where the white man was destroying the game, the new weapons were necessary for survival. But it was safer to find a niche at the station, if one could, than live in the bush where one might be shot as a dangerous myall. New foodstuffs proved especially attractive; and, to those who had an intelligent grasp of catastrophe as well as to the less perceptive who were ill, or unhappy because they could no longer achieve purposes with real meaning, or

---

[12] Karl A. Wittfogel, *Oriental Despotism: A comparative study of total power*, p. 110.

SOME RESULTS OF COLONIAL ADMINISTRATION

because they suffered from a deep sense of injustice, or for any of the many reasons arising from rapid dispossession or from being used or destroyed at the whim of men with their own gain as the motive, there was the attraction of alcohol—surely as much a symptom as a cause of the disintegration of Aboriginal society and Aboriginal health. All this, with the rapid depopulation coming from malnutrition, venereal disease, tuberculosis, smallpox, and other diseases not so serious to the European carriers; from warfare, both attacks by the whites and, it seems, a new recklessness in inter-tribal disputes, as well as from the trained Aboriginal killers in the Native Police, meant that as the frontier moved beyond a particular area, what were left were not conquered tribes but dispirited remnants, lacking in the kind of leadership with which an administration might negotiate, lacking even a place of their own which from the European point of view was an axiomatic basis for any kind of civilised or ordered life.

It is not correct to assume, however, that no thought was given to the welfare of the Aboriginal. It was extensively discussed in the early years of each colony, though the end result was much the same in each place. But this discussion, in so far as it affected policies, was mainly a dialogue between the Colonial Office and the governor concerned. It did not become a very serious dialogue, perhaps, until the mid-thirties; but especially after the 1837 Report of the Select Committee of the House of Commons chaired by Buxton, until, in practice, colonial administration ceased in 1850 (except in Western Australia) there was a good deal of discussion. On at least one occasion—the recommendations by George Grey to Russell, at the end of 1840, and Gipps's comment on them[13]— this reached a level of penetration and understanding of the administrative issues involved not to be heard again on the Australian continent for a long time. But the end of colonial administration came with this matter unsolved, even in Western Australia, where Colonial Office control was maintained for a further four decades.

Those respects in which the current situation of the Aboriginal differs from those of the Maori and the Amerindian were determined basically in the period before 1850. When, in the following year, the settler majority in the legislatures assumed greater powers, policy substantially passed into local hands; and no indigenous people have been more completely at the mercy of typical settler democracies, where the standards of parliament are those of the settlers.

[13] See *H.R.A.* (1), vol. XXI, p. 34—enclosure Russell to Gipps, 8 October 1840—and p. 312— Gipps to Russell, 7 April 1841.

There was a high degree of uniformity in the situations and sequences of situations along the frontiers, which, for obvious geographical reasons, swept along coastal areas rather than across the continent. The uniformity in experience that developed as the two racial groups came into contact arose partly from confrontation of only two patterns of land use. Settlement was by people from the same European society, in each colony supervised by the same Colonial Office. Discussions in England about Aborigines produced the same effects in each Australian colony. Aboriginal society had a high degree of uniformity, in religion, economics, and political organisation. The differences between groups described by the anthropologists involve practices like circumcision and sub-incision. Artefacts and the structure of kinship organisation differed through the continent. But these seem minor differences—comparable in importance with religious differences within a single Christian state.

Contact and conquest began while the gap between the middle class and the English villager was considerable, so that the home government showed a tendency to think of the Aboriginal as coming more or less easily into the 'lower orders' of the social hierarchy, an attitude reflected in the earliest 'assimilation' policies. Thus the Aboriginal was just another colonial person who in time would learn to appreciate the benefits of the superior social order into which he had been introduced. The legal device of declaring all land initially Crown land was a matter of administrative convenience, because it is always best to clear the way for policy making by having a *tabula rasa*—especially, as the British well knew, in dealing with land matters. There could have been no foreknowledge of the economic factors which would produce the rush of settlers to displace the Aboriginal nor of the rapidity of this process. Even had there been, no attempt to reserve lands from settlement in the outlying areas could have succeeded, as the attempts which were made indicated. But legal extinction of 'native' rights could, as we have seen, have been a prelude to legal compensation. The conversion to Crown lands did not necessarily extinguish rights which the Crown itself, as the recipient of land purchase moneys, might recognise and compensate. As the settlement of New Zealand shows, an organised warlike resistance of the prior occupants could force the government to recognise some rights.

Things could well have been different. It is one of the tragedies of the Aboriginal that Australia was colonised when Britain was becoming an industrialised nation; that the demand for fine wool should coincide with a combination of cheap land, comparative absence of resistance by indigenous man or by the local fauna, and suitable grasses, all cheaply obtained

SOME RESULTS OF COLONIAL ADMINISTRATION 25

with small capital outlay; that religious restraints on profit making had given way to the Protestant ethic, which in turn was to be supplemented by the best of all sops to frontier consciences—the popular pseudo-Darwinism which could explain the 'passing of the Aboriginal' as a law of nature.

To adjust, Aborigines would have needed long periods of more or less peaceful interaction and sufficient access to their own basic resources to be in the position to make new choices in ways of living. But they had neither the time nor the experience of impersonal government or large-scale organisation to save them. The power of the state was completely outside their experience. Their own 'men of high degree' used no institutionalised and impersonal authority of the kind which a European took for granted. From time to time the settler governments did attempt to identify and deal with such persons, but in their concepts of human organisation the two races were too far apart. The results were the 'King Billys', with their contemptuously-given neck and head ornaments. The white man's contempt has forced these Aboriginal actors to play the fool, as butts for European jests, for the relations between the most insignificant white man and 'King Billy' were jesting relationships in which the tensions could be discharged.

For those accustomed to think in terms of the class structure and officialdom of European society, the apparent anarchy and absence of social order among the Aborigines was both a permissive and a puzzling situation, not made any easier for the early governors by directions from home, which tended to assume at least tribal chiefdoms among the Aborigines. The lack of easily recognised institutions with which the invaders could come to terms, or which they could use for control, and the lack of formal offices borne by persons who exercised official power which could be manipulated, prevented the governments from establishing effective dialogues with Aborigines. The social bonds which held Aboriginal society together required both effort and humility to grasp: and the Christian certainties shared by the settlers were not often compatible with an attempt to do so.

Aboriginal society has been unmalleable for British Australian governments. Aboriginal groups could die far more easily than adapt to the new set of circumstances. White consciences were salved by romanticising high death rates as a graceful making way for the higher race in the inevitable contest for survival. The truth was that the Aboriginal had the same fears and hopes as other men; the same horror of death; the same innate capacity for terror and courage; the same deep bonds of love with those of his own social order. It is becoming better known that in Australia (where the school

THE FAILURE OF COLONIAL ADMINISTRATION

history books have been so dull because nothing ever seemed to have happened), there has been a long-drawn-out process of conquest and of hopeless but stubborn resistance, both material and intellectual. There is a long history of guerilla tactics of a subtle and determined kind where this was possible. There was also the unwilling compliance which mocks the conqueror, and, at least within the warm circle of the in-group, holds to ridicule his later half-hearted efforts to make amends.

This tradition of resistance still remains. The part-Aboriginal groups of the south have inherited it from their tribal forefathers and it may be renewed by what contact they retain with the 'full-bloods', who mainly reside in the more isolated parts of the continent. Well meant but obtuse efforts of missions and government have been held off with ridicule, or with the defence of apathy, often for generations.

EASTERN FRONTIERS:
NEW SOUTH WALES

What the colonists everywhere thought of the Aborigines is easy enough to learn: what we now know shows how great was the misunderstanding. But the moral question of dispossession was probably as clear then as it is now; and though it was blurred by self-interested discussion of what 'occupation' meant, and by stated good intentions of compensation and uplift, the question of justice has been raised in every generation from then till now.

The Aborigines also, of course, had their need for justice, set in a much older human framework of custom and established in the principle of reciprocity between the living and duty to the dead and the unborn. They now saw a new kind of institutionalised violence—in the torture of the flogging triangle and the actions of the soldiers: the degradation of man by official, the linking of men in chains, the drunken orgies where men escaped from their misery. The degradations were all to be theirs in the new society being founded. While governors wrote vaguely of compensation to the Aboriginal in the blessings of Christianity and obedience to the British law, the institutions for harmony and justice were being illustrated in the great occasions of the early days, like the public hangings.

A great attraction, once it became known and available, was probably cash, with its power and the inexhaustible range of choice it conferred. But in Aboriginal morality reciprocal generosity was the basis of economics. The whites shocked those whose lands they were taking by their failure to recognise their reciprocal obligations. Soon the hard niggardliness, as it must have appeared to the Aborigines, backed by shooting in defence of

28 THE FAILURE OF COLONIAL ADMINISTRATION

personal property, had brought retaliation; and the monotonous story of
the Australian frontiers had begun.

THE FRONTILR OUT FROM SYDNEY

Within the first decade of settlement on the Hawkesbury River, the
Aboriginal came to be seen as a depredator and a pest rather than as a
potential labourer. Where there was disciplined convict labour, the
independence of the nomad appeared in contrast as hopeless irresponsibility.
For their part, the Aborigines seem to have looked on the 'croppies' with
contempt.[1] In 1796 Hunter instructed the settlers under penalty to combine
together for their own defence, while at the same time stressing that wanton
killing was murder.[2]

Early governors were instructed to report on how the natives might
become assets.[3] Macquarie reflected that they might be useful as labourers
and 'mechanics' and expressed hopes of the eventual results from tuition.
He foreshadowed his institution at Parramatta to educate the young and his
plans to allot land at Port Jackson to some of the adults.[4] By 1814 some who
had established themselves near the settlements could be described as living
in peace and amity. By then, however, the Aborigines on the fringe of the
settlements had been killing sheep, and for over a decade threatening, and
sometimes killing, settlers and their servants.[5] Killing by settlers appears in
the records mainly as retaliation or defence. Where it was established that
murder had occurred, a military court might sentence the culprit to corporal
punishment. It could happen that the soldier who had been involved in
military action against the Aborigines became the settler and carried on as
though this was war.[6]

Macquarie acted much as Hunter had done two decades earlier, urging
the settlers to form vigilante groups to repel attacks but not to take the
offensive and planning to station troops along the Hawkesbury, Nepean,

[1] N.S.W. V. & P. (L.C.), 1845—Select Committee on the Conditions of the Aborigines,
Evidence, p. 30. David Dunlop, J.P., reports that Aborigines refused convict dress—'No
good, all same like croppy'. This reference is taken from R.H.W. Reece, Diplomacy and
Gifts to the Aborigines of New South Wales 1778-1846 (typescript p. 7, Social Science
Research Council—Aborigines Project (SSRC—AP).)
[2] H.R.A. (1) vol. I, pp. 688-9—Government and General Orders—included in Hunter to
Portland, 12 November 1796.
[3] See for instance Hunter's instructions: H.R.A. (1), vol. I, p. 522.
[4] Ibid., vol. VIII, pp. 367-9—Macquarie to Bathurst, 8 October 1814.
[5] Ibid., vol. III, p. 250—included in King to John King, 1 May 1801.
[6] Ibid., vol. II, pp. 401-22—Report by Hunter to Portland, 18 October 1799, of the trial of
five Hawkesbury farmers for the murder of two Aborigines.

EASTERN FRONTIERS: NEW SOUTH WALES 29

and Grose.[7] He faced the dilemma of every early Australian governor, for the Aboriginal was a British subject, to be instructed and protected. A state of war was seldom recognised as such, and when it was, it was then rather as 'civil war' with the declaration of martial law. The need to develop a sense of 'duty' and loyalty to the Crown was early emphasised. The Aboriginal would, in time and with patience, learn to appreciate comfort and the settled life.[8] In the meantime his sporadic resistance was written off as criminal irresponsibility, only to disappear as he was civilised.

Whatever the types of settler land use—whether small-scale agriculture on the Hawkesbury and then the Hunter (where over 370,000 acres had been taken up by 1826)[9] or depasturing of sheep in the Bathurst district and cattle in the Goulburn—everywhere the very basis of Aboriginal life was at stake. Harmonious relations could be established for a period. Thus Alexander Berry, who had large interest in the Shoalhaven area and combined humanity and restraint, took cattle there. His blend of long-term self-interest with humanity helped to make his fortune and, by employing Aborigines, he offered more of them than usual a place in the new economy. But even such a rare adjustment, in the absence of any provision for a settlement relating to property rights and anchored in the European law, became, in the long run, just another road to unconditional surrender. The descendants of those who were charmed by Berry or other entrepreneurs may have been more numerous; but there is no evidence that they were in the long run any better off than those of groups which had stubbornly resisted to the last.

The extension of agricultural and pastoral settlement across the mountains led to a situation which was to prove typical in many ways of pastoral settlements for the next hundred years. An important episode was the declaration of martial law in the Bathurst district for the last five months of 1824 with results discreetly veiled in Brisbane's reports.[10]

The pastoral industry in the Bathurst-Wellington-Mudgee region, following the new emphasis on sheep raising from the early 1820s, depended upon (often city-bred) convict labour for shepherding. As the stock extended, the killing of a shepherd could be serious economically; and this may have influenced the Sydney stockholders in the station properties and flocks when they pressed the government in 1824 for punitive measures.

After this demonstration of force, there appears to have been no further serious

[7] Ibid., vol. IX, pp. 362 et seq.—Macquarie to Bathurst, 4 April 1817, enclosure 2.
[8] Ibid.
[9] T.M. Perry, *Australia's First Frontier*, p. 41.
[10] H.R.A. (1), vol. XI, p. 409—Brisbane to Bathurst, 3 November 1824.

THE FAILURE OF COLONIAL ADMINISTRATION

trouble . . . Blankets were issued to them in winter, and sometimes clothes and rations were given for special services, such as assisting in the capture of bushrangers, but after 1824 it is the familiar story of a dying race. The settlers introduced the Aborigines to their diseases and alcohol, and their stock drove out the game on which they had depended for their existence. They continued to resist further out, but at Bathurst the battle had been won for the white men by the end of 1824.[11]

From then on, for a decade or so, the main conflict was between master and convict servant; the use of the lash as a labour incentive and punishment for absconding would not stimulate the Aboriginal to seek a shepherd's job. He could only be passive in the violent clashes between bushrangers and police; he may have found special scope in the stock stealing of the first 'squatters' establishing themselves in the bush. He and his women and children would, of course, be completely at the mercy of these brutalised ruffians in the bush, as were the unfortunate Tasmanians. According to Long, there were by 1827 ten unlicensed drinking houses and one with a licence in the Bathurst-Kelso area;[12] and the record of prosecutions for illicit sales shows that the shanty tradition was maintained for more than a decade afterwards.

This state of affairs in race relations repeated earlier ones, and was to be repeated almost throughout the time and the places where the two races and cultures were quite at variance, to a degree where the whites could do much as they wished and at the same time have the defence that Aboriginal morality did not exist. The Aboriginal tradition of using sexual relationships to cement social ties rendered them especially vulnerable in the face of a predominantly male settler group.

The effect of alcohol was the most obviously catastrophic, so much so that observers who are not to be disregarded believed that Aborigines could not resist it. (When rum was currency, there was abundant example of how to escape from one's troubles, and of the link between prostitution and alcohol.) The error in this early but persistent diagnosis was in assuming a physical rather than a social cause; and in seeing, in Aboriginal addiction, a cause rather than an effect of failure in Aboriginal society to adjust to

[11] J.P.M. Long, Bathurst 1813-1940 (typescript), p. 50. Perry (*Australia's First Frontier*, p. 92), states that the demonstration in 1824 was carried out 'without loss of life'. E.G. Docker (*Simply Human Beings*, pp. 84-5), obviously believes differently, but offers no evidence. Especially as martial law enabled settlers and their servants to wage war legally, and in view of what happened elsewhere, my own feeling is that Aborigines would at least have continued to be shot at during the period of martial law. Brisbane obviously believed that there would be deaths to count when he wrote to Bathurst, 'I hope . . . to give Your Lordship a pretty accurate return of all Individuals who lost their lives during these disturbances, but hitherto we have not been able to ascertain it'.—*H.R.A.* (1), vol. XI, p. 431, despatch of 31 December 1824.

[12] Long, Bathurst 1813-1940, pp. 56-7.

EASTERN FRONTIERS: NEW SOUTH WALES 31

changes in a way which offered security to Aboriginal families. This can only be an opinion; but it is based on some consideration of the evidence— that Aborigines suffered the worst effects of alcohol, not only because it offered to individuals temporary escape from what seemed a pointless existence but also because of the vulnerability and nature of authority in Aboriginal society.

That there was no 'law' about alcohol was an initial cause of vulnerability, no doubt; but the fact does not in itself explain why Aboriginal society did not develop controls to deal with it. The reasons are probably the same as those for the failure to develop more effective organisation for physical resistance to the whites. There were, of course, as the anthropologists have shown, social controls in each group; a basis of consensus; and leadership based in this consensus, exerted by the men of high training and status. But social controls of a traditional nature are especially vulnerable when the whole basis of the tradition is in question; even more so when, as in this case, it has been wrecked by rapid depopulation, loss of control of the land, and the obvious disregard of indigenous religious assumptions by the newcomers, not to their disaster but to their advantage; by the new factors which make initiation of the young men, and even correct marriage, impossible; by the complete disregard, by white men who have shared the women or the land, of traditional obligations. Even if political authority had been concentrated in the hands of men with great personal authority in all matters relating to the tribe, and if the tribe had been so organised that the will of such men always prevailed, the political sanctions and social controls would probably have broken down. But there were no such authorities; and probably the first use of alcohol had the effect it has con- tinued to have of reducing the great man to an object of ridicule; and of giving to the doubting and tentatively dissident youth courage to defy him.

Its use by the women must have affected drastically their work of child-raising and socialisation. In a group where the habit had changed quickly from a nomadic hunting existence to limited movement, facing the new health hazards arising from comparative immobility, this must have caused high infant death rates. With ineffective shelter and waste disposal, change of diet, and new disease as well, alcohol must have formed an important link in the chain of causes which so rapidly obliterated whole groups of people. It is significant that, in spite of the theories that Aborigines were British subjects, prohibition is one of the earliest forms of protective legislation. The vulnerability of Aboriginal society has remained where the people have been segregated on missions and reserves and at the same time excluded from access to alcohol; and the early reactions of some groups who now have the right to drink have brought renewed expressions of fear for the future from some missionaries dealing with the remnants of tribal society.

There could be no clearer indication that a society which loses its autonomy completely, loses the power to make satisfactory adjustments to change; and 'satisfactory' here means such as will enable families to live (and children to be reared) in safety, with continuity of tradition to give life point and meaning, no matter how great the change, in each generation. Today, from fringe settlement to mission settlement in the far parts of 'colonial Australia', one can see, in the addiction to alcohol, how the loss of autonomy, so long ago, continued to have the same effects. Those who resist, and object to consequential violence and disorder, may try still to get away from those who are heavy drinkers; in many cases, in vain. Such escape has been one of the motives for attempts to move into the general community. Sometimes, even now, it is a motive for living where there is imposed authority.

In 1966 I received a letter from a missionary working in a desert region of South Australia, to which the right to drink in the nearest town had recently been extended.

Amounts of money spent on liquor off the reserve are out of all proportion to that spent on food and clothing. General living standards have suffered, more families are being wrecked; and the traditional influence of the older natives has all but gone by the board . . . A strange new situation has developed . . . Many of them regard [the mission] as a haven where they can get away from it all, being content with 'outbursts' when off the reserve.[13]

Today the Aboriginal may escape into a controlled situation from the chaos which has not been resolved since the wrecking of his society; or into non-Aboriginal society, if he can find acceptance there. But Aboriginal society in 'settled' Australia has never re-established its autonomy; therefore it has not developed effective leadership to deal with its special problems.

In this respect, the situation as it was at Bathurst a century and a half ago has not changed fundamentally. No one can be positive that opportunities for autonomous adjustment are still possible or that they would have been or would be effectively used. But what is sure is that, without such opportunity, addiction to alcohol and the superficial front of irresponsibility, as aspects of helpless dependency, will continue until there are no longer any

[13] Letter from Mr Barry Lindner, Yalata Lutheran Mission, 19 October 1966. A similar point, with emphasis on the need for some political and social autonomy, was made in a paper delivered to a seminar at Monash University, in May 1966, by Pastor P.G. Albrecht, Field Superintendent of the Finke River Mission, Alice Springs.

EASTERN FRONTIERS: NEW SOUTH WALES 33

people who identify as Aboriginal. The alternative has been restriction by legislation and confinement in institutions, the latter a time-honoured means of avoiding social problems. Where there is inadequate order in human affairs, even the most hated authority may appear better than none. But in the days long ago at Bathurst, as now on any fringe settlement, neither Aborigines with status nor the police and court system could deal with the man who drinks and refuses to help his family. Only consensus, within social institutions with their own autonomy, can support the sentiments for more constructive responses: all these reactions are effects of living in situations where there is little hope of winning prestige in any other way than that of affronting the authority of the whites and the *mores* of the white middle class.

In 1841 the white men of the settler community in the Bathurst district still outnumbered women by more than two to one.[14] Here then must have been developing the pattern of Aboriginal prostitution for alcohol which set the tone of social relationships in so many places; and the beginnings of the part-Aboriginal people—some of whom sprang from permanent liaisons and marriages with whites, and some not; some accepted by their fathers, often no doubt eventually to disappear with their children among the 'whites' and forget their Aboriginal forebears—a process which has been going on ever since. Those rejected by their white relations found their company either in the Aboriginal camps or as true currency lads and lasses with the more improvident element of the frontier population, to find a way of life and attitudes which they shared with the other itinerant workers, perhaps contributing to the developing 'Australian legend' as much as they took from it.

As the sheep multiplied, and the stations were rapidly extended, the enterprises became increasingly vulnerable. At the same time disciplined and cheap labour became harder to secure, so that by the time the first sheep were being depastured on the Clarence River, New England, and the Darling Downs, the killing of a shepherd could involve a serious economic loss. What happened at Bathurst was to happen with monotonous regularity for long afterwards: the initial indifference or even welcome, then the stubborn fight by a few groups for the grasslands, with attempts to hit the pastoral enterprise at the weakest spot. Settler reprisal followed, often with the connivance and sometimes the assistance of the Border Police, which tended to become an attempt to wipe out the Aborigines altogether, since men, women, and children were often slaughtered indiscriminately, and the hunting family was the basis of society.

[14] Long, Bathurst 1813-1940, p. 60.

THE FAILURE OF COLONIAL ADMINISTRATION

This was the pattern of the 1840s. Earlier, as round Bathurst and in Tasmania, martial law had meant that the settlers were led by military officers. Other factors referred to later may have been more important in bringing about the rapid depopulation which occurred, but the settler, with gun in hand facing the Aboriginal warrior, set the pattern of relationships, and this situation tended to define the nature of labour relations with the Aborigines who remained. Stubbornness of resistance can be easily enough accounted for in terms of Aboriginal religion and economics; and the failure of the settlers and governments to grasp the problems they faced possibly arose from failure to appreciate the ties of the Aboriginal with his own land. There were no marks visible to Europeans to indicate these ties, so the shiftless nomad could be assumed to get along somewhere else. As the century progressed, there was the comforting theory of inevitable Aboriginal disappearance to solace consciences. Those involved in their killing naturally enough were ready to equate them with forms of life less than human. Those Aborigines who remained behind the frontier tended to be disorganised remnants of a society: their very hopelessness and the shield of 'apathy' could seem to confirm the frontier views about them.

For the farmer and the small-town businessman the Aboriginal fulfilled much the same role as he did for the pastoralist. He did not become a townsman but, as on the stations, his services would be used as required. There were certain tasks, such as tracking stock or stripping bark for penning in the sheep, for which Aboriginal labour was essential for short periods. On the Clarence and Richmond Rivers, during the first maize boom, the tamed remnants were sometimes employed to gather the cobs and for other seasonal tasks. Aboriginal labour was also used on the upper Clarence in the 1860s for periodical harvesting. So the pattern was much the same: the Aboriginal formed a useful last resort for any kind of labour, and there were some tasks on pastoral stations for which a few were essential. Pastoral stations, however, did not require many labourers. The positions offering were few, as the very effectiveness of extermination of Aborigines and their dogs, and the wild dingo, hastened the conversion to the open range.

The same kind of confrontation marked the extension of agriculture through the coastal scrub as marked settlement on the open range country. There, perhaps, begin the fringe-dwelling communities in the river bends and in other areas not required for whites but offering water and the chance to get some kind of a living from the country town and local farming and pastoral economy. There is, for instance, a marked similarity between the descriptions we have of Aboriginal attack, reduction to a remnant, and

EASTERN FRONTIERS: NEW SOUTH WALES

final relegation to the position of a mendicant caste, in the small farming communities round Sydney in the years just after the turn of the century and the situation round farming centres at Grafton and other Clarence River areas of settlement for maize growing after the mid-century.

The pattern of earlier mayhem, and later fringe-dwelling decline, had become almost uniformly familiar from Tasmania to Wide Bay, and from Port Jackson to the Torrens and the Swan, by the end of the half-century. Official attempts to defend the rights or even the lives of black British subjects involved a kind of open-ended commitment as the frontiers ran away from the limits of effective administration. It was quite possible for men of good repute among the settlers to justify the one good bloody lesson as likely to save lives in the long run, for it might establish the mastery of the settler, and so avoid further clashes. It is easy and quite common in such circumstances for the white settler to assume that fear is the only effective motivation of 'natives'—either to make them keep the peace or to make them work for the whites.

In case of any serious affray ... [wrote W.H. Breton in 1834] it ... would be ... most judicious ... to make upon them at once, a strong impression; for if only one or two be killed, the sole effect is to instigate them to revenge their companions, whereby a series of murders on both sides is the consequence.

The same writer could criticise the 'Christian whites' who 'consider it a pastime to go out and shoot them'.[15]

Just fifty years after the First Fleet, and in the governorship of Gipps, the law on one spectacular occasion was actually carried out, in the well known case of the Myall Creek murders. But this case presented an almost unique set of circumstances.[16] Most such events could not be dealt with effectively because Aboriginal evidence was not valid (since non-Christians could not be sworn). But this case was marked by the unusual circumstances that one of the whites present not only did not participate, but informed the nearest magistrate, one Day, of Muswellbrook. Day took his duty seriously (another unusual circumstance in such cases). There was a governor who realised that, unless the law were to be rigidly applied, there was no hope of control at all. Moreover, the opportunity to apply it came in the aftermath of the Reports of the Select Committee of the House of Commons and of the moves to establish the Protectorate in the Port Phillip District.

Plunkett, the Attorney-General of New South Wales, was determined

[15] *Excursions in New South Wales, Western Australia, and Van Diemen's Land*, p. 176.
[16] The best study of this case I have read is Brian W. Harrison, The Myall Creek Massacre and its Significance in the Controversy over the Aborigines during Australia's Early Squatting Period. (B.A. (Hons.) thesis, University of New England, 1966).

THE FAILURE OF COLONIAL ADMINISTRATION

enough to lead the prosecution himself. Even then, the first jury acquitted the eleven men charged; but Plunkett arranged to have seven of them charged on a further count of murder (hoping that one of the other four might turn Queen's Evidence). All seven were found guilty of murdering one of the children included in the massacre. Killing of women and children was common enough: the children would grow up to cause trouble; the women would have other children. These seven were executed. To the last, no man tried to save himself at the expense of the others—an interesting indication of the bonds of loyalty among assigned servants, which also indicates one difficulty in getting convictions. A reason for not prosecuting the remaining four was that the main evidence against them was that of a 'civilised' Aboriginal who worked on Myall Creek. Because he. was ignorant of the 'ordinances of religion' his evidence was not acceptable.[17]

The massacre on a run held by Henry Dangar was one of a series, and seems to have been undertaken against quite inoffensive people as a routine matter; almost casually, twenty-eight people were taken from the hut of a friendly stockman, tied up with ropes, and slaughtered in the bush. 'In order' wrote the *Monitor*, 14 December 1838, 'that their cattle might never more be "rushed", it was resolved to exterminate the whole race of blacks in that quarter'.[18] ('Rushing' cattle reduced the yield of beef.) That the murderers did not necessarily have support of all station holders in the area is indicated by the action of some of these men, who had refused to tell the party where some of the local Aborigines were. One settler had tried to warn the Myall Creek Aborigines, partly because the activities of the Select Committee and the setting up of the Protectorate had already stirred up controversy.

But a group of graziers in the Hunter District formed a defence fund; and their leader, a magistrate, used his office to get to the accused and exhort them to stick together. Gipps thought this was the reason why not one of them turned Queen's Evidence.[19] As Harrison points out,[20] a significant indicator of the attitude of these pastoralists (the so-called 'Black Association') was that they continued their assistance after guilt had been well established, though they also denied that they were in favour of killing Aborigines. Rumors that the massacre had been in the course of the duties of the assigned servants were repeated in Sydney papers—the *Monitor*, the *Australian*, and the *Gazette*, which supported the prosecutions.

---

[17] Ibid., for an account of the trial and the comment in the press.
[18] Quoted ibid., p. 20.
[19] See *H.R.A.* (1), vol. XIX, pp. 704 *et seq*.
[20] The Myall Creek Massacre, pp. 27 *et seq*.

EASTERN FRONTIERS: NEW SOUTH WALES   37

The contrary view was espoused by the Sydney *Herald*, which in an editorial just before the trial argued that Aborigines had no 'right' to the land: that

this vast country was to them a common—they bestowed no labor upon the land—their ownership, their right, was nothing more than that of the Emu or the Kangaroo. They bestowed no labor upon the land and that—and that only—it is which gives a right of property to it. Where, we ask, is the man endowed with even a modicum of reasoning powers, who will assert that this great continent was ever intended by the Creator to remain an unproductive wilderness? . . . The British people . . . took possession . . .; and they had a perfect right to do so, under the Divine authority, by which man was commanded to go forth and people, and *till* the land. Herein we find the right to the dominion which the British Crown, or, more properly speaking, the British people, exercise over the continent of New Holland.[21]

If the Aborigines had no real right to the land, then the settlers could argue that they were protecting *their* property against alleged Aboriginal law-breakers. Application of the law would have required effective arrests, establishment of identities, and a procedure which made use of Aboriginal evidence—problems faced generally in colonial administration. The Aboriginal was a difficult case, because his skill in the bush made it impossible for Europeans to apprehend him. It was not until the Native Police were developed, the 'black trackers' introduced, and the whites had learned Aboriginal bush lore that arrest became easier; even then, chaining was considered necessary to bring in accused and witnesses. In court, lack of understanding of the procedures and of the nature of the oath could operate both ways; and settlers complained that Aborigines charged were often released because of doubts as to the possibility of a fair trial.

This problem was one of the arguments for violence in self-defence or in defence of property. The executions in the Myall Creek case were attacked as though the killers had been remedying deficiencies of the government in Aboriginal administration. The revolting details could be forgotten in indignation over what seemed almost a breach of faith, after decades of tacit sanctioning of punitive action.

Those who supported the executions, mainly spokesmen of religious and humanitarian groups in Sydney and far from the frontier, formed an influential minority: and their views were well reported in the press.

Yet this incident was no worse than many others; it was one of a series of killings in that region, carried through in the same cold-blooded manner. Earlier in 1838 there had been a publicised massacre of about twice the number killed at Myall Creek, by troops acting as volunteer mounted

---

[21] 7 November 1838, quoted ibid.

THE FAILURE OF COLONIAL ADMINISTRATION

police, in the same area. The circumstances were not favourable for prosecution, and attempts to get evidence were quite unsuccessful. The case did not come to trial.[22] Justice requires efficient auxiliary services, with adequate resources. As Gipps and his predecessors found, these resources might include skills like tracking in the bush, which Europeans did not possess. Gipps's letter to Glenelg in this instance indicates the difficulties. There had to be coronial inquiries to establish the causes of death. Before he could arrange these, the Aborigines were reported to have killed 'several' settlers: he had had to send police and magistrate to the scene of the new outbreaks.[23]

Glenelg's comment is typical of the kind of administration which maintains a correspondence but with no feeling for the distant reality—the bane of colonial administrators for long afterwards. Gipps was told that he should take every precaution to prevent clashes and impress the natives with the justice of the law and its equal punishments irrespective of race. In the meantime Gipps was hesitating to issue such instructions as would make the Lands Commissioners Protectors of Aboriginals and prohibit the forcible seizure of Aboriginal women. His reason, which was to stay his hand, on occasion, later, was that settlers, when incensed, would simply get rid of the Aborigines,[24] for the officials in the frontier regions shared the settler attitudes, and extermination was often possible.

One result of the Myall Creek affair was Gipps's Border Police Act of March 1839. The Border Police would enable the Commissioner to enforce the land legislation, which was the main cause of Gipps's unpopularity, and to protect Aborigines. Taxation of settlers to pay for the police increased their defiance, and the Aborigines probably suffered as a result. Policy could not prevail where such lack of consensus existed. In spite of Gipps's caution, reprisals simply got out of hand. The Commissioners either assisted with their police or took them off elsewhere to keep the reprisal proceedings 'administratively clean'. The Aborigines, with the speed with which information runs through nomadic society, seem to have reacted aggressively all along the frontier.

Colonial administration was to last for a decade after Gipps, at least formally. But, though the dialogue with the Colonial Office continued, government regulation of race relations had broken down in New South Wales. It had been doomed to do so, because in all the conditions there

---

[22] This was the massacre led by Major J.W. Nunn. The story begins in *H.R.A.* (1), vol. XIX, p. 397—Gipps to Glenelg, 27 April 1838.
[23] Ibid.
[24] Ibid., pp. 397 and 678.

EASTERN FRONTIERS: NEW SOUTH WALES

could not be a settlement between the parties. There was no inter-racial negotiation aimed at some limited understanding. The same reasons were to maintain for another century the same kinds of contact in the frontier lands, leaving in its wake dispossessed, detribalised groups of people, some in employment and others in the first fringe camps, and presenting the kind of problem for which charity, institutions, and outdoor relief for the especially needy seemed the only possible answers.

The Myall Creek case highlighted differences which have not altogether receded into the past. On the one hand there is the anger of 'practical' people, who 'know about natives'. These frontier attitudes have been confronted over the decades by the arguments for humanity and, more recently perhaps, for equality.

Frontier prejudice sees the case for equality as the result of inexperience and distance from the facts. This was nicely illustrated in a press account of a meeting of the Australian Council for Native Welfare in 1951, an account which appears to have brought no special reaction then, though it would certainly cause a storm of controversy if it happened today. One of the Ministers, representing a State which has large numbers of Aborigines living in its tropical regions, remarked that most of the criticism was coming from 'people in the southern parts of Australia. Many of the these people would not know a nigger if they saw one'.[25]

The final bankruptcy of frontier policy produced the traditions and the practices of the Native Police, the instrument of 'native administration' which New South Wales, having itself achieved responsible government, handed on to its daughter state of Queensland. This body, originally established in the Port Phillip District, came into its full role in the thick scrub, riverine brush, and the ranges, mainly north from the Macleay and Clarence areas, where the New South Wales government allowed it to operate primarily as a military force to protect settlers. White officers, in charge of Aboriginal troopers, had substantial independence of the local magistracies and operated in accordance with the tradition of the punitive expedition, which was common enough in establishing colonies.

The use of group punishments in retaliation for murders and stock killings had clearly become a standard procedure by the time of the deliberations of and evidence to the Select Committee of the Legislative Assembly of New South Wales in 1856. Officers and Aboriginal troopers were mounted and armed; and when an Aboriginal group took refuge in dense scrub and bush it was the dismounted Aboriginal troopers who did the leading and the killing, with the officer, often vague as to what

[25] *Age* (Melbourne), 4 September 1951.

THE FAILURE OF COLONIAL ADMINISTRATION

his exact duty was, coming on to the scene in time to arrest or otherwise deal with those who remained.[26] It was the troopers who had the essential tracking skills: an officer would have had to show unusual bushcraft to keep up with them. A Justice of the Peace who gave evidence said that there was such a shortage of officers that

a newly appointed Sub-Lieutenant has to proceed at once to his own individual command. As a necessary consequence, he is at the mercy of his troopers, who, taking advantage of his ignorance, do whatever they choose.[27]

The Auditor-General, formerly Inspector-General of Police, stated that 'the principle I have always endeavoured to carry out has been that the duties of the Native Police ought to be confined to the protection of the white population on the extreme limits of the frontier districts.'[28] The same witness stated his preference for what was later sometimes referred to as 'administrative methods' at the discretion of the local officer, and opposed the idea that officers in the north should be placed under the Commissioners of Crown Lands, as they had been in the southern areas. His words indicated a wish to avoid knowing the details of how the discretion was exercised:

The principle I acted upon with them was to place the fullest and widest discretion in the hands of each officer, and to discourage and discountenance referring to me for instructions. I looked to them for the proper management of the men . . . and for maintaining the peace of their respective districts, holding them responsible for the exercise of a proper discretion.[29]

He thought that there was no need for a Commandant of the Force at all.

He opposed the suggestion that units should be controlled by local magistrates, because each would tend to require the Force to operate in his own immediate area, and argued for distant control from the capital. In this he was supported by C. Archer, J.P., who stated that 'I do not think a Bench of Magistrates can know as well as the local head of the Force what ought to be done'.[30] Settler witnesses wanted direct access to the Force, so that they could call on it for reprisals when stock had been destroyed. All seemed to agree that the more remote the headquarters from the scene of operations, the better.

---

[26] *N.S.W. V. & P.* (L.A.), 1856-7, vol. 1, pp. 1157-216—Report from the Select Committee on the Native Police Force, together with the proceedings of the Committee and Minutes of Evidence.

[27] Ibid.—evidence by Francis Nicholl, J.P.

[28] Ibid.—evidence by W.C. Mayne.

[29] Ibid.

[30] Ibid.—evidence by C. Archer.

EASTERN FRONTIERS: NEW SOUTH WALES

Committee and witnesses appeared to accept the 'necessity of making war on' Aborigines; and there was something in the argument that the stronger the patrolling Force, the less likely would clashes be.

This did not mean that due respect to the requirements of the law was quite ignored. Due deference was paid to legal formality. When an Aboriginal was killed, there should always be a magisterial inquiry, and sworn evidence sent to the Attorney-General. But the troopers, being Aborigines, could not be sworn; though their statements were also required, these could have little weight in court. One former officer mentioned cases where troopers had dealt with complaints without an officer present: on one occasion, when a white sergeant in the Wide Bay District had left them to manage a matter of 'inquiring' into 'outrages', they had apparently 'attacked and killed a lot of station Blacks', a serious matter, as it diminished the labour supply and brought disaster to Aborigines known to the settler families as persons.[31] The same witness remarked, 'It is not boys that ought to be placed in command of such men, and for such duty'.[32]

There is a good deal of reticence as to what the killings actually meant, in the occasional references to police severity. W. Forster Esq., a member of the Select Committee, expressed the view of most of the witnesses and apparently of the legislature. Taking up new country would, he said, be slowed down and cost more lives without the Native Police: he had

very little hope of ever civilizing the Aborigines [but the Force would] prevent collision between the whites and the blacks, such as invariably occur in taking up new country. The Native Police being on the spot ... are able, not only to trace the real offenders with more certainty, but to inflict punishment more suddenly, and with greater effect, so as, in the end, to lead to less loss of life and fewer collisions.[33]

This was a clear statement of the practice which had now emerged from all the discussions. Clashes were inevitable, and would be dealt with by military methods.

It is an old tradition of frontiers that punishment must be inflicted at once; otherwise 'natives' do not know what the punishment is for. From this point of view, time spent on getting warrants, on identification of the offenders, on arrests with the use of force limited to that required to make the arrest, was waste of time. In the aftermath of a stock killing, it would also be likely to enable the Aborigines to escape. The cost, obviously, was that the innocent would suffer with the guilty.

---

[31] Ibid.—evidence by R.P. Marshall, paras. 115-17.
[32] Ibid.—re-examination of R.P. Marshall, para. 22.
[33] Ibid.—evidence by W. Forster, paras. 21-3.

THE FAILURE OF COLONIAL ADMINISTRATION

It was usual to talk of guilty 'tribes' or 'mobs'; and the assumption of guilt by association led to massacres of whole groups in the isolation of the scrub. Experience had led settlers to the conclusion that large assemblies of Aborigines were probably planning raids on their property. Forster, advocating a permanently patrolling Force, was all for keeping the Aborigines in a state of uncertainty: 'they never commit a depredation without a considerable degree of consultation and preparation among themselves; they have meetings and long talks over it'.[34] This was the train of reasoning which led to the policy of 'dispersal' by the Native Police of Queensland, maintained for four decades—an argument which assumed that gatherings of Aborigines were planning crime and justified attacks by the Native Police. This, of course, hit at the very core of the Aboriginal social organisation and of the continuity of tradition in the great ceremonies. It could have done more to hasten the disintegration of the old Aboriginal society than all the killings.

No member of the Select Committee questioned the philosophy at which New South Wales settler democracy had finally arrived: that of the one good bloody lesson as the basis for peace in frontier regions. There was also the argument, which was valid enough, that killings on an even greater scale might occur if the settlers were left to deal with matters in their own way. But a few references in the evidence suggest what became even more obvious in the first similar inquiry held by the Queensland government in 1861, that the Native Police was a dangerous instrument, often in the hands of officers who had no real control of their men. Dismissal of troopers for financial or other reasons sometimes left them to prey on the defenceless groups along the frontiers, in the Aboriginal version of the bushranging techniques. The troopers also made their demands on the local women, and there was generally 'trouble' arising from this. With their uniforms and arms, the purchasing power of their wages of threepence a day, and their rations, they seem to have attracted Aboriginal camp-followers in the manner of a professional force. There were references in the evidence to the mounted Aboriginal women who accompanied them, dressed in shirts and trousers, marking, perhaps, the beginning of that frontier tradition of the women who became successful station hands.

Recruiting would be easy enough in the social chaos left behind the frontier; and it was policy as far as possible not to employ a trooper in the area in which he was recruited. He was subjected (except in operations) to a harsh discipline which included floggings; but for this of course

Ibid.—para. 69.

EASTERN FRONTIERS: NEW SOUTH WALES   43

there was plenty of precedent within the settler society. References in the evidence to the recent dismissal of the Commandant for drunkenness indicate how problems could arise: they had in fact been the reason for the inquiry.

The recommendations of the Select Committee were for a more militarily efficient distribution of the Force, with reductions in the area which was to remain within New South Wales, for strengthening units north from Moreton Bay, and for appointment of a Commandant for the areas which were to be included in Queensland (which at that time could have included the Clarence). There was no consideration of the legal and other issues involved in the method of group punishments of British subjects. In the 'troubled districts' the force had 'effected a great amount of good in checking the lawless state of outrage on the part of the native blacks'.[35]

As indicated in consideration of the Myall Creek case, it would be quite wrong to suggest that the view of the legislature was shared by the whole non-Aboriginal community. The expansion of that community was raising moral questions concerning which no answer could be found, except perhaps in the relegation of the Aboriginal to a status less than human. There were always people who refused to make this adjustment, even in the frontier regions. For instance, there were strenuous efforts by missionaries to bring Aborigines into Christian society. A positive secular effort at protection was made by each government, the most notable being the Protectorate in the Port Phillip District. Such efforts were to be continually frustrated, partly by the effects of the earlier events along the frontier.

THE FRONTIER IN VAN DIEMEN'S LAND

The Tasmanian story was played out to its end in about three-quarters of a century; but the decisive actions all occurred within the first quarter. It was inevitable that all useful areas on the island would be stocked rapidly, as the alternative involved transporting flocks to the mainland. There was no vast and easily accessible frontier to attract settlement, leaving interstices and gaps behind for the tribal remnants. The obliteration of the Tasmanians appears spectacular partly because it is comparatively easy to think of them as a separate people. But whole populations on the mainland, of comparable size, were also disappearing.

The story is also useful as indicative of the distance between proposed

[35] Ibid.—Report, p. 5.

THE FAILURE OF COLONIAL ADMINISTRATION

policies and practice and between the white governors and the Aboriginal governed. Here one may see the beginning of the policy of reserves for the unwanted Aborigines, as places where they could be held out of the way. The wide difference between pious platitudes of government proclamations and the facts resulted from dominance of the settler economic interests, especially after the free settlers came. The demands of the whites, immersed in the development of a new system of land use, and in no particular need of Aboriginal labour, meant that even the remnants should, as pests, be sent somewhere off the island or be wiped out. All these situations were to be repeated on the mainland: the resort of the government to proclamation of martial law to deal with Aborigines who were fighting back; the demand of settlers, who did not need their labour, for the removal of the local Aborigines; the undeclared war, never so recognised for any purposes of negotiation and settlement.

From early 1804, the Van Diemen's Land settlement was heavily labour biased, with five convicts for every free person. Many of the convicts became the first bushrangers, partly because of famine in the settlement, which helped to reduce the Aboriginal population to a remnant of refugees. As the stations spread there was little or no control of the actions of the shepherds, a high proportion of whom had been brutalised by the convict system. By the time free settlers were establishing themselves, the gulf was so wide between the settlers and the Aborigines that settlers would shoot on sight. This was one of the practices which Sorrell tried to discourage. He also declared against an apparently established custom of killing the men and taking the children from the women, ordering the Resident Magistrates and District Constables to list all children and youths held by 'Settlers or Stock-keepers, stating from whom, and in what manner, they were obtained'.[36] Those already taken without parental consent were to be sent to Hobart, to be maintained and educated at government expense.

Apparently a few native workers might be useful; but the Aborigines were well on the way to extinction before there was any real place for them in the cash economy. By 1844 the remnants had been on Flinders Island for over a decade, and there were still as many 'bond' as there were free men among the whites. It is significant that the only descendants of the original Tasmanians have come from the unions of sealers with Tasmanian women. These unions often seem to have become real marriages in the sense that each needed the other; the sealer could not manage without his Tasmanian wife to hunt mutton birds and share his hard labour. And often the wife,

[36] Quoted in Clive Turnbull, *Black War: The extermination of the Tasmanian Aborigines*, pp. 57-9—Government and General Orders, 13 March 1819.

EASTERN FRONTIERS: NEW SOUTH WALES   45

even if acquired as a slave, was only able to survive and to raise children because of her isolation.

There is neither need nor space to tell the details here; but an outline of what happened may indicate how similar social ingredients produced similar results on this and other frontiers.

The whole series of events illustrates again the distance in culture and understanding between the races. In May 1804, when the Royal Marines killed near Risdon some forty or so of an armed band, they had in fact dealt with a hunting party, not a raiding party. One of the surgeons wrote the next day to the Reverend Knopwood, 'you will oblige me by X'ening a fine native boy, whom I have, unfortunately, poor boy, his father and mother were both killed'.[37]

Even before white settlement on Van Diemen's Land began, according to Plomley, the 'resident population of seamen, beachcombers, those "free by servitude", those to whom the idea "out of sight, out of mind" was attractive, and runaway convicts', had brought disaster to the coastal people by seizure of their womenfolk. 'Whatever the method adopted by the sealers . . . the results were disastrous for the natives and were undoubtedly the principal cause of the extinction of the tribes of the north coast and, to a less extent, those of the east coast also'.[38]

The best first-hand account of what was happening is probably that of G.A. Robinson, in his notes of events on and round Bruny Island in 1829 and his journal of subsequent expeditions: he spent months at a time on the other side of the frontier, unarmed among the tribal remnants. His remarks, almost *en passant*, shed light on similar situations everywhere, especially on events which conditioned attitudes on both sides. There were the wholesale shooting of marsupials, affecting the Aboriginal supply of food and of furs for warmth; the use of poison mixed with flour to get rid of native dogs, adopted by the shepherds to get rid of their owners as well;[39] the cases of convicts who would cover up their own breaches of the law for which there were serious consequences—killing sheep for a supplement to the ration, for instance—by blaming the Aboriginal.[40] His accounts of the massacres resulting from fear as much as greed ought to be read to bring home the real grimness of this 'passing'.

[37] Quoted in W.E.L.H. Crowther, 'The Passing of the Aboriginal Race', *Medical Journal of Australia*, vol. 1, 3 February 1934, pp. 147-60.
[38] N.J.B. Plomley (ed.), *Friendly Mission: The Tasmanian journals and papers of George Augustus Robinson 1829-1834*, pp. 23-4.
[39] Ibid., pp. 180-203—entries dated 21 and 24 June, 8, 10 and 20 August 1830.
[40] Ibid., p. 245—entry for 10 October 1830. For a typical comment by Robinson, see entry for 23 November 1829.

46 THE FAILURE OF COLONIAL ADMINISTRATION

Against this background the events of the Lieutenant Governorship of George Arthur epitomise the whole story of settler-Aboriginal relationships. As private interests in local investments grew there were always channels past the colonial governor to his superiors; and one had to be strong and determined as well as definite in one's intentions to resist this kind of pressure. Arthur soon succumbed to local pressures, established in his Executive Council. An early declaration authorised resistance by force and allowed for the organisation of the pursuing posse.[41] A year later Arthur exhorted the magistrates to organise these, much in the manner of those on the Hawkesbury thirty years before, and arranged to send out garrison troops to reinforce them.[42]

Already the settlers had made the mental transition characteristic of such situations. 'This land is my land' is the pioneering theme; and the person who has inhabited and humanised it for centuries appears as an inconvenient pest, unless he can be used as labour. There is, I think, little doubt that the rapid disappearance of the Tasmanian had some relationship to the fact that his labour was not really required. In the late 1820s the settlers were beginning to talk of the need for the government to *remove* the natives; otherwise they would all be destroyed. Arthur at this stage preferred

to settle the Aborigines in some remote quarter of the island, which should be strictly reserved for them, and to supply them with food and clothing, and afford them protection from injuries by the stock-keepers, on condition of their confining themselves peaceably to certain limits, beyond which, if they pass, they should be made to understand *they will cease to be protected*.[43]

The italics are mine; and I use them to indicate how quickly the fiction of Aboriginal subjects of the Crown could be forgotten when convenient: once they had been relegated to the reserve it was to be open season, even in law, to shoot Aborigines found elsewhere. Another point worth noting is that the first real attempt to establish a controlled reserve in Australia arose from the twin motives of removing a pest and protecting it from the violence of the white subjects of the Crown, who are assumed to be uncontrollable in this respect. Perhaps one may generalise with some logic: if the first aim is to protect the Aboriginal, some part of his own country will be reserved to him; if it is to get rid of him from valuable land assets, he will be 'protected' somewhere else, and if necessary forcibly removed there. The same kind of thing was done a century later. Here for instance one

[41] Quoted in Turnbull, *Black War*, pp. 73-5—Government Notice, 29 November 1826.
[42] Ibid., pp. 78-80—Government Notice and Garrison Orders, 29 November 1827.
[43] Ibid., p. 83—Arthur to Goderich, 10 January 1828.

EASTERN FRONTIERS: NEW SOUTH WALES 47

recalls the arrest and removal of part-Aborigines from Northam to Moore River;[44] the rounding up of Aborigines from the stations of the hinterland, and their removal to Palm Island;[45] the removal of Aborigines from the valuable goldmining areas at Tennant Creek.[46]

So Arthur was moving toward something which was to set precedents for a long time.

1828 was marked by the Demarcation Proclamation, which purported to order all Aborigines out of the settled districts; the magistrates were to organise for their expulsion; capture without force was to be attempted, but if that failed force could be used.[47]

In the meantime George Augustus Robinson, discounting the fears of those who had no real knowledge of the native people, went unarmed amongst them and had already shown that negotiations were possible. It is hard to read the story of the 'black line' of troops, public servants, settlers, and convicts, which attempted to round up all the Aborigines in the country of the Stoney Creek, Oyster Bay, and Big River tribes, and to drive them into Forestiers Peninsula, without concluding that such administrative and practical absurdity reflects the reactions of the white community under considerable stress. Yet they must have already killed hundreds of the Aborigines, though they had no chance at all of capturing them in this manner. 'One old man and a boy, captured on the way, were the sole trophies of an undertaking that had cost the colony more than thirty thousand pounds'.[48]

While this official bungling was in progress from planning to final failure, Arthur had also, to his credit, backed Robinson's famous mission of conciliation to the Aborigines. Robinson's journal records how he heard of the failure of the 'Line' (earlier predicted as certain in the journal) in November 1830,[49] over ten months after he had first set off, unarmed, to talk and live with the Aborigines, and after having walked almost round Van Diemen's Land. To read this journal is to realise that even incarceration on an island off the coast could fairly seem to offer better chance of survival than any other course of action; and he had in fact by this time begun to win the necessary confidence of a people with whom he had gone far to

[44] *Northam Advertiser*, 18 January 1933; see also vol. II, *Outcasts in White Australia*: 'Policies'.
[45] On Palm Island and other settlements see J.W. Bleakley *The Aborigines of Australia*.
[46] *C.P.P.* no. 237, 1935—'Report on Administration of the Northern Territory', pp. 21-6; Welfare Branch, Northern Territory Administration, *Warrabri Aboriginal Reserve*, p. 4.
[47] Plomley, *Friendly Mission*, Appendix A, pp. 243 *et seq*.—Proclamation, 15 April 1828.
[48] Arthur W. Jose, *History of Australia*, pp. 85-6. Jose probably got his estimate of the cost of this extraordinary example of mass hysteria from H. Melville's *The History of the Island of Van Diemen's Land from the year 1824 to 1835 inclusive*.
[49] Plomley, *Friendly Mission*, p. 283—entry for 25 November 1830.

THE FAILURE OF COLONIAL ADMINISTRATION

establish humane and trusting relationships. It is interesting to find the intuitive realisation of a common humanity in this uneducated bricklayer. His success highlights the timorousness of the settler community as a whole. That Robinson was to lead his people to a doom just as sure as the one from which he hoped to save them was something he could not know.

He had, in his first efforts at least, the assets for this kind of work which no learning can give—absolute control of his fears, continually staking his life on the efficacy of letting it be known that he did not bear arms; and, even more impressive, a humanity which in this context was quite extraordinary. He had taken the trouble to learn at least one Aboriginal language, and while in charge of a small Aboriginal community on Bruny Island seems to have won loyalty and respect.[50] Ostensibly the operations under the Demarcation Proclamation seem to have been for the rounding up and bringing in of those who would otherwise be killed. Robinson had been showing how this could be done without arms and that negotiation was possible. An island in Bass Strait was as far away as it was practicable to put the Aborigines; and Robinson, ignorant of the complex social relationships involved, and possibly more concerned with the salvation of souls than of persons, seems to have agreed with this from the beginning.

The first band of some sixty unfortunates was placed on tiny Gun Carriage Island in March 1831. This was a collection of tribal remnants from far and wide; some from what Robinson calls 'the main', but many were women who had been living with the sealers on islands in this region. Fifteen of these unfortunates had come from Hobart Town: some from Robinson's own house, some from the gaol. Remnants of many different tribes were involved. This was not a community sharing hardship but an assortment of individuals whose world had already been destroyed. (In this respect, also, this first 'establishment' was to be a prototype: and there is a direct line of tradition from Gun Carriage Island to Palm Island.)

Placing the Aborigines on the island was intended to improve on the habit of placing them in gaol, not for a particular offence but to protect them from being shot at sight by nervous settlers and their servants. This is why some of the first to be taken off the mainland were from gaols. (For a long time in Western Australia the main institution for Aborigines was the special gaol for them on Rottnest Island.)

The need to lock Aborigines away to save their lives, in a situation where government was obviously not really interested and lacked power to do very much even if it had been, is illustrated by Robinson's fears

[50] Ibid., for Robinson's account of his Bruny Island experience.

EASTERN FRONTIERS: NEW SOUTH WALES 49

during the expedition which resulted in his bringing in the Big River
people, at the end of 1831. He reproves his Aboriginal followers for
recklessness, not for risking their lives by venturing too close to the alleged
wild savages they were alleged to be pursuing but for crossing a main road
in the dusk, when they could all be taken for Aborigines without a European
in control, and shot. He is angry when they lead him at night too close to
stations or settlements. 'Was the white people to see us the whole country
would be in alarm and parties would be sent out and we should be in
danger of being shot'.[51]

Though great danger was to be apprehended from the hostile natives, still in passing
through the settled districts more danger was to be apprehended from white people,
as their usual practice of attacking natives were heretofore at night and firing upon
them at their encampments.[52]

This made Robinson's mission of persuasion easier; the Aborigines saw
no other way but to trust him. He records some interesting reflections on
the occasion when he has, in September 1831, persuaded one group to
quit their country for temporary sojourn on Waterhouse Island, until they
can be included in the 'institution'. This, he remarks, is really better than
putting them in gaol; but gaol or the island it had to be, as otherwise they
would be killed.

Indeed it was the most humane thing as the only way to save their lives. Here they
can remain and when by a proper discipline their ferocious dispositions are subdued,
they can be brought on to the main . . . and placed under the protection of a
missionary.

He also arranged to send to Waterhouse Island some others who had been
enjoying the sanctuary of Georgetown gaol.[53] This idea, of first catch your
Aboriginal and then lock him away and train him for re-entry to places
where at the time he is not wanted, was to last for a long time.

The results of policy depend in part on its instruments: and the
Aborigines, including the women, were at the mercy of the guards. The
basic cause of the high death rate was not understood, but in retrospect it
appears that failure to make arrangements for hygiene, and conditions
leading to respiratory diseases, were important.

At the end of 1831 the inmates and their guards and mentors had been
removed to Flinders Island.

On 14 June 1832 Robinson led the dreaded remnants of the Big River
tribe into Hobart. By that time they consisted of sixteen men, nine women,

[51] Ibid., p. 488—entry for 21 October 1831.
[52] Ibid., p. 501—entry for 4 November 1831.
[53] Ibid., p. 424—entry for 11 September 1831.

50   THE FAILURE OF COLONIAL ADMINISTRATION

and one child. The convenient conformity of salvation with profit was celebrated in the press statement that

The removal of these blacks will be of essential benefit both to themselves and the colony. The large tracts of pasture that have so long been deserted owing to their murderous attacks ... will now be available. ...[54]

Turnbull quotes the figures available to the effect that in just over a decade of rounding up the remnants, 203 persons were placed on Flinders Island. The settlement was apparently made with a minimum of material preparation, beginning with what became the typical combination of supervised reserve and shanty town. The weather was unsuitable, food, clothing, and blankets short; soldiers of the guard were said to have intimidated the women. It could have been rather more of a shambles than most of these multi-purpose welfare institutions have been at the beginning. It was in fact a prison, and there was a lacuna of policy as definite as that which applied to the first prisons in Van Diemen's Land for white men. Here is the precedent for keeping the inmates busy with instruction in agriculture. A catechist was appointed to teach Christianity and to instruct them in reading and writing. Oddments of European dress were adopted.

Robinson himself took over in 1835. The Aborigines had also set a precedent for these institutions which was not to be reversed for a long time; for by then they seem to have avoided their responsibilities by dying in considerable numbers.[55] With Robinson came the emphasis on ethnocentric tuition which was to mark Aboriginal policy almost everywhere; from the point of view of the bored and bewildered victims, this must often have appeared as some kind of lunacy.[56] 'Though in point of intellectual advancement the Aborigines of this colony rank very low in the savage creation', he wrote in 1829, this 'defect' was 'counterbalanced by many amiable points' which aroused in himself an 'irresistible feeling of sympathy' and an 'urgent desire' for the 'mollifying of their condition'.[57] Later in the same year he is reflecting on the potential of the children whose seizure he strongly opposes: 'the good derived from such a measure is more than counterbalanced by the evil'. But 'Where children can be safely separated from their parents without giving offence to the latter' they should be, 'for the sole purposes of improvement. To the children of these unenlightened creatures we must

[54] *Hobart Town Courier*, quoted Turnbull, *Black War*, pp. 145 *et seq.*
[55] Ibid., pp. 163–4. Over 40 per cent appear to have died.
[56] Ibid.—especially the illustrations on p. 191.
[57] Plomley, *Friendly Mission*, p. 80—entry for 30 September 1829.

EASTERN FRONTIERS: NEW SOUTH WALES 51

first direct our whole study and attention. . . .' On the basis of intelligent observation and experience, he had concluded by January 1830 that

The faculties of those children at present under my care are by no means deficient in strength. God has given them the same portion of understanding as ourselves. Their organs of intellect are as capable of improvement, and I am moreover convinced that they would as readily acquire any of those attainments by which human nature is distinguished, provided they enjoyed the means that are necessary . . . Those who maintain that the savages of this country are nearly akin to the brutes themselves, or that they possess no faculties in common with our own species, oppose their arguments to the dictates of humanity and commonsense . . . Any man that is not born a fool is capable of becoming wise.[58]

It took a long time for the learned men to arrive finally at this verdict —that the chances of parents producing a genius or a fool have no relationship to racial origin. But perhaps this realisation, and the urgent need to save Aboriginal souls, made social change through tuition appear reasonable and possible.

The activity of Robinson and his predecessors on Flinders Island anticipated a long line of similar situations, in which governments have been handicapped by lack of any real knowledge. Of interest here is the readiness of Arthur to hand over the practice of Aboriginal affairs to an uneducated person with strong and conforming views and ready to use his efforts for whatever the officially defined ends might be.

The vacuum in policy, once the Aborigines were out of the way, seems to have worried Arthur. He could hardly plan to move them back into the Tasmanian community; and in 1835, when there were about 130 left, he proposed that these beneficiaries of his government's successful acculturation be transferred to the mainland, in the vicinity of the proposed new colony of South Australia.[59] He seems to have been aware that history would hardly forget the obliteration of a whole people; the remnant could be 'assimilated' somewhere else. In 1838, at the end of Robinson's activities, the number surviving seems to have been about eighty.

The Quaker James Backhouse had visited the island and had looked deeply at root causes rather than at what was in effect the final result. To Buxton, who was chairing the Select Committee of the House of Commons considering native policies, he wrote that land should be purchased by the government (not simply taken and sold to settlers); that missionaries should work with people in their own areas; that

[58] Ibid., p. 93—entry for 1 January 1830.
[59] Turnbull, *Black War*, pp. 168-70—quoting Arthur to Secretary of State for the Colonies, 27 January 1835.

British offenders should be pursued everywhere by the law; and that coroners should hold inquiries into the deaths of Aborigines.

By 1843, the survivors numbered fifty or so; their wants were attended to by a commandant, a clergyman, a medical officer, a storekeeper, a nurse, and a coxswain; soldiers and labourers apparently brought the total staff to twenty-three.[60] Here again one may find the prototype of the Northern Territory or Queensland government settlement, except that Flinders Island had a rapidly decreasing commitment, while these have rapidly increasing commitments. But once staff build up, the result is to bring right into the artificial community all the tensions of the situation outside. Ten children, of whom some were part-European, came back among the forty-odd who returned to the mainland in 1847, to another reserve at Oyster Bay. The account of the last years of these people suggests the same kind of tense recklessness of life and limb which still marks many of the fringe-dwellers; here at Oyster Bay was a prototype fringe.

We are much more aware now of the perils involved in rapid changes of an established way of living; and no change perhaps could be more dangerous for those who are suddenly institutionalised than one such as this was. Adaptation to free roving lives in the bush had little relevance to the situation on Gun Carriage Island, where the nomads were penned in a single spot, for their every need dependent upon the efficiency and devotion of their keepers. The island was small and lacked shelter; rations were short; and people who have lost hope are hardly in the mood to make such an adjustment. Many died there. Chaotic initial administration on Flinders Island seems to have left the Aborigines, especially the women, at the mercy of the guards.[61] But these were only the circumstances making all the more inevitable the effects of the pulmonary tuberculosis which was rapidly reducing the group. The island had been selected not as a place suitable for safeguarding the lives of the Tasmanians but because it was out of the way. Flinders Island was the prototype of the multi-purposed institution—asylum, hospital, training centre, school, agricultural institution, rationing centre, pensioners' home, prison—which was for so long to be assumed to be suitable for Aborigines. It should pay for itself as soon as possible; it should be out of the way of those interested in economic development. A serious attempt to safeguard the welfare of the inmates would have been an enormously complex task, especially in view of the need for real knowledge of the cultural issues involved.

[60] Ibid., p. 225.
[61] Crowther, 'The Passing of the Aboriginal Race'.

EASTERN FRONTIERS: NEW SOUTH WALES

The attempt in this early experiment to establish so lightly another whole way of life for the conquered reveals an innocence of the consequences; with an unacknowledged wish to be rid of the whole matter as cheaply and with as little fuss as possible. It would be comforting to believe that such motives no longer affect practices in Aboriginal administration.

At one stage Robinson's son was left in charge. He reports a ship's visit, in March 1829, which left further disease behind; there were eight deaths in five days. Those affected would leave the houses and go into the bush.

> It would be impossible to describe the gloom which prevails ... from the bereavement of so large a portion of their kindred and friends, and the anxiety they evince to leave a spot which occasions such painful reminiscences is hourly increasing ... the males ... attenuated forms ... proves them to be the greatest sufferers, and that the island has been a charnel house for them.[62]

The habit of leaving the Aborigines out of measures to promote and safeguard public health may be justified, if only on practical grounds, so long as they are living their own separate lives in their own way. But the establishing of special institutions creates new areas of responsibility, which were to be largely disregarded for a long time, irrespective of the finances and skills available. So long as both were in short supply, the priority of such institutions was inevitably very low indeed.

THE PORT PHILLIP PROTECTORATE

The Port Phillip Protectorate was an attempt to adapt colonial administration to the circumstances of Australian land settlement. On the recommendation of the Select Committee of the House of Commons of 1836-7, it was established in January 1838. (The date of the Slave Emancipation Act was 1834; and the Aborigines Protection Society, whose reports and recommendations were to irritate the 'practical' men on Australian frontiers for the remainder of the century, issued its first report in May 1838.)[63]

The Select Committee showed an appreciation of the likely long-term

---

[62] Ibid., p. 155—G.A. Robinson Junior, Report, 29 March 1839.

[63] I am indebted for this reminder to an essay by N.M. Carlyon, G.A. Robinson—Chief Protector (B.A. (Hons.), University of Melbourne, 1960). The authority on this period is Edmund J.B. Foxcroft, *Australian Native Policy: Its history especially in Victoria.* I am also indebted to Dr Diane Barwick for research work undertaken for this project. The material I wish to acknowledge here is (re-written) ch. 2 of *A Little More than Kin* (Ph.D. thesis, Department of Anthropology, Institute of Advanced Studies, Australian National University, 1963).

effects of the relationships which had been developing with indigenous peoples along the frontiers of Empire. It expressed also the confidence that the British Empire had great blessings to bestow, prominent among which was the revelation of Christianity. 'He Who had made Great Britain what she is will inquire at our hands how we have employed the influence He has lent to us in our dealings with the untutored and defenceless savage. . . .'[64] Along with this went a shrewd assessment of what the advantages of the goodwill of native peoples might be worth in the long run: 'setting aside all consideration of duty, a line of policy, more friendly and just towards the natives, would materially contribute to promote the civil and commercial interests of Great Britain'.[65]

With respect to the developments in New South Wales and Western Australia, the Committee noted the inconsistency of practices which had been reported. On the one hand the Aborigines were British subjects; at the same time they had been dealt with on occasion 'avowedly upon the principle of enforcing belligerent rights against a public enemy'.[66] This involved the perennial colonial border problem of relationships with those who do not know or acknowledge the law and who, while living beyond its scope, may act in areas where the law is supposed to run. One method of handling this was to treat with outer tribes, where they could be identified, as bodies to be negotiated with; to have some basis for settlement. But the Committee rejected the idea of treaties, on the ground that native peoples would be overwhelmed by the intruding power. What this amounted to in Australia was *laissez-faire* in practice; while in theory lawbreaking by Aborigines and others would be dealt with by the courts.

Round Port Phillip, settlement produced the same social ingredients as elsewhere. People who took up land on this and other Australian frontiers had to worry about the Lands Department, but not about Aborigines as 'owners'. They did not, as in most colonies, have to go through a form of purchase or get 'natives' to make marks on documents. No relationship was legally established between Aboriginal groups and the land they had occupied. No groups (other than the conjugal family) were dealt with legally as social entities—perhaps because Aborigines generally moved in small extended family groups. Had there been a government-recognised political entity, with which the government

[64] *P.P.* (H. of C.), 1837, no. 425—Select Committee on Aborigines (British Settlements)—quoted Carlyon, G.A. Robinson, p. 76.
[65] Ibid., p. 5.
[66] Ibid., p. 83.

EASTERN FRONTIERS: NEW SOUTH WALES 55

and others dealt and bargained, there could have been a continual process of adjustment to new and changing conditions in a sequence of generations. The political-social group might have had a minimum of protection in law, a legal personality which could be advised or which might have its own 'internal' law and custom recognised, at least in limited areas of conduct. The complete legal atomisation of Aboriginal society into individuals, assumed or exhorted to act and react in the manner of 'reasonable' Europeans, may partly explain consistent failure of administration.

The Protectorate was the first organisation planned for protection. There had been the more or less *ad hoc* arrangements which had enabled a few officials to preside formally over the last days of the Tasmanians, and the appointment of Robinson as Chief Protector at Port Phillip marked the continuity. Governor Bourke had appointed his Crown Land Commissioners as Protectors in 1837, but the Port Phillip experiment was to be an organisation with a positive role and full-time staff. It was established by executive fiat through an instruction to Gipps in January 1838. This by-passing of the New South Wales legislature did not help to win settler support, especially as the costs were to be met from colonial funds.

Only three years before, John Batman, who had tried to compete with Robinson in conciliation in Van Diemen's Land, had on his own account and for his own gain, in an attempt to influence the government, recognised land rights of particular 'tribes' in the Port Phillip area with his gifts of trifles and with treaties which were officially repudiated. Settlement involved overlanding stock from the Sydney area—and inter-racial feuding along the stock routes, similar to that along the Murray to Adelaide. Captain Lonsdale, the police magistrate, was instructed to protect the Port Phillip Aborigines, and 'to settle them in a village where they could be taught to work in return for rations and clothing.'[67] They were to be gently restrained, when necessary, and to be told that they were subject to the laws of England.[68]

At the beginning of 1837 the Church Missionary Society set up the Yarra mission and by the end of that year had thirty-six children in school. But by the beginning of 1839 there were none, and Langhorne, the missionary, had come to the conclusion that it was hopeless to plan for village settlement. When he recommended more gradual change, and the encouragement of hunting, he was rebuked officially.

[67] Diane Barwick, A Little More Than Kin, p. 9.
[68] Carlyon, G.A. Robinson, p. 28—Lonsdale's registry book.

Robinson, as Chief Protector, had four protectors on his staff. Each was to persuade Aborigines in his area to settle down to a life of farming. In the meantime he was to move with them, learn the language, and as far as he could to protect them from encroachments on their property, from cruelty and injustice: he was to make representations on their behalf through the Chief Protector. There was a basic contradiction between the duties of protectors and the situations in law. How, for instance, was the Protector to work effectively to save Aboriginal property while the land itself, the very basis of the social order, could be legally settled and its complete use made over to a white settler?

In this respect the Protectorate foreshadowed the small State organisations established later in the century, with neither means nor power, often to work in direct opposition to the whole trend of government policy if they were to work at all; and to be the repositories of the whole range of unsolved Aboriginal welfare problems. Settlers might in practice take the land and shoot the opposition; but the office of Protector indicated that administratively all was well: for the Protector would 'watch over the rights and interests of natives, protect them as far as he can by his personal exertions and influence, from any encroachments on their property, and from acts of cruelty, oppression or injustice' etc.[69] Major activities of government can still directly decrease Aboriginal welfare and rights, while at the same time these are to be actively promoted by a small department or sub-department of the same government. Thus government so promotes economic development as to destroy Aboriginal welfare—and retains some illusion that Aboriginal welfare is being attended to by 'experts'.

Yet the Protectorate had certain powers. An important one was the demarcation of lands for use by the Aboriginal settlers; and this had a priority above the pastoral leasehold. Each Protector had a district from which Aborigines would finally be settled, and he had vague powers to issue food and clothes as required. The district of William Thomas extended from Western Port to Gippsland. He removed white settlers from his headquarters at Narre Warren; this station was abandoned in 1843. Edward Parker had the Loddon District, which extended from there to the Murray and included the Mallee. For the site of his head station at Mount Franklyn he took over part of a squatting leasehold: the total devoted to Aboriginal needs was over 40,000 acres at this 'Jim Crow Station'. By 1844 there were sixty-six permanent residents, while others would call for rations and medical aid. Ten years later the numbers

[69] Ibid.—Glenelg to Gipps, 31 January 1838.

EASTERN FRONTIERS: NEW SOUTH WALES   57

were smaller, and a local settler reported that 'nearly all the tribes in this district are dead'. The station outlasted the Protectorate; and the remnants were in 1864 transferred to Coranderrk.[70] The reserve itself had been reduced to 112 acres by 1858.

The Geelong District extended to the South Australian border. The Protector, C.W. Sievewright, established a depot at Mount Rouse: inter-racial feuding went on, with the whites complaining that the Protector's presence encouraged the Aborigines. He resigned in 1842. Mount Rouse was a depot for medicines until 1849 but was alienated for white settlement in 1851.[71]

A reserve of fifty square miles was established for the Goulburn headquarters, where James Dredge issued supplies to occasional visitors till he resigned in 1840. His successor, W. Le Soeuf, resigned two years later. The aged and ill, who could get rations, were ready to settle; the others not, but would create trouble when their demands were refused. For nine years after 1842 medical care was available, but the reserve was revoked before 1858.[72]

The establishment of the reserves did not mean that Aborigines had shown a tendency to 'settle down'. In fact, as settlement with stock increased and the game became more scarce, they had to move more rapidly than ever to maintain their food supplies. The Protectors who moved with them had to decide how long they should do so. Should they keep it up until the nomads had changed their way of life? Or could that way in fact be changed until there was some alternative such as a settlement established for Aborigines only? Another consideration was that the longer this was delayed, the more deeply entrenched would the white settlers be. As it happened, some had to be moved, and this must have added considerably to local hostility.

Protectors were not nomads by habit or training; their administration needed a headquarters. The Aborigines were suffering from venereal and other diseases from the first years at Port Phillip; and probably now from some malnutrition. A recognised centre seemed necessary, with facilities to assist the infirm and old, the latter a category which the Protectorate may have helped to increase. The location was sometimes selected where several groups could be associated; but the bringing together of people from different tribes caused inter-tribal feuding to

[70] Diane Barwick, A Little More Than Kin, p. 11. Dr Barwick has identified descendants of this group.
[71] Ibid., p. 12.
[72] Ibid.

THE FAILURE OF COLONIAL ADMINISTRATION

increase under the new and tense conditions.[73] The strong attachment of people to their own 'country' was not fully appreciated, so that Aborigines seemed stubbornly to resist moves in their own interests. White settlers pressed in to the good river bank lands on reserves and complained to La Trobe that Protectors encouraged Aboriginal depredations.

Gipps probably depended a good deal on La Trobe for his assessment of the work; but he was not sufficiently enthusiastic by September 1842 to accept without protest the decision that 15 per cent of the land revenue must be devoted to it. This had already been the practice, administratively established by Russell in 1840: but Gipps was in financial difficulties. By that time the settlers were crying failure. Sydney and Melbourne papers were attacking the Protectors, and talking of pastoralists 'settling the problem' with guns.[74] Three months after he had approved the allocation of 15 per cent of land revenue to finance the Protectorate, Stanley authorised Gipps to use his own discretion for the future.

There had been a parallel experiment with Christian missions, which received government assistance in token of the belief that Christian conversion was essential for civilisation. In his despatch to Gipps of 20 December 1842, Stanley stated that 'the failure of the system of Protectors has been at least as complete as that of the Missions.'[75] He suggested that Gipps might submit some other plan. In 1843 La Trobe was reporting more favourably on what he had seen at Mount Franklyn; but in the event the financial provision was drastically reduced.

Gipps had approved the establishment of reserves in April 1840. When Parker and Thomas set up their head stations, they faced practical questions with which administrators were to be wrestling for long afterwards: how to interest Aborigines in property and in the settled life. Some comments by Robinson show a deep appreciation of the issues, as when he discussed the problem of rationing, which he said was 'prejudicial to the natives whether it be given as a gratuity or in lieu of labour, in the former case it induces to mendicancy, and in the latter, to vassalage'.[76]

Here were plans to make Aboriginal settlements self-supporting, and to produce all the food required. This type of program was to become common on Aboriginal settlements and on mission stations. The Chief Protector and his officers were also involved in religious instruction. They

[73] Carlyon, G.A. Robinson—report by Thomas, 30 November 1844.
[74] Foxcroft, *Australian Native Policy*, p. 65.
[75] *H.R.A.* (1), vol. XXII, pp. 436-9.
[76] Carlyon, G.A. Robinson, p. 69—Robinson to La Trobe.

EASTERN FRONTIERS: NEW SOUTH WALES 59

were the forerunners of the teacher-manager, and their control anticipated multi-purposed paternal government which was to mark so many
government stations and missions in the future. One of Parker's reports
suggests that Aborigines appreciated the significance of the battle for
the children's minds, which was to be at the centre of mission-Aboriginal
and government-Aboriginal tensions for a long time. 'One of them
complained in his anger that I was stealing their children by taking them
away to live in huts, and work, and "read in book" like white fellow'.[77]
Another foreshadowing of the future was in the tendency of the children
to vanish from the first schools at puberty.

All these measures failed to arrest the Aboriginal death rate. This was
not just a matter of killings by white men, of disease, and of the treatment
of Aboriginal women by white men. Tensions within Aboriginal
society itself seem to have increased; deaths and revenge killings probably
increased greatly with access to firearms. That the white man could
break every traditional law of the Aboriginal world, and flourish, must
have had much the same effect on the security of that world as it had in
other traditional societies. Pessimism so generated can have drastic effects
on the survival rates of children, who may die very easily where the
disruption of the established social order has been accompanied, as it
must be, by release of individuals from traditional responsibilities. The
loss of purpose and zest in living can hardly be established as a direct
cause of an increased death rate; but it may well have contributed to
other causes: in villages or in nomadic society the rate of births, and the
relationship of births to deaths, may be less important than the loss of
incentive to undertake all the positive work a culture enjoins in raising
a child and introducing him to the central beliefs and experiences round
which the whole of living is traditionally organised. This loss of incentive
was not just a matter of people suffering under difficult circumstances:
the circumstances would often make it impossible for the parents to go
to the sacred places they had to go to for the ceremonies which in the
culture had direct effects on survival and success. Loss of the ritual may
be believed to involve loss of life itself: the assumption tends to produce
the effect which is accepted as inevitable.

So the inevitability of Aborigines 'dying out' could find credence in
Aboriginal as well as in white Australian society. A whole cycle of
causation was involved. Depopulation itself had causal effects, since it
tended to limit the marriage partners of correct 'skin'. Seizure of the
women by whites increased the difficulties: inevitably children would

[77] Ibid., p. 89—Parker, Journal.

be born who could not, while tradition and traditional leadership survived, be allowed to survive. For a long time the picture of the drunken Aboriginal mother, sitting on the ground and feeding her child, has been used as the symbol of individual degradation. Its more real significance is for the loss of all cultural incentive, of the guidance of tradition, and of autonomy adequate for raising and socialising the child in accordance with rules which enabled this culture to maintain itself for thousands of years under most restricting and difficult natural conditions, and without devastating the resources.

Nor should the effect of Western scepticism on Aboriginal attitudes be underestimated. The Aboriginal has always appeared as a comic figure to the ignorant, who confuse 'civilisation' with the material advantages they have inherited: and the Aboriginal's role as the butt of the white man's jests would not be compatible with lasting confidence in his own inheritance. In the early period of contact, his use of odds and ends of clothing and his dependence on industrial rubbish for building and for other purposes tended to attract scorn and ridicule.

Like many other societies, Aboriginal society had its mechanism for population control through infanticide, inevitable in country affected by droughts. A remark by Protector Thomas in 1844 is suggestive of what was probably happening on a large scale. 'Infanticide I am persuaded is most awfully on the increase though it cannot be detected—their argument has some reason "No good pickaninnys now no country".'[78] The effects of venereal diseases introduced by the whites would be all the more virulent as traditional social controls broke down. The number of half-castes was such that one Protector had to refute the theory that once an Aboriginal woman cohabited with a white man she could bear no more children to a man of her own race.

Earl Grey, writing to FitzRoy in February 1848, suggested more small reserves,[79] pointing out that there was a source of finance for Aboriginal welfare and education and stating that more use should be made of it. The 1842 Act for Regulating the Sale of Waste Land belonging to the Crown in the Australian Colonies had made no specific provision that Aborigines should benefit from the land revenues, although it had done so for immigrants by providing that at least half the gross proceeds be devoted to the expenses of migration. The remainder was to be spent on 'the public service of the said colonies respectively'.[80] Having stated some

[78] Ibid.—Thomas, Quarterly report, 30 November 1844.
[79] H.R.A. (1), vol. XXVI, p. 226.
[80] 5 and 6 Vic., c. 36; sec. 19.

EASTERN FRONTIERS: NEW SOUTH WALES   61

possibilities for Aboriginal development, which from London seemed reasonable, Grey wrote that 'the expense attending any measures of that nature should constitute the very first charge upon the Land Revenue, a principle which Parliament has recognised in the Australian Land Sales Act'. Grey was in error, since migrants, not Aborigines, had been given the priority by Parliament. But he was quite correct in pointing out that the colony could still vote funds for Aboriginal welfare and protection from this source.

That the Aboriginal had some claim to income received from the sale of his land had been recognised by devoting a small proportion of the revenue so obtained to matters pertaining to him. Thus the Protectorate had been financed from this source, as well as half the cost of the Border Police—a nice indication of how what was ostensibly to be used for Aboriginal protection was in fact being used to protect the settlers against him. Russell had authorised Gipps to allocate 15 per cent of the proceeds of land sales to meet the costs of the Protectorate; but this proportion was not established in law or in practice, although Stanley made it mandatory in 1842 for a short period.[81] In 1841, a year when the costs of the Protectorate brought expenditure on Aborigines as high as £18,950, over £322,000 was spent on bringing immigrants into New South Wales—a good indication of the priorities established.[82]

Grey's discussion of the question of reserves had some curiously modern implications. Protector Robinson had echoed the pastoralists' assumption that reserves were necessary because Aborigines would be 'forcibly excluded' from the pastoral leases. Grey was ready enough to put the welfare of flocks before that of Aborigines, by assuming that the 'necessity' for the squatters to spread their flocks over large land areas, and to move them in drought, made the setting aside of large Aboriginal reserves impracticable. Yet he wrote further that

the very difficulty of thus locating the Aboriginal Tribes apart from the Settlers renders it the more incumbent on Government to prevent them from being altogether excluded from the land under pastoral occupation. I think it essential that it should be generally understood that leases granted for this purpose give the grantees only an exclusive right of pasturage for their cattle, and of cultivating such land as they require ... but that these leases are not intended to deprive the natives of their former right to hunt over these Districts, or to wander over them in search of sustenance ... except over land actually cultivated or fenced in for that purpose.

---

[81] *H.R.A.* (1) vol. XX, p. 776—Russell to Gipps, 25 August 1840. Gipps spent so much in the following years on migration, in the face of the depression of those years, that he could not even meet the costs of the usual blanket issue.

[82] See *H.R.A.* (1), vol. XXII, p. 417.

THE FAILURE OF COLONIAL ADMINISTRATION

Here is the beginning of a conflict of interests of long standing. Although the lease in the Northern Territory and Western Australia makes specific provision for rights of this kind, the pastoralist now, as a century ago in the south, acts as the owner when he can. The terms of the lease may acknowledge in a limited way the rights of prior occupation; but the settler quickly comes to the view that the Aboriginal is there for his profit and benefit; that when he does not serve these ends, he has no right to remain.

Grey suggested that the small reserves should be increased in number as 'central depots for the distribution of rations' in seasons when the Aborigines could not get adequate food. This, he wrote, is the practice in South Australia, where 'the success in the management of natives . . . has been greater than in any other colony similarly circumstanced'; if New South Wales did not provide similarly, it should do so. On the small reserves, which Grey thought should each be of about a square mile, there should be schools for the children and education for the adults as well. The Aboriginal should be prepared for his role as a citizen by instruction in the 'Arts of industry' and the 'elements of ordinary and Religious education'; with experience of 'mechanical employment' and 'agriculture'.

FitzRoy put Grey's suggestion for expansion of the Protectorate and additional expenditure on behalf of Aborigines to the Legislative Council. (So the issue was taken from the Executive and put to the legislature.) The Legislative Council set up a Select Committee which recommended that the Protectorate be abolished, and opposed the proposal for further reserves on grounds of management costs. It suggested that displacement of settlers from runs might 'interfere with the good feeling which . . . has sprung up between the white and black population of the colony.'[83] The Protectors were notified that their services would be dispensed with from the end of 1849. But the Colonial Secretary interfered. Thomas was retained to act as Guardian of Aborigines in the counties of Bourke and Mornington. Commissioners of Crown Lands would be part-time protectors. The Council declared that rations might be issued only in emergencies. It recommended that the Native Police be expanded as a 'civilising influence' on Aborigines.

What amounted to *laissez-faire*—the end of any attempt for the time being at 'indoor' relief in institutions, with token sporadic 'outdoor' relief through rations, and the occasional presents of blankets—was to

---

[83] Foxcroft, *Australian Native Policy*, p. 74.

EASTERN FRONTIERS: NEW SOUTH WALES

remain the 'policy' in New South Wales for some time. Before another serious effort was made by a New South Wales government, Queensland had been separated, and the problem of Aboriginal resistance had been settled, mainly by the settlers, south of the Queensland border.

Even after abolition of the Protectorate, methods of institutional relief and management lingered on in what became the colony of Victoria, which was established separately in July 1851. The Colonial Secretary had recommended to La Trobe early in 1850 that small reserves should be established in the less settled districts; but by 1853 only two more had been established—832 acres at Mordialloc, and 1,103 at Warrandyte. The new government voted annual funds for Aboriginal welfare, 'but these were only partially expended, one-third of the vote usually reverting to the Treasury,' for the next decade; of the total amount in 1851-8 of £12,000, over half went on salaries, about one-third on food, clothing, blankets, utensils, etc.; from 1852 to 1858 £11 10s 1d was spent on medical care.[84] Some rations were still issued at the old Protectorate stations at Mount Franklyn and Goulburn; and La Trobe allowed Thomas to issue food and clothing to keep Aborigines out of Melbourne. But over most of the new state, Aboriginal administration meant the occasional blanket.

It is interesting that New South Wales should have passed on to Victoria this kind of emphasis, in contrast with the *laissez-faire* and dependence on the Native Police that were Queensland's inheritance from the mother colony. Shortly after Victoria was established, it dispensed with the Native Police, which had first been recruited from the Aborigines round Port Phillip in 1837. However this 'civilising influence', before it was disbanded in Victoria, had been established elsewhere in New South Wales and in due course played a major part in the 'civilising' of the Aborigines in Queensland.

It seems proper, at this point, to look more closely at what happened in one frontier region. But before doing so, let us look briefly at the results of settlement in Western Australia and South Australia and at the efforts to make Aborigines into Australian subjects of the Crown in all colonies before self-government.

[84] *Vic. P.D.*, 1859-60, p. 204 and *Vic. V. & P.* (L.C.), 1859, no. D8—Report of the Select Committee on the Aborigines—quoted in Diane Barwick, A Little More Than Kin, pp. 17-18.

THE FRONTIER IN
WESTERN AUSTRALIA
FROM 1829

The Aboriginal policy laid down by the home government for the Swan River settlement was substantially the same as in the east—civilisation, Christianity, the status and rights of the British subject, protection of the person. Its outcome was much as in Port Jackson, although there were differences in the style of administration.

The Swan River was not a convict settlement, but the absence of convicts had, according to Hasluck, little effect on race relations.[1] Even as early as 1834 the *Perth Gazette* was complaining of drunken Aborigines and the ill-treatment of Aboriginal women. Yet, despite the insulation of distance, the frontier attitudes of the east and the manners and *mores* of the convicts and pastoral workers became firmly entrenched in the west, brought there, perhaps, by the mobile white working population[2] or ships' crews from Sydney.

Even without such contacts, the same social ingredients would probably have produced similar processes of social adaptation and change and thus similarity in treatment of the Aborigines, whatever the differences in legislative and administrative approach. There were the same good intentions by those in authority in England and in Perth, Stirling warning in 1829 that crimes against Aborigines were crimes against British subjects and would be punished accordingly. Yet by 1834 he was ready to participate personally in the so-called Battle of Pinjarra. On the Swan as on the Hawkesbury, there was a very early concession that settlers were entitled to act in 'self-defence', while at the same time exhortations

[1] *Black Australians*, p. 22. (This authoritative work provided the basis for this chapter.)
[2] Russel Ward, *The Australian Legend*, pp. 7-8.

THE FRONTIER IN WESTERN AUSTRALIA FROM 1829 65

comparable with those addressed to the Governor of New South Wales were arriving from England to treat with severity all acts of injustice (except the taking of the land) against native people: where Aborigines had to be brought to justice, every form was to be observed which would be considered necessary in the case of a white person, and no infliction of punishment, however trivial, should be permitted except by the decision of some competent authority.[3] Such incongruity between profession and practice has been common in colonial administration; and it is especially likely to occur where the native people are themselves quite inarticulate in the terms in which the conquerors converse. What looks like hypocrisy often is; but it is often confusion as well, with lack of imagination or of real understanding of the problem. The distance between the governors and the governed in this case was as wide as it could ever be. In the light of what was happening on each of the New South Wales frontiers, and in the new colony of South Australia; in view of what was by then almost history in Tasmania, the instruction by Glenelg to Bourke, in July 1837, that Aborigines were subjects of the Queen who could not possibly be regarded as aliens against whom a state of war could exist, that in the event of any being killed an inquest was necessary, can be regarded as a prime example of this distance.

When Stirling established the mounted police in 1832, his Superintendent of Natives was in charge of the force, which was involved mainly in punitive work. Hasluck points out that as early as 1833 this force was referred to in the *Perth Gazette* as providing protection *against* Aborigines and he comments that it soon declined in importance as its main functions could be better discharged by military means.[4] Stirling also experimented with an institution to 'civilise' those living near Perth. The idea was for the Native Interpreter to live with those at Mount Eliza Bay; like those established by Macquarie at Elizabeth Bay, these Aborigines were to become fishermen to supply the needs of the town. The interpreter, F.F. Armstrong, devoted most of his life to the cause, but failed to get Aboriginal nomads to sit down in one place. He later became Superintendent of Natives for the Perth area, to act under the authority of the magistrates. Inevitably the emphasis moved from explanation and attempts at conciliation to the maintenance of order in town.[5]

Hasluck has also shown how the good intentions of Hutt, who assumed control in 1839, resulted in the same emphasis on order.[6] Hutt's policy

---

[3] Glenelg to Stirling, quoted in Hasluck, *Black Australians*, p. 50.
[4] Ibid., p. 69.
[5] Ibid., p. 71.   [6] Ibid., p. 77.

THE FAILURE OF COLONIAL ADMINISTRATION

was to remove causes of friction by restraining the Aborigines. Guardians of Aborigines (at Perth and York) were used for this purpose and to modify the application of the law to the unsophisticated. This was sound enough colonial administration; and Hutt seems to have thought more deeply on the problems than Stirling.

He was the first to use the prison sentence for a term of tuition, and established the penal station on Rottnest Island partly for that purpose and partly for health reasons. He set out also to integrate the Aboriginal into the work force, by trying to get settlers to employ them on farms and to train them as workers. His system of bounties for the teaching of farming skills to Aboriginal men and cooking or dressmaking to the women took the form of a remission in the purchase price of land, which was one of the recommendations by George Grey, with whom, as Hasluck points out, Hutt did not always agree. In Western Australia, as in the east, there were experiments with mission schools.

Hutt's philosophy was one of absorption in the settler community. Hasluck points out that in Western Australia segregation came, as a 'policy of despair', later on, and quotes Hutt's view of the range of possibilities for the 'native' (the term still in use in Western Australia) to be

swept off by aggression and disease ... pine away under a feeling of their immeasurable inferiority ... or ... sink into a state little better than the slave, or gradually to be absorbed into and become one people with their intruders? The last, however apparently unattainable, is the result which in our conduct towards them we should ever keep in view.[7]

He advised Stanley in 1842 that only the settlers had the framework of an organised society (!); that Aborigines had no nucleus for a separate community.[8]

It was easy enough then for a governor to think of the Aborigines in time being absorbed into the 'lower orders' of the social hierarchy. Biskup says that in the first years, when the settlers had come to depend to some extent on the sporadic labour available from the Aborigines, the idea of conquest seemed less relevant than that of some kind of coexistence, in which, of course, the Aborigines would be expected to adapt their ways to the needs of 'civilisation'. 'The unexpected hostility of the natives, however, led to a gradual abandonment of this policy and its replacement by one of reprisal and direct action, in practice if not in theory.'[9]

[7] Ibid., p. 57.
[8] Ibid., p. 58.
[9] Biskup, Native Administration and Welfare in Western Australia 1897-1954.

THE FRONTIER IN WESTERN AUSTRALIA FROM 1829   67

Policy notwithstanding, frontier attitudes in the west very quickly became comparable with those in the east, as Hasluck has demonstrated from the diary of George Moore, who settled on the Swan in the first decade. The fight for the land was waged, with the same complete incompatibility between the two systems of land use, in the very first years. Aborigines retaliated in the same ways as in the east, by burning grass and buildings and destroying stock. After four years of this, Moore, who had originally expressed admiration of them, considered that the killing of twenty-five or more at the Battle of Pinjarra was 'likely to be the most humane policy in the end'; this became a very common frontier view. By the end of the thirties, Moore was expressing anger at the English critics of such methods, who demanded use of warrants and other legal safeguards; and by 1840 he was expressing himself as ready to undertake reprisals against those who had carried off his sheep.[10] With such background the next generation of frontiersmen would be likely to consider themselves as experts in 'how to deal with natives'. Hesitation of the first settlers in the west may have differed from the reactions of the ex-convicts in the east for a few years. This, however, was 'but the initiate fear, that needs hard use'. By the time settlement had begun in the Geraldton region, in the early fifties, those who went there were already inured to 'strong measures'; the story is of violence from the beginning, as it was in the north-west a decade later.[11]

Thus, as time went on, it became more likely that the first contact between the races in a new frontier area would be made with the gun; nor was likelihood decreased by the high proportion of the settlers, in the north-west from about 1864 and in the Kimberleys from about 1882, who came from the eastern states.[12] They came with their stock, and by this time their progress across the Northern Territory and into the lands they were taking was likely to be marked by a series of skirmishes, with the Aborigines killing stockmen and cattle when possible, firing the grass, and proclaiming their threats in frontier English.[13] By this time things had moved a long way from the days when a governor could expound 'assimilation' or 'absorption' as the most practical policy. Those who act must justify their actions with some kind of rationale: along the frontier the common justification was the usual colonial code of white supremacy.

[10] Hasluck, *Black Australians*, pp. 175-7.
[11] Ibid., pp. 177 *et seq.*   [12] Ibid., p. 23.
[13] For the story of one of these overlanding expeditions, see Mary Durack, *Kings in Grass Castles*.

68   THE FAILURE OF COLONIAL ADMINISTRATION

This attitude was, in the later nineteenth century, supported by popular pseudo-Darwinism. The takers of the land could see themselves as representatives of a 'loftier race', a view shared in the north of South Australia, the Northern Territory of that State, and in northern Queensland and, to be fair, along the frontiers of empire everywhere. In these parts of Australia, at the same time, settlers were forced by the lack of other workers to make use of Aboriginal labour on a scale much greater than in the earlier settlements of the south. After F.C. Gregory had found the grasslands of the north-west and the first settlers there received land grants from the Crown, they pressed for convict labour. But the difficulties of supervision seem to have influenced the British government to refuse. Convicts and ticket-of-leave men were not allowed north of the Murchison River. By the 1860s the Aboriginal labour camp had become an essential adjunct of the station economy.[14]

Hutt's Guardians of Aborigines quickly became protectors of the settlers' lives and property. In 1849 they acquired the additional title of Protectors of Settlers; six years later, the office was abolished, just after some Aboriginal so-called governors or native chiefs had been appointed to maintain order. Biskup lists some of the best known of these Aboriginal 'kings', who, as a matter of administrative convenience to facilitate contacts between government officials and the Aborigines, were used in many parts of southern Australia for a long time;[15] and who, as Aboriginal status declined, became the 'King Billys' and the objects of ridicule, since no social organisation within which they might have exerted real authority was legally or administratively recognised. What this kind of gesture did indicate was the need felt by administrators for defined Aboriginal groups, and for recognised Aboriginal leadership to deal with.

Hasluck described the process of changing emphasis, from protection of the native to that on order, in the reports of the Guardian Protectors, which were, he says, concerned with decreasing the numbers of 'offences' by Aborigines; after 1855 there are no further reports.[16] Perhaps decreasing offences indicated decreasing resistance to invasion; certainly this must have happened in the south and south-west. But as the frontiers were being rapidly extended in the north and north-west, where resistance remained strong, it might also have indicated a decreasing interest in attempts to apply the law to the Aboriginal case. Offences against

[14] John Wilson, Authority and Leadership in a 'New-Style' Australian Aboriginal Community: Pindan, Western Australia (M.A. thesis, University of Western Australia, 1962); and Biskup, Native Administration, pp. 59 et seq.
[15] Ibid., p. 31.
[16] Black Australians, pp. 77.

THE FRONTIER IN WESTERN AUSTRALIA FROM 1829   69

non-Aborigines were dealt with by the settlers themselves or by police through punitive measures, while those of Aborigines against other Aborigines were simply neglected. As in the east, reprisal and other shootings of Aborigines were reported as necessary action, in self-defence, or as by the police to prevent escape; while the Aboriginal who killed one of his own race tended to have his case dealt with as manslaughter.[17]

George Grey, in 1840, following his experience among the Aborigines in Western Australia, had made the most far-reaching recommendations for the establishment of a rule of law along the frontiers. There could be no peace while two completely opposed social systems competed for the use of the same resources. Grey's solution, for a more thorough application of British law to all British subjects, including Aborigines, he recommended to Russell as the 'best means of promoting the civilisation of the aboriginal inhabitants of Australia'. That Grey should have assumed it possible to supplant indigenous custom with European law illustrates the ethnocentricity of the time. He hoped to break the power of the elders by regulating relationships *between* Aborigines everywhere in accordance with the law. His argument was logical, as far as it went: that all legal breaches must be dealt with, and not only offences against the whites. For this he would provide adequate mounted police, admit Aboriginal evidence (without the oath), and provide for their representation in the courts. The last two were administratively possible: Hutt had been admitting Aboriginal evidence, and having protectors represent the Aborigines in the courts, but he pointed out to Russell the problems involved in dealing with even the more simple matters like homicide by Aborigines against other Aborigines in the bush.[18] The exchange is interesting as illustrating both the practical absurdity of the assumptions on which the frontier situation was being currently handled in each colony and the dilemma already referred to—that unless the law is assumed to apply to all, there can be no restraint to prevent crimes against those who are excluded. One act against the principles of Christendom and western law and morality would seem to involve a whole series of such acts; and the first had been the conquest and complete dispossession of an 'unoffending people'. Hutt saw the point, and asked Russell what there would be to prevent an Aboriginal suing for recovery of land taken from his group and granted to a settler.[19]

Grey's approach was to discount native custom altogether; which

[17] Ibid., pp. 125 and 131-2.
[18] Ibid., pp. 127-8; see also ch. 9, below.
[19] Hutt to Russell, 10 July 1884—ibid., pp. 128-9.

70 THE FAILURE OF COLONIAL ADMINISTRATION

shows how little understood was the tenacity of human groups in adhering to the bases of social relationships which bind them and which give life its enjoyment and meaning. It resembles the approach of the missionaries at that time and for a long time afterwards in Australia: to break the power and limit the influence of the old men, by disrupting the process of indigenous education which passed on the culture from old to young, so that Christian teaching and literacy might replace them. In the century or so since Grey made his recommendations, much more has been learned of the nature of human societies: of the fallacy of applying unitary standards of civilisation and morality and of the resistances to social and political change when the people concerned have not been charmed and enthralled by the encroaching culture. There may well be some problems for which no administrative solution exists. No solution has been found in the meantime for the problem tackled by Grey, in spite of the efforts made since then in the various parts of the colonial world.

In Western Australia there were some attempts to apply the principles of universal law; and a few Aborigines were hanged for the murder of other Aborigines in the fifties. This was after Hutt's time; though Hasluck may well be right when he argues that anything less would make the killing of an Aboriginal look like that of a person of small account, it is also possible that the juries which in time dealt with such cases as manslaughter were influenced by some appreciation of Aboriginal custom, which made killings in certain cases absolutely mandatory on particular persons. In other cases, they acted on the 'principle' that the only good native is the dead native.

After 1859, only the Western Australian policy remained a matter for the Colonial Office and, because the matter of Aboriginal affairs was specially reserved to the Governor in the Constitution Act of 1889, continued so until April 1898.[20] This prolonged control was one reason, no doubt, why there was always some attempt, at least, to go through the motions of legality as the frontier extended into the north-west and then into the Kimberleys. In this respect there is a decided contrast with the situation over the first four decades of Queensland administration. But the contrast in local practice may not have been so great, especially as a substantial proportion of those who took up stations in these areas were overlanders from Queensland and from New South Wales through Queensland.

The introduction of convicts in 1850 was a factor which assisted the rapid expansion into the north and west even though they were not to be

[20] Biskup, Native Administration, p. 56.

THE FRONTIER IN WESTERN AUSTRALIA FROM 1829

employed north of the Murchison. By lessening dependence on Aboriginal labour elsewhere it may have contributed to their rapid decline in numbers.

Comparison of events preceding and following responsible government in other colonies, and of the frontier in the west with others after 1856, suggests that the dialogue with the Colonial Office made little difference. Perhaps the main one was that, under Colonial Office control, a sporadic series of reminders of the person's rights in law came to the Governor. Yet this had already proved compatible with the beginnings of the Native Police in the Port Phillip District. Whether the Colonial Office would have countenanced the use to which the Native Police were put in Queensland is another matter. Yet there are no records on which one may base any theory of whether the Native Police were more destructive of Aboriginal life than the settlers unaided would have been. (They must have been more destructive of social life, because of their practice of hitting at assembled groups.)

In the west, the initial confusion between a state of war and the rule of law, forced on authority by circumstances rather than resulting from any special obtuseness about the issues involved, simply went on. Hasluck's study is completely convincing. From the cases he quotes one can see the usual failure of untrained police to distinguish between the proper use of violence to effect the arrest of a resisting suspect and punitive action against groups which might include the suspect with the clearly innocent. Nor in practice might the distinction have been easy to make. The attempt to arrest an individual, protected by his fellows, might easily have produced the same situation as the outright punitive expedition. Killings occurred when police were arresting individuals and bringing them and the witnesses in on the neck chains for trial, generally for cattle stealing. The pioneers were often convinced (since they had to be if they were men with some degree of responsibility) that the 'one good bloody lesson' was the most humane in the long run. Hasluck quotes the case of one Padbury, a settler in the north-west of high repute among his fellows, who instructed his manager to shoot *at* Aborigines, stating that the police and magistrates had their roles, but that in each district

the pioneers and outside settlers must and will be the people to fight and subdue the natives, and the question is are we or the natives to be masters? And the sooner that question . . . is settled, the less bloodshed there will be—the less expense and the greater security to property.[21]

Hasluck also refers to settlers' requests to government that, for a period

[21] *Black Australians*, p. 178.

72 THE FAILURE OF COLONIAL ADMINISTRATION

after first settlement, a district be free from application of the law, and to a leading article in the *West Australian* in 1886, reflecting on two and a half decades of experience in the north:

As a general rule we have found by long experience that to leave the pioneers to settle their own differences with the blacks we invite them to dispossess is decidedly the most humane course and also the most effectual.[22]

By this time the hard ethic of the pioneer was well entrenched. It has been a commonplace of colonial frontier practice that the settlers hail the government officer who applies the law with 'discretion': he is the man with 'native experience'. What this boils down to is that he goes along with local settler *mores* on this issue and in such cases ignores the law. Hasluck illustrates the fact in his analysis of the case of one Burges, who had shot a 'native' and was tried for so doing. He notes that the killer's belief that he was in danger was taken as justification; that killing was regarded as a justifiable preventive measure even to save property; that shooting to prevent escape was justifiable.[23]

It has been typical of 'settler democracies' that they demand trial by jury as one of their democratic rights—and just as typical that they oppose the right of the 'native' to sit on a jury. Where the latter situation is culturally out of the question, the more liberal colonial tradition was to restrict settler rights theoretically until such time as the indigenes might share them equally. In this way the right to jury trials may be compared with the right to vote. The theory which allowed for communal voting was that it was educative in nature; that real power would not be vested in the colonial legislature until it could be shared by all, on the basis of the common roll. There is little need to stress the degree to which this view of political development has so consistently broken down in the face of settler demands, which tend to leave 'native' rights out of account. The 'rights' claimed by settlers, as British subjects, to trial by their peers enabled the settlers themselves to determine the 'facts' in cases involving 'natives' as well as settlers. Hasluck, who is most restrained in dealing with injustice and atrocity, gives the considered judgment that in Western Australia, as late as the 1890s, 'the court was a process by which [the native] was sent to gaol; not a place where he defended himself against an unproved charge.'[24] Two cases he instances will illustrate how the court protected the accused white men: that of a man acquitted in 1861 of poisoning an Aboriginal child on the grounds that the police had failed

[22] Ibid., p. 181.
[23] Ibid., pp. 181-2.
[24] Ibid., p. 143.

THE FRONTIER IN WESTERN AUSTRALIA FROM 1829   73

to give legal proof of its death; and that, two decades later, of the man who was proved to the satisfaction of the jury to have dragged a 'native' (whose death at that time was also established) by a strand of wire around his neck; the jury found that this act had not caused the death.

These were attitudes which had developed long before the far north of the continent was settled. When it was settled, in the last part of the century, there was a fusion in effect of the frontier *mores* which had been developed in the circumstances of Western Australia, South Australia, and Queensland. But there were no really significant differences between them.

THE COLONY THAT WAS
TO BE DIFFERENT

5

The colony established on the Torrens in 1836 was to be different. The Colonisation Commissioners, pressed by Glenelg, claimed that even should the colony fail otherwise, it would be worth while for the benefits it would bring to the Aborigines.

If the Colony of South Australia can be so conducted as not only to protect the natives in the enjoyment of existing rights but extend the guardianship of legal government, offer them subsistence and comforts of civilized men, win them to regular industry, and secure reserves of improving value for the endowment of schools and Christian teachers; may not colonization on these civilizing and Christianizing principles be extended without limit to other savage lands?[1]

Governor Hindmarsh's Proclamation in December 1836 conferred on the Aborigines the protection and rights of British subjects and foreshadowed punishment 'with exemplary severity' for use of violence or acts of injustice towards them.[2]

Much thought had been given to the place of the Aboriginal in the new colony. The Board of Colonization Commissioners, responsible for land sales and emigration, shared no effective consensus with the anxious humanitarianism of Glenelg or with his determination to be assured that Aboriginal welfare would be guaranteed: any such policy would have jeopardised the experiment in systematic colonisation. From

[1] Kathleen Hassell, *The Relations between the Settlers and Aborigines in South Australia, 1836-1860*, p. 7. This thesis, written in 1921, is a penetrating study of the difficulties involved in extending a frontier while attempting to maintain the assumption that Aborigines had the rights of British subjects. In what follows, I am deeply indebted to this work.
[2] Fay Gale, *A Study of Assimilation: Part-Aborigines in South Australia*—Hindmarsh Proclamation—p. 63.

THE COLONY THAT WAS TO BE DIFFERENT 75

his knowledge of settler claims and humanitarian protests in South Africa, Glenelg insisted in December 1835 that the new colony should be limited to lands which the Board proved to be unoccupied. In reply the Board offered to safeguard the rights of Aborigines to lands 'of which they may be now in actual occupation or enjoyment', guarantee enough if it could ever have been policed. Glenelg then sought a compromise. In return, the Board in its first report announced the reservation of one-fifth of all saleable lands as an endowment of a fund for the Aborigines, a promise that was never fulfilled.[3]

By 1840 there was already an Aboriginal sophisticated enough to point out that some preliminary selections made were within his own country. In the same year a few made application for land, and sixteen 'sections' were reserved involving over 1,150 acres.[4] But this early gesture at establishing Aboriginal small farmers was soon forgotten. Instead, small reserves were set aside for educational or relief purposes: for containment of a 'problem' population. The first of these was the Native Location in Adelaide; and questions for the future were soon being posed by the habit of Aborigines of coming in to sit down round the new town, especially in the cold winter months. The Waste Lands Act of 1842 made it possible for Crown lands to be set aside for reserves. These were almost afterthoughts in the development of the system financed by the sale of the land to settlers, the proceeds of which paid the cost of bringing in progressively more settlers. Furthermore, the Wakefield system of migration involved bringing to the colony a disciplined labour force—thereby completing the process of excluding most Aborigines.

Provision had been made for the appointment of a Protector of Aborigines, and in 1836 there was talk of Robinson going to Adelaide from Van Diemen's Land.[5] With the projected Select Committee on Aborigines, 'protection' was in the air—along with ideas of the Protectorate, of Bourke's Lands Commissioners who were to be made

[3] For a discussion of papers on the settlement of South Australia, see R.M. Gibbs's Humanitarian Theories and the Aboriginal Inhabitants of South Australia to 1860 (B.A. (Hons.) thesis, University of Adelaide, 1959). For an interesting comment on this matter, see second reading speech, S.A. House of Assembly, Aboriginal Land Trust Bill, by Hon. D.A. Dunstan, 13 July 1966.

[4] Kathleen Hassell, *The Relations between the Settlers and Aborigines*, p. 48.

[5] Fay Gale, *A Study of Assimilation*: 'The Protector of Aborigines who we were led to expect would arrive from Van Diemen's Land, has not yet come and . . . there is every reason to believe he will not as we understand he has a better situation where he is'. J.H. Fisher, Resident Commissioner to the Colonisation Commissioners, 1 June 1837 (S.A. Archives). Robinson was offered the appointment through Governor Arthur, but apparently rejected it because the salary was not satisfactory. See Plomley, *Friendly Mission*, p. 930 and Kathleen Hassell, *The Relations between the Settlers and Aborigines*, p. 7.

protectors in 1837, and Hutt's Guardians of Aborigines appointed shortly afterwards. Until 1966, when the title was finally dispensed with in Queensland, the office of Protector was commonly to be held by police officers. As in the other colonies, they were likely to become involved in punitive expeditions in some areas, offering their 'protection' mainly to the whites against the Aborigines. They were also the forerunners, and then the agents, of the small sub-departments of government responsible for Aboriginal welfare. They had responsibility without means: and their vaguely defined duties went so strongly against the general trend of government policies that the pious sentiments of the legislation seem no more than a form of words.

Under Australian systems of protection, 'native affairs' were dealt with other than as central to the objectives of governments. The pietistic phraseology and the objectives for Aboriginal welfare were not necessarily insincere; but it was assumed that the land could be settled and the Aborigines compensated and satisfied at small cost.

In spite of careful planning and an effort perhaps more consistently maintained in South Australia than elsewhere, the results there were to show again that these objectives were incompatible. Whether a more generous arrangement, with large areas retained for Aboriginal use irrespective of their increasing value, might have made a difference is an idle question; settler attitudes being what they were, this could not have happened. It was always a matter of the utmost difficulty to keep quite small areas of land for Aboriginal use. Where political pressures failed, settlers were sometimes willing to drive the Aborigines away or even to annihilate them.

The Aborigines again proved evasive and elusive. The attempts to apply British law to them broke down because of cultural and language difficulties and the problem of establishing identities. They refused to recognise the new boundaries, burning off the grass to get small game, as they had always done. They used sheep and cattle as game: and they soon learned to hit at the pastoral enterprise where it was most vulnerable —at the stores, the shepherds, and the stock. Much of South Australia, away from the Murray (where a comparative abundance of fish meant that Aborigines could survive the stocking of the runs), has limited water. Stock depastured round the wells destroyed game and seed-bearing grasses, leaving no economic basis for autonomous adjustment to new conditions. In spite, therefore, of a more consistent effort to safeguard Aboriginal welfare, South Australian colonial administration arrived at broadly the same results as in New South Wales and Western Australia.

THE COLONY THAT WAS TO BE DIFFERENT 77

There were three temporary Protectors in 1837; and no wonder, for this role was in direct contradiction to the whole purpose of the enterprise of which the Protector was part. The inevitable clashes of settler with Aboriginal spread rapidly over a wide area of the State, especially along the Murray, for the opening up of the new centre at Adelaide attracted pastoralists with their stock from New South Wales. In effect, the area became an extension of the old eastern frontier.

Dr William Wyatt, the first 'permanent' Protector, was 'enjoined' to afford Aborigines 'protection in the undisturbed possession of their property rights, *to such lands as may be occupied in any special manner*'— which could not help nomads without permanent villages or tilled land. He was also to make them friendly to the settlers, induce them to labour, lead them to civilisation and religion.[6] Governor Gawler appointed a committee of colonists and officials at the beginning of 1838 to assist the Protector: it resigned. He approved of another, and the formation of a local branch of the Aborigines Protection Society, in 1839.

One incident illustrates how quickly the settler-Aboriginal relationship moved into one of dependency by nomads who either would not or could not follow the old ways. Kathleen Hassell tells how Bromley, one of the three Protectors of 1837, had to buy flour because the Aborigines (already dependent on rations round Adelaide) refused to eat oatmeal, which was being issued as a substitute. She remarked that 'the first official collision with the natives was farcical. It was not with blood-thirsty savages . . . but with creatures like spoilt children. They would not eat their porridge.'[7]

The European often found the Aboriginal ridiculous in face-to-face situations, mainly when the Aboriginal was experimenting with opportunities offered to him by the European economy and culture: the situation was reversed when the European was moving through the bush. But it is the picture of poor Jacky the Aboriginal that has come down in the literature.

The demand for wheaten flour, by people who had no concept of food as storable wealth, would have been made as a right, so long as there was food. And Aborigines, from their point of view, had the right to a reciprocal relationship with the newcomers. Good wheat flour would have been part of the bargain, for the settlers were using Aboriginal resources; and protest would certainly not have seemed undignified.

---

[6] A Brief Outline of Aboriginal Affairs in South Australia since Colonisation (typescript, Department of Aboriginal Affairs, Adelaide)—Instructions to Wyatt. My italics.
[7] *The Relations between Settlers and Aborigines*, p. 19.

78 THE FAILURE OF COLONIAL ADMINISTRATION

Not only food but principle was involved. Nor would the opinions of the whites have been a matter of concern, except in so far as they affected the source of supply.

The incident, trivial in itself, indicates the extent to which refusal to engage in proper reciprocal relationships could affront the Aboriginal moral code. When stock were depastured on tribal lands, the manager was even more clearly obliged to behave properly. What from the European side of the story looked like fierce and unreasoning aggression must often have been determination to force the newcomers to behave correctly. It was also insistence on the right to eat in one's own country. Perhaps each side was out to teach the other how to behave properly and in accordance with the 'law'.

Some white sealers had been killed prior to the settlement at Adelaide, mainly when the whites took Aboriginal women without observing the basic moral code of reciprocity. For the same reason an Aboriginal killed a white man at Encounter Bay in March 1837, and posed all the problems of how to apply the law to a British subject who had never heard of its provisions and who had acted presumably in strict accordance with his own custom. According to Kathleen Hassell the question was avoided, for the time, when the offender escaped.

But movement of stock into the country near Adelaide raised close at hand questions which no government could ignore. Grass burning, spearing of stock, and then the killing of a shepherd were followed in 1839 by the capture of suspects. Until this happened rations had been withheld, the whites assuming that this would be a 'lesson'. The Aborigines would have considered it moral irresponsibility. Two of the accused were finally executed, the judge and the Executive Council agreeing that the only way to be fair to Aborigines was to apply the British law.[8] There was much earnest discussion between members of the Adelaide establishment. Some of the more thoughtful settlers were already asking whether they had any more right to kill the kangaroos than Aborigines had to kill sheep.

In the same year, police punitive action involved two hangings, without proper trial, of Aborigines in the Coorong, after the passengers of a wrecked ship had been massacred. There had been an inquiry on the spot; and disregard of the formalities and proper procedures of the law would have had no significance for the victims and other Aborigines. But it made a very important difference to the efficacy of the law as a restraint on injustice, since once an officer in such a situation disregards

[8] Ibid., p. 38—Despatch to Secretary of State, 31 May 1839.

THE COLONY THAT WAS TO BE DIFFERENT 79

his own law, there is no restraint at all. This was to be brought home repeatedly, and often in circumstances quite shocking to persons far from the scene and the frontier. Gawler, who had authorised the executions, appears to have suffered a failure in logic rather than in good intentions; but within four years from the foundation of the colony the first authorised punitive expedition had occurred. Gawler was criticised by Matthew Moorhouse, who had been appointed Protector, and was soon replaced by George Grey. Gawler faced possible capital charges for the next five years. But Grey, too, was soon to be involved in what became a punitive expedition.

By this time Aborigines were resisting over wide frontier areas, as they had in New South Wales. Their resistance to the movement of stock along the Murray at times approached guerilla warfare. Much depended on the skill in human relations of the manager of an expedition, and on his view of the 'natives'. But the first overlanders would often have been faced with situations for which there were few helpful precedents. If the indigenous people at first welcomed the invaders, in time other attitudes prevailed, especially as the value of the stock or the goods, and the apparent vulnerability of the new men, was established. Thousands of sheep were captured from one expedition; and in 1841 expeditions were sent from Adelaide, their legal purpose being to arrest Aboriginal British subjects who were suspected of offences so that they might be charged. To have achieved this purpose would have required training and a basic service philosophy administered by professionals.

Grey had arrived in time to recall the Commissioner of Police from what was likely to become a punitive expedition. The Protector, Moorhouse, was placed in charge of a second expedition and given magisterial powers. But a situation can always get out of hand, no matter what care may be taken,[9] and thirty Aborigines were shot. In the aftermath, Edward John Eyre, a person of insight and humanity, was appointed resident magistrate at Moorunde, about eighty miles up the Murray from Adelaide. He established a rationing post, and hoped that the habits of regular work would be learned.

There was a kind of inevitability in this progression, from first contact to violence; from destruction of native food supply, or of the incentives to hunt and gather it, to the establishment of either a government centre for rationing or a pastoral enterprise where rations could be gained in return for minimal labour (this made possible an Aboriginal adjustment in

[9] Ibid., pp. 63-70. The Commissioner of Police, as arranged, took command when the Aborigines attacked.

accordance with the moral principle of reciprocity). Then came the rapid decline in numbers through new diseases, often exacerbated by malnutrition. The loss of freedom to move and of control of the sacred places seriously affected the society in the realm of the man's work, which was intimately involved with places and the spirits and in turn affected the processes of socialisation and the attitude to children. In the long run, it was to be mainly through the kind of enterprise that Eyre and the Protectors in Port Phillip District were pioneering that the Aboriginal population was saved from even more drastic decline.

In 1842 Grey sent soldiers to arrest suspects in a sheep stealing outbreak at Port Lincoln, but the soldiers shot some Aborigines. Arrests were made, and two Aborigines were hanged. When in 1843 the British government authorised colonial governors to approve legislation accepting the evidence of Aborigines, Grey had the Aboriginal Evidence Ordinance passed, a course which Eyre had strongly recommended.[10] This made possible the fair application of the law; and the first white man was hanged for murdering an Aboriginal in South Australia in 1846. By this time, however, the settlers far out were acting as though there were no laws: the more relentless they were, the less evidence there could be. Even where, as at Moorunde, protection was effective and the confidence of the tribes had been won, the result was that the land came more easily into the hands of the settlers. By 1844 there was a chain of stations approaching the New South Wales boundary from Lake Alexandrina along the Murray.

In no Australian colony, in the first decades, was there so sincere and determined an attempt by authority to ensure that justice and law were established. Additional legislation made Aboriginal evidence easier to use; the language and cultural barriers made it hard to get the kind of exact information required. Killing of Aboriginal by Aboriginal should by legal logic have been dealt with by British law: this proved impossible.[11] In practice, there could be no clear differentiation between manslaughter and murder. Furthermore, British legal procedure and rules on inadmissibility of evidence could mean that someone obviously guilty in Aboriginal eyes was acquitted.

By the end of the 1840s many settlers were far beyond the effective reach of the law. The only chance of developing a rule of law would have been within fixed limits of controlled settlement; but this of course would

---

[10] No. 8 of 1844—cited in Gibbs, Humanitarian Theories, Appendix 2. This ordinance was amended in 1846, 1848, and 1849.

[11] Kathleen Hassell, The Relations between the Settlers and Aborigines, pp. 104 et seq.

THE COLONY THAT WAS TO BE DIFFERENT 81

have involved a wholly different set of priorities. By 1844 Grey was driven to the fallacy which was to be shared by most others concerned with the problems: that the best way to promote civilisation of Aborigines was to educate the children[12]—a fallacy which was to be proved such in the long efforts to separate the young from their culture, in north America as well as in Australia; a fallacy for many reasons, including the assumption that the institution is effective in socialising the child, and that the child so trained goes into a society where he is accepted as an equal. It is a fallacy which still survives today in some places. The children, in some of the institutions of northern Australia, are still being processed for 'assimilation' in this way.

Thus the situation was moving precisely in the direction of other colonies and other frontiers with the Aboriginal. With responsible government the attempt at control lost emphasis: from 1856 the protector's office was abolished and the care of Aborigines went to the Commissioner of Crown Lands. By the 1850s the failure of policy was indicated by the chaining of suspects. By 1863, when the vast Northern Territory was placed under South Australian administration, settlement had extended into the dry areas where the few waterholes meant life and death for Aborigines and stock. It was well beyond the control of government, which had, in any case, now become thoroughly infected with the pessimism into which all the efforts of the first settlements had led.

The Wakefield system assumed for the Aboriginal a role in the lower orders of a settled agricultural society, either as an employee or a small proprietor. An important part of the plan advocated by Grey, in 1840, after his experience in Western Australia, was that settlers should be offered incentives, including deductions in the price of land, to employ and train Aborigines. Inevitably there had been some such employment, as part of the process of mastering the bush: all over the continent, and ever since the first settlements, Aborigines have been used to track stock before there were fences, to find boundaries, to show surveyors the way through the bush. This is as true of the first phases of developmental work for Comalco at Weipa in the 1960s as it was for the settlers round Adelaide in the late 1830s. Settlers seem to have paid small amounts in cash. Usually the process began on the basis of the Aboriginal assumption of reciprocity: cash had to wait till he realised its potential. In this earlier stage, he was more likely to demand things like food and steel, which made sense in his own culture; and the denial of need or niggardly

[12] Ibid., p. 115—Grey to Stanley, 7 September 1844.

THE FAILURE OF COLONIAL ADMINISTRATION

withholding appeared a denial of common humanity. So, with the settler intent on making his fortune, conflict was inevitable. In the first stage it was always easy to get sporadic work done for rations and old clothing. The practice was officially discouraged for a time in South Australia, because of the anxiety of the Commissioners in London to avoid anything which could be interpreted as slavery.[13] This may have been a factor stimulating dependence on government rationing; according to Fay Gale, there were four rationing points as early as 1845.[14]

As more dependable labour was available, once the first exploratory work had been done there would have been little regular work for Aborigines: but they would certainly have expected the settler to offer food and other gifts. Aboriginal stress must have increased where stock occupied the waterholes, drove off the game, ate out the seed-bearing grasses, and generally upset the somewhat precarious balance of nature. People under stress react in accordance with their own codes of right and wrong. The situation was typical of a subsistence economy in contact with the world cash economy. The limited range of needs and desires in the subsistence economy, reinforced by the emphases in the culture, may resist for varying periods the attractions of the cash economy. Yet certain foods and weapons, tools and clothes, attracted Aborigines from the first. The centres of supply excited a strong attraction, so that those who died were replaced by others from areas farther out, which in some cases were almost denuded of people. For the remainder, survival was mainly dependent on rationing, as pensioners in a society which had little meaning in the Aboriginal system of belief.

As the Aboriginal made the traumatic adjustment to being a worker for wages or for food or a pensioner of the enterprise, everywhere part-European offspring increased rapidly. Most of them seem to have been classified with the Aborigines as, for instance, in the first South Australian Aborigines Act, in 1844, which related only to part-Aborigines. Part-Aboriginal offspring of the sealers on the coasts and Kangaroo Island pre-dated the foundation of the colony.

In the frontier regions of the future, more Aborigines were to make the transition to become regular workers (even though their working conditions remained for a long time subject to the prejudiced assumptions which had been supported by all this experience) because they had opportunities they would not have had if there had been an adequate

---

[13] Ronald M. and Catherine H. Berndt, *From Black to White in South Australia*, p. 64; Fay Gale, *A Study of Assimilation*, p. 75.

[14] Ibid., p. 76.

THE COLONY THAT WAS TO BE DIFFERENT 83

supply of other workers. This was foreshadowed in South Australia during the rushes to the Victorian goldfields.

Some of the white men [writes Kathleen Hassell] feared that the Aborigines would seize the opportunities to attack the ill-protected stations. On the contrary, they seized the opportunities to get a living by work and not by plunder. Reports from all over the country recorded that Aborigines had stepped into the vacant places of shepherds and other country workers.[15]

New problems then developed which have a modern ring; they spent their wages on liquor and this was said to make them dangerous. In the south-east, in 1852, Aborigines were minding 150,000 sheep; everywhere they were shepherds, stockmen, bullock drivers. But they were paid less than the white workers, and they were said to be unreliable: the prejudices arising from frontier contacts carried over into the employment relationship. This stimulus from the first years of the goldrushes was short lived.

By this time, too, their numbers were decreasing rapidly. In 1842 the Colonial Office had authorised the expenditure of 15 per cent of land sales revenue on Aboriginal welfare.[16] Implicit here was the idea of limited services as compensation for real property. This fund financed the activities of Moorhouse, who was Protector for eighteen years. In 1860 he gave evidence that one-tenth of the land fund had been set aside for two years but that when this revenue had increased it was decided that only what was absolutely necessary would be allocated to the Aborigines and that the 10 per cent charge was not to be maintained. According to Hassell, expenditure had risen from £500 in 1840 to £4,000 in 1854; but by 1860, when Moorhouse was giving this evidence, it had fallen to £2,000 for all medical expenses, supplies, buildings, and the like.[17] As an indicator of the pessimism which came from his long experience, he thought that further reserves should not be set aside because of the difficulties which would arise when the Aborigines became extinct.

Moorhouse's eighteen years as Protector proved mainly that similar causes brought similar results, whether in the eastern settlements, Western Australia, or South Australia. It was only a few months after he had authorised the use of 15 per cent of the land revenue that Stanley authorised

---

[15] Relations between the Settlers and Aborigines, p. 135. Her references are to the quarterly reports of the Protector, 1852 and 1853.
[16] Fay Gale, A Study of Assimilation, p. 68—letter to Grey, 15 September 1842—Governor's Despatches 1842, no. 2, p. 444 (S.A. Archives).
[17] Kathleen Hassell, The Relations between the Settlers and Aborigines, pp. 168-9. Moorhouse's evidence is taken from the Report of the Select Committee of the Legislative Council on the Aborigines—S.A.P.P., 1860, no. 165.

84 THE FAILURE OF COLONIAL ADMINISTRATION

Gipps, in effect, to spend only what he thought necessary on the Protectorate. The impetus which produced the Protectorate and the hopes for South Australia had been lost. Yet in 1848, when much the same pessimism had developed at Adelaide as elsewhere, Earl Grey was holding up South Australian achievements as an example to other colonies.[18] Where the home government outlines a policy based on written reports (often carefully constructed to conceal as much as to reveal), the result is cynicism in the colony. The instructions may be so far from the facts of life in the colony that they become accepted in time as a special form of words and part of the ritual which has to be used in these matters, for the record, and to avoid distressing one's superior officers.

In the end all the great hopes expressed in the founding years had been replaced by the belief that special institutions were needed to protect and 'improve' Aborigines, but that they would soon die out altogether. When colonial administration ended, this view made responsible government less careful about regulating frontier contacts, which were, in any case, now far beyond its effective control. 1856 saw the end of the office of Protector. The Commissioner for Crown Lands, henceforth the person responsible for protection, saw his role as arranging issues of flour and blankets and providing medical attention. Thus the aims of government had, as in other colonies, come to be limited by most pessimistic views of Aboriginal potential.

The idea of charity dispensed (or denied) on small reserves was very different indeed from what had been planned earlier; for there is a profound difference between either a communally held or an individual freehold, and the right to sit down on a small piece of Crown land. The trend was towards segregation from white contacts; and this in turn was to make special protective-restrictive laws inevitable. Such laws suit the needs of the majority as much as the assumed needs of the 'natives'. Prohibition of strong drink for them was introduced as early as 1839. As Aborigines could not stay on most of the reserves, the reserves were commonly rented to whites and the revenue used to pay for relief.

By 1860, forty-two small reserves had been set aside. Of these, only one, at Poonindie, was being used in accordance with any policy of development or social change or of providing new opportunities. Thirty-five were leased to white settlers.[19] Responsible government, and the end of colonial administration, ended the dialogue between Adelaide and the Colonial Office. South Australian race relations had, in under two

---

[18] See *H.R.A.* (1), vol. XXVI, pp. 226 *et seq.*—Grey to FitzRoy, 11 February 1848.
[19] Fay Gale, *A Study of Assimilation*, p. 91.

THE COLONY THAT WAS TO BE DIFFERENT 85

decades, reached much the same point as those to the east and the west. By linking up the new State of Victoria, where the high hopes of the Protectorate had similarly failed, with that of Western Australia, the new colony had filled in the administrative frontier along the south of the continent, linking the best agricultural lands. As in Western Australia, vast expanses of the State were destined to remain frontier lands from then till now.

These areas were to prove unattractive to all but a few white Australians; on them some Aboriginal groups came into a permanent, but so far depressed, place in the new economy, as pastoral workers and dependants. The potential agricultural lands, in terms of the techniques available to the mid-twentieth century, were limited to the south and east of the new State; to the west as well as the north lay desert.

As late as 1965 it was possible to see at the Yalata Mission, well out west of Ceduna, Aborigines of the full descent who still lived in wurlies and spent much of their time in hunting; who thought little of walking north to the railway; whose free movement through the saltbush and over the red earth offered just a glimpse of the exuberance that was once surely the tone of living throughout the continent. The contrast between 'settled' and 'colonial' Australia is nowhere more clearly to be seen than in South Australia today. Only in the last few years has there been any real effort to apply developmental policies to the Aborigines farther out, where they still outnumber the part-Aborigines.

CHRISTIAN SUBJECTS OF THE CROWN: CIVILISATION BY TUITION

6

The society planned for in Australia was much the same whether the outline came from Macquarie or Gipps in New South Wales, from Stirling or Hutt in Western Australia, or Hindmarsh or Grey in South Australia. It was expressed in instructions from the Colonial Secretary. With the exception that it recommended a special code of laws, to embody native custom, the Select Committee of the House of Commons also saw the Aboriginal as a British subject and a person in liberal-legal society. The official views were that there should be a common rule of law for all parties and that the same offence should be dealt with by the same penalty, no matter who the offender. The Aborigines were to attain, as soon as possible, all the advantages of their status as British subjects. The means were to be those which the ethnocentric member of Western society still tends to see as those by which his own civilisation is passed on. One of the most interesting features of this early period, for instance, is the experiment with schooling for the Aborigines.

Macquarie, writing to Bathurst in October 1814, saw the Aborigines as a potential 'asset', as labourers and 'mechanics' who might well find useful roles as members of the lower orders of society.[1] He had found them frank and honest, but they wasted their lives in wandering. Some were living in peace near the settlements, and giving occasional help to the farmers. They required tuition in a sense of duty, which would enable them to advance to a state of comfort. He seems to have regarded the occasional use of armed force against their acts of 'aggression' as part of the teaching process. This is not very different from the attitude of

[1] *H.R.A.* (1), vol. VIII, p. 367.

CIVILISATION BY TUITION

Stirling in Western Australia a few years later. He also believed in the necessary use of military force, as the so-called 'Battle of Pinjarra' may illustrate. Hutt, who succeeded Stirling, had instructions to

promote religion and education ... protect them in their persons ... and in the free enjoyment of their possessions ... prevent ... all violence and injustice ... conversion to the Christian faith ... advancement in civilisation.[2]

Hutt believed that only the Europeans had any worthwhile social organisation—a belief which seems to have been shared by people like Robinson and the other Protectors, and certainly by the makers of policy, and one which made it easy to regard the Aboriginal as something of an untutored child, which is a very common assumption among colonisers. Hutt was a contemporary of Gipps; where Gipps seems to have thought mainly in terms of legal equality attained by enforcement of the law, Hutt could speculate on social integration of the races.[3] 'If', he wrote to Stanley in April 1842 'the Aborigines and the colonists are destined to occupy this land in common as British subjects they ought to be encouraged to mingle together as one people.'[4]

Segregation may, as Hasluck says, have been a 'policy of despair'. But it may also have had something to do with the development, through the century, of the egalitarian society. While there seemed no reason to Macquarie or Hutt why the Aborigines and the 'lower orders' should not mingle, the lower orders and the Aborigines were stubbornly refusing to do so as peaceful British subjects: Tasmanian remnants were, as Hutt was expressing his hopes, going through the terminal stages of segregated misery; and the Port Phillip Protectorate, as an experiment in civilisation, was already an obvious failure. As the century progressed the 'lower orders' continued to share with others the contempt for the Aboriginal. And of course the view of himself held by the Australian worker was to be very different from that foreshadowed by Macquarie and Hutt.

The geographical exploration of the world could be almost complete while at the same time educated men whose profession was the administration of people with different cultures could know little or nothing of what existed across a cultural frontier. This may be illustrated by the supreme confidence of the western European in the basic beliefs of Christendom and its interpretation of reality. What seemed necessary was 'advancement in civilisation', which appears to have been interpreted as increases in comfort and safety for the person, with the habits of sober

[2] Hasluck, *Black Australians*, p. 57.
[3] See p. 66, above.
[4] Quoted ibid., p. 58.

THE FAILURE OF COLONIAL ADMINISTRATION

industry, especially in agriculture; conversion to Christianity; and conformity with British law.

For Christians at that time 'welfare' for non–Christians meant conversion: it did not mean the right of free men to decide what they wanted to do, and then to find opportunities to do it. The historian–archaeologist D.J. Mulvaney has placed this period in its European setting and against the background of attitudes going back to the first settlements in the New World and to the speculation on whether the 'Indians' were also descendants of Adam.[5] Philosophy had already placed the Aboriginal in human society, perhaps even in God's plan, before the theories of Darwin and Huxley were popularised to justify colonial ethics. But there was also the need to save souls; and this, with the conviction of Aboriginal inferiority, ensured that his lot would be tuition, often with emphasis on the next world rather than on participation in such activities as might challenge him to share new wealth.

Mulvaney argues that before *The Origin of Species* was published in 1859 Mosaic chronology was 'the most fundamental limiting factor' in speculation and research into Aboriginal life.

As all varieties of men had developed since Adam, practically no time was left for their differentiations ... As only six thousand years had passed since Adam and as there was evidence of higher civilisation going back almost to his time, any concept of cultural change or progression was impossible. Instead, a retrogression from civilisation was accepted as a norm in primitive societies. Consequently, Aboriginal culture was never envisaged as a dynamic one—the assumption was that it was more complex in its homeland and became simpler after its dispersion ... It had become a truism that the status of Tasmanian Aborigines was the lowest of mankind.[6]

This attitude accounts for the earnest attempts to raise the fallen Aborigines, for the nature of mission activity, and for the idea that only by splitting the generations and interrupting the passing on of the cultural life would it be possible to 'civilise and Christianise'. But the pessimism itself became axiomatic through habit and philosophy. After the *Origin of Species*, the theory of evolution made it possible to account for assumed differences by the further assumption that the Aboriginal, who by this time had begun to appear in the local ephemeral literature as the 'comic savage' (I am again indebted to Mulvaney for the term) was some kind of relic from earlier forms of the human species. Popular pseudo-Darwinism was to be even cruder than this in allocating status, while at the same time salving consciences.

[5] 'The Australian Aborigines 1606-1929. Opinion and Fieldwork: Part 1: 1606-1859.' *Historical Studies, Australia and New Zealand*, vol. 8, no. 30, May 1958, pp. 131-51.
[6] Ibid., p. 150.

CIVILISATION BY TUITION

89

The story of Macquarie's educational institution illustrates the outlook of an educated western man at the time. In 1814 he set out his plan for Lord Bathurst, of a school for the children. Eight years later, writing in London, he thought that it had had some success.[7] But such optimism is possible only in retrospect, since in fact the establishment of the Native Institution had been accompanied with such an outbreak of guerilla fighting and inter-racial feuding that he had to call a peace conference at Parramatta, where the Institution was located; a rum and blanket issue and a parade of the children had marked the occasion.

In the light of what is now known, it is a foolish assumption that the most profitable educational approach to persons of non-literate culture is in the classroom situation; that in fact this situation, in spite of linguistic difficulties and widely differing terms of reference, can be utilised so effectively as to offset the whole indigenous cultural tradition and processes of indigenous education expressed in the parental and extended family influences in socialising the child.

In 1834 Stirling also set up a small institution to experiment in 'civilising' Aborigines, as had Robinson and his catechist on Flinders Island. The same kind of effort marked the first years of South Australia.

Macquarie's Institution was in some ways the beginning of both missionary and educational effort amongst the Aborigines. In his letter to Bathurst of October 1814 he set out his proposal for civilising them, partly through the Institution and partly through the setting aside of reserved land on the shores of Port Jackson. When all education was religious, it was natural that he should be thinking in terms of a missionary enterprise, and he remarked that this was justified at a time when the London Missionary Society was active in Tahiti. The arguments of William Shelley, who was to take charge, were enclosed. Aborigines had been sent to England to spend time in a civilised society,

and on their return relapsed into their former habits and society. They were generally despised, *especially by European females*; thus all attachment to their new society was precluded; they learned neither mechanical arts, nor manual labour ...; long contracted habits recurred with greater force on this account ... No European woman would marry a *native* ... The same may be said of Native Women received for a time among Europeans. A Solitary individual ... educated from infancy, even well, among Europeans, would in general, when they grew up be rejected by the other sex of Europeans, and must go into the bush for companions.[8]

This perceptive and humane comment contained much that was to

---

[7] *H.R.A.* (1), vol. XI, pp. 676-9—Macquarie to Bathurst, 27 July 1822.
[8] Ibid., vol. VIII, pp. 368-71. The italics are Shelley's.

90 THE FAILURE OF COLONIAL ADMINISTRATION

prove prophetic of British colonial relationships, especially in Australia. Shelley advocated a method of education beyond which very few in mission field or government administration have gone in the century and a half since. There should be a public establishment with separate apartments for boys and girls.

Let them be taught reading, writing or religious education, the Boys, manual labour, agriculture, mechanic arts, etc., the Girls, sewing, knitting, spinning . . .; let them be married at a suitable age and settled, with steady religious persons over them from the very beginning to see that they continued their employment . . . The chief difficulty appeared to me to be the separation of the Children from their parents . . .

A gallant effort it was; but of course the Aborigines left their children only as they wished, even though the beginnings were with a modest half dozen of either sex. By 1820 Shelley was dead; and the Reverend Robert Cartwright felt that the Institution could no longer flourish at Parramatta and was stressing the need to keep away from demoralising influences there those who were to be placed out in service. Macquarie forwarded his plan to replace the Parramatta Institution with a whole Aboriginal settlement, with a village and necessary buildings for a settled population, on a reserve of ten thousand acres near Moss Vale.[9] Cartwright was a Church of England clergyman; if his offer to set up and run this new establishment had come to anything, he would have established the first Church of England mission. The project appears to have lapsed on Macquarie's departure.[10]

One matter of some interest is that a government 'institution' to promote Christian education for Aboriginal children should have preceded any such effort by a Christian mission. One reason was that the convict colony, in the absence of old established Church institutions, had been dependent on the government for finance for most of the schooling available—none had been, for the first decade or so. Another was that although schooling was in the main a function of the clergy, those in Sydney and its surroundings had been preoccupied with the condition of an apparently high proportion of orphan and neglected children in the settler community.[11] An early indication is that King on

[9] Ibid., vol. X, pp. 261 et seq.—Macquarie to Bathurst, 24 February 1820.
[10] Ibid., vol. XIV, p. 597—E.S. Hall to Sir George Murray, 26 November 1828: 'The School, I believe, for the sake of a name, and because its public abandonment might be considered a blot on the Government in this religious age, is still alive and lingers; but its spirit, with that of its founder, is departed.'
[11] P.R. Cole, 'Education in New South Wales 1788-1880', Introduction to Kenneth Gollan, *The Organisation and Administration of Education in New South Wales.*

CIVILISATION BY TUITION

his arrival was impressed by the 'wretched and vicious state' of the orphans and abandoned children, and established an Orphan School Fund to be maintained from customs duties and fines. Macquarie, 'having with much regret seen a number of children about the town of Sydney who appear to be wholly neglected in their education and morals', established a school fund from the earlier Female Orphan School and Gaol Fund. By 1824 the Reverend Thomas Reddall, the first Director-General of Education in Australia, was responsible for fifteen schools, one of which was the Aboriginal School at Parramatta. Two years later he was replaced by Archdeacon T.H. Scott, who had been the secretary to Commissioner Bigge. Scott had outlined and had had accepted a plan for Church of England churches and schools in the colony, had entered the ministry himself, and returned to implement his scheme.[12] This of course aroused the bitter opposition of the other sects.

These problems may help to account for the apparent indifference of Scott and his successor, W.G. Broughton, to the call of the mission field among the Aborigines. They had more than they could cope with in the effort to provide a system of schooling. By 1833 there were thirty-five Church of England parish schools with over 1,200 pupils. There were also a few Roman Catholic schools, Lang's Australian College, other Protestant schools, Sydney College, and King's School Parramatta. There were four other schools at Parramatta; but the only Aboriginal school in the country was by this time at Liverpool. It was probably the most highly endowed school in the colony per pupil: it had only four, and the headmaster was paid at the rate of £25 per annum per head.[13]

Because of the importance of precise doctrine in Christianity as practised and taught, literacy has always been at the centre of mission efforts. Schooling played a part of particular importance in missions to the Aboriginal, because almost the only contact by missionaries which could be maintained over the years was with the children. The parents, as food became harder to get and as they had to move swiftly after the decreasing game, were willing enough for the missionaries to look after their children, at least until they realised the implications of the fight for the minds of the children in the missionary efforts to break the continuity of indigenous tradition. That, after so many years of government-sponsored effort, four Aboriginal children should be in school offered no particular promise for the missions.

Peter Cunningham, the naval surgeon who wrote after the demise of

[12] Ibid., pp. 7 et seq.
[13] Ibid.

THE FAILURE OF COLONIAL ADMINISTRATION

Macquarie's Institution of the difficulties of 'civilising' the Aboriginal, probably expressed a common view when he argued that the lack of hereditary chieftainship made such intensive efforts to educate the children essential:

Their mode of government . . . is I think by far the most insuperable bar to their civilisation . . . The first symptom of advancement in a savage body is the establishment of chiefs . . . to whom all pay submission, and to whose protection they trust their persons and properties. But here no such institution exists; might alone constitutes right; and as, consequently, the weak and industrious have no protection for their property against the strong and lawless, they have no inducement to accumulate that which may draw down violence upon their persons.

He saw the advantages of hereditary chiefs for the settlers in places like Tahiti, where

the missionaries, by securing the good-will of the absolute kings and chiefs, and gaining them over to their opinions, not only secured their own persons and property, but ultimately obtained able assistants in converting and civilising the body of the people . . . In countries . . . where absolute hereditary chiefs exist, you have only to gain *them* over to forward your views; but in countries differently circumstanced you must absolutely *secure* the young, wean them from parental influence, and infuse into them new ideas and opinions . . . We had an institution here, in Governor Macquarie's time, where the native children were educated, and turned out of it at the age of puberty good readers and good writers; but being all associated together, and their native instincts and ideas still remaining paramount, they took to their old ideas again as soon as freed from thraldom.[14]

Thus the government interest in Aboriginal education was seen by one intelligent observer as essential for effective colonial administration, which seemed to him to involve an effort to offset the results of parental influence. An effort to capture the minds of the young was basic where a policy, which was in time to become known as Indirect Rule, could not be applied. But, says Cunningham, Goulburn saw the weakness of Macquarie's Institution, and foreshadowed later efforts for assimilation by breaking up the Institution and 'quartering the boys in the Male and the girls in the Female Orphan Asylum, where, mixing with a numerous population of white children, they will gradually imbibe their ideas, and manners and customs too'. Employment by 'humane masters' after schooling should have 'good effects': but 'fixed occupations will probably never answer, for the first and second generations of these young savages, at least; the wild feeling inherent in them must have time to wear out.'[15]

---

[14] David S. MacMillan (ed.), *Two Years in New South Wales*, by Peter Cunningham, Surgeon, R.N., pp. 204-5, letter XX.
[15] Ibid.

CIVILISATION BY TUITION

Macquarie's experience in 'civilising' the Aborigines had included an attempt to stabilise some of them; this also was a precedent for later mission efforts. He had tried to set some of the Sydney people up in a fishing village at Elizabeth Bay; Elizabeth Village was made up of their huts; and he gave them a boat and fishing gear. After his departure Brisbane had the land taken over for a lunatic asylum; but, as one contemporary comment had it, the 'claims of the Aborigines or the lunatics of the colony were forgotten', and the land went in grants to leading members of Sydney society. Here perhaps one may see the first attempt to do something about an urban fringe settlement.

In 1826 Darling informed Bathurst that the Reverend L.E. Threlkeld had been learning an Aboriginal language as a basis for his missionary work; that this was worthy even though many natives round Sydney spoke English; but

it seems impossible for them to abandon their Vagrant habits, or to enter into any pursuit with an appearance of Industry ... The appearance of the Natives about Sydney is extremely disgusting; those, who reside at a distance, are a much finer race, which may in some degree be accounted for by their not having such frequent access to the use of Spirits ... disgusting excess.[16]

He forwarded an unenthusiastic letter from Archdeacon Scott, who was seeking advice on what to do and who had been irritated by the report that the Wesleyans of the colony had located in the Wellington Valley a large group of Aborigines who were keen to become Christians—in which report, he said, there was no shadow of truth.

The first land grant to a mission body was recommended by Brisbane, to the London Missionary Society; he seems also to have signed a deed granting land to the Church Missionary Society. In 1827 both grants were approved.[17] A precedent in the making of reserves, which was to be of great long-term importance, was the provision that if the project failed the land was to revert to the Crown. No one seems even to have considered the eventual vesting of land in the Aboriginal occupiers. The arrangement was regarded as one between the mission body concerned and the government. In the same year the Archdeacon was instructed that, in view of the lack of funds for religious instruction of the colonists generally, he should avoid 'extensive exertions, leading to expense' on Aboriginal conversion; that he should rather inexpensively go on collecting information about them.[18] In the following year the Archdeacon

---

[16] *H.R.A.* (1), vol. XII, p. 796—Darling to Bathurst, 22 December 1826.
[17] Ibid., vol. XIII, p. 14—Bathurst to Darling, 10 January 1827.
[18] Ibid., p. 433—Goderich to Darling, 6 July 1827.

94 THE FAILURE OF COLONIAL ADMINISTRATION

forwarded a plan drawn up by Richard Sadlier, who had been studying the situation west of the mountains. This involved effective mounted police, rationing and clothing issues, travelling missionaries, and three central establishments in the western area—one on the Murrumbidgee, one near Wellington, and one on the Peel. These establishments would be centres for tuition and agriculture. Scott was not enthusiastic. White settlement was expanding too fast; the Church had insufficient funds to promote the spiritual care of the whites; it would be hard to recruit the necessary persons. He preferred a scheme for day schools for both Aboriginal and other children; and the issue of blankets and rations 'on a moderate scale'.[19]

In the meantime, from 1825, John Harper had begun to work for the Wesleyans in the Wellington area, where there was a military and agricultural establishment and trouble arising from military reprisals involving women and children. Also in 1825 Threlkeld commenced an establishment at Lake Macquarie, where he worked for the London Missionary Society until 1830, when the Society relinquished control after a dispute with him. Archdeacon Broughton recommended that his salary from the government continue, with the use of the buildings erected by the Society, along with the land allocated and the use of government rations.[20] But Broughton showed no special enthusiasm for further expenditure on this activity while the profligacy of those in The Rocks area of Sydney was unchecked because of lack of funds for religious instruction.[21]

At the end of 1831 the Church Missionary Society was sending out missionaries to work at Wellington. Goderich instructed Darling to request the Legislative Council for an annual allocation of £500, and this in due course was granted, along with use of the buildings already there. (Fort Wellington had been abandoned, presumably as it had served its purpose.)[22] In due course the mission was established. Interestingly, the impetus for both this mission and the one at Lake Macquarie had come from Britain; and Bourke considered that the running of the Wellington mission should be the responsibility of Church Mission House, London.

An account of the work of this mission, forwarded in 1838 to Gipps by Coates, the missionary in charge, complained that less than the agreed

[19] Ibid., vol. XIV, pp. 54-63—Enclosure in Darling to Huskisson, 27 March 1828.
[20] Ibid., vol. XV, pp. 672 et seq.—Darling to Murray, 9 August 1830 and enclosures.
[21] Ibid., p. 726—Darling to Murray, 20 September 1830.
[22] Ibid., vol. XVI, p. 14—Goderich to Darling, 8 January 1831; Bourke to Goderich, 5 August 1832, p. 691.

CIVILISATION BY TUITION 95

land had been allocated and that the mission had been committed to additional functions without any increase of the government grant. Emphasis was already on those things which were to mark mission effort for long afterwards—on tuition to produce Christian citizens, with attempts at segregation until this could be achieved; on education of children, left there by parents; and on agriculture as the basis of civilisation. A newly appointed Superintendent of Agriculture was instructed to make the mission self-supporting and in doing so to inculcate 'habits of industry, order, and subordination'.[23] By this time Aborigines were employed as shepherds, threshers, gardeners, ploughmen, draymen; they had built two slab huts in the frontier manner, and some had settled down there. One may suppose that the work was mainly seasonal and that rations and the presence of children in the mission school were factors in this stability. The Aboriginal population fluctuated between sixty and eighty.

Already, however, there were seeds of disintegration. (It was to be mainly in northern and central Australia that the mission communities and government stations could settle down on a stable basis.) Land for a mission could be withdrawn when the project was assessed as a 'failure'. And already the pressures for the land for other purposes, which was to be one cause of such failure, had begun. There were now a police station and a post office right at the mission; and the ladies of the mission complained that they had been offended by the sight of convicts stripped to the waist for flogging. (One may fairly speculate here about the daily effect of such examples among those whom the missions were trying to convert to civilisation.) Coates could see that a town would develop there; and he feared that the Aborigines would be 'left as an easy prey to wicked Europeans and must soon become extinct.' Already there were special problems with the women; if only they could be left to the example of the 'female members of the mission', he lamented, they might become 'faithful wives, tender mothers, and useful members of society.' But evil Europeans 'sometimes prevail on them to accompany them to their huts, and remain with them for the night.'

This was the period when the Christian missions in the Pacific were developing the basic techniques of linguistics and translation and laying the foundations for the conversion of the whole Pacific Islands area to the 'lotu'. In the islands, the work was facilitated by the disruption which proceeded apace through commercial and other contacts. Christianity

[23] Ibid., vol. XIX, p. 304—instructions to W. Porter, 2 February 1838—enclosures in Glenelg to Gipps, 26 February 1838.

seems to have been accepted widely and rapidly as part of a 'package deal' by people who felt that the times were out of joint; that the old ways were doomed and that the way to share the material and other advantages of the European world was to make contact through the white man's ritual with the sources of supply. This was a reaction possible to people still in their village communities, and in substantial control of their destinies, whatever hardships they might be facing. As the community continued, social change and adaptation was not necessarily and always completely destructive.

But a mission like Wellington, which was a prototype for so many in Australian history, was not a village; nor even, except potentially and depending on long and stable association within the group and with the place, a community. It is quite basic that in the Australian situation the mission began (as did the stations in the Protectorate and later) with a collection of beaten tribal remnants; and that the whole concept, since the effect of government and other policies and practices had been to reduce the Aboriginal rapidly to the complete economic dependence of the pauper, resembled that of the workhouse. The inmates, or adherents, would have been willing to make use of rations or other facilities where they could, but certainly without gratitude or sense of obligation for what was theirs by right of prior occupation. That their reactions and conduct were so consistently the reverse of what the missionaries wanted was almost inevitable in the circumstances. For if in the world of the white colonist there was no real place for the Aboriginal, there was none in that of the Aboriginal for the white man or his religious beliefs, except as a convenience to be used when possible for Aboriginal ends.

The missionaries were for the most part men of good will and good faith. They certainly had to have great courage and determination. But as for the response they achieved over a very long period, they might as well have been preaching in workhouses full of brawling paupers. And as for the Aborigines, nothing develops more quickly the habit of cynical realism than complete dispossession. There was obvious contrast between profession and tuition, such as could be illustrated where the gospel of love was being preached while white men were flogging each other and shooting black men. These were exhortations to conduct which seemed so pointless that missionaries must have been the butt of the mocking humour which has remained one Aboriginal pattern of defensive behaviour. Some missionaries, confronted with this covert resistance, saw it as another indication of Aboriginal incompetence and lack of intelligence; it could as easily have been the reverse, with Aborigines

CIVILISATION BY TUITION   97

frustrating the attempts to win their children from them. In 1838 at
Wellington, according to Coates, there were six children 'given by their
parents wild from the Bush', averaging seven years of age; he was
impressed with their intelligence, which was admired by some of the
local gentlemen, and claimed that in a few months they had learned to
read and to find pleasure in it. They 'have in the course of nine months
become able to read the Holy Scriptures as well as the Book of Common
Prayer; and to find the Lessons, Psalms, Hymns, etc.'[24] But what strange
things were thus revealed to youngsters reared in the world of the
Dreaming. They had memorised the forms of words with intelligence, and
learned to identify the place in a book whose content could have little
interest or meaning within the indigenous system of reference.

It is unjust to write down retrospectively the efforts of the missionaries,
whose unpromising nineteenth-century efforts in Australia coincided
with the great sweep of conversion across the Pacific. Missionaries
could hope for similar success in Australia, but the contrast is striking.
To men who saw human history as progress towards what they believed
themselves to be, there was nothing unreasonable in persistence with this
barren harvest. The duty of the Christian allowed for nothing less than
continued effort. Missionaries were and are first of all concerned with
conversion and with the salvation of souls. Any measures of segregation
and intensive tuition which appeared to lead in this direction were worth
while. But resistance was determined and prolonged; one looks in vain
for the army of Aboriginal converts risking their lives to convert people
of their own race and culture, a feature of the Pacific story. It is doubtful
whether there was any significant Aboriginal missionary effort until
there were very few people of Aboriginal culture and tradition left;
while those of part-Aboriginal descent who in time were forced or
chose to identify as members of communities separate from the whites
seem to have shown enthusiasm for missionary work mainly within
sects which failed to secure any substantial non-Aboriginal following.

By the mid-thirties there is reference to the need for missions far and
wide, from Moreton Bay to Port Phillip, and in the new states of South
and Western Australia.

The Wesleyans of Port Phillip, with government support, established
the Buntingdale Mission in 1839; but this shared the basic insecurity of the
Wellington and Lake Macquarie missions—termination of the land grant
in case of 'failure', which would be assessed in government rather than

[24] Ibid., p. 660 et seq.—Coates to Glenelg, 31 October 1838—forwarded Gipps, 10 November
1838.

98 THE FAILURE OF COLONIAL ADMINISTRATION

in mission terms. By 1844 the government, under local pressures, and in the face of 'the local settlers' angry criticism of the "waste" of public money on the "fruitless" work,' had decided to close it.[25] The missionaries tried to secure the mission by getting a pastoral lease.

But the Aboriginal population of the area decreased so quickly that even the missionaries despaired. Benson reports in his history of Buntingdale that 'certain tribes' were reduced by 'guns, poison and disease' to one half their number within three years.[26]

When the land was surveyed, the Wesleyan supporters of the mission could not find the funds to buy it; the mission closed.

Troubles within and without may also be illustrated by the Wellington mission. Coates's request for more money and for the land grant in perpetuity was referred to the Land and Emigration Commissioners. They, in 1840, opposed the land grant as waste of the only resource 'from which labour can be supplied', since the land revenues were used to promote immigration (thus emphasising migrants as a priority before Aborigines—a priority still maintained). Furthermore, they said, the missionaries might be making a profit from the lands; and this might well be misconstrued. The basic issue was the same as that which was to bring the Buntingdale mission to a close; and the Commissioners went on to deal with the whole question of reserves. These must be 'carefully chosen so as to remove the necessity of *changing the position* to as distant a period as possible'. Pressure of local settlers, and the missionaries' own desire to keep out of the mission 'Colonists, especially the Stockmen', would of course make removal of any mission in good country inevitable in the long run, or else Aborigines would die out or depart. The government, it was stated, must hold the power to change location of reserves when necessary. In this context the recommendation meant that future reserves should be well away from areas of good land within economic range of the seaports, which was an important consideration that tended to limit the settlement of far inland areas because of the expense of dray traffic. It was assumed that supervision would be vested in missionaries; as they would be spending government money, government inspectors should look at the accounts. The proposed distant reserves should not be large enough to encourage the uncivilised way of life, which depends on hunting, but small enough to put the emphasis on agriculture. Even in the early stages when the Aborigines refused to settle down they could

[25] Diane Barwick, A Little More Than Kin, ch. 2.
[26] Ibid.

CIVILISATION BY TUITION

be persuaded to leave their women there, and the mission in time would become a place of refuge.

As for Wellington and the request for more funds, the Protectorate and missions at Lake Macquarie, Moreton Bay, and Port Phillip were already being supported at a cost of over £5,000 a year; so that £500 was enough, except that the government might establish a small force of troops to keep away persons described by the Secretary of the Church Missionary Society in London as 'stockmen and persons of that class who are looking after the cattle and flocks of the Proprietors' and by another witness as convicts 'quite out of reach and control.'[27]

The inevitability of the process whereby the mission was overwhelmed is evident. In the previous year the Society had requested that either the mission or the police post be moved. Glenelg had asked Gipps to report on the situation. Gipps had referred it to the Executive Council, which had held a detailed inquiry and decided to recommend the removal of the police post to a site eight miles away. The result was an early example of the township with the 'mission' just beyond walking distance. The local settlers had forwarded a petition for a township in the area.

It would be a case of extreme hardship if the interests of the European population . . . were to be compromised in order to prosecute an experiment upon the Natives, which after upwards of Six years' trial has proved a failure as regards the Adults, whatever may hereafter be the effect upon the children at present under tuition.[28]

Internal troubles are indicated in the mission's report for 1838, which stated that since the mid-year the number of adult Aborigines seldom reached twenty and was often below six; and that sometimes there were none at all, except for 'the young men and children who are now strictly speaking members of the mission family'. The 'young men' were probably the products of the school; they did gardening and maize farming work, but because of the drought had been paid nothing. They had been neglecting their religious studies, preferring to work for the police constables for 'trifling remuneration', carrying water and cleaning up round the houses—an interesting reminder that there was an early interest in earning consumption items, tools and cash, and that mission work could be unpaid.

All the mission could say for the interest of their charges in mission efforts was that they were 'not inattentive' when the missionaries read the scriptures to them. The *children* however, looked like making good

---

[27] H.R.A. (1), vol. XX, pp. 737 *et seq.*—Report of Land and Emigration Commissioners to Under-Secretary Stephen, 8 August 1840, and enclosures.
[28] Ibid., p. 614—enclosure in Gipps to Russell, 7 May 1840.

THE FAILURE OF COLONIAL ADMINISTRATION

tradesmen. Possibly they always have done, and missionaries were to be disappointed for a long time by the disappearance of incentives when the children realised the roles which awaited them in Christian society. As for the adults, the contacts made by the missionaries at the station or in the bush were not enough:

they need to be under Continual instruction and training like Children. If, as is almost universally asserted, [they] are more deeply sunk in moral degradation, and possess less intellectual capabilities than those of any other heathen Country [it followed that] continued energy and patience [were] required.[29]

So began the long haul by the missionaries and officials on government stations to 'keep them up to it'.

The mission at Lake Macquarie had fallen on even more evil days, and was closed by Gipps at the end of 1841. The reason was that the Aborigines in the area died out or were exterminated: as on Flinders Island, the congregation vanished. The missionary Threlkeld had to report that his years there since 1824 had proved fruitless 'solely from the Aborigines becoming extinct in these districts'. The few in the neighbourhood could not be assembled for instruction, and 'when seen in the Towns, they are generally unfit to engage in profitable conversation'.[30] By June 1842 Stanley wrote expressing his view that missions were serving no good purpose; and in March 1844 Gipps reported that he had closed down the one at Wellington as well as the Moravian effort at Moreton Bay, which he wrote had had little chance of success, having been located 'too close to the settlement'.[31]

This early pessimism about results of mission work did not of course mark an end but only a beginning, for the missionaries could work a lifetime for very small returns. One saved soul is worth all the effort. Nor did it mean the end of government assistance to missions or even a radical policy alteration. Both government and missions were aiming at the same kind of settled, God-fearing Aboriginal communities; and they made the same assumptions about the means of producing and controlling social change. These assumptions were to remain much the same when State governments later on established their organisations for protection; and the emphasis remained on tuition, with the sober virtues of the middle-class whites as the model.

So far as there was a policy, the Aborigines were being offered the

[29] Ibid., p. 619.
[30] Ibid., vol. XXI, p. 739—Final Report of the Mission to the Aborigines, Lake Macquarie, New South Wales, 1841.
[31] Ibid., vol. XXIII, p. 484—Gipps to Stanley, 21 March 1844.

CIVILISATION BY TUITION

package deal of Christianity and government protection as British subjects within the law. But the protection offered was meaningless where the Aboriginal was the victim of conquest and dispossession; there was nothing much but his life left to protect by the time the law reached him; and even that objective was not effectively pursued. With his property rights already alienated completely, there was no real place left for him in the civil law. It is an important role of colonial government, when indigenous social controls have been rendered ineffective, that its authority be continuously in use by the indigenous people as a means of settling economic and other disputes in their own society, and in matters affecting property rights and social relationships such as marriage. Very often the new authority is welcome in a particular area, especially if it has been approaching for a long time and disrupting the old system of sanctions through the radiation of new ideas and far-reaching economic influences. Had there been large areas of the south-east set aside for Aboriginal use in this first period, similar interaction might have accompanied a process of social change, with erosion rather than wrecking of custom within the Aboriginal area. Change must have been going on anyway, in the regions out from settlement; in fact, there is evidence that Aborigines were constantly attracted from their tribal areas to the stations. But the economic emphasis in western culture, with its assumptions of settled society, produced a regulating legal system which was often irrelevant or inimical to the interests of the Aborigines. In so far as there were native interests in particular areas of land, these had been extinguished by law; and there was no administrative point, it seemed, in trying to establish what these had been.

In any case, for the nomad even more than for the villager practising shifting agriculture, land is as likely to be taken for granted as the sea or the air is. There are rights to certain places and certain associated ceremonies; rights to hunting and gathering in certain areas. None of these was considered worthy of attention, so long as government and the churches saw Aboriginal nomadism as a benighted form of existence. There were no 'native regulations' by which Aboriginal custom could be given a place in the overall framework of law and regulations and by which rights to certain activities involving property (such as rights to use land for their own purposes) and to certain kinds of conduct forbidden to non-natives could be safeguarded. Aboriginal society was elusive and difficult for administrators used to dealing with townsmen, villagers, and farmers. They tried to deal with the Aboriginal by confining him also to a village. Policy was tied to the idea of tuition to change the habits of people who had been so 'settled'.

THE FAILURE OF COLONIAL ADMINISTRATION

Aboriginal social organisation was for very different purposes. When these became impossible, it rapidly disintegrated. Here the new government was not welcomed as offering solutions for a society in crisis, as governments and the mission theocracies sometimes were in the Pacific Islands. Nor could it appear as a restraining and protecting force so long as its agents were involved in conquest and it failed to punish white men for killing and robbing the black.

The contrast of what white men did with what white men taught in the missions would be clear enough. The method of teaching, and the content, assuming as it did the background of the English village, could have little meaning for the children who were left, perhaps to suit for a while the convenience of their parents. But for those Aborigines who thought seriously about it, there must have been something typical and repulsive in the concentration on torture on the Cross. There was plenty of torture in these years wherever there were white men, much of it dealt out to other inferior white men.

The Aboriginal who tried to maintain his Law fought the missionary for the minds of his children. The missions attempted to split the generations and wreck the traditional pattern of socialisation in order to save the soul of the child. It is notable that activities of the cargo cult type have not marked the Aboriginal reaction—perhaps because Aboriginal religion was more than a technology for material advantage and power.

These early policy objectives remain, essentially, in current official formulation and execution of the assimilation policy. There is no provision made for indeterminate separateness at the will of the Aboriginal. Unless he becomes successfully a member of the dominant community he remains a failure and an object of tuition and exhortation. It proved quite possible to leave him, suspended as it were, in this contradictory situation, where the facts of his rapid obliteration conflicted glaringly with the policy of promoting his participation. Commonly, the results were put down to his low performance and intelligence.

The wish that he might merge into the population was a wish to end an intractable problem, the solution of which otherwise would be costly in land, which might have to be given back. But already, by the mid-century, people had become used to the idea that the Aboriginal was dying out rapidly in a particular area. This was a state of mind ripe for the popularised Darwinism of the second half of the century: Aborigines were dying out because of some providential law of nature; the phenomenon illustrated what happened when an inferior race met a superior race. Such ideas of racial superiority justified what white men did as

CIVILISATION BY TUITION

they carried their burdens among the Africans and Asians. Especially did they seem relevant to those who now thought of themselves as the rightful inheritors of the land in Australia, and of the Aboriginal as the last relic of some earlier form of man, while the white Britisher was the last fine flower of evolution and culture. An aura of pseudo-philosophic melancholy was allowed to settle over the facts of murder, starvation, disease, and exploitation. The way had been prepared for those who spoke of the passing of the Aboriginal and the need to smooth (as cheaply as possible) his dying pillow—and for the quiet bowdlerisation of the whole story in the folk histories of the frontier.

This in turn was to lead to administration without hope; to the setting up of establishments where the assumption of 'disappearance' of the 'full-blood' was quite compatible with day-to-day administration. The same basic pessimism marked the efforts of the Christian missions. The Aboriginal would never amount to anything and he would not be here long enough anyway; and by the time the question began to be seen as one of minor national importance, it was essentially not that of the future of the Aboriginal: he was assumed to be fading away. By then the real question, in the long settled areas, seemed to be what ought to be done with the part-Aboriginal.

In South Australia also, when other measures failed, government and missions stressed education of the children. They must be brought up in a new tradition and the sequence of a perverse indigenous education broken. A school for Aboriginal children was begun in Adelaide in 1839; and what the Protector wrote in his next report indicates that the struggle for young minds, between missionary and Aboriginal group, had begun:

Our chief hope now is decidedly in the children; and the complete success as far as regards their education and civilisation would be before us, if it were possible to remove them from the influence of their parents.[32]

In 1844 a second school was opened, for children from the Murray who had come to Adelaide with their parents into an early community of fringe-dwellers; but soon the two schools were merged. The traditional European drills seem to have been used, with Christian training: later there was dressmaking for the girls, some trade training for the boys, gardening, and use of money for all.[33] This effort by the protector was a heroic one, already in the face of prejudice from other whites. Two missionaries began to work there, and they tried to make use of the indigenous languages in transition to competence in English.

[32] Fay Gale, A Study in Assimilation, p. 83—Protector's Report, July 1840.
[33] Kathleen Hassell, The Relations between the Settlers and Aborigines, pp. 118 et seq.

THE FAILURE OF COLONIAL ADMINISTRATION

But the parents used the school, as at Wellington, for their own purposes, not those of the government or missionaries; they took their children away as it suited them. As usual, again, the authorities, including Moorhouse, sought to offset this by separating children from parents. Some of the children were taken to Poonindie from the Adelaide school, when that Church of England mission was established in what was then an isolated location near Port Lincoln; the remainder ran away, and the school in Adelaide eventually had to close. Thus did similar approaches, which assumed that the European schoolroom and literacy formed the best means of cultural *rapprochement*, produce similar results in each colony.

Children had been leaving the school and returning to their people in the bush, under the influence of the parents, as was inevitable; the girls had been going back to the bush as wives to the old men, a custom Europeans found repellent because of the differences in ages. Another threat, from the point of view of mission workers, was the 'vicious portion of the white population'; and in 1850 Matthew Hale, the Archdeacon of Adelaide, with assistance from the Land Fund, set out to establish an institution which would save the children from both threats and 'lead them by degrees into habits of industry and a more settled mode of life'.[34]

This was the establishment at Poonindie which began with fourteen children who had 'graduated' from the Adelaide school. It was a forerunner of two institutions round which Aboriginal administration, in the closely settled areas of South Australia, was to be organised for a century. It was self-contained, as far as possible, with the emphasis on peasant labour and Christian instruction. But the same chain of events as occurred at other mission institutions was to be repeated at Poonindie. Agricultural and pastoral work were well established by the time that Hale left at the end of the colonial period in 1856. There was the same talk of penitence and saving of souls; adults had been baptised. But there were only three births in the first seven years, and twenty-nine deaths up to 1856 from the sixty-seven who had come from Adelaide and others from Port Lincoln. Pulmonary infection seems to have been common.[35] The effort had been 'successful' in all ways but one: those on whose behalf it had been undertaken were rapidly dying out. This could be borne by men of conscience if they had been assured that at least the souls of a dying race could be saved. 'I would rather', said the Bishop of Adelaide in 1860,

[34] Ibid., p. 121.
[35] Ibid., pp. 137 *et seq.*

CIVILISATION BY TUITION

'they die as Christians than drag out a miserable existence as heathens. I believe that the race will disappear either way'.[36]

The Chief Secretary said in Parliament in 1858 that even Poonindie had failed; that the Aboriginal could not be civilised and that when the attempt was made he lost the power to reproduce.[37] In 1858 the grant for Poonindie was reduced by half.

Private interest was tenacious among at least a few. The Aborigines Friends Association, which had been established in 1858, with a grant from Parliament of £500, obtained a grant of land at Point Macleay, and in 1859 the Reverend George Taplin, one of the most remarkable and devoted managers of Aboriginal missions, set to work to found there an institution which still survives as a government station. Poonindie and Point Macleay pointed the way for future policy, and as South Australian settlement extended into the dry lands north and west, welfare had long replaced any consideration of rights. Sparse rations and the annual blanket represented the main government effort for the rest of the century, except for any assistance given to missions. In 1868 Point Pearce mission was established on Yorke Peninsula. The Lutherans and the Moravians were beginning their work in the desert country.

From the earliest times the missions depended mainly on government support, with some from the congregations in England (little being available from sparse settler communities). This raises the question of why the internationally financed missions made so little effort in Australia. One noted exception, in the period of early settlement, was the establishment of a mission at New Norcia, some eighty miles or so north of Perth, by the Benedictines from Spain. It has maintained a continuity from then till now, and since 1907 has been the headquarters for the daughter mission at Kalumburu, on the Drysdale River.

Other efforts, such as that of the Moravian Mission, were shorter lived. Much later, for instance, the founder of the Neuendettelsau Lutheran Mission, Johann Flierl, was working in Queensland before the German government established a Protectorate in New Guinea; but he then transferred his mission, and the support of the Neuendettelsau parishioners, to Finschhafen. There was the founding of the famous Lutheran mission at Hermannsburg: but this, though it is the only mission with a history comparable with that of New Norcia, did not have the independence which came with the financial support of an order like the

---

[36] *S.A.P.P.*, 1860, no. 165—Report of the Select Committee of the Legislative Council on the Aborigines—quoted in Fay Gale, *A Study in Assimilation*, p. 93.
[37] Kathleen Hassell, *The Relations between the Settlers and Aborigines*, p. 157.

Benedictines. On the other hand, it pioneered work in the native tongue, in the true international tradition.

The monastery and chapel at New Norcia are in the overseas Spanish style to be seen in the Caribbean. This must have been an incipient town in the fashion of Ponce or Magaguay or San German. Perhaps its development was arrested by discouragement in the task of building a viable Christian community. Of the forty or fifty pisé houses which constituted the Aboriginal village at the height of the mission's success, a few ruins remain today, dominated by school buildings, some of which are used for non-Aboriginal children. A century ago, this mission was pioneering the technical and commercial education of the Aboriginal; and Aborigines from here held skills which are still rare among part-Aborigines. A close study of its history would be rewarding. Today there are a few houses inhabited by part-Aborigines, a quarter mile or so from the main cluster of buildings. It is still policy, according to the Lord Abbot, to employ no one else on the mission lands. But, he said, they lack basic skills with farm machinery and are unreliable in attendance, so that others have to be employed as well.[38]

Those who explain human 'failure' by race or culture will find support in such a denouement. But one may guess that the mission shelter could not be adequate in the conditions of any Australian colony, for no matter how sincere the administrators of institutions like this one, the Aborigines could be no more than institutional paupers; and the social and administrative pressures tended over long periods to smash the indigenous social structure. No mission effort to the Aboriginal has been so long sustained, and possibly none for a more meagre continuing reward. Missions in Australia did not produce communities which might found indigenous churches. Yet the real results of this work cannot be measured, if one assumes that the individual, in his own lifetime, is an end in himself.

These red-painted multi-storey buildings are still exotic in the Australian setting, beside the old road from Perth to Geraldton. They are a reminder of a colonial situation which often developed, where the foreign mission, staffed with workers with international affiliations, could operate with some independence, because of the basic consensus within Christendom, as the conscience of the colonial government. Later, missions established in the north were able from sheer isolation to wield theocratic powers; but none was in a position to purchase its own lands, as New Norcia was. Therefore, in the last resort, the missions could be used as agents of government policy.

[38] From a discussion with the Abbot of New Norcia, 19 August 1966.

CIVILISATION BY TUITION   107

Missions have maintained a continuing, even if sporadic, criticism of government policies. But lacking the hitting power which financial independence gives, though they have been often most courageous, they had been generally ineffective.

RACE RELATIONS—
A CLOSER LOOK

By 1840 the frontier in New South Wales was advancing in every direction. By the end of the thirties sheep were being depastured up through the New England plains and the Darling Downs, the experienced settlers, well aware of transport costs, tending to divert through the ranges and down to the coast, even with sheep, because the distance from shipping facilities limited the profits to be won and dray transport was slow and very expensive.

THE CLARENCE RIVER, 1840-1860

The Clarence River stations established just before and after 1840 typify the larger enterprises, and were staffed largely by assigned servants.[1] There were a few skilled workers (such as bootmakers) who were in great demand and likely to receive incentive cash payments; but, in the main, employees were shepherds, ration-carriers, and hut-keepers— assigned men who got their 'ten pounds of flour, ten pounds of meat, some sugar and some tea' (rations based on the old convict issue) and clothing; and who would hope for a ticket of leave some day for good conduct.[2] In March 1841 there were 347 white men on the river, many of whom were employed in cedar getting; 85 were privately assigned,

[1] This chapter is based on research undertaken in the late 1930s. The references are, unless otherwise stated, to records of the Clarence River Historical Society; the whole collection is a fitting memorial to R.C. Law who spent much of his later life in collecting and indexing it.
[2] Lectures and reminiscences of Thomas Bawden, who went as a boy to the Clarence with one of the first expeditions to take up land on the River—Ramornie Station—for Dr John Dobie.

RACE RELATIONS—A CLOSER LOOK

11 had tickets of leave, and 10 were convicts in government employment.[3]

But the transportation of convicts was coming to a close, and distance from Sydney increased the difficulty of enticing free labour into the bush. Furthermore, wages for free labour were rising, especially farther out from Sydney. On the Clarence, for instance, a free shepherd was paid £20 per annum with rations in 1846; four years later, after further general rises in cash wages, they could still be hired closer in to Sydney for £16.[4] Squatters from the Northern Districts were prominent in efforts to obtain a new type of convict labour, which led to some shipments of 'exiles' and a few ticket-of-leave men, who were subject to penal sanctions and forced to reside in the districts 'where they were most wanted'.[5] But the scheme eventually came to little, providing only some temporary relief to the squatters of Moreton Bay.

In the first decade stock on the Clarence was mainly sheep, except for the rough back country. Labour and climatic factors combined to bring about the changeover to cattle, which required a less stable labour force. By the mid-fifties the changeover was well advanced,[6] helped by the fact that the Crimean War created a great boom in Australian tallow, so that some of the northern squatters by the mid-fifties could think of trips to England on the profits from grease for the guns.

Here as elsewhere the conditions of the battle for the grasslands and water had not been such as to condition employers, already prejudiced against the Aboriginal as an employee, to look to him to make up the labour deficiencies as the stations extended, although, as elsewhere, his employment in certain tasks was regarded as advantageous, quite often essential. As the value of the product increased so did the importance of labour discipline. But discipline was hardly to be expected from the depredator who in this area had struck back hard at the isolated shepherds and the vulnerable flocks. Here, then, was a typical frontier situation. It merits detailed examination.

The Clarence first became well known as a result of Captain Perry's visit in the *King William* in 1839. He reported to Gipps in June of that year on the very high level of craftsmanship of Aboriginal canoes, fishing

[3] *N.S.W. V. & P.* (L.C.), 1841—Census of the year 1841—Abstract of the returns of the population . . . and in the Commissioners' districts beyond the Boundaries of Location.
[4] Letters of C.G. Tindal, 12 November 1844 and 9 February 1846; *Statistical Register of N.S.W.*, 1859, p. 111—Decennial Return showing average wage rates for the Colony.
[5] *N.S.W. V. & P.* (L.C.), 7 April 1848; ibid., 1850—Renewal of Transportation, papers and despatch—Grey to FitzRoy, 10 November 1849.
[6] A ledger of Yulgilbar Station (E.D. Ogilvie) shows that all but one flock were sold after the disastrous wet season of 1853.

nets, vessels, baskets; forty years before, Flinders had noted the beautifully made circular huts of bark and vines.[7] Those whose country included the Big Scrub along the river had, from the evidence, great skills in fishing and in hunting the small tree animals, in climbing the trees with vines for honey and small game. Lime from the relics of their oyster feasts at the Clarence Heads provided hundreds of tons for the building of the first fine houses on Clarence stations.

Recent research has established two main language groups—the Bandjalang, mainly north and west of the main river; and the Gumbaingar,[8] who lived in the big scrub on the lower Clarence and seem to have depended on scrub products and fish. Most resistance to the settlers apparently came from the Bandjalang, whose descendants still stubbornly adhere, in Tabulam, Woodenbong, Cabbage Tree Island, and elsewhere, to religions with something of the old beliefs—a situation reminiscent of the remnants of the Six Nations at Brantford, Canada, some of whom still profess the 'long-house' religion.

The first intensive contact was between the Gumbaingar and the cedar getters in the late thirties; when Perry got there in 1839 Aborigines were already terrified at the sight of firearms. From the material in the Clarence River Historical Society it is possible to see what had been happening.[9] Cedar cutters set up their pit-sawing centres on the banks. Their employers had depots where they stored expensive flour (costing anything up to £100 a ton and at this time commonly imported from England). The stories of thieving are of course one sided; but here began the usual kind of resistance. Aborigines would take the flour and sugar when they could and spill it along the ground, keeping the bags. The cedar getters, in reprisal, would shoot at any black skin with flour on it. The destruction of valuable food supplies, apparently senseless, may have been no more than that at first; but it went on long after the Aboriginal had learned to use them; it was one possible method of resistance. A few of these cedar enterprises expanded later into pastoral ones, with stock on the open land behind the scrub; and on this open country of the lower river extermination (again of the Gumbaingar) seems to have been rapid. The cedar cutter's licence, like that of the pastoralist, could theoretically have been withdrawn for cruelty; but the Commissioner for Crown Lands tended either to be directly or indirectly involved in reprisals.

Another side of the relationship was the use of the Aboriginal to

[7] David Collins, *An Account of the English Colony in New South Wales*, vol. 2, p. 228.
[8] M.J.C. Calley, *Bandjalang Social Organisation*, map, p. 58.
[9] Reminiscences of Thomas Bawden, W.G. Law, Duncan MacFarlane, and others.

RACE RELATIONS—A CLOSER LOOK

locate cedar trees and crooked timbers for ship repairs. In the scrub there was no complete dispossession until the coming of the maize farmers at the end of the fifties. Some Aborigines were employed at the saw-pits and were paid in rum and tobacco. They and their womenfolk would either join in the carousal round the rum keg in the scrub or be hovering in the shadows; here once again began the association of Aboriginal women with the improvident ticket-of-leave and assigned men who were beginning the frontier tradition. Usually such associations were transient; occasionally they were permanent—with all the possibilities for cross-cultural misunderstandings that ensued when the whites refused the obligations they had incurred to the kinsmen of the women concerned. The cedar men carried arms, and those brutalised by years of the convict system had little hesitation in using them. One can guess the happenings in the darkness of the Big Scrub. By 1840 cedar getters on the river always travelled in armed parties. Two surveyors who had been stationed on the site of South Grafton for six months were censured in 1842 for refusing to move out into the scrub. There was fear on both sides;[10] and the tendency among those armed was to shoot when in doubt.

The process of social erosion along the river banks seems to have been partially mitigated when the cedar was cut out. Intensive and permanent contact, with complete dispossession, came when the farmers moved into the scrub after the passing of Robertson's Land Acts in 1861, which provided for selection before survey (although agricultural settlement on the river had begun as early as 1857).

The Aborigines themselves helped to destroy the protecting brush-woods, men and women joining in felling trees and burning the timber. Some would work seasonally thereafter for employers known to them.[11] This kind of seasonal work for the coastal farmer in the eastern states has been an important Aboriginal activity ever since the destruction of the scrub. But the same hostilities developed here as along the Hawkesbury in the 1790s. In 1848 the *Sydney Morning Herald* published a complaint that residents of the 'Settlement' (Grafton) who were cultivating nearby, were 'sadly plagued by the blacks', who would dig up the potatoes as soon as they were ready. 'The same consequences attended a maize crop, and fowls were articles of peculiar attraction, and further . . . if an angry word was said to them they threatened pulling up, and clasping hand around wrist, made a threatening sign of handcuffs.'[12]

[10] *H.R.A.* (1), vol. XXIII, p. 412.
[11] From Duncan MacFarlane, History of the Clarence.
[12] *Sydney Morning Herald*, supplement, 31 January 1848.

THE FAILURE OF COLONIAL ADMINISTRATION

Here is the beginning of a fringe-dwelling community dependent on the economy of the country town. And here too begin the tensions between townsmen and fringe-dwellers which of course influenced the attitudes of the first municipal councils. Local traditions include the story of the farmer who had twenty-five acres on the site of the Grafton showground; Aborigines camped there ate everything he grew, until the usual punitive measures dispersed them with two lives taken. In the course of a few years rum, disease, loss of their native foods, and disintegration of the organisation which depended so much on free movement and husbanding the game resulted in scant remnants desperately making what they could of their vicinity to the township. To the townsmen they were a source of labour when no other offered.

Gipps's action in the Myall Creek case, just before the first pastoral stations were being stocked on the Clarence, had provoked not only a sensation but a widespread reaction among the Aborigines. Pastoral teams pushing into new lands were often in some tension. Resistance to some of the overlanding parties which brought stock and supplies to the Clarence followed the well established pattern. There was death on both sides when Forster's party was attacked on the Orara in 1840.[13] Intelligently, the Aborigines emptied out the flour and sugar. Here savage reprisal brought further attacks, on the huts and stores and flocks. Forster and Blaxland called their stations Purgatory and Pandemonium; after a few years they had to retire defeated, but others came in. This may help to explain Forster's attitude later, as a member of the 1856-7 Select Committee on the Native Police Force.

Squatters became homicidal maniacs when they found hundreds of sheep butchered. They developed the technique described by Robinson: surrounding a camp at night, attacking at dawn, and massacring men, women, and children. In 1845 at Boyd's station in this area all but 85 of 1,100 sheep were claimed to have been destroyed after the murder of a shepherd and the spilling of the supplies. The report of Mr Commissioner Fry confirms the ineffectiveness of the Border Police in protecting property and the shepherd, and makes no mention of any reprisal;[14] but extermination was practised where possible. In 1848 Thomas Coutts, of Kangaroo Creek, was committed for trial after the poisoning of Aborigines on his station; apparently this happened after they had worked on the station harvest, when he paid them in poisoned damper. But this

---

[13] Reminiscences of Thomas Bawden.
[14] *H.R.A.* (1), vol. XXI, p. 4—Gipps to Stanley, 1 April 1846, enclosure 3.

RACE RELATIONS—A CLOSER LOOK

was not playing the game at all; he was ostracised by local squatters, could not find bail, and had to go in custody to Sydney.

The comments of the *Sydney Morning Herald* on the case illustrate contemporary attitudes. It pointed out that in eight years Coutts's sheep had been reduced from 5,000 to 2,500, though 'he has never sold or boiled down a single head', and two of his men and a boy had been murdered. The crime was, it seemed to the writer, basically due to 'the unprotected manner in which the whole population had been left to fight their own battles.'[15] No evidence can be found that Coutts was tried. Two years later he took his stock to Tooloom, on the upper Clarence; but the Aborigines remembered and again he had to move, this time to the Dawson. Once again the Aborigines killed his shepherds and stock.[16] This suggests that Aborigines were developing guerilla-type patterns of resistance, at least against particular enterprises.

It has long been a minimal tradition of colonial administration that those who go into areas beyond the effective control of the government should be licensed; that this is at least a gesture at control, since the licence can be withdrawn in cases of misconduct. The fact most illustrative of attitudes in this case is that Coutts continued to hold his licence to depasture stock beyond the Limits of Location.

The reprisal sometimes had little to do with the alleged crime. In 1841, while the Commissioner was in the area from his headquarters at Armidale, a group of Aborigines was

found upon the Orara camped in great numbers. A cordon was formed during the night, hemming the camp in with the river behind it. At a given signal at daybreak . . . the camp was rushed and men, women and children were shot down indiscriminately. Some took to the river, and were shot as they swam. Their dead bodies subsequently floated down past the Settlement [Grafton].

This was punishment for theft on Ramornie Station, subsequently found to have been committed by one of the white employees.[17] In the same year J.H. Pagan, finding his blankets missing, had pursued some Aborigines and made the mistake of using his ammunition before he was within range; the Aborigines, from the evidence, had warned him to keep away, and they killed him. At the same time a shepherd was killed on Yulgilbar (as it turned out by another white employee). But the assumption,

---

[15] *S.M.H.*, supplement, 31 January 1848.

[16] Letter of C.G. Tindal; see also J.D. Lang, *Queensland, The Future Cotton-Field of Great Britain*, p. 33.

[17] Reminiscences of Thomas Bawden. Bawden was at the time on Ramornie, where the alleged Aboriginal offence had been committed.

THE FAILURE OF COLONIAL ADMINISTRATION

in the background of tension, was of active hostility. Another river bank massacre resulted, with the Commissioner's Border Police participating.[18]

The theory was that police should be used as civil police to arrest suspects; but in practice the economic system of the conquerors depended on extermination; and group punishments tended always to be justified on practical grounds. The hard lessons were in time well learned, in what was essentially warfare without rules in the first stage of contact. In 1851, F.C. Tindal, writing home from Koreelah Station, told how one Aboriginal had accused some others of cattle stealing. The result was a panic flight of the whole group from the locality, in fear of what Tindal called a 'hostile visit'.[19]

The reports of the Lands Commissioners, who were in charge of the police, varied according to temperament. The most effective of them, in the first years on the Clarence, was one Oliver Fry, a man of known courage and one who could praise the qualities of the Gumbaingar, whose country was mainly the scrub lands of the lower river, and who remained in comparative peace between the cutting out of the cedar and the destruction of the bush for maize farming. But the offences he reports with regret, in 1843 (for the previous year) are of 'outrages connected with Murder' by Aborigines, 'each equally unprovoked ... However ... steps have been taken to prevent aggressions of so melancholy a description in future. . . .'[20] Curiously, in view of the reprisals with which he does not bother the ears of the Governor, he considers the reluctance of the Aborigines to come in to the stations and work for the whites 'a circumstance rather difficult to account for, as I believe them to have been invariably treated with kindness and humanity'.

The method of individual arrests had begun already to assume the shape which was to mark it until after World War II in the far north of the continent: Aborigines were brought in handcuffed to the constable's stirrup.[21] For many decades afterwards, a crude frontier environment

---

[18] Accounts are in the Bawden lectures and in a statement of Alfred Lardner. 'This', Bawden remarked, referring to punitive measures, 'was in reality as merciful a procedure as attempting to capture them, and then to proceed with an expensive and useless trial according to law.' Commissioner Oakes had left the posse before the massacre. According to Bawden, his subsequent inquiries were addressed only to persons who were not there. All was, as William Faulkner would say, 'administratively clean'.

[19] Letter of F.C. Tindal, 29 January 1851.

[20] H.R.A. (1), vol. XXII, p. 652—Gipps to Stanley, 3 April 1843, enclosure 9.

[21] Reminiscences of Thomas Bawden. Bawden saw one in 1840, chained to the stirrup by handcuffs. He was taken thus to Armidale, the headquarters of the Commissioner, 'kept on the chain there for some weeks, but there being no special charge against him, *his whip wounds having healed*, he was presented with a blanket and tomahawk and let loose'. At the risk of being thought 'sensational', one is constrained to repeat that this practice and the others mentioned remained part of the frontier practice for a long time. See for instance the report by Roth on the situation in Western Australia in 1904.

RACE RELATIONS—A CLOSER LOOK

perpetuated similar practices, and the stories were periodically to shock the city dwellers in the south, just as 'southern' criticism was to infuriate the squatters and other whites along the frontiers. Arrest of a suspect was a difficult matter; and getting such a superb bushman back to the police post even more difficult. A development over the decades, and one which also persisted until after World War II, was the use of the neckchain —for suspect and witnesses, male and female. This was most effective against escape and was, at the first conference of Commonwealth and State authorities on Aboriginal policies and practices in 1937, defended (with the reluctant concurrence of representatives from the southern States) as more humane than the handcuffs, since it allowed for free use of the hands.[22]

Arrests could also be made by a pastoralist with a warrant; and this remained a common practice on the Clarence until the Aboriginal resistance petered out. It became something of standard procedure to take out warrants for 'ringleaders' in cattle killing; they could then be shot 'while escaping'. Thus in November 1853 one pastoralist wrote home: 'I have had another nine days hunt, I hope for the last time, after blacks, cattle killers. Two of the ringleaders, for whom warrants had been issued, were shot.'[23]

By the mid-sixties the 'problem' on the Clarence had become no more than Aborigines' dogs frightening the cattle from good pastures. When the Aborigines were seen, their dogs would be shot and their weapons destroyed, thereby making it more difficult for them to live either on the stock or the fast disappearing game.[24] The trend seems to have been from mayhem to incessant harassing of those who still tried to adhere to the old ways. The motive for 'intelligent parasitism' on the station must have been largely the impossibility of existence anywhere else; but the station in these areas was able to find sophisticated labour and would require only a minimum of Aborigines. The familiar pattern of rapid depopulation, from the usual complex range of causes, was repeated here. Cruelty may be less important in this kind of situation than lack of imagination to see across the cultural barriers. Thus in 1850 a squatter and gentleman of goodwill, writing to his father in England who had expressed grave doubts about the massacres and their effects, said that

[22] Commonwealth of Australia, *Aboriginal Welfare: Initial conference of Commonwealth and State Aboriginal Authorities*, April 1937, pp. 31-2.
[23] Letter of C.G. Tindal dated 5 November 1853.
[24] Memorandum of W.A.B. Greaves, of Newbold Station, 16 January 1867, also published in the 1930s in the Grafton *Daily Examiner*: 'Rode to MacFarlane's and the Mares' Run. Saw very few cattle, as blacks were camped on river bed. Killed eight or ten puppy dogs, and fired boomerangs and sticks. Blacks ran away.'

In most parts of the colony, and certainly on the Clarence, the natives are much better off as regards food than they were in former days. At the same time, I must own that their numbers are decreasing, but that is owing to other causes [than the massacres].[25]

The only hope for the survival of the Aboriginal was some kind of agreed settlement to end hostilities, leaving at least some place where he could live. This had to some extent been achieved in the north American situation with the tradition of recognising 'nations' and making treaties which left some lands. And not all the settlers had the imaginative block which prevented them from attempting the parley and peace making. One of the basic difficulties such men faced was the absence of a hierarchical power organisation in Aboriginal society. In practice, the settling of survivors into some recognised 'camp' area on the station went part of the way. This, however, has always been mainly a place to live while some work for rations, and a base from which Aborigines might move out to hunt so long as game remained. The size and permanence of this remnant, unless the pastoral licence contained special and policed provisions for the limited rights of the Aborigines, reflected to some extent the need for labour, as well as the humanity of the pastoralist.

One man so distinguished on the Clarence, among the first settlers, was E.D. Ogilvie of Yulgilbar; and there is a direct result of his actions in the fact that a number of persons of Aboriginal descent still live round Baryulgil, close to his head station of Yulgilbar. His father, at Merton in the Hunter River valley, had taught him his interest in the native languages; in the aftermath of the Pagan reprisals he had taken Pundoon, a young boy, and learned the Bandjalang language. He participated in other reprisals, but looked beyond them. Returning from such an expedition to the head station, some time prior to July 1842, he found a woman with a child of about five, and another at the breast.

They cried out in great fear, and upon our coming close, the woman took the infant from her shoulders, and . . . threw herself upon her knees, and bowed her face to the ground . . . the other child crouched at her side, and hid its face in the grass.

But instead of expected death, they heard their own tongue, 'which I learned from a young boy called Pundoon, who was taken in one of the encounters . . . I addressed the woman, telling her not to fear'. They called the warriors who were hunting over the hill; two appeared above them; one of them cried

Begone! And take away your horses; why do you come hither among the mountains

[25] Letter of C.G. Tindal, 12 July 1850.

RACE RELATIONS—A CLOSER LOOK

to disturb us? Return to your houses in the valley, you have the river and the open country, and you ought to be content; leave the mountains to the black people.

Unarmed, Ogilvie approached him; arms were laid down; Ogilvie's brother presented a tomahawk to Toolbillibam, the spokesman; others approached, among them Pundoon's father. Edward Ogilvie told them that the white men wanted the grass, 'and would leave them their kangaroos, their opossums and their fish. Toolbillibam here interposed, to know if we would not leave them their honey also.' This was promised as well as other small game. Aborigines were to be given bread when they visited the outstations and a tomahawk each if they kept the peace; when they visited the outstations they were to 'walk up openly, and give notice of their approach', not 'sneak from tree to tree'.

To the readers of the *Sydney Herald*, to whom he sent the story, Ogilvie apologises for this fascinating detail; otherwise

I could not have [shown] . . . the very placable disposition and unrevengeful spirit of these people, and . . . convince those who are in the habit of looking upon them as little better than wild beasts that they are mistaken.[26]

The tendency to negotiate continued: Ogilvie's reprisals were not merely homicidal. After thefts of flour and blankets in 1845 he took a prisoner, who escaped (without being shot). 'The blacks all agreed that they should be punished for stealing; but the chief said that he had beaten the man already, and that was enough.'[27] The profound disruption of Aboriginal *mores* reflected in either the giving, or the idea, of such punishment is worth a note in passing: this was indeed forced adaptation.

But by 1850 this phase of extermination was passing on the lower Clarence (though it continued in the back country), and some shepherds had wives and children on the outstations. So long as sheep were run, docile and responsible labour was needed all the year, as well as additional workers of considerable skill at the periods for lambing, for washing prior to the shearing, and for the shearing itself, with quite complicated preparations which illustrate the extent of the adaptation of the industry to the local ecology.[28] Such complete use of what the locale offered made more absolute the dislocation of the Aboriginal economy and religious life, which had humanised the environment for almost irreconcilable purposes.

[26] Ogilvie's story was reprinted in *A Century of Journalism: The Sydney Morning Herald 1831-1931*, pp. 84–6. It appears over the initials 'C.O.' but R.C. Law showed clearly that it was the work of Edward Ogilvie.
[27] Letter of C.G. Tindal, 15 March 1845.
[28] Yulgilbar Station Diary.

The exodus of labour to the goldfields seriously affected the Clarence area in 1851, though shortages were offset by the changeover to cattle and wage rises by the boom in tallow. A married couple paid under contract £27 per annum in 1850 could demand and get £35 in 1851, and £45 at the end of 1852. By 1854, when fencing of paddocks was being introduced, fencers under contract could earn £100 per annum clear. A married couple might get £55 for routine station work, with four rations, in January 1854; by the mid-year they got £90.[29]

The interesting fact is not that there was a disposition to experiment with Aboriginal labour to a greater extent but that the experiment was so limited. The assumption remained that such employment was at the best a temporary expedient. E.D. Ogilvie, for reasons already stated, had on Yulgilbar a sizeable reserve of such labour and in the early fifties began to use Aborigines even as shepherds—a good indication of the change in a decade. 'Sheep station matters go on more smoothly now', he wrote in November 1852, 'and perhaps the black shepherds are somewhat improving in their craft', but he had to exercise constant supervision, and could not take his jaunt to Sydney that year.[30]

The pity is that his methods of training on the job, such as placing an Aboriginal shepherd or hut-keeper on an outstation with a white shepherd, were not more widely used. By this time the Aboriginal station worker generally had a European Christian name for the records; and Ogilvie's station diary indicates his daily inspections of their flocks. So on 11 September 1852 he inspected the sheep under management of Mickey, Billy, and Tommy.[31]

By the middle of the next year another squatter could write that Aboriginal shepherds and bullock drivers were 'coming much into fashion'.[32] Station-grown wheat brought a great saving in ration costs; and in that year the reaping of the harvest on Koreelah Station depended solely on Aborigines. On every station where they had not been wiped out or driven away, there were at least one or two on the permanent pay-roll; and the pattern which is still to be found on the cattle stations in the far north was emerging, since they formed an essential and most profitable, but often unacknowledged, part of the station enterprise,

---

[29] Letters of C.G. Tindal, 10 October 1851, 9 May and 1 December 1852, 9 January and 20 May 1854.
[30] Letter of E.D. Ogilvie dated 30 November 1852 (held in 1938 by a descendant at Grafton).
[31] Yulgilbar Station Ledger. 'Billy' may well have been proud Toolbillibam in his new role.
[32] Letter of C.G. Tindal, 3 June 1853.

RACE RELATIONS—A CLOSER LOOK

working for rations, and sometimes for a cash wage which could be quite comparable with that paid to other station workers.[33]

In addition there would have been what remained of the 'station blacks', people in their own 'country', useful for the wheat or maize harvest, to get bark for building a new outstation hut and sheep pen, and sometimes to build the huts; for finding lost persons and stock, and for other occasional work, especially as guides to explore new country or to find one's way round in the bush. Payment would have been in rations and tobacco.

It is important to note that after a decade of contact there were Aborigines who could earn a full cash wage and whose skills were such as to get it. What we have been looking at in one area was by no means unique. As Docker has pointed out, some wealthy pastoralists like the Imlays and Boyd on the south coast of New South Wales had been employing Aborigines in responsible positions before 1838,[34] while the Australian Agricultural Company north of Port Stephens employed them as stockmen and oarsmen and their wives as domestic servants. They had not made good shepherds there; but Joseph Docker, from the Ovens District, explained to a Select Committee in 1841 that, when his shepherds had been scared away by murders, he had successfully used Aborigines until he went away to Melbourne.[35] What was needed were men like Ogilvie who would concentrate on supervision.

One reason for the system of contracted 'native' labour, in the colonial world, was to get the single man away from his people for the term of the contract. Labour discipline was easier if he was taken so far away as to have no chance of getting home if he ran away. Through the history of the frontier, most of the great overlanding enterprises to take up new stations have operated in this way. Another advantage, of course, was that it enabled the employer to pay only the cost of the single 'unit of labour'. This system was operating to disrupt the native polity well before the opening up of the Clarence; and the very first enterprises

---

[33] In 1853 the Tindal brothers employed three permanently 'as cattle drivers, etc. . . . one of them, who can drive the bullock team, and breaks in the horses [for which his employers received £2 per head from owners] receives seven shillings a week, and his ration. The other two boys are clothed and fed.' Letter of C.G. Tindal, 3 June 1853. Twelve years later, only 8s. was paid to a white worker on a weekly wage at Yulgilbar (Yulgilbar Station Ledger 1865), so that the Aboriginal on 7s. weekly was probably being fairly paid for skill—an indication of what the possibilities were.

[34] *Simply Human Beings*, p. 135.

[35] Ibid., p. 137.

brought Aboriginal workers with them.[36] Those who looked for a new run in the hinterland would take 'boys' from their base.

The proper plan is to procure a black boy from a great distance. They are then afraid to go back through the country of hostile tribes. The parents of a piccaninny will sell him to you for tobacco with great satisfaction if they think you will use him well.[37]

This was one way of getting a worker for life. Another was to save a likely lad taken on a punitive expedition (as in the case of Pundoon). An early tradition in Tasmania was to chase the mother through the bush until she had to leave her children, and then make a selection.[38]

There must have been factors in both cultures which tended to limit the Aboriginal role. Any European or Asian was assumed to be a more suitable, or a potentially more suitable, employee. Thus there was, in the early 1850s, some employment of Chinese as shepherds on the Clarence. But more important was the effect of migration schemes for Europeans. British and other Europeans, especially Germans from Hamburg, were being brought out; and Germans were coming under contract to the Clarence by 1852. Their contracts of employment were not unlike those used in Africa and other parts of the colonial world. Moreover, they could be set up in the bush where they saw no one but the ration carrier once a week; if they did try to abscond they had the language problem to face, and were easily found and returned. The magistrate who dealt out the penal sanction might well be the employer; if not, one of his neighbours. There was the usual co-operation of employers in such circumstances to prevent employees from escaping. As the migrant had to repay the employer's portion of the passage money from his wages, and was bound for two years, it is not surprising that the scheme proved popular.[39]

This was in the tradition of looking away from the Aboriginal inhabitants of an area as a potential labour pool: and of readiness to meet costs of establishing European migrants in preference to those which might be incurred in the motivation and training of an Aboriginal work force. In all the circumstances the trend was inevitable. No one at the time but an eccentric or a person with deep insight like George Grey could have

[36] Reminiscences of W.G. Law—letter to N.C. Hewitt—referring to the Small family, which came to the Clarence by sea to cut cedar: 'When we came to the Clarence, Sydney Billy was the Smalls' slaughter man, and Sydney Mary was Mrs Small's house maid.'
[37] Letter to F.C. Tindal, 12 February 1852.
[38] See Turnbull, *Black War*, pp. 57 *et seq*.—Government and General Orders, 13 March 1819.
[39] The employer had to pay part of the passage money to the Colonial Treasury, but could deduct this from wages.

RACE RELATIONS—A CLOSER LOOK 121

seen as a lost opportunity the failure to find for the Aboriginal a place in the new economy. In the south, this kind of labour crisis was short lived, since the result of the goldrushes was rapidly to increase the work force, even while ending forever the docility of labour.

So, in south-east Australia, the problem did not have to be faced of gearing development to the rate of social change of indigenous people. Attitudes to the Aboriginal worker had begun to harden round the stereotype of fecklessness and unreliability; and, as usual in complex human relationships, one effect of these attitudes was to produce in generation after generation the expected result. With Aboriginal populations left on the economic fringe, the gap could widen as the whites became wealthier. In the 1860s, Edward Ogilvie of Yulgilbar, who may fairly be regarded as the employer best equipped and disposed of those on Clarence River stations to use Aboriginal labour, had only one Aboriginal, Billy Cobie, regularly on the payroll.[40] This emphasises one aspect only in complex intercultural reactions. Cash economics, in contact with a subsistence economy, always tend to wreck the whole pattern of social relationships on which the traditional, kinship-oriented society depends. Yet cash may not be effective for a long time as an incentive for the indigenous worker, for many reasons: that it is used to supply only minimal demand, and on purchases which are distributed in accordance with traditional obligations; that the man who would turn his back on his traditional obligations, if he could, finds himself working to maintain his relatives. Fundamental is the tenacity of *mores*, especially where the culture lays little emphasis on comfort or material possessions, as was the case among the Aborigines. Another factor, in any one area, was that after the initial displacement the Aborigines disappeared with startling rapidity as the physical environment was speedily and completely transformed to suit a way of life which left decreasing opportunities for the traditional activities of the still stubborn black man.

In this north coastal area of New South Wales, however, something of the old life could be lived for a few more decades. The Bandjalang of the upper Clarence, Richmond, and Tweed River country could still wander through pastoral areas and retire to the mountains, until with farming and closer settlement they were to be confined to reserves or the town fringe areas.

When some gestures in Aboriginal policy did develop, they had little to do with the access of the Aboriginal to the economy either as a

[40] Yulgilbar Station Ledger.

THE FAILURE OF COLONIAL ADMINISTRATION

consumer or a producer. The keynote was not opportunity or even exploitation, which would probably have been far less destructive in its effects than the propensity of governments to regard Aboriginal affairs as an area of cheap charity.

Until the setting up of a government-sponsored body for protection, the most effective positive step taken for Aborigines seems to have been the blanket issue on each 24th of May. By 1889, just 402 blankets were required for the Clarence River Police District.

Perhaps it is as well to indicate here that there is another side to the story, of which there are some signs in what we know of the settlement of the Clarence. There has been, throughout, the attraction of the tools, food and store goods for the Aboriginal. There were, for instance, no tales of embattled tribesmen holding out against all comers in the wild country of the watershed, although this kind of thing sometimes did happen elsewhere: Aborigines were *attracted* to the sources of industrial goods and food. Especially in areas later depastured, and farther north, where the enterprise had to get along with Aboriginal labour, this becomes more clear. As someone had said of Africans in contact, they were not only forced to change their ways of living; they 'resigned' from tribal life. There must have been something of a symbiotic relationship from the beginning. Those who joined in the carousals of the cedar getters when they could would also rob and plunder when they could. The Aboriginal was almost everywhere ready to resign from his hard life as a hunter once he realised the possibility of becoming a pensioner, or of adapting to the new situation with a minimum of the work which to him was more or less pointless exertion. By 1860 one finds references in the records to the 'station blacks'; and there must have been fringe camps round most of the commercial settlements along the river banks, which went back to earlier ways of exploiting the settlements by robbing the neighbouring farms, working for rations and alcohol and probably, in view of the shortage of women for the whites, prostitution.

These references to the Clarence River situation may indicate how little the facts had changed in half a century. The instructions to the early governors of New South Wales were intended to regulate the relations of a small penal settlement with the Aboriginal subjects of the Crown. The rest of New South Wales, as defined, constituted in effect, and up to the stage of the overlanding of stock and the excursions of cedar getters beyond the boundaries of the Nineteen Counties, one great Aboriginal reserve. But once the grasslands outside called to capital invested in stock within the Limits of Location, administration, ineffective as it inevitably

RACE RELATIONS—A CLOSER LOOK

123

was, could never catch up with the facts. An attempt to do so presupposes a real will to protect Aborigines, consistently maintained and in the forefront of government policy. Perhaps, in looking for indications of such a will, one is in danger of applying the professions of the mid-twentieth century to the practices of a hundred years ago, and tends to forget how far the patterns of conduct were set by a particularly brutalised group of social outcasts from the hard society of newly industrialised England.

From the majority of those who made up this new settler community, one could hardly expect much concern for 'savages'.[41] When we look at the policy statements from the home government, we have to remember that those who framed them were not only isolated from the distant facts but also from other basic emphases in policy. For instance, there could be no serious thought, in the social and political context of the time, of putting the welfare of heathen savages before economic development. And even the best-intentioned Australian governors saw the future of the Aboriginal as becoming an asset in the developing cash economy. A governor who saw him as having something of his own to contribute, or as entitled to use his land in his own way, might just as well have abdicated his main responsibilities, among which Aboriginal rights were hardly in the first order of priority. Even the effort to establish and protect minimum rights to life itself could lead, as Gipps learned, to hysterical enmity from settlers.

With the establishment of colonial legislatures there was the classic situation developing of settler democracy, hungry for the land. As for the protection, by the Governor, of Aborigines in lands still unsettled, the home government had already had the experience with the American colonies and Indian lands.

The problem of a cultural frontier in the colonial situation is basically the same everywhere. If the frontier is expanding, law and order depend on the government leading the way and taking charge of the processes of trade, settlement, recruitment of labour; and establishing by use of superior force the best approximation to a rule of law possible in these very difficult conditions. This has happened only rarely in colonial history, for a colonial government can generally be by-passed with appeals to the home government or to influential quarters in the colonising country. In any case, more 'development' is necessary for more revenue.

[41] Writing of early Tasmania, Turnbull (*Black War*, p. 44), remarked that 'Compared to the men now come among them, the inquiring Frenchmen of a few years before were mental and social giants, a century in advance of their time. For to those now in occupation of their land the natives were rather less than the strange new birds and beasts and of considerably less economic value.'

Development involves the taking of land: and in spite of legal theories about certain lands being 'waste and vacant', practically all land is the object of indigenous claims to ownership. There may be violent resistance, and reprisals by the settlers taking the law into their own hands. Efforts by police to keep the peace tend to come later. In practice, the police will go where there is 'trouble'; and the nature of the trouble will be described for them by the settler community. So the first contact of the Aboriginal with the police has been characteristically in the role of an avenging force; and the tradition of Aboriginal hostility to police has continued ever since. Queensland, in taking over from New South Wales the Native Police dispersal squads, accepted dispossession by force as inevitable; the methods of the Native Police were those of military conquest without attention to rules of warfare.

One other aspect of colonial administration is relevant here. Every act and every policy of the conqueror has some relevance for those whose lands have been overrun and occupied, since from now on they have no separate future. In Australia, the basis of the new set of property relationships was *all* the land, so that every decision of the new government had either remote or immediate consequences for the Aboriginal. In any colony, every 'affair' is potentially a 'native affair'—not only land use and tenure but policy on matters as diverse as the law of evidence, criminal law, taxation, education, marriage, local government. From the first landing, therefore, the fates of the settler and the Aboriginal were interlocked; the situation was recognised in the theory which established for the Aboriginal the status of a British subject. From that point onwards, laws on labour, land, housing, education, police, civil rights, health, affected him directly or indirectly, or by the implication of his being omitted from any thought or consideration at all. So every act of administration became in effect a piece of colonial administration. Yet Western European colonialism was marked by the distance between administrator and 'native'. This exclusive tradition profoundly differentiated it from some earlier traditions. It is not difficult to see why the British settlers in Australia failed to charm their subjects with the attractive force of their civilisation. Where the 'coloured' subjects were in the great majority, the problem could be shelved by the assumption that the White Man's Burden was to rule 'the silent sullen peoples' more or less for ever. Where they were such a small minority, and were rapidly being exterminated, it was easy to shelve the whole question of the future with the assertion that there would not be one. The Aboriginal was dying out. Local experiences like that in the Clarence area confirmed the assumption.

THE FAILURE OF
COLONIAL ADMINISTRATION:
RETROSPECT

Policies and practices which result in the rapid disappearance of the subjects may be fairly described as failures. In relation to the Australian colonies one reason lies in the contrast between a policy of protection and its practice.

The policy itself can be seen, with the advantage of hindsight and in the light of what we now know of the nature of man and his relationship with human society, to have been doomed to failure. One reason was the vulnerability of a nomadic society, without hierarchical organisation or multi-purposed leadership. The other was underestimation of the effect on the mature person of socialisation in his own culture. It was regarded as something like a bad habit, which could be shed with training. Because of contemporary beliefs about the origin of mankind, Aboriginal differences were thought to exist because the Aboriginal had had no chance of becoming like a European; it was believed that human change and development was a unilinear process with possibilities of 'progress' or 'regression' to civilisation or savagery; that the 'highest' stage reached was to be seen in the civilised European. Thus it should have been possible to 'civilise' the Aboriginal by schooling, by revealing to him the 'truths' of a 'higher' religion, by offering to him equality before the law, and by teaching him, by application of the law to his case, what it was and what his 'duty' was.

If the older people proved to be too set in their habits to change, then their children could be changed. Here, too, it is easy in the light of what is now known to see the fallacy: that people cannot be 'civilised' in institutions, especially when the first years of life have been lived in a culture which has turned their minds in other directions. We also know now that constructive adaptation to changing circumstances requires some degree of group autonomy; that the process is slow, resulting from the decisions of individuals and the groups of which they consider themselves members; and that it is as likely to be retarded as hastened by exhortation, threats, force, or legal enactment.

The problems, as they appeared to an experienced, intelligent, and well-informed officer shortly after the Select Committee of the House of Commons had made its report, and before he became Governor of South Australia, were defined by Captain George Grey in a letter he sent to Russell from Mauritius in June 1840.[1] Part of this we have already discussed; but worth stating again in this context is the argument that one reason for failure to civilise the Aboriginal had been failure to enforce British law universally. The law had been applied

as far as European property and European subjects were concerned . . . yet, so long as they only exercised their own customs upon themselves and not too immediately in the presence of Europeans [it was assumed that] they should be allowed to do so with impunity.

He conceded Aboriginal intelligence; the differences lay, he argued, in 'barbarous customs', which he says would degrade even civilised men—an interesting reference to the theory of reversion to savagery. Aboriginal customs should not be given the status of indigenous 'law', and were not comparable with indigenous custom recognised by British law in other colonies.

(Where British law had been applied to village societies, it had undermined traditional authority and in other ways operated as a factor for social disintegration. But village authority had enabled villagers to continue to make many decisions of their own. The disintegrative effects were gradual, extending over long periods.)

Grey thought that there should be very serious effort to make impossible the practice of Aboriginal custom where this offended against the law, not only under the noses of Europeans but everywhere. Such custom was the reverse of humanity; only the rule of law could bring a complete fulfilment of their potential humanity. Aborigines who broke customary rules should be protected from the traditional enforcers using violence 'in the execution of their own laws', for otherwise the old men could prevent individuals from attaining civilisation.

Little was known of the imperative nature of custom and of the

[1] *H.R.A.* (1), vol. XXI, p. 34—Russell to Gipps, 8 October 1840, with enclosure Grey to Russell, 4 June 1840.

RETROSPECT

significance of status and security obtained through initiation and ritual contact with the spirit world. There was little appreciation of the weight of traditional religion or sorcery; little realisation that basic concepts of reality and causation may be culturally determined. There was a facile assumption that the individual psyche was basically that of a frustrated liberal Englishman, and that individuals could be levered by legal and administrative means out of the social matrix.

It is interesting to see where this argument led Grey. Already in his day Aborigines were congregating in the towns, where it appeared comparatively easy to apply to them the full range of the law. But out in the bush and the sparsely settled areas, there would have to be mounted police numerous and efficient enough to arrest Aborigines even for petty law breaking. Only so could the larger crimes, which led to the massacres, be prevented.

There is an assumption here that the benefits of the imposed law are self-evident and attractive; Grey argued for an educational method of dealing with offences by relating the sentence to the degree of sophistication. We know now that people subjected to alien codes of conduct, which may be immoral in terms of the indigenous culture, will resist strenuously. The idea of placing the whole of Aboriginal life under supervision, when one considers what kind of persons were available for police work and the great difficulty of executing justice where it is so difficult to establish individual identities, was quite impractical. It would have been difficult to recognise 'native custom' in Native Regulations, because it rapidly withered away. But another reason was expressed in Grey's argument: to Europeans there was something especially 'savage' in Aboriginal custom. He was repelled by cases where young Aboriginal girls went out of the institutions and into the bush with their betrothed.

Grey discussed the difficulty of getting convictions for massacres of Aborigines because of the legal situation that Aborigines were not competent to give court evidence, and recommended that this might be accepted without the formality of the oath, provided that there was also circumstantial evidence. That Aborigines were already beginning to define the injustice of their lot in European terms is suggested by his statement that they regarded the current situation as a great hardship. It was not simply that the survivors of killings could not give evidence against the killers (which greatly facilitated the task of extermination) but that an Aboriginal charged could not call on others in his defence. As white juries might be involved, there was good reason for counsel to be retained.

In 1839 the Legislative Council of New South Wales had passed an

THE FAILURE OF COLONIAL ADMINISTRATION

act to accept Aborigines as competent witnesses in criminal cases:[2] this was disallowed by the British government, as to allow heathens to give evidence would be 'contrary to the principles of British Jurisprudence'.[3] But in 1843 the home authorities having thought again and adopted an Imperial Act (6 Vic. Ch. XXII), it was put to the New South Wales Legislative Council, and rejected.[4] It was put to the Governor of South Australia also, and in legislation was adopted accordingly. Western Australia had already adopted such legislation in 1841 and the Imperial Act confirmed it. But in New South Wales the rejection meant maintaining a legal situation which enabled the settler to act much as he wished so long as he used a limited amount of discretion. In the other colonies the settler had to depend more on the attitude of the white jury. In 1849 the New South Wales Legislative Council again rejected a measure which would have enabled the Imperial Act to apply.[5] The barrier to Aboriginal evidence was not removed until the Evidence Act 1876 enabled a judge to take evidence otherwise than on oath. Victoria provided for affirmations from Aborigines and part-Aborigines in 1854. Queensland accepted affirmations only from 1884.[6]

There was no doubt [writes Professor A.P. Elkin] about the real issue in the debate on the 1849 bill [in New South Wales]. The arguments centred on the clash in the marginal regions. The Attorney-General . . . considered that the bill, if made law, would stop collisions there, for white men, 'knowing that evidence would be allowed by the black man' . . . would refrain from coming into hostile collision with him. Members, opposing the bill, disagreed, even suggesting that it would recoil adversely on the natives, on the principle 'that dead men tell no tales'. This was inherent in the main argument of such members as Lowe, Hamilton, Wentworth, Fitzgerald and James Macarthur, that 'the wisest policy was to let the blacks and the settlers fight it out between themselves', and that 'it was not the policy of a wise Government to attempt the perpetuation of the Aboriginal races . . . by any protective measures. They must give way before the *arms*, aye! even the diseases of civilised nations'. The Colonial Secretary . . . pointed out that an accused white man would be tried by a jury of his peers . . . Could they have seen ahead, they would have realized that with such a jury and counsel system a white accused would seldom be found guilty, whether guilty in fact or not.[7]

[2] 3 Vic. No. 16 (N.S.W.).
[3] *H.R.A.* (1), vol. XX, p. 368—Gipps to Normanby, 14 October 1839; and p. 756—Russell to Gipps, 11 August 1840, enclosure no. 1.
[4] *N.S.W. V. & P.* (L.C.), May and June 1844—quoted in Carlyon, G.A. Robinson, Chief Protector, p. 99.
[5] See A.P. Elkin, 'Aboriginal Evidence and Justice in North Australia', *Oceania*, vol. XVII, no. 3, March 1947, pp. 189-94.
[6] Ibid. The Victorian Act was the Law of Evidence Further Amendment Act 1854; the Queensland Act was the Oaths Amendment Act 1884.
[7] 'Aboriginal Evidence and Justice', p. 191.

RETROSPECT

Perhaps a main weakness of Grey's case for strict application of law to Aborigines was that he assumed too much for the power of the law to control the settlers. He had his real experience later. Gipps's comment is that of a governor who realised this situation very well. But the basic assumptions of Grey's arguments are more important than the arguments themselves. For they are humane; and the effort is made to distinguish between culture and Aboriginal potential. One implication of this humane approach is that, having the protection of the law, the Aboriginal who had learned to use it could sue and be sued, and so have the hitting power of the civil law. In theory the Aboriginal had had this from the first. Grey's assumption that with education he would learn to use it implied one other: that he would remain in full exercise of civil rights. Perhaps, had he been a villager or a member of a tribe led by a chief, this exercise of civil rights would have been his, whatever else happened, as member of the village or tribe, which by treaty, or statute, or by use of the ordinary process of law for incorporation, could exercise the rights of a legal person. In no other way, in the practical circumstances where black men risked being robbed or killed with impunity, could he be sure of these rights.

Grey did not see this; nor was it likely that any one of his time could have done so. His emphasis on the individual who might progress or regress arose from the assumptions of his day. By contrast, the intuition of the untutored ex-bricklayer Robinson is all the more extraordinary for his time. In 1841, reporting as Chief Protector he wrote that 'the want of a code suited to the Aborigines is now strongly felt and of . . . vital importance to the welfare and existence of the natives.'[8] His was the experience of day-to-day contact with the real problems facing the Aboriginal, such as the right to hunt, which meant one's very life, but was never clearly established in law or within a definite area. Without a code, the protector could use only 'personal influence', and he could not prosecute any who prevented exercise of the 'right'.

Here he was in sympathy with those who faced a situation which could not be very clearly defined at that time. Perhaps nothing is more likely to disintegrate a social order based upon status and duty of young to old, women to men, uninitiated to initiated, than the application through the courts of the colonial power of the principles of abstract justice. For the way is open for the constant challenge to established customary authority: society, already under tremendous stresses, is further atomised when any offender against the tribal law can appeal

[8] Carlyon, G.A. Robinson, p. 97—Report of Chief Protector, 1841.

THE FAILURE OF COLONIAL ADMINISTRATION

past the men of status to the courts. Thus every attempt to enforce the principles of British justice among the Aborigines would merely add to the stress and lead to more complete disintegration. For such ethnocentricity there is always the excuse of ignorance and good intentions. It was to have its effect throughout the British colonial world; and Furnivall dealt with its effects in Burma in telling fashion as the colonial system was coming to a close.[9]

The Aboriginal's lack of power to operate in the law was to remain as long as he was dealt with as an individual who had the 'rights' of individuals in European liberal society. These rights depend on the knowledge and the resources of the individual, except in criminal matters. A recognised group, with assets, would inevitably have developed some functions of the legal person, if only because it would have been necessary for the government to negotiate with its spokesmen; this in turn would have enabled spokesmen, concerned with matters of real interest, to be chosen or to opt for the role. Thus a leadership involved in the process of interaction, and geared to the promotion of Aboriginal interests, would probably have developed, at least to the extent that it has done in other colonial situations.

The lack of such opportunities meant that the remnants seemed especially helpless; as indeed they were in this impossible situation. This was a reason for the policy of 'protection' which marked the latter part of the nineteenth century. Involved in protection were cumulative legal restrictions—against Aborigines, and sellers of alcohol, those who sought the women, those who might still kill, and so on. Protective-restrictive laws, applicable to people defined in racial terms and in practice to those with dark skins and Aboriginal features (since genealogies were not available), made any later incorporation of rights or claims impossible; and they often placed these people, including those of mixed descent who were or appeared to be within the legal definition, in out-of-the-way institutions, under authoritarian management which was supposed to educate individuals to be members of European society. These measures in turn lowered still more the prestige of Aborigines and made them still more helpless.

Hasluck's is a classic study of the steps by which the *legal* status of the Aboriginal declined, partly through the application of special legislation to meet the demands of expediency and partly through his omission from legal provisions for the services provided for other citizens. The study

[9] J.S. Furnivall, *Colonial Policy and Practice: A comparative study of Burma and Netherlands India.*

RETROSPECT 131

is limited to Western Australia, but it is typical of what happened every-where. He says that in Hutt's 1841 Bill, providing for Aborigines to give evidence, there were provisions that they might be flogged on the summary order of two magistrates. Russell refused assent to these on the grounds that

the delegation to justices of the peace of summary powers of punishment over the inferior race, from which the colonists of European descent are to be exempted, is a measure dangerous in its tendency as well as faulty in principle. By thus establishing an inequality in the eye of the law itself between the two classes, on the express ground of national origin, we foster prejudices. . . .

Immediate convenience, he says, must be sacrificed.[10] This was the crux of the matter.

The sanctions of European society were largely meaningless, especially where a gaol sentence might be hailed as a pleasant change from the search for a living. For this reason it has often been argued that flogging serves the purpose better than a gaol sentence. Another reason was that flogging was assumed to be good labour discipline; a gaol sentence might involve the nuisance of court appearance and loss of the time of the worker under sentence.

Colonial history illustrates the inevitability, in the circumstances of domination of 'natives', of a lower legal status for them. This operates in a complexity of multiple causation: the different status flows from the facts of discrimination, and then operates to justify the prejudices, leading to further discriminatory practices and judgments—as Russell had so clearly seen. On this issue, expediency prevailed when in 1849 two Justices sitting together were given power to sentence to twenty-four lashes.[11]

Special legislation was not all punitive. No special law could operate without some basic legal definition of those to whom it applied; and one of the purposes for such definition was that special protections might be applied—such, for instance, as the prevention of legal access to alcohol, which in Western Australia was initiated under the Publicans' Act of 1843. Later came regulations which prevented others than Aborigines and officials from living on reserves. Such laws have always the overt justification of special welfare measures, although, as in the case of drunken-ness, there would obviously be other motives. Thus there was tending to grow up from the first decades, in each colony, a legal definition of a special kind of British subject, and other, restrictive, laws which applied

[10] Hasluck, *Black Australians*, p. 136—quoting Russell to Hutt, 30 April 1841.
[11] Ibid., pp. 139 *et seq.*—quoting 12 Vic. No. 18 (W.A.).

to these persons and were generally justified as protective. As time went on, such legislation was in each colony applied also to persons of prescribed degrees of part-Aboriginal descent.

The Australian situation resembled that of the United States and Canada in that the future lay with the whites, who so greatly outnumbered the others. Where this was not the case, as in Africa, the restricted citizenship for the native people exacerbated all other 'colonial' sources of friction. In the north American and Australian situations, the restrictions produced resentful but powerless minorities.

Australia differed from the United States in that this legislation was introduced by the separate colonies during the nineteenth century and, after federation, Aboriginal affairs remained a State responsibility. So the basic definitions of Aboriginal (or, in Western Australia, 'native'), have remained different. The resultant confusion, as traffic and travel between the States have increased, added to the other problems arising from this special legislation.

Other processes of declining Aboriginal legal status were by omission of the Aboriginal, as defined, from consideration in law-making, by failure in practice to apply the law to his case, and by specific exclusion. Thus, when the first provision was made for compulsory education, his children could be excused—in some areas they were much later actually expelled from certain schools, by administrative action—or schooling could be missed because no schools were built where Aborigines lived. Another example is the exclusion or the excusing of the Aboriginal from military or other national service. These things operate as links in a chain of causation. In the case of schooling, for instance, Aborigines might be excluded because of an implicit assumption that they were not suited to it; the fact that their descendants are not educated tends to reinforce unthinking people in their belief that they lack the capacity for education.

The processes of debasement of legal status were to proceed apace under each of the colonial governments, after the failure of the first attempts (half-hearted as they were) to apply the law equally to all. It is interesting that in Western Australia, as in New South Wales, the half century marks a turning-point in Aboriginal affairs—not in the practices so much as in attitudes of governments. To some extent this illustrates the growing power of the settler community in politics. The governors were, in the colonial tradition, the safeguard of the indigenous people against the settlers—how effective, we have seen. The growth of elected legislatures inevitably tended to push concern for the Aboriginal into the background.

RETROSPECT   133

That history was to render the thoughts of Grey so far off the mark is a warning to those who try to establish the thread of causation in human affairs today; for perhaps our certainties also will seem quaintly unreal to our successors.

Russell had sent Grey's letter to Gipps, who commented on it.[12] Although it shows the impatience of the old colonial hand with the tyro, it indicates the same preoccupation with producing Aboriginal citizens by enforcing the law. Aborigines are 'Her Majesty's Subjects' fully entitled to the protections, and subject to the penalties, of the law. Practice in New South Wales was 'as far as possible' in accord with the principle. There is the same idea of unilinear cultural change, to be promoted by tuition, with the law used educationally. Obvious offences against 'society', like murder, were severely punished, since there could in such cases be no doubt that they 'should be regarded alike by the Savage and the civilised man, as deserving of punishment'—which indicated the same ignorance of Aboriginal cultural imperatives. That Gipps was justified in his claim that the courts were applying, as opportunity offered, the same law to white and black may be verified by reference to the case of R. v. Jack Congo Murrell in 1836; the decision that an Aboriginal was not a member of a 'free and independent' tribe placed him in the category of British subject without qualification.[13]

This case is an important precursor of the Myall Creek case two years later, in that it stressed the Aboriginal's right to the protections of the law. But it is mainly significant as indicating that, in the view of the court, the position adopted by Grey—that Aboriginal 'offences' against other Aborigines should be dealt with as though they involved Europeans—was correct. Jack Congo Murrell was charged with the murder of another Aboriginal. Stephen, for the defence, on demurrer argued that the court had no jurisdiction; that an Aboriginal was not bound by law which did not protect him; and that the position of the law in New South Wales had features of extra-territoriality, in that it applied only to the Britons to whom it offered protection; that New South Wales had not been conquered, ceded, or effectively settled. Therefore the court had no jurisdiction in this case. The Attorney-General claimed that New South Wales was held on the basis of occupation; that the law therefore

---

[12] H.R.A. (1), vol. XXI, p. 312—Gipps to Russell, 7 April 1841.
[13] R. v. Jack Congo Murrell (1836), 1 Legge (N.S.W.) 72. I am indebted to Dr J. Hookey for pointing out the significance of this case, which is cited in Biskup, Native Administration and Welfare in Western Australia. The state of Victoria, in 1860, applied the principle to at least two other cases—R. v. Peter (June 1860) and R. v. Jemmy (September 1860). I am indebted to Mr J.R. Mattes, who located these cases in the Melbourne Argus Law Reports.

THE FAILURE OF COLONIAL ADMINISTRATION

applied. The court (Burton J.) ruled that Aboriginal tribes had no sovereignty at the time of taking possession; that the offence had been committed within the area of the court's jurisdiction; that the British government had exercised its rights over a long period; that offences against an Aboriginal must be punished to protect his civil rights; that there could be no distinction from the situation which would have arisen if the victim had been a white man.

Neither Gipps nor Grey saw good reason why the Aboriginal should not become an effective British subject. Gipps reminded the Colonial Office that his 3 Vic. No. 16 of 1839, to admit Aboriginal evidence, had been 'disallowed at home'; and claimed that his government had been appointing counsel to defend Aborigines so effectively that settlers complained that they were 'almost invariably acquitted'. This, he wrote, had been one cause of white atrocities like the Myall Creek massacre. This reference is a reminder of just how far from the facts of frontier contact all this theorising was. But the end of British colonial administration brought the end of such administrative consideration of principle and justice.

Grey argued that the Aboriginal could become an effective citizen if he learned to work effectively in the cash economy. His analysis of the situation could be applied to many areas today. The demand for such labour was irregular and uncertain; an employer would use the Aborigines' services when he needed them, and then they would 'go bush'—necessary for them because the wages were inadequate. He saw that once a man had committed himself to employment the wage must be adequate to purchase the food and equipment for himself and his family which he would have obtained in his own way. He criticised the failure to teach skills and the different values of different skills. He put the case for training institutions and schools, but his purpose was not indefinite deferment of the Aboriginal place in society.

He argued also for apprenticeships. After the end of slavery, the 'indenture' system was taking its place elsewhere for 'native labour'. This was an adaptation of the old apprenticeship system to cases where employers demanded assurance of a permanent labour force. The only Australian gestures at this system were to be made by governments interested in the pearling and the pastoral industries, mainly in 'colonial Australia' and where no other than Aboriginal labour was available. Grey argued that a settler who trained an Aboriginal worker added a labourer to the work force as definitely as one who brought out a migrant and that such a settler should be rewarded by grant of additional land or

RETROSPECT   135

by remission of part of the land purchase price. This would be far better
than dependence on training in a few institutions; and it would be in the
settlers' own interests properly to 'encourage and reward' the Aboriginal
worker.

Such an objective could have been set and was in fact temporarily the
aim in Western Australia. Difficulties would have been great, because real
organisation and control would have been needed, with assessment of
what 'training' meant, and fixing stages in efficiency. Perhaps Grey over-
estimated the power of logic in the employer and the force of enlightened
self-interest to overcome prejudice. But the position has always been that
policy could only be a choice between difficult objectives. The problem
of selecting realistic and satisfying objectives remains.

In the settled areas, he recommended the use of Aboriginal road
building and maintenance gangs, with their own hunters to supply meat,
and proper standards of management. Any Aboriginal who had been
employed for three years should be given a grant of land in his own
country, with a sum of money from the land revenue to enable him to
stock it.

Gipps supported Grey's emphasis on employment, with a shrewd
assessment of the effectiveness of cash in the process of change. Next to
Christian instruction, he wrote, the use of money is 'the most effectual of
all means that can be resorted to in advancing civilisation'; and (disre-
garding his inevitable ritual emphasis on Christian conversion) colonial
policy was not to get much further than this anywhere. He had, he said,
tried to get the settlers to employ Aborigines but had rejected a system
of rewards for so doing as liable to abuse. This was understandable; where
he could not trust his officers in the field to refrain from helping the
settlers kill the Aborigines, there was not much chance of using them
effectively to administer a scheme of employment.

This practical side of the problem was not yet well experienced by
Grey; but the fact was that wherever the two races were in contact,
Aborigines rapidly lost their lives. Gipps points to the cogency of the
argument that the Aboriginal could only survive if he were removed
away from the whites (the obvious alternative being unthinkable).
'Missionary and other Establishments for the Education of the Aborigines
should be placed as far as possible from the resort of ordinary settlers.'
Here was a dilemma; and he had compromised, he said, at Port Phillip;
the establishments of the protectors were not so far from the settlers as to
prevent employment, but far enough for refuge.[14]

[14] This seems the gist of Gipps's meaning, but his words are not clear.

I consider that it is by contact with White Men and by being placed as nearly as possible on a par with them, that the civilisation of Aborigines is most likely to be advanced. It must be admitted indeed that this will frequently expose them to temptations which they may not be strong enough to withstand, the men to the use of ardent spirits, the women to be seduced from their husbands or natural protectors.[15]

This practical dilemma had already resulted in some special protective and restrictive legislation; so that while two noted colonial administrators were theorising about the necessity of legal equality, restrictions of this theoretical citizenship had begun. The growth of these restrictions was to be supported after the end of British colonial administration for the benefit of the settlers—and for the assumed benefit of the Aborigines. Gipps, for instance, refers in this letter to 2 Vic. No. 18 section 49, which made supply of spirits to an Aboriginal an offence with £5 penalty; and he was considering asking for legislation to protect Aboriginal women. On the other hand protective laws, with law enforcement as it was, were almost all the protection Aborigines were to get. 4 Vic. No. 8 had already made it illegal, even where settlers constantly bore arms, for Aborigines to do so.

It is interesting to compare the assumptions of the civilised men participating in this discussion of 1840 with those of the participants in the first conference on Aboriginal policies, between the Commonwealth and the States, in 1937. In the Grey-Gipps dialogue there was a good deal which we might well question in the light of later knowledge. But the basic assumptions are humane in the wider sense; and the objective an eventual equality. By 1937, a further ninety-seven years of practice in Aboriginal affairs had established the Aboriginal in the minds of administrators as a person of inferior innate capacity. Much of the discussion at the Commonwealth-States conference in that year was on the crude assumptions of the stock breeder. The same dilemma, outlined by Gipps in 1840, exercised the minds of the members of the 1937 Conference— how to make a useful worker and member of society, and at the same time protect the Aboriginal from contacts which no government had been determined or able to control. The 1937 solution was to place the part-Aboriginal in white society and the 'full-blood' on reserves as isolated as possible. Gipps and Grey had assumed, in the face of facts, that the Aboriginal still had full *rights* as a member of legal-liberal society. By 1937 it was assumed that his admission to that society would depend on his racial origin and the colour of his skin; that if the breed was right,

[15] *H.R.A.* (1), vol. XXI, p. 312—Gipps to Russell, 7 April 1841.

RETROSPECT   137

progress could be made, through special treatment, towards 'assimilation'. This retrogression from principles of humanity to those of animal husbandry was by no means limited to Australia.

Colonial administration may be said to have come to an end with the introduction of responsible government in 1856, in eastern and South Australia. Only in Western Australia, thereafter, was it possible for this kind of dialogue, involving the Colonial Office and the local executive, to continue, since the executive now became more effectively the instrument of the settler democracy. The special condition of Aboriginal affairs in Queensland probably owes something to the fact that this colony was shortly afterwards (1859) excised from the New South Wales frontier, without those gestures at policy which the Colonial Office was wont to make. For over thirty years thereafter, Queensland's main activity in Aboriginal affairs was that of the Native Police, mainly an instrument of extermination which Queensland had taken over, fully blooded, from New South Wales.

It is worth noting that the year of publication of *The Origin of Species* was the year of Queensland's independence. As interpreted into the frontier folk lore, this could be used to justify the worst offences by the whites, as members of the 'superior race' before whom the inferior ones would melt away and die out. Murder could be romanticised and abstracted; and depopulation by disease and other factors could be seen as the convenient operation of both immutable law and divine providence. This poor race would make way for the fine flower of British civilisation.

From this point on, as the frontier was rapidly extended, the Aborigines were largely at the mercy of persons who saw their best interests in taking the land and getting rid of Aboriginal incumbrances. What saved the remnants in the north was the lack of any other source of labour; so the 'native' was hardly used and heavily depended on, while the value of his services was continually denied and decried.

The time has come to draw the broad outlines of this story, on the continental scale, even though this must depend heavily on secondary sources. The most important and significant trains of events seem to have been:

The further expansion over, and settlement, for stock raising of, nearly all watered and grassed areas of the continent, progressively until even the sparsely scattered wells of the Musgrave Ranges had been fouled by stock; destruction of game; breaking of resistance by force and the threat of force, very often with free use of the gun; and support of these activities by the police and other frontier agencies of government, with punitive expeditions, mounted by the police themselves, as late as the 1930s.

The establishment of special institutions for Aborigines, in general multi-

THE FAILURE OF COLONIAL ADMINISTRATION

purposed and for all ages; and the development of special departments of government to manage those inside and those outside the institutions. This, like frontier practices, continued methods established in the days of colonial administration, through missions, and directly by governments, as with the institution on Flinders Island and the stations of the Protectorate.

The development, in each state, and in the Northern Territory after 1911, of a body of special law relating to Aborigines—law which was professedly protective, and generally so in intent, but which, like all such special protective legislation, became restrictive of rights and created a special body of 'offences' such as drinking or sexual intercourse between white and black.

A complicated process of legal definition follows from this, and the limits set in defining who is an Aboriginal, by different governments for different reasons, have operated to render any logical approach to statistics or other measurement of the population and its problems almost impossible for Australia as a whole. The position of legal definition is still chaotic.

Rapid and heavy depopulation of the nomadic people, with the survival of those who managed to adapt to the restrictions, to get through the period of starvation and violence and the effects of introduced diseases, and to raise children. The invaders of frontier areas tended to be men without their women. A pattern of adaptation within the *mores* of tribal custom was to make the women available—they would have been taken in any case, with all the things and services needed. The numbers of Aboriginal people were so rapidly replaced by part-Aborigines that special theories about it were common on both sides of the cultural frontier. Some whites maintained that Aboriginal women were far more likely to conceive from sexual activity with whites than with men of their own race. Some Aborigines had theories about the effects on the next generation of parents eating white flour. Both are in accord with what was possibly dominant sentiment. Here the white man saw the effects of contact with the superior race; and the black, the bitter fruits of having to depend on the food of strangers who had displaced him.

The new skin colour in the camp must often have been the mark of a new type of man, to whom the secrets were not passed on, perhaps because they were no longer relevant, nor the ritual possible in the new circumstances, perhaps because he could not be classified in the kinship system. (On this point, A.P. Elkin has informed me that such classification was possible.) Race prejudice would operate to favour the part-Aboriginal, where employers assumed that he must be of 'higher intelligence' than the 'full-blood'. How often he went into the family of the non-Aboriginal, parent no one knows; but where he moved from the Aboriginal camp to the homestead, he moved mostly out of Aboriginal society. What the proportion of Aboriginal descent in the general population of Australia is, no one will ever know. The lower, the less honour to our frontier ancestors. From the first parental decisions, this kind of social mobility would be determined largely by the skin colour of the child: and such colouration has determined 'passing' ever since.

RETROSPECT   139

Thus, out of disaster, arose the Dark People of the continent: descended from both parties in the conflict but increasingly identified in legislation as Aboriginal. Their failure or refusal to conform to middle-class *mores* has been monotonously explained as due to the stubborn resistance of Aboriginal 'mentality' or custom, or culture, to 'civilising influences'. By the 1960s this was the most rapidly increasing group of Australians. The 'full-bloods', mainly in their secluded institutions and on equally inaccessible pastoral properties out in 'colonial Australia', were also increasing much more rapidly than the non-Aboriginal population (both of course exclusive of migration).

For a long time before this point was reached, the existence and obvious increase of the part-Aboriginal population presented a dilemma to governments. A dying race could be nicely institutionalised and allowed to fade away; but what had this group of people to do in White Australia? Discussion of this issue, on the most blatant racist assumptions (as they seem to us today) of superiority for the 'white race', preceded the adoption, by Commonwealth and States, just prior to World War II, of a scheme to 'absorb' the 'half-castes'. The offending characteristics of the Aboriginal could and should be 'bred out' in successive generations. The 'full-bloods' should be isolated on their reserves, while the 'half-castes' were to be processed sufficiently to attract marriage partners of impeccable white 'blood'—or dispersed in situations where, nature being assumed (wrongly as it proved) to be reliable in such things, they would have whiter children with each generation. It was implied that the 'full-bloods' would either die out or, through the breakdown of the efforts to isolate them, be replaced by part-Aborigines. Absorption through miscegenation was to 'solve' the 'problem' by removing the Aboriginal as a separate identity.

There is an awkward matter of definition involved here. In estimating statistics we so often tend to talk as though the disappearance of the black-skinned people marked the end of a 'race'. Perhaps it marked the end of a culture; and the cause of this was the kind of culture clash which occurred. The descendants of the Aborigines include three groups as defined by themselves or by others. There are the remaining 'full-bloods', those known as part-Aboriginal (popularly as 'half-caste'), and those who make up an unknown proportion of 'white Australians'—European and Aboriginal Australians have been cohabiting under various circumstances along the frontier, from one side of the continent to the other, for nearly two centuries. Part-Aborigines and others have been doing the same thing behind the frontier as it extended beyond each area. Those of us who do not bear some Aboriginal genes may yet bear some traces of Aboriginal culture; for interaction between cultures cannot all be in the one direction.

It is possible, I think probable, that just as the Negro and the Indian have contributed to the American culture, so has the Aboriginal to our own: especially perhaps in the first contacts along the frontier. What to the newcomer seemed Aboriginal anarchy may have contributed something to the stubborn independence of the 'nomad tribe' of the frontier, along with Irish intransigence. Who, one may ask, taught Irish potato farmers to adapt to the bush, and who developed the opposition of the frontier worker to the squatter who wanted all the land? Perhaps too little has been made of the Aboriginal contribution to what makes us 'Australian', even if the 'main contribution has come through his part-Aboriginal descendants. Aboriginal intransigence may have matched that of the ticket-of-leave men. In *The Australian Legend* Russel Ward defines a pattern of frontier *mores*, and Jeremy Beckett has pointed out how closely the part-Aboriginal *mores* conform to earlier frontier traditions.[16] Is it correct to assume that the white frontiersman was always the teacher and the Aboriginal or part-Aboriginal always the pupil? Why not the reverse? Only by prejudging the issue do we consistently assume that Aborigines are always the learners. In the first years in the bush, the reverse *must* have been the case; and the evidence of what goes on on a cattle station in the far north today reinforces the argument.

Cultural change and adaptation do not mean that the Aboriginal population is to disappear. No one can affirm or deny this. For generations Aborigines have been intermarrying with others: and there are many Australians whose Aboriginal ancestry is forgotten. But this does not mean that the part-Aboriginal community disappears as a social entity. It has often maintained a long continuity, in some cases perhaps going right back in tradition to the Old People. Because of what we have described it would be impossible for the Aboriginal culture to have been handed down; but there could be a continuity of adaptation, with the changes in each generation reflected in socialisation of the child. No one can say that the special value these people place on kinship, their 'country', seasonal work, and sharing has any more to do with the Aboriginal heritage than with the economic and social necessities which make this way of life imperative. To take one case: the emphasis on seasonal work, commonly attributed to the cultural urge for 'walkabout', is at least as

[16] A study of a mixed-blood Aboriginal minority in the pastoral west of New South Wales (M.A. thesis, Australian National University, 1958).

RETROSPECT

likely to be due to the fact that other work is not easily available for the Aboriginal. But in all these cases, it would be just as dogmatically foolish to deny that the habit has anything to do with the Aboriginal culture. It is as impossible to deny that general Australian culture owes a good deal to the Aboriginal.

THE DESTRUCTION
OF ABORIGINAL SOCIETY

II

THE FRONTIERS AFTER 1856

By the mid-century the frontier had extended to almost everywhere where there was good water and grass. Only in the Northern Territory and the north of Western Australia were there large Aboriginal populations as yet uncontacted. The future held for them nothing very different from what had been happening elsewhere. From the establishment of the colony of Queensland in 1859 to the first inter-governmental conference on Aboriginal affairs in 1937, the questions raised by the first settlements continued to be raised, but in areas farther and farther away from seats of government. Moreover, only three of the colonies were directly and administratively involved in frontier questions. Tasmania was left with only a small minority in the islands of Bass Strait, descended from the sealers and their Aboriginal womenfolk. In Victoria and New South Wales frontier questions became more and more remote from policy, although the basic moral issues were posed so long as *any* descendants of the Old People remained living in isolation from the general community; and these issues became more complex with the passage of time. For Queensland, South Australia, and Western Australia, however, the frontiers posed immediate questions, involving the law and its application, rights arising from prior occupation, and basic human rights.

But as the frontier clashes became geographically more remote from Brisbane, Adelaide, and Perth (and from Melbourne-Canberra after 1911, when the Commonwealth took over the Northern Territory), they tended to take on more of the aspects of distant colonial questions, towards which the attitudes of thinking people in 'the south' now

THE DESTRUCTION OF ABORIGINAL SOCIETY

became openly critical; and as time passed the kind of criticism which had formerly come mainly from interested groups in Britain began to come from the capital cities and to be expressed in the southern press.

AUSTRALIAN FRONTIERS AND 'NATIVE' ADMINISTRATION

Characteristic of colonial settlement was the prominence in frontier regions of the Christian missions, which in some colonies attempted to discharge the traditional colonial function of jogging the consciences of the Europeans, and which governments began to recognise as the protectors of 'natives'. The management of cattle, mining, and pearling industries, and the tendency for the services of the indigenous inhabitants to assume greater value, since other labour was not available, were also typical of the colonial world. In the cattle industry of the sub-tropical and tropical areas the Aboriginal worker could well have come into his own at last, had the markets been nearer and greater, had management operated with something more than minimal levels of efficiency, and had the value of the local work force been less obscured by decades of prejudice.

The continental frontier did not move evenly from south to north, nor from east to west. From the settlements in the south, stock were overlanded to unclaimed grasslands almost irrespective of distances, so that the last to be claimed and stocked tended to be the fringes of the drier desert country of the centre. This envelopment of Australia contrasts with the westward movement in north America.

The distant frontier region also had something of a 'colonial' relationship with the southern governments in the special labour legislation, which made ineffective gestures at establishing working conditions for the Aborigines. It began in Queensland and Western Australia with attempts to regulate the conditions in the pearling industry in order to protect the tribes from the grosser abuses arising from recruiting for service on ships. Western Australia had to deal with Asian workers and employers as well as Aboriginal workers; Queensland with Asian employers and Melanesian as well as Aboriginal recruits. This aspect of the distant frontier was heightened, for Queensland, by inclusion of the Torres Strait Islands within its boundaries. Only Queensland, of the states, has had typical colonial responsibilities, involving the administration of people of a different culture *overseas*. It was partly the lack of the 'salt-water component' of colonialism which made the difference between colonial administration and that of Aborigines as far from the centre of

THE FRONTIERS AFTER 1856   147

government as the Kimberleys or Cape York Peninsula. The existence of the sea barrier made it easier to see a separate eventual development for the distant controlled region; if the region was in the same continent, the assumption was that it would remain for ever under the same government.[1]

The popular ideas justifying expansion were those of extending the boundaries of the British Empire—a convenient identification of self-interest with extension of 'civilisation'; of profit with justice and the gift of the British law. The empire would go on indefinitely bringing the 'natives' under its beneficent control. This concept of the indefinitely extending frontier was not seriously questioned by a settler society itself the product of such a concept. The relationship of white men to coloured men seemed permanent, both internally and in the Pacific and Asia; very few Australians challenged it, even when Hughes during World War I proclaimed his 'Munroe Doctrine in the Southern Pacific'.[2] His intransigence at Versailles on the matter of the New Guinea Mandate would have been impossible except on the assumption that European domination of this area of the world was a very long-term arrangement indeed. The granting of the Mandate to Australia finally extended the frontier to the equator, presenting a challenge to 'native administration' experience and resources which the experience with Aborigines had made the country especially unfitted to meet.

By the end of the nineteenth century the racist attitudes which were to be the core of 'colonialism' had long been reinforced by the developments in popular education. The picture of the lone white man controlling by his influence (and his gun) thousands of coloured men had become part of the reading of the schoolboy.

Of the whole Australian frontier, the one area where there was a serious attempt to apply a colonial policy, based in the law and on principle, to the process of extending control, was Papua. This is not the place to enlarge on that story, but the granting of the Mandate was important in this context. It introduced Australian administrators to the best of the international colonial tradition. It also made the Commonwealth Government answerable to the Permanent Mandates Commission, at least to the extent of having to justify each year what had been done. Hughes showed in his first report to Parliament that he expected these reports to be no more than the form of words which disguised a situation

---

[1] Quincy Wright, *Mandates under the League of Nations*, pp. 4 *et seq*. deals with the effect of natural barriers on the concept of a colony.
[2] See *Argus* (Melbourne), 1 June 1918; *C.P.D.* (H. of R.)—11 June 1918, p. 573.

THE DESTRUCTION OF ABORIGINAL SOCIETY

tantamount to annexation.[3] But things did not develop that way. How far the Commonwealth Government was influenced by its involvement in the Mandate system remains to be studied, for its effects on Aboriginal policy at least. Perhaps the main influence was through reinforcing those protests by humane persons and organisations which mark the history of Aboriginal affairs, by giving greater prestige, if not force, to their arguments. But there is a great contrast between the kind of expertise in traditional cultures and the traditions of government which formed the background of members of the Permanent Mandates Commission and the expertise and traditions largely shaped in the 'feed back' from frontier conditions, which are preserved in the records of the first conference of Commonwealth and States, in 1937.

By that time the last Aboriginal resistance was over and the period of punitive expeditions had almost come to a close.

THE PROBLEM OF DEFINING FRONTIER CONFLICTS

Although it is tempting to refer to 'warfare' and 'guerilla war' in relation to frontier conflict, the concept of warfare involves a hierarchical social structure, with the leaders and the led; armies, and those who command them; and these in turn require a certain size in the warring population. There must also be some concept of possession of land, with advantages to be seized or defended with it.

War, in effect, was born out of agrarian civilisation. Previously there had been murders and vendettas, occasionally collective, but most of man's aggressiveness was slaked by hunting. A real war, with battles, requires that a society attain a certain critical size. Above all, it must play a role in the economic development of societies. War made its appearance when the bounty was no longer game but the soil and the men who worked it.[4]

The economic role, the hierarchical organisation, the 'critical size' which made possible a *campaign* with an end in view, serving the economic and other interests of the social group, were lacking from Aboriginal society. Resistance was easily swept aside, since it did not have leaders to organise campaigns. Furthermore, the Aborigines were particularly vulnerable in that the tribal units comprised small family groups of men, women, and children, who were easily overtaken and slain by posses of mounted

[3] *C.P.D.* (H. of R.), 10 September 1919.
[4] André Leroi-Gourhan—interviewed by Tanneguy de Quenetain—Realités du Pacifique, August 1966.

THE FRONTIERS AFTER 1856　149

pursuers, often with the evidence of their marauding—white flour on black skin—still upon them.

British nationalism had been geared to this role for centuries; so that one finds the events of the frontier continually justified in the terms of warfare. War had conditioned the minds of white men to a special fear of the stranger. The tradition of the frontier fighter was well established. The identification of the economic interests of the adventurer with the spreading of civilisation produced the kind of popular story already referred to.

So this was war on one side, with all the suspending of morality involved in war, until the objective was gained. Methods of warfare lasted into the 1930s. Only on occasions did the victims manage to use some of the techniques of war in their own defence. We can possibly use the term guerilla *action*, where the Aboriginal uses the tactics of hitting the white man's enterprise and organisation where it is most vulnerable, by slaughter of key manpower, stock, and the destruction of stores. But we cannot, I think, fairly write of guerilla *war* waged *by* Aborigines (except in the service of the whites: it was easy for the attackers to use Aboriginal manpower against other Aborigines)—only of war waged *against* them.

The compromise seems to have been to treat armed defence or attack by the whites as warfare (with a few exceptions such as the trials and executions which followed the Myall Creek affair) and Aboriginal armed defence or attack as warfare before arrest or where no attempt was made to arrest and as a criminal offence where the arrest was made. The lack of effective leadership was a handicap not only for physical resistance but for treaty and discussion. Such grave injustice could at least have been made more clear to authority, had the Aboriginal groups affected been articulate. Lacking this, the *conflict* was never clearly defined in terms of the law. To the extent that individual actions were, the rules of evidence were heavily weighted against the Aboriginal; the jury system even more so.

POLICE AND THE FRONTIER

When the conquerors do not recognise a state of war, there is confusion between the facts of warfare and the theory which extends potential citizenship with conquest.

In such situations, two approaches seem logical. The first is to treat conquest as such, and to expedite it by military means: reduce the inhabitants to complete submission, and only then impose the law, with full machinery of enforcement. Only at this stage are the conquered admitted to whatever legal status the conqueror determines. Those conquered and within the controlled area are then protected by military means from warlike non-citizens across the newly extended frontier.

The other approach is to acknowledge common citizenship for all, whether 'controlled' or not. This involves the use of civil police to keep the law and good order, at least wherever there are settlers, missionaries, traders, and the like. But the only way to do this is by the government itself being first into new areas, establishing control, and only then admitting settlers.

In such a situation the problem arises of what action should be taken when a 'native', acting in accordance with his own custom, kills or injures someone within the area of control. J.H.P. Murray, who retained the position of Chief Justice of Papua when he became Lieutenant Governor in 1907, formulated the principles that officers should act as civil police only and should pursue and arrest suspects without the use of force except for that purpose. It was Australia's only really humane frontier policy—and it was also often in violent contrast with practice, both because of the very high degree of discipline and imagination required for its execution and also because government forces going into new areas were resisted as attacking forces or the attempt to seize an individual was resisted as an attack.

There is a difference, nonetheless, between the practices that arise from a policy based on reprisals and those that arise from the breakdown of a principle based on the rights of the person. The purpose in the policy of extending legal protection and safeguards to all leads to the practical situation that the officer who fails to do so must explain why or evade the facts in his report. He may be charged for breach of the civil law, even when his life has been in danger. This offers some hope of better race relationships and of common respect for law in the long term, and of more thoughtful practice in the short term, among the more able and perceptive officers. It is the reverse of the situation where lip service only is paid to the law, and where the government, in weakness or confusion, accepts the punitive expedition as unavoidable; and in practice or by default of control assists with the police, thus helping to develop a whole system of adminstrative double-talk about the facts. No matter how inapplicable the law may be to the circumstances, once it may safely be assumed that the law does not bind the officer and settler on the frontier there can be no barrier against the worst tyranny and crime.

THE FRONTIERS AFTER 1856

It is, then, hardly good enough to justify the Australian frontier facts as 'inevitable'. British colonial tradition and practice had become better than this: and the Papuan tradition for some time remained an exotic in Australian cross-cultural administration. There was a distinct difference between the tone of Papuan colonial administration in Murray's day and that which continued in Australia well into the 1930s. It is ironic, but significant, that a more humane policy was developed where resistance of settled village communities was so much more difficult to overcome.

The attempt to maintain law and order by use of civil police against individual lawbreakers demands that the force be effective. Also required is a 'controlled' area within which whites and 'natives' learn to know each other, under the control of the government. This is why government must *precede* others, to regulate the first contacts. Realisation of this led to the restricted areas policy in Australian New Guinea, introduced in the mid-1920s. Along the Australian frontier, even from the first settlements along the Hawkesbury and out of Hobart, the reverse was the case. In *no* case was pacification established before settlement.

The more widely the stock was depastured, the more impossible the problem became. The situation is well illustrated in despatches from Gipps. Back in 1838 he was trying to control a dispersed situation by use of the Mounted Police, who were mainly volunteers and shared settler prejudices. He wrote to Glenelg in July that he had to resist pressures from squatters, interested in the overlanding of stock to Port Phillip, to allow them to form their own 'militia'. (This would have been a way of keeping their punitive expeditions 'administratively clean'.) If, he wrote, 'Proprietors, for the sake of obtaining better pasturage . . . will venture with them to such a distance from protection . . .' it must be at their own risk, since the government had not the resources for their protection. The occasion was the killing of eight members of an overlanding party in the Ovens River area.[5] He deferred a policy announcement on such incidents because things had got out of hand some 500 miles to the north in the New England area, where he had just heard of a massacre of twenty-two Aborigines.[6]

But his policy could never catch up with events. It did have some effect in encouraging resistance from the Aborigines—and thus increased the fear and determination of the settlers. In February 1841 he reported continued fighting in the Ovens River area. The Aborigines were now using firearms. The stations of the Protectorate offered, he thought,

[5] Docker (*Simply Human Beings*) says that this was near the site of Benalla.
[6] H.R.A. (1), vol. XIX, pp. 508-10—Gipps to Glenelg, Despatch No. 115, 21 July 1838.

centres of refuge for them, since with all their lands taken for stock they must fight or have somewhere to go and some way to get food. He was still trying to have Aboriginal offenders captured and brought to trial. In the same letter he mentioned the capture of two 'tribes' near Melbourne, but at the cost of two (disclosed) Aboriginal lives.[7]

The relationship of Aborigines to particular areas, and the nature of their society and economy, were not well enough known to provide the facts on which intelligent application of any policy could be based. In any case, the Border Police which succeeded the Mounted Police, partly to enforce Gipps's Land Act, formed an equally inefficient means of executing consistent policy, being recruited largely from former convicts.

The Native Police had begun to operate in the Port Phillip District during the Protectorate. Bourke had instructed Lonsdale to establish the force at Port Phillip. Something of the confusion which has marked thinking in Aboriginal affairs may be noted in the plan, since it concentrated on the effects of good food, discipline, employment, status, and the like on the Aboriginal troopers. Their families were to be established in villages and educated for settled agriculture.[8] Some settlers were moved away from the Dandenongs to make way for these settlements. Maconochie, who first raised the idea, seems to have had the precedent of the Sepoys in mind. One is struck by the lack of consideration of what impact such a dread weapon could have on Aboriginal society.

The necessary detribalisation which made the troopers into an effective fighting force must also have been a process of brutalisation; and it would have been effective enough among young men whose world was collapsing and who felt no particular loyalty to Aborigines from areas far away from their own: a 'foreign legion' at the disposal of the whites along the eastern frontiers.

The association of Aboriginal bushcraft with European discipline made such a force invincible in the bush. A group of Aborigines would be tracked, located, and surrounded; armed sentinels would be posted to prevent them breaking out of the trap; and then the group would be charged. As James Collier, a devotee of the theory of white supremacy, has written, 'they soon made short work'.[9] This use of the Native Police as a military force was in the earlier tradition of using troops; but in the earlier cases, as in the Bathurst area in 1824, the killing had occurred after declaration of martial law.

[7] Ibid., vol. XXI, pp. 208 *et seq.*—Despatch No. 35, 3 February 1841.
[8] See Foxcroft, *Australian Native Policy*, ch. 4.
[9] See James Collier, *The Pastoral Age in Australasia*, p. 129.

THE FRONTIERS AFTER 1856

There were no separate Native Police in South or Western Australia, but the police were made more effective as a fighting force in the bush by the use of the black trackers. Under South Australian administration in the Northern Territory, one group of trackers with their white constable did operate for a time as an unofficial punitive squad.

So no overt policy for extending control was defined in law and applied in practice. In law, the Aboriginal continued to enjoy his legal status as a British subject, while in every part of the frontier, at some stage or other, the private punitive expedition was possible. This set the tone of relationships between the races and affected labour relations between white employer and Aboriginal worker. The story of the frontiers is monotonously the same: when prosecution did occur, the penalty for homicide was inflicted almost exclusively on the Aboriginal offender. From first to last, until the whole continent was occupied (with the dubious exception of the large reserves of the north and centre, established in areas which were inaccessible or useless for grazing) the first contacts were made by unrestrained settlers, with subsequent and variable efforts at control, involving use of police in situations which were out of control and in which police duties were seen as primarily to protect white settlers.

Only the reverse order of events could have offered some hope of better relations. This would have required some real interest in the Aboriginal, even if only as an economic asset to the pastoral industry and mining, an effective police force, and a liaison between the government and the Aboriginal as against the settler interests—the kind of liaison which could develop in other colonies, in very different circumstances in Papua for instance.

The same dilemma can be seen along the Murrumbidgee and the Murray in the late 1830s and early 1840s and in the Kimberleys and the Northern Territory half a century later. In February 1839 James Coutts Crawford, having passed the last station on the Murrumbidgee on the way to South Australia with stock, had his first bullock speared—'a wanton and malicious act'. This led him to reflect that

All our colonies are more or less plagued with so-called Philanthropists . . . who like to hear the sound of their most sweet voices at Exeter Hall and elsewhere . . . The Australian blacks have been for long great pets of theirs. Now I have as much liking for the Australian Aborigines as perhaps any of the Exeter Hall gang . . . But I consider that any race is safer in any hands than in those of the philanthropists . . . The protectorate . . . has only tended to the exasperation of the whites and the consequent annihilation of more blacks.[10]

[10] D.H. Pike (ed.), The Diary of James Coutts Crawford: Extracts on Aborigines and Adelaide 1839 and 1841, *South Australiana*, vol. 4, no. 1, March 1965, p. 4.

154 THE DESTRUCTION OF ABORIGINAL SOCIETY

The chain of causation assumed is interesting for its premises: that non-Aboriginal land claims override Aboriginal rights to life. The point is subsequently expanded in a very clear analysis of the current dilemma.

A stockholder is in want of a fresh run for his stock, and therefore proceeds with them *outside his neighbours* [the italics are mine] and therefore in contact with an uncivilized tribe of blacks. He erects his hut and stockyard and takes up his residence. A day or two after his first arrival one or two blacks drop in, they are well received and entertained, get some meat and damper fare offered, a little tobacco, which never having used before they look at with disgust ... in a week or so the whole tribe is domesticated with the squatter ... Soon however they see an ox killed, cut up and prepared for eating and they eat part of him themselves. That evening out of curiosity they kill one for themselves ... The blacks are remonstrated with, they then proceed to spear some every day. The squatter at length takes up arms, the blacks spear him or any of his stockmen when they find them with their backs turned and war commences and often continues for months and years.[11]

It is interesting that as early as this an exasperated settler puts together as the object of his anger the government's organisation for protection, and the philanthropists. As time went on and frontier life moved far from the centres of close settlement, people in the towns of the south were joined with these 'do-gooders'. Such efforts, wrote Crawford, merely create jobs and plague the settlers.

The true way to protect the blacks is to prevent them from injuring the whites. *Of course the colony might be tried to be kept within limits so as not to be brought in contact with more wild tribes* but anyone who is acquainted with Australia knows that such restraint is totally impossible. Let the blacks then be fairly restrained by a border police, who will treat them with kindness but at the same time with determined firmness and who can at the same time keep their eye upon the white settler and then [*sic*] at all events be some probability of safety for the Aborigines.

He repeats his view of the Protectorate; accuses the protectors of staying in towns and settled areas, 'palavering much in ... religious phrases. They might as well have been in England.'[12]

It is worth comparing with this situation one far removed in space and time but not very different. Mary Durack's story of her family contains some most revealing evidence of these same views, more or less inevitable in the circumstances, held by the pastoralists who settled in the Kimberleys. Her father, she says, would have been embarrassed to have been thought 'unrealistic' about Aborigines by those who expressed the majority sentiment among the Kimberley squatters. But he made the point that conquest of a country involved at least some limited responsibilities; and

[11] Ibid., pp. 4-5.
[12] Ibid., p. 5. My italics. This would involve a restricted areas policy—C.D.R.

THE FRONTIERS AFTER 1856

advocated some integration of the Aboriginal, as a matter of government and economic policy, within the station work force. He was well aware that this was essential for the best economic returns where labour was in short supply.

I would like [he says, in reply to the criticism coming from Perth and other Australian capitals] to ask our critics how else they would have us deal with the situation . . . other than by remaining out of the country altogether . . .? My father, a pioneer of western Queensland, held it as an ideal to absorb the aborigines into the whiteman's economy and trained many natives successfully . . . Others in the district pursued the same policy and the fact that so few aborigines now remain in those parts was in spite of their efforts. Had they been encouraged and subsidised to bring in and train many more natives the situation might be very different today for it was the behaviour of the outside or bush blacks who, in failing to co-operate with the new regime, in killing cattle, horses and sheep and committing a number of unprovoked murders that led to the settlers *having to call in the protection of the police*. I speak therefore from some experience and would regret to see the situation in Kimberley reach a point where the wholesale extermination of the aborigines would become inevitable.[13]

The italics are mine; they may serve to emphasise what were normal assumptions of a frontier station owner; that the police were not called in just to arrest suspects and that their intervention, at least in Queensland and the Kimberleys, was likely to lead to extermination of Aborigines. The argument that the station owner is the possessor of the land (even though the terms of lease from the Crown protect Aboriginal rights to use water and to hunt) and that the Aboriginal is the intruder has been maintained by pastoral interests to the present day. The other fact of interest is that the frontier could not be divided into 'settled' and 'unsettled' or 'restricted' areas: the tribes farther out refused to 'co-operate' in helping the pastoralist to make money.

What the facts in the Kimberleys could be is illustrated by Miss Durack's reminiscence of the Aboriginal Ulysses and his sister Maggie,

the only survivors of a raid on a big encampment of blacks around the Ord River after the spearing of Tudor Shadforth. Without a trace of rancour, in fact with the suggestion of a reminiscent chuckle, the genial old man in his pensioner's camp on the river told how he and his sister had been discovered crouching behind a tree. 'Better shoot 'em', one of the whitemen said. 'This little boy only gonna grow up to put a spear in some poor whitefulla and this little girl—well she gonna breed more blackfellas'. Then big Duncan McCaully come up. 'I can do with a boy', he says, and he put me up on his saddle and somebody else take Maggie. . . .[14]

[13] *Kings in Grass Castles*, p. 290.
[14] Ibid., pp. 314-15.

THE DESTRUCTION OF ABORIGINAL SOCIETY

Half a century had elapsed from the reflections of Crawford in his diary to the time when Durack wrote of the problem of the Aborigines farther out who refused to 'co-operate'. In that half century no alternatives had been found to the complete defeat of Aboriginal resistance and complete domination of the remnants. Solutions were being sought to problems inside the frontiers; but the first contacts profoundly affected attitudes of both races, confirming the whites in their superiority and bringing progressively to the blacks the hard lessons of defeat and loss.

THE QUEENSLAND FRONTIER,
1859-1897

Two decades of violence, from the opening up of the Moreton Bay District, preceded the establishment of the colony of Queensland. The first settlers on the Condamine and the Macintyre faced difficulties like those in the hinterland of the Clarence about the same time; as there, some stations had to be given up; and there were punitive expeditions of the same type.[1] The reminiscences of Tom Petrie, which appear circumstantial and which, according to Walter E. Roth, show 'an intimate and profound knowledge of the aboriginals with whom they deal',[2] indicate the extent to which violence and injuries to the person were believed by one who knew them well to be in-built in the traditional culture. Perhaps this was an Aboriginal reaction to the violence of the convict settlement on the Brisbane River. What seems to have been a large-scale massacre by poisoning on Kilcoy Station in 1842 was known among the tribes far and wide; it appears to have been merely the biggest of many such attempts. Petrie tells of the flour being poisoned and left in the shepherds' huts; and, perhaps more significantly, of the instant recognition by the poisoned Aboriginal of the white man's treachery. Petrie's Aboriginal friends could imitate for him the symptoms of arsenic poisoning. Of an attempted poisoning on Nindery Station (near Maroochy) he wrote: 'Before eating much, however, fits came on, and

---

[1] *Q.V. & P.*, 1861, p. 389—Select Committee on the Native Police Force and the Condition of the Aborigines Generally, Report; see also Winifred Cowin, European-Aboriginal Relations in Early Queensland 1859-1897 (B.A. thesis, University of Queensland, 1950). I would like to acknowledge here that my references to the organisation of the Native Police were greatly facilitated by access to this work.

[2] Foreword, in Constance Campbell Petrie, *Tom Petrie's Reminiscences of Early Queensland* ...

THE DESTRUCTION OF ABORIGINAL SOCIETY

knowing at once what was wrong, they ran to the river and drank a lot of salt water, which made them very sick, but cured them.'[3]

Petrie also recalls the early use of troops against Aboriginal 'thieves and murderers'; and the mixture of brutality and ridicule in dealing with some of these Aborigines convicted of murder, for acts which if committed by whites were regarded as self-defence or a part of warfare. In this context the execution of Aborigines publicly in Brisbane had something of the expediency of punishment for war crimes.[4] Murders in cold blood by whites could be brought to trial, with a chance of conviction, only if witnessed by other whites willing to testify, since Aboriginal evidence was not admissible. Petrie tells of a quite shocking series of murders of Aborigines on the run next to his own, where his father knew the facts but, because he had to depend on Aborigines' evidence, saw no point in laying information.[5] Old Dalaipi, who worked for Petrie for a long time, summed up the whole story as the Aboriginal saw it.

we were hunted from our ground, shot, poisoned, and had our daughters, sisters, and wives taken from us . . . what a number were poisoned at Kilcoy . . . They stole our ground where we used to get food, and when we got hungry and took a bit of flour or killed a bullock to eat, they shot us or poisoned us. All they give us now for our land is a blanket once a year.[6]

By the time of separation, the *Moreton Bay Courier* was monotonously reporting inter-racial clashes.[7] The Native Police, first introduced into these northern areas in 1848, under Lieutenant Frederick Walker, with headquarters at Callandoon on the Macintyre, had become the main instrument of Aboriginal administration, making it possible for the settlers to spread quickly into new areas without heavy stock losses. In Queensland the Aboriginal seems to have come closer than hitherto to true guerilla warfare, hitting more consistently at the isolated shepherds' huts and killing the shepherds and the stock. By the time of the 1861 inquiry into the Native Police, even the Lutheran mission at Brisbane and the Catholics on Stradbroke had been discouraged. New frontier contacts tended to be with armed settlers, without active missionary work, and with police who went there to maintain order, often in practice by striking first. Thus Queensland frontier policy came close to

[3] Ibid., pp. 208-9 (my italics), see also pp. 148 *et seq.*
[4] Ibid., ch. XX, on the careers of Millbong Jemmy, Dundalli, and Ommuli.
[5] Ibid., pp. 6-7.
[6] Ibid., pp. 182-3.
[7] Select Committee on the Native Police 1861; and Winifred Cowin, European-Aboriginal Relations, p. 4.

THE QUEENSLAND FRONTIER, 1859-1897

the alternative of complete conquest before introduction of the rule of law.

But as the frontier went farther north, there was increasing need for Aboriginal labour. Petrie, on his run at Lone Pine near Brisbane, depended almost completely on Aboriginal workers. Yet the leaseholder before him could not work it because of the stock losses; and Petrie tells how on one occasion he came through the bush to find the white officer and the Native Police with a group ready surrounded, about to commence the massacre.[8]

The Aboriginal, lacking the type of social organisation and background which enabled the whites to regard all strange black men as enemies, seems to have often persisted in regarding whites as possible friends, until he knew otherwise from experience. This of course continued to render vulnerable one group after another. Settlers included men of all kinds, good and bad; but many were blinded by their own system of belief, by fear, and the ethic which accepted expansion of frontiers of 'civilisation' as justifying the means. Their relations with the Aborigines varied as greatly as those of any group of men who in practice were vested in the absolute power of the gun. It would be wrong to suggest that all contact was of the type which is highlighted in the criticisms and in the well-documented accounts of brutalities by members of the Native Police. Obviously, and especially as the cattle runs extended, there was a common adjustment between the pastoral station and the group much like that elsewhere. But the Native Police set the tone of Aboriginal administration: it emphasised the sanction of force in labour relationships; and it was for over three decades the main instrument of government policy. It was the only instrument of 'native administration' which the new government inherited from New South Wales.

Public criticism of the spectacular injustices involved in its operations was one of the reasons which led to the appointment of a Select Committee of the Legislative Assembly, in May 1861, not only to inquire into the organisation and management of the Force but also to look at the whole question of 'how far it may be practicable to ameliorate the present condition of the Aborigines of this Colony'.[9] The specific questions concerned the 'present condition and organisation' of the Force: 'the charges of unnecessary cruelty brought against their officers when dealing with the Natives, and protecting the settlers against their aggressions' and 'the prospect of civilising, or in any way improving the

---

[8] *Reminiscences*, pp. 7-8.
[9] Report and Minutes of Evidence of Select Committee, p. 1 (*Q.V. & P.*, 1861, p. 389).

condition of the aboriginal population'.[10] It was very much a pastoralists' Committee. Pastoralists gave most of the evidence and 'the whole weight of the evidence' was found to justify the system.

any want of discipline . . . or any excesses that are attributable to the Troopers, have arisen mainly from the inefficiency, the indiscretion, and the intemperate habits of some of the Officers, rather than from any defect in the system itself.[11]

The main recommendations, therefore, were for a more efficient Force—with cadet officers, stations outside the towns, adherence to the policy of using troopers away from their own country; with a monthly report from each detachment to the commandant, 'who would furnish a general abstract thereof to the Colonial Secretary, or the head of the Executive Department, under which he may be placed'.[12] This appears to have maintained a tradition of secrecy. In the absence of Aboriginal evidence (a situation which continued until 1884), the only source for a coroner's inquiry, except very occasionally, would be the officer himself. Even his report to the commandant could be suitably treated before it was sent to the departmental head.

How a disclosure might occur was illustrated by the evidence of a commercial traveller, Henry Babbitt, who had given assistance to the detachment in the Dawson District by allowing them to use his carriage to take an Aboriginal named Gulliver, hopelessly drunk and bound, and wanted for murder. He was quite sure that the man could not have tried to escape from under the tree where he was placed, while he, Babbitt, accompanied the officers to the homestead nearby. When he came with the officers to get the prisoner, he was told 'He no keep away any more'. Babbitt had apparently been disturbed when he heard the official report that Gulliver had been shot while attempting to escape. But the tenor of the questions put to him suggest a view that the prisoner had been a murderer in any case: in fact, in this and other cases the attitude of the Committee was almost that of counsel for the Force:

'Are you aware that there was a warrant out against Gulliver?'
    'I had heard there was.'
    'Are you aware that when a warrant is out against a person, and he attempts to escape, it is justifiable to shoot him?' 'Yes'.[13]

With respect to the 'charges against the Officers', the Committee claimed to have investigated them 'as far as practicable', in face of the

[10] Report, p. 2 (ibid., p. 394).
[11] Ibid.
[12] Report, p. 3 (ibid., p. 395).
[13] Minutes of Evidence, p. 34 (ibid., pp. 439–40).

THE QUEENSLAND FRONTIER, 1859-1897 161

difficulty 'where depredations are committed by the blacks to make them amenable to British Law'. It claimed that it 'could not countenance the indiscriminate slaughter which appears on more than one occasion to have taken place'. One lieutenant appeared to have 'acted with indiscretion', and a reprimand was recommended. 'Were it not that in other respects he is a most valuable and zealous Officer' members felt that he should be dismissed.[14] Dismissal was recommended in another case, where the bodies of participants in a bunya feast were left lying about a station after a more or less routine 'dispersal', but drunkenness of the officer was the main reason. One who in the town of Maryborough shot an Aboriginal in the river (and was subsequently presented with a sword by a committee of the citizens, a matter which led to protests in the local press) was commended as a 'zealous and efficient officer', even though the act was witnessed by town dwellers and although an arrest would have been easy enough. There is simply no point in giving lengthy details; one requires a strong stomach, even at this point in time, to read the lengthy evidence.

But that of the 'valuable and zealous officer' who should be reprimanded has to be recounted, because it shows without any question that contact was completely out of legal control. The officer had received letters from station holders in the Logan River area telling of Aborigines killing cattle, robbing huts, stealing sheep, and threatening shepherds. He finally found tracks near Mount Lindsay and found a group in the Dugandan scrub.

'Had you any direct evidence to shew that they were the blacks who had committed the outrages complained of?'

'The shepherds at Mr. Compigné's told me that the blacks had come down from the Telemon side of the range . . . I only dispersed the Telemon mob . . .'

'Were there any warrants out against those blacks?'

'No. Warrants are never given out against the blacks for cattle-stealing, which is done by the whole tribe.'

He stated that he was in control of his men, but not when they 'go into the scrub; they then dismount and take off their trousers'. He went round the scrub to warn another 'mob': the troopers were out of sight for half an hour. Asked what his orders had been, he said: 'I told them to surround that camp of Telemon blacks, and to disperse them.'

'What do you mean by dispersing?'

'Firing at them. I gave strict orders not to shoot any gins. It is only sometimes, when it is dark, that a gin is mistaken for a blackfellow . . .'

[14] Report, p. 3 (ibid., p. 395).

THE DESTRUCTION OF ABORIGINAL SOCIETY

'Do you think it is a proper thing to fire upon the blacks in that way?'

'If they are the right mob, of which I had every certainty.'

'. . . Was there any necessity for such an indiscriminate slaughter?'

'I don't think there was any indiscriminate slaughter: there were only two blacks shot.'

'. . . What induced you to give those orders?'

'The letters I had received from several squatters . . .'

Asked if he had seen any cattle killed, he replied that he 'could not waste time to see whether a cow or a bullock had been speared'.[15]

He said that he had never received written or printed instructions from the commandant, other than the general instructions (which dealt with reports, the discipline of the camp, care of horses; and the duty of 'dispersal').

It is the duty of the Officers at all times and opportunities [states this routine order] to disperse any large assemblage of blacks; such meetings, if not prevented, invariably lead to depredations or murder; and nothing but the mistaken kindness of the Officers in command inspired the blacks with sufficient confidence to commit the late fearful outrages on the Dawson River. The Officers will therefore see the necessity of teaching the aborigines that no outrage or depredation shall be committed with impunity—but on the contrary, retributive justice shall speedily follow the Commission of crime; nevertheless the Officers will be careful in receiving reports against the blacks, as it frequently happens that mistakes are made as to the identity of the aggressors.[16]

Some reports of 'clashes' were appended to the Committee's Report, as they passed through from the commandant to the Colonial Secretary. One, of twelve lines, dated April 1861, dealt with 'outrages' by Aborigines at the time of the 'bunya bunya' (where large numbers came together they would often raid the stations for food), the purchase of horses, patrolling at Wide Bay, the officer's own encounters with Aborigines, and the fact that 'on two or three occasions I found it necessary to fire upon them before they would disperse'.[17]

It was clear enough to the 'zealous and efficient officer' what he had to do; and he was probably being more candid than his superiors in his disclosure that 'I act according to the letters I receive from squatters'. He had no time to look through the difficult cattle country for the allegedly dead beasts, 'but we can generally tell whether they have been rushed or not'.

[15] Minutes, pp. 16-18—evidence of Lieutenant Fred Wheeler (ibid., pp. 423-5).

[16] Minutes, Appendix A, pp. 151-2 (ibid., p. 559).

[17] Minutes, Appendix B, p. 152—E.V. Morisset to Colonial Secretary, from Rockhampton, 10 April 1861 (ibid., p. 558).

THE QUEENSLAND FRONTIER, 1859-1897　　　　163

'Do you not think there is any other way of dealing with them, except by shooting them?'

'No, I don't think they can understand anything else except shooting them; at least, that is the case, as far as my experience goes.'

Should he pause to call on them to surrender, they would get away. Perhaps the most revealing remark came when he was asked whether the establishment of the Force headquarters at Sandgate had helped to 'civilize' Aborigines:

'That is a question I am not prepared to answer, I know so little of the blacks. They run before me—I never see them.'[18]

There is much other evidence to confirm the administrative arrangements and methods revealed in this evidence, on which it seems unnecessary to dwell further. The Committee did hear evidence from A. C. Gregory, on the need for a higher proportion of white officers, as in Western Australia, who should know the local language; but he admitted that in the open country of Western Australia the task was easier. There was also discussion of the possibility of a non-Aboriginal mounted force, which the nature of the country appeared to rule out. But there was no consideration at all of an approach in which police used in a military fashion did not form the main agency of policy. The system was working, the stations extending; and, so long as the facts were shrouded by 'discretion' and reticent reporting, there could even be evidence that the Force was the instrument of peace and order—for the settler.

As for the prospect of civilising the Aborigines,

The evidence taken by your Committee, [says the Report], shews beyond doubt that all attempts to Christianize or educate the aborigines of Australia have hitherto proved abortive. Except in one or two isolated cases, after being brought up and educated for a certain period, the Natives of both sexes invariably return to their savage habits. Credible witnesses shew that they are addicted to cannibalism; that they have no idea of a future state; and are sunk in the lowest depths of barbarism. Missions have been established amongst them at different periods with but partial success; and the same may be said of the schools established in the different Colonies.[19]

No more bitterly prejudiced statement, one hopes, has ever been used of the indigenous people by a responsible body representing a settler parliament. Fear, abhorrence of activities which were little known and less understood, exasperation caused by economic loss where the Aboriginal hit back or cheerfully and recklessly sallied out from the bunya feast to supplement it with beef or mutton, and some defiance to boot, had all helped to lead to this.

[18] Minutes, pp. 29-32—evidence of Lieutenant Fred Wheeler (ibid., pp. 435-8).
[19] Report, p. 4 (ibid., p. 396).

164　THE DESTRUCTION OF ABORIGINAL SOCIETY

The reports of addiction to cannibalism had in fact come from at least one 'credible witness' in Tom Petrie: this is a good example of a cause of cultural aversion. Yet the Aboriginal cannibal, on evidence now known, was a ritual one where he was a cannibal at all: and consumption of the body, or parts of the body, of a man whom Elkin would describe as one of 'high degree', appears to have been a way of conserving his greatness within the group.[20] The millenia of literate tradition had, with the intellectualisation and sublimation of such religious ritual, transformed ritual cannibalism for the European into another kind of sacrament— either a token eating of flesh and drinking of blood or a miraculous one, in which the bread and wine became the flesh and the blood. The spiritual significance of ceremonies which appeared the grossest of animal material-ism only became known much later. We know more now about such symbolism, expressing filial piety and love of the group. It seems reasonable to assume that what Stanner wrote of the Murinbata religion much later would apply broadly to most Aboriginal religions. That of the Murinbata

centred on inexorable events of human life ... the inexorables were thought of as being in sequence along a stretch of a cycle with two parts, one corporeal and determinate, one spiritual and less determinate. *The spiritual part of man had by necessity to move through that cycle even as fleshly man.* The principle of the religion was to make fleshly, determinate and social life correlative with the spiritual cycle. But life in human, wordly society was at all times a function of that cycle, and subserv-ient to it.[21]

Adherence to such a religion, and the early socialisation within it of those who appeared to the Committee as hopeless 'drop-outs', partly explains the failure of attempts to Christianise, and to educate in schools. Nor does it appear to have occurred to the Committee that the events so clearly established in the evidence might interfere with motivation. Who could envisage religion without God, Sin, Salvation, and Church?

Evidence included a series of letters from the Moravian missionaries Spieseke and F. A. Hagenauer, from the Wimmera mission in Victoria, purporting to strengthen the argument that missions had been successful; but these, since they were mainly concerned with death and salvation, could have little relevance to those seeking an answer to practical problems faced in Queensland.[22] But there was another submission, from the

[20] I have checked this statement with Professor A.P. Elkin, with relation to the Queensland area.
[21] W.E.H. Stanner, *On Aboriginal Religion*, Oceania Monograph no. 11, p. 267, reprinted from *Oceania*, vol. XXXIII, no. 4, 1963. My italics.
[22] Minutes of Evidence, p. 160—Appendix B—Missionary Success Among the Aborigines (*Q.V. & P.*, 1861, p. 566).

THE QUEENSLAND FRONTIER, 1859-1897

Reverend W. Ridley, who argued that there were numerous cases to prove 'the capacity of the Aborigines for social and spiritual improvement'. He had met Aboriginal shepherds in the Namoi and Barwon areas who had been taught at the old Wellington mission, and he claimed that some trained there as children had lived and died as Christians. He outlined a program to introduce tribesmen gradually to regular employment; and argued that there should be an isolated training centre like Poonindie.[23]

Ridley was supported by Dr Challinor, M.P., who was also the Coroner of the Ipswich Police District and whose letter to the Attorney-General, following his discharge of his duty on bodies which the 'valuable and zealous officer' and his detachment had failed to destroy, was one of the reasons for the appointment of the Committee. Challinor objected not only to illegal killings but to the molestation of those fishing or camped on station properties, with the shooting of their dogs and the destruction of their blankets and opossum rugs. The point was an important one, since Queensland did not safeguard hunting and fishing rights on pastoral leaseholds. Challinor argued (in vain) that either such rights or other sustenance were essential. He claimed, against the 'weight' of the evidence, that Aborigines were capable of formal education, and that they should be included in the new scheme of 'general instruction' for other children. He was well ahead of his time when he argued that they should be included in schemes for secular, but not religious, education. 'I entirely object to any interference by the Government in matters of religion'. He quoted cases of very good Aboriginal station workers—and chess players as well.

Both as doctor and coroner he had had to deal with the aftermaths of official killings, where his findings had confirmed the reliability of Aboriginal informants. When asked whether he thought that 'the life of a white man ought to be placed in any danger whatever by such evidence?', he replied that he considered 'the life of a black man to be quite as valuable in itself as that of a white man'. He therefore argued for the admission of Aboriginal evidence. 'I would take his evidence, and leave it to the jury to judge of its value'. Assemblies, he said, should be 'dispersed' only where it was proved that the meetings were for illegal objects. Instead of dependence on police, white or black, he thought that there should be a system where acts of war followed only on warnings through interpreters.

The Committee put to him the analogy that reprisals were currently part of the method of keeping order in the Pacific:

'Have not the murders of merchantmen by savages in different islands always

[23] Minutes, Appendix C, p. 165 (ibid., p. 571).

THE DESTRUCTION OF ABORIGINAL SOCIETY

been held to be a *casus belli*, and have not men-of-war invariably been despatched to retaliate upon the murderers?'

'I cannot say that I altogether approve of such a course; I would make the authorities upon the island find out the perpetrators.'[24]

The confusion between a state of war and the assumption that Aborigines were subject to the law was evident throughout the deliberations.

Challinor's evidence is an indication of serious questioning by men of good will and intelligence. In a submission to the Committee made later, he developed his ideas and outlined a scheme for Aboriginal Protectors, who should instruct the 'chiefs' in what the law was. He also proposed that Aborigines should be encouraged to investigate offences against them and report these to Protectors. 'If the charges are sustained by legal evidence, of course the perpetrators ought to be dealt with according to law'. He could see no hope of justice until Aboriginal evidence could be admitted in the courts; and he referred to the evidence of Chinese being admitted to British courts in China. 'Why should it not be the case with regard to the Aborigines in this colony?' Each Protector should operate within a defined district. The Protective Force, the agency of law enforcement, should be composed of white men with black trackers; and should be strong enough to prevent crime.

If, however, the sole object of a Protective Force is to pursue the aborigines into scrubs and there slaughter them without discrimination or remorse, I think no force could be better adapted for that work than the present Native Police Force . . . This mode of protection appears to me as utterly repugnant to British law as it is to every principle of justice and equity.[25]

This statement makes one wish to know more of Dr Challinor. It also suggests that there were others in Ipswich and Brisbane who were deeply concerned with what was happening; as, indeed, there were among the pastoralists. Men like Tom Petrie were showing how effective Aboriginal station labour could be. New factors were, in time, to increase the questioning. One was the increasing shortage of Aboriginal labour, as the stations extended and the Aborigines disappeared. Another was the rise of a new kind of demand for labour, in the first sugar industry, which was a family crop in the south but which in the northern sugar lands was organised on the plantation system. This was anticipated in some evidence and in one of the recommendations of the Committee. Because 'any

[24] Minutes, pp. 2–6—evidence by Challinor (ibid., pp. 408–12); and pp. 12–16 (ibid., pp. 418–22).
[25] Minutes, pp. 166–7—Appendix D, Letter from Challinor addressed to the Chairman of the Committee (ibid., p. 572).

THE QUEENSLAND FRONTIER, 1859-1897   167

improvement in the social condition of this benighted race is an object so desirable of attainment', it recommended a proposal by a Mr Zillman for a 'Missionary Cotton Company, who, receiving land and other assistance from the Government, would endeavour to educate the children while employing the parents in the necessary work of the plantation.'[26] In the background were the experiments with cotton from the Clarence northwards; the boost was to come from the interruption of United States exports caused by the Civil War. Australian production was to collapse when it ended.

Another factor in change was to be the increasing political weight of the townsmen and their isolation from the harsher conditions of the frontier. The immediate cause of some interest among them would be the fringe-dwelling populations; and it was inevitable that the direction of policies supported would be towards institutionalisation and the relief of poverty of a 'dying race'. One of the reasons for early development of the town fringe-dwelling group was that the harried Aboriginal had often nowhere else to live in comparative safety from the Native Police. One Lieutenant Wheeler, asked during his evidence to the Select Committee whether the 'blacks' in the Moreton district were better behaved than they used to be, said 'Yes; we have driven them almost entirely away from the Logan. They generally go to the islands in the Bay, over the Dividing Range, to the boiling-down establishments, and to the townships.'[27] He mentioned groups which had fled to Stradbroke and Bribie Islands. He said also that many went to the Tooloom diggings, on the upper Clarence. (Such settlements round the goldmines became common all the way from Cape York to Kalgoorlie.)

The reference to the boiling down of cattle is a reminder that tallow was the main export from cattle runs, not beef; and that the industry had recovered from the great depression of 1842 through the boiling down of both sheep and cattle for tallow. There would always be food available round the 'boiling-down'; perhaps the habit of throwing the offal to the Aborigines began there.

Tom Petrie's evidence referred to the rapid depopulation round Brisbane, which he attributed to alcohol: not only the 'small settlers' round the new capital but the businessmen and others in town paid in 'grog'. He also referred to the danger of disbanding the Native Police in this kind of situation, saying that they would form a nucleus of Aboriginal anti-European organisation, as had happened some years before. Something

[26] Minutes, p. 5 (ibid., p. 397).
[27] Minutes, p. 18 (ibid., p. 424).

THE DESTRUCTION OF ABORIGINAL SOCIETY

of the tension of these early fringe-dwellers is indicated in his statement that drunken men 'cut one another'. He gave instances of his own employees refusing clothing and issues, demanding cash, and 'drinking it all out'.[28] The Committee had refused to recommend that Aborigines be granted hunting rights on stations, and this refusal must have been a factor in the influx to the towns, the diggings, and the boiling-down sites.

Before the Select Committee was appointed, the *Moreton Bay Courier* had stated in an editorial of 19 February 1861 that the white officer could do just as he liked, since the evidence neither of the victims nor his troopers was legally admissible.[29] The passing of the Oaths Amendment Act of 1884 did not end the tradition, because it was maintained by administrative means. 'Discretion' in disclosures was emphasised in regulations issued in 1866, which in effect prevented an officer from disclosing what had happened on a punitive expedition.[30] Yet the same regulations required civil police methods, including the arrest of any Aboriginal for whom a warrant had been issued—another indication of the confusion in frontier policy. No training except in camp and on the job was required of the 'Sub-Inspector', which was now the title of the junior officer. He had to be able to shoot and ride. His instructions remained vague for a long time, so that in a report presented in 1897, W E. Parry-Okeden, the Commissioner of Police, expressed the need for 'a clause distinctly legalising punitive action on the part of the police when deemed by proper authority to be necessary'.[31]

The Native Police offered a perfect niche for the sadist; and the Parry-Okeden Report clearly enough indicated, if this was necessary after nearly four decades of doubt and uncertainty in parliament and the press, that there had been officers who were 'cruel, cowardly or inefficient'. Winifred Cowin, who has studied the Native Police in detail, makes it clear that the uncertainty about the limits of its functions and powers remained throughout its existence. It was constantly involved in action which was illegal for police, though not for a military body under conditions of martial law (which never seems to have been declared). She cites the case of Chief Inspector Murray, sent to report on the shooting of Aborigines at Morinish, which had led to protests from the miners who were in theory being protected. 'I cannot see that the officer could have acted otherwise

---

[28] Minutes, p. 111 (ibid., p. 517).
[29] Quoted in Winifred Cowin, European-Aboriginal Relations.
[30] Ibid., p. 27.
[31] *Q.V. & P.*, 1897, vol. 2, p. 16—Report on the North Queensland Aborigines and the Native Police.

THE QUEENSLAND FRONTIER, 1859-1897 169

... it is very much to be regretted that he did not do so more quietly'.[32] She quotes, from officers' reports, complaints about the squatters who sheltered Aborigines on their runs from the police; for it continued to happen that an enthusiastic officer, in the pursuit of his duty, would 'disperse' the station labour force as well as the myalls.[33] In 1876 the *Brisbane Courier* stated that it was 'notorious' that some officers were 'influenced in the execution of their duty by unnatural ferocity'.[34]

The continued striking at the heart of the Aboriginal social order, on the occasions of large assemblies, made dangerous and difficult the renewal of social ties and the enforcement of the sanctions on which Aboriginal society depended. This in turn must have increased the desperation of the influential men and probably helped to provoke resistance on a scale resembling guerilla warfare.

The size of the Force was never over 250 men—mostly it was between 100 and 200—but firepower made a larger force unnecessary. The biggest extensions were made necessary by the goldrushes of the early seventies. Charters Towers, the Palmer, Cape River, Mount Morgan, Etheridge, Ravenswood, Normanby, Broughton River, all had to be 'protected'. By this time the Aboriginal resisted as far as he could all newcomers, even the miners who had the protection of numbers and who were not competing for the grasslands. In 1880 the Commissioner of Police stated that no Aboriginal had been known to enter the camp of any white man in the Palmer or Cook districts; and the press was referring to 'a sickening and brutal war of races'.[35]

By this time the conduct of Aboriginal affairs was being handed over to the ordinary Queensland police (assisted by Aboriginal trackers) in the 'settled' districts; and the Native Police were able to concentrate on spreading civilisation in the northern and western regions. Winifred Cowin states that there was a short-lived effort to use methods of conciliation in 1877—no doubt a reaction to the protests from areas now becoming remote from danger or fear. In 1880 the *Queenslander*, which was lending its columns to some of these protests, stated that in Cape York Aboriginal resistance had been intensified by police methods; that either new methods should be used or 'settlement must be delayed till the work of extermination is completed'.[36]

---

[32] *Q.V. & P.*, 1867, vol. 2, p. 983—quoted in European-Aboriginal Relations, p. 38.
[33] *Brisbane Courier*, 26 June 1865—Report of Sub-Inspector Peacher—quoted ibid., p. 41.
[34] 6 April 1876.
[35] Winifred Cowin, European-Aboriginal Relations, quoting *Queenslander*, 1 May 1880, editorial.
[36] Ibid.

Desperation had on occasions led to real battles. One such instance occurred in the 'Battle of Mitchell', when Jardine, the government resident, was attacked on his way to set up a shipping settlement at Cape York in 1864; firearms ensured that all the casualties were Aboriginal. In 1875 the Palmer River goldrush began, and according to Arthur Laurie the Aborigines put up there a more stubborn armed resistance than anywhere in Australia, maintaining a guerilla-type campaign for seven years, at the cost of hundreds of lives.[37]

In 1895 W.E. Parry-Okeden became Commissioner of Police. By this time Aboriginal society seems to have been shattered everywhere but in Cape York. Here they were resisting so effectively that the Colonial Secretary sent him to tour the area and to recommend a better police system. At the same time he was to consider how to 'ameliorate the condition of Queensland Aborigines'. His report in 1897 is clear enough indication that it was the remnants of the tribes which needed the protection of the police, against 'some of the blackest scoundrels alive'. He stated that the time had come to use the police to promote justice for white and black. The settlers could best be protected by conciliation of Aborigines. He saw a continuing need for punitive action, but he wanted the conditions for this defined in law.

There is a good deal yet to be learned of Queensland society in the early country towns which serviced the pastoral stations. They tended to be at the limits of deep sea navigation, where the drays brought wool and tallow for the sailing ships. Here round the mid-century congregated the ex-ticket-of-leave men and other 'squatter-haters' who were establishing themselves in business: and there could well have been something in these townsmen's attitudes which made possible a readiness to criticise the treatment of the Aboriginal on the stations: though to be sure, Aborigines in the fringe settlements growing up round the towns faced destruction in other ways. Real opposition to the pastoral interests had to wait for the growth of towns which did not depend on them economically. Even a large town like Ipswich was in the last resort dependent on the station business.

As time passed, the frontier was more widely separated from parts of the settled areas: the problems were different. After the goldrushes, some of the squatters' towns became mainly farmers' towns. Thus there was a range of situations, from mayhem and violence in Cape York, back to the streets of Brisbane and the country towns where Aborigines

[37] See 'The Black War in Queensland', *Royal Historical Society of Queensland Journal*, vol. VI, no. 1, September 1959, pp. 155-73.

THE QUEENSLAND FRONTIER, 1859-1897   171

and part-Aborigines had come to be regarded as harmless nuisances. Only occasionally was the question of the Aboriginal future seen as an urgent matter for government action (in any colony). He was becoming part of the background, and his depressed condition tended to be taken for granted.

As for the future, the general assumption was that there would not be one. He would disappear: and the main argument for some time in Queensland became one of what action should be taken to preserve the lives of individuals and to ameliorate their lot. But it is hard to tell how much public opinion was changing or how much of the change was due to the strengthening of other than the pastoral interests, to a degree that their opinions appear in the press.

Winifred Cowin quotes from the *Courier* and the *Queenslander* columns and correspondence to show how, by about 1870, the division of interest between frontier and town was showing itself in expressed opinion. Labour for the sugar plantations was urgently required by the mid-seventies; townsmen and farmers were better represented in parliament; and one result was a short experiment with a reserve system.

Something of a turning-point came in 1873, when some residents of the district of Mackay, the centre of the growing sugar industry, presented a petition relating to protection and employment of Aborigines in that district. By this time the big mining fields to the north had been opened up, and far northern Queensland had been proved suitable for cattle. The frontier had moved farther on and with it the Native Police. Aboriginal remnants had provided labour for the sugar plantations useful enough to rouse interest in their possibilities. Probably they were at least as efficient as many of the Pacific Islanders brought in as indentured labour. The Governor in Council appointed four Commissioners to deal with the petition; and further, generally to enquire 'what can be done to ameliorate the condition of the Aborigines of this Colony, and to make their labor useful to the settlers and profitable to themselves.[38]

They sent a circular to people in all parts of the colony, asking for population figures and opinions. The Aborigines Protection Society sent a draft Bill with recommendations. The Commissioners reported with tolerable unanimity on the rapidity of decrease in numbers, on addiction to alcohol, easy to obtain in spite of the law saying that 'diseases which

---

[38] Q.V. & P., 1874, p. 439—Report from the Commissioners appointed to Enquire into the Employment and Protection of the Aboriginals in the District of Mackay, and Generally to Enquire into What Steps can be Taken to Ameliorate the Condition of the Aborigines of Queensland (p. 1).

172   THE DESTRUCTION OF ABORIGINAL SOCIETY

have been introduced by Europeans are committing fearful ravages amongst the young and middle-aged'. They declared that although Aborigines were sometimes and in some places 'satisfactorily employed by settlers and others', generally they showed an 'unconquerable aversion' to 'persistent labor' (there is no reference to wages or incentives); that for the old and middle-aged little could be done but provide food and shelter, 'but that by education and training much may be done for the young'. (The last recommendation, after all the efforts of this kind, is enough, perhaps, to point the significance of history for government administration.) That opinion was changing is indicated in their statement, apparently based on the 'more than one hundred replies' received to the circular: 'it appears to be pretty generally held that justice and humanity alike demand that no effort or expense should be spared in doing what lies in our power for the welfare of the Aborigines.'[39]

Apparently the exceptional cases of satisfactory employment were in the Mackay District, whence C.F. Bridgman, of the Association for the Employment and Protection of Aborigines,

speaking for himself and neighbouring sugar-planters, represents that the Aborigines of that district, for certain classes of industry, are as good and reliable as ... any other colored laborers—not excepting South Sea Islanders.

They were being employed also as indentured labourers; and were

said to understand both the terms and period of an agreement, and faithfully to adhere to it, working diligently, and giving their employers little trouble; and the Commissioners are satisfied that the employment of these particular Natives is honestly conducted, and attended with considerable advantage both to employers and employed.

The Commissioners, although equally satisfactory results were not, they thought, generally to be expected elsewhere, were 'yet of opinion that Aboriginal labor, especially for short terms of service, might be far more generally and profitably employed than it has hitherto been'.[40]

Here is the beginning of the idea of the contract of service in its special Queensland form. There is also the beginning of hope, in a new possibility of Aboriginal welfare and settler self-interest lying in the same direction. But administrative moves in this direction did not come until 1897, when the Aborigines had been exposed to two more decades of a policy centred on the Native Police. Had they come earlier, Queensland might not have reacted so far into such rigid protective measures.

The legislation of 1897 was foreshadowed in further recommendations

[39] Report, p. 2 (ibid., p. 446).
[40] Report, p. 2 (ibid.).

THE QUEENSLAND FRONTIER, 1859-1897

from the Commission. One was for the appointment of Protectors of Aborigines for specified districts. They were to inquire into cases of ill-treatment and they were also to see that all contracts with Europeans were equitable and were fulfilled; and if necessary to sue for wages and to enforce agreements. This suggests that many of the Aborigines were finding their way into the cash economy. Reserves were recommended, exclusive to Aborigines, and on these the Protectors were to reside. Aborigines were to be excluded from towns and from places where liquor was available and 'induced' to stay on the reserves (which raised a long-standing contradiction between segregation and the need for employment). Housing, rations, clothing, implements, and medical aid were recommended for the reserves, along with employment there in cultivation of tropical and sub-tropical crops and in stock raising. Special efforts were to be made to 'improve, educate, and Christianise the young', in schools on the reserves. Stringent laws to prevent the sale of liquor were recommended. In fact this sounds very like a statement of Queensland Aboriginal policy for at least the next nine decades.

It was recognised that 'considerable sums' would be required. A statement which shows that public opinion was changing (one of the Commissioners had given evidence, with very different emphasis, to the Select Committee of 1861), was that settlement had been 'the source of great evil to the Aborigines', though this was qualified by the remark that 'at any rate in the settled districts' they 'receive much kindness and forebearance'. A question raised long before was raised again: that money received from the sale and lease of Crown lands was for an asset which the Aborigines 'originally occupied'. The right of prior occupation was obviously in mind when the Commission recommended as 'no more than just and reasonable that some small portion of this large sum should be set apart and held by the Government in trust for the benefit of those who are left of the tribes which formerly held these lands in possession'.[41]

They recommended that the proposed system be established tentatively in five districts—Moreton, Darling Downs, Wide Bay-Burnett, Port Curtis, and Mackay-Bowen.

There was a special recommendation that 'any measure for bringing the Aborigines under the special protection of our laws and ensuring to them justice and fair treatment' must also impose restrictions and penalties for breach of the law. Court records showed very few prosecutions for anything but personal violence against Europeans (in itself indicative of Aboriginal attitudes). Difficulties in getting proof and unsuitable penalties,

[41] Report, pp. 2-3 (ibid., p. 442).

they said, meant that many victims either submit to loss, 'or take the administration of punishment into their own hands'. This sounds very like one aspect of the discussion between Gipps and Grey. Here it was an argument for special sanctions, since so far there had been no segregation in prisons. It was recommended that Aborigines when convicted be separately confined, in institutions where they could be employed out of doors.

It would scarcely be practicable to have a prison on the mainland which would combine security with sufficient space for the employment of the prisoners in cultivating land, but there are several islands off the coast which meet the requirements of isolation combined with ample area of land adapted for agriculture.[42]

There seems a degree of inevitability, in retrospect; for one can see the chain of causation from this document to Palm Island. It was inevitable that any expenditure, on such a location, would be for a multi-purposed institution, given the degree of Aboriginal priorities from government; that a prison would also be training centre, old people's home, village, and the rest. It was also inevitable that where the settlement was established, it would in at least some respects serve the function of a prison in troublesome cases. From here, one may look forward to Palm Island or back to Flinders Island.

In 1875, reserves with ration depots were established, one in the Mackay area, one at Bowen, and one on Bribie Island, to which the fringe-dwellers of Brisbane were to be moved. But no new legislation was passed; and the experiments did not last long. The petition and the report are mainly significant as indicating a growing unease in the settled areas, while the Native Police proceeded much as before on the frontier. Probably the kind of policy outlined by the Commissioners was too obviously at variance with these facts.

The admission of Aboriginal evidence in the courts, in 1884, was probably more a by-product of secularism than a move for Aboriginal rights. It merely moved the hindrance from procedure to the white jury. Yet the pressure of mission and humanitarian interests, in Britain and at home, was growing. A sensitive political nose of the day might have detected 'Exeter Hall' and British colonial pressures behind the refusal of the British government to allow Premier McIlwraith, in 1883, to extend the Queensland boundary into the island of New Guinea (although the deal with Germany in African affairs was a more important cause). When the British government declared its Protectorate in the following year, there was a guarantee that the land would be preserved

[42] Report, p. 4 (ibid., p. 442).

THE QUEENSLAND FRONTIER, 1859-1897   175

in the hands of the native people. But the *de facto* Australian frontier had
been pushed across the Torres Strait; and Queensland was to have a role
in New Guinea administration.

That same year, 1884, saw a British Protectorate proclaimed in New
Guinea, and the adoption into Queensland legislation of the Native
Labourers' Protection Bill 'to prevent improper employment of Aboriginal
natives of Australia and New Guinea on ships in Queensland waters'.
Although this Bill was rendered almost innocuous by reduction of the
penalties for breach, it suggests that the British presence in New Guinea
may have affected Queensland policies. In the background, and in this
year, was the Berlin Africa Conference, which was to set some minimal
international standards for the treatment of 'native' peoples. But the
debate in the Queensland Legislative Council on this Bill is a good
indication of how far professed morality in a settler democracy can be
moulded by economic interest and the need to cover up awkward facts.
Some members strongly criticised the government for assuming that
Aborigines needed any special protection. The Fisheries Act (which
fixed a maximum penalty of £10 for ill treatment of natives), they said,
was good enough. Persons with Aboriginal standards of morality should
not be protected (a criticism of the provisions to protect women from
seizure by force). The provision that employment should begin with a
proper attestation before a government officer involved a principle which
might be extended to pastoral employment, which would be quite
absurd. One member suggested that the Native Police were being used
to destroy Aborigines as a matter of policy, and he accused the government of inconsistency in this legislation. If the Bill were adopted the
same police authority would be used both to destroy Aborigines in the
north and to protect them by inspecting conditions of employment on
ships along the coast. The Postmaster-General, who had charge of the
Bill, indignantly declared that the suggestion was a gross untruth. There
were occasional rumours of misconduct by the Native Police, he said,
but these were rumours only.[43]

By this time the last frontiers in Queensland had been breached by
settlement, by miners, and by sugar planters as well as by pastoralists.
Successful miners in the Charters Towers area invested their earnings in
the pastoral industry after 1870. Graziers moved into the Cape York
Peninsula with the prospect of new markets for meat, following the
goldrush to the Palmer River. G.C. Bolton refers with good reason to

[43] *Q.P.D.*, 1884, vol. XLII—Debate on the Native Labourers' Protection Bill (L.C.: Committee).

the 'conquest' of the tribes beyond the Palmer and the Mitchell. 'On sparsely stocked and unimproved country these nomadic battlers [the squatters] held the land by a tenure scarcely more secure than that of the Aborigines themselves.' In the 1870s, he says, Aboriginal resistance in the great coastal scrub between the Tully and Herbert Rivers involved such frequent attacks on sugar plantations, maize farms, and homesteads 'that by 1872 the Resident Magistrate of Cardwell thought an attack on the port itself not unlikely'.[44]

There was now more variety in the frontiersmen, but the technique of extending control had not changed much. There were the same stories of murdered settlers, of punitive expeditions which shot the 'wrong' tribesmen, including women and children, of Aborigines in times of drought reduced by the destruction of game to emaciation and starvation; the stories were to continue in Cape York Peninsula till the end of the century. Here the cattle industry thrived, so that mayhem at Aboriginal expense was bound to be displaced in time by concern for Aboriginal labour. For by the middle eighties there were three-quarters of a million cattle in north Queensland: by the mid-nineties, just under 1,400,000. Adaptation of men and beasts to the tropics, in the last three decades of the century, meant that only a few pockets of tribal life remained in Queensland. 'Though the wealth and population of North Queensland were chiefly derived from the mining and sugar industries,' writes Bolton, 'the pastoralists could claim to have made productive a wide region which would otherwise have remained a mere hunting ground for Aborigines.'[45]

The value judgment here, that western economic 'progress' is the justification for other consequences, indicates how a frontier like this resembled others in Africa, where similar kinds of expansion were being justified on the same grounds. The process was not long afterwards to be given the respectability of colonial doctrine by Lugard, in the theory of the Dual Mandate, that the colonial power should 'develop' an area for the indigenous people and the world. The variation on his theme, in the Australian situation, is that development is for all Australians; and that when the Aborigines are ready. . . . But this was still to come. The emphasis did mean that there was no serious consideration in Queensland of a solution other than one which removed Aboriginal hindrances from areas of development (for their own good) where their labour was not

[44] G.C. Bolton, *A Thousand Miles Away. A History of North Queensland to 1920*, esp. ch. 5, 'Squatters and Aborigines, 1879-90', and pp. 93-5.
[45] Ibid., p. 108.

THE QUEENSLAND FRONTIER, 1859-1897

required. The controlled institution, on the distant reserve, was inevitable once a genuine concern with Aboriginal welfare developed. This in turn produced a new climate for the missions, to which government was ready, in the eighties, to provide new opportunities and in a few cases even minor financial assistance.

One sign of the changing times was, as it were, a second call to missions to go to the Aboriginal. By the time of Archibald Meston's epoch-making report to Tozer, the Minister responsible for Aboriginal matters, in 1896, there were missions south of the frontier area—at Myora (on Stradbroke Island) and at Mari Yamba, near Proserpine. But of the four missions in the far north, only Bellenden Ker (now Yarrabah) on Cape Grafton, near Cairns, which John Gribble had just established for the Church of England (on a site which Meston helped to choose), had soil suitable to maintain a settlement. That of the Lutherans at Cape Bedford (Hope Vale), some thirty miles north of Cooktown, was criticised by Meston as mainly on rock and sand; and, he thought, far too close to Cooktown for the policy of segregation in which he saw the only hope. Bloomfield River, established by the Lutherans in the same year, south of Cooktown, was so badly situated that he reflected that 'some evil genius must have presided over the selection of sites for all mission stations in Queensland', for Mapoon, which the Moravian missionaries had established for the Presbyterians in 1891, was also on a notoriously poor site. It was not an evil genius but the low priority of Aboriginal requirements that fixed these sites, since Aboriginal claims meant little politically against pressures from settlers for good land.

These mission settlements were in effect anticipating the protection policy which Meston was to recommend.[46] All four had been established partly in response to a call from the Moravian missionary, F.A. Hagenauer, who visited north Queensland in 1885.[47] The Queensland government in 1896 was paying an annual grant of £250 each to the Mapoon and Bloomfield River missions. That at Cape Bedford received nothing, being supported by funds from Germany. The Church of England supported the Bellenden Ker Mission, where the community was made up of the tribal remnants left after the struggle for the Bellenden Ker Range country.

The alternative to this kind of enforced adjustment for a doubtful

[46] Q.V. & P., 1896, vol. IV, pp. 723 et seq.—Report on the Aboriginals of Queensland by Archibald Meston to Home Secretary H. Tozer.
[47] Notes of a Missionary Journey to North Queensland 1885, with Report of the Aboriginal Mission at Ramahyuck, Victoria, 1885.

178   THE DESTRUCTION OF ABORIGINAL SOCIETY

salvation lay in integration into the pastoral enterprise, for which in north Queensland there was a range of possibilities, once Aborigines had been subjugated completely. Robert Christison of Lammermoor Station established real contact with the local group, in the manner of E.D. Ogilvie on the Clarence half a century before: there was an understanding, as in Ogilvie's case, that they should hunt on the station but not attack stock. John Fulford of Lyndhurst, west of the Bellenden Ker Range and scrublands, established terms which enabled him to use Aboriginal station labour when the white stockmen went to the Palmer rush. According to the family tradition it was the Aborigines who built stockyards of basalt on the station.[48] Such station owners would protect their Aboriginal employees from ill-directed punitive expeditions and from the worst excesses of the Native Police. But such social skills and foresight were rare: most pastoralists remained hostile or indifferent.

Although there was now a law which prevented employment of Islanders beyond thirty miles from the coast, and although some Aboriginal labour had become essential, there was not employment for all in any one area until only dispirited groups remained. For the others there seemed the choice either of a segregation which would provide a degree of physical security or obliteration.

Some there were who regretted that the white man's penetration of the country had caused such hostility and wrought such destruction among the natives. Most authorities agreed, however, that the Aborigines were a dying race. They were to be clothed and fed, and might make themselves useful around the stations to the best of their ability—so limited in most respects, so remarkable when their powers of observation or memory were called into play. Their children and the station children might join in each other's games whole-heartedly, until they reached the age of self-consciousness. But as the world evolved, an 'inferior' race had to give way to those who were better able to develop the land and its resources; such was the thought of the times, and in truth the Aborigines who lived under the paternalism of a North Queensland cattle station were not, in 1890, the least fortunate of their race.[49]

The remnants, flotsam and jetsam of Aboriginal society, had already created a 'nuisance' for the first townships of the north. Cooktown imposed a formal curfew after dark in 1885. This first attempt at urbanisation was, as usual, catastrophic. Bolton tells how the Bumburra people haunted Bowen; and how, when they were got together for a corroboree in 1900, there were only 200 left in the whole district.

In 1889 Meston, in a report on the Bellenden Ker Range country, mainly concerned with flora and fauna, had added some remarks on

[48] Information from Mr J.A. Fulford, a grandson of John Fulford.
[49] Bolton, *A Thousand Miles Away*, p. 108.

THE QUEENSLAND FRONTIER, 1859-1897

Aborigines there. Some had worked in prospecting for the diggers on the Russell; others on sugar plantations on the Johnston. At that time Meston considered the settler who trusted his life to the tribal Aboriginal as quite foolhardy, remarking that the human savage differed little from other wild animals in this respect. Yet, he wrote, the savage is a far nobler animal than the 'lowest type' of white man; of the two races, the whites had been the more unscrupulous and deliberate murderers; wholesale murder by whites for the sake of economic gain was continuing, and for every killing of a white man there had been fifty blacks killed.[50] (The far northern missions appear to have provided a sanctuary at a critical time.) But Meston was to come to realise a common humanity. His interest in the whole problem led him into a situation where he found himself entertained as a visitor to the last tribes of Cape York Peninsula. This was part of the preparation of a report which proved the most decisive in the Queensland history of Aboriginal affairs; it formed the basis of the Queensland legislation from 1897 almost to the present time, and was the foundation of policy.

The extent of the reaction to what had been happening along the frontiers for so long is reflected in the rigidity of the restraints assumed necessary to save the race from extinction. This is a very good example of how the events of the frontier, in those states which still had within their boundaries areas of conflict, set the pattern of legislation for the state as a whole. As the first basic legislation arising from this kind of circumstance, the Queensland Act set the pattern for the Western Australian Act of 1905 and for the South Australian Acts of 1910 and 1911—the 1910 Act providing the basis for early Commonwealth administrative effort in this field, in the Northern Territory, from the beginning of 1911, the 1911 Act being the first comprehensive legislation for the State of South Australia.

Meston had travelled through Cape York Peninsula quite extensively, and claimed to have made friendly contacts with about 2,000 Aborigines, distributing presents and occasionally killing a bullock for them. Such was the background, he said, that old women warned the men not to go where the bullocks were killed; that this offer was a ruse to get the tribe together for a massacre (as had happened to groups on the Batavia and Ducie Rivers). At that time, he wrote, there were only six stations occupying the grasslands north of the 13th parallel. The contacts that had been made with the Aborigines had been made by the Native Police,

[50] A. Meston, Report on Government Scientific Expedition to Bellenden Ker Range, 1889, p. 20.

bêche-de-mer and pearl-shell crews, those constructing the telegraph line to the Cape, and later by the staffs of the telegraph stations. The Native Police should be re-constituted; many were unfit for the task, and for economic as well as humane reasons the emphasis should be on making peace. He said that outrages by the pearling and other crews continued (in spite of the earlier legislation, which was tepid and ineffective), with the usual results, in prostitution of women and abduction of boys and girls. Disease and violence were common along the coasts, and even the populations of the missions were not safe.

The Cape, from Newcastle Bay north, being closest to the pearling fields and the Straits, had been most seriously affected. Meston wrote that twenty-five years before there had been twelve tribes and 3,000 people there; and now there were only a hundred or so. He reported on the strife arising from the disputes about women and the kidnapping of children in Cape York—both customs of long standing, from the days when the sealers on the islands off Tasmania kidnapped the women, while the settlers seized children in the bush. But the whole eastern watershed of the Peninsula north of the McIvor was still tribal country, with only a few miners moving through it; on the western side, tribal society still dominated the area from the Mitchell to the Jardine.

He pointed out that there had been no attack on the telegraph line, although the posts had been built with spear-proof gates and loop-holes in the walls; and suggested that overtures might be made to end the current hostilities by offers of food, including the occasional bullock. The report shows that people still living under tribal conditions had developed trading relationships with ships along the coasts, and that, when there was nothing else to sell, or as a matter of hospitality, they would make the women available for the flour and tobacco which they must have once they had formed new habits.[51]

Meston's reaction, understandable enough in one who now saw the Aboriginal as a man rather than an unpredictable and dangerous savage, was in the direction of strong paternalism. He recommended absolute prohibition of employment in the pearling boats, even though he admitted that some pearlers had treated their Aboriginal employees well; his argument was that otherwise it was impossible to maintain any control once a vessel had left port. This was consistent with his recommendation for absolute exclusion from towns of all but those in rigidly controlled conditions of employment.

Another recommendation was for the abolition of the Native Police.

[51] Q.V. & P., 1896, vol. 4, p. 725n.

THE QUEENSLAND FRONTIER, 1859-1897

Police duty should be undertaken by the Queensland civil police with *unarmed* trackers where necessary. Meston's report was made shortly after W. E. Parry-Okeden had become Commissioner of Police. It caused the Colonial Secretary to send the Commissioner to tour the Cape York area, to recommend a better police system; and to consider how to 'ameliorate the condition of the Queensland Aborigines'. This resulted in Parry-Okeden's Report of 1897, in which the Native Police Force was finally damned by its own most senior officer, which made easy the transition to use of civil police in the new policy after 1897.

Meston's report also throws some interesting light on the growth of a mixed population in tropical Queensland, south of Cape York Peninsula. Here, in the areas where sugar farms had replaced the first big estates (which had been established in their day with the aid of the Native Police), Chinese, Malays, South Sea Islanders, and others were establishing themselves, some with wives they had obtained in various ways from the Aborigines: Meston said they had usually been abducted without the consent of the tribe, and that spearings had resulted.

He reported also on the ration stations. On the Barron River there were two, at Atherton and Kuranda, and another at Thornborough. He recommended that the police stations should be supplied with food for gifts, to show that police could be protectors as well as avengers. He heard from the police, in three of the small townships, how Aborigines would come in at night and beg for protection against white men who came to their camps with guns and demanded the women. The other phase of Aboriginal administration which had long become traditional (along with rations to the needy) was the annual blanket issue; so many went into the possession of the whites as to call for special recommendations.

In addition to drunkenness, the long-standing symptom of social breakdown, there was an allied problem. In northern Australia, where there had been considerable contact with Chinese miners and others, opium dross—the ash left from smoking—had long been an item of trade with Aborigines; the results seem to have been even more obviously disastrous than those of alcohol addiction. According to Meston, opium was being used widely through Queensland as a work incentive and in order to tie the restive Aboriginal worker to the enterprise.

He recommended the removal of abuses by abolition of the causes as far as possible. In addition to his recommendations for abolition of Native Police, and against employment in shell fishing, he wanted imprisonment for selling alcohol or opium to Aborigines and severe penalties for the whites found with government blankets. He also advocated that the

182 THE DESTRUCTION OF ABORIGINAL SOCIETY

Aborigines, except those in regular employment, should be totally excluded from the towns and that those employed should be registered, with wages and conditions carefully regulated. The missions should be centres for distribution of rations. Maize, he said, was better than white flour, and had kept the convicts in good condition (another interesting indication of how the Aboriginal sometimes stepped, as it were, into the convict's shoes). Most important was the recommendation for the creation of reserves in the south, centre, and north of the colony, into which Aborigines could be gathered to set up permanent homes, free from European influence as far as possible: segregation, he assumed, was the only way of saving their lives. There should be appointed a Chief Protector and an Assistant Protector, whose sole employment should be in Aboriginal affairs. An indication of how far Meston's thinking was dominated by the conditions of the frontier was his recommendation that the Chief Protector should be stationed in the north, his assistant in the south. Implicit in this recommendation was the assumption of disappearance of the problem in the south.[52]

In addition to the mission settlements, the government had now established another at Deebing for those in the Moreton and Darling Downs areas to live when not employed. It was, said Meston, too close to Ipswich, and had a defective water supply and inadequate land. Either it should be moved or a farm should be purchased to be worked with the labour from the settlement. The collecting and concentration of those who otherwise would live round the towns, looking for employment or other ways to get food, clothing, and shelter, into areas controlled by missions, had already begun. Mission settlements had made possible a policy of segregation under strict control, except for those in employment. For the latter, the colonial-style contract of service was to be adapted as a way of establishing Aboriginal identities and maintaining them in the records as well as making possible at least some control of the conditions of work. The ruthlessness with which, after the Act was passed, the Aborigines were rounded up, suggests at least a concern by authority with the reputation of the government: and a conviction that there was no other way to avoid extermination.

An Act to make Provision for the better Protection and Care of the Aboriginal and Half-caste Inhabitants of the Colony, and to make more effectual Provision for Restricting the Sale and Distribution of Opium

[52] Ibid.

THE QUEENSLAND FRONTIER, 1859-1897   183

received assent in December 1897.[53] It was to be a model for basic legislation of the other States with frontier situations, and for the Northern Territory —legislation that illustrates how far things had moved in the direction of a low-caste status since the days when Grey and Gipps wrote of legal equality. In this Act, protection involved new restrictions in law. There was a penalty of £50 for supply of liquor; twice that for opium. The special provisions (sections 19-25) against possession of opium, the right of police to break into premises if necessary to search for it, and other measures to control its distribution indicate that it must have become a really serious destroyer of Aborigines. These provisions also operated as restrictions on the actions of white men, though applicable only in Aboriginal cases.

Queensland now set a new example, by defining in rigid racial terms those who were to be the main concern of the Act—to be directed where to live, to be 'drafted' there where necessary; to be limited to the life of the institution at the will of the official. The special category of persons to whom the Act applied included Aborigines, and half-castes married to or children of Aborigines, or who 'habitually' associated with Aborigines (see section 4). Also subject to the Act (section 3), in certain respects, was any other half-caste, defined as 'any person being the offspring of an Aboriginal mother and other than an Aboriginal father' (Aboriginal father and non-Aboriginal mother being then unthinkable). So legal rights were dependent on racial origin: and the legal basis for institutional and separate management of Aborigines as defined became, until World War II, a basic principle of all Aboriginal policies. This probably saved many lives: but it was to leave the legacy of an institutionalised and legally restricted minority.

There were to be superintendents in charge of reserves, and Protectors of Aborigines off them. Reserves were to be controlled under regulations. Aborigines, by administrative direction and without appeal, could be 'removed to' and kept 'within' the reserve boundaries, unless they were lawfully employed or married to white men. This did not apply to the 'half-caste' not 'habitually' associating with Aboriginals; but in practice who would know the difference? Here begins that confusion and authoritarianism which has marked Queensland Aboriginal administration ever since. Half-castes shared with legal Aborigines exclusion from liquor and opium. Both must be employed only under permit of a protector, renewable every twelve months and subject to revocation. It was a serious offence to have Aborigines on any premises except as prescribed, in

[53] No. 17 of 1897 (Qld).

consequence of a written labour agreement attested by police officer or justice. The labour agreement was to specify the term of employment, wages, and accommodation. A protector could inspect the conditions of employment and sue for unpaid wages on the Aboriginal's behalf. The Minister could exempt a half-caste person from the provisions of the Act and regulations. The cost of this protective measure was to place the Aboriginal at the mercy of officials. There were no provisions for appeal. No matter how lofty the intentions, its execution would reflect the attitudes of the police and others who now had to administer it. These would vary a good deal, but the background made certain a tight pattern of authoritarian management. At least it can be said for Queensland that, having at last adopted a policy, very strong efforts were made to carry it through. Aboriginal affairs remained an area sheltered from public interference, since an Aboriginal, once removed to a settlement (a reserve under a superintendent) could only be seen henceforth by persons author-ised under the regulations. Aboriginal administration in these places became an issue as remote as that of gaols or asylums. The settlement has illustrated the classic ills of the institution under authoritarian management, but one more or less out of sight, as well as largely beyond the interest, of other Queenslanders. In time the full-time staff of the small Department of Native Affairs came to concentrate its efforts on these places, leaving the other areas of activity in the outside world to the police protectors. Up till 1966, for instance, there was no staff for labour inspection: this was a matter for police protectors.

Tozer, the Home Secretary, introducing the Bill, argued for the efficacy of the police, whom the Aborigines, he said, no longer feared; and he read some police reports to prove it. There were a few objections, in committee, to the use of the police as protectors—not surprisingly, in the circumstances. One member tried to have the missions undertake the main tasks. But this was the time for secular control. The consensus in parliament was that the *missions* had failed to carry out the protection of the Aborigines. The government would make the reserves so attractive that the inmates would not want to leave them. At least no harsh comment in opposition, of the kind which had marked similar debates, was now heard. Perhaps there was some uneasiness about what had been done, perhaps now that all resistance had passed there was a realisation that the cost of reserves in areas not required for settlement was a cheap price to pay for a 'final solution'. The interest of the station holders in retaining a supply of cheap labour was safeguarded. One member even advocated 'a fair wage the same as the white man' for pastoral employment, though

THE QUEENSLAND FRONTIER, 1859-1897

Tozer had promised that not a word in the Bill would attempt 'to interfere with the rate of wages'.[54] Seventy years later, the Aboriginal as defined and 'under the Act' could hope soon to receive the white man's wage in pastoral employment.

The impact of frontier events had been severe. Obviously, Aborigines would be conditioned against believing in official goodwill. Profound distrust of government measures must have been increased by their exclusion, after 1897, in considerable numbers, from the only chances of constructive change left to them. Hostility and resentment must have flourished in the settlements and missions to which they were confined.

Yet this was only one colony and one government administration. The same trends were developing everywhere else to different degrees. Every area has been a frontier area. From the point of view of the whites, most of whom obtained superficial views and impressions from the 'old hands' who had ground their own axes in the frontier conditions, the policy of control seemed the only reasonable one. Not for a long time was it to be very widely questioned.

Only now are there signs of a change of practice, as distinct from professed policy, in Queensland, for a system becomes bound up with the whole rationale of the public service. Officials and politicians become committed to produce certain easily promised social changes by established methods, to fit in nicely with government plans, generally while saving the taxpayers' money. Ambitions may be achieved and promotions made, with Aborigines as the raw material for careers. The system has to 'succeed'; and where there are signs that 'trouble' lies ahead, information may for many reasons be distorted or suppressed—and especially so where outside inquiry is involved. To raise the issues by reference to the facts may be to 'make trouble'—really for the government or the public servants, but ostensibly for the Aborigines.

The background of injustice has weighed on the minds of thinking Australians for a long time. The care taken to suppress the past, or to misrepresent it in respectable language, or to slide over it with linguistic avoidance, illustrates this sensitivity. The school history books avoid it. Serious historians have said that the Aboriginal contacts form a side issue, as though to deny a basic moral question. In the long run, questions of justice, more clearly grasped when raised in areas where some frontier conflicts remained, gave to the Aboriginal question the status of a national issue. In some ways the frontier issues have been decisive.

[54] *Q.P.D.*, vol. LXXVIII, 1897—quoted by Winifred Cowin, *European-Aboriginal Relations*, p. 75.

THE DESTRUCTION OF ABORIGINAL SOCIETY

It seems that this past is something Australians must learn to live with; that it will be a perpetual reminder that in race relations we have reacted just as ruthlessly to serve our mainly economic interests as have others of European culture. In May 1965 an oil survey group near Bedourie, in the far south-west of Queensland, found eight skeletons in two groups, with

several .32 calibre cartridges near one group of the bones ... Mourning caps, normally used by Aboriginal women after the death of the men, were found near one group of skeletons. Drought conditions and strong winds have combined to cause large areas of earth and sand to shift in the Bedourie district.[55]

It seems possible that the growing interest in Aboriginal archaeology will lead to revelation of a recent catastrophe and the relics of the policy of dispersal.

The rapid expansion of Queensland pastoral activities and the decades of attack on Aboriginal social gatherings appear to have reduced the society to remnants far more rapidly than occurred in either the Northern Territory or Western Australia—or even in the dry areas of South Australia. By the time that frontier conditions and the questions arising from spectacular injustice were raising organised protests, in the 1930s, Queensland had most Aborigines under control. Even on the reserves of Cape York they were, or could by then be claimed to be, controlled by the missionaries, as agents of the government. The government had, in the meantime, established a reputation for expertise in the Aboriginal problem, and was commonly regarded as setting an example to the others. It was the source of expert advice for Western Australia in 1904; and for the Commonwealth Government, in the Northern Territory, in 1928.

[55] *Sun* (Sydney), 7 May 1965.

THE EXTENSION OF
SETTLEMENT IN
WESTERN AUSTRALIA

Although, as Biskup points out, the pastoralists in the north-wes of Western Australia, and later in the Kimberleys, because of their fear and isolation 'often felt particularly unsafe, and . . . inclined to see in every native a thief and a potential killer', they had been forced by the ban on convict labour in the north to depend on Aborigines. R.D. Sturkey says that the De Grey station at one stage employed Aboriginal shepherds only, for a mob of 2,000 sheep.

Gradually groups of natives became permanently associated with the various stations. They gave up their roaming habits, took to wearing white man's clothes, ate his food and smoked his tobacco, and some even learned to speak his language. Only once a year, during the slack period, would they disappear into the bush to go 'walkabout', and to reforge their ties with the eternal dreamtime.[1]

This involved a degree of trust beyond that generally accorded by management on most cattle stations today, if one may judge from what management in the Northern Territory has been saying about Aboriginal labour.

In practice most settlers could deal with Aborigines as they liked, though one important piece of British colonial administration, the Land Regulations gazetted in 1864, preserved the right of Aborigines to enter freely all unenclosed leasehold lands east of longitude 121 and north of the Murchison, which includes all the Kimberley area.[2] As in Queensland, some of the harshest contacts along these northern coasts were made by

[1] Biskup, Native Administration and Welfare in Western Australia 1897-1954, p. 38; quoting R.D. Sturkey, Growth of the Pastoral Industry in the North-West 1862-1901.
[2] Biskup, Native Administration and Welfare, p. 40.

the pearling luggers, which preferred Malays for the work, using Aborigines only when necessary.

One interesting difference from Queensland was that in the west policy measures continued until 1897 to be subject to the most experienced of all the colonial authorities, Great Britain; legislation in the west was, then, different from that of Queensland. In 1871, employment of women and children in pearling was forbidden, and that of the men had to be in the typical colonial contract of employment, attested by a justice or police constable. Under the W.A. Pearling Act of 1870 conditions of employment were also regulated, and diving by Aborigines limited to certain times of the year.

In 1873 this Act was repealed and replaced by the Pearl Shell Fishery Regulation Act, which expressed the best principles of colonial 'native labour' legislation at that time. It is in marked contrast with the later first efforts of the Queensland government to control this trade. There had to be a written contract in each case, subject to endorsement; and the term of service was limited to twelve months. A justice or police constable could endorse the contract only if he was satisfied that the Aboriginal was a free agent, without fear or coercion; that he understood and agreed with the terms of the contract; and that he was physically fit for the work (sections 3-5). (In failing to provide for some kind of medical examination, this fell short of the best legislation of its kind, such examination being in the economic interest of employers as well as a safeguard for the workers.) No deposit was required from the employer, as a guarantee of the return of the Aboriginal to his home at the end of the contract; but a penalty of up to £50 was involved for failure to do so. There was no ration scale, but rations and issues of clothing were included in the agreement (Schedule A). But this legislation applied only to the pearl shell trade. Even in Western Australia, legislation for the pastoral industry tended to have its teeth drawn, as occurred in the adoption of the Aborigines Protection Act of 1886.

Before considering this, let us briefly refer to the background of Western Australian practice with Aboriginal labour. Hasluck has noted employment of Aborigines in the south-west of the colony from 1840. There were similar instances in the east, even before the goldrushes, and increased dependence on Aboriginal workers as settlement went into the northern areas. In the west there had always been some use made of the contract of employment—mainly, it seems, because of the legal sanctions established under the Master and Servant legislation. An Aboriginal under contract who absconded from employment could legally be brought back

THE EXTENSION OF SETTLEMENT IN WESTERN AUSTRALIA 189

by the police and penalised for breach of contract. I can find no evidence of this in the 1840s and 1850s in New South Wales, but the same kind of legislation was used there to hold the German migrants who were brought out from Hamburg. Hasluck says that as from 1854 the government had established a 3-months agreement for Aborigines; the colonial flavour is indicated by the use of the term 'indentures'.

Aborigines were employed as shepherds and herdsmen and for reaping the station crops. As settlement went north, the station labour pool of Aborigines was essential. But there would have been some employed under Master and Servant legislation, in the Gascoyne district in the eighties, with cash wages of five shillings per month.[3] Their conditions were, however, worse than those in colonies where labour was recognised as a valuable resource by paying attention to ration scales, accommodation, and the length of contract terms, and where systems of labour inspection were established. Individual contracts, where the conditions are not subject to regular inspection, are mainly of value to employers. In Western Australia they enabled the settler to call on the police to round up absconders.

As in Queensland, protective legislation for Aborigines arose partly from a growing realisation of the need to conserve the labour force in the northern areas. Therefore, the Aborigines Protection Act of 1886 is also, in some respects, typical of colonial labour legislation.[4] The contracting age is the convenient one of fourteen years (in practice established by indications of puberty); the fourteen-year-old contractor must be a free agent; he 'made paper', as the New Guineans put it, by making his mark on the contract (probably by putting his finger on the pen while the government representative at the signing on made the mark). At the signing on there were the employer or his agent, the recruit, and the government representative to ensure willingness of the recruit. But the government was represented not by a full-time administrative officer but by a Justice of the Peace (in practice probably another employer) or a Protector (in practice a policeman). This made all the difference; for detailed knowledge of the implications and real impartiality are required to ensure a genuine agreement. The Schedule, setting out the form of the contract, did not provide for any statement of cash wages. It provided for medicine and medical attention 'when practicable and necessary', for

[3] See Hasluck, *Black Australians*, p. 151.
[4] An Act to Provide for the better protection and management of the Aboriginal Natives of Western Australia, and to amend the Law relating to certain Contracts with such Aboriginal Natives (50 Vic., No. 25) 1886. The provisions governing the contract of service appear in Part II.

flour, tea, a blanket, and 'one pair of trousers'. There was no limit stated
to the term of service and no provision for compulsory periods of leave,
though the worker might get two weeks off in a three-to-six months
contract, and three weeks for a longer one. Most serious of all, the Act
did not provide that the contract *must* be used.

The section on labour was, in fact, a form of words which could bind
the Aboriginal indefinitely to a master. That it could be cancelled for
non-fulfilment on either side meant little without expert and regular
inspection—which is needed even for economic advantage, as a means to
conserve willingness to work. There was no provision for the health of
the worker beyond the vague ones in the Schedule; even the medicine
and attention did not need to be provided if the worker's illness was
'caused by his own improper act or default'. Lack of provision for the
return of the worker to his own country probably reflects the fact that
most of them belonged, or had established themselves, in the station area
where they were employed. Lack of provision for cash wages shows that
no thought was given to the important matter of labour incentives—or
to the future of the work force as a market. That little attention was given
to the progress of individuals into the cash economy hardly needs to be
said. According to Hasluck, even the age of contracting was a compromise;
the squatters had been advocating that ten years be the age of manhood
for workers.[5]

The Roth Royal Commission of 1905 found that only 369 Aborigines
were employed with the doubtful protections of the contract;[6] that even
these included some under fourteen years; that the limited provisions for
medical care, and the time limits stated in individual contracts, were
ignored; and that no proper records of the contracts had been kept. And
as for the 4,000 or so employed *outside* the contract system (for the Act
did not discriminate between casual and permanent employment, or make
it obligatory to have all permanent employees under the 'protections'
established), Roth asserted that no legal grounds existed for action by the
police to improve conditions. There were no minimum conditions for
those not signed on; yet it had been the practice to bring back absconders
by force as though they were contract-breakers.

Roth also reported that no wages at all were being paid to those employed
without contracts.

Thus although this labour legislation has a colonial flavour, and

[5] *Black Australians*, p. 155.
[6] *W.A.V. & P.* (L.C.), 1905, vol. I—Report of the Royal Commission on the Condition of
the Natives (Roth Report).

THE EXTENSION OF SETTLEMENT IN WESTERN AUSTRALIA 191

resembles real protective legislation in the form of words, the loopholes in law and in practice made it no more than a convenience to be used by the occasional employer. That this was not only an adjustment to the frontier and its hard conditions but applied to those long within the settler community is indicated in the definition in the Aborigines Protection Act of 1886 (section 45) of 'Aboriginal' as including 'every Aboriginal Native of Australia, and every Aboriginal half-caste or child of a half-caste, such half-caste or child habitually associating and living with Aboriginals. . .' It thus applied to the part-Aboriginal people of the south-west if they lived with Aborigines as defined. A Resident Magistrate could, in the matter of employment, ignore parental wishes, even of 'half-caste' children, and could bind the 'half-caste' or his child to a master in apprenticeship (section 36).

Even though the 1886 Act operated to protect pastoral enterprises, in which over 2,000 were employed in 1881, it also indicates an acquaintance with what were at the time advanced colonial policies: and it is interesting that Western Australian Aboriginal administration even today has retained something of this colonial flavour. After World War II, it looked again to the colonial world, this time to Papua-New Guinea, for a new assessment of the Aboriginal question. Perhaps one reason for the fact that there were more effective protests in Western Australia than in Queensland, from the town and city dwellers in the south, was a greater awareness of the standards of 'native administration', since legislation approved by the Colonial Office would have to express these. But this did not alter the basic facts of the frontier areas, where the Aborigines by this time seem to have known well what they were up against, and to have resisted to the best that the social organisation would allow. There is a wider gap between the northern pastoralists and the critics from the south than in Queensland, due perhaps to the greater awareness of standards elsewhere. The gap is well defined by Mary Durack in *Kings in Grass Castles*. What was resulting in the distant regions of the far north was a forced adjustment, with considerable employment on pastoral properties.

This situation in the north had come from conquest by the gun, in the last resort. By 1890 the main area for this was in the Kimberleys, where things were not so very different from those in Cape York Peninsula.

Just before the end of colonial administration, the police had led a punitive expedition against an Aboriginal group led by one 'Pigeon', who had acquired the name and his knowledge of tactics as a tracker; and there is also ample evidence that, when in doubt, settlers were

THE DESTRUCTION OF ABORIGINAL SOCIETY

for years inclined to shoot on sight.[7] So far as one can judge, however, the characteristic situation in this area, as in the Northern Territory, was of an adjustment to the station property by a group still in their own 'country', a group that may have been forced in to the station by the danger of being caught out in the bush by armed settlers or attracted in by the chance of beef, sugar, flour, tea, tobacco, clothing, and steel, and one that may have been augmented and renewed to a varying extent by others from tribes farther out. After the efforts of the Native Police, this kind of situation did not exist to any marked degree in Queensland, even in Cape York Peninsula, where what tribal remnants remain do so mainly on the missions and government stations from which they move out to the stations as required, leaving their families behind. The Kimberleys type of adjustment led towards a type of peonage, if the term may be applied to those who were not previously tillers of the soil. In Queensland it led rather in the direction of colonial-type migrant labour, with the contract of service and the single man's wage.

This was curious, because the Western Australian legislation had led the way with typical colonial regulations for an indenture system. There were, however, as Roth showed in his report, no effective controls in frontier regions, despite the fact that the Aborigines Protection Board had been established in 1886. It was Roth's opinion in 1905 that while there was no evidence of actual physical cruelty in the settled areas, the cruelties and abuses in 'unsettled' districts 'cannot be longer hidden or tolerated'.[8]

The main hope in the situation described by Roth was the emphasis on the Aboriginal as a unit of labour. He might not be paid, and might be shot on sight with impunity where the squatter was in doubt or afraid, but at least he had an acknowledged importance in the station economy; and this was to lead to the present (mid-1960s) type of adjustment. In the Kimberleys up until 1967, for instance, wages were not fixed by law, and the amounts paid often make the much publicised minimum wage under the Wards Employment Ordinance of the Northern Territory look attractive. Roth recommended a minimum wage of 5s per month, which was comparable with the lowest contract wage paid in the Pacific (by the German administration of New Guinea) and about half that in Papua: this was, of course, the cash component, with rations and accommodation to be provided. There were squatters even then who said that they would 'get rid of' the station groups if they had to pay money wages, since they kept

[7] See authorities quoted by Biskup, Native Administration and Welfare in Western Australia, p. 48.
[8] Roth Report—conclusions.

THE EXTENSION OF SETTLEMENT IN WESTERN AUSTRALIA 193

them there only for charity and to ensure that they did not kill the cattle. Roth found that in some areas the settlers had got round the provisions that enabled the Aborigines to hunt on the runs by placing stock on all water, by destruction of game, and by killing the Aborigines' hunting dogs. Such measures placed the tribe quite at the mercy of the station management. He found that small children were being indentured, some for pearling; the Chief Protector of Western Australia thought that six years was a suitable age for indenturing a lad. No more shocking document marks this story: it should be read by all who question the reluctance of Aborigines to respond to current policies. Demoralisation on the shell boats and round the ports was inevitable, as the social organisation was largely destroyed: and here again is the grim story of venereal disease, drunkenness, and prostitution. Those who ran away from a particular employer were often brought back by police as a matter of course, even where there was no contract.

But the main bone of contention with the police was cattle killing. Roth says that on occasion the pastoralists themselves objected to police actions. Perhaps it was the absence of the Queensland tradition of 'dispersal' which placed greater emphasis on arrest on this part of the frontier. Regulations allowed the use of the neck-chain to bring in prisoners in special circumstances; but by this time its use had become so much of a commonplace that its cruelty was likely to be denied and it was usual for the constable, with his trackers, to 'bring in' not only the persons charged but a line of 'witnesses' chained together in this way. Roth says that even children of fourteen to sixteen years might be so treated; that women were chained with the men; that they might be completely at the mercy of the police in this way for weeks, with the chains never removed, especially as the female 'witnesses' taken were often young. He stated that the connecting chains between prisoners or witnesses might be no more than two feet in length. (Chains were still in use after World War II.) Some nine-tenths of those arrested by this time were charged with cattle killing: Roth mentions the case of a child of ten years sentenced to six months for this offence. The number on the chain, he suggests, had some relation to the fact that the policeman got maintenance money for those arrested, since the constable received between 1s 6d and 2s 5d per day for rationing. Roth says that this was a source of profit, as the police would save on the rations.[9] A patrol of this kind through rough country and

[9] One constable had received £462 in nine months at these rates. Aborigines, more articulate these days, sometimes complain even in western New South Wales that they are gaoled for the ration money; it may seldom be true, but there is good historical reason for this kind of suspicion.

THE DESTRUCTION OF ABORIGINAL SOCIETY

across rivers, with several people linked by the chain, is unfortunately a commonplace of the tradition; the chain used as a club could also be a cruel weapon. Roth found that those sentenced might spend years chained to objects, to one another, and working on the chain, since the only gaol in the north was at Roebourne. The application of the old convict methods to the Aboriginal, at a much later stage, is clear.

Theoretically, this system involved the arrest of suspects for breaches of the law and the bringing in of those British subjects who were law-breakers to be tried. Chains were to be justified for a long time afterwards as necessary because Aborigines were so adept at slipping the handcuffs, but the difficulty about establishing identities, the treatment of possible witnesses in the same way as the suspects, the probability that there would be bitter resistance to such cruelty and humiliation from the tribes, all helped to make the frontier conditions much as they had always been.

Roth recommended that prisons should be built; that where chains were used, they should not be attached round the neck. By this time the status of the Aboriginal in the law was such that a Justice of the Peace, sitting alone if there were no other within ten miles, could sentence him to a flogging and to three years imprisonment. Roth points to the effect of alienating large areas without making any provision for Aborigines: especially in dry country, all the waterholes would be stocked and this led to a rapid decrease of native animals. He recommended large reserves, both for humane reasons and because otherwise there would be continued bloodshed and counterattacks. The Aborigines should, he thought, be allowed to retain the areas they still occupied.

Roth's recommendation that handcuffs should be used instead of chains was probably dismissed by practical men. In 1935 H. D. Moseley, another Royal Commissioner, recommended that there should be no change, because of the 'difficulties' of the police in 'escorting' native prisoners; and he quoted the words of a missionary of whom he expressed approval, to the effect that a neck chain is the most humane way of 'restraining native prisoners'.[10] It seems incredible that, three decades after Roth's report, another report solemnly discussed the difficulties of the police in acting as Protectors.

Another aspect of the relationship between police and Aborigines was due to the arming of police trackers and the system whereby, being un-paid, they were completely dependent on the constable, but rationed by

[10] *W.A.V. & P.* 1935, vol. I, p. 23—Report of the Royal Commissioner Appointed to Investigate, Report, and Advise upon matters in relation to the Condition and Treatment of Aborigines.

THE EXTENSION OF SETTLEMENT IN WESTERN AUSTRALIA 195

him on the basis of an allowance for the purpose. Roth wanted them to be 'signed on', on agreement, paid a minimum wage, and disarmed; and to be issued with uniforms. The constable selected his own trackers. In practice, under such a system he could wield the power of.life and death without much real restraint.

Moreover, the old confusion between arrests and punitive action remained; and acts of brutality in the bush by others than police went on.[11] Continuation of cattle killing by Aborigines in the Kimberley region finally, in 1909, induced the government to compensate leaseholders and resume an area of over one million marginal acres in the upper reaches of the Margaret River, to establish the first self-supporting station for Aborigines whose food supply was disappearing. On Moola Bulla they could work at raising their own beef—the first really positive step in frontier policy; but while cattle killing seems to have diminished in this region, it still went on, and Aborigines continued sporadically to be shot by settlers.

As in Queensland, this background largely explains the hard protective authoritarianism of the comprehensive legislation introduced in Western Australia in the Aborigines Act of 1905.[12] Western Australia had already set up general legislation with the Aborigines Protection Act of 1886. Though the main concern had been with labour legislation, that Act had established the Aborigines Protection Board, of five persons to be appointed by the Governor. Its duties were to spend the money voted by the Legislative Council for Aboriginal relief; to recommend to the Governor steps for the care and education of Aboriginal children; to provide 'as far as practicable' medical care and rations for the old and infirm; to manage reserves, and to exercise a general protective function (sections 3-11). All Board members were Protectors, and the Governor could appoint others on their recommendation (sections 15-17). Their function as Protectors was to protect the rights of Aborigines in the courts and report to the Board. A function specially stated was protection of Aborigines in employment. The inclusion of certain categories of 'half-castes' (section 45), as being Aboriginal for legal purposes was necessary because of their increasing numbers, especially in the south-west. But the Act was mainly concerned

---

[11] Biskup, Native Administration and Welfare, p. 119—citing F.W. Bateson, 'The Story of the Canning Stock Route', *Journal of Historical Society of Western Australia*, 1942. This was an attempt to find a suitable route from the Kimberleys to the Eastern Goldfields. Hugh Mahon, who brought the matter to the notice of the Prime Minister, was Member for Coolgardie at the time and later was to provide important political support for J.H.P. Murray's efforts to establish a humane native policy in Papua.

[12] Act No. 14 of 1905 (5 Edw. VII, No. 14); proclaimed April 1906.

with the kind of employment which was most common in the northern regions of the colony. It is significant in that it precedes the Queensland legislation of 1897 as a generally applicable measure arising mainly from frontier conditions.

The Act of 1905, following the exposures of the Roth report, continued this emphasis while greatly increasing the legal restraints. Powers vested in the new office of Chief Protector over Aborigines and those defined as half-castes in the Act were considerable. Henceforth, he had protectors in all districts, but as these were members of the police force, the power of the Chief Protector in dealing with whites was in practice only really effective, especially in the frontier regions, where it happened to coincide with police policy and suit the consensus generally established between the police and settlers in such areas.

One provision of some importance required employers of Aborigines to hold permits, to be renewed each year (or eight months for employment on vessels); the power to grant, withdraw, or renew was vested in a protector, which meant placing considerable power in the hands of the local policeman. To anyone with knowledge of the quite detailed labour legislation at that time applicable in colonial situations, these later provisions also seem vague and ineffective. On the other hand, it was difficult to legislate for the settled areas of the south-west of the State in the same Act which dealt with the frontier situations of the north and north-west.[13] One humane provision forbade the employment of women, and of children under sixteen years, on vessels. But there was no limit on the age of employment of Aborigines in the pastoral industry, male or female; the only restriction was that all Aborigines, half-caste males under fourteen years, and half-caste females had to be employed under permit. Theoretically, the permit system might have worked if it had required a substantial deposit against breaches of the basic conditions of employment such as affected wages and rations. But there were no precise conditions laid down. A permit implies that its recipient is a man of suitable character who has the confidence of the government in dealing with those under protection; but this Act provided, for instance, that on the death of a permit holder, it might continue to be exercised by the legal representative of his estate—which is a clear enough indication of where the emphasis lay.

The Act retained, in an 'agreement' system, the written labour contract. The employer thus retained, where necessary, a legal control of un-sophisticated workers and the right to recruit from a distance and be sure

[13] Aborigines Act, 1905 (5 Edw. VII, No. 4), sections 16-32.

THE EXTENSION OF SETTLEMENT IN WESTERN AUSTRALIA 197

of getting his money's worth. This Act included formal safeguards at 'signing on', but among those who could attest the contract were Justices of the Peace, police officers, and others authorised, as well as protectors, none of whom was in a position to develop a professional competence in these matters. The Aboriginal must have had the agreement explained and 'appeared fully to understand the same, to be a free and voluntary agent, and physically fit for the work specified'. There was a general, but no specific, provision for rations, blankets, clothing and medical care.[14] Like the permit, the agreement could be cancelled by a protector. One humane provision, which fitted in well with the pastoral working year, was that a worker on a 6-months agreement must on request be granted fourteen days leave and thirty days where the agreement was for a longer term. Since he worked without pay, he could fairly be awarded leave without pay.

Ineffective as this all was as labour legislation, it may well have been pointless in the circumstances for the law to have been more specific. The effect of legislation depended on the attitudes and the authority of protectors and employers. In colonial areas, governments could often depend on the big companies to support minimum labour standards. The workers often had to be recruited from distant areas, which was costly; and there were professional recruiters who risked their lives on the reputations of the employers for whom they worked. But here there were no professional recruiters. In frontier areas, the labour was mostly on the spot; where it was not, the police might be used to recruit. Where they were also protectors, the situation was farcical. The only advantage of the agreement system over the general permit seems to have been to enable a pastoralist, in an area where Aborigines were scarce, to bind legally those he could get from farther out; and perhaps to hold workers with any special skills. (A permit was necessary to participate in an agreement.)

The Act included provisions (sections 10-15) for establishing reserves on Crown land, but not more than 2000 acres for any reserve could be taken from land already held under lease, in any one magisterial district. This effectively safeguarded the position of the settlers and ensured that any large reserves would be in the worst areas.

Difficult if not impossible to police were the provisions against miscegenation (sections 36, 40, 43) which made it an offence to be within five chains of a place 'where Aborigines or female half-castes are camped', for Aboriginal females to be within two miles of creeks where pearling luggers came, between sunset and sunrise, and, curiously, to 'habitually'

[14] Ibid., section 22.

live with Aborigines, or to cohabit. At the time, it was not un-common for settlers to employ females as stockmen, and it was thought suitable to presume that any male person other than an Aboriginal who travelled with an Aboriginal woman was cohabiting with her.

Another provision was for the licensing of guns held by Aborigines. Guns held without licences were to be confiscated, and it was made unlawful to sell a gun to any Aboriginal without a licence. No fewer than six sections (47-52) are devoted to provisions about guns, an indication of the nervous-ness in the frontier areas. But the effects went further than to protect the settler and his stock, since the custom of shooting the Aborigines' dogs made them dependent on other means of hunting game. The trusted station Aboriginal would generally be armed, and the effect of such a provision must have been to make labour more docile and Aborigines more dependent on the station economy.

Such were the relevant legislative and administrative provisions. They were to be somewhat but not substantially amended in 1911,[15] as the last of the Western Australian grasslands were settled. Other sections of the Act illustrated the very different circumstances which had developed in the areas long settled, so that the Act as a whole was an awkward com-promise concerned with the two types of situation at the extremes in space and period of settlement and attempted to deal with the range of situations in between.

By this time the racism of the white pioneer on the frontier was commonly justified by a bastard melange of pseudo-Darwinism and the assumptions of the stock-breeder. Not that all settlers were inhumane, but, like any other human group, they included all kinds of men; and their actions on the whole were no better, no worse, than those of other persons of western European culture in unrestrained colonial situations. Where men noted for kindness and good management employed Aborigines whose land they had settled, the position was basically the same; the same fear would be there in the background. Those who themselves did not use the gun to maintain their domination still owed their power to it. In 1914, one who had participated in subduing the north-west wrote of the pioneer of his generation that

were it not for his superiority as a race he would never have had these superior weapons (firearms), and should he degenerate . . . that savage race, through higher teaching may ascend and improve—and then our very instrument of defence may perhaps participate in the degeneration and become retrograde.

[15] Aborigines Act Amendment Act, 1911 (1 Geo. V, No. 42).

THE EXTENSION OF SETTLEMENT IN WESTERN AUSTRALIA   199

The pioneer, he wrote, 'feels himself both intellectually and morally superior to the savage tribes . . . and at once, almost as an instinct assume(s) the superior tone of command'. To avoid cases of homicide was 'utterly impossible . . . when a strong and masterful race comes in contact with an inferior ignorant and savage race'. In 'well meant ignorance' the authorities had allowed 'unwise, often personally prejudiced police, to put the natives up to all sorts of moves, incite to insubordination . . . thus relations between natives and employers began to get more difficult . . .' Reaction to the Roth Report was

worked up by excited and ignorant writers in newspapers . . . thousands of city residents headed by . . . clergymen who had never taken the trouble to ascertain the facts . . . yelling shame on a considerable body of respectable settlers, most of whom are far higher in moral standing and social life than hundreds of those who are denouncing them.[16]

Australian States, after the foundation of the Commonwealth, remained sensitive to criticism from England. In 1907, there was agitation on the matter of neck chains, and representations were made by the Secretary of State for Colonies to the Governor. The annual report for the new Aborigines Department for that year states that medical and other evidence had indicated that this was the best method. The chain was fastened just below the chin, to allow the hands to be free: to chain by wrist or ankle would mean chaining tightly because of Aboriginal agility, as would chaining round the waist. Four were usually chained together; the constable might have as many as twenty on the chain, and his safety had to be considered (etc.)[17] Thirty years later it was still being defended on the same grounds by the first conference of Australian authorities in Aboriginal affairs, and the practice remained for years after that. It may still be resorted to unofficially: as late as 1958 there was a report of Aboriginal prisoners kept on the chain at Halls Creek, the Western Australian Police Commissioner stating in defence that the Aboriginal prisoner preferred chaining to being locked up.[18] For a long time the brutality of the chain has dominated the relationships of police and Aborigines in 'colonial Australia'. During the research for this project I learned on irrefutable evidence of a case (not in Western Australia) where

---

[16] A.R. Richardson, *Early memories of the Great Nor'-West, and a Chapter in the History of Western Australia*, quoted by John Wilson in Authority and Leadership in a 'new-style' Australian Aboriginal Community: Pindan, Western Australia. There is a copy of Richardson's book in the Mitchell Library, Sydney.

[17] *W.A.V. & P.*, 1907, p. 6—Annual Report of Aborigines Department.

[18] See articles by Douglas Lockwood in the *Herald* (Melbourne), 19 March 1958 and reply by W.A. Commissioner of Police, quoted on 20 March 1958.

THE DESTRUCTION OF ABORIGINAL SOCIETY

the constable, in an area of rapidly developing mining activity, was at a loss because he had found some Aborigines drinking alcohol, but had no gaol. What else could he do but chain them to the trees?

Frontier conditions tended to set the standards elsewhere, since they affected attitudes profoundly. There is not much discussion of what is suitable for British subjects or for human dignity in such cases. Police protectors, the officials most closely in contact with the Aboriginal people in these frontier regions and responsible for their welfare, naturally enough developed the attitudes better suited for animal husbandry; criticism of what they had to do sounds like the kind of thing we hear from the R.S.P.C.A. about movement of stock or neglect of pets.

The whole system came under public attention, and contributed to the awakening of national public opinion, when yet another Royal Commission inquired in 1927 into the 'Alleged Killing and Burning of Bodies of Aborigines in East Kimberley and into Police methods when Effecting Arrests'. A man called Hay, on Nulla Nulla Station, was killed by Aborigines; the arresting party, which consisted of two constables, two 'special' constables, Hay's partner, and seven armed Aborigines was, in the opinion of the Royal Commissioner, G.T. Wood, S.M., much more like a punitive expedition than one to bring in the murderers. The Reverend E. Gribble, from the Forrest River Mission, thought that his regular Aboriginal visitors had been reduced by thirty. Evidence found at the camps of the expedition suggested that an unknown number had been shot and burned, probably while 'on the chain', and the Commission established that this had happened in at least eleven cases. There was evidence that Overheu, Hay's partner, had subsequently shot his Aboriginal employee, who had been a witness. Wood mentions this carefully but states that there is not enough evidence to prove it. It is a long and sickening story, with justice defeated by the fact that although it was told freely in Wyndham, it proved impossible to get adequate evidence from the whites there. The missing thirty could have 'died of influenza'.[19]

Police methods also came in for more discussion, and it is clear that the trackers were not only still armed but that they were being sent into the bush somewhat in the manner of the old Queensland Native Police. The technique of surrounding the camp while the Aborigines slept was similar; the Commissioner found that in this case the trackers had been

[19] *W.A.V. & P.*, 1927—Report of the Royal Commission of Inquiry into Alleged Killing and Burning of Bodies of Aborigines in East Kimberley and into Police Methods when Effecting Arrests.

THE EXTENSION OF SETTLEMENT IN WESTERN AUSTRALIA 201

armed and at the time of arrest not accompanied by the constables. An interesting feature of the inquiry is the obvious disagreement between the Aborigines Department and the Police Department on the matter of how arrests should be made. The sergeant at Wyndham stated that he had 'always sent natives out armed when they are scouting. You could not induce them to get the horses unless they had them'. The constable from Turkey Creek told how, when the camp had been surrounded, some of the whites stood guard while the 'boys' 'put them on the chain'. 'We chained those whom we thought capable of running away and the remainder were left loose.' The comments of Neville, the Chief Protector, make it clear that in his view the system of using trackers had extended to

the engagement of mobs of blacks to accompany the police, round up camps, and as has been done on some occasions, promiscuously shoot . . . unfortunately, when we arrest a black, we do not treat him as we would a white . . . the taking of trackers from prison, the making of a man who has murdered someone into a tracker of his own kind, is . . . wrong, more especially if the man comes from the same part of the country . . . .[20]

The mission's role in the situation is comparable with that played by missions in colonial situations in early frontier times, in Africa or the Pacific, with the mission trying to act as the conscience of the government and as the confidant of the indigenous people. Yet the mission in these areas was as vulnerable to Aboriginal cattle raiders as the pastoral property. In 1925 Gribble had reported to the Minister for the North-West an extensive raid by Aborigines from the Drysdale River. Neville was reported to have said that such a raid was 'only to be expected': in the meantime the police had arrested the 'chief offenders'.[21]

In the triangle of tension—mission, settler, and government—it is typical of the continental frontier of Australia that the government role is weak. Weakness in this case was shown in the split between the Aborigines Department and the police. For the police, the government was a settlers' government, as it had always been; for the Aborigines Department the problem remained that most of its agents were members of the police: and this restriction on attempts to implement policy continued.

This incident, or rather, the publicity arising from the Royal Commission, seems to have marked a turning-point in Aboriginal affairs. It was extensively reported in the capital city press.[22] The Australian Board

[20] It had long been established practice in Western Australia to employ Aboriginal prisoners as trackers on completion of their sentences. A.C. Gregory referred to this, in evidence to the Select Committee of the Queensland Legislative Assembly in 1861 (see ch. 10).
[21] *Argus* (Melbourne), 4 August 1925.
[22] See, for instance, *Sydney Morning Herald* for 9-12. 15, 16, 19, 23, 24, and 26 March 1927.

202 THE DESTRUCTION OF ABORIGINAL SOCIETY

of Missions had publicised a report of the incident in October 1926; and this may have influenced the decision of the Western Australian government to hold the inquiry. When the constables were subsequently reinstated, Collier, the Premier, received protests from the Association for the Protection of Native Races in Sydney; and from the National Missionary Council of Australia.[23]

An interesting indication of the way in which the part-Aborigines in the settled areas were beginning to seek an identity with those on the frontier is indicated by Peter Biskup. 'The murders', he writes 'led to a crystallisation of the smouldering resentment among the educated natives and mixed-bloods [of Western Australia] who in November 1926 formed a union "in order to obtain the protection of the same laws that govern the white man".' William Harris, the organiser, made history when he wrote to the *Sunday Times* that Aborigines objected to being 'robbed and shot down and run into miserable compounds'. He was concerned with land rights, segregation, arrests without warrant, the right to drink in hotels, the use of government reserves as, in effect, prisons, education, the dormitory system, the rigid paternal controls at Mogumber and Carrolup Aboriginal settlements. In March 1928 the first deputation of part-Aborigines to see a Minister of the Crown put their protests to the Premier.[24] In other ways this incident was a turning-point; we will return to it later.

Conditions in the Western Australian frontier lands were to play their part in stimulating the agitation, mainly in the capital cities and maintained by academic, religious, and humanitarian bodies, which led to some reappraisal by governments in the 1930s. For the most part, this national agitation was focused on the situation in the Northern Territory, in which all citizens had a direct interest.

[23] See *Argus* (Melbourne) 9 October 1926 and 21 March and 14 April 1928.
[24] Biskup, Native Administration and Welfare in Western Australia, p. 228.

THE SOUTH AUSTRALIAN FRONTIER,
1860-1911

In 1860 a Select Committee appointed by the Legislative Council of South Australia heard evidence from the experts on the condition of Aborigines and considered what ought to be done. As background to its pessimistic report, the frontier was rapidly being extended. It was easy for the gentlemen who considered the results of over two decades of settlement to assume that reasonable effort had been made and that all positive steps had failed: that Aborigines defeated welfare policies by dying out. In the 2800 square miles round Adelaide, according to Moorhouse, numbers had declined from 650 in 1841 to 180 in 1856. Under 10,000 acres had been set aside as reserves; but against the background of a vanishing people, why complicate the land laws by setting aside any more? What use had Aborigines made of the small allotments? It seemed wrong to feed persons who did not work—only the old and ill should be rationed: the others should work for the settlers. Not only did the gathering of Aborigines from different areas to central points for rationing increase disputes; but the Aborigines did not think the supplies issued were worth the long journeys to get them! Issues of clothing, the Committee said, only increased ill health, as clothes would be worn while wet. The causes of decline in numbers were thought to be infanticide, initiation rites, alcohol, intercourse with settlers, disproportion of the sexes, and syphilis— an interesting list, since all but the second appear to be as much the *results* of dispossession and white settlement as causes of the decline.

The Committee's recommendations were attuned to the belief that the 'race' was 'dying'. The Chief Protector's office, closed in 1856, should be restored. He should adjudicate in cases where law clashed with native

THE DESTRUCTION OF ABORIGINAL SOCIETY

custom; the injustice of applying the law to actions governed by native custom was increased by the necessity of bringing in witnesses, as well as the accused, in chains. He should be assisted in rural areas by part-time sub-Protectors appointed from the government officers and settlers, who might teach 'steady industrial habits and the manners of civilised life', morals, and Christianity. The settlers should be used to distribute food and clothing where required—a foreshadowing of the role of pastoral station managements in the Northern Territory, maintained at least until 1966, when they were still the agents of the Commonwealth Department of Social Services. Reserves should be increased, not for Aboriginal use but for leasing, in order to raise revenue to pay for Aboriginal sustenance and meet other costs. Educational effort should be based on the principle of separating children from parents.[1]

These recommendations illustrate that when in the original establishment of race relations justice on the major issues was ignored (no matter how inevitable it may have been), only some effective resistance, of the kind the Aborigines were not organised to offer, could have brought about even that minimum of consideration which came after resistance by the Maori people and others in similar case. As the Aborigines were 'dying out', the expediency of allowing the process to continue, and of being as kind as possible in the meantime, became here (as in other colonies) the basis for practice. The one really humane and liberal recommendation was that for tempering the administration of the law where indigenous custom was involved, by enabling the Protector to adjudicate, in colonial administrative fashion: it came to nothing.

From now until the early twentieth century there was to be limited outdoor relief for those outside the mission institutions; otherwise they were to be left to the settlers and the police protectors. They could not wage effective war to resist; but they did continue, even within the northern regions of the colony, in a stubborn intransigence where they were ill-treated. It was here that the last punitive expeditions in all Australia seem to have occurred as late as the early 1940s.[2] Educational effort of the type which had been tried at Poonindie, maintained at the missions of Point Macleay and Point Pearce (founded in the Yorke Peninsula in 1868), was to preserve there institutionalised populations which are only now being dispersed. Point Macleay is among those most noted in Australia for practices that illustrate the extreme ethnocentricity

[1] S.A.P.P., 1860, no. 165—Report of the Select Committee of the Legislative Council on 'The Aborigines'.
[2] Information from Professor R.M. Berndt, based on his knowledge of the police records.

THE SOUTH AUSTRALIAN FRONTIER, 1860-1911   205

of some Christians: it was here that Taplin deliberately, and in fervent
good will, set out to smash a culture pattern he could not understand.[3]

A Protector was again appointed in 1861, though by this time, with
the frontiers rapidly receding beyond the control of the government, he
was faced with a problem even more difficult than Moorhouse had. The
police, as the officials most common in the areas out beyond the towns,
generally became the protectors. Thus a pattern in Aboriginal administration was established for what was to become the Northern Territory
also, where, for the usual frontier reasons, the interdependence of the
settlers and the police, as well as their common attitudes, meant that race
relations were a matter for the settler and the local Aborigines without
effective government interference.

In the 1860s towns were established at the copper mines in the Yorke
Peninsula. There, too, the Aboriginal fringe camps became part of the
mining scene, as they inevitably were everywhere in the dry areas, from
the eastern goldfields of Western Australia to the far reaches of the
Northern Territory and north Queensland. Mining activities required
water; and the use of sparse water resources for mining and other purposes
made the Aborigines even more dependent than the depasturing of stock
on the waterholes had done. The period produced the pastoralist 'battlers',
who moved not only into the South Australian desert but across into the
Northern Territory with their stock. To this day, the resultant relationships between settler and Aboriginal have survived in these dry regions
of South Australia; and it is only recently that the government has
established an active policy in the areas north and west of Port Augusta.
The southern region of the Northern Territory was settled as an extension
of this movement out of the better regions of the colony, but the northern
region of the Territory was settled mainly by overlanding expeditions
from Queensland.

Except for the help given to mission effort at Point Pearce and Point
Macleay, rationing for the aged and ill, and the annual blanket issue, the
only positive government effort seems to have been encouragement for
new missions. The Moravian Brethren and the two Lutheran Churches
established the Kopperamanna and Killalpaninna Missions, both on
Cooper Creek, west of Lake Eyre, in 1866. According to Fay Gale, who
has made a careful study of the development of South Australian policy,
there was no further effort within South Australia until the Lutherans
established a mission at Koonibba, west of Ceduna, thirty years later.

[3] For an account of Taplin's efforts, see R.M. and C.H. Berndt, *From Black to White in South
Australia.*

But in 1877 the famous Hermannsburg Mission was established in the Alice Springs area by Lutherans who had overlanded their stock to the site. By 1900 most mission work was being devoted to part-Aborigines in the areas of closer settlement.[4]

South Australia beyond the farming areas and the Northern Territory formed another whole region where the settlers were subject mainly to their own consciences for many decades. No legislation at all followed the Select Committee report in 1860. The lack of any serious purpose is well indicated by the fact that the first Bill on Aboriginal Affairs to be considered was presented in 1899; it was rejected. There was no legislation from the beginning of responsible government until the Acts of 1910 and 1911. One reason for the 1899 Bill was the reports of cruelty which were coming back from the frontier regions, and especially the ill-treatment of women and girls; so one of the provisions of the Bill was to limit contact with Aborigines to persons licensed to have them on or near their premises.[5] Later, it was to become an offence in South Australia to be found without authority within a certain distance of an Aboriginal camp; but the real effort to protect the women does not seem to have been made until the part-Aborigines were being seen as a 'problem' in their turn. Then the legislation aimed to limit the 'problem' by preventing miscegenation.

THE NORTHERN TERRITORY OF SOUTH AUSTRALIA, 1863-1911

In July 1863 the Northern Territory was separated from New South Wales by the Imperial Government, to become a territory under control of South Australia. In 1864 the first sales of Northern Territory lands were held in Adelaide; and two years later the settlers had reached the Macdonnell Ranges. Before 1870, when the Administration was formally set up in Palmerston (Darwin), cattle and horses were being established on the waterholes in the Alice Springs area. This stocking of waterholes, more or less at will, without more than token interference from the South Australian government, had especially drastic results in the drier regions. Here highly developed arts of conservation had enabled a light population to preserve, with sanctions emphasised by religious belief, a favourable balance of nature. T.G.H. Strehlow has shown how the 'land-based religious institutions' of the Aranda people included in each 'section'

---

[4] Fay Gale, *A Study of Assimilation*, pp. 90 *et seq.*
[5] Ibid., p. 103—quoting *S.A.P.P.*, 1899, no. 77—Minutes of evidence, p. 21.

THE SOUTH AUSTRALIAN FRONTIER, 1860-1911 207

area (the section being a local group) the storehouse (cave or tree) for the 'local sacred objects'. The precincts of this formed

a prohibited area, whose edge was generally about a mile (or even more) from the sacred cave. Within these sacred precincts all hunting and food gathering was forbidden. Even wounded animals could not be pursued into this forbidden zone, which could be entered only for ceremonial purposes.

Even in drought times, he says, the Aranda were prevented from using

many of the best permanent waters in their territory ... In drought times the animals and birds from thousands of square miles of drought-stricken country found refuge at these pmara kutata; and when the drought broke, the surrounding country-side was restocked with game as quickly as it became covered with food plants.[6]

The same writer's sensitive description of the emotional attachment of men to their totem animals, and to those of their kindred, suggests something of the shock when settlers began to shoot the game as well as depasture on to the sacred places.

In the old days it was common to hear remarks of compassion uttered by men who saw a hunter returning to the camp with a killed animal of their personal totem. This compassion for animals, even if it had not first created the game reserves in Central Australia, certainly helped to protect their integrity in times of droughts.[7]

It is only occasionally, where an anthropologist has worked in an area early enough in the process of contact and settlement, that we have such a glimpse of this harmony with the environment as it was, of its deepest meaning, so that it served for the Aboriginal the functions that home, town, garden, library, theatre, school, and church discharged in the western culture; and those of farm and factory as well. Here too was the close integration of religion with economic life. When the Aboriginal lost this relationship with his 'country' he lost everything. This kind of loss was repeated progressively everywhere, until the last efforts were made to establish the extensive reserves.

The lack of multi-purposed leadership of the kind required for extensive political organisation meant that the same range of situations, varying to some extent with the attitudes of settlers, occurred as on innumerable earlier occasions. In larger regions, the same sequence of race relations developed. The Northern Territory includes some of the worst of the desert country; and in time stock were to be depastured even on the rare waterholes there, with the very serious results which Charles Duguid,

---

[6] 'Culture, Social Structure, and Environment in Aboriginal Central Australia', in Ronald and Catherine Berndt (eds.), *Aboriginal Man in Australia: Essays in Honour of A.P. Elkin*, p. 143.
[7] Ibid., p. 144.

with the advantages of an observer at first hand over a long period, has effectively described.[8] This situation was characteristic of the 'centre' of the continent, where big droughts are inevitable; so that here the small-scale resistance had something of the character of a struggle for life itself.

The likelihood of violence in the early stages of contact, between a particular settling enterprise and a local group, was so great that when he generalised about the stages of contact, A.P. Elkin, a really perceptive observer of frontier situations in Australia, included 'clash' as one of the stages.

The Aborigines feel justified in resisting the white man both by non-cooperation and by physical means, until they learn through punitive expeditions and police action that the intruder's power is paramount, that clash means defeat and death. They have nowhere else to go, for they are tied by spiritual bonds to their tribal and horde country, now possessed by another. They must therefore accept the changed position ... and adapt themselves to it according to the circumstances ... and according to the personality of each white person with whom they have to deal.

Elkin stressed this adaptation to the particular man and his enterprise by reference to his experiences in Central Australia in 1930. In each case there was a keen assessment by the Aborigines of the man with whom they must deal; and in most, it is implied, the terms of the adjustment reached, even as late as 1930, had not become complete submission:

All the white men over a large area were classified by the natives according to whether they kept their word or not, fulfilled or did not fulfil their spoken or implied social and economic obligations (to the Aborigines); in the first case they were good, in the second, bad. The second were in danger of being speared ... For the very adaptation they are compelled ... to make is both general and particular. It is not only to a changed economic environment and organization ... but also to a particular expression of the change, as mediated through the settler, station manager or employee, prospector, missionary or official who has become the focus and point of contact with the change.[9]

Elkin's most famous observation on these situations relates to those where, perhaps after violence which has not been completely destructive and which has left the Aborigines with access to their sacred places and with sufficient resources to carry on their own ceremonial life, there is an unstable state of 'intelligent parasitism'.[10] This is possible where other labour is inadequate or unavailable, so that the manager must have the work of some of the men for at least some of the time. This is supplied without enthusiasm or interest, in return for supplies of food and the

[8] *No Dying Race.*
[9] A.P. Elkin, Reaction and Interaction: A Food Gathering People and European Settlement in Australia, *American Anthropologist*, vol. 53, no. 2, 1951, pp. 167-9.
[10] Ibid., p. 172.

THE SOUTH AUSTRALIAN FRONTIER, 1860-1911 209

few implements which fill the needs of the group as a whole, with the men of status in the background organising the Aboriginal side of the arrangement. Also in these frontier areas, and on the scale of the individual European enterprise, access by the 'boss' to the women as required was often part of the implicit bargain; and this implied reciprocal obligations on his part. Failure to fulfil obligations undertaken by accepting either sexual partnership or economic assistance might lead to a spearing.

It is worth noting that among the Aborigines employment did not, as contract employment in the Pacific Islands did, take the place of initiation as a socialising experience, providing a substitute way for the man to win prestige by supplying trade goods. There are many reasons for this, no doubt; one may be the comparative lack of interest by Aborigines in material artefacts beyond a narrow range with immediate appeal. More important, I would guess (because cash, in the long run, with the offer of universal exchangeability and an inexhaustible range of possible purchases, breaks down customary duties and preferences), was the fact that Aboriginal labour was not rewarded in the first stages with cash; that the worker remained under the control of the group and in the camp. He did not win the prestige of the traveller and the man with new experiences. Also, the services of the women, either sexually or in the homestead or both, were often as highly rewarded by the 'boss' as the work of the men with cattle.

This adjustment could last for a long time, work on the station forming, from the point of view of the Aborigines, a means of acquiring food somewhat easier than hunting. Elkin has described the resumption by station workers of the ceremonies and the dancing at night as a regular renewal of the real interests of the group. (Some years ago I was able to hear and observe the nightly ceremonies at Mainoru Station, in Arnhem Land.) In some regions, as in the Kimberleys, the off-season in the yearly routine of station work could be so adjusted as to fit in with the need to visit the sacred places, perform the initiation ceremonies, and the like—the 'walkabout'. Yet it was always bound to break down into a hopeless dependency in the long run, for many reasons—the attractions of the cash economy for the younger men, and the consequent breaking down of social controls; or as the result of depopulation, which could so easily follow drought in the dry regions, once the old balance of man with nature had been altered; and commonly the employer's refusal of opportunities for a greater share in the enterprise which caused those who might have developed real interest to withdraw into what remained of their own tradition. Their 'apathy' would disguise from the employer

210   THE DESTRUCTION OF ABORIGINAL SOCIETY

the emotional response to frustration. The old savour and excitement had gone, with nothing comparable to replace it. Nineteenth-century Australian pastoral management was not equipped to deal with such situations, even in its own long-term interests. Often the labour force was decimated by poor feeding and by the effects of conditions in the camps, which were to remain to this day, either for efficiency or humanity, a disgrace to the industry. The pastoral enterprise did not operate on cash, but on credit at the station store. Besides making truck payment easy and profitable to this day, this maintained a lack of sophistication in money matters. The surprising thing is not that there should now be a movement by Aborigines for equal wages in the Northern Territory but that this has been so long delayed.

Another factor delaying the confident movement into cash economics has been that lack of demand for meat produced in the areas farther out has enabled poor management to survive there—management largely based on prejudices of 'how to treat natives', which helps to give these regions their colonial air. This is by no means universal; but it has been possible because stations far out have long been regarded and managed as sources of store cattle to be fattened in areas closer to the southern markets. Big firms which took over large stations tended to hold rather than develop, especially where they had similar interests in other countries closer to the European markets.

Elkins's 'intelligent parasitism' is essentially, as he makes clear, a transitional stage. The autonomy remaining, expressed in the nightly ceremonies when the people return to the important business of life, would have to be preserved, and opportunities offered for continued adaptation while maintaining the integrity of the group, if Aborigines were to come to better terms with the new things. Such opportunities did not come along the frontiers; and the drift was to pauperism in the end.

Elkin saw other possibilities. Where the first settlements were established, pauperism came very quickly as tribes became landless: for here landlessness involved lack of access to the 'country'. Some punitive measures were so severe as to leave only a few remnants. Out on the later frontiers, he says, most of the settlers came to learn where their own interests lay—in some kind of adjustment which left them with the labour they required.[11]

The early settlement of the north of South Australia and of Central Australia appears to have involved at least some who were conditioned to take drastic action. The history of Queensland and Western Australia

[11] Ibid., p. 181.

THE SOUTH AUSTRALIAN FRONTIER, 1860-1911 211

as well as the Northern Territory suggests that there was a stage when the attitude to the local labour supply was reckless because there seemed to be plenty of Aborigines; in the less fertile regions the drift from farther out, in to the stations, motivated partly by economics, partly by fear, partly by curiosity, had been noted by several writers; and the process was to be accelerated until restrained later by administrative controls. Even the Aboriginal trained to control his curiosity could not resist this kind of experience and with the breakdown of the old system of socialisation, curiosity gained a freer rein. It seems that in many areas the regions farther out were first denuded of people as they moved into the spaces left by those who had perished from the new diseases and other causes. The South Australian frontier, extending over to the Macdonnell Ranges, seems also to have been the locale for harsh ill-treatment of the Aboriginal women and girls, to such an extent that 'gin-busting' was one of the reasons for the introduction of the Bill of 1899.

One reason why this Bill was rejected was that the problems of violence were over in the more heavily settled areas. The frontier problems seemed different from the residual problems round the towns and among the farms of the south, where people were becoming concerned about part-Aboriginal prostitution, disease, and drunkenness. The difficulty of devising a policy applicable both in the vicinity of the Overland Telegraph Line and also in the south may have contributed to the neglect. Yet, even within the northern regions of the colony, as R.M. and C.H. Berndt's study of race relations makes clear, the native police trackers, recruited in the usual way from other regions, were being armed and used to deal out summary 'punishment' for 'trouble' which they had helped to foment.[12] Little wonder, then, that the Northern Territory was the frontier area where for a long time the government interfered least in relations between settlers and Aborigines.

South Australian administration of the Northern Territory had begun with the first survey expedition led by Finniss to Palmerston in 1864. There was a part-time Protector, who was also the medical officer, whose instructions were to win the confidence and respect of the Aborigines and make them aware of their legal rights as British subjects, as well as to prevent sexual intercourse with them or the sale of liquor to them; and to use the law against settlers who ill-treated them.[13]

The means for Aboriginal administration were those set up for South

[12] *From Black to White in South Australia,* p. 71.
[13] *S.A.P.P.,* 1864, no. 36, p. 154—Instructions to Boyle Travers Finniss Esq., Government Resident, in April 1864.

Australia after the Select Committee of 1860 and applied in the same spirit of pessimism, as an extension of the colony's administration, except that there was an additional part-time Protector in Darwin. The same system of sub-Protectors was used in the Territory as in the colony.

The Northern Territory Act of South Australia, in 1863, had provided for the appointment of a Resident responsible to the South Australian Commissioner for Crown Lands. South Australian law applied in the Territory, and parts of it there only. Between 1863 and 1911, when the Territory was handed over to the Commonwealth, its administration was handled, as an additional responsibility, by twenty-seven ministers in thirty-eight cabinets. The fluctuations in the cattle industry and repeated failure of hopes for mining and tropical agriculture increased unwillingness to incur considerable expenditure. One of the first activities undertaken was the construction of the Overland Telegraph Line from Darwin. The first cattle were brought there to supply meat for the workers. Pastoral settlement of the 'Top End', including the sub-tropical grasslands, came mainly with the overlanders through and from Queensland but appears to have remained partial and scattered until the 1930s.[14] According to J.P.M. Long, most of the groups of Aborigines living in the pastoral regions of the Territory have been at least in touch with stations from about 1920 at the latest.[15]

There was a real absence of government control of any kind over wide areas for a long time. One-fifth of the 523,600 square miles had been occupied by pastoral leases by 1880, and nearly two-fifths by 1890; but many of these stations had been abandoned by 1900, largely owing to the depredations of the blacks, and a tradition of hostility between whites and blacks had been definitely established.

Some of this settlement was by large pastoral companies, whose role in the Territory and in northern Western Australia was to be of special importance in the attitudes of management and of Aboriginal employees. In the Territory, in these years, there was no government effort to regulate the conditions of labour. As labour must be had, the methods amounted to forced labour, unless the Aborigines were able to make the kind of adjustment described by Elkin.

In a 'colonial' situation, labour relations form what Barbara Ward has called, in another context of race relations, the 'neuralgic point'. By the

[14] F.H. Bauer, *Historical Geography of White Settlement in Part of Northern Australia*—Part 2: *The Katherine-Darwin Region*—CSIRO, Division of Land Research and Regional Survey—Divisional Report No. 64/1.
[15] J.P.M. Long, Note in SSRC-AP file.

THE SOUTH AUSTRALIAN FRONTIER, 1860-1911

end of the century, stories from the Northern Territory were raising the same indignation in Adelaide as those from other areas of the northern frontier were receiving in other capital cities. One of the reasons for the failure of the South Australian legislature to pass the Bill of 1899 (which followed reports of fighting and punitive expeditions on the Daly, on Brunette, Newcastle Waters, Elsey, and the Roper) was that it proposed use of the written contract of labour—a measure which, to judge by a similar one in Western Australia, the pastoralists should not have feared. The position was shocking, even from the point of view of the minimal requirements of cross-cultural administration as generally conceived at the time in colonies. The only provisions for the special situation and rights of Aborigines were in the part-time office of Chief Protector, the use of a few sub-Protectors, and scattered ration depots. The police, who did the patrolling, held their positions by their ability to 'deal with natives' in accordance with the settler ethos.

One of the most damning comments, because it is made by a student of historical geography who was concerned not with social problems so much as with the utilisation of resources, is that by F.H. Bauer, an American student of the Australian frontier. Of the years 1869-89 he wrote that while the Aborigines

probably suffered somewhat less than did the native population of many parts of the world when Europeans began to take over their country ... By the end of the period, the aboriginal problem was still unsolved and the Government was not anxious to grapple with it ... this failure to face the issue squarely cost both Europeans and aborigines dearly in later years, for it merely compounded the difficulties by delay.

... The aboriginal problem was to prove one of the thorniest passed on to the Commonwealth in 1911, and much of the later difficulties may be traced directly to the complete lack of regard for the rights and responsibilities of this people during the early years.[16]

There is no point in repeating here details of ill-treatment, and of the sometimes very effective retaliation: in retrospect and in view of the understandable reticence of literate persons involved at the time, it is very difficult even to guess at the *scale* of violence. To go through the literature carefully looking for incidents is to assemble a horrifying picture of murders by irresponsible whites. It may well be that the whole loss of life involved in settlement of Australia, judged alongside what happened in the Americas or elsewhere, amounts to comparatively small-scale homicide; even a minor war involving civilian bombing might involve physical suffering on a greater scale. The main points are that here again

[16] *The Katherine-Darwin Region*, pp. 141-2, 194.

214 THE DESTRUCTION OF ABORIGINAL SOCIETY

the land was settled either at the point of the gun or against the background of Aboriginal knowledge of what the gun can do; and that the same wide gulf between the cultures helped to produce justifications for settler consciences in the same pattern as elsewhere and earlier; and that these justifications in their turn, purporting to establish for the Aboriginal a status somewhat less than human, sustained and increased prejudice which blinded all but the imaginative to their plight. Thus Alfred Giles of Springfield, in 1887, could maintain that those in the south who expressed concern were deluded with ideas of the 'noble savage'; that if the Aboriginal

lacks one thing more than another it is virtue. Moral laws they have none; their festive dances and corrobbories [sic] are of the most lewd and disgusting character, their songs, rites, and ceremonies utterly revolting and fiendish ... if we add a few of the white men's vices, and then ask the question as to the possibility ... of chastity among their women, the idea at once becomes preposterous ... preposterous, therefore, is the idea of the black women being outraged, unless it is by stopping their supply of tobacco.

The white man, he says, is often seduced by the Aboriginal woman, 'and therefore they justify ... killing him, whereas ... in nine cases out of ten, the blackfellow sends and insists—often against the woman's will—on her acting as a decoy'.[17]

As in north Queensland, mining was another reason for going to the Territory, although the heavy expense soon tended to limit mining enterprises to company activities. The first finds of gold were made during the construction of the telegraph line; and one may fairly speculate that had race relations been established on any kind of reasonable basis, the Aborigines could have made a very great contribution in this kind of development, especially in prospecting. According to N.F. Gamble whose study of the mining industry in the Territory is a basic document, the first white miners lived so badly at Pine Creek that the conditions improved somewhat when the Chinese miners came in from Singapore in 1875.[18] It was South Australian policy to develop the industry with Asian labour; and for over thirty years Asians outnumbered others by twelve to one, with over 2,000 in the fields in 1894-5.[19] Although the Chinese were themselves subject to restrictive laws, liable to be ordered off any goldfield, and after 1895 prohibited from being granted mining

[17] Ibid., pp. 139-40—quoting *S.A.P.P.*, 1887, no. 53.
[18] Mining in the Northern Territory 1861-1961, Department of Territories File 62/1116 (typescript). I have to thank the author and the Department for access to this document.
[19] Ibid.; and Bauer, *The Katherine-Darling Region*, p. 164, Table 18.

THE SOUTH AUSTRALIAN FRONTIER, 1860-1911

leases, they filled the need for disciplined labour which made it unnecessary even to consider seriously the employment of Aborigines. The use of Asians in this way was typical of the colonial world. Such labour was cheap and efficient, and saved management from costs of training workers whose culture did not differentiate between 'work' and other activities and was not geared to cash economics.

When later it became the policy of the Commonwealth to ensure preference for white labour, there was to be no significant problem of the place of Aborigines in the industry. The chance of an Aboriginal to make his mark as a prospector belonged to the period 1870 to 1910, when mining was organised on the basis of wide-ranging alluvial activities. In the north there was the area from Pine Creek to Maranboy and the Daly River for gold, and the Daly River for copper. In the south there was the goldfield at Arltunga, and mica at Harts Range. But as current developments show, the future lay with deep mining by the heavily capitalised enterprise, which renders out of date both the old-time miner and the Aboriginal, along with the settlers who have adapted to the environment, and which transforms the environment and creates within an enclosed construction the conditions for heavy industry.

Round mining towns like Pine Creek and Tennant Creek, the Aborigines lived, often in fringe camps which were among the worst in the continent. Miners of both races, white Australian and Chinese, interfered deeply by their demands on the women, and probably were no more under government control than the pastoral employers and workers. The plight of Aborigines in areas of scarce water, where mining was carried on, has been referred to already. One of the first reports of the first Commonwealth Administration sheds some light on the limits of 'native administration', where parties could go where they wished without any real effort at control. Before 1913 there was a system of encouraging prospecting by giving money and rations to prospectors, which they would sometimes accept and then go 'into the bush close to good fishing and shooting, where they had a tribe of black gins waiting on them'.[20]

The few police through this vast area, even had they been trained for the task of protection, would have had little chance of standing against the traditions. In the northern areas subject to the monsoon, most cattle stations were cut off in the wet even from the telegraph. The solitary policeman was similarly isolated. This situation emphasised the unity of

[20] Gamble, Mining in the Northern Territory, p. 97—quoting Annual Report of Administration 1912, C.P.P., 1913, vol. III, pp. 227 et seq.

216 THE DESTRUCTION OF ABORIGINAL SOCIETY

the whites, to maintain 'supremacy'; the white man's burden was mainly to issue the traditional blanket on occasions and when available; and the role of the police 'protector' was in practice to do what he could to assist the pastoral industry. The 'good' official, as throughout the colonial world, was the man who knew when to ignore the law and when to allow or assist the whites to take it into their own hands: in the Territory, to deal promptly with cattle spearers and to assist in the control of unwilling station labour. In this environment (as in most colonies) the government official and the white settler were interdependent. In the Northern Territory the missionary had less chance than in most of these situations of prompting or restraining either.

The policeman was dependent on the pastoralist for social acceptance and approval. Patrol officers of the Northern Territory Welfare Branch were dependent in this way in the 1950s. The long tradition of employers making their own rules, actively assisted by an Administration which placed the pastoral industry above all else, and which considered it the foundation for northern 'development' almost irrespective of efficiency or markets, formed the background of a partnership which has proved durable indeed. How durable, is well illustrated by the recent developments in the matter of Aboriginal wages.

While it is easy to criticise the current situation of Aboriginal administration in the Territory, recent achievements have to be assessed against this background and the continuing power of very powerful interests, which are in the classical situation of the big firms in a colonial area on which 'development' is assumed by governments to depend, and which can always, through their political and social contacts, go straight to the central or colonising government. Such interests are in a position to frustrate good intentions of local officers or to corrupt them with social acceptance, in order to undermine their efforts; and even to refuse openly to be bound by the law which the junior officer in the field may try to enforce.

The South Australian system of appointing sub-Protectors, who might be police officers or officers in charge of the telegraph stations, began in 1877 to be used for the management of a limited number of ration depots, mainly to feed the old and ill. It was possible for a man of insight and ability like F.J. Gillen, the sub-Protector at Alice Springs, to acquire specialist knowledge of Aboriginal custom, but most of the first contacts were made by the settlers. In their wake came the patrolling police, often on a punitive expedition resulting from the earliest contact by settler or prospector. The custom of using armed trackers, often to go into

THE SOUTH AUSTRALIAN FRONTIER, 1860-1911

the bush without control, was first introduced in the centre and then extended; and it developed much the same way as in Western Australia and northern Queensland (before Queensland policies changed in 1897). The literature abounds with the details, from the early exploring contacts and the construction of the telegraph line, on through the period when overlanding parties were coming into the north from the south and east, especially in the period from 1878, when Glencoe was taken up near the site of Katherine, to the early 1890s, during which time land on the Victoria, Roper, and Macarthur Rivers was stocked, some by the big pastoral companies. These companies, had the industry needed many labourers, and had they themselves placed the highest priority on efficient development of the stations, might have pressed the government for more effective husbandry of the indigenous labour resources. But the Aboriginal was often seen and treated as a pest. Labour was required periodically, but it was seemingly plentiful because of the drift from areas farthest out from the stations. The industry lacked sure markets for beef, which might have hastened improvements and developed an interest in higher standards of management.

Perhaps most destructive of the balance of nature on which the Aboriginal depended was the 'battler', the man with his own few cattle who was ready to settle in a marginal area and 'defend' the one or two waterholes on which his whole enterprise depended. Attack and reprisal led to a monotonous (in retrospect) series of punitive expeditions, by police, by settlers, by both together, some with the open, some with the tacit, support of the Resident; and some of which he would not know. Among the most damning evidence are the boastful accounts of his bloody adventures on the fringe of empire by a Constable Willshire, who, with his band of trackers, seems to have been able to commit mayhem at will, at the expense of the tribes in the central desert.[21]

Yet one has also to account for situations where Aborigines have lived, for several decades now, under paternal management; for the kind of situation, which for a long time had elements of hope in it, where a group of Aborigines had both adjusted to the station requirements and maintained that minimum of autonomy which gives meaning to 'intelligent parasitism'; and which illustrates that many of the settlers, at least after they had established supremacy, were able to reconcile humanity with their own long-term self-interest. Having seen something of this situation on a station like Mainoru, on the fringe of the Arnhem Land reserve, where the homestead seemed to operate as the place of resort for those with

[21] See W. Willshire, *Land of the Dawning*.

troubles in the camp, as well as the school for the children, verifies for this observer the reminiscences of Mrs Aeneas Gunn decades earlier. And if she saw the situation mainly through the eyes of the women employed as household servants, and of the men who had come to identify themselves with the enterprise, there is other evidence that even in the hardest economic conditions some autonomy could be retained. Even the fact that groups acted in unison, in 1966, by walking off the stations at Wave Hill and Newcastle Waters, and referred to themselves by tribal names, suggests that some autonomy remains. It is easy enough to list the numerous atrocities and injustices; but without discounting these it seems necessary to point out that the same wide range of relationships was possible here as along other frontiers, within the limits set by dispossession, the paramountcy of western economics, the paternalism of the enterprise, and the pattern of race relations.

SOUTH AUSTRALIAN LEGISLATION, 1910 AND 1911

Until the Territory became a Commonwealth responsibility, from the beginning of 1911, it shared with South Australia a common method of administration of Aboriginal affairs and a common lack of basic legislation. When South Australian legislators passed the Aborigines Act 1911,[22] almost twelve months after the separation, its terms showed the influence of the Queensland Act of 1897, and especially of the Western Australian Act of 1905. It established an Aborigines Department, and a Chief Protector to administer it (sections 5, 9), and gave him very wide powers over the Aborigines and those half-castes who fell within categories established for the first time under this Act. It provided specifically for assistance to institutions, for leases of up to a thousand square miles of Crown land to any one of them, mission or other. There was power to segregate on reserves. Much of the Act is not of special interest in this frontier context, but a reference to the provisions governing employment will help to explain why the pastoralist in the South Australian semi-desert regions has until very recently been subject to rather less government control in his use of Aboriginal labour than those in other outlying areas.

The pastoralist had to allow the protector or police officer access to his employees, inform the protector of the death of an Aboriginal employee, and send to him any wages owing, as well as any property

[22] An Act to Make Provision for the better Protection and Control of the Aboriginal and Half-caste Inhabitants of the State of South Australia; No. 1048, December 1911.

THE SOUTH AUSTRALIAN FRONTIER, 1860-1911 219

of the deceased. He was forbidden to entice away labour from other employers, but the same clause protected his own labour (sections 27-9). An interesting provision (clause 34) may refer to the frontier custom of 'employing' female stockmen. Should an Aboriginal or half-caste woman be found 'in male attire and in the company of any male person other than an Aboriginal or half-caste', both were guilty of an offence. Such a clause indicates the nature of demands on Aboriginal society—for work and for sexual services. Though the Act conferred power on the Governor to make regulations on matters of welfare and discipline, conditions of employment were not included.

In fact, what was included in the Aborigines Act 1911 is less significant than what was omitted, for there had been a previous Act dealing with Aborigines, assented to exactly a year earlier, in December 1910—not, however, the Aborigines of South Australia but those of the Northern Territory. What was omitted from the Act which was to apply in South Australia illustrates the pressure of vested interests. The Northern Territory Aboriginals Act 1910 provided a somewhat more complete cover of the employment conditions, though inadequate enough by contemporary colonial standards.[23] Employers had to be licensed; the licence was to be issued by a protector in the district, but with appeal to the Chief Protector of the Northern Territory. Asians were specifically excluded from the issue of licences to employ—an effective way of keeping them out of the pastoral industry in the north. (The German New Guinea administration used similar means to keep them out of the plantation industry and the import trade.) Six-monthly returns of employees and payment of wages to a protector (since the protector could recommend cancellation of the licence to the Chief Protector) could be a nuisance to the employer. These clauses, and that for licensing employers, did not appear in the Aborigines Act 1911.

The handing over of the Northern Territory might well have seemed like shedding the worst of the frontier problems, to making possible a concentration on the problems of an increasing part-Aboriginal population. A Royal Commission reported in 1913 that 'while the number of full-blood aborigines is certainly decreasing . . . the aboriginal half-castes are on the increase'.[24] Experience with the enormous frontier region had brought no solutions, partly because the pessimism with which the task had been approached tended to bring the expected results. There had

---

[23] An Act to Make Provision for the Better Protection and Control of the Aboriginal Inhabitants of the Northern Territory, and for other Purposes: No. 1024 of 1910.
[24] Fay Gale, *A Study of Assimilation*, pp. 104-5—quoting Royal Commission of 1913.

been no solution to the basic questions of justice and of the place of the Aboriginal in the law; and now it seemed that the question could become redundant as the Aborigines of the full descent died out in the State.

In the meantime, the Protector for the State of South Australia appears to have been mainly concerned with the issue of rations to the indigent and with the relations of government with the missions. Before the Act of 1911 he had very little power. Perhaps it was inevitable that policy should be debased to the level of segregation of the Aboriginal and the half-caste, since there was no power to protect them in the world of affairs. With the missions minding the inmates, and in effect determining the real practice, the reaction of Protector W.G. South, once the Act was passed, was to press the government to take control of Point Macleay and Point Pearce as going concerns.[25] By this time other State government authorities had their institutions and strong control of the inmates. The situation was not very different from that of the first Aboriginal institutions, in terms of human relations; but perhaps secularisation, with governments taking over, tended to reduce the level of aspiration. The discrimination in the law was very far indeed from the early preoccupation of the South Australian government with equality and justice.

The title of both Acts had stressed protection and control. By this time it seemed, on very good grounds of experience, that humanity could only be satisfied through protection, preservation, control, and institutions. This of course was making it more necessary to be specific in the definitions of who was to be protected and preserved; and the answer was again to include *all* those of full descent, while attempting a workable division (on *ad hoc* racial lines) between those of part-Aboriginal descent who should be included in the group to be protected and those who should not. The Queensland model was used, as adapted for Western Australia in 1905.[26]

With the advantage of half a century we can assess something of what the great cost of institutional living was to be—and what it had already been. But judgments have to be tempered: without the establishment of the institutions there could well have been even greater loss of life. Frontier experience, in circumstances where every area had within a few decades been a frontier area, showed that drastic means were necessary to save Aboriginal lives: to save them from others, and to save them from their own despairing excesses, which seemed to verify all the assumptions

---

[25] Department of Aboriginal Affairs, A Brief Outline of Aboriginal Affairs in South Australia since Colonisation—quoting Report of Protector, June 1912.
[26] Northern Territory Aboriginals Act 1910, section 3; Aborigines Act 1911, section 4.

THE SOUTH AUSTRALIAN FRONTIER, 1860-1911   221

of incapacity and inferiority. Men of good will could and did believe that there was no alternative but the institution for those who were not employed; and very close control of those who were.

Control meant further restriction of rights. This was the continuation of a process of lowering legal status (though, as with the laws of evidence, there had been some moves towards liberalisation) which had been cumulative from the times of first contact.

The 1911 Act in South Australia dealt with such matters as who was an Aboriginal to be controlled; who might remove or confine Aborigines; who might visit them, and the penalties for 'enticing' them away. There was extensive provision for the problem of venereal disease, with separate hospitals and lock-hospitals, which illustrates one of the reasons for concern and control, since there is nothing like a threat to public health to arouse interest in that of a minority. Aborigines could be ordered to move their camps away from a municipality, town, or township; and such towns could be proclaimed 'prohibited areas'. The Chief Protector was the legal guardian of every Aboriginal or half-caste child, overruling parental authority, until twenty-one years of age; and could take over the property of an Aboriginal or half-caste. Here was the compromise of almost absolute control with a degree of apartheid; and, as usual, of good intentions to protect, with economic interest. Those in lawful employment, for instance, could not be directed to live on a reserve. (This was also the case in the Western Australian Act of 1905.)

It is interesting to see the logic of economics operating to produce a truly colonial labour situation. The reserves were inevitably to become enclaves where the Aboriginal family produced in safety the labourers of the future. From here they were to go into rural employment, and here they were to return when not required. To the extent that they left their families on the reserve, they could be paid the wage of a single man, since the government or government-subsidised mission management was there to ensure that the family was maintained. The system could thus operate as a subsidy to the pastoral and other industries. Perhaps only in Queensland was this economic integration into the economy fully realised. There were no qualms where there was no doubt that Aborigines were inefficient workers.

THE COMMONWEALTH ENTERS THE FIELD OF ABORIGINAL ADMINISTRATION

The year 1911 was something of a turning-point, as it began with the transfer of responsibility for the Northern Territory to the Commonwealth Government. Inevitably, involvement of the Commonwealth in Aboriginal administration of a particular area raised the wider question of whether it should take over all responsibility. But the Constitution had established a nation of white Australian citizens, among whom Aborigines were not to be counted in the census. It had established a federation of States, each of which retained the right of managing its own Aborigines, so that the Commonwealth Parliament could make laws for 'The people of any race, other than the aboriginal race in any State, for whom it is deemed necessary to make special laws' (sections 127 and 51 (xxvi)). Both provisions remained until 1967. Even allowing for other issues involved in framing the Constitution, and for the practical difficulties of census taking, exclusion of Aborigines from the census indicated the strength of attitudes arising from frontier experiences.

Only four years earlier, the Commonwealth had taken over control of Papua, which now had the status of an Australian Territory; in 1911 the Northern Territory was given the same status. Of the two, Papua was probably the more accessible from the seat of government in Melbourne, although the overland telegraph to Darwin facilitated administrative communication.

Because of the superficial similarity in Territorial status, and although the circumstances of white settlement were profoundly different, the Territories tended to be associated for administrative purposes. In the files of the small Department of External Affairs, of which Atlee Hunt was

COMMONWEALTH AND ABORIGINAL ADMINISTRATION 223

the permanent head, one set of 'native' matters could look much like the other. The similarities were mainly those which were imposed by the relationship of each Territory in law and administration with the Commonwealth—a common predicament, as it were, to the extent that each was now exposed to Commonwealth administration. It was inevitable that the centralising tendencies of the small Commonwealth public service, which had no expertise in the control and administration of people of other cultures, would go hand in hand with the basically economic concepts of growth and progress for the nation as a whole. The Territories would be developed by white settlers, as assets for the people of Australia. The association of Territories administratively under the management of the one department was sometimes discontinued and sometimes renewed. More recently, administrative semantics were to overcome administrative realities when the Commonwealth Government established a Department of Territories; but reversal has again placed the Northern Territory under the Department of the Interior.

A NEW INTELLECTUAL INTEREST IN ABORIGINAL AFFAIRS

Yet, from the point of view of Aboriginal administration in the Northern Territory, and indirectly in Australia as a whole, there were potential advantages in the association: during the period of Papuan administration by Sir William MacGregor some of the more advanced principles of British colonial government had been introduced, inherent in which was the view that the native inhabitant was a potential citizen with rights to be protected until he was in a position to assert them for himself. This was the antithesis of the kind of administration which assumed the disappearance of the native race in some kind of final solution of the problems it now presented to conscience and government. This clash was from 1907 well illustrated by differences between Atlee Hunt and J.H.P. Murray, the Australian Lieutenant Governor of Papua. Murray's academic and professional interests linked him with the intellectual life of Australia: his work must have been a factor stimulating a new interest in 'native administration'. The motive of protests up till that time appears to have been humanitarian: the fruit of liberal, Christian, and humane opinion rather than of informed knowledge of just what had been destroyed. Not until the early 1930s, with A.P. Elkin's analysis of his field experiences, were the anthropologists to make clear the scope of destruction: that it had involved far more than wholesale loss of life, in the obliteration of a unique culture.

224 THE DESTRUCTION OF ABORIGINAL SOCIETY

Officials like Meston and Roth, the first Protectors for Queensland, had been in the forefront, with church leaders and others, round the turn of the century. Meston was largely the architect of the Queensland protective measures, while the Roth report was a turning-point in Western Australia. It received publicity in the capital city press of other States. Biskup shows how, after the report and the 1905 Act, politicians in Western Australia began to claim in their policy speeches that progress had been made in improving the circumstances of 'natives'.[1] In 1906 seventy Perth citizens signed a petition to parliament, urging action against the few pastoralists who were bringing discredit on the citizens of the State.[2] In 1907 the Secretary of State for Colonies wrote to the Governor of Western Australia about the effects of the new legislation, especially on the treatment of cattle killers.

In the later part of the nineteenth century the process of cultural exploration had been well established. Fison and Howitt, Baldwin Spencer and Gillen had commenced the careful description of Aboriginal society, providing material for speculation by scholars overseas. In 1911, when the Commonwealth took over control of the Northern Territory, Spencer in Melbourne and Herbert Basedow in Adelaide seem to have been consulted by Atlee Hunt. Basedow was appointed Chief Protector for the Territory in 1911, and Spencer as Special Commissioner for one year. One reason for medical interest in the problem may have been that public health is one and indivisible, but there were wider scientific issues also: for instance, from 1893 the Department of Anatomy, University of Sydney, had begun at least sporadic research into what was to become the science of physical anthropology.

There seems no need here to trace the development of anthropological studies in Australia. But 1911 may be regarded in another way as something of a turning-point in the story, with the conjunction of humanitarian and scientific opinion. In that year, coinciding with the Commonwealth assumption of authority in the Territory, there was a conference in Melbourne of members of the Australian and New Zealand Association for the Advancement of Science, members of the Linnean Society, and politicians and church leaders. The conference recommended that the Commonwealth establish new reserves and a special department to deal with native affairs.[3] It would be interesting to know whether Murray had been consulted. The view seems to have been

[1] Biskup, Native Administration and Welfare in Western Australia 1897-1954, pp. 153 et seq.
[2] Ibid., p. 154.
[3] Melbourne Argus, 25 January 1911, p. 210.

COMMONWEALTH AND ABORIGINAL ADMINISTRATION 225

that the Commonwealth should take over Aboriginal affairs from the States.

The idea that a non-literate culture could have values which charmed and held those socialised within its framework, in spite of what seemed the obvious advantages of comfort and Christianity, took a long time to develop. But as the pioneer observers in Australia began to publish their findings, there developed some realisation of this unique view of the world, of the complexity of the social organisation, and the more recognisable perfection of artefacts and adaptive skills. Yet the obvious failure of the Aboriginal faced with Western man had so bolstered the religious and cultural prejudices, even among the scholars, that the early students of Aboriginal life accepted as an axiom that they were dealing with people of limited intellectual capacity. The social scientist has arrived the hard way at the conclusion that there are no measurable differences of intellect or capacity between the races of man. He began from the assumption that differences in capacity exist, seeing the obvious results of these in the lower achievements in European society of 'coloured' races and has explained differences in status as due to differences in intelligence. The honest attempt to measure and understand the differences has always raised doubts as to their existence; and then the evidence has consistently failed to support the initial assumptions.

But in the meantime a whole corpus of racist theory had been established in the folk lore, supported by the emotional reactions of the whites against an obvious out-group. Stanner has commented on the way in which contempt for Aboriginal inferiority in cultural achievement made it possible for early students to describe their rituals without taking the further step which would have discovered the depth of meaning expressed. The missionaries could well be blinded by their own preconceptions of what was essential to constitute a religion. Moreover, rituals which expressed human relationships, for instance through sexual intercourse, types of mutilation, and other means, repelled Christians who lacked understanding of both the symbolism and the social bonds thus cemented and renewed.

Scholars, writes Stanner, were

unable to see, let alone credit, the facts that have convinced modern anthropologists that the Aborigines are a deeply religious people. That blindness ... profoundly affected European conduct toward the Aborigines. It reinforced two opposed views—that they were a survival into modern times of a protoid form of humanity incapable of civilization, and that they were decadents from a once-higher life and culture. It fed the psychological disposition to hate and despise those whom the powerful have injured ... It allowed European moral standards to atrophy by tacitly exempting from canons of right, law, and justice acts of dispossession, neglect, and violence at

226 THE DESTRUCTION OF ABORIGINAL SOCIETY

Aboriginal expense. It was instrumental in defeating plans for their welfare because every postulate and procedure of action collided with what Emile Durkheim was to call 'the profoundly religious character' of their culture.

Blindness, he writes, was 'organic with the European mind of the day. Religion without God? Without creed or church or priests? Without concern for sin or sexual morals? Without any material show?' He quotes Baldwin Spencer as saying, in 1902, two years before the fruits of his work with Gillen were published, that 'the Central Australian natives have nothing whatever in the way of a simple, pure religion'.[4]

In 1911 Radcliffe-Brown was studying social organisation of the Aboriginal tribes in the Gascoyne, Murchison, and De Grey regions. When, after a recommendation by the Second Pan-Pacific Science Congress of 1923, and a decision by the Commonwealth to support it, Sydney University established a chair in anthropology, he became the first professor.[5]

By this time anthropological studies of the Aboriginal were already well established as of basic importance for the understanding of culture generally. A young Australian clergyman of the Church of England, A.P. Elkin, back from London with specialist anthropological training, did more perhaps than any other to reveal to other Australians the rigid morality and complex social obligations of Aboriginal life. He carried out his first field work in the Kimberleys in 1927 and 1928, some of it in the Forrest River area just after the massacre already referred to, and further field studies in the northern areas of South Australia in 1930, and in 1933 he became Professor of Anthropology at Sydney University. From the beginning of the 1930s he was committed to agitation: he himself says that at first he had not fully realised the implication of his field observations. Perhaps it was in the polemics of Aboriginal affairs that he worked these out and revealed for himself and others the whole complexity of organisation, the richness of the system of belief, and hence the full enormity of the destruction which had been repeated in each area.[6] He remained the scientist in what he wrote, in spite of his activity as a publicist.

Although this more informed intellectual appreciation came mainly in the 1930s, it was developing in 1911. Such appreciation was bound to

[4] Religion, Totemism and Symbolism', in Ronald M. and Catherine H. Berndt (eds.), *Aboriginal Man in Australia*, pp. 208-9, 218.
[5] For details of this see Ronald M. and Catherine H. Berndt 'A.P. Elkin—the Man and the Anthropologist', in *Aboriginal Man in Australia*, pp. 7-14.
[6] 'Australian Aboriginal and White Relations: A personal record', *Royal Australian Historical Society. Journal and Proceedings*, vol. 48, 1963, pp. 208-30.

COMMONWEALTH AND ABORIGINAL ADMINISTRATION 227

increase pressure on administrators and politicians to examine the question of Aboriginal legal status. There is always a lag in such processes; legal status has become a political issue only in the last decade. Just what the lag may be is well illustrated by comparing anthropological writing of the 1930s with the kind of assumption made at the first conference of Commonwealth and States on these matters in 1937.

PROBLEMS OF JUSTICE, LAW, AND ABORIGINAL CUSTOM

By 1911 every State but Tasmania had adopted special Aboriginal legislation, with the emphasis on protection and restriction. Tasmania made no special laws for the tiny minority of part-Aboriginal descent who lived mainly in the Furneaux Group. The Victorian government, which seems to have been bound to some extent by commitments acknowledged in the Protectorate, had established a Central Board to promote Aboriginal welfare as early as 1860; a further Act, in 1869, transformed this to the Board for the Protection of Aborigines. New South Wales had appointed a Protector in 1881, and a Board for the Protection of the Aborigines in 1883. But its first general Aboriginal legislation was the Aborigines Protection Act of 1909.[7] This legislation, along with that of Queensland, Western Australia, South Australia, and the Northern Territory, formally limited the rights of the subject. The process had been a long and piecemeal derogation of status in each colony: its results were reflected in the special clauses of the Commonwealth Constitution.

This detailed legislation expressed the determination to save from abuse people who, as experience was showing, could not protect themselves. The Aboriginal had proved himself a failure in society, and could now be removed from it. But in States which still had frontier problems and large 'full-blood' populations, those who were useful in European employment were not to be removed to reserves. This was provided for in the 1897 Queensland Act, and the provision was subsequently written into those of Western and South Australia and the Territory. The situation in Victoria and New South Wales had long been different. There, tribal life had almost disappeared. The main concern was with the Dark People of part-Aboriginal descent which placed them within the extended categories of the Aboriginal legislation.

At the other end of the scale were Aborigines still only occasionally in contact. These, by 1911, lived mainly in Arnhem Land and in the area

[7] Act No. 25, 1909: An Act to provide for the protection and care of Aborigines, etc.

of Central Australia west of Alice Springs and north of the 29th parallel. About the same time as the Commonwealth was preparing to move into the Northern Territory, humanitarian and learned opinion was developing in favour of saving such people indefinitely from catastrophe by sealing them off, as it were, in inviolable reserves. This idea was by no means new. Missions which had gone out into areas ahead of settlement had had the idea of protecting people in their own environment, without clearly realising what profound change their own activities could bring. But it was not until June 1919 that a deputation to the South Australian Minister for Lands asked that an area of 40,000 square miles in the north-west of the State adjoining the Western Australian border be set aside for this purpose. The Minister stated that joint action with the Western Australian government would be necessary, otherwise disease, the greatest killer, would come into the proposed area across the border: he expressed the opinion that some 70,000 square miles should be reserved by joint action of the three governments concerned (for this foreshadowing of the Great Central Reserve included also a substantial part of the Northern Territory), and he hoped that the Commonwealth government would act on his submission.[8]

These goals were limited and pessimistic. Vague hopes for a new kind of Aboriginal administration in the Territory came to little. The basic frontier issues were brought no nearer to any legal-administrative solution which could appear just to well-meaning white Australians. The problems of administering justice remained as baffling as ever: Western legal systems do not lend themselves to adjustment to traditional systems of settling disputes in 'folk' societies, partly because the objectives of the respective efforts differ. The Westerner is concerned with abstract principle and justice. The member of the small pre-literate group is involved rather in processes which discharge tensions and restore harmony. In Aboriginal society this discharge of tensions was often through ritualised violence, involving ceremonial or actual killing which was deemed to restore the balance of obligations and duties. Settlers and other intruders, wherever they incurred obligations or broke rules of conduct, were inevitably caught in this web of reciprocal violence.

Thus justice was one of the most perplexing matters involved in colonial administration and in that of non-literate minorities. In Papua, and later in Mandated Territory, the problem was approached by recognising 'native custom' in 'native regulations'. This involved a separate 'native' status within the statutory law, and of course such

[8] Reported in the *Argus* (Melbourne), 11 June 1919.

COMMONWEALTH AND ABORIGINAL ADMINISTRATION 229

protective law and separate status, once the 'native' acquired sophistication and to the extent that it was used to protect European privilege, was to appear increasingly discriminatory. Once the indigenous means of settling disputes had broken down or had been forbidden as 'repugnant to humanity', field officers had to spend a great deal of time in adjudication. In practice they often operated outside the law, but frequently with the advice of indigenous elders.

The lack of any such service tradition, while the autonomy of the Aboriginal group was rapidly being destroyed, was another factor for chaos in Aboriginal society. The Aboriginal who attempted to restore harmony by the only means he knew could become a criminal in British law. Yet the destruction of Aboriginal authority left from his point of view only British power: and this imposed power operated under British law. Thus, for the Aboriginal, it was British law or no law at all. Very serious breaches of his moral code, and of the rights and obligations it supported, might not be breaches of the British law. The resultant denial of acceptable settlements has been a basic cause of social disintegration. It helps to explain the high rate of homicide within Aboriginal society at the time of disintegration, which the officers of the Port Phillip Protectorate had noted long before. The breaking down of social controls could perhaps have been arrested, had enough autonomy remained for those groups which still followed the precepts of Aboriginal custom to adjust their mutual obligations by a continuity of decisions arrived at in their own way. A basic problem, in 1911 as today, has been the assumption of an absence of 'law', a legal vacuum, as it were, in Aboriginal society. This was one reason why there were no 'native regulations' in Australia.

Social change is not regulated by 'native regulations', which are rather a concession to the colonists' desire for a show of order. Whether Aboriginal regulations might have improved matters in 1911 is hardly capable of decision now. Aboriginal groups lacked both the power and a recognised means to assert the legitimacy, for them, of their own traditions.

Such possibilities were implicit when the United States government made a treaty with a tribe which left it with some assets; and also where a colonial government failed to interfere deeply into the social life of a village. In either case, even if in a very restricted way, the tribe or village survived as such because it was still possible to maintain a coherent inner life of its own and assert the legitimacy of tradition. Whether or not the law, by 'native regulations', conceded the right to decide within certain limits what was right or wrong and what sanctions should be used, the

230 THE DESTRUCTION OF ABORIGINAL SOCIETY

village and the tribe often did so. The government often ignored actions of questionable legality because if it prevented unofficial 'native courts' from restoring harmony and settling disputes, a whole mass of unwanted litigation was likely to flood the courts. To satisfy the purists, such settlements could be regarded as applying to civil matters 'settled out of court'.

There must have been hundreds of individual cases, in the Northern Territory alone, where the British law has been applied because an Aboriginal action came to the courts as a case of violence between individuals, the court having no power, precedent, nor perhaps understanding to take other matters into account.

Let us look briefly at the case of Guragi of the Nungubuya in Arnhem Land, reported in the southern press in December 1966. The court knew that as a tribal elder it was his function and duty to discharge tensions by spearing a younger offender; the offender did not resist, but stood and awaited the ceremonial spearing in the leg. Confusion (i.e. confusion in a situation unresolved by statute) which has continued for nearly two centuries is clear in the reported remarks of the judge that 'this man had an obligation to take some action as a leading member of the tribe, but at the same time I think he knew he should not have done what he did'.[9] Perhaps because of His Honour's opinion about what Guragi knew he 'ought to have done', he was sent to prison for three months.

NORTHERN TERRITORY LEGISLATION, 1911-1953

The Northern Territory Aboriginals Act of 1910, passed by the South Australian parliament in preparation for the Commonwealth administration, shows the strong influence of the Queensland and Western Australian models. The emphasis is on rigid protection, with control of individuals defined in racial categories and legislated for as passive recipients of special treatment, much in the manner of prospective inmates of institutions—minors, mentally ill persons, the sick, or the aged. Nothing could be further removed from concern with autonomy and the opportunity for groups to live in their own way, in time to acquire power to protect their interests.

Such legislation for a long time embalmed official assumptions about Aborigines. When an area of human relations is so defined as to provide conservative public service authority with definitions and directives, administrative habit tends to confirm basic assumptions, and departure

[9] *S.M.H.*, 1 December 1966.

COMMONWEALTH AND ABORIGINAL ADMINISTRATION

from the principles established involves something of a revolution. The officials who carry out duties so laid down cannot fairly be blamed for retention of administrative relationships which have become obstacles to achieving new objectives. The danger is that new objectives tend to be sought by the old means: that people are kept in institutions while being made 'ready' for assimilation into the community. So the concept of 'readiness' is used to explain the contrast of means with ends.

In the Act, the definition of 'Aboriginal' (section 3) included 'half-castes' with Aboriginal spouses or habitual associates and those under sixteen years. 'Half-caste' meant anyone with an Aboriginal parent or grandparent. In addition there was a special category of 'half-caste' including any offspring of an Aboriginal mother and non-Aboriginal father; this would include a person whose mother had an Aboriginal grandparent. The Chief Protector, represented by a protector in each Protector's District, was to be the legal guardian of 'every Aboriginal and half-caste child, notwithstanding that any such child has a parent or other relative living, until such child attains the age of eighteen years'—a provision based on South Australian legislation of 1844. The implications of this were quite definite, and in due course it became usual for a protector to remove the children with light skins from their mothers.

The Act established an Aboriginals Department under the Chief Protector. Provision was made for the declaration of reserves, for superintendents to be appointed to reserves, for leases of Crown lands to missions, for removal to and retention within a reserve of any 'Aboriginal or half-caste', except that employed persons and females married to non-Aborigines could not be so dealt with. Only Aborigines and authorised persons could enter reserves. A protector could order Aborigines to remove their camps from any township (or public house). Any police officer could expel an individual Aboriginal for loitering; and any township could be declared a 'prohibited area', as in Western Australia, for unemployed Aborigines. The Chief Protector had control of their property and estates.

Marriage between an Aboriginal and a non-Aboriginal was subject to Ministerial authority (section 22). Similar control was established in the Queensland and Western Australian legislation by this time, indicating the view that a population of mixed origin was a 'problem' which should be avoided. Hardly anything could better illustrate ponderous official paternalism than the Protector having to explain to the Minister responsible in the Commonwealth Government why he had used the delegated authority to permit such a marriage. As he did not have to report a case where he refused consent, he would be likely to refuse.

The effort to keep Australia legally white merely meant that Northern Territory 'comboism' might be more legal under this Act than a union blessed by the church in ignorance. But it was an offence to be found without permission within five chains of a 'camp' where there were 'Aboriginals or female half-castes' (section 42). A further deterrent to increasing the part-Aboriginal population was the provision that a Protector could take to court the 'alleged father' to show reason why he should not contribute to the upkeep of a half-caste child in an institution. If the child remained with the mother, there was no claim on the father, and this may have been another reason for the later common practice of taking light-skinned children from mothers—a practice which in various ways and for various reasons has marked race relations in Australia from early times. The practice has at times gone further than this, as when missions have taken all the children at school age from the parents in the attempt to split the generations, offset the effects of socialisation in the Aboriginal culture, and build a godly Christian society. 'Forget the older people, and concentrate on the children' is still a common folk remedy for assumed social ills.

The permit system of controlling employment, already established in Queensland and Western Australia, was established in this Act for the Territory. The licence to employ could be granted by the Protector of the district in which the employer lived, with the proviso that no Asian could be granted a licence. The licence could be cancelled by the Chief Protector. As elsewhere in the frontier regions, such a general provision, without the individual contract and regular labour inspection, could have little effect on conditions. There was no provision that wages must be paid, though the Chief Protector might have some show of control of the conditions through the annual return of employees and wages paid. As in Queensland after 1901, a protector could direct that the wage or portion of it be paid into a trust account, through him or a police officer. Regulation of employment aboard ship was on the Western Australian model. A protector had access to employees and premises. The section on control of firearms in Aboriginal possession was taken from the Western Australian Act of 1905.

The duties of the new Department were both charitable and protective. It was to 'exercise a general supervision and care' over *all* matters affecting Aboriginal welfare, so that it could theoretically have insisted on basic standards in employment, supported by the sanction of the licence. But

COMMONWEALTH AND ABORIGINAL ADMINISTRATION 233

the difficulties in practice and the political influence of the settler meant that effective control of employment conditions on pastoral properties was not even established or enforced even under the Welfare legislation in the decade after 1953. Other duties were to manage reserves, to control, maintain, and educate children 'where possible', to provide care for the aged and infirm, including medical care as far as practicable, and to give relief or assistance to others, including the inevitable blankets which formed the one tangible compensation for the dispossessed Aboriginal in every colony from the days of first contact when the blanket was a diplomatic gift.[10] There were the usual penalties for the sale or exchange of blankets, which along with the bedding or clothing issues remained 'the property of His Majesty'.[11]

Commonwealth Regulations under this Act were gazetted in September 1911.[12] They suggest the practical difficulties. An application for a licence to employ should go forward with a reference from a government officer or Justice of the Peace: but the Chief Protector, where no officer or justice was available, had to make his own assessment from a distance. He had power to refuse a licence where either wages or conditions were not satisfactory. One regulation must have alarmed the pastoralists who heard of it—that all wages must be paid in money, that the Chief Protector could demand that such wages be paid to him or his representative, and that no deduction for items issued could be made without his consent. But there was no provision for a specific minimum wage or other means of fixing it; all that the Protector could do was to fix it in each particular case of an applicant for a licence. This meant that some paid cash wages while others did not. In the event cash wages began to be paid where the work force had been depleted—for economic reasons rather than because of policy decisions.

A minimum wage for all Aborigines was introduced first in Queensland in 1919. The effect there was to freeze their employment conditions at the level of frontier standards, so that economically those in New South Wales and Victoria who might not be paid, but legally could claim, wages common in the industry, were better off, with more chance of economic integration. But the Northern Territory, in a sense, was all frontier; and pastoral management, notoriously diffident when it came to cash wages, was able to avoid them in some areas for over three decades longer.

The Aboriginals Ordinance 1911 (gazetted in January 1912) incor-

[10] R.H.W. Reece, Diplomacy and Gifts to the Aborigines of New South Wales 1770-1846.
[11] Northern Territories Aboriginals Act, 1910, section 34.
[12] Commonwealth Gazette, 16 September 1911.

234 THE DESTRUCTION OF ABORIGINAL SOCIETY

porated the South Australian Act of 1910. It also gave power to the Chief Protector to take any Aboriginal or half-caste into custody. He could delegate this power to police officers, i.e. the police, in the main, would be his agents. The implications of this legal power were profound, however necessary it might have been for protection. The power of the Chief Protector to cancel licences to employ at any time was included in the Ordinance, and the grounds for doing so were extended. The power under the Act for the Governor to declare towns and other places prohibited areas for Aborigines was vested in the Administrator: *any* place could be so declared, and grounds for action were established against whites who took Aborigines into such areas. The Regulations of 1911 were repeated in the Schedule of the Ordinance.

Had this legislation been applied extensively, the government would at least have been in some control of what was happening. But the early flurry of Commonwealth activity had little result. In April 1911 Basedow began a survey of the situation in the 'north end' of the Territory, with Baldwin Spencer as Special Commissioner. There was a staff of three Inspectors of Aboriginals and two medical inspectors. But Basedow resigned after six weeks or so, after a clash with the Administrator. Spencer held the position for a year, in conjunction with that of Special Commissioner; but his recommendations for managed reserves appear to have been rejected as too costly, as they 'would involve an annual expenditure for each reserve of about £2,000'.[13] By 1916, only one of the original Inspectors of Aboriginals remained. But two years earlier, even the full-time appointment of Chief Protector had been abolished, with the Government Secretary taking over the management of the Aboriginal Department. Part of the trouble had been due to disagreements between the anthropologists and the administrators.

The location in Darwin of an Administrator with responsibility for Aboriginal affairs might have seemed to promise something like colonial standards of native administration, but the powers of Administrators, both in the Territory and New Guinea, have always been limited, in a fashion perhaps inevitable in a federation. Some Commonwealth departments have always operated directly in the Territory, outside the control of the Administration. The local Administration has been under direct financial and policy control, in a way which would have been impossible in the earlier period of colonial expansion. The Administrator has not been the initiator of new policies; he has had a

[13] *C.P.P.* 1914, vol. II, no. 30, p. 675—Northern Territory. Outlines of a Policy—by the Honourable P.M. Glynn, Minister for External Affairs.

COMMONWEALTH AND ABORIGINAL ADMINISTRATION 235

most awkward role, as both ceremonial figure and the spokesman for the government.

Gilruth, the first Administrator, was actually expelled from Darwin by people who seem to have resented the Commonwealth authority which replaced the South Australian. One reason, no doubt, was the lack of representative institutions, which provide for catharsis. All legislation at this time was by the Governor-General in Council—in effect, by the Department responsible when the Minister did not care or lacked knowledge, or by the Minister when he was interested. With or without the support of the Administrator, the Chief Protector was in an impossible situation if he tried to implement the protective clauses of the legislation. He had no means of supervising Aboriginal welfare over vast distances, which made regular communication between the Administration and the pastoral stations almost impossible, and quite so during the 'wet' in the northern area. The isolated frontier attracted lawless whites from the south. Government deferred to pastoral interests. Police and other officials shared the pastoral and mining communities' prejudices.

But the concentration on western economics and the assumption that Aborigines presented only the temporary problem of a race doomed to disappear meant that this legislation became a form of words to placate the outsider and the critic of government. The concern of many public servants was to keep out of trouble; and one sure way into trouble would have been a serious attempt to regulate the conditions of labour. The duties of Protector were additional, part-time ones, for officials conveniently situated, generally police, secondary to duties of serving the settler community.

The trend went further than in Queensland and Western Australia, with the abolition of the separate office of Chief Protector in 1914. Before this, there had also been two protectors at what seemed important points to control race relations. Their duties were transferred to the managers of government farms at Oenpelli, Batchelor, and the Daly River. They distributed rations to the needy who happened to be there, and saw that employers of Aboriginal labour were licensed. Police officers discharged this function.

Whatever hopes seemed possible in 1911 were forgotten during the 1914–18 war. But, for other reasons, changes in the legislation which followed had little to do with the facts of race relations, beyond being a response to the more obvious signs of Aboriginal social disintegration. Thus a comprehensive Ordinance of the Northern Territory (No. 9 of 1918), which replaced all previous legislation, and which formed the basis for subsequent legislation until the Welfare Ordinance of 1953, extended the category of those to be protected: the definition of 'Aboriginal' now included all female half-castes, unless legally married to persons of 'substantial' European descent, and all half-caste males under eighteen years (previously sixteen).

If the Aborigines were to die out, what was to happen to the half-castes? As far as possible the policy was to prevent them being conceived; and to give to those who were special tuition as children, in institutions, since their white blood offered hope that they would make useful citizens. The Commonwealth had established institutions for this purpose in Alice Springs and Darwin; they probably served to remove embarrassing evidence of infidelity from some of the pastoral stations.

The 1918 Ordinance provided for an arrangement with the missions like that in Queensland. Any mission station (or other private institution) could be declared an Aboriginal institution for the care of Aboriginal and half-caste children. Where a child was committed for care and education, he was under the control of the superintendent. Half-caste children seem to have been the major concern, and caring for them became one of the main activities of missions, though the government subsidy remained very small. What one missionary termed the 'production of half-castes' had been ostensibly regulated by the control of marriage and by the law which made it an offence to approach an Aboriginal camp. But the first had probably prevented permanent unions from leading to marriage; the second, in that environment, must have been regarded as something of a joke. It now became an offence to 'habitually consort', keep an Aboriginal or half-caste mistress, or 'unlawfully' have carnal knowledge of an Aboriginal or half-caste woman (which was probably nothing more than a way of lessening the penalty for rape by providing an alternative charge). The penalty was £100 or three months gaol, and loss of the licence to employ in the case of an employer; and the onus of proof was on the defendant. The cause of the stringency (by frontier standards) seems to have been the growing half-caste problem. But such a law could not be enforced; in so far as it could, it would have emphasised the casual relationship and penalised the more or less permanent union. The incidental effect on the status in law of the Aboriginal woman was to lower it further, by purporting to control her intimate life.

In the earlier legislation there were careful limitations on the Aborigines' use or possession of firearms; these were repeated, but relaxed in one interesting way. An employer could issue a firearm to his Aboriginal employee for 'protection', but it had to be surrendered whenever the

COMMONWEALTH AND ABORIGINAL ADMINISTRATION 237

holder was within two miles of a township. What protection might mean out in the bush there could be no way of knowing very well, but mayhem was to be kept out of the centres of white settlement.

An important change was in the separation of town from country districts. One effect was to clear the way for regulating employment, in the town, of Aborigines from the town fringe, without disturbing the all-important pastoral stations. Employment of town Aborigines by persons living in towns—but not on stations—had to be under agreement. This meant that a protector could fix a wage and have a form of contract which identified the employee precisely enough to enforce his rights. In these circumstances the full-time protectors had insisted on cash wages in the first couple of years of Commonwealth administration; but these pressures had lapsed. The greater need, of course, was out on the stations, where an agreement system would have been resisted. It would also have been difficult to enforce use of agreements and payment of wages where the employer was wont to maintain a camp to draw labour from it.

This is interesting evidence of growing town problems. At the same time there was need of the Aboriginal in town for domestic and manual work. He could be employed in a hotel, but only those employed could be in the vicinity of one. Specific penalties for supplying alcohol or opium were included. Aboriginal camping grounds could be declared in a town district, since the 'unit of labour' had to live somewhere adjacent to his place of employment. But the old penalties on white men who approached within five chains remained. The presence of the Aboriginal in town was to be as far as possible in his role as a unit of labour.

Legal powers of protectors and police were defined. For breaches of this Ordinance they could arrest without warrant—an indication, perhaps, that there was little expectation of other arrests than those of Aborigines. But Aborigines could plead guilty only with the consent of a protector, and provision was made for appeal to the local court, and for that court to state special cases for the Supreme Court. Here was a definite channel through which some of the perplexities arising from the conflict of law with custom could have been considered and referred to the legislative process. But it is clear that Commonwealth administrative control had been mainly limited to the vicinity of the townships, to the special treatment of part-Aboriginal children, and mainly in the 'north end' of the Territory. Out from the townships application of the law could have helped protect both those who worked for drovers and who might be left far from their country without resources and those employed on ships and similarly treated. There was provision for recognisances, but the fact that Dr C.E. Cook, when he became Chief Protector a decade later, had such trouble in trying to safeguard Aboriginal drovers, teamsters' assistants, and those working for prospectors and other itinerants suggests that not much was achieved.

Government of this vast area was so difficult that from 1926 to 1931 there were two Territories, North Australia and Central Australia, involving separate but parallel legislation in Aboriginal affairs.[14] This was not of great consequence, except that it indicates a tendency to extend the scope of legislative control and protection where a situation was out of effective administrative control. For instance, from 1924 a half-caste retained Aboriginal status until he was twenty-one. From 1927 he retained Aboriginal status if, in the opinion of the Chief Protector, he was incapable of managing his own affairs.[15]

At the time of the Commonwealth takeover, Asians were excluded from those to whom employers' licences might be issued. This might have been racist prejudice or an attempt to limit the use of opium and opium dross as a means of payment, but the exclusion had not been repeated in the 1918 Ordinance, though of course the Chief Protector could exclude any person. In the Aboriginals Ordinance of 1928 it was provided that no person of Asiatic or Negro race could be licensed to employ Aboriginal women and that only the Chief Protector could issue a licence to employ Aboriginal men. The trend of this legislation was to increase legal control of part-Aborigines, and one reason for it was to decrease the likelihood of other than 'European' half-castes being born. By this time the transition from the philosophy of a Gipps or a Grey, with their worry about human equality before the law, to a situation where those in control thought mainly in categories of racial origin, had been long since completed.

The habit of legislation for rigid restriction had by this time become so deeply ingrained that much later, when the aim was more generally optimistic, it was pursued by the same legislative means. The old assumptions as to the relations between government and Aboriginal society remained implicit in the Welfare Ordinance and the Wards' Employment Ordinance of 1953. The intentions of these later ordinances, hailed at the time as beginning a new era (as was the beginning of Commonwealth administration in 1910) were certainly different. The legal draftsmen, with linguistic avoidance of racially defined categories, replaced the term

[14] Northern Australia Act, 1926 and Northern Territory (Administration) Act, 1931.
[15] Northern Territory Aboriginals Ordinance (No. 2) 1924; and Aboriginals Ordinance 1927, Territory of North Australia and Territory of Central Australia.

COMMONWEALTH AND ABORIGINAL ADMINISTRATION 239

'Aboriginal' with the new term of 'ward'. But wards were restricted as Aborigines had been. They had to be *managed*. Institutions and special legislation were implied in the term and provided for in the ordinances and, in due course, regulations. There were laws for the management of institutions, providing for special conditions of employment outside them and including special wages. The Director of Welfare in 1953 was given basically the same kinds of power as the Chief Protector of Aborigines had wielded since 1910. The power was now more detailed and explicit, and the administrative and financial means much more adequate for their effective exercise than they had ever been.

The Director became the guardian of all wards. He controlled their movements, where they might live, and their property. He retained the power to segregate them on reserves, which might only be entered with government authority. He could prevent wards living together and refuse consent to a marriage involving a ward.[16] In fact, substantially what had been considered necessary for 'protection' in 1910 and in ordinances from 1918 onwards was considered to be necessary for 'assimilation' in 1953 and for a decade afterwards. The old means were to be used to attain new ends, through the addition of more services and by intensive education and training. No provision was made in the later legislation for areas of Aboriginal decision, for autonomy adequate for the development of effective leadership, for Aborigines to adapt to new circumstances. By basically the same methods as before, they were to be processed individually for assimilation, which indicates humane intention, but little attention to the background and social context.

It is always difficult to change old habits and methods of administration which express class and caste relationships and status. The four decades of Commonwealth control had by 1953 seen the transition from rationing points to settlements on reserves, and to institutions which had their own authoritarian logic. The settlers' and the officials' attitudes had been confirmed in the old patterns, and by now a difficult barrier to change was the settled and institutionalised Aboriginal group, with the special resistances and suspicions which such a situation produces in the inmates. Moreover, protection had involved isolation, which also conformed with white settler prejudice. Some institutions were on land without known economic potential. Means determine ends, and as the wards' legislation brought greater effort, higher expenditure on bigger and better institutions (including the Christian missions), and more effective controls, the result was the large pauper community of the Northern Territory

[16] See Northern Territory Welfare Ordinance 1953–1960.

settlement. Yet the whole purpose of this later effort was to get to grips with a situation where Aborigines were already largely institutionalised; and the objective was to train and educate the inmates for a full role in the general community. That this effort has met with so little success must raise serious doubts about the means used. At the same time, one has to concede the great difficulty, politically and administratively, of making a complete break with the past, especially as large detribalised communities were already in existence.

If the intentions have been better than the methods, it must also be remembered that it is very difficult to innovate and get funds from Treasury; and comparatively easy to waste funds year after year in accordance with a precedent, which in this case went back to the first period of colonisation. The social and political models of institutions under authoritarian control had long been a guarantee that the money provided would be 'properly' spent. One may guess how difficult it might have been to get funds, for instance, for Aborigines to manage. So the same kinds of institutions confirmed daily the prejudices which officials shared with other whites: training of staff for democratic methods of working had to be irrelevant to the situation on a settlement. Moreover, new aims for a public service department have to be pursued with staff already on strength. The location and nature of staff housing in relation to Aboriginal housing on any settlement makes the point. So, for the attainment of assimilation, the old means remained and formed barriers to change in a complicated situation of which they had long been part.

The Welfare legislation was an attempt to use the old methods intensively to produce the changes desired: intensive efforts were in fact made. In the event, the legislation was repealed. In 1966, the Queensland government also began a new effort, with new legislation, to hasten 'assimilation'; and the means were also the old and tried ones. Here too, one suspects, they appeal because they are old and tried, not because they have produced encouraging results. Eventually the Queensland government will probably fall in with the current trend and repeal all special restrictive legislation and control.

The fallacy is in the assumption that social change can be controlled within an authoritarian institution, so as to produce the democratic citizen of western society. It was one thing to collect all the Aborigines in need of protection and help and to segregate them. This was at least logical in the circumstances; and it can be argued that otherwise the destruction of individual lives must have been greater. The current

COMMONWEALTH AND ABORIGINAL ADMINISTRATION 241

rapid increase of populations on these settlements indicates what regular feeding, with some basic hygiene measures and medical attention, can achieve. But institutions set up their own resistances among the inmates, presenting the current problems of how to develop Aboriginal leadership, with what a political scientist might call 'legitimacy', for Aboriginal organisations, which might work out, with technical assistance, agreed solutions for their own problems. A technical assistance operation of a very special kind seems to be called for in the case of every settlement and mission in 'colonial Australia'; but this implies assistance to people with some institutional autonomy, so that they may be advised and helped rather than directed. The way for this may have been cleared in the Northern Territory by the repeal of the Welfare Ordinance.

Perhaps one of the most significant advances lies in what was left out of the Welfare legislation: it excluded from institutionalisation or control those of Aboriginal descent entitled to vote. The effect of this was to exclude from wardship part-Aborigines not defined as Aboriginal in the Aboriginals Ordinance 1918-1953.

Under this Ordinance a part-Aboriginal was not under control unless he 'lived after the manner of' an Aboriginal, or was already under control as a minor under twenty-one years, or had been specially declared to be Aboriginal. Presumably the repeal of this Aboriginals Ordinance would have prevented any further declaration of a part-Aboriginal as an Aboriginal. Under the Welfare Ordinance, status of wardship depended on one's name being entered in the Register of Wards, with the effect that not only the part-Aborigines of the Territory but also the few full-bloods whose names were missed were not 'declared'. Perhaps this freeing of the part-Aboriginal people from control will be seen in retrospect as the greatest gain in the 1953 legislation, with the repeal of the Welfare Ordinance, in August 1964,[17] as the second important step towards Aboriginal equality. It meant that Aborigines were no longer wards except for wages in the pastoral industry. But the managed settlements and missions remain, as do enough of the powers of the Director to control entry to the reserves on which they are located and to enable the officials in control to maintain discipline among the Aboriginal inmates.

Northern Territory legislation is of interest in that the Commonwealth was inevitably looked to by informed opinion, if not by State governments, to set the best example to the States, a fact which suggests how far thinking about Aboriginal affairs remained enmeshed in the problems of frontier situations.

[17] By the Northern Territory Social Welfare Ordinance 1964.

242   THE DESTRUCTION OF ABORIGINAL SOCIETY

The Commonwealth also had to bear the main brunt of international pressures. But until World War II these were minimal, stemming mainly from private organisations like the Aborigines Protection Society in Britain. A world-wide colonial system seemed to justify the internal pattern of race relations. The only breach which could admit criticism by international organisations was in the relationship of the Commonwealth to the Permanent Mandates Commission as Administering Authority for the Mandated Territory of New Guinea, from 1921. It might have been expected that, in the national interest, the Commonwealth would take the initiative for a concerted policy; and in fact this had begun with the Commonwealth-States conference of 1937.

SOME NEW LIGHT ON OLD DIFFICULTIES

In the Northern Territory the old frontier situations that were being reproduced continued into quite recent times, when they could be examined somewhat more objectively by scholars and others without local interests and in the light of increased knowledge.

According to J.P.M. Long, although pastoral settlement was quite scattered until the 1930s, most Aborigines had been in touch with the stations by the 1920s. By 1930

the only areas in which there were substantial numbers of Aboriginals with no contact or only limited contact and pursuing a hunting existence were Arnhem Land Reserve, Fitzmaurice River, and the South West Desert. Substantial numbers from these areas had already moved in to Darwin, Alice Springs and other centres, or had filled the vacuum created by depopulation in the pastoral districts.[18]

Thus the populations at the township compounds were not composed solely of those who had nowhere else to go. Contact history was being repeated in the far north in the early twentieth century, and had been in process there for a long time, involving the obliteration, especially by respiratory diseases and introduced epidemics, of the original groups in the areas of white settlement. Such diseases 'flourished in the unsanitary camps of Aboriginals who abandoned a nomadic life'; while venereal disease, which proved probably far more harmful even than the squatters and the police, was limiting the birth rate.[19] In the centre and the desert areas there were severe droughts in the years 1926-33, causing many deaths. 'Actual violence, shootings and poisoning' writes Long, 'has in the Northern Territory probably played a relatively minor role in depopulation.'[20]

[18] Notes on Contact History of Northern Territory Aboriginals.
[19] Ibid.   [20] Ibid.

COMMONWEALTH AND ABORIGINAL ADMINISTRATION 243

Stanner, while working among the people of the Daly River in 1932 as a student of Radcliffe-Brown, saw the constant search for food. He described, long afterwards, the very good sense of the nomad who decided to opt for the chance of regular meals at somewhat less effort.

The life of a hunting and foraging nomad is very hard even in a good environment. Time and again the hunters fail, and the search for vegetable food can be just as patchy. A few such failures in sequence and life in the camps can be very miserable. The small, secondary foodstuffs—the roots, honey, grubs, ants, and the like, of which far too much has been made in the literature—are relished tidbits, but not staples. The aborigines rarely starve but they go short more often than might be supposed when the substantial fauna—kangaroos, wallaby, goannas, birds, fish—are too elusive. The blacks have grasped eagerly at any possibility of a regular and dependable food supply for ... lesser effort ... There is a sound calculus of cost and gain in preferring a belly regularly if only partly filled for an output of work which can be steadily scaled down. Hence the two most common characteristics of aboriginal adaptation to settlement by Europeans: a persistent and positive effort to make themselves dependent, and a squeeze-play to obtain a constant or increasing supply of food for a dwindling physical effort.[21]

He described the white 'battlers' on the peanut farms on the Daly, living on bread, tea, and wallaby stew. Their Aboriginal workers and other dependants received no cash, but poor handouts of clothes and other items. 'Pitiably small as this real income was, it attracted far more natives than could be employed.' Those with skills played one employer against another; while the settler who formed a union with a native woman found that her affines soon appeared, 'and every artifice and pressure was used to make themselves part of the protector's estate'.[22]

One enterprise after another had failed on the Daly before Stanner was there; it was, even in 1932, after repeated failures since 1870, 'a barbarous frontier—more, a rotted frontier, with a smell of old failure, vice, and decadence'. But each attempt had drawn more Aborigines; and after each failure many had set off

to look for the new wealth and excitements—to Pine Creek, Brock's Creek, the Victoria River, even to Darwin itself. In places where no European had ever set foot, or was to do so for many years, a demand had grown up for iron goods, tobacco, tea, sugar, and clothes. There was also a hankering for a sight of such marvels as houses, machines, vehicles, firearms, and bells, one of the most alluring things of all. Unrest and covetousness had drawn in people from tribes on the outer marches ... Whole tribes ... had migrated, and large tracts had thus been emptied decades

[21] 'Durmugan, A Nangiomeri', in Joseph B. Casagrande (ed.), *In the Company of Man*, pp. 69-70.
[22] Ibid., pp. 72-3.

244   THE DESTRUCTION OF ABORIGINAL SOCIETY

before the authorities or settlers were aware of it. Some of the small tribes of the Daly ... had ceased to exist. Those members who had not died from new diseases (such as measles, influenza, tuberculosis, and syphilis), or from bullets, or from debauchery by grog and opium, or in the jealous battles for possession ... had been dispersed by migration or else absorbed into larger tribes ...' The dwindling in total numbers, so far as they were visible on the Daly, had been concealed by the inward drift ... There were then no more tribes to come, except the Murinbata of Port Keats, and all that held them away was the opening of The Sacred Heart Mission ... in 1935. The authorities, in all good faith, could well imagine that the hinterland was still densely populated, for the Daly river seemed to keep on breeding *myalls* continuously.[23]

Note how this statement confirms the analysis of early contact made by Elkin. It also confirmed the good sense of the recommendations by Spencer, at the time when the Commonwealth was establishing a policy and administration, for substantial reserves out from the settled regions, with supervision from a centre on the reserve where Aborigines might make some kind of controlled contact with the industrial and cash economy.

I think no one has set out more sympathetically and convincingly than Stanner the drastic effects upon the Aboriginal culture of this sudden and overwhelming appeal of hope for material advantage, for in these places, farther out than the fringe settlements round Darwin, Brocks Creek, Pine Creek, Barrows Creek and Tennant Creek, the basis for orderly life was being wrecked by the sudden loss of the traditions. His friend Durmugan was typical of Marginal Man, except that, being of outstanding moral quality, he managed to salvage for himself enough of the Law to live out his life, as far as possible, in accordance with meaningful principle. But even he faced the situation where the tribal Law, as it had been reconstructed for him and as it had been deeply rooted in his personality by what he had of true Aboriginal socialisation, constantly went unenforced for the lack of the traditional sanctions; while attempts at enforcement meant a clash with British law.

Stanner poses the problem of justice for such men. What alternative was there but the use of traditional violence or retribution, where the younger 'spivs' and lesser minds, the true marginal men growing up out of their 'country' and without any law at all, recklessly and for their own immediate pleasure brought catastrophe to him and everything for which he had stood all his life? A very gifted police protector might have involved himself in some process of adjudication, at the risk of being accused of aiding and abetting action which was illegal under the British

[23] Ibid., p. 75.

COMMONWEALTH AND ABORIGINAL ADMINISTRATION 245

law. But on the Daly at that time, Stanner suggests, there was no great effort even to enforce the British law.

Part of the catastrophe is that oral tradition is lost with a frightening ease. The process is likely to be expedited by the tradition of the pioneer who goes where he wishes, selects the land he wants, and is supported by an all-powerful government.

14

MISSIONS AND EXTENSIVE RESERVES

Destruction of Aboriginal populations was eventually arrested, partly by the efforts of missions on the large reserves. One example is the Port Keats mission referred to by Stanner. It was not established until 1935, a comparatively late foundation among those missions of the North and Centre which have contributed to physical survival and to maintenance of cultural continuity in the great reserves farther out. (An earlier mission on the Daly had failed.) The reaction of the Aborigines, recorded as seen by the missionaries, was much the same as it had been at Fort Wellington or Lake Macquarie long before, or at the rationing posts established by governments, or round the homesteads of innumerable pastoral properties. They wanted food, especially in times of drought; they wanted neither religious instruction nor work.

At the beginning of the century Hermannsburg was the only mission in the Northern Territory surviving. In 1908, with a small grant from the South Australian government, the Church Missionary Society founded the Roper River mission in Arnhem Land, well before the declaration of the great Arnhem Land Reserve. In 1910, just before the Commonwealth took charge, the Order of the Sacred Heart began its work on Bathurst Island, which became a reserve in 1913. These missions saw their social and educational function as preparing the people, by their efforts in tuition and conversion, to participate in European society. In practice their great material achievement was to present, within the tribal lands, enough of the counter-attractions needed in food supplies, clothes, steel and other industrial goods to keep people there. By so doing they made possible an interim process of adjustment based on Aboriginal

MISSIONS AND EXTENSIVE RESERVES

decisions for Aboriginal purposes. The less effective the missionaries were at this stage in destroying Aboriginal religion and belief the better would seem to have been the prospects of some satisfactory adjustment. The dilemma thus posed for the missionaries, which perhaps the less rigid and more penetrating minds among them came to realise, led a few of them to give less immediate attention to the salvation of souls and more to the problems of social change.

In so far as there was a model for Commonwealth legislation and practice, at least up to 1928 when the Queensland Chief Protector was asked to report on Aboriginal administration in the Territory, it was the Queensland administration. The trend there was towards closer association with the missions in the frontier regions. The Commonwealth introduced similar measures, though on a more niggardly basis, with the legislation of 1918.

The Queensland policy was well founded before the Commonwealth took over the Territory. By 1907 there were eight reserves in the state; of these, six were in the far north and their administration was under mission control. The Presbyterians, already established at Mapoon and Weipa on the Gulf coast of the Cape at the time of Meston's survey, set up another mission at Aurukun, on the Archer, in 1903. Government and missions seem to have had a gentlemen's agreement which enabled the missions to use the substantial reserves also established at this time for pastoral and farming enterprises—which, as the value of some of this land increased with the approach of more settlers, led to the usual tensions between mission and white settler.

In 1904 the Church of England established the Mitchell River mission on the same basis. According to J.W. Bleakley, who became Chief Protector in 1913 and remained in charge of the Department until 1940,

it followed the now recognised rule of segregation from alien influences. Continuity of policy and control, study of native culture and language, development of settled village life, religious and secular education and training in productive industries with the aim of self-dependence.[1]

These missions resembled those of the colonial world in that they conducted economic enterprises for profit to help meet the expenses incurred. From the time of the first missions in Australia, government had contributed to mission costs, even if only by making land available. But the Queensland government was paying small subsidies for education. After the establishment of the Mitchell River mission, the reserves on the western shore of the Cape were so extended as to form one great reserve,

[1] *The Aborigines of Australia*, p. 116.

extending thirty miles inland from the Mitchell to the Batavia. The missions were there in permissive occupancy; no Aboriginal tenure right was legally established. It was, like all other reserves in Australia, created by declaring Crown lands within its limits to be reserve lands for use by the department responsible for administration of the Aboriginal legislation.

The help given to missions by Queensland offered hope of similar help from the Commonwealth and thus led to new interest in mission possibilities in the Northern Territory after 1911. But Spencer had wanted government, not mission bodies, in control of the reserves he recommended, and the policy statement of Glynn, the Minister in 1914, included no promise of a situation like that in Queensland. Under the Queensland legislation of 1897 and subsequent amendments, missionaries in charge were able to exert quite strict control over the Aborigines. Any difference from a prison farm was not marked.

The Queensland policy was emphasised by an amendment to the State Children Act in 1911, which enabled the executive to approve an 'industrial school, reformatory, or training home established by private benevolence for the maintenance, custody, and care of aboriginal and half-caste children'.[2] The mission, then, was to become a multi-purposed institution through which the government could deal with some of its pressing problems by isolating them together. This enabled the removal of the part-Aboriginal child from the town fringe to a mission in Cape York—a power by no means unused—and such a decision would often be made on the basis of assumed Aboriginal descent.

There was some confusion in official objectives. For the large reserve, of the kind which Indian tribes had retained under treaty in north America, there was a very sound argument. This is what Australian scholars had already begun to advocate, for there was possibly more knowledge of the American Indian situation then than at any time until the last decade or so. Large areas of the kind which Queensland had set aside in Cape York were needed. So, also, was some governing body—which the Indians had, in the tribal system, to a degree which the Aborigines had not. But indigenous representation of some kind, in decision making on important issues, was essential. Another problem was how to keep Aborigines on the reserve, which seemed insuperable without rigid control. The Queensland Government had placed the Aborigines in the lap of the mission, on the simple assumption that instruction in Christianity and 'industry' was the best which could be offered.

[2] Aboriginals Protection and Restriction of the Sale of Opium Acts, 1897 to 1934, section 7A.

MISSIONS AND EXTENSIVE RESERVES

Perhaps, if more had been known about the way in which traditional societies re-settle themselves, there could have been a different approach. The person who opts for change does not necessarily intend to cut himself off for ever from his ancestral country; if he can he will generally go back when he has seen the world. In such a process of movement, there will be a good deal of mixing of peoples which had not occurred in tribal life. Only when they have attained possession of assets (economic or social or other) in the new place are they likely to opt to make that the main place of abode; the old home will still be visited. This process can be seen currently in the urbanisation of persons of Aboriginal descent in southern Australia; it would probably have reached a more advanced stage than it has but for the earlier control exerted by the missions and government settlements over movement of the inmates.

Autonomy on reserves, proper camps at the towns, and freedom to move at will from one situation to the other might have prevented much social disruption. With real attention to wages and work incentives, such a policy would have made choices possible: workers would have been attracted into the cash economy without meeting complete frustration in any attempt to get beyond the very poorest of working incentives and conditions. It would also have assisted economic development of the Territory and use of its established human resources more effectively, by maintaining the willingness to work.

That such change can be made without complete loss of the old identity has been well argued in a study by Catherine Berndt.[3] She describes the camps established during World War II between Larrimah and Darwin, to which Aborigines travelled from all over the Territory. One of the apparent contradictions of army life is its egalitariansim. As the army was in control, hygiene and health measures were the same for all. Aborigines were rationed and paid regularly for their work. Those in control of the camps were generally determined to give Aborigines a 'fair deal' and had no families there to complicate the relationship. The result was constructive resettlement, because when the army went, many lived on in the new situations, with visits home from time to time.

This process is consistent with the progressive integration of the home areas into the cash economy which centres on the towns or other places of employment—in this case, the army camps. Yet in both types of area— that of resettlement and the old tribal region—justice would require that traditions could be maintained continuously while persons make

[3] 'The Quest for Identity: The Case of the Australian Aborigines', *Oceania*, vol. XXXII' no. 1, September 1961, pp. 16-33.

their own decisions on how they will live. At the same time security of the possible retreat is required, including cultural security of a kind which cannot exist on an authoritarian type of mission or government settlement and still less on a cattle station where the Aboriginal is treated as a unit of cheap and expendable labour. As Catherine Berndt points out, this social and personal autonomy would be quite inconsistent with the policy of assimilation as officially stated and applied a few years ago, when she wrote this study.

One argument for the large reserve, set out here with the wisdom or unwisdom of hindsight, was that it could offer basic security for those whose 'country' it was, and perhaps for others whom they might welcome there. By the time when the matter was being seriously considered, only areas generally considered of little economic value remained, and when the large reserves were gazetted they were in regions both remote and apparently useless. But this did not tempt any government to a reckless recognition of the right of prior occupation in any area. All reserves remained Crown land, and the classification could be administratively revoked. Even then, there was no security for those who lived there. The boundaries meant little, and from then till now the search by whites for economic assets has been little impeded. When such assets have been found in a spectacular way in the last decade, the insecurity of the Aboriginal or mission tenure has been amply demonstrated, as in the excisions from the Arnhem Land and Cape York reserves in the 1960s.

I think it is fair to say that generally governments have been more keen to keep the Aboriginal in the distant reserve than to keep the prospector, dogger, or other entrepreneur out. The legislation was generally very strict about entry to reserves but it could only be applied to the institutional centre of such an area, the Aboriginal camp or village site.

The step taken in Queensland in 1911 to use the reserve institution, generally a mission, for neglected or delinquent children of fringe areas, indicates the general change of administrative emphasis. The main concern was now with the half-caste. But dependence on the institution to meet government's needs, in difficult cases, remained; there had been really little variation from the time of the early mission experiments round Sydney, Melbourne, Adelaide, and Perth. When governments were concerned, they established or supported institutions; when they were not, they let them run down. The ingrained habit was to take people from fringe areas to institutional camps. But the problems of the fringe areas were but facets of a much bigger one; and there was a real relationship between the situations round the townships and those

MISSIONS AND EXTENSIVE RESERVES 251

of the rural regions. Where there are still tribal lands in occupation, the fringe may be seen as an indicator of the gap between hopes and possibilities in those more distant areas. The situation called for better employment conditions, with incentives; better hygiene measures in proper camping areas round the townships, and autonomy on the distant reserve to ensure that at least those still there could make a constructive adjustment to change. The agent of government on the distant reserve should be there mainly to offer advice, to adjudicate where required, and to ensure that visitors genuinely not welcomed by the people be escorted off the reserve. It was, however, much easier and cheaper to delegate difficult functions to the missionaries, who were ready to assume them. It was also easier where former nomads had 'sat down' and come to regard living off the land as a hardship, to drift into the institutional situation where the mission set up, legally or otherwise, a theocracy on the reserve, so that eventually it controlled the people by controlling the assets, and especially the stores and rations.

In the wake of the Queensland decision on the large and distant reserves and of the agitation in South Australia already mentioned, the Central Australian Reserve was created by the Commonwealth, Western Australian and South Australian governments in 1920. This was one of the factors productive of inter-governmental co-operation in Aboriginal affairs: and in this respect Commonwealth policy cannot be considered apart from that of the other three governments with commitments in central and northern Australia. Also in 1920, 2,400 square miles were set aside round Oenpelli, in Arnhem Land. Three years later the Daly River reserve, of over 4,000 square miles, was proclaimed. Pressure for a reserve to include the greater part of Arnhem Land came from the Australian and New Zealand Association for the Advancement of Science in 1926. Its gazettal (over 31,000 square miles) in 1931 was in part due to the report by Bleakley, who was brought to the Territory in 1928 by the Commonwealth.[4]

South Australia's main contribution was its share of the extensive but otherwise apparently useless Central Australian Reserve. By 1929, in addition to the Western Australian part of the Central reserve, there were others at Admiralty Gulf (just under 1,000 square miles) and Drysdale

---

[4] For the present situation of these and other big reserves in the Territory, see a statement by the Northern Territory Director of Lands in Debates of the Legislative Council, 11 August 1964. The reserves mentioned above appear to have been extended, perhaps when re-gazetted under the Welfare Ordinance; the Arnhem Land reserve is stated to be over 37,000 square miles.

River (about 500 square miles) both in the North Kimberleys. In the East Kimberleys were Moola Bulla (about 1,700 square miles), Marndoc (nearly three times the extent of Moola Bulla), Violet Valley (under 400 square miles), Forrest River (then only about 150 square miles); in the West Kimberleys, Collier Bay and Munja together amounted to over 1,500 square miles; and there was a similar expanse of reserve at Mt Hann, in the Central Kimberleys.[5]

The declaration of the large reserves formed a challenge for governments and missions. The missions which were established in some of them, or on the fringes, were there mainly to save souls; governments made more or less half-hearted efforts to assist them in their roles of charitable institutions, rationing points, and educational and training centres. It was inexpensive to set up the reserve, but the Aboriginal had not the priority for expenditure which would have made some rational policy for using them possible. The nearest approach was that of the government of Queensland, which was making more use of the missions than either the Commonwealth in the Territory or the governments of Western and South Australia.

By 1929 there were six missions in the far north of the Territory, most of them in Arnhem Land. In addition to those previously established on Bathurst Island (Catholic) and Roper River (Anglican), others on Goulburn Island (1916) and Millingimbi (1921) had been established by the Methodists, and Groote Eylandt (1921) and Oenpelli (1925) by the Church Missionary Society. Four of the six were on islands off the coast: this was a well-established Pacific mission practice in earlier years, allowing as it did for a safe base close to the larger populations and a place to train the indigenous mission workers who made most of the first contacts and provided most of the martyrs. But the Aboriginal of Arnhem Land seems to have been no more enthusiastic to learn how to spread the Gospel than those elsewhere. The mission island became rather a means of isolating Aborigines from non-mission contacts. In the Centre, Hermannsburg was still the only mission.

Though the Commonwealth had provided in 1918 for the use of the missions as training institutions, the partnership seems to have been less close than in Queensland. Western Australia shared the reluctance to delegate government authority to religious bodies.

Mission policies will vary with the bodies which sponsor them. The existence of a religious policy will create problems for any secular

[5] Biskup, Native Administration and Welfare in Western Australia 1897-1954, Appendix X, p. 462.

MISSIONS AND EXTENSIVE RESERVES

administration. These problems will be increased by the opposition of settlers and pastoral companies, whose interest in the control of native labour may lead them to oppose all missions as unsettling to the labour force. The common view among such employers is that the 'cheeky' mission 'boy' is not to be trusted. If he is educated enough to count and to write, he will not only get to know his rights but he may also tell the other employees. Government also faced the fact that the management of a mission far out, especially in those days, was almost completely in the hands of the person in charge, who might be a man of great perception and sympathy or an ignorant bigot willing to use constraint and even violence to promote what he considered proper conduct and the saving of souls.

A.O. Neville, who was the Chief Protector in Western Australia from 1915, and who had a tenure in that office comparable with that of Bleakley in Queensland, attempted to provide for the holding operation out in the distant reserves by establishing more cattle stations under departmental control.[6] One of the constant causes of violence in the early 1920s had continued to be cattle raiding by the Aborigines. Neville did secure funds to purchase a property, additional to Moola Bulla, on Walcott Inlet in 1926; there he established Munja Station.[7] His opposition to the use of missionaries as administrative agents was partly due to the difficulties of implementing a consistent policy through voluntary bodies which had their own priorities, partly to what he thought was their tendency in staffing to confuse zeal with efficiency and qualifications. His argument that missions should limit their work to the religious sphere, while the government took full responsibility for material welfare, was in accordance with the principles of the secular state. He was to complain later that in his first years of administration a policy of 'hands off missions' prevented effective supervision of their secular work,[8] encouraged missions to retain support by optimistic reports, and enabled governments to assume too easily that, where there was a mission, all could be assumed to be well enough. He believed that priority should be given to training Aborigines for employment, and this was one of the objectives of the departmentally-managed cattle stations.

No government regarded its own operations as of high enough priority to embark on a comprehensive scheme. Whatever might have been the shortcomings of particular missionaries, these were not likely to

---

[6] *Australia's Coloured Minority: Its place in the community*, p. 77.
[7] See Biskup, Native Administration, pp. 202 *et seq.*
[8] *Australia's Coloured Minority*, p. 98.

be avoided by use of untrained secular officers and managers. Moreover, the use of missions could be secured at very small cost, since they would depend mainly on their sponsoring churches. Neville's doubts seem to have caused some difficulties for them in securing land after World War I, but those already established in the far north were able to maintain and consolidate their positions, partly because there was nothing to replace them, but mainly because of the political support that religious institutions can always secure, of the willingness of missionaries to give their lives to this work at no direct cost to the taxpayer, and willingness of their congregations to support them.

There were six missions in Western Australia's north by 1930. The Catholics had established Beagle Bay in 1891, north of Broome. The 'secular mission' established by Hadley on Sunday Island was taken over by the United Aborigines Mission in 1924. In 1907 the famous old Catholic mission of New Norcia, which has maintained a continuous history longer than any mission on the continent, set up another station at Drysdale River, north-west of Wyndham, which has since been removed to Kalumburu. Lombadina, another Catholic mission, was founded north of Broome in 1911; Kunmunya, a Presbyterian mission, north of Derby, about the same time; and Forrest River, near Wyndham, by the Anglicans, in 1913.

No others were established in the north after Neville took office in 1915. But the establishment of the Central Reserve attracted missionaries to work along the fringes of the desert, and in spite of Neville's doubts, the United Aborigines Mission was established at Mount Margaret, near Leonora, in 1921.

All this amounted to considerable change in a decade or so. The apparent uselessness of the large reserves for any economic purpose, so that few non-Aborigines would want to use or visit them, meant that they were to be used for the purpose of Aboriginal administration from then until now, when in the mid-1960s their hidden wealth is being revealed. In the meantime, they formed an asset which allowed for some flexibility in policy making.

EXPERT ADVICE ON
NORTHERN TERRITORY
PROBLEMS

By the end of World War I the smaller reserves in the south and the big ones of the north had become a supplementary source of labour, especially in the pastoral industry. According to Bleakley, the demand from the pastoral industry during the war had exceeded the supply in Queensland; and one result was that he was able to arrange for a standard wage for Aborigines, applicable throughout the State. He says that care had to be taken so that these rates 'should not place them at a disadvantage in competition with white station hands'; and at the end of the war he arranged that Aborigines should not be included in the pastoral award and that the department should frame its own. Here a real chance was missed, as the Australian Workers Union was pressing for equal pay. On Bleakley's own statement he at least agreed with a general assessment of the Aboriginal station worker as lower in efficiency than others. This kind of generalisation was to be maintained in the industry for long afterwards and to make nonsense of the whole principle of a living wage and a minimum award. It is one more example of how by regulation and law the rights of Aborigines continued to be further restricted. But Bleakley managed to have both union and management in the pastoral industry accept his suggestion of a wage 'at approximately two-thirds that of Award men'.[1] He regarded the 1919 Aboriginals Employment Regulations as the basis of the special rates which have applied in the pastoral industry of Queensland for those Aborigines 'under the Act' (falling within the racial definitions and not exempted).

This principle of an Aboriginal minimum wage (with other conditions,

[1] See Bleakley, *The Aborigines of Australia*, p. 171.

which were seldom enforced as there was no effective method of inspecting Aboriginal working conditions on station properties) formed the basis for integration of the reserve into the cash economy. This integration, while setting limits to Aboriginal earnings, at least involved an economic role for reserve Aborigines. In Queensland they could plan to move out from the mission or other reserve area to work; they could fix the times they wished to be away, and then could return. Travelling expenses were covered and wages were protected, as far as protectors could be depended on for this.

The reserve served some of the functions of the village in the colonial system of contract labour and was a source of labour over which management could assume control for defined periods. Despite all the breakdowns in this system it served to some extent the need of the Aboriginal for cash and experience while making it possible for him to leave his family in a protected situation.

The system made possible the payment of a single man's cash wage, without destruction of the worker's family and the future work force. The biggest brake on incentive was probably the control of earnings, by compulsory payment of what was generally most of the wage to the protector, and compulsory banking and saving. The wage rates fixed in the 1919 Regulations were 40s for adult station workers, 40–45s for male cooks; 15–25s for female cooks, and 15s for farm labourers.[2] The higher rates for pastoral workers indicated a skill margin recognised in the industry and the importance of the Aboriginal worker in the pastoral economy.

The 1920s saw the development of the Provident Fund, from a levy of 5 per cent on single workers and 2½ per cent on married ones. This pattern of rigid control was at least a logical and comprehensive effort in protection. By using the fund, part of the costs of improved living conditions on the missions and settlements could be met. Thus the Aboriginal worker was contributing directly to the cost of his management and protection.

It was at least a realistic effort not only to establish the Aboriginal permanently in the national economy but also to ensure his safety and mobility. The Queensland Aboriginal, even if he came out of the most remote reserve along the Gulf, had definite rights to a cash wage and some basic economic security, both on the pastoral station and on the reserve. The development of an apartheid-type of reserve economy, the movement of the single man without his family, the restrictions which

[2] *Queensland Government Gazette*, 6 June 1919.

EXPERT ADVICE ON NORTHERN TERRITORY PROBLEMS 257

meant that he could not learn to speak for himself or to organise, were all to emphasise other consequences of institutionalisation. Fundamentally, the premises were those now widely condemned as the basis for apartheid policies; and the inefficient paternalism involved in depending on police for protectors must have made the position of the 'native' under the Act a frustrating one. But, economically at least, the frontier Aboriginal was much better off in Queensland than on the pastoral stations and reserves of the Territory and Western Australia. In time the drift of Aborigines across the northern regions of the continent into Queensland was to become marked.

Neville was apparently impressed by the provisions of the 1919 wage regulations in Queensland, and in 1922 he had recommended that the Queensland system of uniform wage rates for Aborigines should be introduced in Western Australia. This would have been possible since pastoralists in some areas, even then, had already found it advisable or necessary to pay in cash from 10s to 40s plus rations.[3] He persisted, against political opposition and the effects of droughts; but a uniform wage for Aborigines was one advance which was not to be achieved in Western Australia. The payment of wages in cash, in the north of the State, remained until 1967 a matter between the local employers and the Aborigines, although these days some cash component seems to be almost universal.

This may serve to indicate that by 1928 the problems of the frontier areas were changing from those of first contact to those of how to maintain the comparatively large Aboriginal populations remaining, what their future in Australian society was to be, and what institutions should be established for them. Both Queensland and Western Australia, in their small specialist departments and Chief Protectors, despite their tendency to reflect the general prejudices of the day in their assessment of possibilities for Aborigines, and despite the very low priority that governments gave their work, had at least a core of continuity in administration, with considerable experience behind it. Even so, the time of the punitive expedition had by no means passed; the quite obvious and spectacular injustice of these operations had been publicised by the Royal Commission inquiring into the Kimberley massacre in 1927. Less publicised violence in employment and outside it went on all over the frontier regions. It is the often implicit background to discussions on the role of missions, the function of the large reserve (which in practice was open most easily to those most likely to exploit and ill-treat), and the fixing of minimum wages.

[3] Biskup, Native Administration and Welfare in Western Australia, 1897-1954, p. 194.

258 THE DESTRUCTION OF ABORIGINAL SOCIETY

A quite grim understatement by Elkin indicates the basic reason why, by the end of the twenties, the employer had to pay cash wages in some areas outside Queensland. Of the situation where no wages were paid, he writes that

this modus vivendi did not prevent the Aborigines from dying out; not enough future stock-boys were born on the various pastoral stations, with the result that stations sometimes competed with each other for native employees, and accused each other of enticing their 'blacks' away.[4]

Malnutrition and disease, affecting the reproduction of the work force in the north, seem to have provided opportunities for economic advance for fit males who remained, because the cash wage would be one means of 'enticing' labour.

Elkin's writings show how these conditions in the far north stimulated agitation in the cities. In what seems to be a reference to his own pioneering work of the early thirties, he writes of the growing opinion of humanitarian and mission bodies that proper administration could 'save the Aborigines'; that the main activity at the end of the twenties was still expended in protesting against abuses, in a situation where abuses were inevitable until all governments accepted a new, positive policy which 'would take for granted that the Aborigines had a future', but 'must be based on a knowledge of Aboriginal life and of the contact process, and must include education in the wide sense of the term'.[5]

There were thus good reasons why the Commonwealth should, by 1928, look to Queensland for an expert to advise it. The invitation was also a confession of failure. Not only in relation to Aborigines, this was about the nadir in Commonwealth control of the Territory. When in 1926 separate Territories, of Central and North Australia, had been established, the result was to create one more ineffective administration. This period saw the beginning of one of the great droughts; and there followed press accounts in the south of the effects of the droughts on Aborigines. If the Commonwealth was now moved to consistent effort, it was sensible to get some advice. Consistency so far had been notably lacking, partly because there had been so many changes in the Ministers responsible for Northern Territory matters.

Against this background, the optimism of the Association for the Protection of Native Races, in its advocacy of federal control of Aboriginal affairs might seem ill founded; yet the Commonwealth could hardly

[4] 'Reaction and Interaction: A Food Gathering People and European Settlement in Australia', *American Anthropologist*, vol. 53, no. 2, 1951, p. 184.
[5] Ibid.

EXPERT ADVICE ON NORTHERN TERRITORY PROBLEMS 259

avoid its responsibility to lead. The Association had recently been pressing for a national inquiry. The invitation to Bleakley was a way of opening up the matter without risking provocation of State jealousy by seeming to interfere in State matters.

One local turning point had been the transfer of the duties of the Chief Protector from the Commissioner of Police to the Government Health Officer, in the Territory of North Australia, in 1927. The holder of this office was Dr C.E. Cook, who had long experience of health matters in the north and who had some years before conducted a survey of Aboriginal health in northern Western Australia. But in Central Australia the duties of Chief Protector were discharged by the officer in charge of police: one result was that the pastoralists of the Centre continued without real interference. Cook, who had the courage to refuse some police as protectors, and who had his medical officers to use in supervisory welfare duties, insisted on the minimum responsibility of the pastoral station to maintain the Aborigines' dependants as well as the workers. So bad were the conditions that, had standards of proper nutrition been established with a ration scale for Aboriginal employees, this would have been a major advance. But though ration scales had been adopted as a minimum protection of the 'unit of labour' in Papua and New Guinea, it was good enough for the government to trust the manager in the Northern Territory.

Cook's report for 1931, when he had taken over responsibility for the area which had been Central Australia, mentioned the opposition by pastoralists and others there. Apparently they were objecting to maintaining tribal dependants; and Cook explained the reason for the provision— that the stock depleted water and food supplies, that stations employed (without wages) the able-bodied men, who were compelled to work on the pastoralists' conditions. Maintenance of dependants, he said, took the place of payment of the money wage, except for the Aboriginal drover, who had to have cash to keep his dependants while he was away.[6]

When Cook reported in this vein, it was in train of events which illustrated how labour relations constituted the 'neuralgic point' of inter-racial contacts, and of relations between government, economic, and mission interests. A turning-point was reached with the visit to Central and North Australia in 1928 of J.W. Bleakley, Queensland's Chief Protector, at the invitation of the Commonwealth Government. Bruce, who had had to deal with the most unfortunate events which had marked

[6] C.P.P., 1932-4, vol. III, pp. 2075-9—Chief Protector of Aborigines, Report on the Administration of the Northern Territory.

260 THE DESTRUCTION OF ABORIGINAL SOCIETY

the early administration of the Mandated Territory of New Guinea, was no stranger to this kind of question: apparently frustrated by State governments in his moves for a Royal Commission to inquire into the conditions of Aborigines throughout the nation, he borrowed the services of Bleakley to report on those in the Commonwealth Territories of Central and North Australia.[7]

Bleakley reported to the Prime Minister in 1929.[8] He said that there was no way of estimating the numbers of myalls remaining. The figure he gives for the 'nomadic tribes', of 14,000, and a total of 21,000 including 800 'half-castes' must be taken as an informed guess and subject to the tendency to overestimate. (The 1921 Census estimate was 17,831, and that for 1947 was 15,147.)[9] More accurate would be his estimate of 2,500 in regular or casual employment, with 1,500 of their 'camp dependants', 'usually old, indigent, and young', of 1,450 'full-bloods' and 200 'half-castes' as inmates of Aboriginal Institutions, with a further 1,350, approximately, visiting or 'influenced by' institutions. He mentions the problem which still, even in the settled areas of the continent, faces the worker who attempts any wide survey of Aboriginal conditions— that he may spend weeks in the search 'and then see very few of them'.[10]

He described a range of employment situations. Those best off for wages and conditions were employed either in the towns or adjacent to the railway. Town employees, in domestic or labouring work, were entitled to 5s per week—3s in the hand and 2s in the Trust Account— plus food and clothing. He criticised the use of a fixed rate instead of a minimum rate, arguing that some servants were worth much more than this; and it is quite true that the wage which operates as a maximum as well as a minimum offers no inducement to efficiency—with results which employers still attribute to Aboriginal stupidity or 'tribal elements' in the culture. The sleeper-cutters' 'assistants' (who often did all the work) received 10s along the railway, where they could no doubt bargain; but out in the bush the licence fee of 10s per month allowed the sleeper-cutter or other employer to hire as many as he wished for food, clothing, and shelter, the supply of which could not possibly be checked without

[7] See A.P. Elkin 'The Background of Present Day Aboriginal Policies', in J.W. Warburton (ed.), *Proceedings of Conference on Welfare Policies for Australian Aborigines*.
[8] *C.P.P.*, 1929, vol. II, pp. 1159-225—The Aboriginals and Half-Castes of Central Australia and North Australia: Report by J.W. Bleakley, Chief Protector of Aborigines, Queensland, 1928.
[9] Statistician's Reports on the 1921 Census, pp. 112-22; and on the 1947 Census, pp. 153-65; quoted by F. Lancaster Jones, *The Structure and Growth of Australia's Aboriginal Population*.
[10] *C.P.P.*, 1929, vol. II, p. 1163.

EXPERT ADVICE ON NORTHERN TERRITORY PROBLEMS 261

means of regular inspection. In this, such employees shared the lot of the 80 per cent of all employees who were on the pastoral stations. Though the licence to employ provided for a weekly cash wage of 5s, of which half was to be banked monthly in the Trust Account, 'As employers on pastoral holdings have claimed that many more natives have to be fed than are employed by them, the payment of wages has not been insisted upon, at any rate in North Australia'.[11]

In Central Australia, however, he was told by some managers that they paid up to £1 weekly for men and 5s for women, the Aborigines buying their own clothes and tobacco—an interesting indication of the need to pay cash where there might be more jobs than effective workers. Wages in cash above the minimum were also being paid by 'a few stations on the Barkly Tableland . . . to their more capable employees'. No doubt this was to offset, in the case of the efficient worker, the attraction of the Queensland stations, which were paying up to £2 weekly for competent stockmen; and Bleakley argued cogently that even the western regions of North Australia were in no worse situation for transport and markets than the Gulf country of Queensland, where the Queensland minimum cash rates applied and were supervised.

He found that 'at very few places' had the pastoralists provided 'reasonable shelter' for the Aboriginal work force. The usual excuse was Aboriginal preference to live in the 'camp'; but the only evidence was the fact that a few huts of galvanised iron were not occupied—and no wonder, he wrote, in that climate. He also noted the attempts to provide effective shelter for themselves, from old bags, tents, and other 'waste material given to them'. The nomad once stabilised needs the same kind of shelter as other men: Bleakley noted the attempts to make beds and tables. But here was the fringe settlement again—'mere kennels and most insanitary'. On the other hand, the workers seemed well enough nourished and clothed; though he noted that 'one large firm', having paid in clothing for work done, took this back when the workers were sent on 'walkabout' in the off-season. He also mentioned that managers would 'stop the rations' as a labour discipline, and remarked that the loss of their traditional means of subsistence meant that the Aboriginal group must 'yield to circumstances'. On the other hand, the pastoral industry in the Territories was

absolutely dependent on the blacks for the labour . . . If they were removed, most of the holdings . . . would have to be abandoned . . . It is remarkable that . . . there has been no attempt . . . on these holdings to elevate or educate them, though this

[11] Ibid., p. 1164.

should enhance their value as machinery. It seems to be the conveniently accepted notion that they are beyond redemption, that education spoils them, so there is no encouragement for ambition and the blackfellow, naturally lacking initiative and given no opportunity, has a hopeless outlook.[12]

The range of situations he described, with cash wages paid mainly in towns and along the railway, suggest that few would be attracted to the pastoral property as a transitional situation leading to employment elsewhere. They would probably be actively discouraged as not required, where there was already a captive work force, tied to the job by economic dependence and attachment to their 'country'. The cash wages of the town probably attracted men from far out in the tribal areas. Five shillings per week was twice the wage paid in Papua, and four times that in the Mandated Territory at that time, though in the overseas Territories much more care had to be exercised to maintain the recruiting rate by attention to ration scales and accommodation; and to ensure the safe return home with useful items of trade. The Aboriginal received little of this kind of consideration. As he was in most cases a captive in the main industry, at the mercy of an all-powerful management, the threat of force or starvation could remain the chief incentive used by those who expected no more from him than a bare minimum of interest and productivity.

Bleakley found good as well as bad managements. That some paid cash wages, some even above the fixed wage in certain cases, he used as an argument that their neighbours in similar economic circumstances could also afford to do so. Bleakley was long enured to the harsh circumstances of the Aboriginal station work force and had few illusions about how far owners and managers might be pushed by governments. His criticism of the situation is thus all the more telling: there was the failure to provide even elementary village conditions for the work force; the lack of water and sanitation; the contemptuous attitude to the children, whose education would only make them 'cunning and cheeky', and who grew up without either European or true indigenous education. There were the stations where owners refused to acknowledge any responsibility for dependants (although they did not pay cash wages to the workers). On such stations, 'the only food received is the offal of the beasts on killing day and whatever is contributed by the working natives from their own food or an occasional marsupial caught by them'. Starvation in the camp forced the women into prostitution.

[12] Ibid., p. 1165.

EXPERT ADVICE ON NORTHERN TERRITORY PROBLEMS 263

As practically all public roads lead through the stations ... these simple women are an easy prey to passing travellers, who, at times, are low enough to cheat them by paying them with bogus money ... It was complained that motor car loads of men from bush townships or construction camps bent on 'ginsprees', in other words drink and prostitution orgies, had given trouble on stations even 100 miles distant.[13]

He stated also that non-Aboriginal station staff, who (to save expense for housing) were mainly single men, would use the camp for the same purposes. Bleakley's evidence of underfeeding was supported over a decade later, during World War II, when R.M. and C.H. Berndt found a similar situation on a group of large stations.

In this respect the government in 1928 was setting no good example. There were the other 'indigent camps' not on cattle stations, where relief was issued by police, telegraph employees, and by some approved cattle station managers. Rations, clothing, and medicines could be issued; but especially when drought had killed off the game, this was insufficient even for those who were legally entitled to it; issues to the old and ill would be shared with the young and fit; only a few were needed in government employment, by police or the telegraph service. 'The majority of the inmates of these camps are in an emaciated miserable condition ... an easy prey to the unscrupulous.'[14] Officers in charge of the telegraph stations had no power to keep out travellers.

The real need, he thought, was for relief camps with motherly women present. He was much impressed by the work of married police protectors, and especially with what their wives did out of the kindness of their hearts. He was moved to comment on the children with yaws and eye complaints; he suggested that missions should establish relief camps. Through the report one can see the effect of the hard niggardliness of distant government in setting standards for people whose living conditions were not well understood by the public servants or politicians. He made recommendations for improved conditions for workers and for their dependants in camps outside Aboriginal institutions.

In considering wages, he was caught to some degree in a dilemma, since he wanted on the one hand a fixed minimum wage scale, and on the other that spending of wages be controlled by government officers or representatives. As the only possible representative in many situations was the employer, he left his suggestions and recommendations open to some doubt in the matter of the cash wage: and this enabled the pastoralists later to suggest an interpretation convenient to their interests.

[13] Ibid., p. 1167.
[14] Ibid., p. 1168.

264 THE DESTRUCTION OF ABORIGINAL SOCIETY

Although he had, in the body of the report, suggested a scale of wages from 5s to £1 according to efficiency, his recommendation was for 'a definite scale of wages ... according to value of services' without indicating who was to assess this value. He also recommended that 'as far as possible, cash payments direct ... be discontinued, and wages be drawn in goods ... through the employers or the local Protector'. Part of his dilemma was that station wages could generally be spent only in the station store; and he had been concerned in Queensland with ensuring that wages were not wasted. His recommendation assumed some system of accounting, in the Queensland manner, so that a Protector could make some check on issues of goods from the store; and he recommended the deduction from the cash value of a portion for compulsory saving.

This was the one point on which, if his plan was implemented, management could be effectively pressed to make over cash into the workers' accounts.

Bleakley also recommended better living conditions for employees. His outlook was rigidly paternal. He obviously thought that employers should pay cash: but his concern for saving by Aborigines was also strong. This was in accord with Queensland policy, which ignored the fact that the only way to learn how to handle money is to have the right to decide how to spend it. He considered the living conditions so bad that any 'allowance made for cost of maintaining dependent blacks' should be withdrawn from leasehold conditions and the rents fixed again, with the government taking over responsibility for relief. He recommended also that the laws against prostitution and abuses be extended; that pressure be placed on employers to enforce morality and to engage married employees. For camps off the stations, he recommended better police protection from construction camps and other sources of exploitation; relief depots under mission control; and appointment of married men as police protectors.[15]

Part of the impact of this Report lay in the obvious understatement of the conditions on pastoral stations, and of the inadequacy of relief for a people whose nutrition and health had been seriously impaired by destruction of their economic life. By implication at least, what he had to say of conditions in the town compounds, of the adequacy of health measures, and of staffing for Aboriginal administration was equally telling. He also considered the Commonwealth provision of £1 10s per annum paid to missions for each inmate maintained to be far too low.

The Report also contains snapshot pictures of the Aboriginal

[15] Ibid., p. 1169.

EXPERT ADVICE ON NORTHERN TERRITORY PROBLEMS 265

Institutions as they were in 1928: the Kahlin Compound in Darwin, and the special 'half-caste homes' there and at the Bungalow, Alice Springs. The site of Kahlin Compound had been chosen by Baldwin Spencer as well out of town; but now it was close to a suburb. Bleakley accepted the need for white housewives in the tropics to have domestic servants at cheap rates. The compromise, for protection of male and female servants, was to shut them up at night in the compound and enforce a curfew in town: at that time Aborigines were excluded from the town between sunset and sunrise. The 'white neighbours' were concerned by the possibility that venereal and other disease might spread from Kahlin, where, in accordance with the tradition of the multi-purposed Aboriginal Institution, the Aboriginal clinic was located. The galvanised iron huts of the clinic were 'in the same block' with living huts for the 'working natives'. 'The patients are locked in the wards at night, the verandahs enclosed with "K" wire'; but as the manager and matron were not there at night, 'there is nothing to prevent contact between the diseased and healthy ones'. He did not go so far as to recommend integration of Aboriginal with other health and medical services, but did say that the clinic should be near the general hospital; that Aborigines could be trained as assistants to the nursing staff. The half-caste home was only a hundred yards away; and the management had quarters in between. There are hints of 'immorality with the women'; and no wonder. There was only the nightly 'corroboree' for entertainment, as the curfew and film censorship kept the inmates away even from the Darwin cinema. There was not even religious instruction. Bleakley was all for maintaining segregation; but he recommended recreation facilities, full-time supervision, and a canteen store. Dreary as the place so obviously was, it could easily at the time have been matched in most of the government stations of the States. Queensland must be given the credit of at least giving consideration to increased comfort and recreation within the segregated settlement.

Even the half-caste homes were multi-purposed, and not for children only. Ages ranged from four months to adulthood. Bleakley classified the inmates according to 'strain' and 'breed', and as 'half-caste', 'quarter-caste' 'octoroon'. In this he spoke as a man of the time, when 'breed' was assumed in administrative circles to determine competence. Those with '50 per cent or more Aboriginal blood or a preponderance of other dark blood' should be trained for station work with 'the civilised Aboriginal children' on the missions at Bathurst Island or Goulburn Island. But those with higher potential, with 'preponderance of European or Chinese

266 THE DESTRUCTION OF ABORIGINAL SOCIETY

blood' should go to the Darwin convent or other 'European institution'. He made similar recommendations, on similar grounds, about the half-caste bungalow at Alice Springs. Those with a 'preponderance of Aboriginal blood' should go to the mission at Hermannsburg, since 'no matter how carefully brought up and educated' they would 'drift back to the Aboriginal'. Some of the others should go to Salvation Army homes in Adelaide; and for some a new 'industrial home' should be set up by the Administration, well out of Alice Springs, because of the proposed establishment of the railway construction camp there. This would involve special grants to the missions. But in addition he analysed the costs of each mission, and maintained that the government should increase the subsidy to each to meet costs of food and education, leaving the mission to bear that of its religious work. In time this principle, as he partly foresaw, was to make the missions more and more the agents of government. Since government funds have to be accounted for, government was to interfere in how the missions spent the grants; while increasing costs, with the drying up of the traditional sources of mission funds, were to render them more dependent on government.

Bleakley rather spread himself on the problem of the part-Aborigines, about half of whom, he thought, were employed on stations, being often the offspring of the management or staff members; others remained still with their mothers in station camps. One way of evading the law on cohabitation was to pay an Aboriginal 'to pose as dummy husband'. The recommendations he had made for the future of those in the two 'homes' were in accordance with principle which had formed the basis of his Queensland policy. Thus the 'crossbreed with a preponderance of white blood' had to be controlled and guided and trained to become a member of white Australian society, and kept rigidly from his relatives with greater strains of 'dark blood', to 'avoid the dangers of the blood call'.[16]

This is what the greatest official expertise had come to from the time of the speculations by Grey and Gipps; nor has this kind of racist nonsense been forgotten in the officialdom of Aboriginal administration. Bleakley thought that the 'problem' should be attacked at the roots, as it were, 'to check as far as possible the breeding of half-castes', by 'protection and control' of 'female Aboriginals', by getting white women into the Territories, and by having married men in positions of authority over Aborigines. This discussion belonged to a wider one which had been going on in the States for a long time, as the Dark People who, by their

[16] Ibid., p. 1187.

EXPERT ADVICE ON NORTHERN TERRITORY PROBLEMS 267

increasing numbers, obviously threatened the basic assumptions on which all policy was at least implicitly founded, had to be provided for. He stood for absorption by intermarriage, obviously for those with the right 'blood', into the 'white' community; and absorption into Aboriginal society for the others. It may be worth a note here that government officials are seldom in a position to develop policies on assumptions too far from the folklore of the day, and that Bleakley expressed the views which were almost axiomatic in Aboriginal affairs, and which were only then being questioned by scholars.

His essential humanity is indicated by his consideration of the plight of the tribal people, both those in the outlying parts of the enormous company stations and those on land not yet alienated. At the time of his report the Commonwealth was inquiring into the circumstances of a massacre of men and women of the Kaitish group in Central Australia. Part of the background was conflict with the pastoralists over use of waterholes during the drought. Land Ordinances of both Territories provided that in pastoral leases rights of access to, and use of, game and natural water should be reserved to the tribes in the terms of the lease—a condition omitted, he wrote, from recent leases in Central Australia. But in drought, water and game supplies became critical; cattle spearing increased, station hands carried guns, and the few police protectors could not control the situation. Bleakley's remedy was the reservation of areas excised from properties, with missions set up on them, and more police to patrol and relieve distress; and he suggested that the pastoralist who killed an occasional beast for the Aborigines could win them over.

In the unalienated lands he thought there could be about 5,000 people all told, of whom 3,000 would be in the watered coastal areas of Arnhem Land. He guessed at another 1,000 based in the Macdonnell and Petermann Ranges, whence they had been forced in to the station waterholes by droughts. In these areas he suggested missions, not to control but to win trust and offer help. The whole of Arnhem Land should be reserved and the Commonwealth part of the Central Reserve extended. He recommended that the Lutherans should be helped to set up a mission at Lake Amadeus for people in the Central Reserve; that there should be two additional missions to serve those in Arnhem Land; that the Catholics should have another mission on Melville Island under control of the Bathurst Island mission, and set up yet another on the Daly.

By this time even Arnhem Land was well in contact with the industrial economy; in fact it was an area where foreign contacts, with trepangers from the north, were of long standing, anticipating those with white

Australians. The trade items for which there was demand are interesting, partly because the list Bleakley gives is so suggestive of what had been the trade of the Arafura Sea for a long time, drawing even the coastal villages of western New Guinea into the area of Islamic influence and stimulating them to sell members of other villages as slaves to the traders from Ceram Laut—wire, iron, knives, fish-hooks, axes, and cloth. The mission boats had been used on coastal patrols; and the tribes traded into the mission stations their turtle shell, eggs, fish, fibre rope, and bags. He saw the possibility of extending the trade to include bêche-de-mer, trochus, sponges and the like. But this was a coast where unscrupulous whites made hard use of the tribesmen for labour; and there was trouble, as usual, about the women: he mentions murders at Caledon Bay. Tribal society in Arnhem Land was already in that state of disruption which was bound to raise the whole range of issues in the clash situation. The stage was set for spectacular incidents raising again, in a much more obvious way than issues related to fair employment practices, the question of justice; and by this time there was in the capital cities of the States growing concern with justice among few but influential persons and associations.

Bleakley advocated the appointment of more full-time staff; so far there had been only clerical members. He wanted two senior full-time officers in North Australia, and one for the Territory of Central Australia; and more police protectors. While recognising the clash of duties, he thought naturally within the limits of the priorities of that time, and of the cost which to any government then seemed reasonable. He pointed to the incredible situation in Central Australia, 'where no medical help whatever is available': he recommended more blankets and relief. The biting cold of the winter nights of the Centre must have been hard on the old people in the camps. He saw the injustice of trials in the British Courts for 'crime' committed for 'tribal' reasons; and suggested special courts. He even suggested motor transport for protectors, a useful reminder that much of the obvious inadequacy of administrative controls was due to the fact that Aboriginal administration through the vast northern regions still went on at the pace of the policeman's horse.

The publication of this report came at a time when interest was growing in stories about ill-treatment of Aborigines. The report represented what were considered enlightened views, backed by Queensland experience and expertise. Australian isolation is illustrated in the contrast in its tone and assumptions with those of the Meriam Report of 1928 on the condition of the American Indian in the United States, which was to lead to the abandonment, as outmoded and disproven, of

EXPERT ADVICE ON NORTHERN TERRITORY PROBLEMS 269

many of Bleakley's assumptions. The limitations of this report are also evident by comparison with the humane criticism of Australian policies in the Mandated Territory of New Guinea, which came to the Commonwealth each year from the Permanent Mandates Commission. The Meriam Report outlined the depressing results of decades of the kind of protection Bleakley was advocating. The Permanent Mandates Commission politely indicated each year that autonomy and self-determination were more than formal expressions to justify colonial exploitation.

What really seems to have shocked the pastoralists was Bleakley's suggestion of a minimum cash wage (well below the Queensland level) of from 5s up to £1 per week plus rations. Experience of cash in hand had for a very long time been especially provided for in all colonial labour legislation, including that applicable in New Guinea. One good reason for this is the self-interest of management, concerned to provide the only work incentive which does not flag with accumulation, since cash opens up a range of potentially limitless demand.

As we shall see, the Northern Territory Pastoral Lessees resisted. The North Australian Workers Union, on the other hand, wanted a higher cash wage. The missions were interested in promoting more humane working conditions. It should be remembered that while in Queensland there was a good deal of organised movement out of the protected reserve into employment, and back again, most station labour in the Territory and Western Australia was settled permanently on the station—a situation which had been less characteristic of Queensland since many Aborigines had been rounded up and 'transferred' to reserves. In the long run, and with ordinarily humane management and minimal legislative protection and enforcement, those living on stations should have been better off; there was at least a range of management skills, which included the very good managers, men with a personal interest in the property and in those who lived there. Perhaps the greatest handicap was in the holding operations of large companies, producing erosion of the work force as well as of the land.

Bleakley's recommendations for the Territory were mainly for the introduction of Queensland policy there. The subsequent declaration of the Arnhem Land reserve was probably expedited by his recommendation for the reservation of tribal areas. He wanted more missions for 'protective supervision' and more assistance to the missions to pay for care and training. Even in the frontier areas, by this time, there was a growing 'half-caste problem'; and a public servant used to thinking in terms of the racial categories on which his own administration was based (as they were by this time in all States) would naturally regard them as a special case. In fact this had been a major matter of concern in the Territory for a long time; the first government institutions established had been for the half-castes at Alice Springs and Darwin. Bleakley criticised these and their lack of facilities for training. He advocated greater 'moral protection' of Aboriginal females (which would prevent increase of the 'half-caste problem').

He was concerned with the effect of the droughts in the Centre; and one reason for his support of missions was that they could be trusted as the agents of government relief: the pastoral manager might too often use government relief to feed the work force, and let the old and infirm fend for themselves. Following his report, the Administration stopped using the pastoral station to issue government relief. In the Centre, this duty was assumed by the Hermannsburg mission. The government sent the fringe-dwellers of Alice Springs out to Jay Creek.

The Bleakley Report presented some awkward issues, especially in the matter of wages. It appears to have become widely known; and such was the growing public concern that in April 1929 C.L.A. Abbott, Minister for Home Affairs, found it necessary (mainly for other reasons stated below) to convene and chair in Melbourne a conference of his own departmental officers, representatives of the Northern Territory Pastoral Lessees Association, and voluntary bodies, to discuss the report. The missions were strongly represented—the Australian Board of Missions, the Methodist Missionary Society, the Church Missionary Society, the National Missionary Council, Catholic delegates from New South Wales and Western Australia, missionaries from the Territory and all States but Queensland and Tasmania. Other bodies represented were the Aborigines Friends Association of South Australia, the Association for the Protection of Native Races of Australasia and Polynesia, which was based in Sydney, the Aborigines Protection League of South Australia, the Australian Federation of Women Voters, and the National Council of Women, as well as women's organisations of South Australia and Victoria; and the Anthropological Society of South Australia. There was even an 'Aboriginal missionary' named James, who was probably the first to raise his voice in such an assembly. He was, in fact, the son of a school teacher of Indian descent, whose work at Cumeroogunga on the Murray is still remembered by those part-Aborigines who regard themselves as Cumeroogunga people.

The meeting is important as indicative of growing pressures, because of the wide interstate representation of the voluntary organisations, and

EXPERT ADVICE ON NORTHERN TERRITORY PROBLEMS 271

because it was called by a Commonwealth Minister. The discussion, limited to a single day by the Minister, showed enough division of opinion to enable him to get most of his own way; but important criticism was voiced. Some representatives came with carefully prepared submissions. Abbott had his own agenda, of five items—nomadic Aborigines, those in employment, those camped on stations, those housed in institutions, and half-castes. Committees were to be set up to continue consideration of points not settled during the meeting.

The agenda suggests how the frontier dominated the thinking of that time. Atrocities were still occurring, and still made spectacular appeals to those concerned with justice. Abbott was inclined to dismiss these as inevitable—as they were, so long as policy was based on assumptions that there would soon be no Aborigines. Speaking of the 'very severe criticism' his government had received from 'certain societies' over the recent killing of seventeen Aborigines, he dismissed such events as part of a long history, now past, and of an inevitable process. 'I say it quite frankly—these things end the same way—in the domination by the whites.'[17]

The Minister mentioned as evidence of Commonwealth achievement the expenditure for 1927-8 of just under £5,000 on Aboriginal welfare in North Australia, and just over £3,000 in Central Australia. A former cattle man from Queensland, he made the handsome admission that Aboriginal workers were 'almost vital' for the industry; cattle stations were apparently a civilising force to 'weaken the grip of the dead hand of the past, which has kept in existence those dreadful tribal customs' of the two Territories and Western Australia.

The South Australian group pressed for a common control of the Central Reserve, partly because the South Australian government had granted prospectors' rights in its own area. Genders, of the Aborigines Protection League, made a radical recommendation, which was not to become part of the argument about Aborigines until over three decades later, when he said that the large reserve should have natural boundaries known to the Aborigines and should be allotted to them in perpetuity; that they should be helped to govern it for themselves; and that no whites should enter without permit. Questions of development should be 'left to the Aboriginals'. This was opposed by enough missionary opinion for Abbott to get the motion withdrawn.

A Catholic missionary questioned the possibility of 'a State within

[17] Commonwealth of Australia, Department of Home Affairs: Conference . . . Convened by the Minister of State for Home Affairs . . . 12 April 1929 (typescript).

a State governed by the natives'; and one from the United Aborigines Mission could not see any hope in giving 'the power of self-government to the Aborigines . . . if the natives are to be allowed to govern themselves in the manner adopted by them in the past'. While such a suggestion was unthinkable for missionaries and others on practical grounds (although it was not so very different from what happened within the boundaries of South Africa in respect to the High Commission territories and the Transkei), it was already part of the currency of ideas about the Aboriginal situation. The idea of a 'Native State' had been discussed and rejected in the Bleakley Report. In the previous year the Communist Party of Australia had formulated the objective of 'complete self-determination . . . inclusive of the right of state separation' for the Aboriginal 'national minority'. A draft policy statement in 1963 (still as far as I know under consideration) included among the objectives for Aborigines 'the right to control their own affairs as a distinct national minority within the Australian nation'.[18] Probably one effect of Communist advocacy of national autonomy has been to discredit moves for Aboriginal *social* autonomy in the eyes of politicians and public servants. The rigid paternalism of government policy, on the other hand, must have been playing into the hands of the Communist Party, by conditioning Aborigines to listen to the only real criticism of that policy over a considerable period. Thus, as early as 1929, one can see the present set of political complications taking shape. The Communists have in fact been more alert than any other political group, over a long period, to the potentially critical nature of the Aboriginal issue.

Bleakley had recommended that Arnhem Land be reserved. Pastoral interests merely demurred; the Commonwealth had already begun to move in this direction, and the Minister spoke of compensation for any interests in leases. Burton, of the Methodist Missionary Society, told of how an oil prospecting company had been permitted to erect a plant 'right at our front door' in the area, and asked that no miners' rights be granted.

Jennison, of the Anthropological Society of South Australia, moved that the Commonwealth control Aboriginal affairs; that the States be approached to transfer their rights; and at Abbott's suggestion recommended that the matter should be referred to 'the forthcoming conference

---

[18] *Communist Policy on the Aborigines of Australia* (Draft for Discussion) Sydney 1963. The only summary of the Communist Party's policies since 1928 on this question known to me is from the Catholic viewpoint. See W.G. Smith S.J., 'Communists and the Aborigines', *Social Survey* vol. 12, no. 8, September 1963.

EXPERT ADVICE ON NORTHERN TERRITORY PROBLEMS 273

of the States and the Commonwealth'. He spoke of the unfairness of different methods of 'control' in the States; of the difference between South Australian parsimony and the situation in New South Wales; of the Aborigines 'transferred' across State boundaries who were forgotten and could not get home again.

Though Morley, of the Association for Protection of Native Races, supported Commonwealth control, some missionaries opposed it. Burton was one; and his reason indicates the high reputation of the Queensland administration, 'where such excellent management has been displayed in regard to the Aborigines . . . to ask Queensland to hand over its control to a body which has not yet been tried, is asking for something which is not likely to be granted'. There were references by Jennison to Aboriginal opinion, an interesting indication of the growing sophistication in the settled areas and the emergence of the part-Aboriginal communities as potential pressure groups. He maintained that they favoured Commonwealth control of all Aboriginal affairs; and on this point he was supported by James, the missionary from Cumeroogunga, who mentioned the case of an Aboriginal girl who had completed a business college course but could not get employment other than as a domestic. But James was dealt with expeditiously, from the chair, by the Minister.

The most contentious issue was that of employment in the pastoral industry. Thonemann, one of the pastoral representatives, admitted that Aboriginal workers were 'essential to the progress of the Territory'; but argued that payment of workers in cash would attract to the stations an 'undesirable class of paupers' who would take it from them. In the event of a wage in cash being fixed 'we would have no option but to move the whole of our cattle to Queensland and abandon the station'. (His interest was in the famous Elsey Station.)

Apparently the effect of cash payments in Queensland had been to make them necessary on the Barkly Tableland, where the wage varied from £1 to 30s per week: but he argued that neither the Queensland nor Barkly stations had to maintain dependants. To be fair, many dependants in Queensland would be maintained by missions on the reserves. He moved that 'payments should usually be otherwise than in cash' and that 'due regard should be given to the economic position of the white settlers'. He claimed that the wages suggested by Bleakley, of 5s to 20s plus rations, would force the Territory stations out of business —the kind of argument which played on the overwhelming concern of government for the pastoral industry, a concern which was not for a long time to include the major asset of the Aboriginal work force or the need

274 THE DESTRUCTION OF ABORIGINAL SOCIETY

for incentives to develop and maintain its efficiency. The situation on the Barkly was probably easier than farther west, since the northern industry depended on getting store cattle in to the fattening areas close to the markets and sea ports.

Bleakley, having in mind the Queensland system, had recommended that wages be not paid to workers direct, but drawn in kind. When one of the missionaries pointed this out, it appeared that what the pastoralists wished to avoid was the supervision and checking of actual payments. Moreover, the setting aside of part of the wage as enforced saving for the worker would involve money payments which could be checked and enforced. They tried to avoid definiteness in wages; in fact Thonemann remarked that Bleakley's recommendation '"for a definite scale of wages" although it is to be "according to the value of services", to my mind, [is] too definite for a conference to pass. We would like to adopt the principle and deal with the details in committee.' What he really meant was that he wished to avoid the principle and settle for the *status quo* in committee.

The Reverend John Jones, of the Australian Board of Missions, resisted this move. He asked how workers were ever to save, if paid in kind; and questioned the justice of suggestions that the wage should be determined only with regard to the economic situation of the station as interpreted by the management. (And it was in fact, as it has remained, curious that such a situation should be tolerated in a country where the tradition of the basic wage has been so strong.) 'Would we', he asked, 'regard that as a fair way of reckoning wages in any other community, or in any other branch of life in Australia?' Thonemann had argued that it was unfair to make the station pay cash wages unless the missions paid equally. Jones pointed to the basic differences between an enterprise managed for profit of owners and an institution managed for the inmates; he offered to produce mission balance sheets if the pastoralists would produce theirs. 'I do not think', remarked the Minister of State and initiator of Commonwealth policy, from the chair, 'you should go too much on those lines. Things are pretty bad up there.'

But other missionaries had supported Thonemann; and one, W.J. Eddy, of the National Missionary Council, suggested that what Bleakley had meant was that 'cash payments should be discontinued as a general principle'. Genders then advocated free movement of Aborigines in employment, and the licensing of employers, with cancellation of licences where conditions were bad. This of course was already law, but not practice.

EXPERT ADVICE ON NORTHERN TERRITORY PROBLEMS 275

In the event, the conference carried a motion supporting Bleakley's somewhat contradictory recommendations, that for a definite *scale*, and one submitted by the pastoralists with some mission support, agreeing with 'the principle of the payment of Aboriginals employed, but it is considered desirable that such payments should be usually otherwise than in cash'.

Mission paternalism had, with exceptions, been rallied to the support of the *status quo*. The record suggests that a reaction to the Bleakley Report was to call this conference, so that it could be argued that the issues raised and recommendations made had been 'considered'. This was the process of interpreting them for government action. Not the report, but this woolly superstructure, would constitute the plan of action.

Abbott promised to investigate the situation of the Kahlin Compound, where Bleakley had recommended maintenance of the curfew but more attractive and healthy apartheid conditions. But most of the discussion on institutions arose from his recommendations for those catering for the part-Aboriginal children, who were part of a growing part-Aboriginal population in the Territory. There was no questioning of Bleakley's assumption of the need to base policy on racial origin, or of the different treatment recommended for part-Aborigines of different 'breeds'.

Bleakley had offered the fruits of his experience in Queensland, where he differentiated between 'superior' and other half-castes on similar grounds. When the matter was raised of what future lay ahead in Australian society for either, or for the full-bloods, there was vague talk of a conference with the anthropologists, as though the problem lay wholly in the nature of the Aboriginal. Perriman, of the Church Missionary Society, spoke with pride of the 'rather unique work on Groote Eylandt in segregating these people' (the half-castes) who in accordance with the law became 'whites in the eyes of the law and have a vote' at the age of twenty-one; the conference approved Bleakley's recommendations. But the pastoralists wanted to retain those half-castes whom they were 'training'; they liked to start them young as part of their program of 'uplift'; and Thonemann mentioned with some pride the case of one of his own 'stock-boys' who 'has been trained from the beginning. When he was 5 or 6 years old, he could ride. . . .'

A committee set up to deal further with employment stated that until the government set the example at Kahlin Compound, it was 'impossible' to expect employers to improve living conditions! As for the licensing of employers, care should be exercised 'while not interfering with the efficient working of reputable stations'. Station managers should be trusted to issue licences, on behalf of the government, to their own white employees. Efforts by managers to 'uplift' their Aboriginal workers and 'generally improve their conditions' were 'more important than the question of monetary payments'. While boys should not be used for station work, 'they should be permitted to accompany their parents or natural guardians round the station, for by so doing they are fitting themselves for their future occupations'. The pastoral spokesmen could hardly have hoped for more. Bleakley's shocking and revolutionary suggestions about cash seemed to have been pushed into the vague future, with the blessing of some at least of the missionaries.

Nonetheless, the appointment of more protectors was recommended, their duties to include the inspection of labour and making of recommendations to the Chief Protector on wages and conditions. Abbott promised also to act on a suggestion by Jennison that protectors should be placed at key points on the route of coastal and pearling vessels—at Victoria River, at Bowen Straits (south of Croker Island), and at Cadell Straits, south of Elcho Island. Jennison described a situation along the coasts of forced recruitment without wages or reference to any protector. There had been a protector at Bowen Straits from 1911 till 1914 during the short period when there were full-time protectors, but apparently none since; the recommendation, then, was, like many others at this conference, for reforms long established in law, and sometimes provided for in administration, and long forgotten.

But the chaotic conditions along the coasts of Arnhem Land had been contributing to the other causes of tension as the last remaining tribal areas, especially in eastern Arnhem Land, were brought into the magnetic field of the cash economy. Further spectacular injustices were yet to embarrass the Commonwealth as never before, and raise again, for the last time on a large scale, the basic issues of the frontier. At the same time, there was a growing realisation that these issues were national in their importance and relevance; and this conference may be seen as a step in the direction of Commonwealth-States consultation on Aboriginal affairs. The issue of Commonwealth control had been raised; and this conference recommended that 'at the next Conference of Premiers with the Prime Minister they take into consideration the whole question of the proper co-ordination and adjustments with a view ultimately to Commonwealth control'.

Implicit in Bleakley's arguments for a minimum wage and a range of wages (though this seems not to have been recognised clearly by him) was the general question of the admission of the Aboriginal into Australian society as a consumer and producer, even if not as a friend and neighbour. Once a wage is fixed with increments for skill, pressures inevitably follow for equality in wages, partly because the trade unions will in time become anxious to avoid competition of their members with 'cheap labour'. In the long run, so long as the government does not cushion the employer against the operation of economic forces, the need to use the wage as an incentive becomes clearer, even to the most obtuse management. But at the conference of 1929, there was no questioning, except that implied by the Reverend Mr Jones, of the pastoralists' assumption that Aborigines and even part-Aborigines born on the station property would live out their lives there as dependants of the management—a beautiful arrangement not to be spoilt by sordid issues of money. The pastoralists, with their threat of leaving the stations if they must pay cash, were doing very much what their successors were to do thirty-five years later: threaten to expel the Aborigines from the stations if the Conciliation and Arbitration Commission introduced award wages. By implication, even in the view of the Court, the Aboriginal worker had not by 1965 attained the right to immediate wage equality: he must wait for a period before he received the award wage. He, and not the taxpayer or the employer, should be temporarily deprived of what he was admittedly entitled to, so that the industry could have time to adjust.

The immediate result of the 1929 conference was a further conference in Darwin in 1930, of the officials with the pastoralists, the North Australian Workers Union, and the missions. The pastoralists were not so secure, because the Bruce-Page government had gone; Scullin and Labor were in power. On the other hand, the great depression had begun. This Darwin conference did no more than interpret the recommendations of 1929. The pastoralists had managed to sidestep the threat of the cash wage; and now the whole country was feeling the effects of the world-wide depression. There was thus some excuse for the fact that the short-lived Scullin Labor government proved no more sensitive to the needs of the Aboriginal worker in a Commonwealth Territory than its predecessor. The excuse cannot fairly be made, however, by anyone who has looked at the history of labour administration in Papua and New Guinea before World War II; the political party in power made as little appreciable difference there as in the Northern Territory. Bleakley himself has attributed the sidestepping of his recommendations to 'political change';[19] but it seems that the pastoral interests had managed to have his report relegated to conferences, and to prevent it from

[19] *The Aborigines of Australia*, p. 243.

278 THE DESTRUCTION OF ABORIGINAL SOCIETY

becoming the basis of new legislation, before the change of government occurred.

When the Northern Territory was again united in 1931, it had just about all the restrictive legislation which operated in Queensland, but without Queensland's very great advantage of the fixed minimum wage for all Aborigines, to be reckoned and assessed in terms of cash. Cook seems to have been the prime mover for a fixed cash wage for half-castes in the pastoral industry, and especially for all Aborigines employed as drovers, for whom cash would be essential to support their families. The most important legislative gain, after reversals due to pastoral pressures and ministerial intervention, was made in 1933, when for the first time the Commonwealth assumed the power to prescribe Aboriginals' wages and conditions of employment by regulation.[20] That Cook's pressures formed a new factor in the situation may be illustrated in an oblique but interesting way. Under the 1918 Ordinance, it was an offence for an *employee* to obstruct entry on to a property of an officer acting for the Chief Protector—one would think, an obvious misprint; if it were not, a protector could enter only with the consent of management; if it were, the provision for inspection had long been something of a dead letter. But in 1933, 'employer' was substituted for 'employee'—after fifteen years.[21]

For Aborigines in the pastoral industry Cook was insisting on the responsibility of management to feed, clothe, and house employees and dependants—as the current situation shows, with limited success. But he did insist on the licence, and on agreements, as far as possible, in the town areas. In 1931, for instance, 261 employers were licensed; and there were individual agreements for 302 individual workers, mainly in Darwin itself. He had set the wage of £1 10s to £3 per week for Aboriginal drovers, and refused to authorise the employment of half-castes on this work. The Commonwealth legislation had always provided for an apprenticeship system under regulation; and it was Administration policy in North Australia, and after 1931 in the Territory as a whole, to develop a system of regulated cash wages for half-caste apprentices. The Ordinance of 1927 had given power to the Chief Protector to define as Aboriginal any half-caste, even if he had passed the age of twenty-one years, probably with the intention that he should be able to intervene on the employee's behalf. As we have already seen, the Pastoral Lessees Association's representative hoped that such workers would be uplifted by remaining

[20] Aboriginals Ordinance 1933, section 13.
[21] Ibid., section 5.

EXPERT ADVICE ON NORTHERN TERRITORY PROBLEMS 279

on the stations where they were born; long afterwards Dr Cook mentioned the difficulties he had met with on this matter; he found that his rates of pay were disallowed by a Labor Minister.[22]

Cook's attention to the half-castes and his effort to promote higher standards of living for them may have been a shrewd assessment of the possible at the time. But the Administration reports also indicate a concern with the numbers of persons of mixed race; and the general background of assumptions for the White Australia policy are quite obvious. Thus the 1932 report expresses concern because they constituted a third of the 'European' population; their standard of living must be 'elevated' to that of the whites. To this end, those of 'half-caste and less' were taken from mothers in the camps, placed in institutions, and educated in accordance with the 'State' syllabus (of South Australia). The girls were then trained in domestic work to fit them for 'a higher station as the wives of higher grade half-caste males or whites'. It was the boys thus prepared who went to the pastoral industry as apprentices, and for whom Cook was trying to get suitable cash wages.[23]

After 1933 the Administration was operating in Queensland style, except for the vast majority of workers—i.e. the Aboriginal workers on the stations. Yet there was a real gain for Aboriginal drovers and for the small number of part-Aboriginal workers, in the careful regulation of employment in the Town Districts. In this respect, the Aboriginals Ordinance of 1933 embodied the practical result of the Bleakley Report and the subsequent negotiations. Within the limits mentioned, the protector could, as in Queensland, direct payment of part of the cash wage to himself, and careful arrangements were made for the payment of this into a trust account (section 6). This was the same ordinance as made it possible to fix a wage rate by regulation. It was also now possible to regulate the general conditions of employment, incredibly, for the first time, since up till then the law gave the protector the right to refuse a licence in a particular case, but set no standards.[24]

---

[22] Statement to the author, 9 January 1967.

[23] *C.P.P.*, 1929, vol. II—Chief Protector of Aboriginals, Report on the Administration of Central Australia and Northern Australia.

[24] See Aboriginals Ordinance 1918, section 67(g); and Aboriginals Ordinance 1933, section 13, which was the basis for Cook's efforts later. But this kind of legislation is like colonial labour legislation, where very great pressures can be brought to bear by employers' interests on the metropolitan government. It is rather like locking the gate and lowering the sliprails somewhere else. Thus Ordinance No. 5 (Aboriginals Odinance 1930) had already provided against any danger from an enthusiatic Chief Protector by transferring the power to make regulations from the Administrator to the Minister. Hence the complaint of Cook, mentioned above, about his frustration by a Labor Minister.

280   THE DESTRUCTION OF ABORIGINAL SOCIETY

It now became possible for the Minister to set the standards by regulation.

In 1933 Cook summed up the results. The dependants on pastoral stations had to be maintained by management, which also had to contribute to a medical fund for employees, and in cash; to the embattled pastoralists in the midst of the depression, this must have seemed the thin edge of the wedge, but the depression was probably also the reason for the 20 per cent reduction in that year of minimum cash wages for the Aboriginal drovers and workers in the Town Districts.[25] Over one hundred drovers were employed under contract. The Chief Protector was getting to grips with part of the employment situation; but with a staff of a couple of clerks, and the part-time services of protectors, he could not hope to make much headway beyond the Town Districts.

The 1933 Ordinance tightened the law against miscegenation outside marriage, maintaining the same heavy penalties which had already proved ineffective (section 11); and provided against inter-racial soliciting or procuring (section 12); drinking or possessing strong drink became an offence for Aborigines and half-castes (section 10). In 1936 the legislative effort at control went further. It had been lawful to employ Aborigines on licensed premises up to 1933: the law against this was further extended by the 1936 Ordinance (section 3), which established penalties for Aborigines and half-castes found on licensed premises, for those who supplied them with liquor, and for Aborigines found drinking. The Ordinance also provided (sections 3-5) that the Court must cancel the licence to employ Aborigines held by any person convicted of sexual intercourse with an Aboriginal outside marriage.

Thus the general trend, in the years following the Bleakley Report, was to establish control in the legislation; but this process went on without any increase of staff or the appointment of full-time field staff who might have made it effective. One potentially important provision in the 1936 Ordinance (section 2) enabled the Chief Protector to exempt a part-Aboriginal from the provisions of the Aboriginal Ordinances; this was in accordance with legislation in the States. It did not go all the way, however; since the declaration in the *Gazette* could be revoked.

Cook saw a potential threat to the development of a White Australia in the North if the increasing part-Aboriginal group became a dissident minority. From the reports, he appears to have been vigorous in the program of taking the part-Aboriginal children from the camps to the

[25] *C.P.P.*, 1932-4, vol. III, pp. 2110-14—Chief Protector of Aboriginals, Report on the Administration of the Northern Territory 1933 (Paper No. 203, pp. 6-10).

EXPERT ADVICE ON NORTHERN TERRITORY PROBLEMS 281

'homes'. In 1932 he described a housing scheme he had set up on the basis of subscriptions from the Trust Accounts, for half-castes in employment. In 1934 he stated that unmarried females not in employment had been moved into institutions, and that the half-caste illegitimate birth rate had fallen. This was very much in line with the Bleakley recommendations, as was his announced policy of sending those with a 'predominance of native blood' to missions on Bathurst Island and at Oenpelli. His reports also refer each year to the part-Aboriginal women who had been married.[26] After the 1936 Ordinance, he exempted thirteen, and partially exempted nineteen more, presumably of the seventy-six he had in supervised employment. Exemptions seem to have been under twenty in each of the report years until 1939-40, when sixty-two were freed from the legislation, almost certainly as a result of the wartime changes in the Territory.[27]

Thus, except for the provisions for exemption (which applied to part-Aborigines only), the main effect of the discussions which followed the Bleakley Report was in tightening protective legislation, perhaps with the main emphasis on prohibition of strong drink; and in measures designed to limit the increase of part-Aborigines. The main effort for social change was to bring about conditions in which the part-Aborigines who looked like being of at least half European descent would be absorbed among the whites; while those with darker skins were to be relegated to the Aboriginal group. That skin colour would be the determining factor in the fates of these people was certain enough, since few genealogies would have been taken by police and other protectors. Obviously such objectives raised long-term issues, especially in the north, which became clearer, in time, when it became evident that minimal provisions for health and protection would tend to halt depopulation of the full-blood communities. These developments in Territory policy and legislation made the situation superficially more like that in the States, where also the 1930s saw legislation reach the high tide of control and protection, with the other effect of restricting Aboriginal rights.

One of the effects of the great depression, all over Australia, seems to have been a more rigid containment in institutions, where conditions were probably worse than ever before, with enduring effects on Aboriginal attitudes. Elderly Aborigines in 1965, for instance, spoke bitterly of the

[26] The Reports of the Chief Protector for the 1930s appear in the Reports on the Administration of the Northern Territory, *Commonwealth Parliamentary Papers.*
[27] 1939-40 Report on the Administration of the Northern Territory. Abbott was the Administrator. The last of Cook's reports published as a separate section was that for 1937-38.

conditions on the New South Wales government Aboriginal stations in those years, when the reward for a day's work might be a poor ration. It is hard to estimate the effect of the hard times on Aborigines employed in the Territory; but I can find no evidence of any decrease in the Aboriginal labour force, though there was a decrease in the cash wage payable in the Town Districts.

A policy statement by the Department of the Interior of 1934 outlined the objectives of protection for the Territory, and included the interesting statement that State governments opposed Commonwealth control, on the grounds that Aborigines in the States were 'properly and humanely treated'.[28] Cook at that time had forty-six protectors, most of them police officers but including medical officers and some others. The attempt was made to maintain individual records—medical histories, offences, and employment. It would be unfair not to stress the very definite efforts made to promote health. All police stations had their first aid posts. Employers were bound to notify illness and take the sick worker to hospital, maintain first aid posts, and pay into the medical fund for Aborigines in proportion to the number employed. Efforts were being made to control malaria; and the final results of such efforts have probably done a very great deal to promote Aboriginal health. Here was something with which a determined professional man could get to grips.

In Town Districts, payment had been established as 3s in the hand and 2s to the trust account, with the employer providing food, clothing, tobacco, and shelter. Again there was genuine concern with what was tangible; here was a way of preventing the untutored from wasting their money or being deprived of it by others. When the worker's savings reached £20, a bank account was opened in his name, and there was the same kind of supervision of withdrawals as in Queensland.

Other protective provisions already described are referred to. There is the statement that 'in practice, no permission is given for a white or half-caste to marry an Aboriginal woman'. The matter of whether a half-caste girl could marry a white man was then 'receiving consideration', indicating the concern with basically the same kinds of question as were at the basis of the immigration policy.

The background of hopes and ideas affecting Territory policies is well exemplified in the Payne-Fletcher Report of 1937. Like the Bleakley Report it was the result of Queensland expertise, both W.L. Payne and J.W. Fletcher having made their careers in that State, the former as Chairman of the Land Administration Board, the latter as a pastoralist.

[28] Department of Interior file no. 40/1/626, referred by courtesy of Department of Territories.

EXPERT ADVICE ON NORTHERN TERRITORY PROBLEMS 283

They were to inquire into land tenures, conditions of settlement, investment, land use, transport, and other matters involved in economic development.[29] Their lack of interest in the Aboriginal role is indicated by their relegation of this 'problem' to a group of subsidiary matters; they do not see the Aboriginal worker as economically important, even in prospect.

By this time there were four different sets of conditions under which a pastoral lease might be held—the old South Australian, the Central Australian, the North Australian, and those established from 1931. The Commonwealth had gone so far as to offer tenures up till 1965, and consolidation of older leases where held by one owner, to find a way out of the tangle. The very big companies were mainly in the north: on the Barkly, the Victoria River, the Gulf, and round Darwin. The long-held belief that northern development depended on the pastoral industry, and the obsession with 'development' on the occasions when policies for the far north came up for review or renewal, make it easy to see why the pastoralists had managed to avoid paying cash wages to their Aboriginal station hands. Payne and Fletcher did not even concede the vital part played by cheap Aboriginal labour in establishing the industry. They pointed out that central Australia was mainly in the hands of small holders; the Aboriginal appears only in passing, as one of the minor assets.

Rents were low, the aboriginals assisted in the stock work and droving, and there was little other expense apart from living costs . . . In few parts of Australia could men have made a start as graziers with so little capital and without financial backing . . . progress . . . is mostly due to the resolution and perseverance of the men themselves.[30]

Dr Duguid has sketched the other side of this story;[31] and the drought of the late twenties had illustrated the consequences of stocking the few waterholes in marginal country.

An interesting part of the report praises the well-built yards and other improvements of Rosewood Station, and the effective personal supervision by its management; but it was J.H. Kelly, a decade and a half later, who indicated that the labour so supervised, and the efficient yard-builders, were Aboriginal.[32] Payne and Fletcher quote Cook to indicate

[29] *C.P.P.*, 1937-40, vol. III, no. 4, pp. 813-925—Report of the Board of Inquiry appointed to inquire into the Land and Land Industries of the Northern Territory of Australia: 10 October 1937.

[30] Ibid., p. 864 (Report, p. 40).

[31] *No Dying Race.*

[32] Report on the Beef Cattle Industry in Northern Australia (Bureau of Agricultural Economics, Canberra 1952).

that 3,500 were in employment by this time, with only 1,400 dependants maintained. (For some time, the white Australian basic wage had assumed three dependants at least per worker.) There were 2,500 on missions, and under 10,000 were guessed to be self-supporting in their 'native state'.

They quote the statement of the Chief Protector, probably expressing more humane purposes in economic terms for the Board of Inquiry, that the aim of government is to change the Aboriginal fringe-dwellers of the town 'from a social incubus to a civil unit of economic value'. (Although the town worker enjoyed a cash wage of 5s, less the compulsory saving, there was neither precise ration scale nor precise provision for his dependants.) In the Country Districts, off the pastoral runs, Cook hoped that government policy would change the Aboriginal 'from an un-productive nomad to a self-supporting peasant' (which in view of the history of small-scale farming in the Territory seemed a hopeless objective). He should be 'so reared and educated that he may be competent to engage in profitable occupations which do not bring him into conflict with the white population, but which enable him to provide for himself and his dependents, and increase the wealth of the Territory'.[33]

Even this modest hope for some kind of low caste status in economic apartheid received only conditional approval from the Board of Inquiry. It was wrong to use female labour in the Kahlin Compound when the same women could be placed in the domestic service of white women, 'who are expected to maintain the White Australia Policy', but 'are forced to carry out, unaided, all the heavy and enervating duties of household management. . . .'[34] As one of the purposes of the Compound was to house domestic servants, presumably they thought that unpaid domestic labour of this kind would be fitting. In the meantime the men should be employed to plant trees and to clean the streets in Darwin; the unionists of Darwin who had begun to agitate against cheap labour could not object, they said, as this was not 'the class of work on which award wage men could be employed'.

Modest as the changes after the Bleakley Report had been, they led this Board of Inquiry to the conclusion that the government was develop-ing a tendency to make 'all industries revolve round the Aboriginal question'. It was true enough that from the first settlement every attempt at development had raised questions of Aboriginal rights (and frequently of life itself); that every 'affair' was at least in its implications an Aboriginal affair. But the immediate cause for complaint was the Aboriginals

[33] C.P.P., 1937-40, vol. III, p. 894 (Report, p. 70).
[34] Ibid.

EXPERT ADVICE ON NORTHERN TERRITORY PROBLEMS 285

Ordinance, gazetted in April 1937, which prevented unauthorised vessels entering into territorial waters of an Aboriginal reserve, the penalty being seizure of the vessel. The reasons for this were the troubles in Arnhem Land referred to below.

Indeed it would seem [stated the Board] that if anything occurs to the administration calculated to help the aboriginals, it is proclaimed immediately without regard to its effects on industries ... of value to the Territory. This occurred in connexion with the Ordinance prohibiting the Darwin pearling fleet from watering at any place in Arnhem Land ... There have been cases also where the tenures of lands actually in occupation have been cancelled in order that the lands might be added to an aboriginal reserve.[35]

They also criticised the power of the Chief Protector to prevent a police officer, in cases where only Aborigines were concerned, from making arrests until he had decided whether the alleged offence was a 'tribal' matter. They thought that the police should arrest in the first instance; that otherwise the law would be brought into contempt. The efforts made by Cook within the modest limits set by policy had obviously led to much of this oblique criticism. To the settlers the 'good' officer in this kind of situation was the man who knew when to shut his eyes—the 'experienced practical man' whom colonial settlers have so often tended to praise for what he does not see and what he fails to do.

Work on the pastoral stations, it seemed, offered the greatest opportunities for Aboriginal fulfilment. They saw 'some really skilful workers, delighting in their work and the conditions under which they lived. Inquiry always showed that these individuals had been trained on the stations, and that they had not been subjected to other influences'. They 'seemed well nourished and contented'—a common defence of 'colonial' labour conditions, which puts forward the physical condition of the worker as justification for the system, without mentioning the condition of the dependants or the social effects—an argument based on alleged sound animal husbandry. More of this practical effort by experienced employers was needed.

We recommend that a greater effort be made to apply practical principles to the ethical ideals of the aboriginal service and that industries be not unnecessarily interfered with. To this end we suggest that an Aboriginal Board, composed of local men, experienced in the various industries, be appointed to guide the activities of aboriginal labour in the Territory, to advise on the issue of Ordinances, to supervise the methods of training, and generally to see that the lives of these people are lived in a useful and happy manner with benefit to themselves, and without detriment to the well being of the community.[36]

[35] Ibid.　　　[36] Ibid., p. 895 (Report, p. 71).

286 THE DESTRUCTION OF ABORIGINAL SOCIETY

The Report makes it very clear that when they write of the 'community' Payne and Fletcher mean the community of White Australia in general and its extension into the north in particular; feelingly they proclaim the

inviolability of the national policy of a White Australia. This is something which the Australian people regard as sacrosanct ... all sections of the people are united in an ardent desire to maintain racial purity. Cheap or coloured labour cannot be allowed to become permanently established in Australia.

Yet there was their plan to legislate for and control cheap Aboriginal labour. To Payne and Fletcher this was quite compatible with the goal of White Australia, so long as they assumed that the Aboriginal was a disappearing 'problem' of whom the best use might in the interim be made. History showed that Aborigines 'died out'. As for the part-Aborigines, 1937 was the year in which the first conference of States and Commonwealth saw their future as absorption in the 'white' population; and in this sense 'assimilation' seemed to offer the final solution of the 'problem'. Aborigines would continue to 'die out': the problem then was to limit half-caste births, turn those with 'dark blood' back to Aboriginal society to share its fate, and absorb those with 'lighter blood' into White Australia.

The aims of the Aboriginal labour policy recommended by Payne and Fletcher had nothing to do with Aboriginal welfare or rights. What was needed was a 'virile' white community. Yet the census returns showed that adult white females were less than 30 per cent of adult males. The problem, then, was to attract white women to the Territory, by providing amenities and comforts 'enjoyed by all white people in all tropical countries except North Australia'. What they had in mind, of course, was the situation of the whites in the colonial tropics. This led them to the extraordinary conclusion that it was necessary to bring in Chinese gardeners and other Asian servants to safeguard the health and leisure of white Australian women; such measures 'would, paradoxical as it may seem, help to strengthen the White Australia policy by guarding the health of females on whom the success of that policy depends'.[37] One feature of this ponderous nonsense was the underlying assumption that the Aboriginal would not even make an effective servant—this at a time when most of the pastoral homesteads were run with their labour. Bleakley had made the point that the Aboriginal woman was the mainstay of the Territory.

This underlying assumption, by 'practical' men, that the Aboriginal

[37] Ibid., p. 896 (Report, p. 72).

EXPERT ADVICE ON NORTHERN TERRITORY PROBLEMS 287

was less than an effective human being, had rationalised the frontier practices from the days of first settlement. What I have outlined in the development of policy and administration, from 1911, had amounted to no great change; though change was in the wind since the Bleakley Report. All this formed the background for more spectacular events, which seem to have made a more direct appeal to the consciences of thinking persons, mainly in the capital cities, with nothing to lose.

16

REACTIONS TO SPECTACULAR INJUSTICE

Just after Bleakley's report was ordered to be printed, another paper was presented to the Commonwealth Parliament; this was ordered to 'lie on the Table' and was never printed. It was the report of a Board of Inquiry into killing of Aborigines in Central Australia 'by police parties and others' and was part of a chain of events which brought to a close the overt destruction of Aboriginal society by violence in frontier regions.[1] What was involved and of long custom was not merely the killing of Aborigines by settlers, but killing by police, an 'administrative method' known to their superiors but condoned. Apart from its inhumanity, it was a practice which made farcical the professions of concern about illegal acts by Aborigines and about Aboriginal respect for law.

What was new about the events leading to this inquiry was the public outcry. On 8 November 1928 the *Sydney Morning Herald* published the news that police from Alice Springs had killed eight Aborigines alleged to have been implicated in the murder of a white 'dogger' named Brooks. On the following day the figure had grown to seventeen. Constable Murray, who was charged, had stated that he shot to kill because he did not know what to do with the wounded out from 'civilisation'. A missionary named McGregor, who had been in Alice Springs, stated that the original killing had resulted from the starvation of Aborigines in drought country, and that not only police conduct should be investigated but also the system of land settlement which made

[1] *V. & P.* (H. of R.), 1929, No. 2—Central Australia: Finding and Evidence of Board of Inquiry concerning the killing of natives in Central Australia by police parties and others: Paper presented and Ordered to lie on the Table, 7 February 1929.

REACTIONS TO SPECTACULAR INJUSTICE 289

such happenings inevitable. The Department of Home and Territories promised an inquiry to ascertain why the Aborigines were hostile. An Aboriginal witness stated that Brooks had been killed for his food supplies.[2]

The Association for the Protection of Native Races asked the Prime Minister, S.M. Bruce, for an inquiry by tribunal. (At this stage two of the Aboriginal survivors were being tried for the killing of Brooks.) This was supported by the Presbyterian Assembly, the Aborigines Inland Mission, the Australian Board of Missions, and other bodies. Bruce, after consultation with Abbott, the Minister for Home Affairs, announced his decision to appoint an independent board. It comprised a magistrate from Cairns (who was to preside), the Government Resident of Central Australia, and a police inspector from South Australia.[3] The A.P.N.R. protested against the 'official' constitution of the Board, and asked for representation, which Bruce, who had had experience of handling matters of this kind arising in New Guinea, refused.[4]

The inquiry did not open until January 1929 (by when there would have been little hope of first-hand Aboriginal evidence), and the report was completed by the end of that month. The trend of settlers' evidence was that the Aborigines were not starving or ill treated. A missionary gave evidence to the same effect, even criticising other missionaries who were too familiar with the Aborigines—a comment which brought a letter of appreciation from an 'outback settler' in Western Australia, where the embattled settlers had no redress because of the ill-advised system there. A woman living on a station out from Alice Springs gave evidence that it would be dangerous if news got about that a policeman could no longer shoot an Aboriginal.[5] The correspondence columns of the 'southern' press carried replies critical of settler attitudes to Aboriginal rights. The Board's report criticised missionaries, stressed the need for more police, stated that there was no evidence of starvation, and admitted that thirty-one Aborigines had been shot—justifiably, in self-defence. The police had given no provocation.[6]

A meeting of the A.P.N.R. was so critical of the whole procedure that Abbott stated its language made more difficult the task he faced of getting more 'public support' for Aborigines. This meeting had criticised the composition of the Board as not suitable for independent inquiry;

[2] *S.M.H.*, 12 and 13 November 1968.
[3] *S.M.H.*, 14-16, 23-4, 27-8 November and 4 December 1928.
[4] *S.M.H.*, 5 and 6 December 1928.
[5] *S.M.H.*, 2, 3, 9, and 12 January 1929.
[6] *S.M.H.*, 31 January 1929.

the Prime Minister's Department for refusing to provide legal aid for the Aborigines concerned; the lack of evidence to establish that those killed were the killers of Brooks; the facts that the shootings occurred not at one time, but on four different occasions, and that the Aboriginal tracker, a key witness, had 'gone bush' and was not available.[7] A meeting of the Australian Board of Missions passed similar resolutions, stated that the evidence should be published, and claimed that the report was biased against the missions and had failed to comment on provocation by the settlers.[8]

In February, Abbott promised to summon to a conference in Melbourne representatives of the missions working in North and Central Australia. He wanted to deal especially with a charge made at the inquiry that missionaries were preaching unadvisedly the doctrine of equality; that some, including women missionaries, were causing 'trouble'. But before that conference was held, the Bleakley Report had been published. As we have seen, Abbott devoted the conference to discussion of the Bleakley Report, after only a passing reference to the atrocity. Had there been no protests, it is doubtful whether a conference on this report would have been held.

This was no isolated case of violence; nor, it seems, were all missionaries better than other men on this score. When in 1927 three Aborigines were tried for attacking Methodist missionaries on Crocodile Island, their claim was that they had been whipped by one of them.[9] As in the Pacific missions, paternalism could easily go with the whipping of people regarded as children, for the good of their souls or as a desperate measure to protect mission Aborigines from intruders. Aborigines had little recourse, except to violence, for protest.

TUCKIAR AND THE KING

After 1930 the main area of publicised violence was Arnhem Land, where tensions within Aboriginal society appear to have been increased by the greater activities of the missions, and of pearling and trepanging expeditions from Darwin, Thursday Island, and the Japanese Trust Territory, with Japanese divers and crews operating even for Territory enterprises. They also operated off Port Keats, where three Japanese fishermen were killed in 1932 by a group of Aborigines led by the

[7] *S.M.H.*, 7, 8, and 29 March 1929.
[8] *S.M.H.*, 9 April 1929.
[9] *Argus* (Melbourne), 10 June 1927.

REACTIONS TO SPECTACULAR INJUSTICE 291

well-known Nemarluk. But the problems of justice which led to most publicity and forced the Commonwealth government to reappraise the whole question began with the slaying of five Japanese crew members at Caledon Bay, in 1933. Such attacks were nothing new, but the social climate was. A decade before, Aborigines at Cape Hawke, near the Elcho Island mission, had attacked while the Japanese were diving, and captured the guns and boats; this was announced in the Melbourne press, with a laconic statement that a punitive expedition of twelve who 'knew the country well' had set out to deal with the attackers, though these had apparently killed nobody.[10]

In August 1933 a Constable McColl was speared and killed at Woodah Island. The press announced that police were standing by in Darwin for a punitive expedition; that officials feared a 'general massacre' of the whites unless such action were taken.[11] The announcement of this intention, with the government stating the need for a 'display of force', brought an outcry beyond any previous experience. The missionary bodies and others held protest meetings. There was a new concern with international opinion. Finally the Commonwealth accepted the offer of the Church Missionary Society, which sent two members to parley with the alleged killer. The party, financed by public donations and even a government grant of £150, talked to Tuckiar, the Aboriginal alleged to have killed McColl, promised a fair trial, and brought him and the others in to Darwin. From press accounts of their conduct in Darwin, it appears that Tuckiar and his fellows had interpreted the mission approach as a peace-making expedition: they had come in to Darwin to show their goodwill, and the chaining and locking up in cells naturally terrified them and made them feel betrayed.[12]

Of the five brought in, three were tried for the murder of the Japanese and convicted in August 1934.[13] As the offence was a capital one, they were tried by jury. The Commonwealth government had been reconsidering the question of cross-cultural justice, partly, it seems, because of representations by the A.P.N.R., and a year earlier had abolished the use of juries except for capital offences.[14] As Elkin pointed out over a decade later, the trial of a native person by a jury of settlers was almost

[10] Ibid., 6 March 1923.
[11] Ibid., 17 August; and *Herald* (Melbourne) 1 September 1933.
[12] *Herald* (Melbourne), 11 April 1934.
[13] *Argus* (Melbourne), 2 August 1934.
[14] Criminal Procedure Ordinance 1933.

THE DESTRUCTION OF ABORIGINAL SOCIETY

certain to lead to conviction where a white person had been killed.[15] Just about the time of this trial an amendment to the law enabled a court of the Northern Territory to take into account the cultural background of an Aboriginal offender in deciding the sentence—also the result of public agitation.[16]

By this time, those in the distant capitals who knew something of these matters were not the only ones ready to agitate. An interesting indication that concern for white supremacy did not necessarily rule out concern for justice had come from Darwin, when in April 1933 a panel of sixty jurors petitioned the Supreme Court there that Aborigines, where serious offences were 'of a purely tribal nature', were 'merely meting out justice to delinquents according to their . . . customs', and should therefore be tried in accordance with those customs.[17] Hasluck and Elkin have both remarked on the tendency of white juries to bring in verdicts of not guilty for tribal killings of Aborigines. Such a way of avoiding what appeared injustice (so long as the death of a white man was not involved) was no longer necessary. Whether the Japanese victims fell into this category was no longer relevant.

Mr Justice Wells sentenced the three who had been found guilty to twenty years gaol; and some of his reported comments added to the indignation of bodies concerned with justice to Aborigines. He was reported to have discounted the plea that interference with their women was a provocation and to have indicated his view that the kindest way to treat black criminals was to hang them. Yet he had refrained from the death sentence, remarking, in respect of the twenty years, that anything less would enable them to learn the tricks of hardened criminals and to introduce these to their tribes.[18] The charges in these cases did not involve killing of a white man.

His Honour's statements on this occasion seemed to defy the critics from 'down south' and to indicate either strong prejudice or intolerance of change, even when embodied in law. But the issue was brought to a head when Tuckiar was tried, and sentenced to death by the same judge,

---

[15] See A.P. Elkin, 'Aboriginal Evidence and Justice in North Australia', *Oceania*, March 1947. This penetrating discussion of the problem of justice for tribal Aborigines is still as relevant as it was in 1947.

[16] Ordinance to Amend the Criminal Law Consolidation Act (1876) South Australia (already amended, as Elkin points out in 'Aboriginal Evidence and Justice', by the North Australia Crimes Ordinance 1928).

[17] *Daily Telegraph* (Sydney), 13 April 1933—quoted in Elkin 'Aboriginal Evidence and Justice', p. 199.

[18] *Herald* (Melbourne), 17 May 1934; *Argus* (Melbourne) 12 July and 2 August 1934.

REACTIONS TO SPECTACULAR INJUSTICE 293

also in August 1934. The delay in the trials was partly at least due to the failure to catch the necessary witnesses to establish a case against Tuckiar. Significantly, the Church Missionary Society, whose missionaries had brought in Tuckiar, was being criticised in July 1934 for refusing to assist in the search for witnesses. The whole system was obviously in question among men of conscience.[19]

Without such witnesses, and in view of Tuckiar's misunderstanding of the mission expedition and the complicated trial procedures, the obvious injustice of proceedings which had been maintained for so long was becoming clear, partly because of the greater understanding of the cultural differences involved, partly through a growing and more genuine concern than at any time since the end of British colonial administration. The evidence used included two conflicting statements which Tuckiar was alleged to have made to two Aboriginal witnesses. These spoke to the court interpreter, who translated into Aboriginal pidgin—a language which in the absence of a full-time field service, and of any real interest in management of Aboriginal employees, had reached nothing like the precision of Melanesian pidgin, the *lingua franca* in Melanesian society. The stories could be regarded either as conflicting or complementary. The second of them, repeated through the interpreter, was a claim that Tuckiar had surprised McColl with one of his wives: the court appeared more concerned to discredit this than to establish the truth. Tuckiar's own counsel co-operated, stating that Tuckiar had withdrawn the story with its implications against McColl's reputation.

As Elkin stated later, both stories could have been true.

The important question is: why did he deny the second story? No doubt because he was by then indeed 'too much worried': 600 miles from his country; kept for weeks in gaol at Darwin; told that one of his statements was a lie; and that he should say which one, and why. And what hint did the interpreter give him? Perhaps that his second story had lost him sympathy. At any rate, his only aid would be to say the 'right thing'—that is, what was wanted, and so obtain that fair treatment which the Peace Mission had assured him, and get free.[20]

The death sentence, coming so soon after the sentencing of the killers of Japanese to imprisonment, could only have been determined in relation to the fact that McColl was a white man. In fact, press comments were that at first Tuckiar did not understand the sentence; that when he did, he understood that Aborigines could not kill white men.[21] Mr Justice

[19] See *Argus* (Melbourne), 12 July 1934.
[20] Elkin, 'Aboriginal Evidence and Justice', p. 182.
[21] *Herald* (Melbourne), 7 and 11 August 1934.

THE DESTRUCTION OF ABORIGINAL SOCIETY

Wells took the opportunity to criticise government weakness; and the difference in the sentences clearly showed his unwillingness to take cultural background into account in Tuckiar's case, especially as in the other cases he had indicated the possibility of reducing the sentences when the Caledon Bay people were brought under control.

Protests against both procedure and verdict had a background of discussions between the A.P.N.R., the Department of Home Affairs, and the Lieutenant Governor of Papua. The difference from the situation in Papua and the Mandated Territory was that, while in matters of justice the Northern Territory presented a 'colonial' situation (as it still does where Aboriginal custom remains), it lacked the machinery and provision for colonial justice in native regulations and in special courts for native affairs in which procedure could be simplified, which could be held in the area of the alleged crime, and in which field officers with training or knowledge of custom could elucidate the cultural issues involved. In 1931 Blakeley, Minister for Home Affairs, had told the A.P.N.R. that he was thinking in terms of such courts;[22] and Parkhill, his successor, now consulted with J.H.P. Murray.

Elkin was in the centre of the agitation. Nobody knows more of the issues then involved; and as he is himself in the process of writing the history of the discussions of government, other voluntary bodies, and missions at this time, it would be foolish to attempt here to elaborate on the details. He says that Murray advised Parkhill in 1932 that as British law must prevail in the end, he would 'view with alarm' any attempt to abrogate it. This advice was consistent with Murray's comments on the report by John Ainsworth eight years earlier, which had recommended recognition of the luluais' courts in the Mandated Territory.[23] But, Murray advised, native regulations made it possible to take custom into account, both for the defence and in the sentence.[24]

Before the Tuckiar trial the issues had also been discussed in the press. Missionary and other bodies in 1932 and 1933, recalls Elkin,

made representations to the Commonwealth Government on this subject as well as on the need for ... a general positive policy for the Aborigines ... Thus, the National Missionary Council arranged in December, 1933, a conference of a few men with special knowledge and experience

which recommended that in Aboriginal cases 'full justice' required 'full

---

[22] Elkin, 'Aboriginal Evidence and Justice', p. 199.
[23] See C.D. Rowley *The Australians in German New Guinea*, pp. 227-8.
[24] Elkin, 'Aboriginal Evidence and Justice', p. 204, quoting letter form Murray to Parkhill, 29 June 1932.

REACTIONS TO SPECTACULAR INJUSTICE

consideration . . . [of] tribal traditions and customs', with field officers to interpret these and explain the requirements of British law to Aborigines; and that cases should be tried in the areas where offences occurred.[25] Such moves were developing a concept of frontier situations long ignored within Australia—that here was a colonial situation, that justice in a bi-cultural situation demanded the methods of colonial administration, and that the application of British law, in the philosophy of white Australian settlement of the frontier regions, involved profound injustice to the tribal remnants remaining. The fate of these people was to be institutions and poor-law type relief; their treatment, to be as 'units of labour' without the protection of colonial labour legislation or native regulations.

The agitation was by no means limited to Sydney, though it was mainly from the capital cities. Protests came from academic, mission, and humanitarian circles in both Melbourne and Adelaide; there were protests in Perth, but mainly about conditions north of Carnarvon. The list set out above of the bodies represented at the earlier conference called by Abbott to consider the Bleakley Report gives some idea of the range of interests involved. But the intervening years had seen a wider interest among scholars in the Universities of Melbourne and Adelaide. Both Donald Thomson from Melbourne and T.G.H. Strehlow of Adelaide were to play noted parts in the field in the Territory, for which support from government came largely as the result of the events surrounding the Tuckiar case.

Wells's refusal to take cultural factors into account where the death of a white man was involved produced such a spate of protest and pressures on the Commonwealth government that an appeal was arranged.

A report of a meeting held in the old King's Hall, Sydney [said Elkin much later] was published next day in England. Emphasis was placed on my own speech regarding the unsatisfactory nature of court proceedings in Aboriginal cases. Authorities in England inquired through our High Commissioner there whether the position was as reported. He rang the Prime Minister, who rang me. He was given the facts.[26]

The meeting, attended by representatives from many organisations, was held on 6 August 1934. It was a reaction not only to the Tuckiar case but to at least four others which in 1934 had posed the questions of cross-cultural justice and involved a series of death sentences. The meeting

---

[25] Elkin, 'Aboriginal Evidence and Justice', p. 200.
[26] 'The Background of Present Day Aboriginal Policies', p. 11; also A.P. Elkin, 'Aboriginal Policy 1930–1950: Some personal associations', *Quadrant* vol. I, no. 4, Spring 1957, pp. 29-30.

demanded the release of the prisoners and the removal of the judge. Subsequently the A.P.N.R. collected money for an appeal by Tuckiar. It appears, however, that this appeal was arranged by the Commonwealth.

In November 1934 the appeal on behalf of Tuckiar was upheld by the High Court of Australia and the conviction quashed, with the appellant to be discharged. The reasons against either reducing the sentence or a second trial were stated by the High Court in terms which condemned completely the procedures and directions of Mr Justice Wells. The whole Court held that one of Wells's comments on the 'failure' of Tuckiar to give evidence was in itself enough to invalidate the whole proceedings and that his charge to the jury 'denied the substance of fair trial to the accused'.[27] In addition, Gavin Duffy, C.J., and Evatt and McTiernan JJ. ruled that the defendant's counsel had failed to press fairly for acquittal or manslaughter.

The whole court also agreed that Tuckiar's counsel had acted improperly when he stated in court that Tuckiar had admitted to him that one of the reported statements attributed to him by witnesses was true and that therefore the story of McColl's adultery with Tuckiar's wife was false.[28]

The reasons offered by the Chief Justice for the majority judgment form a condemnation of the 'kangaroo court' methods by which white supremacy had been upheld, and of the use of the court system to pervert justice, from the days of the first frontiers. It was pointed out that no defence witnesses had been called. The jury had even asked the judge what they should do if they felt there was not enough evidence; and Wells in reply had suggested that a 'not guilty' verdict would be a slander on McColl. The judge had practically directed the verdict of guilty.[29]

Defence counsel's extraordinary statement in court, that Tuckiar had, by admitting one story, by implication admitted that the one accusing McColl of sexual intercourse with Tuckiar's wife was a lie, had shown that counsel shared the judge's concern for white supremacy: 'I think this fact', he had stated, 'clears Constable McColl'.[30] Equally irrelevant to the legal matters to be settled was Mr Justice Wells's admission of evidence about McColl's good character.

[27] (1935), 52 C.L.R. (High Court), p. 335.
[28] Ibid., p. 336.
[29] Ibid., p. 342.
[30] Ibid., p. 344.

REACTIONS TO SPECTACULAR INJUSTICE 297

Mr Justice Starke, in a separate judgment equally condemnatory of the trial judge, pointed out that it had been quite wrong for Wells to direct that the jury should accept one of the two stories and reject the other (which was the one discreditable to McColl). Wells had also erred when he told the jury that, if they accepted the story he indicated they should accept, the verdict was necessarily murder; Starke J. stated that a not guilty or manslaughter verdict was equally open. He quoted the hearsay story, told by the Aboriginal witness Parriner, which was the one less discreditable to McColl. This was in the interpreter's pidgin, and one does not have to be a lawyer to see that it could have offered grounds for a self-defence plea. Finally, both judgments agreed that there could be no further trial. Wells had made this point himself. The High Court, with a nice irony here (only) agreed with the learned judge.

But neither Tuckiar nor his people were to know that there was a great set of institutions for justice somewhere behind the hard front of settler democracy. Wells and the defence counsel took white supremacy for granted. There should be no slur on the good name of a good police-man, who had died on duty. Tuckiar, where the leaders of the community thought in this way, had little chance, because the executive simply did not control the situation sufficiently to ensure that he resumed the 'rights' and the life which the High Court had legally defended for him. He was to be sent home of course; and may have had the thrill of expectation and setting out. But he never reached his home, and there have been stories of foul play ever since. That he was murdered is highly probable.

The action of the missionaries in bringing Tuckiar and his companions to trial, probably with the help of a trepanger named Grey, whom the Aborigines trusted, would hardly win confidence at Caledon Bay. There was, of course, a whole range of competence and understanding among missionaries in any large organisation. On a matter such as this there was no clear line of division between missionary workers and others; and the bringing in of Tuckiar and the others cannot necessarily be taken as indicating that the Arnhem Land Aborigines were looking to the missions for their salvation. The historical and social forces operating in Arnhem Land were very complex indeed, and may serve to remind us that no overall survey of culture clash in Australia can purport to do more than to suggest the main lines of a theme on which there are almost infinite variations within each local or regional situation.[31]

[31] For the Arnhem Land situation as it was up to 1947, see Ronald M. Berndt and Catherine H. Berndt, *Arnhem Land: Its History and its People.*

THE MOSELEY REPORT

In the meantime, the response to events in the Territory were having their impact in Western Australia, strengthening the case of those who wanted a 'positive policy' and an act of faith in the common humanity of the Aboriginal. Biskup has pointed out that S.D. Porteus, a psychologist from the University of Hawaii and a pioneer of the 'culture free test' of intelligence, worked in the Kimberley, Central Australia, and at Moore River in 1929.[32] In the United States at this time the new science of psychology had become involved partly in the effort to measure racial differences in intelligence.

As is not uncommon in the unveiling of truth, an axiom from which arose the attempt to compare intelligence of different 'races' became more and more subject to question as the means of measuring the assumed differences were more critically regarded; the effort to isolate 'intelligence' from cultural factors increased the doubt. The process was to culminate in the famous UNESCO declaration that racial differences have no known relation to differences in intellectual capacity.

It is interesting to read now, with all this hindsight, a review by Elkin in 1932 of Porteus's *Psychology of a Primitive People*.[33] It is interesting because it is a good example of how the process worked. Porteus had, on what would seem now very slight evidence, attributed to the Aborigines of the central deserts intelligence superior to that of Aborigines of the north. But Elkin had first hand knowledge of both the Kimberley peoples and the Central Australians.

The ordinary sociological investigator who has spent months discussing the most intricate matters of native law and belief, and indeed of civilized life, too, with natives in the Kimberleys and other parts of Western Australia, of Central and South Australia, certainly fails to detect the difference in intelligence.

Elkin suggested that, especially in view of the small numbers 'tested', the differences might well have been explained by differences in acculturation and experience and that more suitable tests might have reversed the findings. And this of course had implications for the main thesis that Aborigines could not adapt to a 'civilised environment', which was one of Porteus's conclusions. Elkin suggested that there are many different kinds of civilisation. As a scientist, he paid due respect to opinion of the current experts that 'there are racial differences and inequalities', but he

---

[32] Biskup, Native Administration and Welfare, pp. 275 *et seq.*
[33] 'The Social Life and Intelligence of the Australian Aborigine: A Review of S.D. Porteus's "Psychology of a Primitive People",' *Oceania*, vol. III, no. 1, September 1932.

REACTIONS TO SPECTACULAR INJUSTICE

wrote of cases he had known of 'individuals who have shown great power of abstract reasoning'. He also interpreted Porteus's findings as evidence that Aborigines could become effective in western civilisation. 'What they lack in speed they make up for in quiet and concerted deliberation . . . Their deficiency, according to the tests, in rote memory is made up for by their quite extraordinary memory for . . . all matters concerned with their environment'.[34] His cautious conclusion was that attempts at civilisation might not be successful, but were not 'necessarily foredoomed to complete failure'.

Such speculation was to demolish the reasoning on which Aboriginal policies, assuming a 'lower' intelligence and ability in the coloured races, were based. But policies are also framed by politics: and a lot had happened since the days when the early British administrations could envisage the Aboriginal passing into the society of the lower orders. Any Aboriginal policy had to be adapted to the automatic assumption of Aboriginal ineptitude, which had now become deeply ingrained into popular culture. The protests of the 1930s arose from considerations to which questions of comparative ability are only marginally relevant, if at all— that all men need justice and that human equality is an equality of rights, not of achievement. The consideration of achievement by Aborigines, as indicating unfitness for equality, illustrated the self-fulfilling prophecy. A basic reason for low achievement was that low expectation by whites was a major factor limiting opportunity—as in the matter of cash wages, which, it was assumed, would merely be wasted on gambling and strong drink. There was an implication of this in Elkin's remark on Porteus's work, that high intelligence scores in areas of long contact could reflect better opportunities: that the Aborigines in such areas 'may have learned to adapt themselves better to our more hurried way of doing things'.[35]

In October 1932 an Australian Aborigines' Amelioration Association was established in Perth. A series of articles by Mrs M.M. Bennett in the *West Australian* was attacking the administration of Aboriginal affairs and the pastoralists' attitudes. Her survey of the situation, discussed in London by the British Empire League in 1933, was publicised in England and Australia. In 1932 R. Piddington, a research worker sponsored by the Australian National Research Council, was so critical of the conditions on pastoral stations in the Kimberleys that the Council was advised that future workers would be required to give an undertaking not to criticise the Aborigines Department or its administration.[36] In February 1934,

[34] Ibid., pp. 109, 113. [35] Ibid., p. 112.
[36] Biskup, Native Administration and Welfare, p. 279.

300   THE DESTRUCTION OF ABORIGINAL SOCIETY

following a vote in Parliament, R.D. Moseley, a police magistrate, was
appointed by Cabinet, with the status of a Royal Commission, to inquire
into and report on the 'social and economic conditions of Aboriginals
and persons of Aboriginal origin'; the relevant legislation; the administration of the Department; and the recent allegations of ill-treatment.[37]

Much of this report covers aspects of the situation in the south-western
region, and does not concern us in this context. Moseley had been supplied
with a set of the critical press cuttings dating back to July 1930; some, he
said, were too old to be investigated. One of the objects of criticism had
been the conditions under which leper patients had been taken by lugger
from Broome to the Commonwealth leprosarium in Darwin, following
Cook's earlier recommendations for their isolation. There is a guarded
admission of 'unfortunate' circumstances on one such voyage. As for
allegations of 'slavery', so much depended on the point of view; and
Moseley's was obviously sympathetic to the employer. He did make the
point that though no wages were paid north of the Pilbara, Aborigines
on the stations were free to move at will (which from other evidence
seems doubtful in many cases). He regretted that Western Australians
should have promoted discussions in London, when greater good might
have come from bringing matters to the attention of the local authorities.

When he said that he saw no cases of cruelty, he wrote the truth as he
saw that also; but then he thought, from what he was told and saw, that
chaining by the neck was a necessity which meant no hardship and that
it was the most humane method of restraint. He could even quote a
missionary who agreed with this view. Perhaps the critics were justified
in associating chaining and work without pay with slavery; but slavery
had a legal definition. Several decades before, a Sydney court, in the
Daphne case, had acquitted the master of a vessel, arrested by the captain
of a British warship, for illegally seizing South Sea Islanders and offering
them as indentured labour at the best market in Fiji.[38] A weakness of
emotional attacks, made far from the facts, is that attacks on government
administration require precision and legal hitting power. Another is that
persons making their livings where the whole environment is obsolete by
the standards of industrial society will generally defend the standards of
right and wrong they consider necessary for success. Better labour
conditions, one must admit (in the good company of the I.L.O.) flow

[37] *W.A. V. & P.*, 1935, vol. I—Report of the Royal Commissioner appointed to Investigate,
Report, and Advise upon matters in relation to the condition and treatment of Aborigines,
Paper no. 2, p. 23.
[38] See Captain George Palmer, *Kidnapping in the South Seas*, Appendix B.

mainly from more effective application of technology than from the sources of human kindness. The chaining of prisoners, and the reasons for it, reflect basically the conflict for limited resources between the new settler community which was transforming the environment and the long established one which had developed incredible skills in *adapting* to the old and in conserving what it offered of flora and fauna, without change. The degree to which the Aboriginal remained adapted to a disappearing economic base rendered him to that extent useless to the settler, as well as helpless. Moseley's report took the needs of his own society as imperative and as setting standards for logical conduct.

Yet without inquiring into its causes, he was shocked at the health situation among those in contact, especially in the region north of the 25th parallel. Those who managed pastoral properties, he said, did all they could; but the Aborigines died. There was no hospital accommodation for Aborigines at Wyndham, Broome, Roebourne, or Onslow, where there should be; there should also be a clinic on the government pastoral property at Moola Bulla. Derby was the assembly point for lepers brought in (on the chain) to be sent to Darwin. He recommended that the Sunday Island Mission be taken over for a leprosarium.

Of 10,000 Aborigines in the Kimberleys known to the Department, no fewer than 2,000 were in employment; it is probable that the health situation had some relation therefore to the conditions of employment. What was happening here was repeating the oft-experienced and drastic population decline. Yet he describes, and with authenticity, the adjustment of the two interests on the cattle station: the men and some women working; the station assumed at least to support the dependants; and the walkabout in the wet season. The Aboriginal, he said, is free because he can go elsewhere if he wishes (which again depended on the employer). He was not paid, even the equivalent of a minimum wage expressed in cash. Clothes and dwellings were suitable to Aboriginal needs. The situation seems to have been comparable with that which Bleakley had described more perceptively in the Northern Territory. Wages were paid from the Pilbara southward, but the Kimberley at this time was, as one would expect, less 'developed' in this respect than even the northern part of the Territory away from the Barkly Tableland. Moseley claimed that Aborigines had no use for money; and apparently deplored the fact that wages had been paid for twenty years in the Pilbara for the natives to 'waste'—too long to be changed. Like the Territory pastoralists, those of the Pilbara said that Aborigines had no idea of the value of money; they gambled and spent it with unscrupulous hawkers.

Moseley was worried about the 'production of half-castes' in the State as a whole, but in the north saw them as an asset to the pastoral industry; those born on the stations should be left in their own country and become efficient workers. He was also concerned with the cruelty involved in taking the part-Aboriginal child from the mother; he wanted the families to be taken from the camps to new settlements where the children could be educated while the parents worked.

He was critical of the missions and of the three government cattle stations in the north, but he believed that lack of funds was the main cause of deficiencies. He was also critical of the system of police protectors and of that whereby the Chief Protector tried to control the situation from Perth through 102 'honorary protectors'. By this time, the idea of area administration was in the air; and he thought that there should be two Divisional Protectors, one for the Kimberleys and one for the north-west, with the Chief Protector concentrating his energy on the southern areas of the State. He criticised especially the low priority given to the Department's needs. Funds were inadequate for its work and the Chief Protector could not even get a car allowance for inspections.

On the matter of justice, Moseley stressed the incompatibility of the role of the policeman as a person who must both arrest and protect. He was a fair-minded person, within the limits of what one might expect from a magistrate at the time. He could not agree that tribal custom had any relevance for legal defence, but he did suggest a different kind of tribunal for Aboriginal offences against Aborigines. This he thought should comprise the nominee of the Chief Protector, a magistrate, a nominee of the Minister, and the 'head man' of the accused man's tribe. (The last indicates how far out of touch with the situation of Aboriginal society he was; but implicit in it was the sensible idea of an Aboriginal assessor who should be a man of status in Aboriginal life.) He also thought that punishment should be other than imprisonment, and advocated flogging, in the presence of the 'tribe'. To see what was involved here, one has to remember that the 'tribe' in many cases would be the group on the pastoral property and also that employers in 'colonial' situations have tended to advocate corporal punishment because of the loss of time when the worker is imprisoned. A Labour Commission in the Mandated Territory, which met in 1939, heard evidence from employers and even missionaries who advocated the restoration of flogging for 'natives'. Moseley seems to have been an honest man who got his evidence honestly where he could; and in the frontier the only sources other than official ones would be employers and missionaries.

REACTIONS TO SPECTACULAR INJUSTICE

In Western Australia, as elsewhere, the discussion of the 1930s had resulted from reports of spectacular injustice. In spite of the limits in this report, it hit shrewdly at some abuses. Immediate results were the appointment of a specialist in tropical medicine in 1935, the establishment of a leprosarium at Derby, and 'native' hospitals at Broome and Wyndham. Moseley had recommended that employers should contribute to a medical fund like that in use in the Northern Territory, which was interesting in view of his defence of employers in the Report. This fund was provided for in the legislation of 1936.[39] Holders of employment permits had to contribute to a fund to be used for medical and hospital expenses; where required, provide free transport to hospital; and maintain a first aid kit. The absence of such elementary provision from earlier legislation indicates how different was the situation of the Aboriginal worker from that of a colonial indentured labourer: it may suggest why Moseley commented on the rate of deaths on stations in spite of the kindly ministrations of the employers.

The most important result, however, was the Aborigines Act Amendment Act of 1936, which completely reorganised the Department and considerably extended its powers. Moseley had suggested, and parliament finally agreed, that greater control of the 'half-caste' was required. The old categories were replaced by the new and more extensive one of 'native'. The Commissioner of Native Affairs now had power as guardian of all natives up to the age of twenty-one years. The laws against miscegenation were extended to apply even to that of whites with part-Aborigines; and the Commissioner could now control marriage between part-Aborigines. Thus the reaction to protest was towards greater control, as happened elsewhere; and in Western Australia the first ideas of assimilation were ideas of the absorption of the part-Aboriginal, to be made easier by restricting miscegenation.

Moseley's recommendations for a special court were established in the new Act, with modifications. Such a court had to be specially constituted in each case. It consisted of a special magistrate, and a protector nominated by the Commissioner, with a 'headman of the tribe' if 'practicable'. It was limited to offences of native against native. Custom could be taken into account. The limits of sentence were ten years, even for offences which had involved the death penalty (section 31 (59D)). At the same time there was a provision which took away from the white jury cases where whites had assaulted natives; such cases were to be tried summarily by magistrate (section 31 (59C)).

[39] Aborigines Act Amendment Act 1936, section 21 (33B).

The dilemma is clear: protection involved the progressive lowering of status in the law. Hasluck, in *Black Australians* (pp. 160-1) referred to this Act as confining 'the native within a legal status that has more in common with that of a born idiot than of any other class of British subject'. But the scholar, much later, had to approve in the Northern Territory the kind of legislation which would promote assimilation and be acceptable to his party and colleagues in the Commonwealth Cabinet: the Welfare Ordinance of 1953 illustrated the dilemma and resulted in the same kinds of control. What Hasluck did achieve, on that occasion, was the omission of all but Aborigines of the full descent from restriction and control.

Events in Western Australia illustrated the general trend of the 1930s to establish Aboriginal administrations on the basis of even more rigid control, for their 'good' and for their education, and to include more and more of the problem group of part-Aboriginal descent within the scope of the special legislation. The spectacular injustices of the frontier had produced a real reaction, but the effort was to be channelled into more extensive and more rigid control of individuals. At the same time, one effect of the great depression was pressure to remove Aborigines, some long established, off reserves, and move others, who had never lived on reserves, on to them. Aborigines in areas long settled tended still to be approached with the stereotype frontier Aboriginal in mind, their skills and potential as underrated as were their needs. In desperation, as Elkin has pointed out, the part-Aboriginal of the south tended at this time to 'return to the mat', and to seek an Aboriginal identity in lieu of the equality which was being denied him.

THE COMMONWEALTH LOOKS
FOR AN ABORIGINAL POLICY,
1934–1948

The trial of Tuckiar had posed in spectacular fashion for the Commonwealth basic questions of justice. Similar questions had led to the adoption of a 'restricted areas' policy in Papua and the Mandated Territory of New Guinea. This involved limiting contacts with groups still living under traditional conditions on their tribal lands to an officer with a general responsibility for area administration. It also involved special courts operated by the same officer, with special powers to take indigenous custom into account in minor offences, and adjudication in disputes. As we have seen, some provision had been made before the trial of Tuckiar to temper law with a consideration of the Aboriginal cultural imperatives.

But in most of the Northern Territory it was now impracticable to delimit regions for a 'colonial' area administration. This was not so difficult in the great Arnhem Land reserve, though it is significant that the disorders with which the government was mainly concerned occurred at the points of contact with the industrial economy, mainly at the re-fuelling and watering points along the coasts. The work of Dr Donald Thomson, in extensive patrols through Arnhem Land, seems to have been supported by the Commonwealth with an area administration of the colonial type in mind. The other area considered was the Territory portion of the Central Reserve. Here the boundaries had not included some of the waterholes, without which the Aborigines there could not survive, especially in the droughts which had marked the late 1920s; while the attraction of beef, flour, tea, tobacco, and steel had greatly reduced population on the Northern Territory part of this reserve. The first and only Patrol Officer, T.G.H. Strehlow, established his base at Jay Creek and began to patrol, but without the powers of the colonial field officer. There were a few hundred only in the reserve and the movement out to the cattle stations and towards Alice Springs was already marked. There was an established trade in dingo scalps with white 'doggers' who operated officially along the fringe of the reserve and unofficially wherever they wished, so that even the boundaries of the reserve did not delimit an effectively restricted area. Some Aborigines were getting better payment (in kind) for scalps by trading them at the Hermannsburg Mission.

In the event no patrol staff was appointed to Arnhem Land, though colonial administrative methods were foreshadowed by the appointment of a Director of Native Affairs with anthropological training and with experience in New Guinea. The role of a patrolling field officer concerned with 'native affairs' would inevitably lead to a clash with that of the police officer concerned with law and order. Frontier tradition was that the policeman always 'got his man'. (The colonial arrangement was that the patrol officer exercised police powers.) In 1938 two control stations manned by police officers were set up in Arnhem Land, one at the mouth of the King River and one on Croker Island, to control the contacts of the Aborigines with the fishing fleets. These stations had little effect, since the Aborigines depended heavily on the trading of their women and other services for tea, sugar, and limited trade goods.

The war with Japan cut off these mainly Japanese contacts. The coasts were patrolled by the navy, with the new Native Affairs Branch of the Administration participating. Men were attracted out of Arnhem Land to the large army establishments set up along the new road from Darwin to Alice Springs. Employment there offered the new experience of an environment comparatively devoid of discrimination. The army, whatever the limitations of its discipline for man management, tended to treat the Aboriginal as a soldier, who needed the army ration scale to keep fit for his work, training for the tasks required, and a money wage. This part of the situation changed, while the war brought to an abrupt end the discussion of policies which had only begun between government and the academic, mission, and humanitarian bodies interested.

This discussion had involved attempts to reverse trends, long established, for the Aborigines to come into the centres of pastoral, mining and commercial activity, and finally to the destructive conditions of the compounds. While these trends might conceivably have been checked by the establishment of area administrative and commercial centres, out beyond the pastoral stations, where trained officers might have established a constructive and adaptive interaction with the indigenous leadership, it was

COMMONWEALTH LOOKS FOR AN ABORIGINAL POLICY 307

becoming too late. The checks were to be imposed during the war by restricting Aboriginal movements, but without any compensatory rewards for those held back. In any case, the traditional society tended to disintegrate with the touch of the cash economy and industrial trade goods. Considerable power would have been needed, again on the colonial model, to restrain the resort to destructive warfare between Aboriginal groups and persons competing for material advantage. This may have been one reason why Cook, the Chief Protector, referred in 1936 to the possibility of creating a Native Police—not, in this humane context of discussion, on the earlier New South Wales and Queensland models, but in the tradition of Papua.[1]

The problem had not been entirely ignored by governments. The compromise was to meet the need by encouraging or allowing missions to set themselves up either in the reserve itself, as happened in the Cape York Peninsula and Arnhem Land, or in a strategic situation between the settled areas and the reserve, as in the case of Mount Margaret Mission, between the Western Australian part of the Central Reserve and the Eastern Goldfields. Bleakley's recommendation for a mission at Lake Amadeus, just off the Central Reserve, had it been acted upon, would have resulted in a mission performing the second function, of offering a trading point which might have checked to some extent the movement into settled areas. As already noted, the Port Keats Mission was set up in the Daly River Reserve in 1935. The Presbyterians of South Australia, stirred by Duguid's indignation about what was happening to the people in the Central Reserve, established Ernabella Mission in 1937; and the policy has been ever since to work in indigenous language, and to offer economic opportunities in what was selected as a strategic area between the reserve and the settlers. Four years earlier the United Aborigines Mission established itself at Ooldea, where Daisy Bates had worked for a long time with the desert people of the Nullarbor.

But this had the result of further complicating the task of getting any real administrative grasp of the situation. This abdication to religious bodies illustrates the low priority allocated to Aboriginal needs. There were special problems involved in the particular policies and methods of each mission, and in the individual missionary's view of his role. Most mission effort and energy continued to be spent on the thankless task of building Christian communities. This and the charitable work subsidised by governments (with exceptions) tended to be handled in the traditional

[1] *C.P.P.* No. 63, 1937—Report on the Administration of the Northern Territory 1936, pp. 12-16.

schoolmasterly fashion with the usual results. The missions must certainly be credited with the survival of Aboriginal populations. The cost was institutional living, under paternal management, comparable with that on government-controlled reserves in the settled areas of the States. This kind of control, especially where the missionary was insensitive to the imperatives of Aboriginal culture, and driven hard by conscience to save souls, was almost as destructive of Aboriginal autonomy and leadership as seizure and use of the land or use of the group as a source of labour on the cattle station. Thus quite different intentions, and quite different methods, could result in institutional situations which were basically similar. The pastoralist could regard himself as a philanthropist comparable with the missionary: and could justify poor housing and feeding by comparing the conditions on his property with that on the neighbouring mission settlement.

The gap between mission aims and achievements was by no means peculiar to Australia. The Aboriginal, having been especially deprived, was perhaps more prone than members of mission communities elsewhere to see the mission as a source of economic assistance. No socialised Aboriginal would seek to learn morality from a missionary; and to the extent that he adhered, it would be for material advantages. The limited supplies handled by the missionary became essentials, and aroused all the covetous desire which has marked the impact of the industrial West on subsistence economies the world over. The establishment of more mission centres in Arnhem Land thus possibly added to, rather than decreased, the dissatisfaction with the old ways, which was tearing Aboriginal society to pieces in its last stronghold.

Elkin argued for administrative arrangements for order and justice and to enable Aboriginal leadership to operate with an essential minimum of autonomy, within which the traditional society could make progressive adjustments to rapidly changing conditions. In two articles written in 1934 he went to the heart of the matter[2], pointing out for the politician and the lay reader that Aborigines had the same inherent capacity to adjust to change as other people but that adjustment, made by a process of decisions arrived at in ways which Aborigines recognised as valid, required a degree of autonomy for the society within which leadership and decision-making could operate. Elkin hoped for the kind of administration in tribal areas which would cushion the impact of the encroaching economy. He

[2] 'Anthropology and the Future of the Australian Aborigines', *Oceania*, September 1934, vol. V, no. 1, pp. 1-18; and 'The Aborigines, Our National Responsibility', *Australian Quarterly*, no. 23, 1934, pp. 52-60.

COMMONWEALTH LOOKS FOR AN ABORIGINAL POLICY 309

described the economic life ordered on the principle of reciprocity, the decision-making role of elders, and the religious sanctions for their authority. For that time, especially, his insight into problems of social change was remarkable.

It is therefore obvious that in this time of transition which our presence has forced on the aborigines, we should pay due respect to their secret religious life . . . . Especially should we take care . . . to undermine as little as possible, the authority of the elders and the respect of the rising generation for those beliefs on which this authority is based.[3]

The ideal method, he thought, was for the Aborigines in the 'northern and central parts of Australia' to be controlled and assisted by a single administration. This should be based on the methods of colonial administration used in Papua and the Mandated Territory. He hoped that 'well run' government or mission institutions might provide the points of contact between government and indigenous society which the village provided in New Guinea. He advocated the appointment of an Administrator who knew something of 'the problems of racial contact and clash', a Department of Native Affairs concerned with education, health and employment, and a Department of Native Justice, with district magistrates, assisted by patrol officers, and operating in inter-racial as well as wholly Aboriginal cases, so that they could bring pressure to bear on settlers 'to assist in establishing a workable status quo'. There should be Aboriginal men of status employed as police.[4]

The argument was both practical and humane. Elkin was looking, in a very difficult combination of circumstances, for some way in which the remaining units of Aboriginal society could be allowed to adjust, and be protected against being overwhelmed and smashed by economic exploitation: by the temptation for individuals to throw away their complex but brittle order of duty and responsibility for the industrial mess of pottage; by the effects of the white man's obvious disregard and contempt for the indigenous authority and for the sanctions which upheld it; and by the contagious effects of scepticism, and of scorn of the comic savage. Such an administration would have required quite definite powers of control over the movements and actions of the pioneers advancing the frontiers of White Australia, as well as over the Aborigines in employment or other contact situations. Moreover, colonial history has shown time and again the difficulties of protecting persons who resent the means of protection and who do not want to be protected. Elkin had become responsible for

[3] 'Anthropology and the Future of the Australian Aborigines', pp. 13-14.
[4] Ibid., pp. 16-17.

training field officers of the New Guinea Administration. He hoped for the appointment to the field staff he suggested of officers who had been properly trained for this kind of work.

Such a field staff is essential wherever the basis of consensus and the means of restoring harmony in traditional society have been eroded or destroyed by new influences, for where the traditional leadership is no longer effective, there is no way to settle disputes but through appeal to the new authority. This pointed a basic weakness in the concept of the isolated reserve, without easy recourse to some kind of adjudication. In fact the reserve could not be isolated from the impact of new foods and implements, and new ideas, which increased dissension and weakened the mechanisms for social control. Australian experience in New Guinea had shown for a long time that men in the field could spend most of their time adjudicating in disputes which would otherwise have led to more destructive warfare than had ever plagued native society before contact. This kind of administration, which the Aboriginal never had, might well have led to spontaneous resort to the court where his own problems could be considered. Instead, the mechanism for British justice came to him with an armed police party, generally appearing as an expedition of vengeance for the death of a white man: and what happened thereafter, especially where the court adhered to traditional British procedures, must have been as inexplicable as it was frightening.

Colonial administration on the Australian continent would have constituted a revolution in long-established priorities. It would have involved setting limits to the professed requirements of the cattle industry. It would have raised the spectre, to the fervid apostles of White Australia, of another kind of government, in some cases in separate areas, for black men; it might even have been the thin end of the wedge, the beginning of a chain of events which would lead to the recognition of Aboriginal rights to areas of land (which the method of creating reserves had never done). It might have made labour less docile. Implicit in the idea of special courts was the questioning of the efficacy of British law as the universal source of justice.

All these issues would be raised even if Elkin's suggestions had been limited to the method of controlling large reserves. But tribal people were, it seemed, leaving the reserves, or moving between reserve and centres of white settlement. Their eagerness for the material advantages to be gained may be compared with the eagerness of the whites, who as a group had for so long placed their own economic advantage before Aboriginal lives. To have given Strehlow, from his base at Jay Creek, thirty miles west of

COMMONWEALTH LOOKS FOR AN ABORIGINAL POLICY 311

Alice Springs, power to regulate Aboriginal movements in and out of employment, would have involved control of some aspects of 'white' enterprise. In a colonial situation, where the control of indigenous labour in the contract system came to be recognised generally as in the long-term interests of economic enterprise, quite rigid control over employment was possible. This was hardly so in the Northern Territory or in the frontier regions of South Australia and Western Australia; Queensland came closest, by controlling labour drawn from the missions and government settlements, and by requiring individual agreements of employment.

These discussions in the 1930s did not lead to realisation that frontier problems were becoming a smaller part of the complex of Aboriginal affairs. Away back in time and place behind the frontier, scattered thinly on government stations and fringe settlements round the country towns, and even establishing forward bases as it were in the capital cities, was the detritus of Aboriginal society, the new part-Aboriginal society. The Commonwealth, in the Northern Territory, was the only government with responsibilities still almost wholly of the frontier type, at least to the extent that the Aborigines still formed the majority of the population. The three States with frontier situations had a greater dilemma to face: how to reconcile a system based on the principles of poor relief and the institutionalisation of those deemed incompetent or unsuitable for a full role in the general society with a frontier administration which, if based on the ideas stated by Elkin, would constitute an act of faith in Aborigines and Aboriginal society, with their own special competence and capacity to survive, if given the opportunity.

In the long settled areas it was becoming more evident each year that, although Aborigines might be dying out in the sense that those of the full descent were obviously decreasing, the part-Aboriginal people were not, and could, to administrative minds long conditioned to seeing 'problems' in terms of 'colour', soon present a special problem of their own. This situation, however, was the current form of a historical continuum of contact between the races, of which the frontier conditions formed an early phase. We have already noted the concern of Cook and the Administration with the 'half-castes' in the Territory. Bleakley's expertise in dealing with 'half-castes' was the basis of policy there: it did not prevent the Queensland standards of administration from being regarded as something of a model for other States. Such measures were incompatible with a system of colonial administration, partly because this implicitly assumed that Aborigines need not die out because they were different; that the Australian community was already a multi-racial one,

312   THE DESTRUCTION OF ABORIGINAL SOCIETY

and that there was in fact a Black Australia with values of its own which
were worth respect; that in Black Australia justice had to be worked out
within a bicultural adjustment.

Managing a minority in accordance with poor-law principles and
holding its members within rigid legislative and administrative restrictions
and protections was simply inconsistent with a policy aimed at cross-
cultural justice. This was illustrated in the Western Australian Aborigines
Act Amendment Act of 1936. The special provisions for the establishment
of Native Courts, to take 'tribal custom' into account for serious offences,
seem to have resulted from the discussions over the Tuckiar case,[5] but the
general trend of the Act was to maintain, in some respects to extend, the
already rigid system of administrative controls; and in the exercise of
these there was no provision for any concern with Aboriginal custom.
What happened in court would be a special case; the exercise of these
controls was a matter of daily life, and they were to continue to be
exercised by persons with none of the training for the task which appeared
essential to those who were beginning to think in terms of colonial
administration. This Act expressed the concern with the half-caste situation
and included measures to prevent miscegenation.

In 1939 Queensland provided for the establishment by regulation of
Aboriginal courts, Aboriginal police, even Aboriginal gaols, but only on
the reserves;[6] so that the superintendents of the missions and settlements
both wielded magisterial powers and appointed the 'police'. Thus the
results of the national discussion, filtered through the Queensland system
of Aboriginal management, made for more rigid control than ever in its
institutions. South Australians were active in the agitation of the 1930s;
but this did not, from the evidence in the legislation, lead to any greater
government concern with what must by this time have become the least
known of the frontier regions, out beyond the south-east settled areas of
the State. The Aborigines Act, 1934-1939 was almost exclusively concerned
with the management of Aborigines in controlled situations: it could be
applicable in its terms, and by the principles of paternal poor-law type
administration, to any group assumed to be poor and incompetent.

Preoccupation with the management of institutions, the 'training' of
inmates, was, through a special set of circumstances, taken into the furthest
frontiers by the missionaries. In Australia they could not train evangelists
or catechists and send them into settled villages to make conversions (which
always had to be, to some degree, on the villagers' own terms). Either they

---

[5] Section 31, providing for new section 59D in principal Act.
[6] See the Aboriginals Preservation and Protection Act, 1939, section 12 (3), (4), and (5).

COMMONWEALTH LOOKS FOR AN ABORIGINAL POLICY 313

must manage institutions for people who sat down on the spot or do nothing. To take a random example, the couple managing the Presbyterian mission on Mornington Island in 1940 reported that their Aborigines were by no means useless creatures: they did splendid crochet and other fancy work, made clothing, played games, and the children did well in school.[7] What, one may well ask, had frontier institutions of this kind to do with the other set of problems involved in colonial administration?

In 1935 Paterson, Minister for the Interior, probably in the hope of clarifying the situation in tribal society, invited Dr Donald Thomson, of the University of Melbourne, to go into the Arnhem Land reserve, establish friendly relations with the people, instruct them in the 'gravity of major offences', and report on ceremonial life, morality, and language. Thomson had the status of Protector, and a government grant—a concession that policy making might benefit from knowledge of Aboriginal society. Thomson made two expeditions, in 1935-6 and 1936-7, for a total of twenty-six months in Arnhem Land.[8]

He had already had experience in Cape York; and the friendliness he found from the Aborigines along the east coast of Arnhem Land, notorious outside for their savage treachery, curiously parallels the report by Meston on the people of Cape York four decades earlier. He found the people amenable to yaws injections and other health services he could provide. His first report expressed alarm at the apparent rate of depopulation, in spite of adequate food resources; here his experience accorded with what he had found at places like Mapoon in Cape York. He stressed the drastic effects of contact with the trepangers and pearlers on the coasts, and with the settlers in the Roper Valley. He showed how British justice appeared to Aborigines, as when a cattle station having failed in the Roper Valley, with some of its cattle remaining untended, the Aborigines killed some for food and were tried by local justices from the other stations. He recommended that prisoners from Arnhem Land be released from Fanny Bay gaol to go home with him to their 'country', and some of them accompanied him on his second expedition. He criticised both the efforts of the missions to turn nomads into farmers and institutionalise them and the teaching which alienated them from their own culture and made them hangers-on at the cattle runs and fringe settlements.

[7] *Herald* (Melbourne), 18 April 1940.
[8] Donald Thomson, Interim General Report of Preliminary Expedition to Arnhem Land 1935-6 (to Minister of the Interior); Recommendations of Policy in Native Affairs in the Northern Territory of Australia; *C.P.P.* 1937-40, vol. 3, no. 56, pp. 805 *et seq.*—Report on Expedition to Arnhem Land 1936-37.
to Arnhem Land 1936-37.

On his second expedition he was impressed by the impact of the fishing fleet, which was very different, he thought, from the long-established contacts with the Arafura world through the Malays. He described how the people waited for the ships, their visits to Darwin, their eagerness for cast-off clothing, packs of cards for gambling, and trade supplies. He recommended absolute segregation for tribal remnants still retaining their own culture, wherever these might be found on reserves; and that policy be aimed to preserve Aboriginal institutions and organisation. By this he did not rule out contact with trained patrol officers, who after all would be the instruments of segregation. His concern was with white commercial activities, which he maintained had increased during the period of his contacts with Arnhem Land. Strict segregation, he argued, should be maintained for as long as governments took to work out and prove 'a working policy in the best interests of the Aboriginal, tested and proved by long-term experiences amongst natives already de-tribalised'. Thus he saw the machinery of colonial administration as a means of isolating Aboriginal society wherever it still survived, until governments found a way of justice and prosperity for the remnants where it did not.

Perhaps there was more humanity than practical understanding of the limits of choice for government here; or perhaps Thomson thought that any effort to segregate could be justified in terms of Aboriginal lives ful- filled in the Aboriginal manner, by reduction or restraint of disintegrative forces. He recommended removing protector's powers from police officers; native courts; establishment of a Director and Department of Native Affairs, with trained field staff. The Commonwealth should control all 'native affairs'. In a final report he stressed the incompatibility of Aboriginal concepts of reciprocity, as the basis of morality, with abstract British law: and recommended special courts where Aborigines could explain their motives in a receptive situation.

Thomson claimed to have seen seventy vessels operating off one beach in the Crocodile group, and he accused the Japanese of a policy of giving large presents to Aborigines at a particular spot so that they would continue to assemble there with their women. Aborigines should be kept away from the proposed flying boat base on Groote Eylandt, to avoid what had happened along the transcontinental railway—even to the prevention of the sale of Aboriginal artefacts. He claimed that diseases from Asia had been introduced through contact with fishing fleets; and described the destructive epidemics, from colds to yaws and leprosy. Thomson seems to have hoped for appointment as the first patrol officer for Arnhem Land, but this came to nothing. Frustration continued to be expressed in

COMMONWEALTH LOOKS FOR AN ABORIGINAL POLICY 315

violence. Abbott, who was now the Administrator, found that, following all the agitation, it was no longer possible to deal with disorder by sending in police parties. A new policy was essential.

Police freedom of action may have been limited by an administrative instruction, following a Board of Inquiry in 1933 when an officer was charged with ill-treatment of Aborigines and the shooting of one of them at Ayers Rock. The shooting had occurred, like so many for so long, whilst the prisoner was escaping from custody; the Board's finding was that this was legal, but not morally justified. The Board, which included two Adelaide members, a distinguished scientist and the Secretary of the Aboriginal Friends Association, had made the positive recommendation that the arid areas of the Centre should be patrolled by an officer of the Aboriginal Department who knew the language and customs, instead of by police officers; and that the patrol officer might advise and consult with the men of status, and adjudicate, in the manner of the colonial field officer. There was probably no one competent for this but T.G.H. Strehlow, whose father had been so long head of the Hermannsburg Mission and whose remarkable sensitivity and insight still mark him out, in his writings, as especially gifted for this work along a cultural frontier. But, perhaps because government was mainly sensitive to the interests of cattle men in the area, Strehlow did not get the powers which the Board recommended.

He recommended rationing centres in the Central Reserve where rations could be traded for artefacts and dingo scalps, hoping to attract many of those then wandering round the homesteads of the Centralian 'battlers' back to centres where they could be prepared for employment, and receive health services. Perhaps the only alternative at the time would have been to excise suitable areas from the cattle runs; but one of the problems was to lower the tensions between the Aborigines and the settlers. That his recommendations came to nothing may have been due to the opposition of those who thought that their interests were served best by an over-supply of labour.

Strehlow's plan was to develop his base at Jay Creek into a settlement attractive enough to bring the people from the fringe settlement at Alice Springs; but there was not enough money. Without the necessary priorities, of course, his appointment involved great difficulties. It was his task to try to enforce the Aboriginal legislation in very difficult frontier conditions indeed, where many of the settlers could not afford to meet the minimum conditions of employment, and where he had the thankless task, for instance, of trying to protect young girls from the white settlers

THE DESTRUCTION OF ABORIGINAL SOCIETY

by enforcing the legislation on cohabitation. He was still there when war came, and remained until 1941.

Had his patrol post been established in the Petermann Ranges or other suitable location in the Central Reserve, he was probably the one man who really could have given a fair trial to the ideas Elkin had advocated in 1934. But the priorities remained elsewhere, as the state of Jay Creek illustrates, for, in spite of Strehlow's work, it remained for a long time a typical centre of Aboriginal misery. (One reason for the failure to develop many of these small reserves properly, even as places to live, was that cattle runs or townships were established where there was known water. Thus the Aboriginal Department generally had to depend on an uncertain water supply. Lack of water at Jay Creek finally forced its closing down in 1965.)[9] In 1938 Cook complained that there were no funds for buildings or staffing there. The effect of the low priority for Aboriginal settlements was also exemplified in the discovery of gold at Tennant Creek, and the beginning of large-scale extraction in 1934, when the Aborigines' tenure was affected in the same way as in other 'inviolable' reserves since. They were resettled on the Warramunga Reserve; then at Phillip Creek; but on both sites, as the official statement has it, 'lack of water prevented successful development'. At Tennant Creek there was plenty of water for people, but not enough for people and the big mines. The remains of the Warramunga people and some of the Wailbri were established in 1954 on a new settlement at Warrabri.[10]

Part of the Groote Eylandt Reserve had been taken for the flying boat base there. In this case Thomson's advice was taken, and a protector stationed there to keep the races apart. Even trading activities were to be prevented, and the prohibitions, even of gifts of tobacco, were to be continued. Admitting the impossibility of enforcing such prohibitions, one has to acknowledge the readiness to attempt something new. But in this case there was no problem of affronting vested interests other than those of the mission, which was likely to approve. Cook's 1938 report announces the plan to construct, at last, a new compound for Darwin, on a reserve adjacent to the town, but then not in it—on the Bagot Reserve, which is still occupied, but now surrounded by suburbs.[11]

---

[9] For an interesting account of its history, see statement by D.D. Smith in *Centralian Advocate*, 16 September 1965; for earlier non-official accounts, see article by Charles Duguid, *Australian InterCollegian*, 1 July 1940; *Truth* (Sydney), 30 March 1946; *Truth* (Adelaide), 19 March 1949.
[10] See Welfare Branch, N.T.A.: Warrabri Aboriginal Reserve, p. 4; and *C.P.P.*, 1935, no. 237—Report on the Administration of the Northern Territory, pp. 11-16: Report of the Chief Protector of Aboriginals.
[11] *C.P.P.*, 1937-9, no. 150, pp. 21-6—Report on Administration of the Northern Territory 1937-8.

COMMONWEALTH LOOKS FOR AN ABORIGINAL POLICY 317

Obviously the climate was slowly changing; and the agitation of the preceding decade had not been all in vain. But the same order of priorities was to remain for a long time yet, especially where the assumed requirements of the cattle industry were involved. The planned move to Bagot, like the arrangement at Groote Eylandt and the appointment of Strehlow, would not cost any vested private interest anything.

Too late in the drift into World War II to have any real results, a new system of administration, based on an attempt to adapt colonial administration to the Territory scene and order of priorities, finally began when in April 1939 E.W.P. Chinnery, with long experience as Director of District Services and Native Affairs in the Mandated Territory of New Guinea, began duty as the full-time Director of the new Department of Native Affairs.

Yet District Administration, had the war not interrupted the plan, and even had the new department obtained much higher priorities than it was likely to get, would probably have proved very difficult to adapt to the conditions of the Australian frontier lands. As the subsequent history of the Maningrida government post in northern Arnhem Land showed, the nomads would be attracted to the headquarters established for patrolling, as a source of processed food and trade goods. The gatherings of people waiting for the ships to come, where the conditions had so shocked Thomson, illustrated the irresistible pressures away from nomadic existence which had marked all this history; it was not only the absence of positive policies which led to the institutional situations. Elkin had seen this point in 1934. Thomson's plan for sealing off parts of the frontier, within which Aboriginal life might be maintained indefinitely, until solutions were found for the problems of those already in various conditions of stabilised or semi-stabilised dependency, seems to have ignored one of the main lessons of the history of contact.

Colonial area administration of the New Guinea type was a means of managing stable village communities. Government had to be peripatetic; the travelling representative of the central administration had to establish working arrangements with a village leadership. As there was no multipurposed village leadership in New Guinea, government had established the village constable in Papua and the luluai in the Trust Territory. It was something of a hollow analogy to see the government station, or the mission, as the counterpart of a New Guinea social unit tied to its own land and waters by the routines of subsistence gardening, by use of the local materials for permanent dwellings and artefacts, with social relationships deeply embedded in the concepts of real and personal property, and with complicated patterns of inheritance of particular land areas devoted to food production. Nothing was more inevitable than that the Aborigines would sit down and make the best of whatever offered at any point of supply.

The scholars who had come to appreciate the complexities of the nomadic culture and the spirituality of the religious life which gave meaning to it might regret this and the eagerness of the young for change. But the disruptive power of western culture had been universal. The stable village communities of New Guinea, like those of Asia or Africa, might change slowly; and where there had not been too heavy a use made of them for economic purposes by the invader, they retained enough power of their own to throw off the yoke at the end. But the Aboriginal, once he had sat down, quickly lost the power to do more than supplementary hunting, if only because the processes of hard socialisation in which the Aboriginal personality was formed were so rapidly lost in circumstances where autonomy for the process was lost. It was not lost because of some special tyranny in the white 'boss'. As the history of the best-intentioned of the missions suggests, human kindness which stabilised the nomads in a dependent imitation or a dependent mendicancy had the same effect in the end. Perhaps the answer lay in opportunities for stabilisation in situations where leadership and decision-making for change rested within the Aboriginal society, the whites at the point of contact offering assistance and advice on request.

This was the case, basically, for the rationing point with the opportunity to learn how to *earn* the new foods: for instance, in Strehlow's plan to trade food for dog scalps. But no government had ever been prepared to take the risk; or to set aside from European development the assets required, in the area where the continuity of religious and other cohesive activities retained their meaning. In Central Australia, for instance, some real economic assets, perhaps waterholes for cattle, would have had to be reserved to give Aboriginal groups a chance to adapt while retaining autonomy.

One suspects also that sedentary living brought new tensions. It tended to bring together for long periods people who felt that they did not belong together. Those families which did so belong were now more closely associated, for longer than they had ever been in the dispersed activities which occupied most of the time in the nomadic hunt for food. Moreover, wherever the point of contact was made, the land would have had special meaning for one group and not for the others gathered there. Some would have been intruders more than others—which was another cause for tensions and disputes, the settlement of which required new kinds of social controls and more extensively recognised leadership.

COMMONWEALTH LOOKS FOR AN ABORIGINAL POLICY 319

COMMONWEALTH AND STATE AUTHORITIES CONFERENCE, 1937

The stories of violent injustice from the Northern Territory, where the Commonwealth, all admitted, should be setting standards for the nation, thus led to a somewhat profitless review of frontier policy. There was no drastic reorganisation of administrative methods nor reconsideration of objectives. The tepid experiment with a single patrol officer held no interest for State governments. By this time the major part of their Aboriginal 'problems', even for those with groups still following the tribal life, as in Western and South Australia, had taken its modern form: the camps on cattle runs, the fringe settlements, and the matters related to the management of asylum-type institutions and of who should be allowed or compelled to live in them. The effects of the great depression in the more closely settled areas possibly added both to the obvious poverty of what was becoming more clearly a part-Aboriginal community, excluded from the economic and social opportunities of the country towns, and to the demands by the States for Commonwealth assistance. At the time the Bleakley Report was being considered there was talk of referring the matter of Commonwealth control to the annual Premiers' Conference. The pressure from the voluntary bodies had been continued on this point: and in 1936, at the Premiers' Conference held in Adelaide, it was agreed that, while Commonwealth control of Aboriginal affairs was 'impracticable', periodical meetings of the State and Commonwealth officers responsible for Aboriginal administration were desirable.[12]

The 'initial conference' of the government authorities was held in Canberra in April 1937. That this conference had resulted mainly from the effects of the last publicised clashes between white Australian and Aboriginal society was illustrated in an interesting way by the opening remarks of Bailey, Chairman of the Aborigines Protection Board in Victoria, that 'the problems relating to Aborigines are not acute in Victoria', where only a handful of full-bloods remained; that he had come mainly as an onlooker; and that the real issues were to be faced in Queensland, South Australia, and Western Australia, rather than in Victoria or New South Wales.[13]

Indeed, the basic assumptions of this conference were that after the inevitable frontier catastrophe there were certain things to be done, almost on the analogy of mopping-up operations, before the Aboriginal minority

[12] See statement by Paterson, Minister of the Interior, in *Aboriginal Welfare: Initial Conference of Commonwealth and State Aboriginal Authorities*, p.5.
[13] Ibid., p. 5.

THE DESTRUCTION OF ABORIGINAL SOCIETY

disappeared, this time into White Australia by eventual absorption of the part-Aboriginal. Only Bleakley, with his pessimistic assessment of the potential of the 'inferior' type of 'cross-breed', seemed to envisage a permanent caste of these people. 'Full-blood natives' were divided for the purpose of policy recommendation into three categories—the detribalised living near towns, the 'semi civilised' on pastoral properties, and the 'uncivilised' living in the tribal state. On the one hand there was the need, here again stressed by Bleakley, to check miscegenation and so as far as possible limit the size of the part-Aboriginal population, by the 'moral protection of females'; on the other, the need to promote the new policy, which to those thinking in terms of racial origin as the measure of potential seemed liberal and enlightened: 'that the destiny of the natives of Aboriginal origin, but not of the full blood, lies in their ultimate absorption by the people of the Commonwealth, and it therefore recommends that all efforts be directed to that end'.[14]

Science had indicated that Aboriginal features and skin coloration tended to disappear over a few generations. Bleakley, of course, had his own theories about this. Perhaps we can see here the beginnings of the policy of assimilation; certainly it represents 'assimilation' as popularly understood. Here was a policy based on the assumption of a progression, not of individuals who are thought of as persons and ends in themselves but as successive stages in a breeding program, from the first half-caste resulting from a liaison which the vigilant authorities have been unable to prevent by laws controlling marriage and miscegenation to the disappearance of his descendants into the 'white' community. The full-blood would still 'disappear', but in the sense that his special physical characteristics would be progressively bred out of his part-Aboriginal descendants.

Apartheid, as far as possible without upsetting the current needs of employers, was recommended for the three categories of 'full-bloods'. The children of those established near towns should be educated 'to white standard' for employment 'which will not bring them into economic or social conflict with the white community'. For the 'semi-civilised' on pastoral stations there should be 'benevolent supervision' of conditions, with small local reserves where the unemployable 'may live as nearly as possible a normal tribal life, and unobjectionable tribal ceremonies may continue, and to which employees may repair when unemployed'. The only reference to 'ultimate destiny' in this case suggests that it should be their 'elevation' to the state of those living near towns. The point was implied only—that nature would, in spite of the law, inevitably take its

[14] Ibid., p. 21.

COMMONWEALTH LOOKS FOR AN ABORIGINAL POLICY 321

course: these full-bloods would give place to the part-Aborigines for whom the policy makers felt they could really decide the future. The 'uncivilised' would be kept on 'inviolable reserves' as far as possible: in the background of history and of these discussions, the implicit assumption is that here too segregation would fail; nature would take its course.[15]

In fact Neville, of Western Australia, stated that eventual assimilation of the Aboriginal population was the policy objective of his government. He clearly equated assimilation with absorption through intermarriage, and quoted the Anthropological Board of Adelaide and Dr R. Cilento as authorities for the view that the Aboriginal not being 'negroid', there would be no 'atavism'. With this in mind the Western Australian legislation now used the definitive term 'native' instead of 'Aboriginal'. He was confident that if he could get control of children from the age of six years for training and education he could deal with the problem, which was not a native one, but a financial one. At the level of stock-breeding, perhaps only at such a level, it was possible to bureaucratise the complicated issues of social change. Thus Neville expressed the intention to prevent marriages of part-Aborigines with Aborigines.[16]

Worth noting is the contrast of this approach to frontier problems with the arguments being advanced for a frontier administration of the colonial type. The second were concerned with a humane cross-cultural dialogue, irrespective of the enormous disparity in power between the parties. The arguments at this conference were based on the principles of the stock-breeder and on the pessimism which history seemed to justify: no matter what was done, Aborigines would disappear, giving place to part-Aborigines, so that the real problem was how to bring these into White Australia, with further racial admixture assumed as the process. That this was the real problem, all government representatives at the conference appear, from the record, to have agreed. As a result, the remaining frontier situations tended to be seen as pre-institutional and pre-miscegenation, rather than as arising from the last stand of a very stubborn Aboriginal cultural minority.

This kind of thinking is still common. It is still often assumed, for instance, that one of the advantages of education for the Aboriginal is to promote the hope for mixed marriage and thus for the disappearance of his physical characteristics in his children. This, too, was probably one of the reasons for the recommendation by the conference that the children of town-dwelling full-bloods should be educated 'to white standard'.

[15] Ibid., p. 34.
[16] Ibid., p. 11.

THE DESTRUCTION OF ABORIGINAL SOCIETY

Other recommendations of this conference relate specifically to the disappearing frontier. Both Bleakley and Neville referred to the provision their States had made for native courts. The former made clear that a native court in Queensland was no more than a means of settling minor disputes on the reserve—in fact, a part of the machinery of administering the institution. Neville explained that the new legislation in Western Australia would enable even tribal murder to be dealt with against the background of custom. The conference recommended that jurisdiction of such courts should be limited to cases involving natives only; that natives should be defined as in Western Australia, if the Commonwealth and States did agree on uniform legislation (which illustrates the pressure from the officials to extend controls). But here the incompatibility between the requirements of persons living in tribal society and the classification in terms of descent for purposes of separate administration becomes clear. The native in Western Australia meant any person of Aboriginal descent except one of one-fourth Aboriginal descent or less; while even a 'quadroon' could be classified by administrative fiat as a native.[17] Many natives would know nothing of tribal life: such wide definitions thus confused policy aims and, where there were no real facilities to determine descent (which was almost everywhere), confused attempts to execute policies.

Some of the discussion indicated that the officers were on the defensive against urban critics of 'native administration' in the bush. M.T. McLean, the Chief Protector from South Australia, whose comments showed that his administration was still mainly concerned with what was happening in the settled areas and at the two main settlements at Point Pearce and Point McLeay, remarked that 'in many instances, the points brought forward by organisations in the cities are utterly ridiculous when applied to bush natives.'[18] There was discussion of the use of neck chains—still, let this remind us, common through the northern regions. The Commonwealth Minister had witnessed their use, and was convinced that chains were more humane than handcuffs. In Queensland the matter was left to the police; according to Bleakley the government did try to avoid their use over long distances by providing transport. In fact the custom was so well established as a normal police method that it was still in use after World War II, and still being defended. Cook admitted that chains were still in use in the Territory, for witnesses as well as suspects; and so did Neville, who could quote a Royal Commission of 1934 in favour. The

[17] See Aborigines Act Amendment Act (W.A.) 1936, sections 2 and 5.
[18] *Aboriginal Welfare*, p. 32.

COMMONWEALTH LOOKS FOR AN ABORIGINAL POLICY 323

criticism came mainly from Bailey of Victoria. But the method of chaining was defended in a resolution, that

where, for the safety of the escort and the security of the prisoners, it is necessary to subject the prisoners to restraint, *it is the opinion of the representatives from the States and Territory concerned* that the use of the neck chain while travelling through bush country is preferable to the use of handcuffs, for humanitarian reasons and having regard to the comfort of the prisoners.[19]

Arrangements for native courts to be held in the areas of the offences possibly did not meet the needs, since most cases where the policeman got his man and his witnesses involved crimes against whites.

Another resolution foreshadowed the increased use of the mission as the agent of government policy. Subsidies were to be conditional on the educational standards reached by the natives, measures for health and hygiene, the diet offering, and regular government inspection. It was also recommended that there should be regulations governing all the welfare activities of missions.[20]

These resolutions indicated a trend, which can be followed progressively in the legislation of each State, for the still negligible but increasing funds to be used for increased control and education. If the part-Aboriginal was on the way to obliteration in the bosom of White Australia, he must be assisted by the tighter grip on his activities which more detailed legislation, and more comprehensive definitions, could bring. Here was a matter for public service expertise; and the bureaucratisation of the social questions involved was well established.

The period just before the war was marked by the peak of protective-restrictive legislation. The Northern Territory had served as an arena within which effort could be made to get to grips with some of the problems: it was in many ways a national arena. But there were also the long-established State administrations and policies. Although they had low priorities and status in the State public services and government programs, they were yet likely to be defended, especially against the ever-encroaching Commonwealth authority, as uniquely suited to the requirements within each State. Nor had the Commonwealth, in over two decades of control, set any glowing example of achievement. So the main result of the discussions was to encourage administrators to greater efforts, using the well-established means. When assimilation became the objective, the same means were used: protection was less and less from the bullets of squatters, more and more from evil influences of low white men.

[19] Ibid., p. 32.
[20] Ibid., pp. 29-30.

The development of these administrations, and the emergence of the part-Aboriginal people as a group especially subject to restrictive and protective laws, and especially liable to be located in Aboriginal institutions, cannot be dealt with in this volume. People worried about justice would still be concerned to promote some kind of cross-cultural *rapport* and dialogue; but the assumptions at this conference were of a more concrete exercise in social change, to be worked out not so much in the interplay between two different views of the universe as between blacks and whites in bed.

Decisions about the method of future consultation were made. Carrodus, Secretary for the Interior, stated at the beginning that the press was 'not anxious' to be represented; the sessions were not open ones. The missions would certainly have wished to be represented. There was a session on matters affecting their work, but no report of this was published, except for the resolutions. So the tradition was set of conferences between ministers and the public servants responsible that has been maintained ever since. One effect of this has possibly been to isolate those responsible for policies and practices from serious face-to-face criticism. Even now, there has been no meeting of all groups interested, including Aborigines, at the national level.

Late in the conference another discussion was held about future representation, as so many missionary and other voluntary bodies had wished to attend this one. The decision to keep it to those 'paid to do this work' was justified on the ground that otherwise there would be too many clashing opinions. Better to keep it a cosy affair; and within the bounds which, to be fair, form a very serious limitation on the freedom of action of the Australian public servant, who must not be caught in a situation which might embarrass his minister. And since that time, Aboriginal affairs have presented very awkward issues: but almost any kind of practice can be justified in the very general terms of the policy agreements which have issued from the conferences of the Commonwealth and State authorities.

One suspects, but does not know, that the closed session on missions provided an opportunity for the usual criticisms of these organisations, especially of their tendencies to pursue their own policies. At this time the missions had done more than any other organisations, with their limited financial resources, to establish settled communities. The sparser settlement in these northern regions and round the central desert areas gave the opportunity for long, comparatively uninterrupted contact which had not been enjoyed in the more easily settled regions. Especially

COMMONWEALTH LOOKS FOR AN ABORIGINAL POLICY 325

on the coasts of the north, it was possible for people to maintain themselves, as they had always done, largely from the sea; even where there was a passion in the mission superintendent to make farmers of the nomads, they could always adapt with a gesture and live from fishing. They could also move at will by canoe. Life is easier in the tropics. Perhaps it is significant that the missions came closest to their aims of setting up the Christian communities, on which so much effort had been spent for so long, mainly along the tropical coasts and rivers, where Aborigines did not depend on grass-eating animals to the same extent as elsewhere.

Even today, with all the tensions and problems of which the missions themselves are becoming increasingly aware, there are isolated Christian communities where real security has been enjoyed over several generations. What 'Christian' means in this context need not concern us here; but the long efforts to split the generations and to prevent Aboriginal socialisation of the young people, the mission-arranged marriages, and the other means of isolation from tribal society, which is itself in crisis, have had some real results. There must be many Aborigines for whom there is only a Christian identity. One of the ironies is that the resultant personality has almost obsolete features in the general Australian society. It sometimes happens that the Christian goodness of an Aboriginal person reminds one of the simpler ideals now hard to find in materialistic white Australia.

The resolutions of this conference were concerned with 'practical' affairs and framed to bring the missions under more definite control. In time most missions were to be seen as, some of them were to accept the role of, agents of assimilation; and sometimes a mission has been ready to advance assimilation at the expense of justice, perhaps a result of mission dependence on government for use of land and for funds.

At this conference Bleakley described their efforts to promote the government policy in north Queensland. Here they had powers of protectors (including certain court powers)—suitably, of both Aborigines and Fisheries. They concentrated on training the children; but as these grew up they were 'encouraged to mate and settle in villages'—to help the mission in farming, cattle raising, and fishing, and have their own gardens, pigs, bees, and poultry, while the older people would come in from the bush to get flour, implements, tobacco, and tea. This was a rosy picture, quite in contrast with that painted by Donald Thomson, who had pointed out the heavy depopulation which had occurred. But Bleakley seemed confident that Queensland would set the proper example for all States and the Commonwealth. He opined that the Aborigines Protection Society, which had been advocating developmental activities on reserves, must

326 THE DESTRUCTION OF ABORIGINAL SOCIETY

have gained its advanced ideas from a study of what Queensland had achieved.[21] This was not a defence of missions but an argument for the inviolable reserve.

Neville's criticism of the northern missions in Western Australia was on grounds which do them credit. The mission populations were increasing, he said; and this in itself was an indication of mission success in establishing stability in the distant tropics. But the half-caste population was increasing as the result of marriage between half-castes; the missions would not co-operate in his wish, it seems, to prevent a half-caste from marrying a full-blood: 'they allow half-castes under their control to marry anybody'.[22]

From the remarks of Bleakley and Neville it is possible to confirm that conditions on the northern pastoral properties in their States were not so very different from those in the Territory. Queensland could claim payment for the pastoral worker and enforce this by contract, to the limit of the efficiency of the police protector. But one result of this, said Bleakley, was to make the pastoralists unwilling to maintain the non-workers whose land had been taken up for cattle—the dependants about whose plight Cook had been so concerned in the Territory. Dependence on prostitution for food was common, said Bleakley: and education of children impossible: the only way out of the problem he could see was to transfer all the non-workers to institutions. The suggestion that the pastoralist should pay a wage adequate for dependants did not occur. (The other alternative might have been excision of reserves from the runs: though the necessary expenditure for housing and some rations would have had to be met by government.) He admitted widespread malnutrition: 'even where relief can be given, issues of flour, rice, tea, sugar and beef offal are inadequate substitutes for the native game and fruits of which they have been deprived.'[23]

Neville stated that in Western Australia the full-bloods were 'not, for the most part, getting enough food', though he put down the decline in their numbers to 'decimation by their own tribal practices'.[24] He thought there were 10,000 still not influenced by civilisation. 'No matter what we do, they will die out.' That it was, at least in part, a matter of food shortage is indicated by his next remark that 'on the cattle stations established in the far north' (by his own Department) 'the number of full-blooded

[21] Ibid., p. 7.
[22] Ibid., p. 11.
[23] Ibid., p. 7.
[24] Ibid., p. 17.

COMMONWEALTH LOOKS FOR AN ABORIGINAL POLICY 327

children is increasing, because of the care the people get'. His statement
that infanticide and abortion were the causes of decline may have been
made to avoid embarrassing his government; but the association of beef
with survival may also have been intended.

Neville was no fool, and was pressing for Commonwealth financial
aid. He was the main speaker on this matter ; and his remarks show
that, in his State also, priority remained higher for cattle than for
Aborigines. Even the profits from his Aboriginal cattle stations had to be
offset against expenditure. He could not, he said, provide very much,
even for those under control, on a total of 30s per annum per head—an
amount which had to cover services as well as supplies.

The food is neither sufficient nor of the right kind. It lacks the very things that the
people need. The natives in our State exist on four articles, meat, tea, flour and
sugar. For the most part, they do not get much meat. I am not going to give details
of the ration because I am not proud of it.[25]

There were 18,000 head of cattle on Moola Bulla, but no money even to
house the children there or for technical training anywhere.

The effect of undernutrition on the inland areas, so clearly indicated by
Duguid, must have been especially serious in the combination of drought
and depression years, especially as the ration generally recognised in many
places was first fixed as supplementary, on the assumption that game were
available. As the game were killed out, especially where the fit adult males
were employed for single rations only, and could not hunt, those unable
to go far enough afield to seek more must share the workers' ration or
face starvation. The grim situation in the central desert had led to begging
along the Trans-Australian railway. Both Neville and McLean claimed
that this had become an organised business (which was more than likely).
Neville's department had kept natives away from this source of supplies,
but they had moved into South Australia and operated there. He was
worried about public and international comment; they must be kept
away, or the passengers be prevented from giving them presents. McLean
agreed; some were wont to hang their good clothes on bushes and beg in
rags. The comments were a good indication of the bureaucratic sensitivity
which had limited this conference mainly to officials.

There is a kind of administrative semantics in which the real issues may
be lost or completely misrepresented and which must always limit any
attempt to deal by bureaucratic methods with issues involving social
change. It is not only that officers with no more than clerical skills will
make bold decisions on files which may bind field officers who know

[25] Ibid., pp. 16, 17, and 33.

328   THE DESTRUCTION OF ABORIGINAL SOCIETY

what the problems are. There are also attempts to keep the issues to the level of clerical comprehension. One of the reasons for hostility to missions has been the missionary's often far greater knowledge of a particular group, especially if he is linguistically competent. There was discussion of the 'economic development of reserves', some time after Bleakley had mentioned the pressure from the Aborigines Protection Society. But when the Commonwealth introduced the topic, the reference was to *European* economic activities in reserves; whether miners and prospectors should be allowed to follow Lasseter into the Central Reserve—a suggestion opposed by Cook. But Neville, who badly needed money, said that he would support a request, and pay the royalties towards native welfare.

Even the matter of corporal punishment was introduced by the Commonwealth, because the planters in the Mandated Territory had been pressing for its restoration there as a labour incentive. It is to Neville's credit that he spoke very strongly against this and that he admitted the earlier practice of 'unmerciful flogging' in Western Australia.

THE McEWEN POLICY

That assimilation into the community should be implicitly accepted at this conference as a physical, genetic process indicated the gap between the official Aboriginal welfare organisations and those who had been advocating an intercultural dialogue which should lead to justice and to an accommodation between the cultures. Writing much later of this period, Elkin told how the field workers in his discipline had 'provided first the humanitarian societies, and then the governments, with systematised knowledge of the essentials of native social and cultural life, and of the principles operating in the contact situation, of which both missions and administrations should be aware'.[26]

He was not a member of the 1937 conference, but was later consulted by McEwen, the Minister for the Interior, in the preparation of the first really humane statement of Aboriginal policy since the end of British colonial administration. Early in 1939, in a foreshadowing of the arrangements for a colonial administrative structure which should be based on the principle that the Aboriginal, irrespective of his race or colour, was entitled by right to eventual citizenship, McEwen made a statement in the House about the future in the Northern Territory. The aim would be 'the raising of their status so as to entitle them by right and by qualification to

[26] 'Reaction and Interaction: A Food Gathering People and European Settlement in Australia', p. 184.

COMMONWEALTH LOOKS FOR AN ABORIGINAL POLICY   329

the ordinary rights of citizenship, and to enable them and help them to share with us the opportunities that are available in their native land'.[27] Aboriginal material needs should be met; they should be trained for useful occupations and the settled life (which seemed to overlook the fact that the Aboriginal was the mainstay of the cattle industry); they must be taught to recognise the law and authority, and, of course, rights of property. Religious training was required for 'stability of character to replace that which has been lost by the destruction of their ancient philosophy and moral code....' Thomson's advice was to be accepted on the subject of the myalls in the big reserves; they would be left alone and protected until the policy had resulted in progress for the others; in the meantime there would be no economic exploitation of the reserves. Missions, and headquarters of the proposed District Officers would, however, be established on the fringes of these reserves.

The idea of gradualism in the contact process may, at this stage, have been something of a fantasy: it assumes that the Aborigines would visit these points and return to their country. But the reserves would be patrolled, with medical help and adjudication in disputes. Eventually the Aborigines would congregate round the District Offices where there would be homes for the staff and hospital and administrative buildings; rations to the old and infirm would be issued here; this, it was stated, would offset the drift to towns. Here also recruiting for the stations would be carried on; and here would be the detention camp, instead of the town gaol. There would be training in pastoral crafts for the young, in the hope that the reserves could be developed economically. At a later stage, patrol officers would be assisted by a Native Constabulary on patrols.

The new Director of Native Affairs-elect, E.W.P. Chinnery, was trained in anthropology and had had long experience in New Guinea. He was to have an Assistant Director. Field staff were to be trained in anthropology and law at the University of Sydney, as were those of the Mandated Territory. Officers would later be appointed to educate Aborigines for citizenship; half-castes would be trained as teachers. Government would increase assistance to missions. The District Officer would, as in New Guinea, have magisterial powers in courts of native affairs. These courts would deal with cases involving native and native, seeking justice in accordance with custom 'or along lines prescribed' in later legislation; one means would be the use of native assessors. The half-castes (other than those of half-caste parents only who would generally be

[27] *The Northern Territory of Australia: Commonwealth Government's Policy with respect to Aboriginals.* Issued by the Hon. J. McEwen, Minister for the Interior, February 1939.

330 THE DESTRUCTION OF ABORIGINAL SOCIETY

in family situations) would be trained in institutions; those nearly white would be trained in the States or in separate institutions; from the half-castes, staff could later be recruited.

The document is a curious mixture of humane purposes and the established institutional means. In detail it must have been worked out in the Department of the Interior, after Chinnery and McEwen had looked at the situation in the Territory in 1938. The influence of Elkin is clear in the objectives of policy. Some of the means and some of the assumptions seem bureaucratically naïve in view of what is now known of the processes of social change—such for instance as the hope expressed that the missions might substitute new sets of belief for those assumed to have been lost—when the real dilemma might be as well described as that of people who held to the old beliefs, but were in situations where they could no longer do what they believed to be right.

Nor was anyone (except the taxpayer) to be really hurt. The pastoral industry could be reassured by the statement that Aborigines in employment were protected adequately by the Ordinance; not so much perhaps by the statement that henceforth the Ordinance would be enforced and the conditions of employment inspected. Nor was the urgency of Thomson's recommendations reflected here.

This policy is framed towards a distant objective and should not in its details be condemned as being too ambitious or impracticable. In considering our obligations to raise the status of these people, one must not think in terms of years but of generations.[28]

While conceding the very great advance which had been achieved in this statement of an assimilation policy, an advance which may be clearly pointed by comparison of the objectives stated here with the trend of discussion at the conference which considered the Bleakley Report a decade earlier, it was not a concession of equality *now*; nor did it appear to envisage the possibility of Aborigines, while following their own traditions, holding the full legal rights of citizens. Rather were they to be taught, gradually and kindly, to live like other Australians. The Aboriginal was the pupil; he would have to learn, and have to earn, in some not very clear manner, his civic rights. In fact, the document provided that *individual* Aborigines would move from Aboriginal into non-Aboriginal society. There was the assumption of a common purpose between the teachers and the taught, the governors and the governed, perhaps an inevitable deduction from the assumption that Aborigines could now be

[28] Ibid.

COMMONWEALTH LOOKS FOR AN ABORIGINAL POLICY 331

changed by programs bureaucratically applied. The objective rocked no boats and was compatible with the continuance of the Aboriginal institutions which by now were being maintained by every government. These, as instruments of assimilation (though the objective was not to be generally adopted until after the war), would now be the means of processing individuals to make them acceptable in the general community. The same managements which had been concerned with 'protection' would then be concerned with 'assimilation'. In all the history, this offer to the Aboriginal to make him acceptable to the whites was hardly based on sound psychology.

Had the plan been pressed through in the Territory with more finance than Aboriginal needs were likely to get at that time, the proposed District Officers' townships, the 'centres of hope and refuge', would probably have become secular institutions of the type so well established elsewhere. The very priorities indicated, for buildings for staff in the first instance (quite necessary if there were to be staff there) meant that there would be, round the houses and offices, a 'fringe' of camp-dwellers, recently resigned from the nomadic life, at each station. The effect may have been not so very different from what happened on the big post-war government settlements in the Territory. Once this happens, there is an almost inevitable progression to paternal control and resentful camp-dwellers, who become more and more dependent for rations, and who have to be managed in the interests of hygiene and order.

The McEwen statement foreshadowed two new District Officers' posts—one on the southern boundary of Arnhem Land and one in the Port Keats area or on the FitzMaurice, with Strehlow carrying on his work in the south-west. Had the war not intervened, the location of the present settlements might have been different; but the main advantage would probably have been in their management, provided that their establishment could have been limited to the rate of training staff. They would still have been, as the proposed locations indicate, in areas where there was no demand for land for white settlement and isolated far from the places of economic opportunity.

What would have been a more hopeful approach involved an act of faith and an affront to vested interests which even now seems politically impossible: with what has been spent on establishing settlements out of the way of economic enterprise, perhaps a real stake in the pastoral industry could have been acquired by the purchase of cattle stations offering real chances for training and management. That the idea was not impossible Neville had shown in Western Australia. But the Aboriginal was to remain on the fringe of the economy indefinitely. Having already been largely committed to economic change, and having no other hope, his first need was for employment at a living wage; his second, for living conditions compatible with health, an increasing understanding, and dignity. That his chances of getting these things were so slim was due to prejudice and the limited view of what economic development involves—for here was potentially the settled work force of the north.

That he was offered instead, at least where he heard of it, the goal of assimilation, with these opportunities to follow, was the result of deeply ingrained beliefs about his capacity for change and about what are the true priorities in Australian society. As 'assimilation' implied, to those who adhered to the idea of a monolithic White Australia, that Aborigines would eventually disappear, it was universally accepted. And so the Aboriginal has been left in the situation where he badly needs economic and legal hitting power to confront prejudice and establish his rights in fact. But to exercise such power, he needs his place in the economy.

THE EFFECTS OF WORLD WAR II IN THE NORTHERN TERRITORY

That Aborigines could be effective units of labour in the pastoral industry had long been demonstrated, at the same time as it was being denied. The logic of economics was again to assert itself in the events arising in the Territory from the war with Japan. This effectively prevented the carrying out of the McEwen plan; but it speeded up processes of social change, especially through the attraction of the military establishments. A report of 1943, for instance, refers to the work of Aborigines for the army, where they were being employed on essential tasks of maintenance and construction. Some were working in and round the big motor workshops which kept the trucks rolling along the road from Alice Springs. They soon adapted to 'civilised' ways of eating, it was reported, gave devoted service, and got along well with the troops.[29] Another report in 1945 told how the war and the chance of army employment had 'lifted' Aborigines out of their 'comparative security'; that over a thousand were so employed; that many more depots and patrol posts would be required after the war; and that it would then be necessary to begin the deferred patrol officer system. (Yet the same report could still claim that the large proportion of full-bloods in the Territory was a result of the practice of keeping reserves

[29] Report on the Administration of the Northern Territory 1943 (roneo); section on 'Native Affairs'.

COMMONWEALTH LOOKS FOR AN ABORIGINAL POLICY 333

'inviolate'.)[30] The armed forces had been paying the cash wage, which amounted to 10d. a day; but dependants had been maintained and all were on the full army ration.

This was in many ways a direct reverse of what had been planned for the program of assimilation. The difference in the situation was the presence of an employer with no need to worry about dividends and with plenty of work to offer. There was also the inbuilt services training program. One result of all this was that the standards in government employment had to be raised to 30s per week and keep. But the army withdrew quite suddenly, and the Administration faced a new situation.[31]

There is fortunately one study, by the anthropologists Ronald and Catherine Berndt, of the situation of Aborigines working for one of the big companies, with several stations in the Territory, during the later war years. Their report also includes a description of the conditions in the Australian army work camps.[32] They were commissioned by the firm to make this study: and clearly its interest was to get more labour from the bush to replace the fast-disappearing station work force rather than to invest in measures to halt the decline of station populations. By this time the position was apparently becoming serious. One of the reasons might have been that although the pastoral industry had been allocated a priority to retain labour employed, the army had first priority for workers who were not. This could expedite the inevitable labour crisis which seemed sure to come when the last groups came in from the tribal life to the stations, replacing those groups which would 'die out'. When the Berndts saw the army camps, late in 1945, there were five of them, with some 800 Aborigines. Possibly the end of the war, and the establishment of the settlements, with measures for increasing welfare which have been effective enough to produce an increasing population, saved the pastoral managements from having to make a drastic reappraisal of their employment policies.

The Berndts found that men were employed on the stations in stock work, boundary riding, colt breaking, gardening, wood chopping, driving waggons, assisting the engineer, saddler, blacksmith, carpenter, boring or fencing contractor, cook, mechanic—and in other 'odd jobs'. The women washed and ironed, gardened, worked at fencing and on the

[30] C.P.P., 1946-7, vol. II, no. 13, pp. 1075 et seq.—Report on the Administration of the Northern Territory 1944-45.
[31] C.P.P., 1946-7, vol. II, no. 13, pp. 1083 et seq.—Report on the Administration of the Northern Territory for 1945-46: Report by Carrington, Acting Director of Native Affairs (Paper no. 13, pp. 26-31).
[32] Ronald M. Berndt and Catherine H. Berndt, Aboriginal Labour in a Pastoral Area.

roads, milked cows and goats, pulled the punkah fans, washed up, helped the cook and anybody else, baked and cooked for the stock camp; prepared horsehair for the saddler and hides for tanning, scrubbed and cleaned in the house, shined shoes, sewed, disposed of rubbish and night soil. All worked at some time or other, whether dependants or not. Frequently, children under twelve worked, although this was illegal under the regulations. 'Boys of nine and ten are found in the stock camp, girls of eight and nine in the house'.[33] Every able-bodied person was either in employment or resting. For any special task, the whole camp would be called on, whether classified as dependants or not. Thus the dependants whose maintenance excused the employers from paying the 5s wage were also workers as required.

The Berndts found that the regulations meant little; that the occasional inspection by a patrol officer could not be effective. The difference between what people received in rations and issues and what appeared on the station books would be more marked perhaps, where the company was a large one employing a number of station managers, who are likely to be judged on their annual operating costs and profits rather than on the general condition of the station and the state of the work force. There were often neither full lists of employees and dependants nor birth and death records. Camp dwellings were either bagging and old iron humpies or windbreaks; yet this stable population needed the same shelter from the rains and wind as any other in like case. No sanitation or garbage facilities were provided; not even safe drinking water. The 'usual quota' of food issued to the worker, man or woman, was 'three times daily . . . a hunk of dry bread, a piece of cooked beef, and a pannikin of sweetened tea'. The casual worker received the dependant's ration, generally flour, sugar, and tea, with offal and some bones when a beast was killed. The equivalent of the retirement pension for a worker who survived this to old age was the right to stay in the camp and collect the dependant's ration. It is obvious that there must have been a wide range of current situations: the Berndts, like J.H. Kelly, mention Rosewood Station as one which, by investing in its work force with good conditions and training, had a known record of efficient production.

As in Bleakley's day, prostitution of women for rations and clothing helped to keep the camp going—in clothing, tinned fruit, or jam and tobacco. A contact situation quickly creates the embarrassing awareness of nakedness and the consequent requirements for human dignity. But some stations did not provide underwear and women had to prostitute

[33] Ibid., p. 43.

COMMONWEALTH LOOKS FOR AN ABORIGINAL POLICY 335

themselves to get it. For the children, station tasks took the place of indigenous education; and station experience offered nothing better than what the child began with.

From what they could observe, the Berndts attributed the loss of mothers and children at birth partly to the poor rations. They knew of four births only, on one station; and the loss of life was three babies and two mothers. A woman who usually worked in one station homestead could be desperately ill without the knowledge of the employer's family, thus indicating that Aborigines had their pride, expected little, and often did not report a serious illness. The Berndts also mention the attitudes which kept down the birth rate. 'If there's nothing for them', one man told them, 'it would be better not to have them at all'. To this one might add that bearing a child is only the beginning of the process of producing a worker; that the social facts have to be such as to offer some hope; that mothers without hope cannot make good mothers. But without station population records, the observers could not assess mortality rates.

The lack of other incentives increase or continue dependence on violence, or the threat of violence, especially where management and worker associate only for employment—and, in the special Australian conditions, for the sexual activities of the white males. 'Today, many people in this area maintain that physical violence and threat of violence are the only successful means of keeping the natives under control'.[34] Yet managers could assume that their Aboriginal employees and dependants venerated them—the great colonial illusion. At the end of the war, some managers were still opposing new pressures to improve housing, and also opposing cash wages as likely to corrupt the Aborigines.

The Berndts found contrasting conditions, not only in the army Aboriginal camps but in a new government settlement near Katherine (which could very well have set the pattern for the post-war settlements). The critics of the 'army boys' sounded like colonial critics of 'mission boys': they were, they said, 'spoilt, cheeky, and hopelessly indisciplined'.

Certainly [wrote the Berndts] the Army settlements, with their regular routine, ample diet for all, canteens, showers and latrines, and more friendly atmosphere, were formidable rivals to private employers who could not, or would not, compete in providing facilities for their workers . . . On all these places, generally speaking, there was a feeling of economic and emotional security which had been largely absent from the pastoral areas we had visited.[35]

Men and women were employed. They received only the 5s wage, but

[34] Ibid., p. 62.
[35] Ibid., p. 83.

the difference was that they actually received it and had the right to spend it in the canteen at fair prices. On the stations the investigators found that all hours were either in fact or potentially working hours (except during the 'wet', when the 'walkabout' holiday was taken). But the army worked a five and a half day week, and paid overtime. It provided ample food, tobacco, and clothing; and there were sweets and luxuries at canteen prices for all, with preference for the children. Housing provided good shelter, and the investigators were impressed with the pride in furniture and other possessions, and with the fact that the householders had bought locks to protect their wealth. They had access to laundries, clothes lines, and flat irons; good sanitation, running water, plenty of soap. There was a planned diet, of foods which they learned to cook, some schooling, and medical attention—in fact everything which from their previous experience they would assume to be only for those in the homestead.

Old hands criticised the cost. But a new question had been posed—of whether any industry which could not provide for its workers the basic necessities for a materially safe and civilised life, by western standards, was worth subsidising at the cost of miseries which the workers had never had to endure as nomads. The response to these facilities had indicated the fallacy of the employers' defence that good accommodation would only be destroyed or wasted: and the Berndts pointed out that many of the army employees and their families had come from areas where they had had little work experience. The armed forces, commonly assumed to be authoritarian and conservative, had offered the pastoral industry and the Administration and Commonwealth government a lesson in good and progressive management.

The government came to profit from it. The pastoral managements in general have continued to defend the old *status quo*. Here were the precedents for the post-war government settlements. Whatever has to be said by way of criticism of these, they were and are genuine expressions of a new humanity and concern: the results of efforts to save, and to provide new opportunities for, Aborigines by providing them with those basic necessities for static living which they had not very often found in employment. The further step, of establishing them on good pastoral country, resumed from some of the large companies, would have been politically very radical then, as it would be now. But what is logical but impossible can very quickly become necessary and good politics.

One effect of these armed forces activities (for the Air Force was also providing employment) was to raise the question of what workers in the pastoral industry should be paid, at a time when many managers believed

COMMONWEALTH LOOKS FOR AN ABORIGINAL POLICY 337

that they should not receive a cash wage at all; for what Aborigines had actually received from the armed forces was obviously far more in value than 5s weekly.

In July 1945 V.G. Carrington, Acting Director of Native Affairs, was instructed to investigate the matter of Aboriginal conditions of employment in the pastoral industry. Production of beef was on a high priority, and at that stage it seemed that the war against Japan might be a long one. It is clear from the records that the achievement of Aborigines in Army and Air Force employment had been a revelation to many. When Chinnery returned from war service he took the matter further with the Administrator, the Carrington Report with Chinnery's comments being the basic document. Carrington made definite recommendations for minimum cash wages and conditions, and Chinnery stated that his recommendations were adequate for a conference between the pastoralists and the government.[36]

This was of course a highly political matter. The conference was held at Alice Springs in January 1947. Eventually the wage levels recommended by Carrington were reduced, but a cash wage of from 12s 6d per week, up to £1 for those with over three years experience, was provided for in draft regulations as a result of the conference. An interesting indication of priorities was the fact that the draft was shuttled between Interior, the Attorney-General's Department, and the Administration for two years.

The war may be taken as indicating the end of the process of destruction of Aboriginal society. Questions of economic opportunity and justice were being raised. In 1946 the Australian Workers Union in Western Australia had applied with success to have 'reasonably efficient' Aboriginal workers paid the award wage in rural employment, mainly in the southwest; and though this was to mean very little, it was a straw in the wind.[37] But the Northern Territory continued to be a focus of interest for all Australians who were concerned with Aboriginal affairs—a growing and more vocal minority as post-war prosperity increased and the contrast with fringe settlements all over Australia became more marked. The report of the Western Australian decision apparently stimulated the Aboriginal Advancement League of Victoria to approach the Commonwealth Minister for the Interior, who told its representative, William Onus, that it was up to the unions to apply to the industrial courts to have Aborigines included in awards.[38]

---

[36] This material is in Commonwealth Archives 50/294, files 46/1879, 46/1491, and 46/462.
[37] *Daily Telegraph* (Sydney), 21 December 1946.
[38] *Herald* (Melbourne), 9 December 1946.

338 THE DESTRUCTION OF ABORIGINAL SOCIETY

For a long time yet, however, Aboriginal wages in pastoral Australia were to be excluded from awards. In the Territory an application to the Commonwealth Conciliation and Arbitration Commission to have Aborigines employed in the pastoral industry paid under award was refused by Portus C.C., in 1948, on the grounds that an agreement reached between the pastoralists and the Northern Territory Administration should not be subject to 'interference' by the highest industrial court of the nation.

I must refuse the union's application that the award should apply to Aboriginals. As the result of a conference last year between the Pastoral Associations and the Northern Territory Administration, agreement was reached concerning the terms of employment and the maintenance of Aboriginals living on stations. From a perusal of this agreement it is clear that if the union's application were granted it would interfere with the policy of the Administration. Such an interference would not be justified as the Administration is much better equipped than a court of arbitration to attend to the welfare of the Aboriginals living and working on cattle stations.[39]

This denial, or refusal to use the power of wage fixation which the Commonwealth had,[40] left the way open for the fixing of separate Aboriginal wages later, under the Wards' Employment Ordinance.

Perhaps enough has been said to indicate how the problem had ceased to be one of survival and had become one of equality. Very great differences had been put in train by other steps, taken almost accidentally, such as the extension of social service benefits to various categories of Aborigines, still limited by obsolete definitions in racial terms but inevitably, as in the matter of wages, leading towards equality. These new trends were simply irreconcilable with the rough-and-ready traditions of the frontier methods of administration. And a stage had been reached when it was becoming clear that, next to the part-Aboriginal, the full-blood population was the Australian group with the highest natural increase.

The best use of a patrol service in this post-war period could have been for the policing of definite wage scales and conditions of employment. Such a method of asserting a definite government policy, at the main point of interaction, could under the existing legislation have forced on the pastoral industry the preservation of its own labour force, at least in accommodation and rations. Yet the end of the military occupation had removed a most important alternative source of employment—and greatly strengthened the force of employers' threats to discharge Aborigines.

[39] The terms of the judgment are published in P.J. Sheehan, *Industrial Information Bulletin*, 3 to 8 February 1949.
[40] Since the definition of 'employee' in the Conciliation and Arbitration Act 1904-1964, section 4, has never excluded Aborigines, this seems a good example of the proneness of those in authority to be influenced by their own views on what is suitable for Aborigines.

COMMONWEALTH LOOKS FOR AN ABORIGINAL POLICY 339

It is now clear that the great effort which resulted in the establishment of the large government settlements, to contain those off the pastoral runs and prepare them for assimilation, brought into the frontier, but on a larger scale, the kind of problem of the management of institutions in which every previous effort in Aboriginal administration had ended. The same level of effort, to establish housing and municipal services for Aborigines in the townships, would at least have posed more definitely the social and economic problems which have to be faced; or perhaps there could have been the compromise involved in freedom of movement for all Aborigines, and some choice to elect for living on reserves or in towns.

But the Welfare Ordinance, providing for quite autocratic control of Wards, of where they might live, of their movements and property, was in a long tradition of Aboriginal management. One effect has been to isolate great numbers of the less experienced in institutional situations; and it has intensified the well-established sense of injustice at the hands of the white man, with all the special tensions of institutions isolated from economic and social contacts with other than official Australians. It might have cost less and achieved more to pay unemployment and other social service benefits to all those out of employment; but this would have raised the question of wages lower than pensions, forcing equality in minimum wages. For this, the tradition of paternal management in Aboriginal affairs and the general level of prejudice were probably too strong. The result has been to pose for the Northern Territory, even more acutely than in any of the States where answers are currently being sought, the unanswered question of how to get out of the institutional situations. And, as in Queensland, such an institutional empire inevitably creates vested interests in the *status quo*. The settlements are seen as great 'training' institutions, where the inmates are to be prepared for 'assimilation'.[41]

BY ACCELERATING the processes of social change, World War II probably began a new phase in Aboriginal relationships with other Australians. Passive acceptance of the *status quo*, based on ignorance, could not continue. Open violence by the whites was to become much more rare, if only because governments were more likely to enforce the law. The frontier days were over. Before the war ended, social service benefits had begun to cushion the effects of Aboriginal poverty; and from now on all Australian governments were to be richer in resources than they had ever been. There

[41] For a detailed description of these institutions by a political scientist see C.M. Tatz, Aboriginal Administration in the Northern Territory of Australia.

340 THE DESTRUCTION OF ABORIGINAL SOCIETY

are many political and economic reasons why an increasing gap between respective living standards cannot be accepted by government. Thus the destruction of Aboriginal society, after over a century and a half, would be either arrested and reversed or would proceed by other means. Governments were to accept the assimilation policy as the other means. This policy envisaged that Aboriginal socialisation would give place to some officially approved process which would finally merge Aboriginal social habits in the majority social order. Education and opportunity were to be the means towards this submergence.

Two groups of Aboriginal people will need to be catered for in any policy designed to integrate them into the Australian community—the part-Aboriginal groups in closely settled areas and those, mostly classified as of the full descent, who live in the Centre and far north, retain more their traditional customs and beliefs, and present to the whites a different stereotype from that of the part-Aborigine. They are nonetheless a depressed caste often living in their own 'country' in what is still a 'colonial' society. With the vast mineral discoveries in these areas, important social changes are on the way for them.[42]

The future status and role of the Aboriginal will be a significant indicator of the kind of society which eventually takes shape in Australia. The real question is whether the logic of welfare or the prejudice of White Australia is to prevail—the basic political question which has been so consistently pre-judged in the other vital areas of migration and external affairs.

[42] These two groups form the subject matter of volume II, *Outcastes in White Australia*, and volume III, *The Remote Aborigines*.

APPENDIXES

APPENDIX A

WHO IS AN ABORIGINAL? THE ANSWER IN 1967

Appendix A is an attempt to summarise the problems involved in defining Aborigines, as at the beginning of 1967. It was made because only in this way can something of the complexities be suggested. It had to be at a point fixed in time, because the law is forever changing, and this work was being written in a time of rapid change. The recent trend has been for the special definitions of person as 'Aboriginal', 'native', or 'half-caste', etc. to disappear. It seemed important to look at these definitions as they stood, partly as shedding light on the difficulties facing the census, and partly for their social and political implications.

If by the time this is published, all such definitions have disappeared, it is still important that they should be recorded. For the attitudes of Aborigines and other Australians have been deeply influenced by these laws. Government cannot assume that by abolishing a law it also obliterates memories and consequences of past relationships.

If special laws are to apply to special persons, such persons have to be legally defined. Therefore, from the beginning of legislation restricting and protecting Aborigines, it has been necessary to include definitions indicating who is an Aboriginal person. Sometimes, for part-Aborigines in certain situations, there has been a separate definition, to bring them partly or especially within the scope of the 'Aboriginal' law. This happened, for instance, in Commonwealth law applying in the Northern Territory from 1918 until 1953: 'half-castes', as defined separately from Aboriginal, remained under control until they reached a certain age. But other 'half-castes', including those who were married to Aborigines or habitually associated with them, were, for legal purposes, Aboriginal.

In the definition of who is an Aboriginal there is a history of legislation which is as complicated as legislation in South Africa. Each State, and the Commonwealth after 1911, made its own decisions. One result was that a person might be legally 'Aboriginal' in one State but not in another.

Another result arose from the difficulties faced by those who had to administer this legislation. The easiest way to define the Aboriginal person was to do so in terms of his racial origin—the degree of his Aboriginal descent, or, as the legislation often expressed it (and as the Queensland Act still does[1]) the proportion of Aboriginal 'blood'. This presupposes an official knowledge of the descent of each person to whom the law is applied. But obviously the administering departments of government could have no such accurate knowledge in all cases, especially in view of the limited funds available for Aboriginal administration and the qualifications of those making the decisions. So in practice some rule of thumb had to be used. For generations decisions have been made, and may still be made, on the basis of skin coloration, and of 'Aboriginal features'. The Mendelian law does not operate conveniently to support such a rule of thumb, but the prejudice of white Australians does; the people being so defined have remained largely inarticulate.

Western European settler democracy made use of such laws to define 'native' status in the colonies for many reasons. Sometimes the customs of the natives conflicted with the European law, yet it was necessary to recognise them, *for natives*. Sometimes natives, it was thought, should be protected against pedlars of guns, alcohol, worthless merchandise, and drugs, and against recruiters of labour; or it might be thought good for them to pay special taxes, so that they would have to work for money (and for European employers). For these and many other reasons, it was necessary to define a 'native' person. There was generally a tendency, either in the law or in its application, to pay special attention to the economic requirements or to the social exclusiveness of the settlers, as in the laws which excluded natives from towns, mainly at certain times when they were not needed there for work.

We have to remember that the Australian colonies were settler democracies. Most of this legislation in Australia came after Aboriginal society had been destroyed in all but a few places. Very little of it goes back into the period of British colonial administration. One reason for this was that, having taken over land and other assets for allocation to settlers and for government purposes, the British government vaguely planned that the Aboriginal, as a British subject, should be taught how to acquire a share of the total assets, so assessed, through education. Making him subject to the law was held to be one means of educating him.

In the mid-1960s the trend is for this special Aboriginal legislation to disappear. But it is conceivable that special provisions may have to be made and established in law to assist the Aboriginal minority into a situation of equal opportunity. So the need for defining a category of persons may remain. This is not my main concern at this point; but in passing it is worth noting that racist definitions, leading in practice to decisions made on skin colour or personal appearance, conflict directly with the democratic value-notion that each human being has an equal value before the law. They would merely be absurd, comparable with definitions which set aside for special treatment persons who are left-handed or red-haired, were it not for the long history of discrimination on racial grounds, which in practice resulted in discrimination, in the colonial world and in countries with non-European racial minorities, on grounds of personal appearance. In this context they are insulting, as in the absurd examples used, because they classify persons in terms of things which are quite irrelevant to their potential and their achievements.

[1] See Aborigines' and Torres Strait Islanders' Affairs Act of 1965, section 6 (1) and (2).

WHO IS AN ABORIGINAL? 343

But they are more deeply wounding and insulting because they have been (and are) so often used as the means of classifying a rejected caste group by those who have done the rejecting and who have proclaimed their own inherent superiority.

If, therefore, it is necessary to define Aborigines, for purposes of future assistance, it seems sensible to allow for decision by those who require the assistance. 'Aboriginal' may become a social and administrative category; and those who freely identify as such may claim the special assistance to be provided. This raises the difficulty that many of us who have forgotten our Aboriginal ancestry may be tempted to remember it. But there are ways to get round this, even without requiring the proof of some degree of Aboriginal ancestry; and one of them has often been used in this legislation. Certain persons who have lived with, or after the manner of, other Aborigines, were included, whether they wished it or not. It seems not too difficult to work out a test of inclusion in, or association with, a group in need. Even this may not be necessary. After all, the objective of special laws of this kind must be to promote equality of opportunity for all who share certain handicaps; and the inclusion with Aborigines of some who are not genetically such would be desirable and perhaps useful.

The common administrative practice of using skin colour and facial features to determine who is an Aboriginal is not, to be fair, merely a reflection of the popular prejudice. It is also in part a *consequence* of that prejudice. For the Aboriginal welfare authorities will provide assistance to those who need it; and in Australian society the degree of colour has tended to correlate with the degree of need. It has happened over the whole course of interaction between Aborigines and other Australians that those of light skin coloration have had special opportunities, not available to their darker brothers and sisters, to resign or escape from Aboriginal society and to 'pass' into the general community. Where administrative officers have for a long time been administering laws which apply to people with certain physical features different from those of most Australians, the disappearance of the features which attracted prejudice seemed a solution of the problem. The current policy of assimilation, as commonly understood, involves the 'passing' of people, who (it is assumed) become whiter in each generation, into white Australia.

While this work is concerned with people who, for whatever reason, identify freely, or are identified by society in general or by government, as Aboriginal, the current legal definitions are important. They determine who may be assisted by Aboriginal administrators now. They are also the only basis we have to calculate the size and the distribution of this minority and from which a demographer may estimate the population trends. For this kind of calculation, the definition used by the Commonwealth Bureau of Census and Statistics, a definition administratively derived from the interpretation of the former section 127 of the Commonwealth of Australia Constitution Act, is most important. It provided that 'in reckoning the numbers of the people of the Commonwealth, or of a State or other part of a Commonwealth, Aboriginal natives shall not be counted'.[2]

---

[2]At the time of writing, this section was to be submitted to a referendum for repeal: as a result of that referendum, it is no longer operative.

Except that it is used to fix Commonwealth electoral boundaries, the census definition has nothing to do with the status of individuals. To abide by the Constitution, Aborigines had to be defined for purposes of *exclusion* from the statistics of Commonwealth citizens. The definition used had no direct relationship with definitions used for States' purposes: nor, after 1911, with those adopted in the Northern Territory Ordinances to meet the special requirements of the Territory's Aboriginal administration.

Another reason for defining 'Aboriginal', for legislation by the Parliament of the Commonwealth, related to the enrolment of electors under the Commonwealth Electoral Act. Before the Report of a Select Committee of the House of Representatives in 1961 and subsequent amending legislation, no Aboriginal could enrol unless he was entitled to enrolment in his State and to vote at elections for the State Parliament, or for its more numerous House; or unless he was or had been in the defence forces.[3] A common definition of 'Aboriginal native' used for electoral purposes, and for section 127, was provided in 1929 by the Attorney-General's Department to the Chief Electoral Officer. This memorandum defined an 'Aboriginal native' as one in whom Aboriginal descent *preponderates*: and stated that 'half-castes' were not 'Aboriginal natives' within the meaning of section 127.[4] It may well have been true that, as the Select Committee of 1961 stated, 'no person is excluded from the Commonwealth franchise on the ground of race'[5]: it is equally clear that in determining who were the individuals to be excluded on other grounds, the Commonwealth used definitions related to racial origins and to nothing else.

There were two categories used for the census before the referendum of 1967. One was that of 'full-blood' Aboriginal; these have always been excluded from published statistics relating to the population as a whole. The other was 'half-caste'. Up until the 1961 census, the Commonwealth had to depend on the Aboriginal administrations of the States, with their different definitions of who was a full-blood or a half-caste for figures relating to the more inaccessible areas of State Aboriginal administration. But a special effort to get complete figures was made for the 1961 census. A full-blood, for census purposes, was a person with Aboriginal father and non-European mother. This means that some persons returned as full-bloods were not of complete Aboriginal descent. But the situation remained that a State authority might use its own definition to supply figures for the census. Another problem arose from the definition of the half-caste who is included in the census statistics. Those so identified, by their own decision (on which the census depends as far as possible) or by that of an official, should strictly have included only those persons (very few these days) with one Aboriginal and one European parent. As most part-Aboriginal people are the offspring of part-

---

[3] Commonwealth Electoral Act 1918-1961, section 39. See also Commonwealth of Australia: House of Representatives: Report from the Select Committee on Voting Rights of Aborigines, especially paragraphs 32-41.

[4] Report from Select Committee 1961—paragraph 33.

[5] Para. 21.

WHO IS AN ABORIGINAL?

Aboriginal parents on both sides, the choice facing the conscientious person in such case was difficult; but he might fairly write himself down as 'European'. There is some interesting evidence that in the 1961 census many of these people preferred to call themselves 'full-bloods'. But there is also evidence of 'statistical passing'; and probably considerable numbers have declared themselves to be European although they may be predominantly of Aboriginal descent.

This situation means that population estimates have depended on uncertain information; it was hoped that the results of the 1966 census (in which a new set of questions, based on new definitions of 'race', were used on the census form) would allow for a more correct estimate of the racial origins of the population, so that it would then be possible to say what proportion of the whole, on the basis of how people described themselves, are of Aboriginal descent; and what they have declared the degrees of such descent to be.

This raises the question of why we need to have a question on race at all. The results will certainly assist those who have to form estimates of the size of the Aboriginal population. Without such estimates, only vague plans for amelioration can be drawn up. The Aboriginal population, on known evidence, is at special risk in matters of health and is handicapped in ways reflected in its economic situation, social status, educational attainments and opportunities. To attack these problems we have to know their extent. Perhaps a more accurate estimate, for the purposes of dealing with *problems*, would be made possible by a census question which enables people to identify themselves simply as members of the Aboriginal community, or not; for when, as seems likely, all Australians can be counted as citizens irrespective of race, there will be no particular point in the attempt to establish the *degrees* of Aboriginal and other descent. On the other hand, unless the group which identifies as Aboriginal is statistically demarcated in some way, the Aboriginal figures for such items as infant mortality, infectious disease, educational attainments and the like, are simply lost in the whole. Only by ingenious calculations has it proved possible in the past to separate these from the general statistics of the census. Census figures depend on co-operation of those questioned. Even if all persons of Aboriginal descent co-operated in 1966, there would be no way of knowing how many of those returned as part-Aborigines lived as members of Aboriginal groups. It would be better, therefore, if some means could be found to identify those of some Aboriginal descent who are living in association with others in like case.[6]

No blame can be attributed to the Bureau of Census and Statistics for this situation. The constitutional exclusion resulted in the same kind of absurdity as occurs elsewhere, when special rights or penalties are related to degrees of racial origin. In this case it has meant that the census, in so far as it relates to Aborigines, was a rather inefficient instrument to exclude that proportion assumed by one authority or another, by the Commonwealth or any of the States, to be full-blood.

[6] I am indebted here to a document prepared by Dr P.M. Moodie, Medical Officer (Research), School of Public Health and Tropical Medicine, University of Sydney. 'The Recording of Aboriginal Race for Statistical Purposes' (SSRC-AP).

Yet the figures have a very great value, and not merely as the only ones we have. The main deficiency of the 1961 census was probably in under-enumeration. But the deficiencies indicated would not necessarily affect its validity as a guide to the distribution, and to the age and sex composition, both generally and as between different census districts.[7] In the research for this work, we made two fairly extensive surveys in areas where the population was part-Aboriginal; and the results were very close, in the figures on population trends, to the results of a demographic survey based mainly on the census figures for 1951 and 1961.[8]

In 1967 the only definition by Commonwealth Ordinance which had a current legal relevance was that of a 'ward' in the Northern Territory; and this only for a particular and disappearing purpose—that of defining persons to whom the lower scale of wages under the Wards' Employment Ordinance may be paid. The ward was first defined, in the Northern Territory Welfare Ordinance of 1953, as a person who by his manner of living, inability to manage his affairs, his habits, behaviour and associations, 'stands in need of special care and assistance'; but if such a person was entitled to vote, or would be so entitled at twenty-one years, or was married to a person entitled to vote, he could not be declared a ward unless he so requested.[9]

On this basis of assessment a Register of Wards was established. It seems that some Aborigines of the full descent were overlooked, and that when the move to include them was made later, the Legislative Council successfully resisted. But what concerns us here is that this was the first effort made to define a racial group in need of help in non-racial terms. It would of course have been more logical (though perhaps less practical) to have defined a group in need, irrespective of race. The fact that one who could vote could not be so defined against his will meant that anyone of European or (following a decision by Hasluck, the Minister of the time) of part-Aboriginal descent only became a ward if he so requested. Thus the effect was to bring Aborigines of the full descent under the controls and into the assisted category of the Welfare Ordinance, without mentioning race. The Northern Territory Electoral Regulations were used as the instrument of exclusion.

In passing, it must be conceded that the purpose was the training of effective citizens. That the means used, involving a system of quite rigid controls, did not prove satisfactory, is suggested by the repeal of the Welfare Ordinance in 1964 and its replacement by the Social Welfare Ordinance of that year, 'to provide for the Care and Assistance of Certain Persons'. Who these are is a matter for the discretion of the Director of Social Welfare. It is a category wider than Aboriginal. The term Aboriginal is used to define those who may live on reserves, though by the terms of the Ordinance, the Director may permit others to do so. Thus the

[7] I am indebted here to a short article by J.P.M. Long, during his period as Research Fellow, SSRC Aborigines Project; and to his subsequent paper on The Numbers and Distribution of Aboriginals in Australia, delivered at Monash University in 1965 (both in SSRC-AP files).
[8] Lancaster Jones, *The Structure and Growth of Australia's Aboriginal Population*.
[9] Northern Territory: Welfare Ordinance 1953-1960, section 14.

WHO IS AN ABORIGINAL? 347

exercise in semantic avoidance became less necessary when the controls over the group of persons defined were removed. Although it is now apparently within the power of an Aboriginal to walk off a settlement at will, only officials, candidates for election, and persons with government permits can walk on to them (unless they are Aborigines). Where formerly the Director could take a ward into custody, and tell him where to live, the Aboriginal has legally the power to live where he likes (although he may not know this), unless he is ordered off the reserve for a breach of the law. So, in the new legislation, what was formerly a restriction is replaced by what is legally a special right, to which all Aborigines are entitled.

Before 1953 there was a complicated definition, varied from time to time,[10] of two categories of persons, 'Aboriginal' and 'half-caste' (further complicated by the fact that most female half-castes and half-caste males under a certain age were included as Aboriginal); and after 1936 it became possible for the half-caste to be exempted from the application of the legislation. But the Commonwealth, in the Northern Territory, had the same kind of problem as the States, in the application of its Aboriginal administration to a category of persons defined by degrees of race. As in the States, the practice, as distinct from the legislation, tended to be the rule of thumb which identified the person by his appearance. One result of the tangle of legal definitions was that there had to be an extraordinarily complicated Ordinance in 1953 to simplify the situation with a new definition of Aboriginal (which excluded the part-Aboriginal), before the Welfare Ordinance was introduced.[11]

To illustrate further how these complications can proliferate, even within the one government, the Commonwealth established another definition by ordinance, under the authority of the Minister for the Interior, in 1954. Until that time Aborigines in the Australian Capital Territory had been controlled by the relevant New South Wales Act. It is interesting that a year after the Minister for Territories took such care to define Aborigines in non-racial terms, the Minister for the Interior should define 'Aboriginal' as 'a person who is a full-blooded or half-caste aboriginal native of Australia and who is temporarily or permanently in the Territory'.[12] In 1965 this ordinance was repealed. Such definitions were necessary for protective or discriminatory sections in laws other than in the specifically Aboriginal legislation. Consequently, when it was decided that the A.C.T. Aborigines Welfare Ordinance should be repealed to remove discrimination, a section of the A.C.T. Liquor Ordinance and a regulation under the Fish Protection Ordinance had to be repealed at the same time.

Another effect of having a special category of persons is that an Australian legislature may decide to include or exclude its members from certain benefits, which may not have seemed suitable in the past, so that *all* Aborigines as defined have been excluded. Or *some* Aborigines may be excluded. Thus in 1959 the

[10] See Northern Territory Aboriginals Ordinances 1918, 1924, 1927, 1936, and 1953, section 3 and amendments.
[11] Aboriginals Ordinance 1953, section 3.
[12] Aborigines Welfare Ordinance 1954, section 3.

Commonwealth Social Services Act was amended to allow *most* Aborigines to qualify for age, invalid, or widows' pensions, and for maternity allowances, at the same rates as others. But section 137A, inserted at the same time, provided that 'an aboriginal native of Australia who follows a mode of life that is, in the opinion of the Director-General, nomadic or primitive is not entitled to a pension, allowance, endowment or benefit under this Act'. One has sympathy for the department which has to interpret such a provision. But the decision as to who is 'nomadic or primitive' is easy when compared with the difficulties of payment. It is the policy of the Department of Social Services to pay direct to individuals where possible. But there are legal and administrative obstacles to this. First there are five State governments, each with its own definition of aboriginal or native. Some, which maintain Aboriginal settlements, regard these as benevolent institutions with a claim against pensions paid to inmates. The same claim is often recognised where a mission controls the settlement. Residence on an Aboriginal settlement, whether government or mission controlled, may mean that the legal recipient of the pension receives only a 'pocket money' component, with the management receiving the rest. It is curious that in some parts of the continent the employing pastoralist is still regarded as managing an institution for this purpose.[13]

In August 1966 the Minister for Social Services announced that pensions would be paid direct to Aborigines in the Northern Territory as soon as administrative provision could be made. (The further complication of separate State legislation is not involved there.)[14]

A different result may flow from the fact that a person residing in a remote area is defined as Aboriginal by State law. As an Aboriginal he may not be entitled to the award wage or he may work in an area where the State has recognised, or tacitly allowed, payment of some local wage traditional for Aborigines. Is he legally 'unemployed' if he refuses employment at the 'Aboriginal' wage? How should the Department of Social Services act where State or Commonwealth wages policy is involved? A complication is that the Aboriginal wage may be well below the amount of the unemployment benefit. For instance, although the situation is changing in the Northern Territory, the minimum wage for a Ward, including the clothing allowance, is less than half the unemployment benefit. But as unemployed wards could be sent to institutions in the past, the problem of the unemployed ward did not arise. It did arise in 'remote areas' of Western Australia, where it was assumed that a wage, paid to Aborigines only, 'normally applied' to them within certain districts and types of employment. The definition of who is Aboriginal may be relevant in another way. For some good legal reason, which the Department of Social Services (often through the agency of the Department of Labour and National Service) must accept, a claimant, because he is defined as Aboriginal, may be rejected because the welfare action in his case belongs to the State department responsible for Aborigines.

[13] See Report of the Director-General of Social Services 1959-60, pp. 5-6 for a discussion of the problem then faced by the Department.

[14] *Sydney Morning Herald*, 3 August 1966.

WHO IS AN ABORIGINAL? 349

Of course, being defined as Aboriginal may have advantages other than access to the special services available for Aborigines only. The Aboriginal youth, for instance, is exempt from being called up for military service under the National Service Act, though he may volunteer.[15] Presumably the Commonwealth definition for census purposes would apply here in any legal action. But the administrative procedure is to make a general announcement of the requirement for persons in the age categories to register, without mentioning Aborigines; and any who do register are subject to call up. It appears that if a person of Aboriginal descent, otherwise liable, does not, the matter is not pursued—probably for the very sound reason that it would be very difficult to decide whether a particular person had the 'preponderance' of Aboriginal descent. Perhaps also it is a tacit recognition that the whole question of Aboriginal status involves injustice. The matter was the subject of some agitation in 1965, mainly by persons other than Aborigines concerned with the principles of civil rights.[16] But in a background of exclusion, on occasions at least (the last blanket exclusion seems to have been from the Occupation Force which went to Japan in 1946), the removal of the provisions from the Act, without corresponding amendment of the other special laws, might well create injustices.

Thus the Aboriginal citizen of the Commonwealth, especially if of part-Aboriginal descent, must find his situation confusing; for he may be treated as Aboriginal, or in a special way applicable to some Aboriginals only, in one context but not in another. He may also be angry, since the same loyalties are legally mandatory for him as for persons for whom there is no special legislation. The last decade has been marked by considerable change in these laws, with the trend, for the nation as a whole, towards equality. Each of the governments involved (all but Tasmania, where there are a few people who would be Aboriginal if they went to certain other States to live, who may be legally Aboriginal for certain Commonwealth purposes, but who are not separately defined for Tasmanian purposes) has proclaimed the objective of equality; but there are differences on what this means and how to get it. Each legislating body goes its own way; and State jealousies of their powers are involved. The resultant confusion has been increased in the period of changing legislation, which has also been one of greater personal mobility, probably involving Aborigines as well as other Australians in more frequent movement across State borders. Since the differences in the methods of bringing Aborigines into the exercise of full citizenship have involved differences of definition, some persons who are legally Aboriginal in one part of the Commonwealth are not so in another. Thus it seems that a Queensland Aboriginal of the full descent who goes across the border

[15] National Service Act 1951-1964; see sections 18 and 30.
[16] See, for instance, editorial in the *West Australian*, 22 February 1965; and debate in the Legislative Council of the Northern Territory, 17 and 18 February 1965. In March 1965 the Minister for Labour and National Service mentioned the difficulties involved in drafting an amendment (*Sydney Morning Herald*, 25 March 1965).

into the Northern Territory, or who goes to Tasmania, ceases to be Aboriginal while he is away.

It seems fair to say that the Government of Queensland, in its very recent legislation, has retained the basic principle of tight control of Aborigines deemed to be 'in need of care', or simply 'declared' to be 'assisted Aborigines'. The legislation continues the restrictive tradition which marked Queensland effort to save Aborigines from extinction from 1897 onwards.

The Aborigines' and Torres Strait Islanders' Affairs Act of 1965 establishes categories of *Aborigines*, of *part-Aborigines*, and of *assisted Aborigines*.[17] The terms in which the categories are expressed are as unscientific as they are obsolete. An 'Aborigine' may be a 'full-blood descendant of the indigenous inhabitants of the Commonwealth' (a definition which would strictly include any Papuan who strayed into Queensland); a 'person who has a preponderance of the blood of an Aborigine'; a 'part-Aborigine who lives as spouse with an Aborigine' (as already defined); or 'a resident of a reserve for Aborigines other than an officer or other person (having no strain of Aboriginal blood) authorized. . . .' A legal *part-Aborigine* has one parent who is an *Aborigine* (as defined) and one parent with 'no strain of the blood of the indigenous inhabitants . . .'; or is a person 'both of whose parents have a strain of the blood of the indigenous inhabitants . . . other than a Torres Strait Island [*sic*] and who himself has a strain of more than twenty-five per centum of such blood but who has not a preponderance of such blood.' Thus are established the categories of persons whose 'assimilation' is the declared objective of the Queensland Government.

Some of them may, in the opinion of the authorities, be making their own way in that direction, or successfully avoiding the ministrations of the Department of Aboriginal and Island Affairs. Thus it becomes necessary for the *Aborigine* or *part-Aborigine* who is assisted to be specified in some way, so that the controls necessary to process him may be exercised over him. Once he is so 'declared', whether he is *Aborigine* or *part-Aborigine*, he is included in the category of 'assisted Aborigines'. He is included in this category if he resides on an Aboriginal reserve; if he is declared by the Director of the Department, or is named in the declaration as the child of a person declared to be an *assisted Aborigine*; if he is declared by a magistrate to be 'in need of care', in which case also the declaration may include his children; or if in his case a judge or magistrate orders that 'care' be provided. Having set the limits expressed in terms of racial origin, the Act embodies an earnest effort to ensure that none who need it may have to go without, or may avoid, assistance. *Any* person 'having a strain of Aboriginal blood' may be declared by the Director, along with such children as are named; or a magistrate's court may declare such a person 'in need of care' and include any or all of his children. This means that legally any trace of Aboriginal ancestry in one's 'blood' may, in conjunction with other circumstances, lead to a situation where one becomes an *assisted Aborigine*.

[17] See sections 6 (a) and (2) and 8 (1). The Act establishes parallel categories of Torres Strait Islanders. Henceforth italicised terms are in accordance with the legislation.

WHO IS AN ABORIGINAL?

The important point here, however, is the inevitable confusion as to who is Aboriginal. Clearly, under this Act it is possible, though perhaps not likely, for a person who has forgotten his Aboriginal ancestry to become an *assisted Aborigine*. Moreover, the definitions in themselves are enough to indicate that the Queensland government and that of the Commonwealth are miles apart and looking in different directions in the promotion of Aboriginal welfare. It is true that a person who does not want the 'assistance' can appeal. The right of the Director to declare those who live off reserves was to expire after one year from commencement of the Act; those so declared might 'institute a reference' to a court, but if the reference were allowed (i.e. the appeal is upheld), this did not render unlawful any action taken in the meantime following the declaration. As there appear to be no safeguards, other than the common sense of the Director and the accuracy of his records in determining who has the strain of Aboriginal blood, this legislation seems dangerous. But it also makes for yet more confusion.

After the expiry of the year, 'admission' of a person to the privileged status of assisted Aboriginal, unless he himself applied, involved a 'complaint' by the Director to a justice that he had a 'strain of Aboriginal blood', and 'should in his best interests, be declared to be in need of care'. The complaint could include 'any number of persons who . . . are included in one family unit'.[18]

Thus it was, for a period of twelve months, legally possible for anyone to be an *assisted Aborigine*, at least until he successfully 'instituted a reference': in the meantime he might have had his property taken over and managed for him by the Department, and have been directed to move his home from Brisbane to a mission on Cape York. If his reference succeeded, he would appear to have had no claim on the Director for his fare home. I would not expect this to happen to many Australians; but it is sobering to realise that it could have happened legally to one who looked like an Aboriginal. It also illustrates the ultimate absurdity of the attempt to define all the members of a group, some of whom need assistance, in detailed racial terms purporting to classify people in accordance with their descent. While there was a period, then, during which *anyone* could be an assisted Aboriginal in Queensland, nobody can be an Aboriginal of any kind, except for Commonwealth purposes, if he lives in Tasmania. The Director in Queensland, of course, is a responsible public servant: but the good sense of an official is hardly an adequate protection for the rights of the citizen.

Up until 1936 Western Australia used categories, largely based on what was then Queensland legislation, of Aborigines and half-castes, but since that year has had one extensive category of *native*. A native includes 'any person of the full blood descended from the original inhabitants of Australia', and any person of less than full descent, 'except a person so descended who is only one-fourth or less than one-fourth of the original full blood', with certain exceptions. These are persons who have served overseas in the defence forces, or who have served for six months in the defence forces anywhere, and who have been honourably

---

[18] Ibid., sections 17, 20, and 25.

discharged.[19] Yet, as in Queensland, any person of Aboriginal descent who falls outside the category so defined may, at the discretion of the Minister, be brought within the scope of the Act. There is however, a decisive difference, in that the Minister may take such action only if the person concerned 'establishes to the satisfaction of the Minister' that he is of part-Aboriginal descent, which appears to envisage the action coming from someone who applies to be treated as a native.[20] That only the benefits of such classification are envisaged seems to be confirmed by a provision in the Western Australian Land Act that the Governor (i.e. the Executive), if he is of the opinion that any person descended from the 'original inhabitants' is at any disadvantage in applying for, or acquiring land under the Act, may grant or lease to him any area of Crown land not exceeding the area prescribed for a selector.[21] This is an example of how the attempt to liberalise administration involves breaking down the categories, when they are based on racial assessments only; so that some persons may be treated as Aborigines in Western Australia for a particular purpose, without being *natives*.

Perhaps at the other end of a scale of racial definiteness is the Victorian definition, made, it appears at first sight, almost as an afterthought in legislation which defines the functions of the Aborigines Welfare Board, but which is pointedly not included in the section which includes other definitions.[22] The dilemma is here clearly indicated; how to define a class of persons for whom the government considers it must make some special provision, and who have in common only their Aboriginal descent, but without doing so in racial terms. It was done simply by including anyone of Aboriginal descent 'not only full-blooded aboriginal natives of Australia, but also any person of aboriginal descent'. A great deal, of course, depends on the social and historical context of the legislation. The 1957 Act which established this broad definition was introduced at a time when there were very few Aborigines of full descent in Victoria. There had been a great deal of protest because the authorities responsible for the administration of the previous Act, which had stood since 1928, were attempting, as they were perhaps legally bound to do, to limit the services of the Board and the right to live at Lake Tyers, the last remaining Aboriginal station, to those legally entitled. These were defined in 1928 as an Aboriginal native, a half-caste living with or associating with an Aboriginal and who was thirty-four years of age in 1887; a female half-caste married to an Aboriginal before that year; an infant child of an Aboriginal parent, and who was unable to earn his own living; and any other half-caste who held a written licence from the Board to live in a place prescribed for Aborigines.[23] Most of those entitled would obviously have been dead long before 1957. Those who considered themselves Aboriginal would in many cases be of less than half Aboriginal descent. But they naturally enough regarded the homes in which they

[19] Native Welfare Act, 1963, section 4.
[20] Ibid., section 10.
[21] Land Act, 1933-1963, section 9.
[22] Aborigines Act 1957, sections 2 and 6 (1). Later legislation refers to the 1957 definition.
[23] Aborigines Act 1928, section 5.

WHO IS AN ABORIGINAL?

had grown up as places where they were entitled to remain. Therefore, the curious result of liberalisation in 1957 was to extend the category. The background was an attempt to promote 'assimilation' by forcing people out of the reserves because they were less than half Aboriginal and therefore, it was thought, should be in the community finding their own way. The 1957 Act represented second thoughts.

Victorian Aboriginal legislation began almost with the separation of that State from New South Wales; and the earlier definitions reflect what was then in many ways a colonial situation. 'Natives' should be protected from abuses; and this required definition of those to whom special laws should apply. A difficulty arose from the rapid growth of a part-Aboriginal population, members of which tended to be excluded from the settler community. Most of them were offspring of Aboriginal mothers, in a situation where the settler group was preponderantly male. How many were taken into the settler homes cannot now be known; nor, for that matter, how many there were. But most seem to have been socialised by Aboriginal mothers in the conditions of the camps from which the present fringe settlements round the country towns have developed. Aboriginal culture was largely and very rapidly lost; but a part-Aboriginal camp-dwellers' sub-culture was taking its place when this kind of legislation began.

As time passed, the details of racial mixture would have become more confused. The records of descent available to the authorities which had to administer the law would not have been adequate to make accurate decisions of the kind envisaged in categories which distinguished, for instance, a person of less than half Aboriginal descent from a 'half-caste'. Therefore, even where there were precise categories in the law, the action taken was often, perhaps commonly, on the basis of skin coloration. This was especially serious for the part-Aboriginal in Victoria, because from time to time there were doctrinaire policies applied on who might live on reserves. Some families established for long periods on reserves formed attachments to these poor communities; but in the later generations, through intermarriage or other miscegenation, more children of light complexion were born. The rule that no one of less than half caste could live on the settlements, when translated into practice, resulted in the expulsion of persons with white skins or with skins which indicated to the 'experts' that they did not come within the provisions. Families with both white and dark children might be split, some allowed to remain, others forced away; or a family with some white-skinned children might leave its old home and attempt to establish itself elsewhere. The idea of 'assimilation' which involves absorption is not new; it is as old as white settlement.

So, in Victoria, the interesting situation developed that extension of the definition, to include all people of Aboriginal descent, was, in the circumstances, a way of providing within the law for greater flexibility, which would make it legally possible for persons of Aboriginal descent to remain where their families had lived for generations. Yet before this happened, many had established themselves outside the scope of government agencies. Others belong to families which may never have lived on the reserves; many want nothing to do with the Welfare Board.

This is true of a considerable part of the Aboriginal population in each State. Thus Queensland authorities have been stating in Annual Reports for years that over 20,000 Aborigines are 'outside the Act', though this seems to be a considerable overstatement. These are additional reasons why the only meaningful definition of an Aboriginal is that of a person who identifies as one or who lives as a member of an Aboriginal group. As urbanisation proceeds, with greater mobility, the old racial definitions become pointless. They are also the basis for administration which tends in practice to relate government action to skin colour. Officials, especially because their records cannot provide full genealogies of their charges, think in terms of people of 'very light caste', of 'light caste', 'half-caste', and so on. It has happened that services or assistance have been refused because an official considers that someone in need is of such 'light caste' that he should be going to the general welfare authority. It is also possible that an official of a general welfare authority, doubtful of how far he should go without reference of an 'Aboriginal' case to the 'Aboriginal' authority, will refrain from what may be interpreted as interference in the province of another department. Thus, even with a general and inclusive definition, the doubts about who is an Aboriginal may have quite unintended and unfortunate consequences.

There is a special danger of this where a State maintains institutions for Aborigines which parallel the institutions for others. At the beginning of 1967, for instance, New South Wales still retained, though it was considering the closure of, separate institutions for Aboriginal children, to which an Aboriginal child might be committed by a court as a neglected or uncontrollable child under the Child Welfare Act.[24] If the definition of Aboriginal is a wide one, including in effect all of Aboriginal descent, the court will tend to depend on expert advice as to whether the child should go to a general or an Aboriginal institution. I have myself heard, on more than one occasion, discussion between the Child Welfare and Aborigines Welfare Board officers, in a country town, on what the decision ought to be; and the matter of advising the court settled on the basis of whether the 'caste' is 'light' or 'dark'. In this context also it is possible that two members of the same family, both 'committed', will be administratively separated. This, of course, is not the fault of the officer but of the system. The New South Wales definition of *Aborigine* is 'any full-blooded or half-caste aboriginal who is a native of Australia and who is temporarily or permanently resident in New South Wales'.[25] Even if the officer has a very detailed genealogy, which is most unlikely, he will find difficulty in deciding who is half or more than half-caste; and who is less. He will fall back again on the rule of thumb and make a guess on skin colour; either he or the local court will do so.

Even where the definition is racially precise, as in Western Australia, the problem is really no easier, because the border line cannot be determined. The

[24] Aborigines Protection Act, 1909-1963, section 13A.
[25] Ibid., section 3.

WHO IS AN ABORIGINAL?   355

answer lies not in the area of definition at all but in the provision of equality in access of all Australians to common services. Then there can be such additional services which people who identify as Aboriginal may need, and which it is in both their own and the national interest to provide. Where this is the situation, reference to racial origin may be less insulting, especially as access to additional services can, and as far as possible should, be optional, on request. If New South Wales does dispense with the separate establishments for Aboriginal children, it will avoid the need to make the arbitrary and wounding decisions which such establishments have involved. As cases of serious delinquency by youths are eventually dealt with by confinement in Child Welfare institutions, the Aboriginal youth in an Aboriginal institution, who resents this special treatment, may well be tempted to such action as will force the court to transfer him. From his point of view this may well seem a reasonable way of obtaining equal treatment.

In South Australia there are two categories—*Aboriginal* and *person of Aboriginal blood*. An *Aboriginal* is a person 'of the full blood descended from the original inhabitants of Australia' unless his name has been removed from the Register of Aborigines. If his name has been omitted from the Register, he may still be legally Aboriginal. This provision illustrates the fact that in 1962, at least, when this legislation was adopted, the South Australian government did not have the staff, in the Department of Aboriginal Affairs, to establish all identities in what remained an awkward frontier region, in the north-west of the State, where some movement across the borders of the Northern Territory and Western Australia continued.[26] A *person of Aboriginal blood* is one with any degree of Aboriginal descent, other than the full descent, except that removal from the Register of Aborigines of any Aboriginal makes him a *person of Aboriginal blood*.

Before 1962, an *Aborigine* was a person of full or part descent who had not been especially exempted. It was thus a blanket provision which included all people of Aboriginal origin, no matter how distant in time the Aboriginal forebear, except for the few who had been exempted from the operation of the Act.[27] The setting up in 1962 of two categories where there had been one added further to the national confusion; but the reasons may be sought in the fact that in South Australia there is a whole range of situations, from the nomadic people of the Central Desert to the sophisticated groups of some Aboriginal descent living in the south-east of the State, some on the two Aboriginal Stations of Point Pearce and Point McLeay, which have been in continuous occupation from the time of their establishment as frontier missions; others in and round country towns and in Adelaide itself. The 1962 Act allows *Aboriginals* to enter or remain on reserves where there are 'Aboriginal institutions'; but *a person of Aboriginal blood* requires special permission. Even the *Aboriginal* may be refused such permission by the Minister. For *Aboriginals* there are special provisions relating to employment, to compulsory medical examination, and to representation by a departmental officer before a court, which do not apply in the case of a *person of Aboriginal blood*. But

[26] Aboriginal Affairs Act, 1962, sections 4 and 17.
[27] Aborigines Act 1934–1939, sections 4 and 11A.

other protective-restrictive legislation applies to both categories. The 1962 Act amended the Licensing Act, partly to make it possible to allow access to alcohol in certain parts of the State but not in others. Probably because of the difficulty of using racial distinctions in this matter, the amendments to the Licensing Act were such as to include *persons of Aboriginal blood* among those who would be restricted in the areas where the restrictions apply. Thus whether any person of Aboriginal descent could buy a drink in a hotel depended for a time on where the hotel was; one could be treated as an Aboriginal legally in one part of the State but not in another, for one purpose only. This particular discrimination has now been removed throughout the State. But the legislation was a very good example of the difficulty faced by governments in operating on the basis of racial categories.

One important feature of Aboriginal legislation, which tended to the confusion of definition, but acknowledged the potential equality of the Aboriginal, was the provision for exemption of individuals deemed to have indicated their fitness for full or partial civil rights.

The Commonwealth, in the Welfare Ordinance which created the category of *ward* in the Northern Territory, provided for appeal by a person 'declared' to be one.[28] The tribunal to which he might appeal made its decision solely on his capacity to look after his own affairs. While at first the onus of proof was with the appellant it was, in 1962, in effect transferred to the Welfare Branch of the Administration.[29] By this provision the *ward* was treated as a potential citizen, whose rights could be safeguarded by the courts. In the earliest Commonwealth legislation for the Territory, the only 'exemptions' had been partial, to suit the convenience of employers: enabling the Aboriginal to carry firearms in his employer's service; or preventing him from being removed from his place of employment to a reserve. In 1936, the Chief Protector was given the power to exempt half-castes as then defined from the operation of the Aboriginals Ordinance;[30] and thereafter the *Commonwealth Gazette* published notices of exemption. But not until 1953 could an *Aboriginal* be exempted;[31] and this was preparatory to the legislation on *wards*.

The Ordinance operating for the Australian Capital Territory provided for exemption, but, like the earlier Northern Territory Ordinance, it provided also for withdrawal of the rights so granted; in this case, by cancellation of the certificate of exemption.[32] Commonly, Aboriginal men have referred to the certificate of exemption as the 'dog-licence', reacting as such niggardly legislation probably deserved, but prizing it in the then state of the law mainly as admitting them to the hotel bar, which in the country town was tantamount to admission to the town club. It did of course make for opportunities for the barman to humiliate the person holding it; and where it was open to cancellation, often led

[28] Welfare Ordinance 1953-1960, sections 30-6.
[29] Welfare Ordinance 1961, No. 12 of 1962, section 14.
[30] Aboriginals Ordinance 1936, section 2.
[31] Aboriginals Ordinance (No. 2) 1953, section 4.
[32] Aborigines Welfare Ordinance 1954, section 16.

WHO IS AN ABORIGINAL? 357

to just that, where the holder of a certificate was convicted of obtaining liquor for members of his family or for his friends.

In practice, so far was the question of liquor the core of the matter that, when the Victorian government liberalised the law in 1957, by repealing the old Aborigines Act, it removed the special clause preventing Aboriginal access to liquor at the same time.[33] Up to 1967 the New South Wales Act still provided for the Certificate of Exemption; but also for cancellation.[34] Since the repeal of the New South Wales Supply of Liquor to Aborigines Prevention Act, in 1963, exemption has lost much of its meaning.

In Queensland, there has since 1965 been an interesting reversal of the procedures. For each *assisted Aborigine* there is a certificate of entitlement, which admits him to the special benefits of being legally Aboriginal. This may be cancelled by the Director of Aborigines' and Torres Strait Islanders' Affairs, either on his own or the Aboriginal's initiative; there is also provision for appeal to a magistrate.[35] The first Queensland Protection Act, in 1897, had provided that the Minister could issue a certificate exempting a half-caste (only);[36] four years later, provision was made for the certificate to be withdrawn at any time, even though it had always been issued subject to whatever conditions were thought fit in the particular case.[37] In 1939 it became possible for any Aboriginal as defined to become exempt, though still subject to whatever conditions the Director thought fit; and the exemption was subject to withdrawal.[38] In Queensland, where there are certainly large numbers of persons of Aboriginal descent who have never been 'under the Act', the annual reports of the responsible department have claimed this to be the effect of exemptions in the past. It is more likely to reflect the fact that the department did not, over a long period, have the resources to bring under control all those then within the categories, for the descendants of those exempted in the past would hardly account for more than a fraction of the numbers (in excess of 20,000) claimed officially not to be 'under the Act'. In the year ended June 1965, for instance, the total exempted (including children) was 292.[39] Nor can I find any real evidence of a population of this size in addition to those 'under the Act'. On the other hand, for reasons already outlined, it cannot be refuted on the basis of census figures alone.

The story of exemptions is somewhat reminiscent of that in the colonies formerly administered by the French and Belgian governments, which used the concept of the *evolué* or *assimilé*—the person who, though of 'native' origin, had proved that he was a civilised man and therefore fit for full civic rights. The standard tended to be set in the Australian States, as in the French and Belgian colonies, by the official view of what the white man ought to be, rather than of

[33] Aborigines Act 1957, section 11.
[34] Aborigines Protection Act, 1909-1963, section 18C.
[35] Aborigines' and Torres Strait Islanders' Affairs Act 1965, sections 23-5.
[36] Aboriginals Protection and Restriction of the Sale of Opium Act 1897, section 33.
[37] Ibid., 1901, section 6.
[38] Aboriginals Preservation and Protection Act of 1939, section 5.
[39] Annual Report of Director Native Affairs 1965.

358   WHO IS AN ABORIGINAL?

what he was likely to be; the ethnocentric concept of 'advancement' leading towards what the official considered true civilisation lent itself to schoolmasterly handling of the situation. And where in Australia there remained the cautious provision for cancellation, the effect must have been that the 'freed' Aboriginal could not feel really free: he was subject to a special penalty, of being re-declared as an Aboriginal in law.

But the holder of the dog-licence, the Australian counterpart of the *evolué*, was a comparatively rare person, as was the *evolué*, for instance, in the Congo. Patrice Lumumba once pointed out that at the rate at which Congolese were achieving this status, it would take centuries of colonial rule to complete the process.[40] There, as in Australia, once the tide of population turned, 'assimilation' at this rate has probably been less than the increase in the population being tutored, processed, assimilated, integrated, civilised, or what you will.

In the 1905 Act, the Western Australian government followed the example of Queensland by providing for the exemption of half-castes, by certificate; but this could be withdrawn.[41] In the Act of 1936, which established the category of 'native', the certificate of exemption became possible for all in the category. Moreover, the native was given the right of appeal to a court from any adverse decision by the Minister resulting either in the refusal or withdrawal of the certificate.[42] But the nearest approach to legislation based on principles comparable with that which produced the colonial *evolué* is in the Natives (Citizenship Rights) Act of 1944, as amended.[43] This provided for local Boards, each of one official and a 'district representative' who should be nominated, to consider applications for a Certificate of Citizenship.

It seems to have been introduced to deal with the anomaly that Aborigines had been serving in the armed forces but could not vote or obtain civic rights. It also provided for a distinction between persons who ceased to be legally *natives* and others who were exempted from the restrictions of the Act (as in access to alcohol) but remained *natives* to retain its benefits. The application had to be supported by evidence of war service, with honourable discharge, or with evidence of suitability for citizenship. There also had to be evidence that the applicant had 'dissolved tribal and native associations', except for those with his immediate family, for a period of two years.[44] This was insulting enough; even more so was the requirement that the Board must be sure that he did not suffer from certain diseases. Even his children were to be citizens only until they reached the age of twenty-one years. Worst of all, the Certificate could be revoked, on the initiative of the local Board—two convictions for drunkenness, a belief by the Board that he was 'not adopting the manners and habits of a civilised life', or the contraction of leprosy, syphilis, granuloma, or yaws were enough.[45]

[40] See *Congo My Country*, pp. 29–68.
[41] Aborigines Act 1905, section 63.
[42] Aborigines Act Amendment Act, 1936, section 34.
[43] Natives (Citizenship Rights) Act 1944–1951.
[44] Ibid., section 4.
[45] Ibid., section 7.

WHO IS AN ABORIGINAL? 359

An amendment in 1958 repealed the provisions for revocation, that which made certain diseases a barrier, and that which caused the child of such a citizen to revert to the status of *native* at twenty-one.

The implication, which is at the heart of the assimilation policy and was the basis of the colonial system which produced the *evolué*, is of a transition from a lower order of living to a higher. This is especially pointed in the provisions for breach of social ties with all but immediate relatives in the *native* community as a pre-requisite for citizenship. It seemed safe to assume that as the right to drink was extended to more regions of this State, fewer would wish to take advantage of this kind of opportunity. That the government itself considered the need for this Act to be mainly to control drinking by *natives* was indicated by a remark in the annual report of the Commissioner of Native Welfare for the year ended June 1964, just as the current legislation was to come into effect. This new legislation was accompanied by removal of some discriminations from other laws—provisions for whipping *natives* from the criminal code, for requiring *natives* north of the 26th parallel to have a special gun licence, for special conditions concerning *native* evidence, for exclusion of *natives* from certain protections in the Mining Act. But receiving or supplying liquor remained an offence in cases involving *natives*; and it was stated that the Natives (Citizenship Rights) Act 'will be required until liquor restrictions have been removed in all parts of the State'.[46] Thus the accolade for the *evolué*, Australian style, was the entree to the pub.

The Commissioner's Report for the previous year stated that the total number of applications for citizenship made in Western Australia to that time was 2,600, of which 1964 had been granted; 72 had been granted and then withdrawn, 404 refused, and others were deferred or pending. As the known *native* population at that time in the State was about 20,500, the average of about 130 applications in each year since the legislation was introduced probably did not keep up with the population increase. On the other hand the movement was enough to create further doubts about statistics, especially as additional citizen rights were established for 1180 children on the same certificates.[47]

Exemption tends to lose point when the disabilities of the Aboriginal status are reduced. One of the greatest inducements existed when Aborigines could not get certain social service benefits. Thus the New South Wales Annual Report for 1961 stated that there had been only 68 applications (57 granted) in that year; that there had been 125 applications approved in the previous year. The Report explains this decline in applications as due to the action by the Commonwealth in liberalising the conditions attached to pensions for Aborigines. Before this 'it was necessary for those seeking this assistance, who resided on Stations or Reserves, to be in possession of an Exemption Certificate'.[48] By 1963 the Board could comment that in the past the main purpose for applications had been to get access

---

[46] Western Australia: Commissioner of Native Welfare: Annual Report for Year ended 30th June 1964, pp. 7-8.
[47] Ibid., 1963, pp. 55-6.
[48] Report of the Aborigines Welfare Board for the Year ended 30th June 1961, p. 11.

360   WHO IS AN ABORIGINAL?

to liquor; that the few requests made in the 1963 report year 'were for the purpose of prestige only'.[49]

Yet so long as there are any restrictions at all, the Certificate may be a useful document—as when, for instance, the father of a 'neglected' child may wish to ensure that the child is sent to a Child Welfare Home rather than to one of the special Aboriginal establishments. In theory it involves important differences in those parts of Australia where by law or by local custom the Aboriginal is paid a lower wage than others—situations to be found in 1967 in South Australia, Western Australia, Queensland and the Northern Territory. On the other hand, in these frontier areas especially, where by the nature of an immense country sparsely occupied, the agencies of government can be only partly effective, legal status may be less important than the colour of a man's skin: a very dark part-Aboriginal may be entitled to rights of which he is ignorant. Even in New South Wales and Victoria, the same result follows where only the Dark People may be employed for particular tasks, such as pea- and bean-picking, for which there is no award. Perhaps a reason why there has been no great pressure for exemption in the past is that legal equality is one thing; actual equality, and especially social equality, another matter altogether.

South Australia also provides for exemption, by removal of the name from the Register of Aboriginals, with provision for appeals. Before 1962, the conditions were set by legislation passed in 1939, under which the Aborigines Protection Board could declare a person to be exempt, either conditionally or unconditionally. If the latter, the declaration was irrevocable for the person and his descendants. If the exemption was conditional, it could be revoked within three years, but not thereafter. This Act also had provided for appeal.[50]

Over various periods, then, the exemption provisions had been providing for a limited degree of mobility out of the Aboriginal category, in some cases on the uncertain basis of a certificate which could be cancelled. The provisions, as far as they went, and although their limited results reflected official pessimism, at least envisaged a place for the Aboriginal in the general community. That so often this was much easier for the part-Aboriginal than for the full-blood indicated the prejudice of the time, but it was also a rule of thumb for the hard-pressed official who had to assume that the darker the skin, the more restricted the possibilities. Such an assumption was supported by the greater difficulties facing the darker person in white Australian society.

The exemption provisions were also based on the assumption of a monolithic 'white' community sharing a culture which should be common for all citizens. The outlines of this culture were so vaguely defined that those who had to interpret the provisions were always cautious. The Aboriginal exempted had to conform to the official view of how good Australians behave. There was no concession of the possibility that an Aboriginal or part-Aboriginal culture, changing in accordance with its own laws, might produce leaders who might

[49] Ibid., 1963, p. 13.
[50] Aborigines Act 1934-1939, section 11a.

WHO IS AN ABORIGINAL? 361

win status in a multi-cultural society. Even today, the full import of immigration as tending in this direction has not been grasped. The more ambitious Aborigines of the southern settled regions, in the meantime, had begun more and more, especially over the last decade, to escape from the effects of the restrictive laws which remained by migrating to the capital cities. Urbanisation has probably been a more decisive factor in social mobility than all the cautious processing based in legislation. It has also greatly increased the difficulty of establishing just who are Aborigines, and where they are.

Any attempt to define Aboriginal status on a nation-wide basis leads into the kinds of complications outlined. There were in 1967 Commonwealth and State definitions which varied considerably. We are in a period of such rapid legislative change that much of what has been outlined here could be out of date before it is published. The trend is, in general, towards legal equality; but this means reversing a whole history. The tangle posed in the varying definitions is merely indicative of a wider confusion involving rights. Thirty years ago, when the Commonwealth and State Aboriginal authorities met in conference for the first time, the matter of a common definition was raised, but because definitions flow from policy, and because, while there has been agreement on the very broad objectives of policy and on what it is to be called, there has been no agreement on methods, the definitions simply reflect the differences. The case for a common national policy is clear enough. This may be facilitated by the result of the 1967 Referendum on the Constitution, which enables the Commonwealth to legislate for all Aborigines. This in itself makes a single basis for definition legally necessary.

In the meantime, the Aboriginal who is commonly the object of long-established prejudice is a person who looks like one. If he does not, his chances of being accepted socially as an equal by other Australians are very good. So far as I can judge, there is none of the anxiety in the Australian community about a possible strain of Aboriginal 'blood' in one's ancestry or in that of one's friends which a corresponding situation might give rise to if the locale were Mississippi or Cape Town. When one condemns, with the advantage of hindsight, the emphasis on absorption, and on the disappearance of the Aboriginal appearance, in the past programs of 'assimilation', one should also concede that prejudice does not seem to have reached a stage as in itself to render the objective impossible. Such an objective was comforting for those who could think of the 'problem' disappearing in later generations; and might have seemed feasible when it appeared that Aborigines were dying out, but is quite impossible now that we know that they form a rapidly increasing minority.

The real argument against such a view is that it disregards the need of the individual living *now* for justice and equality; and that it is deeply insulting in its implications. A belief in Aboriginal disappearance has been the basic reason for the survival of legislation of the type which defines rights in terms of race; and it is no defence to say that a comparatively mild apartheid, not capable of really effective administration, is meant to lead to equality in the end. It applies to human affairs the principles of the stock-breeder; and on quite unscientific grounds it justifies restrictions on persons now so that other persons in the future may be more acceptable to the majority.

For the research worker, the problems of definition are a very real hindrance. For there is no way in which the population with which he is concerned can be accurately defined; therefore a sampling technique is almost impossible. Moreover, the racial questions involved are sensitive ones, to a degree that many persons, who are known to other co-operating Aborigines to be of Aboriginal descent, find, or at least believe, that they must deny their origin to 'get on'. On the other hand, the proper subject for the research involved in this project was the community whose members identified as Aboriginal. This, however, does not solve the problem of statistics, or of defining the 'universe' for research, since there is no way of establishing any relationship between the identifying group and the basic statistics in the census or those maintained by the relevant State government departments.

There is another and very important area of government, where decisions affecting Aborigines may be made without any other than visual definition—that of local government. Members of municipal and shire councils, and of roads boards in Western Australia, have been making decisions for a long time which affect locally based Aboriginal communities. The fringe settlement is in many ways the ultimate effect of the long history of local government discrimination. It is here especially that the refusal of the white Australian to include the Aboriginal in his circle of friends and neighbours has been reflected in the way in which the local Aborigines live; where, in relation to the town, they live; and in the kind of municipal services which have been considered suitable for them. Local government protests have frustrated central government housing schemes: sometimes the treatment accorded the Aboriginal minority reminds one of the attitude by an English parish to its poor in the time of the Poor Laws. The tendency, inevitable where the tangle of definition remains but especially so because of all the history which has produced an unthinking prejudice, is for the shire or municipal body to include with the Aboriginal minority anyone who looks like an Aboriginal. There is another tendency, limited, as it has been, mainly to very small townships, which it would be unfair not to mention: to include in the town social activities families of Aboriginal descent, and to maintain that in some way they are 'different'. They are likely to be 'different', not because they do differ from many others who are excluded from local society elsewhere but because they have become known and respected. They may differ not so much from the other Aborigines as from the stereotype Aboriginal.

When we look at the situation at the level of local government and the society of country town or suburb, another complication becomes evident, for Aborigines are not the only minority with dark skins in Australia. There are people of Asian descent in the north-west and north-east; of South Sea Island descent in the north-east. Often they have intermarried with persons of Aboriginal descent, as well as with persons of European descent. Where such persons form a small minority they may for social purposes be classed by the whites as Aboriginal; by force of

WHO IS AN ABORIGINAL? 363

circumstances, or by choice, they may form part of the Aboriginal social group socially. This may be especially likely in Queensland, where the Department of Aborigines' and Torres Strait Islanders' Affairs exercises administrative controls over certain Islanders.

In this case there are some interesting indications of attitudes produced by the different histories of these two groups. In one field excursion between Brisbane and Cairns I found that almost universally officials maintained that efficient and sober folk in the group under control must be 'islanders'; those who gave 'trouble', Aborigines. Also along this coastal region, and down to about the Clarence River, the limit of the sugar industry, there were other Islanders, mainly of Melanesian descent, whose descendants are one of the reminders of the importation of indentured labour in the last century: these people may or may not identify with the local Aborigines. It is thus quite possible for a person to be socially classed as Aboriginal without having any strain of Aboriginal descent.

He may even be so classified for administrative purposes where neither he nor anyone else may know the precise details of his descent. This can easily happen, for instance, when a widow or widower with non-Aboriginal children takes an Aboriginal spouse and moves on to an Aboriginal reserve. The same kind of situation is possible where persons of part-Asian origin have lost their traditions, especially where the accident of skin colouration has prevented them from moving into 'white' society. All this not only adds to the difficulties of an 'Aboriginal' survey: it means, as one of the research teams found when piloting a questionnaire in Brisbane, that many people may themselves be confused as to how they can or should identify.[51] It also demonstrates the futility of the racial categories as a starting-point for administrative programs: that even irrespective of the purposes of the administrative effort and the assumptions implicit in racial categorisation, the categories cannot in fact be efficiently established. The drift will always be to special administration based on appearance of the individual.

The complications of definition may be removed, as a tedious task of legal drafting, in two ways. The simpler, and the way to ensure that there is no legal basis for differentiation between citizens for rights and duties, would be to excise all such definitions and all legislation which applies to persons so defined. A general question on race, couched in terms of general usage—e.g. 'European', 'Asian', and 'Aboriginal'—would allow for self-identification as member of a sub-group as required for the purposes of the statistics in the census. This could easily be confidential, so that only the statistics, and not information about individuals, would be available for those who are concerned with the size and distribution of the populations, Aboriginal and other, which may be in special need or risk, the real extent of which is otherwise lost in the general statistics.

Yet there will be another need, on the part of persons who have special problems because they are Aboriginal, and therefore subject to social discriminations. It does

[51] Hazel M. Smith, Ellen H. Biddle, and C.M.R. Cornwall: Social Survey of Persons of Aborigine and Torres Strait Island Descent Residing in Brisbane, Queensland 1965-1966: Progress Report (typescript)—SSRC-AP File.

not seem possible, however desirable on theoretical grounds, to place all Aborigines immediately in the situation of having to compete in the market, or satisfy the financial or other requirements for services like housing where their poverty would place them in a hopeless situation, for their need, as a group, even with the special welfare services for them, is far more acute than that of other Australians. They have been administratively and legally restrained, to a high degree and to varying extents, as no other group has. It would be unreal not to allow for the need for compensatory assistance. But this raises the same question: who is to be an Aboriginal?

The end aimed at, I think, should be definition in terms of the group with which a person identifies. There are other reasons, quite apart from definition, for the endeavour so to organise special assistance that the request for it, and the management of it, are delegated to groups, perhaps companies or other corporate bodies. If ever this stage were reached, all we would need would be a definition of such an 'Aboriginal' corporate body: as having certain special rights and responsibilities beyond those which Aborigines would have as full citizens in their individual capacities. But such a group definition depends on an evolution in the situation. It has to be seen as an objective; and in the meantime there has to be some definition of Aboriginal. Assuming that all restrictive laws were repealed (an obvious necessity), a proper step would be to include anyone who claims or can establish that he is of Aboriginal descent or who in the opinion of the administering department is such, provided that he does not desire otherwise. Probably any individual monetary or other special benefits, beyond those already available to him as a citizen, should be subject to a means test. Both registration and removal from the list of Aborigines should be facilitated, on request by the individual. Even when all people of Aboriginal descent have all civic rights, it would be unfair not to allow for some lag in their knowledge of what they are entitled to, and of what they have to do to get it. One special service available, for instance, should be advice on how to acquire the actual benefits of a citizen; and for this alone there has to be a definition of who is entitled to the advice. It can be argued that such advice should be generally available to all who need it. Yet if the Aboriginal does not need special help, there is no problem and no need for a special definition at all.

Also useful in this context is the idea of a register of those who are to have some special additional rights. This might well be compiled with the assistance of representatives of the Aborigines, who could be elected if necessary. The very discussion of who should have the right to Aboriginal status and registration, once this had definite advantages, would help to clarify the situation for each Aboriginal welfare authority and for the Aborigines. Where only benefits can flow from a special definition and from registration, these should tend to lose the historical connotation of inferiority, especially if registration or de-registration is made easy and dependent on Aboriginal initiative as far as possible.

APPENDIX B

THE ABORIGINAL POPULATION

HOW MANY ABORIGINES?

As there is no definition of 'Aboriginal' to suit all purposes, there can be no absolute figure for an 'Aboriginal' population. We can reasonably accept the figures from the 1961 census as a minimum, and they can be used to calculate population trends and to indicate comparative distribution by census districts. One reason for taking the figures as a minimum only is that the question asked on the 'race' of non-Europeans, in the censuses of 1954 and 1961

almost certainly led to an understatement of the number of persons of mixed racial background. The instructions suggested that only the offspring of first generation intermarriages between Europeans and non-Europeans were to be described as 'half-caste'. Thus a person both of whose parents were . . . half-caste Aborigines would be in some dilemma as to whether he was Aboriginal or European.

Dr F. Lancaster Jones, who made this comment, found evidence that some disliked the term 'half-caste' and described themselves as Aboriginal.[1] Other research has confirmed this.[2] For instance, in the map (pp. xiv-xv) which shows the relative distribution of Aborigines and part-Aborigines for Australia as a whole, on the basis of 1961 census figures, it will be noted that the proportion of Aboriginal to part-Aboriginal in capital cities is higher than in many of the more remote census divisions of the States concerned: we know that this was not so, and it is relevant as indicating an unwillingness to identify as 'half-caste'. Many part-Aborigines must also have described themselves as 'European', probably many more than those who opted for 'Aboriginal'. Some used a category of their own—'Australian'.[3] It is certain, then, that the figures for *half-caste* were considerably below the number

[1] *The Structure and Growth of Australia's Aboriginal Population*. I am heavily indebted in this chapter to Dr Lancaster Jones's work.

[2] Dr D. Barwick commented on the approach to the census of 1961 by persons who identified as Aboriginal in Melbourne: 'Despite my explanations of the intention of these forms, a number of Aboriginal people insisted that they were fullbloods since "my mother was Aboriginal then I'm black too". I heard of only one case in which a woman classified her children as Europeans. Her own father was white, as was her husband. Her maternal relatives, while admitting the accuracy of this classification, criticised the woman for "being ashamed of what she is".' (A Little More than Kin, p. 25.)

[3] Lancaster Jones, *The Structure and Growth of Australia's Aboriginal Population*.

THE ABORIGINAL POPULATION

of those who have some degree of Aboriginal ancestry and who identify with other 'Aboriginals'. One reason is that where the father is stated to be 'European', the children of a part-Aboriginal mother are not included with half-castes.

'But it is equally clear', writes J.P.M. Long, 'that the enumeration of half-castes included great numbers who were not strictly of half-Aboriginal descent.' Yet the same writer argues that while a total in the 1961 census of just over 40,000 'rather overstates' the numbers of full-bloods (partly because he feels that the census, in allowing for just under 4,000 in the remote regions beyond the operation of the census, in the Northern Territory and Western Australia, made an overestimate of about 3,500), the figure of just under 40,000 *half-castes* 'is substantially less than the actual total of people with some recognizable trace of Aboriginal ancestry'. Long feels that the 1961 census got close to the true size of the 'problem' population at about 80,000, and that allowing for increase by 1966 'the "problem population" may be about 90,000 Aboriginals and part-Aboriginals in the country'.[4]

The actual census count was 75,309, made up of 36,137 enumerated *Aboriginals*, and 39,172 enumerated part-Aborigines (*half-castes*). (These figures do not include the 5,217 Torres Strait Islanders enumerated.) But the census also included an estimated 2,000 out of touch with the collectors in Western Australia, and a further 1944 in the Northern Territory. Long has probably had as much experience of the remote areas concerned as anyone competent to make such estimates; he suggests a total of under 500 for these remaining nomads. But the estimate of the census authorities brought the total figure to 79,253.

Long's estimate, that the 'problem population' was by 1966 about 90,000, was challenged by people of experience who have worked in Aboriginal affairs.[5] When in 1964 Lancaster Jones collected estimates from the State authorities, the Director of Native Affairs for Queensland offered a figure which was 41 per cent higher than the 1961 census figure; the Victorian Aborigines Welfare Board's estimate was 67 per cent higher, and the South Australian estimate 23 per cent higher. Lancaster Jones's careful summation is partly a comment on the unknown difference between the census figure and the total of those 'of Aboriginal descent who think of themselves, or are thought of, as Aboriginal or part-Aboriginal'; but he thinks that the difference is considerable.[6]

To establish the numbers of people who identify, or are identified as members of a minority which is scattered and unorganised, requires more than the completion of a census form, especially where the census questions are confusing. A careful count involves the getting of names. As these are nowhere registered in such a way as to show whether or not they belong to persons who are Aboriginal, they have to be established by reference from one person or family to another; as even names are likely to be repeated, and addresses may quickly change, the best method

[4] See 'The Numbers and Distribution of Aborigines in Australia', in Ian G. Sharp and Colin M. Tatz (eds.), *Aborigines in the Economy*, p. 2.
[5] See, for instance, Sharp and Tatz (eds.), *Aborigines in the Economy*, p. 13, remarks by P.E. Felton, Superintendent, Aborigines Welfare Board, Victoria.
[6] *The Structure and Growth of Australia's Aboriginal Population*.

THE ABORIGINAL POPULATION

is to take out genealogies. This, fortunately, is likely to win the co-operation of Aboriginal people, who are themselves intensely interested, as a rule, in family relationships; and this is just what Dr Diane Barwick, in co-operation with the Aborigines Welfare Board of Victoria, managed to do. As a result it was known that by March 1962 there was a total of 2,989 persons who were members of the Victorian Aboriginal community.[7] The figure given to Lancaster Jones at the end of 1964 must have been this one; so that his information of an effective Aboriginal population 67 per cent over the census figure was conservative in that it ignored the natural increase since 1962. Such a large discrepancy, so well based, could suggest that even the figures made up of a total of the State and Commonwealth departmental estimates are conservative. They amounted to 106,000 in 1964.[8] On the other hand, these are often based on departmental returns from the field, of figures arrived at by some kind of count by busy officers. Long has drawn attention to the fallibility of the system of 'counting heads' as a basis for estimating population numbers, since the tendency is for each officer concerned to include all those with whom he is 'in touch'. As each is likely to count persons who move from one centre of enumeration to another, unless names are counted the result is likely to be over-enumeration.[9]

Table 1: *Estimated Aboriginal population, 1961 and 1964*

State or Territory	Estimate by Relevant Authority*			Result of 1961 Census		
	Aboriginal	Part-Aboriginal	Total	Full-blood	Half-Caste	Total
Australian Capital Territory	(not included)				143	143
New South Wales	235	13,163	13,398	1,488	13,228	14,716
Victoria	Nil	3,000	3,000	253	1,543	1,796
Queensland	11,445	27,994	39,439	8,686	11,010	19,696
South Australia	2,250	3,850	6,100	2,147	2,737	4,884
Western Australia	9,411	11,579	20,990	8,121†	8,155	16,276
Northern Territory	19,334	4,000	23,334	15,442‡	2,318	17,760
Tasmania	(not included)			Nil	38	38
Total	42,675	63,586	106,261	36,137§	39,172	75,309
Total all Aboriginal			106,261			75,309

* *Source: Assimilation in Action: Progress.* Statement by C.E. Barnes, Minister for Territories.
† Plus 2,000 est.   ‡ Plus 1,944 est.   § Plus 3,944 est.

Table 1 sets out the figures from the 1961 census and the departmental estimates published by the Department of Territories in 1964.

That estimates by the various Aboriginal administrations, taken as a whole, must be regarded with considerable caution may be demonstrated by the fact that

[7] Personal communication from Dr Barwick, Department of Anthropology, Institute of Advanced Studies. Australian National University.
[8] See *Assimilation in Action: Progress.* Statement by C.E. Barnes, Minister for Territories.
[9] 'The Numbers and Distribution of Aborigines in Australia', p. 15.

368   THE ABORIGINAL POPULATION

the Queensland figure of 27,994 part-Aborigines is just over the 27,847 reported
officially for the year ending 30 June 1964 as the total coming under the special
legislation—a figure which included all the Torres Strait Islanders. The annual
report, however, mentions also that 'Approximately 21,150 have full citizenship
rights and live as ordinary members of the community'.[10] This figure of 21,150
appears to have originated in a guess some years ago and to have been progressively
adjusted to allow for natural increase. The 1964 Queensland report mentioned an
approximate 50,000 for 'controlled and non-controlled Aboriginals, Half-Bloods
and Torres Strait Islanders'.[11] Even if we subtract from the 50,000 the 5,217 Torres
Strait Islanders, this does not explain the total figure set out in Table 1. At the time
of writing one is forced back to the 1961 census.

In 1967 the results of the 1966 census were not known. As the questions and the
categories have been changed, these results would require expert analysis to indicate
population trends. No one could foretell what would be the degree of Aboriginal
co-operation in that census. It seemed, therefore, wise in the meantime to use the
figures we had, taking an adjusted 1961 census figure as indicating a minimum
population of round 90,000 for the census categories: and expand this to around
100,000 for the number of those who are identified as Aboriginals in ordinary life
if not at census time.

DISTRIBUTION

The actual distribution, by census districts for each state and the Northern
Territory, of all persons returned as *Aboriginal* and *half-caste*, are indicated in
Maps 1-6. A warning is necessary against accepting the census figures for any
metropolis, although we have had to depend on them for these maps. One
reason for caution is that an increasing number of Aborigines come to the city,
having committed themselves to change. They have already demonstrated a special
independence and will be especially suspicious of a government form which
invites them to identify themselves in the new environment as 'half-caste'. Because
the process of urbanisation of Aborigines seems to have been accelerating in the
1960s, the distribution of the population as between rural and metropolitan urban,
and rural and other large urban areas, has possibly altered a good deal since 1961.
Another reason for using the census figures for 1961 in these maps was that the
estimates by State authorities in Table 1 do not indicate distribution; and in any
case, with each State adhering to its own definition or making its own estimate,
from such figures there could be nothing like the degree of exactness one can
expect from the census.

Perhaps it is necessary to indicate how it is that, in spite of exclusion from the
Commonwealth census of those with over half-Aboriginal descent, such figures as
we have used, including the 'full-bloods' excluded from the census, are available.
Since 1921, census collectors have been instructed to collect as much information

[10] Queensland: Annual Report of the Director of Native Affairs for the year ending 30 June
1964, p. 3.
[11] Ibid.

369

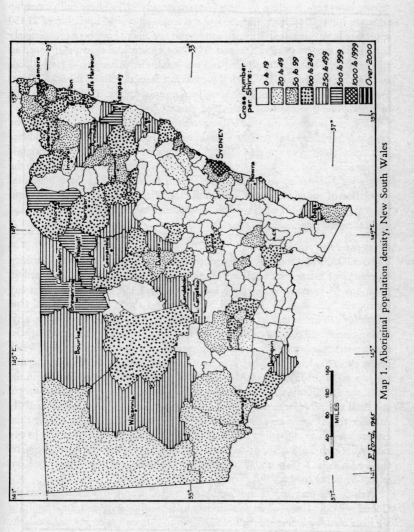

Map 1. Aboriginal population density, New South Wales

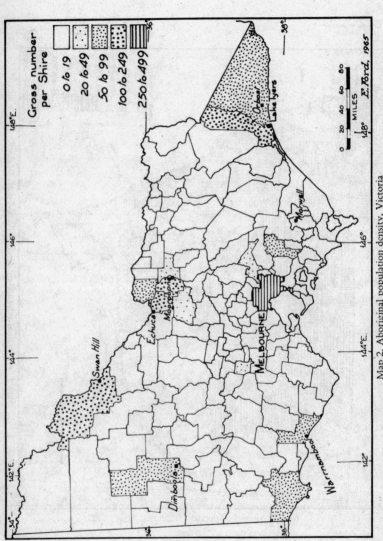

Map 2. Aboriginal population density, Victoria

371

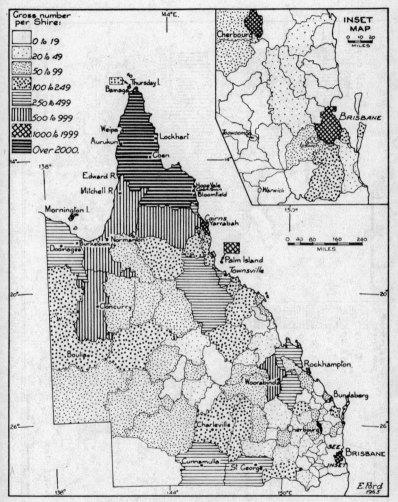

Map 3. Aboriginal population density, Queensland

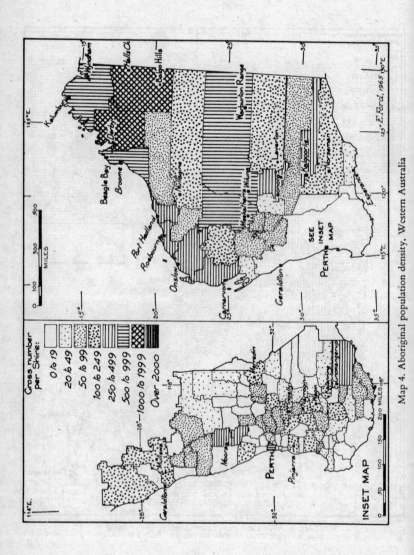

Map 4. Aboriginal population density, Western Australia

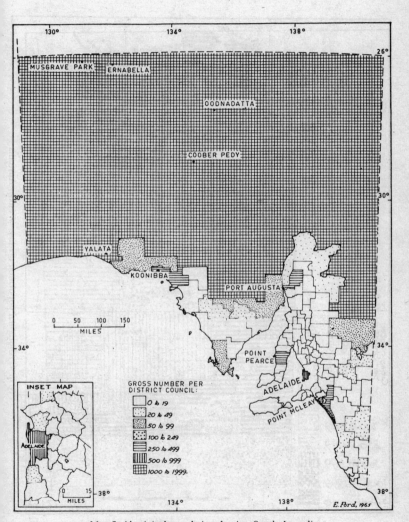

Map 5. Aboriginal population density, South Australia

374

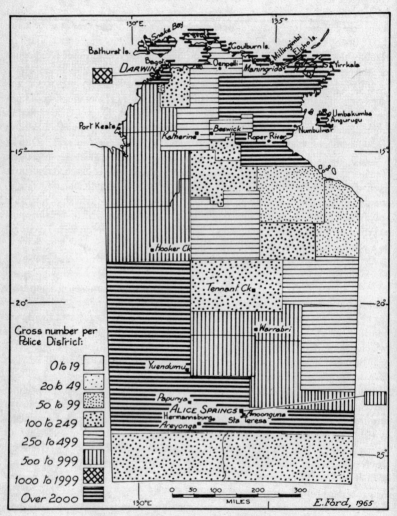

Map 6. Aboriginal population density, Northern Territory

THE ABORIGINAL POPULATION 375

as possible about full-blood Aborigines, although the figures were excluded from statistics of the population as a whole. By 1961 this count was considered to be complete except for Western Australia, where it was thought to have included 80 per cent, and the Northern Territory, where it was estimated to have included 89 per cent, of the totals. As indicated above, Long considers that instead of some 4,000, the official estimate of those missed, the number would be under 500. The result of the 1967 Referendum will lead to more effective measures for a full count of all Australians; and those measures should be successful.

If there has been some under-enumeration, there is no reason why, outside the large cities at least, figures from the 1961 census relating to census areas should not fairly indicate the distribution. It will be noted that in Maps 1-6, to give an impression of the overall situation, the census areas have been grouped into shires (for Queensland, New South Wales, Victoria, and Western Australia), District Council areas (for South Australia), and Police Districts (for the Northern Territory). This method of presentation has its problems, because a large shire, even if Aborigines were established evenly throughout the whole population, would appear at first sight to be more heavily populated by them than a smaller subdivision. But, with the figures available, this was thought to be the most effective way of indicating where, in relation to the State (or Northern Territory) as a whole, the greater concentrations of Aborigines are.

On pages xiv-xv we have used in each State and in the Territory the Statistical Divisions of the Commonwealth Bureau of Census and Statistics, and within each of these attempted to present impressionistically the total number of Aborigines returned at the census, with the relative proportions of *Aboriginal* and *half-caste* (to be as exact as possible, it is necessary here to use the terminology of the census form). Also on the basis of the census material, we have divided the area within which *half-castes* outnumber *Aboriginals* from that in which the reverse applies: it will be noted that this line of division runs roughly from Cooktown to Fowlers Bay on the Bight, and thence to about Exmouth Gulf.

The absolute strength and relative size of the population of full Aboriginal descent may be understated for Western Australia and the Northern Territory; and for reasons already given the total Aboriginal population is probably understated. The full-blood segment of the circles south of the line is probably an overstatement. This line was drawn as accurately as possible to separate local government areas in which enumerated *half-castes* outnumbered enumerated *Aboriginals* from those in which the reverse was recorded at the census. A confirmation that this line was meaningful was the fact that in some areas along it the numbers for the two groups were about equal: the line was drawn approximately through the middle of such local government areas.

The great area north of this line I have called 'colonial Australia' (one reason being the existence throughout this region of some at least of the social relationships typical of a plural society of the colonial type; while the Aboriginal group is relatively numerous enough to pose some of the problems which have been traditionally dealt with in colonies by the methods of colonial administration). In

376   THE ABORIGINAL POPULATION

most of the 'colonial' area, enumerated *Aboriginals* outnumber whites as well as
enumerated *half-castes*. Long, who made these calculations, states that 'only in the
towns did whites outnumber Aboriginals, and in one of the towns at least
(Laverton, W.A.) Aboriginals outnumbered whites'. Throughout this area, if we
exclude the towns, the Aboriginal population predominates.[12]

As Table 2 shows, *Aboriginals* outnumber *half-castes* in 'colonial Australia' by
between five and six to one.

Table 2: *Distribution of Aboriginal population in 'Colonial Australia' and in the more
closely settled areas by States (30 June 1961)*

	Full-blood Aboriginals	Half-caste Aboriginals	Total
Northern Territory	15,442*	2,318	17,760*
Western Australia	6,840†	1,959	8,799†
Queensland	4,566	1,242	5,808
South Australia	1,300	435	1,735
Total	28,148 (32,092)	5,954	34,102 (38,046)

* Plus 1,944   † Plus 2,000

Note: 'Full-bloods' comprised 82·5 or 84·3 per cent of the population of Aboriginal descent. As in all
tables, Torres Strait Islanders are not included; had they been, the great majority of Queensland's 4972
Islanders would have been in 'Colonial Australia', giving Queensland a total of over 10,000 people of
indigenous descent in the north.

Perhaps we could refer to the region south of our dividing line as 'settled
Australia'. Within this region, the *half-castes* outnumbered the *Aboriginals* at the
census by just over four to one—see Table 3.

Table 3: *Southern and Eastern areas ('Settled Australia')*

	Full-blood Aboriginals	Half-caste Aboriginals	Total
New South Wales and Australian Capital Territory	1,488	13,371	14,859
Queensland	4,120	9,768	13,888
Western Australia	1,281	6,196	7,477
South Australia	847	2,302	3,149
Victoria	253	1,543	1,796
Tasmania	—	38	38
Total	7,989	33,218	41,207

Note: 'Half-castes' comprised 80·6 per cent of the population of Aboriginal descent. The full-bloods in
'Colonial Australia' comprised 77·9 per cent of the total full-blood population and the half-castes in
'Settled Australia' comprised 84·8 per cent of the total half-caste population.

[12] The data for these maps were assembled, with the co-operation of the Bureau of Census
and Statistics, by J.P.M. Long, during his term with the Social Services Research Council's
project, Aborigines in Australian Society. The maps were prepared by Mr Edgar Ford, of the
staff of the Australian School of Pacific Administration. I am also indebted to Mr Long for
demographic details of the Aboriginal populations north and south of the line in the map on
pages xiv-xv, and for Tables 1-7.

THE ABORIGINAL POPULATION

In Map 7, the line dividing 'colonial' from 'settled' Australia is superimposed on a general land-use map of the continent. It will be noted that 'colonial Australia' corresponds mainly with the areas which are very sparsely settled and that, except for mining developments, which have of course acquired very great significance over the last few years for the economy as a whole, white settlement of this region has been based mainly on large-scale cattle grazing and on raising sheep for wool along with some cattle grazing. Some of the sheep-raising areas of Western Australia and South Australia fall to the north of our dividing line, but this is not so in Queensland, a fact which may partly reflect the results of Queensland government policies in the past, which involved more drastic action in the removal of Aboriginal populations.

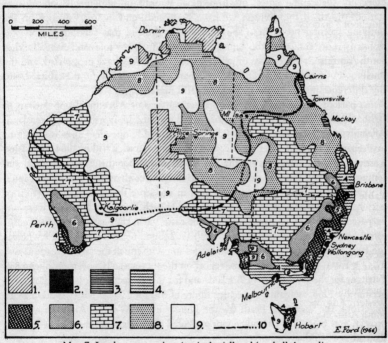

Map 7. Land-use map, showing 'colonial' and 'settled' Australia

Key. 1. Large Aboriginal reserves in 'colonial' Australia, 1966.
2. Large urban and industrial areas.
3. The sugar coast.
4. Dairying, beef cattle and crop farming.
5. Meat animals, sown pastures, orchards, vegetables.
6. Wheat, sheep, pastures.
7. Large-scale wool sheep grazing and some cattle.
8. Large-scale beef cattle grazing.
9. Thinly settled or unoccupied.
10. Boundary between White and Aboriginal areas.

378   THE ABORIGINAL POPULATION

It may also be noted that the very large reserves for Aborigines fall within areas either unoccupied by white settlement or adjacent to those stocked with cattle. This reflects the adjustment of Aborigines of the full descent to the cattle-raising industry. It is also a reminder that the very large reserves were established at a late stage in the process of extending white settlement; that even then, with the possible exception of the Arnhem Land reserve, they have been in areas not suited, as far as was known, for other purposes.

While one of the problems facing the research worker is that of a very sparse Aboriginal population, scattered over great areas, Aborigines do tend, with the exception of a few hundred still following the nomadic life, to congregate in and round country towns, to some extent in the inner suburbs of the big cities, especially the capital cities, on Aboriginal stations or settlements, on mission stations (north of the division we have suggested), and in small groups on the outlying pastoral properties. The 1961 census showed that this population was distinctly more rural than the Australian population as a whole; and even allowing for the significant indications of urbanisation as the 1960s have progressed, and the likelihood of under-enumeration in urban areas, and especially in the capital cities, this difference in distribution is probably still marked.

As part of the research for this project, surveys of Aboriginal populations in Brisbane, Adelaide, and Perth were organised with the Universities of Queensland, Adelaide, and Western Australia. The University of Sydney had already begun to investigate the situation in that city; and Dr Diane Barwick had in 1964 completed a survey of the Aboriginal population in Melbourne for the Australian National University. The results of these surveys so far is to confirm the belief that capital city populations were under-enumerated, in the sense that a high proportion of persons of Aboriginal descent who identify as such for other purposes were not prepared to identify as Aboriginal or half-caste when they completed the census form: Dr Barwick, for instance, in March 1962 found 653 in Melbourne,[13] whereas the 1961 census figure (which would be dealing with much the same situation) was 391. Dr Fay Gale, in a preliminary report on the survey she has been conducting in Adelaide for the University of Adelaide and for this project, records a total of 1,474 persons by 1965, as against the census figure of 512 for 1961.[14] Mr C. Makin, who undertook the survey in Perth for the University of Western Australia and the project, and who, like the other workers, used the referral method, concluded at the end of 1966 that the

total number of people of known Aboriginal descent in this Region [i.e., the Perth Metropolitan Region] and more or less permanently domiciled there, is . . . estimated to be about 1,000 consisting of some 130 to 150 families and about 100 or so individuals living as single people in hostels, hospitals, or other institutions.[15]

[13] A Little More than Kin, Table 1, pp. 26-7.
[14] Summary of Preliminary Findings on Aboriginal Migration to Adelaide (SSRC-AP file).
[15] A Socio-Cultural Anthropological Survey of People of Aboriginal Descent in the Metropolitan Area of Perth (SSRC-AP file).

THE ABORIGINAL POPULATION

But in this case the 1961 census figure was 773; and it seems reasonable to allow for substantial urbanisation in the interim period.

There are no comparable figures for Sydney; but the work undertaken by Mrs Pamela Beasley for the Department of Anthropology gives at least a hint. In the period November 1963 to January 1964 she selected an area, including part only of Redfern and part of Chippendale, both inner city areas known to have substantial Aboriginal populations, and was able to record the names of 501 persons living there at that time. High mobility in these urban populations presented problems for all the workers involved; this was one reason why 54 of the 501 could not be verified as established at a particular address in the time. The area surveyed did not include even the major part of the inner city region; it 'is contiguous with the rest of Redfern, Surry Hills, Waterloo, Alexandria and Erskineville, all of which have comparable Aboriginal populations which in turn merge with similar, if perhaps smaller, populations in neighbouring suburbs'.[16] From some knowledge of the area, one would guess that in the suburbs mentioned there are at least 2,000 persons who identify as Aboriginal. But Aborigines are scattered widely through the enormous extent of the Sydney metropolitan area. For instance, in a thesis completed in 1965, Miss R.R. Iredale, a geography student who also assisted with this project, located 382 persons, in sixty-three households, located close to the railway line from Dundas to St Marys, mainly areas newly 'developed' for housing and well out from the centre.[17] An estimate of at least 5,000 living in Sydney seems on this and other evidence likely to be most conservative at the present time. The census figure for 1961 was 1,397.

In Brisbane, where the census data led to the expectation, by a University of Queensland team headed by Miss Hazel M. Smith, that they would find 1,057 persons, the use of a 'network-referral' system led after great difficulty to the location of 330 dwellings, a high proportion occupied by two or more families; and the preliminary report by the team in 1966 indicated that this was a sample—that while they thought that they had found most of the families established on some permanent basis, there was a mobile population of unknown size. Actually counted were 2,403 people: 'easily another thousand' refused interview or could not be located because of movement, wrong addresses, etc. Thus 3,400 would be a very conservative figure for the total. The research team tentatively suggested that the difference from the census figure was due to migration into Brisbane since 1961.[18] At the same time, it is probable that numbers of Torres Strait Islanders included in these figures may have been separately returned in the 1961 census.

The 'urbanisation index' (i.e. the urban-dwelling percentage of the total)

[16] Pamela Beasley, Draft Preliminary Report on the Redfern-Chippendale Area of Sydney, February 1964. Typescript (SSRC-AP file).
[17] The Enigma of Assimilation: The position of the Part-Aboriginal in New South Wales (SSRC-AP file).
[18] Social Survey of Persons of Aborigine and Torres Strait Island Descent Residing in Brisbane, Queensland 1965-66: Progress Report; also memo from Hazel Smith, 11 April 1967 (SSRC-AP file).

THE ABORIGINAL POPULATION

indicated in the 1961 census, taking only the capital cities of the mainland, was only 9·1 per cent for Aborigines as compared with 56·1 per cent for the population of the five States and the Northern Territory.

Table 4: *Populations of the Capital Cities excluding Canberra and Hobart*

	Sydney	Melbourne	Brisbane	Adelaide	Perth	Darwin
Total population	2,183,358	1,911,895	621,550	587,957	420,133	12,326
Full-bloods and half-castes						
male	657	186	492	248	367	569
female	740	205	567	264	406	554
total	1,397	391	1,059	512	773	1,123
% of Aboriginal population of State	9·5	21·8	5·4	10·5	4·7	6·3
Full-bloods	316	116	220	136	150	461
% of Aboriginal population of city	22·6	28·9	20·8	26·6	19·4	41·1
Approx. Aboriginal % of city population	0·06	0·02	0·17	0·09	0·18	9·1

Note: Excluding Darwin, the capitals rank by gross Aboriginal population in the order—Sydney, Brisbane, Perth, Adelaide, Melbourne. The order of greatest to least proportion of Aborigines is Brisbane, Perth, Adelaide and, a long way behind, Sydney, Melbourne. Note the high proportion in these urban Aboriginal populations identifying as of full descent at the census.

Supposing, however, that we try to allow for possible under-enumeration in 1961 by taking an outside figure of 12,000 for Sydney, 5,000 for Brisbane, along with the other figures based on research by the 'referral' method, and accept an outside estimate of 20,000 persons who identify as Aboriginal in the capital cities. Suppose that at the same time we take the census figure for 1961, and allow for a rate of increase which brings this to a total of 90,000 by 1966. The capital city urban dwellers even then amount only to about 22 per cent of the total, well below half the proportion for the population of the mainland as a whole. It would be less if we took the higher total of Aborigines based on the State estimates. It does seem possible to conclude that, although there are current indications of increasing attempts by Aborigines to establish themselves in the capital cities—efforts which will inevitably be accelerated with the increases in educational opportunity and the increasing awareness of the possibility of escape from the social situation of the country towns into the more impersonal social-economic milieu of the capital city—the population remains a predominantly rural and country town population.

The Bureau of Census and Statistics regards as urban areas towns of more than 1,000 inhabitants, except for Tasmania, where the figure is 750. If we take the 1961 figures, which are the only ones we have to show this kind of distribution, for all *Aborigines* and *half-castes* together, the urbanisation index for all Australia (see Table 5) is just over 23 per cent.

THE ABORIGINAL POPULATION   381

Table 5*: *Aborigines—Urban and Rural (excluding Tasmania)*

	Urban	Rural	Total	Urban %
New South Wales and Australian Capital Territory	5,825	9,034	14,859	39·2
Victoria	873	923	1,796	48·6
Queensland	5,201	14,495	19,696	26·4
South Australia	1,186	3,698	4,884	24·3
Western Australia	2,567	13,709	16,276	15·7
Northern Territory	1,868	15,891	17,759	10·5
Total	17,520	57,750	75,270	23·3

* The estimated 2,000 in Western Australia and 1,944 in the Northern Territory not counted in the census are ignored for the purposes of this and other tables.

Of the Australian population as a whole, 82 per cent were returned as urban in the 1961 census.

As would be expected from the predominance of part-Aborigines in the settled areas, the indications are that they are far more likely to live in towns (as defined by the census) than the Aborigines of the full descent. For the purposes of Table 6 we have regarded all Aborigines returned in New South Wales and Victoria as part-Aboriginal; but for the other mainland States, where the Aboriginal category was substantial, only the figures of half-castes were used.

Table 6: *Part-Aborigines—Urban and Rural*

	Urban	Rural	Total	Urban %
New South Wales and Australian Capital Territory	5,825	9,034	14,859	39·2
Victoria	873	923	1,796	48·6
Queensland	4,281	6,739	11,020	38·8
South Australia	827	1,910	2,737	30·2
Western Australia	2,117	6,038	8,155	25·9
Tasmania	20	18	38	52·6
Northern Territory	1,251	1,067	2,318	53·9
Total	15,194	25,729	40,923	37·1

Table 7 indicates the urban and rural distribution of those returned as *Aboriginal* in the three States with substantial full-blood populations, and in the Northern Territory. It is necessary to remember, however, the tendency already noted for part-Aborigines in urban areas to claim that they are of the full descent.

THE ABORIGINAL POPULATION

Table 7: *Aboriginals—Urban and Rural*

	Urban	Rural	Total	Urban %
Queensland	920	7,766	8,686	10·5
South Australia	359	1,788	2,147	16·7
Western Australia	450	7,671	8,121	5·5
Northern Territory	617	14,825	15,442	4·0
Total	2,346	32,050	34,396	6·8

It might be noted that the Northern Territory, with the greatest absolute numbers and proportion of Aborigines of the full descent outside the towns, is the area of the greatest contrast between Aboriginal and other Australians in the relative degree of urbanisation. This may be due in part to the emphasis on controlling Aborigines of the full descent, to the extent that until recently they had to live in government settlements and on missions—some of these so large that they might almost be regarded as 'towns' of a special segregated kind, into which even in 1967, only Aborigines might go without a permit from the Administration.

This lag in urbanisation may have social as well as economic causes. In a total economy which requires only 18 per cent to be employed in the rural areas, it is one indicator of an economically depressed rural situation. Rural labouring and seasonal work, with a high proportion of unemployment and under-employment, go with a high proportion of people who live on reserves which are in some areas (especially Queensland and the Northern Territory) still segregated, in others not segregated by law, but only recently removed from this situation, or, at the time of writing, about to be removed. Many of such rural groups of dwellings occupied entirely by Aborigines are isolated by distance from towns, and have nothing like the range of services which make the town what it is; therefore they cannot themselves be regarded as towns, even where the population may in itself be large enough to qualify. The housing shortages elsewhere, long custom of living in one place, the mental carry-over from long institutionalisation in the one spot, all help to restrict these people to the sites of these former institutions and to the present reserves in 'settled Australia'. The problem of housing is especially acute for a group which generally, because of poverty, prejudice, and the effects of other causes, finds itself especially handicapped in competing for this scarce commodity, so that it is only by some administrative action that a house in any kind of repair is likely to be vacant in one of these reserve settlements, whatever the distances which must be travelled for employment.

Better known, and at least as characteristic, is the fringe settlement adjacent to the town. It may or may not be a reserve, or even a managed settlement on a reserve. Where it is either, it is probably treated as lying outside the boundaries of a town, so that the 'rural' proportion may to this extent be inflated, where the reserve is sufficiently close to the town for the inhabitants to regard themselves, even where not so regarded by the shire or municipal council, as part of the town

THE ABORIGINAL POPULATION

community—which they will often be economically, both as labour supply and market, but not socially. This is merely one of many examples of the difficulty one faces in attempting to apply to this situation the forms of statistical measurement which assist in delineating meaningful concepts when one is dealing with the white population, or even the population as a whole. In a sense, because of the past exclusion from the census, and because of the degree to which rural Aboriginal living conditions and standards diverge from those of the population as a whole, their situation is beyond statistics.

POPULATION TRENDS

It is important to know not only the size and distribution of the Aboriginal population but also population trends, for if this population is rapidly increasing, government policies have to allow for this fact. For a long time policy was based on the assumption, based soundly enough on observation, that the Aborigines would die out. As for the part-Aboriginal, the idea of his absorption into the white community is of very long standing; and policies formulated in all States, and expressed in the legislation from early in the century, to be agreed upon at the first policy conference held between Commonwealth and State government authorities concerned, in 1937, were aimed to hasten this process. One of the reasons for the long-standing effort by governments to prevent sexual intercourse between Aborigines and others was to keep the half-caste problem within manageable proportions, though it was generally justified in terms of morality.

Estimation of population trends is very difficult for the government authorities as well as for the research worker, partly because the basic records of births and deaths maintained by Commonwealth and States do not include statements concerning race. Even when, as a result of the 1966 census, figures of the population become available, with indications of the degrees of Aboriginal descent, these will not help very much in this connection. First, they will refer only to those of Aboriginal descent, rather than to the 'population at risk', the group which is identified socially and economically as Aboriginal. Second, they will provide no more than a base for future calculations; and these will remain impossible on a large scale without similar racial categories being included in the registration forms for vital statistics. Third, they will be in effect a different set of figures, and will, it seems, shed no additional light on what the trends are now, until the following census. We must therefore do the best we can with the various figures and past estimates we have.

In the broadest terms, and extending over the whole period of white settlement in Australia, these indicate a rapid decline from what may have been a population as high as 300,000 in 1788 to about 62,000 at the time of the 1921 census, with a trend to increase indicated in subsequent census figures. The whole problem of making the best guess from available information has been discussed in *The Structure and Growth of Australia's Aboriginal Population* by Lancaster Jones. He has taken the minimum estimate of the original population, as stated by Professor Radcliffe-Brown in an article published in the *Commonwealth Year Book* for 1930

384   THE ABORIGINAL POPULATION

and related it to a reconstruction of the distribution of Aboriginal tribes made by
Norman B. Tindale in 1940. On this basis he has preferred to use Radcliffe-
Brown's minimum figure of 251,000 rather than his 'quite possibly, or even
probably, over 300,000'. The result is shown in Table 8, which he has prepared
with the caution that 'all figures shown except those for 1961 (and to some extent
1954 and 1947) involve considerable guesswork, are of uncertain reliability, and
in some cases omit sections of the Aboriginal population'.[19]

Table 8: *Some Estimates of the Number and Distribution of Aborigines in the States and
Territories of Australia, 1788 to 1966*

	1788*	1901†	1921†	1947‡	1954§	1961‖	1966¶
New South Wales	40,000	8,065	6,067	11,560	12,214	14,716	13,613
Victoria	11,500	521	573	1,277	1,395	1,796	1,790
Queensland	100,000	26,670	15,454	16,311	18,460	19,696	19,003
South Australia	10,000	3,070	2,741	4,296	4,972	4,884	5,505
Western Australia	52,000	5,261	17,671	24,912	16,215	18,276	18,439
Tasmania	2,500	0	0	214	93	38	55
Northern Territory	35,000	23,363	17,973	15,147	17,157	19,704	21,119
A.C.T.	**	**	0	100	172	143	96
Australia	251,000	66,950	60,479	73,817	70,678	79,253	79,620

Source: F. Lancaster Jones, *The Structure and Growth of Australia's Aboriginal Population*, Table 1.
* A.R. Radcliffe-Brown's estimates in *Official Year Book of the Commonwealth of Australia*, No. 23 (1930),
pp. 687-96.
† *Official Year Book of the Commonwealth of Australia*, No. 1 (1901-7), p. 145; No. 17 (1924), pp. 951-61.
‡ *Statistician's Report on the 1947 Census*, pp. 153-65.
§ *Official Year Book of the Commonwealth of Australia*, No. 46 (1960), p. 328.
‖ *Census of the Commonwealth*, 30th June, 1961: *Census Bulletin No.* 36 (Race of the Population), Table 3.
¶ *Census of the Commonwealth of Australia*, 30th June, 1966: The Aboriginal Population (Revised
Statement), Canberra 1967.
** Included in N.S.W.

In the main, Lancaster Jones has had to depend on guesses as to how many
people the land in different areas could sustain and on what was about the average
number of members in the Aboriginal tribe—guesses made by people with great
expertise, but of their nature such that small variations in the basic figures made a
considerable difference in the totals. Lancaster Jones points out that 'nobody
knows how many tribes were extinct and unrecorded at the time of Tindale's
survey'; and that even when we take his tribal map and assume that the average size
of the tribe was round 500, the effect is to suggest that the figure for the mainland
should be reduced to about 215,000 in 1788.[20]

Calculations of this type are necessary to give some general idea of what
happened; but they can never be more than rough indicators. Similar attempts
have been made to estimate the changes in the north American Indian populations.
Here also there are indications of a spectacular decrease in the indigenous population,
a turning point, and a recovery. But the recovery and its extent depend a good
deal on interpretation. Do we, for this purpose, include all or some of part-

[19] Lancaster Jones, *The Structure and Growth of Australia's Aboriginal Population*.
[20] Ibid.

indigenous descent, and if some, how many? The Australian calculations are ingenious, and probably get us as far as we can ever get in estimates of the numbers in 1788. But all we can say is that the original Aboriginal population was very light by the standards of settled agricultural society: that it might have been 200,000 or 300,000. Even the bases for such guesses are likely to be brought into question by current discussions about the nature and size of the original social groups occupying particular areas.

The trend since 1921, says Lancaster Jones, is indicative of 'moderate growth' overall through the four decades until 1961. But there were distinct trends within this pattern. Aborigines declined from 82 per cent of the total of *Aboriginal* and *half-caste* in the 1921 census to 51 per cent in 1961; and the decrease in *Aborigines* was of the order of 20 to 25 per cent, while the *half-castes* increased by 238 per cent. But the evidence indicates that the decline of the full-blood population was arrested by the early 1950s, and 'the best available evidence suggests that Australia's full-blood Aboriginal population is now steadily increasing'.[21]

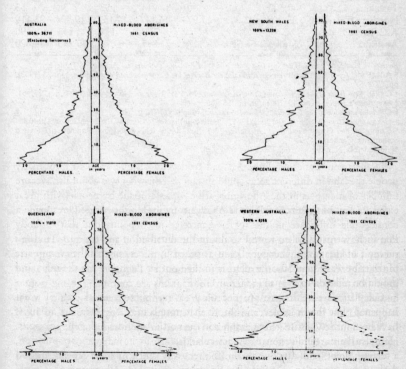

Fig. 1. Age distribution of mixed-blood Aborigines by single years of age: 1961 Census

[21] Ibid.

The more spectacular increase has been within the part-Aboriginal group. The situation for *half-castes*, in the 1961 census, as set out by Lancaster Jones, is indicated in Fig. 1 and that of *Aboriginals* in Fig. 2. I have already stated

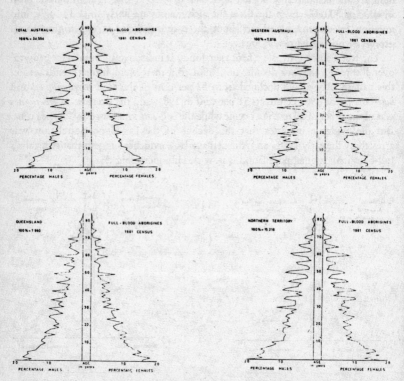

Fig. 2. Age distribution of full-blood Aborigines by single years of age: 1961 Census

that there seems to be no reason to doubt the distribution and the age-sex composition of the Aboriginal population as stated in the census; and some support for the figures of population structure worked out by Lancaster Jones, with some indication that the trends suggested in his diagrams are continuing, came from a household survey conducted as part of this Project within two areas—country town and rural New South Wales, and the Eyre Peninsula of South Australia, in 1965. In New South Wales 183 households co-operated in completion of the questionnaire; and in the Eyre Peninsula, 62 households.

In the New South Wales households there was a total of 1,283 persons; but of this number, ten were non-Aboriginal male spouses and two were non-Aboriginal female spouses. We did not establish age for seventeen females and nineteen males. Excluding these, we had a group of 1,235 persons, whose ages had been established,

THE ABORIGINAL POPULATION

at actual interviews in the homes. The households where interviews occurred were as far as possible representative of situations in non-metropolitan areas of the State, falling into the census categories of 'other urban' and 'rural'; and the attempt was made at a representative selection based on the tenure of the land on which the house was built—town block, government Aboriginal station, town common or crown land other than Aboriginal reserve, unmanaged Aboriginal reserve, or other land privately owned.[22]

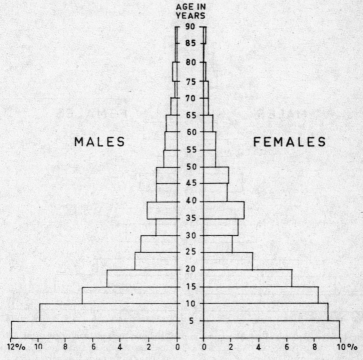

Fig. 3. N.S.W.: Part-Aborigines in rural and non-metropolitan urban areas, 1965

The age-sex structure of this group of 1,235 part-Aborigines is set out in Fig. 3. In this group no less than 55·8 per cent of the whole were children under fifteen years, and 80·1 per cent were under thirty years of age. That the proportion under fifteen years is higher than the 50-53 per cent found by Lancaster Jones may indicate that more children in these large families are surviving than in 1961. It may be influenced by other factors. For instance, if the thirty-six persons whose

---

[22] For details of this survey, see C.D. Rowley, The Aboriginal Householder (Paper read to ANZAAS, Section G, Thirty-ninth Congress, January 1967).

ages are unknown were all over fifteen years, the proportion under fifteen years falls to 53·7 per cent; or there may have been a movement to the Sydney metropolitan area of persons over fifteen years. Again, the probability is that this group is in some ways not representative of the part-Aboriginal population of New South Wales as a whole. If we apply to the 55·8 per cent of these 1,235 persons the standard error calculations, the result confirms that the trend shown in the 1961 figures was still maintained at least in 1965 in New South Wales. An adjust-

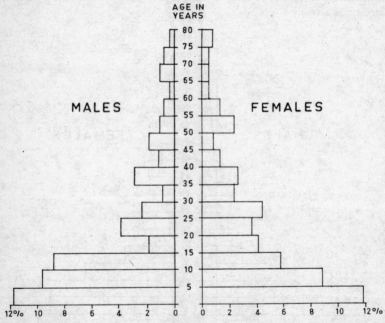

Fig 4. Eyre Peninsula: Part-Aborigines in rural and non-metropolitan urban areas, 1965

ment of twice the standard error either way suggests that part-Aborigines under fifteen years formed somewhere between 53 and 58·6 per cent of the total. Taking into account the other factors mentioned which affect this group, one can go no further than to say that the figures confirm the age distribution indicated in the 1961 census; if they are suggestive of any more, it is that the proportion under fifteen years is more likely to be greater than less than it was in 1961. This in turn confirms in one respect the basis on which predictions of a rapid increase in the part-Aboriginal population depend.

Of the sixty-two Eyre Peninsula households co-operating, forty-two were on town building blocks, mainly in the urban areas of Port Lincoln, Whyalla, and Port Augusta. Others were in the hinterland, along the railway line to Maree, and

THE ABORIGINAL POPULATION

at Iron Knob and Coomunga. The group of 400 persons included one non-Aboriginal wife and nine non-Aboriginal husbands (all Caucasians), who were excluded from the calculations involved in Fig. 4. There were two women and one man whose ages were not established; and the total of thirteen exclusions left a comparatively small group of 387 persons. It seemed worth while to look at the age and sex structure of this group, again with a view to any light which might be shed on Lancaster Jones's findings from the 1961 census. The decision to work in the Eyre Peninsula was due to the possibilities offering to have the questionnaire administered, with the other incentive that here was a group which had been to a large extent recently urbanised.

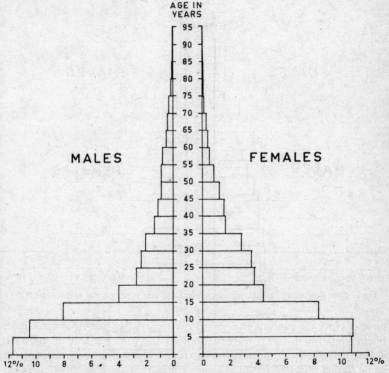

Fig. 5. Aborigines in New South Wales, 1958-63

Figure 4 shows the kind of irregularities one would expect in view of the small numbers involved. But the fact that in this group 56·3 per cent were under fifteen years, and 76·5 per cent under thirty provides at least minor confirmation of the youthfulness of the part-Aboriginal population indicated by the survey in New South Wales.

Dr Peter Moodie, a research worker at the School of Public Health and Tropical Medicine, University of Sydney, who has been engaged on the study of Aboriginal health, recently made a preliminary survey of the age-sex structure of rural Aboriginal communities which had been subjected to Mantoux and X-Ray tests by the New South Wales Department of Public Health. Information on age and sex was available from the departmental records for 6,454 individuals from forty-six communities covering most parts of the State. Moodie tentatively rejected seven of these communities because of a noticeable absence of adult males, whom he presumed to be away at work, and two communities where the figures showed a noticeable absence of school-age children. But he did include the suspect groups in a supplementary, total, analysis. His analysis of the thirty-seven

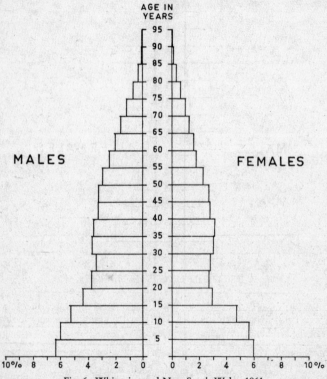

Fig. 6. Whites in rural New South Wales, 1961

communities which appeared 'normal' in that the total number of 5,116 individuals 'showed no unexpected gap in any age group', showed that 60·2 per cent were under fifteen years. When he included the apparently atypical communities, the proportion was very slightly higher, but not significantly different. (The proportion under thirty years was 81 per cent.) Moodie's diagrams, one setting out these results and one indicating the sex-age structure of the total New South Wales *rural* population as shown in the 1961 census, have been reproduced in Figs. 5 and 6. The contrast of the New South Wales *total rural* population (in Fig. 6) with that of New South Wales part-Aborigines as indicated in Fig. 1

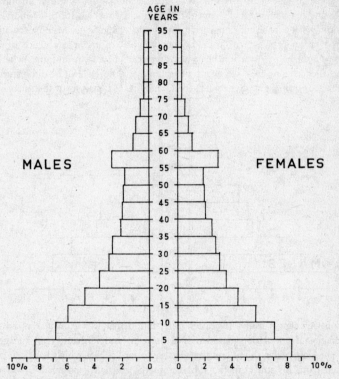

Fig. 7. Indians in the United States of America, 1960

(which portrays census figures) and with the patterns indicated in Figs. 3-5 is clear.[23] For comparison with the part-Aboriginal situation, one may look to the Indians of the United States (as in Fig. 7) and the Maoris (Fig. 8).

This emphasis on youth seems common enough in the cases of indigenous minorities in wealthy nations. It is also, as a rule, in marked contrast with the situation of the European populations which hold the economic power: for instance, the 1961 census showed that in Australia as a whole the proportion of persons under fifteen years was only 30·23 per cent and that 50·7 per cent were under thirty.

[23] P.M. Moodie: Draft report: Aboriginal Health, New South Wales: The Aboriginal Population of New South Wales (in SSRC-AP file).

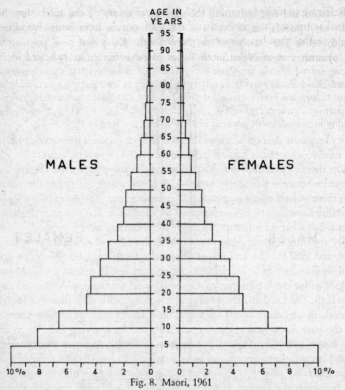

Fig. 8. Maori, 1961

From his census study, Lancaster Jones found that, for Australia as a whole, the *Aboriginal* population included 38·2 per cent under fifteen years of age and 62·4 per cent under thirty and that (as shown in Table 9 which has been partly adapted from his study) in the 1961 census the *Aboriginal* population was more youthful than the Australian population as a whole, occupying a position in this respect in between the *half-caste* and the Australian populations.

Table 9: *Population Age Structure—Part-Aboriginal, Aboriginal, and Australian, 1961*

Age Group	Half-caste	Aboriginal	All Australian
0-14	51·1	38·2	30·2
15-29	24·0	24·2	20·6
30-44	14·0	18·5	20·8
45-59	7·2	11·4	16·1
60+	3·7	7·7	12·3
Total	100·0	100·0	100·0
Median Age	19·6	22·6	29·4

Source: Adapted from Lancaster Jones, *The Structure and Growth.*

THE ABORIGINAL POPULATION 393

Referring to his age pyramids for *half-castes*, Lancaster Jones comments on their general symmetry, suggesting that the main factor in the situation has been high fertility rather than heavy mortality in the older groups.

This symmetry suggests that mortality at older ages has probably been fairly stable among mixed-bloods for some time. The little evidence that exists suggests that mixed-blood fertility has been relatively high for at least twenty years, and that the major change has been a gradual decline in infant and childhood mortality. Thus the proportion ... under fifteen ... was already high in 1947 (45 per cent), but has steadily increased, to 48 per cent in 1954 and 51 per cent in 1961.

Lack of separate data on births and deaths, he says, makes it impossible to estimate the relative importance of declining mortality and increasing fertility.[24]

On the age pyramids for Aborigines of the full descent, he comments that 'the steps between the age groups 0-4, 5-9, and 10-14 are rather more marked than those at later ages, again probably reflecting some decline in infant and child mortality since about 1950, or perhaps a little earlier'.[25] It is not possible, however, to establish what the infant or the child mortality rates have been.

By applying to these figures the New Zealand Maori mortality rates for 1955, 1956, and 1957 (63, 54, and 58 per thousand respectively), he estimates a possible total fertility rate of 7·25 children per woman at the end of the child-bearing period, with a crude birth rate of 43 per thousand for the part-Aboriginal population. If the child and infant mortality rate were in fact higher than that for Maoris (something we cannot know, but which the evidence we have on living conditions for the part-Aboriginal suggests could be possible, ignoring here the results of few surveys of very limited populations of fringe-dwelling part-Aborigines), then, Lancaster Jones argues, we have to assume an even higher level of fertility. If the mortality rates were lower, we can settle for lower fertility rates in accounting for the census figures. But his assumption of a fertility rate resembling that of New Zealand Maoris seems to be sensibly conservative; and even on this basis, by working out the age-specific fertility rate for each woman in each of the five-year age groups in the child-bearing period, he has forecast that the part-Aboriginal population will more than double itself between 1961 and 1981 (see Table 10).

This, he writes, means a natural increase of from 3·8 to 4 per cent per annum, comparable with that of New Zealand Maoris. A conservative estimate, he says, would be 3·5 per cent: but even this means that the population doubles itself in the two decades after 1961.

In dealing with fertility and mortality rates among the *Aboriginals*, he had the advantage of being able to compare the figures taken from the Register of Wards, maintained by the Welfare (now Social Welfare) Branch of the Northern Territory Administration, with the census figures for the Territory. Using both sources, he worked out age-specific fertility and mortality rates. Once again, he limited the period of his population forecast (sensibly, since the rates so painfully deduced from inadequate data are of course subject to change) to the period 1961-1981.

[24] Lancaster Jones, *The Structure and Growth of Australia's Aboriginal Population.*
[25] Ibid.

394   THE ABORIGINAL POPULATION

Table 10: *A Projection of Population Growth Among Mixed-Blood Aborigines in Australia, 1961 to 1981*

| | Age Group | | | | | | |
	0–14	15–29	30–44	45–59	60+	Total	Total No.
1961							
Males	25·5	11·9	7·0	3·8	2·1	50·3	19,713
Females	25·6	12·1	7·0	3·4	1·6	49·7	19,459
Persons	51·1	24·0	14·0	7·2	3·7	100·0	39,172
1966							
Males	25·2	12·5	6·9	3·6	2·0	50·2	23,845
Females	24·9	12·9	6·9	3·5	1·6	49·8	23,667
Persons	50·1	25·4	13·8	7·1	3·6	100·0	47,512
1971							
Males	24·8	13·3	6·5	3·5	2·0	50·1	29,002
Females	24·5	13·5	6·6	3·6	1·7	49·9	28,900
Persons	49·3	26·8	13·1	7·1	3·7	100·0	57,902
1976							
Males	25·0	13·5	6·2	3·5	1·8	50·0	35,500
Females	24·8	13·6	6·3	3·5	1·8	50·0	35,461
Persons	49·8	27·1	12·5	7·0	3·6	100·0	70,961
1981							
Males	25·3	13·2	6·4	3·4	1·7	50·0	43,501
Females	25·0	13·1	6·6	3·5	1·8	50·0	43,514
Persons	50·3	26·3	13·0	6·9	3·5	100·0	87,015

Source: Lancaster Jones, *The Structure and Growth of Australia's Aboriginal Population*, Table 8.

As Table 11 shows, he predicts an increase of from 36,000 to 55,000 for Australia as a whole, on the basis of those actually counted in the census, or from 40,000 to 61,000 if the additional estimates made by the Bureau of Census and Statistics are included. But since these figures assume an annual growth rate of only 2 per cent over the two decades, and since there is a trend to better conditions, he suggests what seems a properly optimistic growth rate of 2·5 per cent from 1966 to 1976; and of 3 per cent from then till 1981, which would result in a total of around 66,000.

Taking the analysis for the enumerated *half-castes* and *Aboriginals* together, his prediction from the census figures is that

by 1981 Australia's total Aboriginal population will almost certainly number 150,000 persons, and possibly more. If these trends are continued there is every possibility that by the turn of the century Australia's Aboriginal population will have recovered to the number estimated by Radcliffe-Brown to have been in Australia at the time of first European settlement.[26]

[26] Ibid.

THE ABORIGINAL POPULATION

This finding must be assessed in the light of the fact already referred to—that some part-Aborigines did not choose to describe themselves as *half-caste* at the time of the 1961 census, while they continued to identify as members of part-Aboriginal groups; thus the numbers involved could be much greater.

Table 11: *A Projection of Population Growth Among Full-Blood Aborigines in Australia, 1961 to 1981*

	\multicolumn{5}{c}{Age Group}						
	0-14	15-29	30-44	45-59	60+	Total	Total No.
1961							
Males	19·4	12·7	9·5	6·3	4·4	52·3	18,899
Females	18·8	11·5	9·0	5·1	3·3	47·7	17,238
Persons	38·2	24·2	18·5	11·4	7·7	100·0	36,137
						Scaled	40,081*
1966							
Males	19·8	12·5	9·0	6·3	4·4	52·0	20,747
Females	18·9	11·5	8·7	5·5	3·4	48·0	19,130
Persons	38·7	24·0	17·7	11·8	7·8	100·0	39,877
						Scaled	44,224*
1971							
Males	19·6	13·1	8·7	6·2	4·1	51·7	22,926
Females	18·6	12·4	8·2	5·8	3·3	48·3	21,408
Persons	38·2	25·5	16·9	12·0	7·4	100·0	44,334
						Scaled	49,166*
1976							
Males	19·8	13·4	8·7	5·3	4·0	51·2	25,097
Females	18·7	12·9	7·9	5·9	3·4	48·8	23,909
Persons	38·5	26·3	16·6	11·2	7·4	100·0	49,006
						Scaled	54,348*
1981							
Males	19·8	13·6	8·4	5·6	3·9	51·3	28,204
Females	18·8	13·0	7·7	5·6	3·6	48·7	26,767
Persons	38·6	26·6	16·1	11·2	7·5	100·0	54,971
						Scaled	60,963*

* To allow for the number of Aborigines estimated not to have been enumerated in the 1961 census.
Source: Lancaster Jones, *The Structure and Growth of Australia's Aboriginal Population*, Table 9.

Even from the figures for half-castes in the two censuses of 1954 and 1961 he found that there had been a substantial disappearance of persons who were aged over five years in 1954 and that the loss was far too great to be accounted for by deaths in the intervening years. A substantial proportion of these young people must have been describing themselves as either *Aboriginal* or *European*. There is no proof, as he points out, that the 'statistical passing' accompanied social 'passing' into the white group; but this seems more probable than the claiming of *Aboriginal* identity. What makes it more probable is the whole background in which the chance of social equality has depended on whiteness, or comparative whiteness, of the skin; and on absence, or comparative absence, of the recognisable 'Aboriginal' features. In fact, the cruder apologists for 'assimilation' have for a long time been advocating this kind of absorption. It seems impossible to estimate the extent of 'passing' which has occurred since 1788; but there must be a substantial proportion of the Australian population which is of part-Aboriginal descent. Historically, this has had more to do with cosmetic inheritance than with other qualities, or with tolerance.

SOME IMPLICATIONS OF THE ABORIGINAL POPULATION TRENDS

One implication of persons 'passing' as 'white' into 'white Australian' society is that Aboriginal society here has resembled Negro society in the United States. Colour-prejudice has so overwhelmingly dominated the value system as to restrict the opportunities of dark-skinned persons, irrespective of ability, while opening the way more easily for those of fair coloration. Thus the fair-skinned member of the family may be urged or tempted to 'pass', to forget loyalties to the group; or a whole family may either manage to do so or be strenuously trying. Those trying to escape from their Aboriginal lot or those who have succeeded may be very sensitive on the point. Those who have no chance to do so, some of whom may feel that they have greater abilities or worth than those who have succeeded, will often regard this action as a kind of desertion or capitulation. This is one of the causes of the tension which is a noticeable feature of part-Aboriginal society in the 'settled' areas of Australia; and while there seem to be few of the desperate attempts to alter personal appearance which have led to the development of special beauty industries in the metropolitan cities of the United States, the limitation placed on ambition and hope by the accident of personal appearance has for generations been harsh reality for the adolescent dark Australian.

Typically, this involves a degree of social rejection by 'white' members of his age-group, at the sensitive time of puberty, which also tends to correspond with the later years or the end of compulsory schooling. At this point the dark child must be strongly influenced by those of his elders who, having shared some of these experiences, share also a realistic pessimism. His own experience confirms their argument, that for the person who cannot 'pass' there is nothing in Australian society but unskilled work and membership of a socially depressed caste. That such a large proportion of part-Aboriginal children leave school as soon as they can is one indication of this situation. It is also an indication of where the basic difficulty lies. Often the 'solution' of the Aboriginal 'problem' is assumed to depend on some special effort on his part to become house-trained in some way, so that he will be 'acceptable'. Assimilation programs have involved the careful selection of 'good' families, often specifically stated to be 'of light caste', to be placed in houses 'in town'. The basic problem, of course, is in the prejudice expressed in the myth of 'white Australia'. Unfortunately, education is unlikely to reduce racial prejudice significantly.

It seems that the Aboriginal has to find opportunities to gain the economic power, irrespective of the colour of his skin, to make his way into all strata of Australian society, and to gain the political strength to confront prejudice, rather

THE ABORIGINAL POPULATION   397

than defer to it. To assist in this process, governments must recognise that
Australian society has always been, and can only be, a multi-racial society.

That this population, as indicated in the census, is likely to double itself in a
comparatively short time has clear economic implications. Irrespective of what the
1966 census figures might show, it was clear in 1967 that costs involved in establishing the basis for equality of economic opportunity and social mobility, in a society
where economic status has a close relationship to class, are likely to double in two
decades or so, even if we think only of Aborigines attaining the range of living
standards which the 'white' population enjoys now. This argument is not really
offset by the fact that many Aborigines now may be better off than some categories
of non-Aboriginal Australians who live in poverty, like the old-age pensioner
group.

If there is a 'hard core' to the problem in 'settled' Australia, it is probably
in the fringe-dwelling groups round the country towns and on the reserves and
Aboriginal stations in the rural areas, where the evidence is of very rapid rates of
increase. These must be due in part to the considerable decrease in mortality rates
arising from the increasing concern of governments, and extension of rights to
social service benefits. Increases in urbanisation, a process which seems to be in the
initial stages and still involving high mobility between the old home and the
centres of industrial growth, will almost certainly contribute to economic strength,
since the logic of industrial production tends in time to erode prejudices which
affect efficiency. Greater sophistication and urbanisation can be expected to have
the same effect on increase rates as in the community generally; and measures
which facilitate urbanisation may help to strengthen Aboriginal economic power
(provided that they are responses to Aboriginal choices), not only by increasing
earnings but by tending to reduce the numbers of dependants. Yet the real
challenge is presented by the fringe settlement from which those newly urbanised
have come, for confidence and security in the home base is required for success
in the wider society. The crux of the matter here lies as much in the relationship
of the fringe-dweller to local as to central government.

In 'colonial Australia', as we have somewhat roughly defined it, the question
of how to develop mobility and greater equality of economic opportunity, and a
greater range of choice, appears not so hopeless as it seemed even a decade ago.
The very great mining possibilities which are being revealed pose in a more
sophisticated context the old questions of the rights of prior occupation which
have been disregarded in the development of the pastoral industry. The Aborigines
of the north form a potential labour force and market already deeply rooted in
their 'country'; and a more subtle question, almost completely ignored in the
history of contact, is that of what concessions, in the way of shares in the new
wealth, are to be made to them. Here I have in mind not only opportunities
to work, but to obtain shares in the enterprises. The problems of large pauper
populations without access to effective training for participation in the cash
economy and production, and very often without anything like full-time employment, can hardly be ignored in the face of the evidence that they are increasing

rapidly, and possibly at an accelerating rate. As in 'settled' Australia, the longer the delay, the greater the likely costs for remedial measures, irrespective of questions of justice.

The passage of time could also be marked, in both cases, by a widening of the gap between the living standards of the white middle classes and the coloured poor. This of course will tend to increase costs of action, in the areas of housing, education, health, and spatial and social mobility, to close the economic gap. This same gap, so far as it repeats within Australia that between the rich 'white' nations and the poor 'coloured' ones, will tend to attract increasing international attention: the issues arising from the social and economic status of the Aboriginal have already been taken into the arenas of international diplomacy:[27] and have been linked with Australian immigration practices and control of Australian New Guinea in criticism of Australian racial policies.[28] Any increase of Aboriginal population will, with the trend to greater organisation, increase Aboriginal political pressures, which are still minimal. In situations where economic and social differences tend to coincide with racial ones, as there is plenty of evidence to show, the transition to overt intransigence can be rapid.

There would seem, then, to be some arguments for allocating a high national priority to the promotion of Aboriginal equality and welfare.

Irrespective of what may happen, there is now the annual bill for the maintenance at an often very inadequate level of welfare, of a group of people who compare in size with the annual migrant intake and who are operating well below their efficiency potential as producers; and an increase in their earning power would form an important stimulus to the local market. In the present level of dependency there are many vested interests—political, religious, perhaps especially administrative; nor is the matter made simpler by the fact that each State has claimed sovereign power as well as a special competence in dealing with Aboriginal people. From the time of the early settlements until now, the first priority in stimulating population growth and economic development has been allotted to European migration. The Aboriginal population has probably greater economic potential on a per capita expenditure basis. They are already here, and most of them want to live and work where few migrants will stay. The question of a comparable level of priority, on the grounds of the most hard-headed economic self-interest, can hardly be avoided. The alternative is to face increasing costs for an increasing, largely dependent, group.

[27] Pressures could arise in the context of relations with Asian nations; and the shaping of an administrative entree to what governments may choose to regard as their own business may be seen for instance in the Declaration on the Elimination of all Forms of Racial Discrimination, unanimously adopted by the General Assembly on 21 November 1963.
[28] See statement by Tom Mboya on return to Nairobi from Australia in The Sun (Sydney), 9 September 1964. A full account in the Irish Times (9 September 1964) makes the line in his statement clearer. The Kenya government subsequently (and pointedly) invited a mixed party of Aborigines and New Guineans to Kenya (see S.M.H., 4 December 1964).

REFERENCES

I. GOVERNMENT AND OFFICIAL PUBLICATIONS

AUSTRALIA

COMMONWEALTH

The Aboriginals and Half-Castes of Central Australia and North Australia. Report by J.W. Bleakley, Chief Protector of Aborigines, Queensland, 1928. *Commonwealth Parliamentary Paper (C.P.P.)* no. 21, 1929.

Aboriginal Welfare: Initial Conference of Commonwealth and States Aboriginal Authorities, April 1937. Canberra, 1937.

Annual Report of the Administrator of the Northern Territory, 1912. *C.P.P.* no. 45, 1913.

Bureau of Agricultural Economics: Report on the Beef Cattle Industry in Northern Australia, by J.H. Kelly. Canberra, 1952.

Bureau of Census and Statistics: *Census of the Commonwealth of Australia*, 30th June, 1961.

Central Australia. Finding and evidence of Board of Inquiry concerning the killing of natives in Central Australia by police parties and others. *Votes and Proceedings (V. & P.) (H. of R.)* 1929.

Commonwealth Parliamentary Debates (C.P.D.) (H. of R.) 1918-19.

Department of Home Affairs, Conference Convened by the Minister of State for Home Affairs, 12th April 1929.

Department of the Interior, Notes of a Conference of Commonwealth and State Aboriginal Welfare Authorities, Canberra, 3 and 4 February, 1948.

Historical Records of Australia, Series 1, vols. I-XXVI.

Nineteenth Report of the Director-General of Social Services for Year 1959-60. *C.P.P.* no. 65, 1960-61.

Northern Territory. Outlines of a Policy—by the Honourable P.M. Glynn, Minister for External Affairs. *C.P.P.* no. 30, 1914.

Recommendations of Policy in Native Affairs in the Northern Territory of Australia. *C.P.P.* no. 56, 1937-40.

Report from the Select Committee on Grievances of Yirrkala Aborigines, Arnhem Land Reserve, 1963. *C.P.P. (H. of R.)* no. 311, 1962-3.

Report from the Select Committee on Voting Rights of Aboriginals, 1961. *C.P.P.* (H. of R. 1 and 2), vol. II, 1961.

REFERENCES

Report of the Board of Inquiry appointed to inquire into the Land and Land Industries of the Northern Territory of Australia, 1937. *C.P.P.* no. 4, 1937-40.

Report of the Chief Protector of Aboriginals, in Report on the Administration of the Northern Territory, 1932-3. *C.P.P.* no. 124, 1932-4.

Report of the Chief Protector of Aboriginals, in Report on the Administration of the Northern Territory, 1933. *C.P.P.* no. 203, 1932-4.

Report of the Chief Protector of Aboriginals, in Report on the Administration of the Northern Territory, 1935. *C.P.P.* no. 237, 1935.

Report on the Administration of the Northern Territory, 1936. *C.P.P.* no. 63, 1937.

Report on Administration of the Northern Territory, 1937-8. *C.P.P.* no. 150, 1937-9.

Report on the Administration of the Northern Territory, 1944-45. *C.P.P.* no. 13, 1946-7.

Report on the Administration of the Northern Territory, 1945-6. *C.P.P.* no. 48, 1946-8.

Report on the Administration of the Northern Territory, 1946-7. *C.P.P.* no. 53, 1948-9.

Welfare Branch, Northern Territory Administration, *Warrabri Aboriginal Reserve.*

NEW SOUTH WALES

Census of the year 1841. *N.S.W. V. & P.* (L.C.), 1841.

Report of the Aborigines Welfare Board for the year ended 30th June, 1961. *N.S.W. P.P.* no. 90, 1961.

Report of the Aborigines Welfare Board for the year ended 30th June, 1963. *N.S.W. P.P.* no. 241, 1963.

Report from the Select Committee on the Native Police Force. *N.S.W. V. & P.* (L.A.), 1856-7.

Select Committee on the Conditions of the Aborigines. *N.S.W. V. & P.* (L.C.), 1845.

Statistical Register of N.S.W., 1859.

NORTHERN TERRITORY

Debates N.T. (L.C.), 11 August 1964, 17 and 18 February 1965.

Report on the Administration of the Northern Territory, 1943. Northern Territory, *Reports*, 1933-55.

QUEENSLAND

Annual Report of the Director of Native Affairs, Queensland, 30th June, 1964. *Q.P.P.* no. A.42, 1964.

Annual Report of the Director of Native Affairs, Queensland, 30th June, 1965. *Q.P.P.* no. A.48, 1965.

Debate on the Native Labourer's Protection Bill. *Q.P.P.*, 1884, vol. XLII.

Report from the Commissioner appointed to Enquire into the Employment and Protection of the Aboriginals in the District of Mackay, and Generally to Enquire into What Steps can be Taken to Ameliorate the Condition of the Aborigines of Queensland. *Q. V. & P.*, 1874.

Report on the Aboriginals of Queensland by Archibald Meston to Home Secretary H. Tozer. *Q. V. & P.* no. CA.80, 1896.

REFERENCES

Report on the North Queensland Aborigines and the Native Police. *Q. V. & P.* no. CA.10, 1897.

Select Committee on the Native Police Force and the Condition of the Aborigines Generally, Report. *Q. V. & P.*, 1861.

SOUTH AUSTRALIA

Department of Aboriginal Affairs: A Brief Outline of Aboriginal Affairs in South Australia since Colonisation, 1963.

Half-Yearly Report on Northern Territory to December 31st, 1886. *S.A.P.P.* no. 53, 1887.

Instructions to Boyle Travers Finniss, Government Resident, 14 April 1864. *S.A.P.P.* no. 36, 1864.

Report of the Select Committee of the Legislative Council on the Aborigines. *S.A.P.P.* no. 165, 1860.

Select Committee of the Legislative Council on The Aborigines Bill, 1899. *S.A.P.P.* no. 77, 1899.

VICTORIA

Parliamentary Debates (V.P.D.), 1859-60.

Report of the Select Committee on the Aborigines. *Vic. V. & P.* (L.C.) no. D8, 1859.

WESTERN AUSTRALIA

Aborigines Department. Report for Financial Year ended 30th June, 1907. *W.A. V. & P.* no. 9, 1907.

Annual Report, Commissioner of Native Welfare for year ended 30th June, 1963. *W.A.P.P.* 1963, vol. III.

Annual Report, Commissioner of Native Welfare for year ended 30th June, 1964. *W.A.P.P.* 1964, vol. III.

Report of the Royal Commissioner appointed to Investigate, Report, and Advise upon matters in relation to the Condition and Treatment of Aborigines. *W.A.P.P.* no. 2, 1935. Commissioner, Henry Doyle Moseley.

Report of the Royal Commission of Inquiry into the Alleged Killing and Burning of Bodies of Aborigines in East Kimberley and into Police Methods when Effecting Arrest. Commissioner: G.T. Wood, Esq., S.M. *W.A. V. & P.* ho. 3, 1927.

Report of the Royal Commission on the Condition of the Natives. Commissioner: Walter Edmund Roth, Esquire. *W.A. V. & P.* (L.C.) no. 5, 1905.

UNITED KINGDOM

HOUSE OF COMMONS

Select Committee on Aborigines (British Settlements). *P.P.* (House of Commons) no. 425, 1837.

II. BOOKS AND ARTICLES

Attitudes and Social Conditions (S.S.R.C.: Aborigines in Australian Society). Canberra, 1970.

BATESON, F.W. 'The Story of the Canning Stock Route', *Western Australian Historical Society, Journal and Proceedings*. 1942.

BAUER, F.H. *Historical Geography of White Settlement in part of Northern Australia. Part 2—The Katherine-Darwin Region*. CSIRO, Division of Land Research and Regional Survey, Divisional Report No. 64-1, Canberra, 1964.

BEASLEY, Pamela. 'The Aboriginal Household in Sydney', in *Attitudes and Social Conditions*. Canberra, 1970.

BEAZLEY, K.E. 'Dispossession and Disease—or Dignity?' Australian Labor Party, 1964.

BERNDT, Catherine H. 'The Quest for Identity: The case of the Australian Aborigines', *Oceania*, vol. XXXII, no. 1, September 1961.

BERNDT, Ronald M. and BERNDT, Catherine H. *From Black to White in South Australia*. Melbourne, 1951.

—— and ——. *Arnhem Land: Its History and its People*. Melbourne, 1954.

—— and —— (eds.). *Aboriginal Man in Australia: Essays in honour of Emeritus Professor A.P. Elkin*. Sydney, 1965.

BLEAKLEY, J.W. *The Aborigines of Australia*. Brisbane, 1961.

BOLTON, G.C. *A Thousand Miles Away: A history of North Queensland to 1920*. 2nd impression. Canberra, 1970.

BRETON, W.H. *Excursions in New South Wales, Western Australia, and Van Diemen's Land*. 2nd ed. London, 1834.

CASAGRANDE, Joseph B. (ed.). *In the Company of Man: Twenty portraits by anthropologists*, New York, 1960.

COLE, P.R. 'Education in New South Wales 1788-1880', Introduction to Kenneth Gollan, *The Organisation and Administration of Education in New South Wales*. Sydney, [c. 1926.]

COLLIER, James. *The Pastoral Age in Australasia*. London, 1911.

COLINS, David. *An Account of the English Colony in New South Wales*, vol. 2. London, 1802.

CROWTHER, W.E.L.H. 'The Passing of the Aboriginal Race', *Medical Journal of Australia*, vol. 1, 3 February 1934.

DAWSON, John L.M. 'Aboriginal, Attitudes Towards Education and Integration', in *Attitudes and Social Conditions*. Canberra, 1970.

DOCKER, E.G. *Simply Human Beings*. Brisbane, 1964.

DUGUID, Charles. *No Dying Race*. Adelaide, 1963.

DURACK, Mary. *Kings in Grass Castles*. London, 1959.

ELKIN, A.P. 'Aboriginal Evidence and Justice in North Australia', *Oceania*, vol. XVII, no. 3, March 1947.

——. 'Aboriginal Policy, 1930-1950: Some personal associations', *Quadrant*, vol. 1, no. 4, Spring 1957.

REFERENCES

——. 'The Aborigines, Our National Responsibility', *Australian Quarterly*, no. 23, 14 September 1934.

——. 'Australian Aboriginal and White Relations: A personal record'. *Royal Australian Historical Society. Journal and Proceedings*, vol. 48, 1963.

——. 'The Background of Present Day Aboriginal Policies', in J.W. Warburton (ed.), *Proceedings of Conference on Welfare Policies for Australian Aborigines*. Armidale, 1960.

——. 'Reaction and Interaction: A food gathering people and European settlement in Australia', *American Anthropologist*, vol. 53, no. 2, 1951.

——. 'The Social Life and Intelligence of the Australian Aborigine: A review of S.D. Porteus's "Psychology of a Primitive People".' *Oceania*, vol. III, no. 1, September 1932.

FOXCROFT, Edmund J.B. *Australian Native Policy: Its history especially in Victoria*. Melbourne, 1941.

FURNIVALL, J.S. *Colonial Policy and Practice: A comparative study of Burma and Netherlands India*. Cambridge, 1948.

GALE, Fay. *A Study of Assimilation: Part-Aborigines in South Australia*. Adelaide, 1964.

HAGENAUER, F.A. *Notes of a Missionary Journey to North Queensland 1885, with Report of the Aboriginal Mission at Ramahyuck, Victoria, 1885*. [n.d., n.p.]

HASLUCK, P.M.C. *Black Australians: A survey of native policy in Western Australia 1829-1897*. Melbourne, 1942.

——. *Native Welfare in Australia: Speeches and addresses by the Hon. Paul Hasluck, M.P., Minister for Territories*. Perth, 1953.

HASSELL, Kathleen, *The Relations between the Settlers and Aborigines in South Australia, 1836-1860*. Adelaide, 1966.

JONES, F. Lancaster. *The Structure and Growth of Australia's Aboriginal Population*. Canberra, 1970.

JOSE, Arthur W. *History of Australia*. 10th ed., Sydney, 1924.

LAGASSÉ, Jean H. 'Community Development in Manitoba', *Human Organization*, vol. 20, no. 4, Winter 1961-2.

LANG, J.D. *Queensland, The Future Cotton-Field of Great Britain*. Sydney, 1850.

LAURIE, Arthur. 'The Black War in Queensland', *Royal Historical Society of Queensland Journal*, vol. VI, no. 1, September 1959.

LONG, J.P.M. *Aboriginal Settlements*. Canberra, 1970.

——. 'The Numbers and Distribution of Aboriginals in Australia', in Ian G. Sharp and Colin M. Tatz (eds.), *Aborigines in the Economy*.

LUMUMBA, Patrice. *Congo My Country*. London, 1962.

McEWEN, J. *The Northern Territory of Australia: Commonwealth Government's Policy with respect to Aboriginals*. Canberra, 1939.

MACMILLAN, David S. (ed.). *Two Years in New South Wales, by Peter Cunningham, Surgeon, R.N.* Sydney, 1966.

MELVILLE, H. *The History of the Island of Van Diemen's Land from the year 1824 to 1835 inclusive*. London, 1835.

MERIAM, Lewis, and Associates. *The Problem of Indian Administration*. Washington, 1928.

MESTON, Archibald. Report on the Government Scientific Expedition to Bellenden Ker Range, 1889, in Annual Report of the Department of Agriculture, Queensland, 1889-90.

MULVANEY, D.J. 'The Australian Aborigines 1606-1929. Opinion and Fieldwork: Part 1: 1606-1859.' *Historical Studies, Australia and New Zealand*, vol. 8, no. 30, May, 1958.

NEVILLE, A.O. *Australia's Coloured Minority: Its place in the Community*. Sydney [?1948].

[OGILVIE, Edward.] In *A Century of Journalism: The Sydney Morning Herald, 1831-1931*. Sydney, 1931.

PALMER, George. *Kidnapping in the South Seas: Being a narrative of a three months' cruise of H.M. Ship Rosario*. Edinburgh, 1871.

PERRY, T.M. *Australia's First Frontier*. Melbourne, 1963.

PETRIE, Constance Campbell. *Tom Petrie's Reminiscences of Early Queensland . . .* Brisbane, 1904.

PIKE, D.H. (ed.). 'The Diary of James Coutts Crawford: Extracts on Aborigines and Adelaide, 1839 and 1841', *South Australiana*, vol. 4, no. 1, March 1965.

PLOMLEY, N.J.B. (ed.). *Friendly Misssion: The Tasmanian journals and papers of George Augustus Robinson 1829-1834*. Hobart, 1966.

Realités (Paris), August 1966.

RICHARDSON, A.R. *Early Memories of the Great Nor'-West and a Chapter in the History of Western Australia*. Perth, 1914.

ROWLEY, C.D. *The Australians in German New Guinea*. Melbourne, 1958.

SHARP, Ian G. and TATZ, Colin M. (eds.). *Aborigines in the Economy*. Brisbane and Melbourne, 1966.

SMITH, W.G., S.J. 'Communists and the Aborigines', *Social Survey*, vol. 12, no. 8, September 1963.

SOUTER, Gavin. *New Guinea: The last unknown*. Sydney, 1963.

STANNER, W.E.H. 'Durmugan, A Nangiomeri', in Joseph B. Casagrande (ed.), *In the Company of Man*.

——. *On Aboriginal Religion*, Oceania Monograph no. 11, reprinted from *Oceania*, vol. XXXIII, no. 4, 1963.

——. 'Religion, Totemism and Symbolism', in Ronald M. and Catherine H. Berndt (eds.), *Aboriginal Man in Australia*.

STREHLOW, T.G.H. 'Culture, Social Structure, and Environment in Aboriginal Central Australia', in Ronald M. and Catherine H. Berndt (eds.), *Aboriginal Man in Australia*.

REFERENCES

TAFT, Ronald. 'Attitudes of Western Australians Towards Aborigines', in *Attitudes and Social Conditions*. Canberra, 1970.

THOMSON, Donald. Interim General Report of Preliminary Expedition to Arnhem Land 1935-6.

———. Report on Expedition to Arnhem Land, 1936-7. Canberra, 1939.

TURNBULL, Clive. *Black War: The extermination of the Tasmanian Aborigines*. Melbourne, 1948.

WARBURTON, J.W. (ed.). *Proceedings of Conference on Welfare Policies for Australian Aborigines*. Armidale, 1960.

WARD, Russel. *The Australian Legend*. Melbourne, 1958.

WILLSHIRE, W. *Land of Dawning*. Adelaide, 1896.

WITTFOGEL, Karl A. *Oriental Despotism: A comparative study of total power*. New Haven, 1957.

WRIGHT, Quincy. *Mandates under the League of Nations*. Chicago, 1930.

III. NEWSPAPERS

Age. Melbourne.
Argus. Melbourne. 1911-57.
Brisbane Courier. Brisbane, 1865.
Centralian Advocate. Alice Springs, 1965.
Daily Examiner. Grafton.
Daily Telegraph. Sydney, 1946.
Herald. Melbourne, 1933.
Irish Times. Dublin, 1964.
Moreton Bay Courier
Northam Advertiser.
Sydney Morning Herald. Sydney, 1848-1968.
Sun. Sydney, 1965.
Truth. Adelaide, 1949.
Truth, Sydney, 1946.
West Australian. Perth, 1965.

IV. UNPUBLISHED MATERIAL

BARWICK, Diane. A Little More than Kin (Ph.D. thesis, Department of Anthropology and Sociology, Institute of Advanced Studies, Australian National University, 1963).

BEASLEY, Pamela. Draft Preliminary Report on Redfern-Chippendale Area of Sydney 18 February 1964. Social Science Research Council—Aborigines Project.

REFERENCES

BECKETT, Jeremy. A study of a mixed-blood Aboriginal minority in the pastoral west of New South Wales (M.A. thesis, Department of Anthropology and Sociology, Australian National University, 1958).

BERNDT, Ronald M. and BERNDT, Catherine H. Aboriginal Labour in a Pastoral Area. Hallstrom Pacific Library, Mosman, Sydney.

BISKUP, P. Native Administration and Welfare in Western Australia 1897-1954 (M.A. thesis, University of Western Australia, 1965).

CALLEY, M.J.C. Bandjalang Social Organisation (Ph.D. thesis, University of Sydney, 1960).

CARLYON, N.M. G.A. Robinson—Chief Protector (B.A. (Hons.) essay, University of Melbourne, 1960).

CLARENCE River Historical Society. Records.

COWIN, Winifred, European-Aboriginal Relations in Early Queensland 1859-1897 (B.A. thesis, University of Queensland, 1950).

GALE, Fay. Summary of Preliminary Findings on Aboriginal Migration to Adelaide. SSRC-AP.

GAMBLE, N.F. Mining in the Northern Territory 1861-1961. Department of Territories File 62/1116.

GIBBS, R.M. Humanitarian Theories and the Aboriginal Inhabitants of South Australia to 1860 (B.A. (Hons.) thesis, University of Adelaide, 1959).

HARRISON, Brian W. The Myall Creek Massacre and its Significance in the Controversy over the Aborigines during Australia's Early Squatting Period (B.A. (Hons.) thesis, University of New England, 1966).

IREDALE, R.R. The Enigma of Assimilation: The position of the Part-Aboriginal in New South Wales (B.A. (Hons.) thesis, University of Sydney, 1965). SSRC-AP.

LONG, J.P.M. Bathurst 1813-1940. SSRC-AP.

MAKIN, C. A Socio-Cultural Anthropological Survey of People of Aboriginal Descent in the Metropolitan Area of Perth. SSRC-AP.

MOODIE, P.M. Draft report: Aboriginal Health, New South Wales: The Aboriginal Population of New South Wales. SSRC-AP.

——. The Recording of Aboriginal Race for Statistical Purposes. SSRC-AP.

REECE, R.H.W. Diplomacy and Gifts to the Aborigines of New South Wales 1778-1846. SSRC-AP.

ROWLEY, C.D. The Aboriginal Householder. ANZAAS, Section G, Thirty-ninth Congress, January 1967.

SMITH, Hazel M., BIDDLE, Ellen H. and CORNWALL, C.M.R. Social Survey of Persons of Aborigine and Torres Strait Island Descent Residing in Brisbane, Queensland 1965-1966: Progress Report. SSRC-AP.

STURKEY, R.D. Growth of the Pastoral Industry in the North-West 1862-1901 (B.A. thesis, University of Western Australia, 1957).

TATZ, C.M. Aboriginal Administration in the Northern Territory of Australia (Ph.D. thesis, Department of Anthropology and Sociology, Australian National University, 1964).

WILSON, John. Authority and Leadership in a 'new-style' Australian Aboriginal Community: Pindan, Western Australia (M.A. thesis, University of Western Australia 1961).

INDEX

Abbott, C. L. A., 270-2, 275-6, 289-90, 295, 315

Aborigines, uncontacted, 228

Aboriginal administration (general), 2, 53; areas of development (Qld) 176-7; armed forces employment, 306, 333, 336; arrests, 168; assimilation, 231; assumptions, 230-1; Central, 315; Commonwealth, 186, 215-16, 223, 227, 251, 258, 259, 271-2, 288, 314, 317; Commonwealth-State relations, 319-21, 324; comparisons, 9-15, 19, 23-4, 132, 191; conditions, 170; contract of service, 172; contact, 161; control, 161, 185, 323; descent and special legislation, 343; education, 323; emphases, 4; expenditure, 63, 271, 327; frontier conditions, 317; failure, 2-26; handouts, 181; inadequacies, 268; indigent camps, 263; injustice and administrative methods, 319; institutions (controlled) 177; labour incentive, 328; legislation (protective-restrictive) 323, 343; Meston Report, 177-8; mining and prospecting, 328; missions as agents, 323, 328; Native Police, 159, 172; part-Aborigines, 323, 384; police (as agents) 163, (as protectors) 181, (system) 170; principles, 223; priorities, 3, 253-4, 316-17, 323, (Aboriginal needs) 307; protection, 172; punitive expeditions, 168; race relations, 343; Register of Wards, 347; resettlement, 316; reserves, 173, 328; Strehlow proposals, 316; TPNG model, 310; 'Wards' (definition) 347

Aboriginal administration (by States and Territories), 19, 21, 299, 305-7, 317; area, 302; Central and North Australia, 238, (administration) 258, (Bleakley Report) 259-60, (employ-ment) 261, (expenditure) 271, (pastoralists) 259, (police) 259; Commonwealth, 1-9, 177, 222, 257-8, 281, 307, 310, 317, 327, (and States) 319, 324, (indigenous citizens) 223, (N.T.) 219, 222, 237, 305, 323, (part-Aborigines) 320-1, (principles) 223; N.S.W., 18, (areas) 28-9, (dilemma) 29, (Director of Native Affairs) 306, 329, (frontiers) 41, (law and justice) 37-8, (martial law) 29, (native labour) 18, (Native Police) 39, (Protectors) 38, (vigilantes) 29; N.T., 211-13, 216-59 passim, 278-82, (Aboriginal rights) 284-5, (Aboriginals Dept.) 322, (Administrator) 234, (area) 238, (Asians) 238, (changes) 239-40; Commonwealth, 219, 222, 237-8, 305ff, 323, (control) 234, 305, (costs) 240, (delimitation) 305, (Department of the Interior, 1934) 282, (Director of Native Affairs) 306, (District Offices) 331, (education) 279, (employment) 279, 338, (expenditure) 271, (failure) 213, (frontier-type) 311, (gradualism) 329, (improvement) 279, (industrial awards) 338, (institutionalisation) 239, (justice) 228, (land tenure) 285, (legislation and policy) 281, 235, 237-41, (McEwen policy) 328-31, (Papua and) 222-3, (part-Aborigines) 279, (pastoralists) 218, (patrols) 305, 306, (pearling) 285, (pensions) 349, (police) 213, (policy development, 1911-) 287, 314, 323, 328-32, (population) 281, 305, (priorities) 317, (problems) 211, (progress) 239-40, (protection and control) 213, 218, 230, 232, 278, (reprisals) 217, (racial categories) 348, (reserves) 239, 305-6, (separation) 238, (settlements) 331, 339, (settler-police relationship) 205, (wages) 278, 339, (welfare) 238–41, 282 (white Australia) 279; Qld, 157–86, 312, 325, (Assisted Aborigines) 358, (categories) 351, (confusion and authoritarianism) 183–4, (control) 186, 312, (crimes by and against) 158, (definition and status) 350, (employment) 171, 184, 256–7, (expertise) 186, (hunting rights) 168, (influence on N.T.) 269, (injustice) 158, (isolation) 167, (labour) 255–6, (legislation) 179, 351, (Meston Report) 179, (murders) 158, (native courts) 322, (protection) 170–2, 184, 264, (punitive action) 170, (reserves) 184, 248, 250, (social conditions) 167, (status) 166, (troops and warfare) 158, 166; S.A., 203–21, 312, (control) 220, 312, (cruelty) 206, (health) 356, (land) 77, (legislation) 206, (missions) 205, 220, (protection) 220, (range) 356, (rationing) 205, (reserves) 356, (resistance) 204, (segregation) 206, 219, (settled areas) 322, (settlements) 322, (settler-police relations) 205, (women) 206; Tas. (destruction and disruption), 44, (marriage) 44–5, (policy) 48–51, (protection) 46, (relations with whites) 44; Vic., 63, (assimilation) 354, (Lake Tyers) 353, (legal provisions and racism) 353, (protection) 39, 53, 55, 62, 354, (reserves) 354; W.A., 66, 187–92, 195–8, 253–4, 257, 303, 312, 321, (administrators) 312, (assimilation) 360, (citizenship) 359–60, (control) 304, 312, (costs 327, (cruelties and abuses) 192, (deficiencies) 327, (education) 304, (employment) 188, 191, 257, (imperial) 188, (indenture system) 192, (legislation and administration) 198, (marriage) 321, (part-Aborigines) 359, (policy) 321, (principles) 188, (priorities) 327, (protection) 189, 195, 302, (rule of law) 71, (weaknesses) 201–2

Aboriginal affairs: charity, 122; colonies concerned, 145; Commonwealth-State control, 132, 225, 272–3, 276, 282, 350–1; definition (common), 362; inter-governmental co-operation, 251; labour force, 399; maintenance costs, 399; national policy, 362; Referendum (1967), 362; special services, 356

Aboriginal Advancement League (Vic.), 337

Aboriginal Affairs Act 1934–1939 (S.A.), 356n.; 1962 (S.A.), 356, 357n.

Aboriginal Board (N.T.), 285

Aboriginals Department: N.T., 218, 231, 234; S.A., 231–3

Aboriginals Employment Regulations 1919 (Qld), 255–6; and W.A., 257; wage rates, 256–7

Aboriginal Evidence Ordinance (S.A.), 80

Aboriginal Friends Association, 315

Aboriginal Law, The: and Missions, 102; British law and, 244–5; traditional sanctions, 244, see also Religion, Social system, Society

Aboriginals Ordinance 1911 (N.T.), 233–4

Aboriginals Ordinance 1918–1953 (N.T.), 241, 278, 348; 1928 (N.T.), 238; 1933 (N.T.), 278–80; 1936 (N.T.), 286, 357n.; 1937 (N.T.), 285; 1911 (S.A.), 233–4

Aboriginal School (Parramatta), 91

Aboriginals Preservation and Protection Act of 1939 (Qld), 358n.

Aboriginals Protection and Restriction of the Sale of Opium Act 1897 to 1934 (Qld), 182–5, 227, 248, 358n.

Aborigines Act 1844 (S.A.), 82; 1910 (S.A.), 205, 219, 230–3; 1911 (S.A.), 218–21; 1934–1939 (S.A.), 312; 1928 (Vic.), 353n.; 1957 (Vic.), 353n., 358; 1905 (W.A.), 195–8, 218, 224, 359n.; Amendment Act 1911 (W.A.), 198, 205; 1936 (W.A.), 303, 312, 359

Aborigines Amelioration Association, 299

Aborigines' and Torres Strait Islanders' Affairs Act of 1965 (Qld), 351, 358n.

Aborigines Friends Association (S.A.), 105, 270, 315

Aborigines Inland Mission, 289

Aborigines Protection Act, 1909–1963 (N.S.W.), 227, 355n., 358n.; 1886 (W.A.), 189–91, 195–8

Aborigines Protection Board (W.A.), 192, 195, 319

Aborigines Protection League of South Australia, 270, 271

Aborigines Protection Society (S.A.), 53, 77, 171, 242, 328

INDEX

Aborigines Welfare Board (Vic.), 353, 368

Aborigines Welfare Ordinance 1954 (N.T.), 348, 357n.

Act for Better Protection and Care of the Aboriginal and Half-caste ... 1897 (Qld), 181-2, 218

Act for Regulating the Sale of Waste Lands ... (1842), 60, 61

Administration, cross-cultural: A.P.N.R., 289; Asia, 22; British, 151; concern, 293-5; controls, 312; custom, 303; dialogue, 321; frontier situation, 123, 321; law and justice, 293; marriage, 321; Native Courts, 312; New Guinea, 294; obligations, 111; Papua, 147-8, 150, 151, 222, 223, *see also* Custom, Frontier policy, Law and justice, Social organisation

Admiralty Gulf, 251

Africa: colonial administration, 13, 19, 132; pattern of settlement, 13-14

Ainsworth, John, 294

Alcohol, 23, 30-3, 131, 167, 171, 182-3, 193, 203, 237, 280, 357, 358; Certificate of Exemption, 358; Qld, 182-3; S.A., 84, 203

Amerindians, 23

Anthropological Society of S.A., 270, 272

ANZAAS, 224, 251

Arafura Sea, 267

Aranda, 206-7

Archaeology, 186

Archer, C., 40

Armed services: amenities, 336; army work camps, 333; and assimilation, 333; constructive resettlement, 249; employment, 332-3; health and hygiene, 249; hours worked, 336; housing, 336; schooling, 336; wages, 333, 336-7

Armstrong, F. F. 65

Arnhem Land, 276

Arnhem Land Reserve, 217, 246, 251, 267-9; administration, 305-6; Bleakley proposals, 272; contact, 313 (Japanese) 314; Crown land, 250; depopulation, 313; health, 313, 314; justice, 313; leases (compensation), 272; missions, 313; police, 314; preservation of Aboriginal institutions, 314; prospecting (oil), 272; segregation (tribal remnants), 314

Arthur, Lieutenant Governor George, 46, 47, 51

Asian labour, 214-15, 286, (Chief Protector, N.T.), 218

Assisted Aborigines (Qld), 351-2

Assimilation, 18-20; Aboriginal institutions, 331; and autonomy, 249-50; and education, 92; and justice and equality, 362; and schooling, 81; and 'wards', 239; and White Australia, 332; armed forces, 333; assumptions, 2, 136-7; by legislation, 240; goals, 2-3; institutionalisation, 339; Lake Tyers, 353-4; lower orders, 66, 81; 'passing', 344; physical genetic process, 328; protection, 323; social mobility, 361, 362; rights in terms of race, 361-2; theory, 2-5, 102-3

Assimilation policy, 2-5, 20, 24, 102-3, 239-40, 328-31; Bleakley Report, 320; genesis, 320; McEwen, 330; N.T., 330-2, 333, 340; official, 102; part-Aborigines, 340; W.A., 321

Association for the Employment and Protection of Aborigines, 172

Association for the Protection of Native Races of Australasia and Polynesia, 202, 258-9, 270, 273, 289; Brooks case, 289-90; cross-cultural justice, 291, 294, 296

Attitudes: Aboriginal (frontiers), 185, 186, (institutionalisation) 281-2, (missions) 96-9, (retaliation) 28, (settlers) 27-8, (status) 86-7, (to whites) 159, *see also* Missions, Pastoral industry, Protection, Reserves; European, 6-7, 11, 25, 59, 60, 66, 68, 77, 87-9, 102-3, 112, 198-9, 203-4, 214-15, 225-8, 309, 364; pastoralist, 155; settler, 7, 35-8, 163, 165, 166, 178, 239, (beliefs, fears, and ethics, Qld) 159, (control) 42, 153-4, (crimes by and against) 64, 65, (employment) 175, (frontier) 338, (land) 16, 154, (law and justice, W.A.) 73, (pastoralists' and townsmen's) 170, (protection) 153-5, (reprisals) 33, (S.A.) 76, 80, 206, (Tas.) 44, 46, 47, (W.A.) 67, 198-9, 200

Australian Agricultural Co., 119

Australian Board of Missions, 201-2, 270, 274, 290

Australian Capital Territory, 348

Australian College, 91

Australian Council for Native Welfare, 39

Australian Federation of Women Voters, 270

Australian National Research Council, 299

Australian Workers Union, 255

Aurukun Presbyterian Mission, 247

Autonomy, 32, 33, 60; and assimilation, 250; and land/group use, 308; and leadership, 308-9; and missions, 308; ceremonies, 210; destruction, 229; leadership, 308; pastoral labour, 218, 308; Newcastle Waters, 218; N.T., 230; spread of settlement, 22; Wave Hill, 218, *see also* Political organisation, Religion, Social Structure

Babbitt, Henry, 160

Backhouse, James, 51

Bagot Reserve, 316-17

Bandjalang, 110, 121

Bailey, 319

Barkly Tableland, 270, 301

Barwick, Diane, 368, 379

Basedow, Herbert, 224, 234

Batavia River, 179

Batchelor government farm, 235

Bates, Daisy, 307

Bathurst, Lord, 19, 86, 93

Bathurst (district), 29, 32, 33, 89; land use, 29; martial law, 29

Bathurst Island Catholic Mission, 252, 265, 267; Bleakley Report, 281

Bathurst Island Reserve, 246

Batman, John, 55

'Battle' of Mitchell, 170

'Battle' of Pinjarra, 7, 64, 67, 87

Bauer, F. H., 213

Beagle Bay Catholic Mission, 254

Beasley, Pamela, 380

Beckett, Jeremy, 140

Bellenden Ker *see* Meston Report

Benedictine Missions, 105

Bennett, M. M., 299

Berndt, Catherine, 211, 249-50, 263, 333-7

Berndt, R. M., 211, 263, 333-7

Berry, Alexander, 29

Big River people (Tas.), 49

Birth rate, *see* Population

Biskup, P., 68, 187, 202, 224, 298

Blakeley, A., 294

Bleakley, J. W., 247, 251, 255, 259-70, 286-7, 307, 311, 321, 322, 325-6

Bleakley Report, 260-70, 290, 319-20; and Meriam Report, 269; and Permanent Mandate Commission reports on New Guinea, 269; Conference (Abbott), 270-5; employment, 260-4; housing, 261, 263; missions, 265-6, 271-2; population (N. Aust.), 260, 267; recommendations, 263-70 passim; wages and conditions, 255, 260-2, 269, 270, 276-7, 279, (recommendations), 263-4

Bloomfield Lutheran Mission, 177

Board of Colonization Commissioners (S.A.), 74-5

Board of inquiry into Brooks killing, 289; procedures and criticism, 289-90

Border Police, 18; Aboriginal protection, 38; activities and functions, 114; colonial policy, 151, 152; financing, 61; land legislation, 38, (taxation) 38; massacres, 114; property protection, 112; reprisals and reactions, 38; use against Aborigines, 33

Border Police Act 1839 (N.S.W.), 38

Bourke, Governor Sir Richard, 55

Bowen, 174

Bowen Straits, 276

Breton, W. H., 35

Bribie Island, 174

Bridgman, C. F., 172

Brisbane, Governor Sir Thomas, 29

Broughton, W. G., 91, 94

Bruce, Lord, S. M., 259-60, 289; and Mandated Territory of New Guinea, 260

Bruny Island, 45

Bumburra, 178

Bungalow, 265

Buntingdale Wesleyan Mission, 97-8

Burton, Rev. J. W., 272, 273

Bushrangers, 30

Buxton Report, 23, 119, 126

Cadell Straits, 276

Caledon Bay, 291

Canada, 9, 10, 132

Cannibalism, 164

Cape Bedford Lutheran Mission, 177

INDEX

Cape Hawke, 291

Cape York Reserve, 192, 250

Carnarvon, 295

Carrington, V. G., 337

Carrodus, J. A., 324

Carrolup Aboriginal settlement, 202

Cartwright, Rev. Robert, 90

Cash economy: Aborigines and, 123, 134, 309; and institutionalisation, 249; attractions, 276, 317; disintegration (social), 307, 309; effects (S.A.), 82; impediments, 210; incentive, 212, (wage), 190, 269; Qld, 173; subsistence economy and, 81, 121, 308; traditional society and industrial goods, 307

Cattle, 17, 176; stations, *see* Pastoral industry

Catholic Mission, Stradbroke, 158

Cedar cutting, 110, 111

Census: and States, 345; definitions, 344, 345; exclusion of Aborigines, 344-6, 384; 'full-bloods', 345; 'half-castes', 345; inclusions, 345-6; race, 346

Central Australian Reserve, 227, 228, 251, 254, 267, 271, 307, 315-16; control, 271, (compared with S. Africa) 272; prospecting, 271; rationing and trading centre, 315, 316

Certificate of Citizenship (W.A.), 359-60; status of children, 359

Chaining, 37, 81, 115, 199-200, 204, *see also* Neck chains

Change, process, 68

Chief Protector, *see* Protectors

Child Welfare Act (N.S.W.), 355

Children: control and training (S.A.) 221, (W.A.), 321; delinquent (Qld) 250; education, 335; guardians, 231; removal (from parents), 231, 232, (to missions) 248, (to Child Welfare or Aboriginal Welfare Departments), 355, 356; status (W.A.), 359; work force, 193, 334-5, *see also* Education, Missions, Pastoral industry, Pearling

Chinese, 214-15

Chinnery, E. W. P., 317, 329-30, 337

Christianity, 10, 25, 54, 91; Aboriginal attitudes, 96-7; basic beliefs, 87-8; welfare and conversion, 88, *see also* Education, Missions

Christison, Robert, 178

Church Missionary Society, 246, 252, 270, 275, 291, 293; Wellington, 93, 94, 99; Yarra, 55

Church of England Mission, Pt Lincoln, 104

Cilento, R., 321

Civil rights, 1, 20, 202

Clarence River, 33-5, 108-16; population (1841), 108-9; stock, 109

Collier Bay, 252

Collier, James, 152

'Colonial Australia', 377, 378; land areas and use, 378; plural society, 376; populations (Aboriginal) 377, (relative) 376; reserves, 378-9

Colonial doctrine, 176

Colonialism: Australian, (New Guinea) 147, (Pacific) 146-7, (Queensland), 174-5, (racist) 147; European, 10-11

Colonial policy and administration (imperial), 19, 38, 70-1, 83-6, 123, 188; Aboriginal Affairs (1856), 137; Aboriginal subjects, 18, 19, 53-4, 65, 86, 122-3; assimilation policy, 102; attitude, 132; cessation (1856), 137, (W.A.) 137; 'colonies of settlement', 10; comparisons, 132; context, 123; controls, indigenous social, 101; cross-cultural, 321; customs, 127; education, 19; frontiers, 321; Governors' Instructions, 19, 23, 28, 38, 64-5, 86, 122; land, 60-2, 75, 83-4, 174-5, 189 (occupancy) 124; law and justice, 65, (evidence) 80; pre-literate societies, 228-9; legislation, special, 131, 343; N.S.W., 18; N.G. village organisation, 317; pacification and settlement, 151; principles, 19, 64; protection, 18-19, 62, 152, (S.A.) 84; regulations, native, 127; religion, 19; reserves, 63; responsibility, 101; rule of law, 71; S.A., 74-5, 84; safeguards, 132; Select Committee of the House of Commons (1837), 20, 23; settler legislatures, 23; status, 54, 124, 343, (legal) 18, 19, 65, 122-3, 131, 132; technological change, 11; W.A., 23, 64-6, 71, 137, 188, 191, 201-2

Colonies of settlement, 16

Colonisation: administration, 21; conquest, 21; frontiers (extension), 21; lands, tribal, 11 (rights of occupation), 11; principles, 18; treaties and restitution, 11

Commissioners of Crown Lands: as Protectors, 62, 81, 84

Commonwealth-State Conference (1937), 115, 136, 148, 227, 242, 319-28, 384

Commonwealth-State responsibilities, 323-4

Community misgivings, 43

Communist Party of Australia, 272

Conciliation and Arbitration Act 1904-1964, 17, 45

Constitution (Australia), 222; Constitution Act, 344

Constitution Act 1889 (W.A.), 70

Contact, 23; Aboriginal resistance, 208; Armed Services, 306; culture, 31, 140, 305; fishing fleets, 306; history, 185; industrial areas, 305; land, 207-8; legal control, 161; spread of settlement, 124; trade, 306; trepangers, 267-8; W.A., 187-8

Contract of service, 172; W.A., 189-91, 196-7

Controls, Aboriginal, see Society

Convicts: introduction (Swan R.), 70-1; cessation, 109; payment, 108; ticket of leave, 109, see also Work force

Cook, C. E., 238, 259-80, 284-5, 307, 311, 316, 322, 326, 328

Cook Report: chaining, 322; employment, 278; housing (part-Aborigines), 281; Jay Creek, 316; Native Police, 307; part-Aborigines, 278-9; police, 259; reserves, 328; staff, 282; summary, 280; wages, 278-80, (licences) 278, (rates) 278; White Australia policy, 280

Cooktown, 178

Coutts, Thomas, 112; poisoning, 112; reprisals, 113

Cowen, Winifred, 168-9, 171

Craftsmanship, 109-10

Crawford, James Coutts, 153-6

Croker Island, 306

Crown as trustee: 'native rights', 19

Crown Land Commissioners (as Protectors), 55

Crown lands, 14-16, 24

Culture, 4-5, 22, 24, 31, 34, 60, 70, 88, 92; Aboriginal Law, 102; achievements, 140-1, 225; adaptation, 140; and environment (spread of settlement), 22-3; basis (religious), 225-6; compared with immigration, 362; children (effect of removing), 232; contacts, 140; contribution to Australia, 5, 140-1; frontier traditions, 140; influence, 5; kinship, 140; land and, 22, 34; material advantages (impact on) 244; morality and social obligations, 27-8, 34, 77-8, 226; multi-cultural society, 361-2; reciprocity as moral imperative, 27, 77-8, (and British justice) 314; religious and cultural prejudices, 225; unique, 225; value, 225; 'walkabout', 140, see also Missions, Political organisation, Religion, Social organisation, Society

Culture clash, 17, 22, 45, 92, 116, 229, 297, 308; and spread of settlement, 17; depopulation, 31; destruction, 205; initiation, 31; marriage, 31; moral irresponsibility, 78; religion, 31; political authority, 31; S.A., 76, (wages and slavery) 82; Swan R. indigenous custom and European law, 69, 204, 224; Tas. (Risdon massacre), 45; Robinson, 45, 47, see also Administration, cross-cultural, Law and justice, Missions, Social organisation, Political organisation.

Cultural determination, 127

Cultural exploration, 224

Cultural frontiers, 123

Cultural imperatives, see Social system

Cultural misunderstandings, 125

'Culture free' test of intelligence, 298

Cunningham, Peter, 91, 92

Custom, 24, 45, 69, 101, 126-7, 129, 312; disruption, 117; indigenous, 214; Law, 68, 102, 229, (British) 294-5; Native Regulations, 127; reciprocity, 27-8, see also Culture, Religion, Social change, Social organisation

Daly River, 235, 251, 307

Dangar, Henry, 36

Dark People, see Part-Aborigines

Darling, Governor, 93-4; instructions, 19-20

Darling Downs, 33

Darwin, Charles, 88

Darwin, 206

Darwin conference (1930), 277

Death rates, see Depopulation

Deeping, 182

Definition: Aboriginal, 348; advantages, 350; and alcohol, 357; and children, 355; and disadvantages (W.A.), 353; and social services, 348-9; by colour, 343-4 (N.S.W.) 355; by descent (Vic.) 353, (S.A.) 356, (W.A.) 352; categories, 344-5, (S.A.) 356, (Vic.) 354, (special) 348-9; census, 344-5; common, 362; 'declared', 351; electoral responsibility, 349; employment (W.A.), 189-91; exemptions, 357; extension, 354-5; 'half-caste', 139, (absorption) 139, (assimilation) 139, (legal identity), 139, (miscegenation) 139, (population increase) 139; legal, 13, 183, 342, (N.T.) 230, (Tas.) 46; local government, 363, 364; need for, 365; non-racial, 347; 'outside the Act' (Qld), 355; 'passing' and, 354-5; precise, 355-6; racial, 355; Qld, 351; racist, 343-4; Register of Aborigines (S.A.), 356; self-identification, 344, 345, 355, 365; State, 345; 'ward', 347; Vic., 354, *see also* Legal status

Demarcation Proclamation, 1828 (Tas.), 47, 48

Democratic rights: Aborigines', 72; electoral, 72; jury trial, 72; settlers', 72

Department of Home Affairs, 270-7, 294

Department of the Interior, 223, 338

Department of External Affairs, 222

Department of Native Affairs (N.T.), 317

Department of Social Services, 349

Department of Territories, 223

Depopulation, 7, 19, 31, 34, 137, 138; cultural significance, 59; death rates, 59; Clarence R., 115-16; decimation (Bumburra), 178; disease, 60, 211; infanticide, 60, 203; N.T., 242, 281; Qld, 167, 180; S.A., 80, 82; settlers' views, 203, *see also* Population

Depredations, 28; W.A., 67

Director of Welfare (N.T.), 239

Disease, 258; S.A. 203, *see also* Health, Welfare

Dispersal, 42, 161-3, 169, 186, 193, *see also* Native Police

Dredge, James, 57

Drysdale River, 201, 251-2

Drysdale River Catholic Mission, 254

Dual Mandate, 176

Ducie River, 179

Durack, Mary, 154-6, 191

Durkheim, E., 226

'Dying race', 83-4, 102-5, 178, 203, 235, 286, *see also* Depopulation, Population

Economic system, 27; and environment, 117; contact with trepangers, 267-8; cultural needs, 81; impact on Aborigines, 24-5; incentives (N.T.), 249; labour (and incentives, W.A.), 189-90; rationing, 82; reciprocity, 27, (and wages) 81-2; role, 123; S.A. (and 1911 Act), 221; stock depasturing (S.A.), 76; subsistence (stresses), 82; trade and trade goods, 268; wages and incentives, 81, *see also* Employment, Wages, Work force

Eddy, W. J., 274

Education and training, 86-94, 134-5, 163-5, 172, 335; Aboriginal School, 91; aggression and, 86-7; agriculture, 50; assimilation, 81; attitudes, 90, 104; children, 97, (separation of), 50, 204, (socialising), 81, 89, (struggle for minds of), 59, 91, 103-4; Christian education, 90; Church of England contact, 91; C.M.S., 93; civilising by, 81, 93; comparisons, 81; contact, 91; custom and, 127; schools plan, 91; duration, 59; fallacy, 81; financing, 60; government views, 90, 103, (and colonial administration) 92; indigenous, 89, (language) 103; legal status, 132; L.M.S., 93; Macquarie's Institute, 86, 89, 90, 91; missionary, 90, 100, 103, 106 (and employers) 253, (failure) 106, (literacy and doctrine) 91, (pupils) 91, (Qld) 248; non-literate cultures, 89; orphan, 90-1; parents' attitudes, 59, 91, 103-4; Parramatta, 28, 89-91; Poonindie, 204; Pt Jackson, 28; reserve (Qld), 173; schooling, 86, 103-4; S.A., 81, 103, 204; Shelley's proposals, 90; social change, 125; training, 103; 'tuition' (V.D.L.), 50-1, *see also* Children, Social system

Elcho Island, 276

Elizabeth Bay, 93

Elkin, A. P., 8, 22, 138, 164, 210, 212, 244, 294, 309-12, 316-17

Employment, 33-4, 95, 146, 198; accommodation, 217 (W.A.) 301; adaptation, 8, 115, 192, 208-9, (intelligent parasitism) 8, 115, 208, 210; Agreement (written), 184, 196-7; armed forces, 306, 332-7; Asian, 214-15, 219, 238; bushcraft, 81; Central Australia, 259; child (W.A.), 189-91, 196; Clarence River, 110-11, 117-21; conditions, 184, (N.T.) 232, 279, (W.A.) 189-91, 196-7; conservation (W.A.), 189; contract of service, 120, 172, 188-92, 213, (N.S.W.) 184, 189, (N.T.) 213, (W.A.) 188-9, 196-7; control, 311; country (N.T.), 234, 282, 284; Daly River, 243; dependants, 284; domestic, 265, (N.T.) 284; enforcement (W.A.) 188-9; female (N.T.), 218-19, 284, (W.A.) 196; geographical spread (W.A.), 188; herdsmen (W.A.), 189; income (N.T.), 243; indentured, 16, 172, 189, 192; licences, 219, (N.T.) 232-3; Mackay, 171-2; management, 311, (native labour) 17-19; necessity for, 243-4; N. Australia, 259 (wages and conditions) 260; 'neuralgic point', 212; N.T., 68, 209-10, 212-15, 219, 232-3, 237-8, 243, 279, 282, 284; pastoral, 192-3, 326-7, (control) 311, (McEwen policy) 330, (N.T.) 212, 219, (Qld) 159, 166, (W.A.) 187, 189, 301, 337; pearling, 180, (W.A.) 188; permit, 183, (N.T.) 196, 232, 236, (W.A.) 196; protection (W.A.), 189, 195-6; protective legislation (N.T.), 282; protector's duties (health, wages), 173; Qld, 171, 233, 257; recruitment (N.T.) 212; registration, 182; regulations (N.T.), 232, 279, 311; reserves, 173; S.A., 81-3, 218-19; segregation, 178; settlers, 175; shepherds, 187, 189; ships, on, 175, 178; social pressures, 243; socialising force, 209; station economy, 192, 209, (W.A.) 187, 189; town and country (N.T.), 218-19, 237, 282, 284; trust a/c (N.T.) 282; unions, 284, 337; units and labour, 192; urban (N.T.), 282, 284; wages, 173, 184, 192-3 (and reciprocity) 81, (N.T.) 233, 279, (pastoral) 192-3, (Qld) 233, (Wakefield system) 81, (W.A.) 189, 197, 301, 337; welfare and, 301, *see also* Armed forces,

Economic system, Mining, Missions, Pastoral industry, Work force
Environment, 117, 206-8
Ernabella Mission, 307
Evidence, Aboriginal: legislation, 128, 129, *see also* Law and justice
Evidence Act 1876 (N.S.W.), 128
Exemptions, Certificates of: compared with French and Belgian colonial practices, 358-9; N.S.W. 360-1; S.A., 361
Eyre, E. J., 79, 80

Female Orphan School and Gaol Fund (N.S.W.), 91
Finding ... of Board of Inquiry concerning the killing of natives ... by police parties ... (1929), 288
Finke River Mission, 32n.
Firearms, 197, 198, 199, 214; N.T., 232, 236-7
Fisheries Act (Qld), 175
Fison, L., 224
FitzRoy, Governor, 60, 62
Fletcher, J. W., 282, 286, *see also* Payne-Fletcher Report
Flierl, Johann, 105
Flinders, Matthew, 110
Flinders Island, 51-3, 174
Food supplies: Aboriginal, 57, 77, (destruction) 79, (depreciations) 111, (effect of scrub clearing) 111, (hunting) 79, (malnutrition) 80, (reciprocity) 79-80, (search for) 243; European (destruction), 110, 112, (right to) 77, (storable wealth) 77
Forrest River, 252
Forrest River Church of England Mission, 254
Forster, W., 41, 42, 112
Fringe settlements, 52, 168, 319, 337; Alice Springs, 270; and institutions, 250; and reserves, 251; civic rights, 398; Clarence River, 112; colonial administration, 21; conditions (N. Aust.), 261; economic dependence on towns, 112; housing, 383, hunting, 168; increase, 398; mining, 205, 215; N.T., 215; police, 167; potentialities, 251; S.A., 205; station, 331; status, 331-2; townsmen and, 112, 167-8, transitional stage, 251

INDEX

Frontier conflict, 5; Aboriginal vulnerability, 148-9; and warfare, 148, (injustice) 149; conquest and war, 149-50, 154, (common citizenship) 150, (imposition of law and order) 150; definition, 148, 149; destruction of Aborigines, 176; duration, 149; food, 152; guerilla warfare, 148-9; justification, 149; police, 150; policy, 150; troops, 158

Frontier policy and practice, 35, 67, 123-4, 150-2, 311; Aboriginal employment, 85, 146, 176; Aboriginal society (extermination) 155, (vulnerability) 148; administration problems, 6, 21, (Commonwealth-States dilemma) 311, (comparisons) 6, 22, 147-8, 150, 151, (cross-cultural) 213, 321; and settled areas, 170-1; attitudes, 67, 200; citizenship, 150; civil police, 150, 151, 155; clashes, 145; Commonwealth, 306, 307, 311; conditions (compared with Africa), 22, 176, (impact) 185, (N.T.) 242; conquest, 21, 149-50, (responsibilities) 154; contract, 24, 84, 158 (control essential) 151, (first) 153; control, 21, 42, 70, 84, 157-9, 161, 176, 179, 185-6, (default) 150, (policy for extension) 21-2, 123-4, 153; controlled areas, 151; cross-cultural administration, 321, (Asia) 22, (Britain) 151, (Papua) 147-8, 150, 151, (S.A./N.T.) 213; cultural frontier, 123; dilemma, 153-4; expertise, 148; extension, 70, 145, 146; Gipps, 151-2; Hawkesbury River, 28; humane, 150; homogeneity, 24; industry, 146; indefinitely expanding frontier, 147; integration (economic) 155; Kimberleys, 153, 154; labour (Asian) 214-15, (value) 146; land use, 24, 67; land rights, 155; law (rights) 145, 150-1, 153, (special legislation) 146; mining, 146; missions, 146, 152, 254; Murrumbidgee, 153; native custom, 150; Native Police, 152, 153; N.T., 205, 211-14, 306, 311, 321, (areas) 212, (Commonwealth) 306, (S.A.) 212; punitive expeditions, 150; Qld, 70, 145-6, 157-9, 168, 179, (control) 185-6; restricted areas policy, 151; S.A., 145, 153, 211, (and N.T.) 205; settlement (expansion) 21, 145-7, (limits) 6; settlers' views, 151, 154; sovereignty, 5-6; stock, 151; W.A., 70, 145, 146, 153; warfare and citizenship, 5, 148-50, 155, 159, 169; pearling, 146; police, 149-55, 306; policy, 147-50, 168, 195, (Papua) 147, (prerequisites) 148; problems, 145, 311; protection (legal) 151; race relations, 34, 39, 137, 147, 150, 156, 203, 210-11, 214; walkabout, 140

Fry, Oliver, 112, 114

Fulford, John, 178

'Full-bloods', 320-1; isolation on reserves, 139

Furnivall, J. S., 130

Gale, Fay, 82, 205, 379

Gamble, N. F., 214

Gawler, Governor George, 77, 79

Geelong, 57

Geraldton, 67

Giles, Alfred, 214

Gillen, F. J., 216, 224, 226

Gilruth, J. A., 235

Gipps, Governor Sir George, 5, 6, 23, 35, 36, 38, 84, 86, 94, 133, 134, 136, 151, 174, 266; colonial principles, 18; land revenue, 58, 61, (Pt Phillip) 58; legal equality and law enforcement, 87; missions, 58, 99; Myall Creek, 112

Glenelg, Lord, 38, 74, 75, 99, 151

Glynn, P. M., 248

Goderich, Lord, 94

Goldmining: Qld, 169-70; S.A., 213

Goulburn, Lord, 92

Goulburn (district), 29, 57

Goulburn Island Methodist Mission, 252, 265

Governors' Instructions, 28, 65, 86, 122

Grafton, 35

Gregory, A. C., 163

Gregory, F. C., 68

Grey, Captain (later Sir) George, 23, 66, 79, 86, 120, 126, 129, 133-6, 174, 266; Aboriginal custom, 69, 70, 126 (education and) 127; law (application) 69, (indigenous) 126; social change and enforcement of law, 126-9; training Aborigines, 121, (S.A.), 81

Grey, Earl, 60-2, 84

Gribble, John, 177

Gribble, Rev. E., 200, 201

Groote Eylandt, 275; C.M.S. mission, 252; flying base (exclusion of

Aborigines), 316; reserve, 314, 316, 317

Guardian of Wards (N.T.), 239

Guardians of Aborigines (Swan R.), 68, 76

Gulliver, 160-1

Gumbaingar, 114

Gun Carriage Island, 48, 52

Gunn, Mrs Aeneas, 218

Guragi: tribal elder's duty, 230

Hagenauer, F. A., 164, 177

Hale, Matthew, 104

Half-castes, *see* Part-Aborigines

Harris, William, 202

Harrison, Brian, 36

Harper, John, 94

Hasluck, Sir Paul, 7, 65, 66, 68, 70-2, 87, 130, 188-9, 292, 304

Hassell, Kathleen, 77, 78, 83

Hawkesbury River district, 28-9; contact, 151

Health, 327; and warfare, 23, 244; Arnhem Land, 313; Daly River, 244; disease, 23, 52, 53, 80, 203, 228, 242, 244, 258, 314; hygiene, 49; infant, 335; Kahlin Compound, 265-6; Kimberleys, 301; malnutrition, 23, 57, 80, 242, 326; N.T., 242, 244, 263, 265-6, 301, 314, 335; Pt Phillip, 52, 53, 57, 60; public, 265; Qld, 167, 171-2; S.A., 80, 203; Tas. 49, *see also* Welfare

Hermannsburg Lutheran Mission, 105, 206, 246, 252, 265, 270, 306, 315

Hindmarsh, Governor Sir John, 74, 86

Hobart, 151

Housing, 3, 334, 383; living conditions, 153, 210, 262, 334; N.T., 334, 383; pastoral, 210, 261; reserves, 173; station, 261, 334-6, 383; settlement, 240

Howitt, A. W., 224

Hughes, W. M., 147

Humanitarian influence, 174, 258

Hunt, Atlee, 222-4

Hunter River, 29

Hunting rights, 155, 165; Qld, 168; W.A., 193

Hutt, John, 65-6, 68-70, 76, 87, 131; and Grey and Stirling, 66; education,

66; integration into work force, 60; law as applied to Aborigines, 66; policy, 66; social structure, 66

Huxley, Julian, 88

Immigration: and Aboriginal work force, 120, 134-5, 399; land revenue, 58, 60-1

Indentured labour, 16; W.A., 192, *see also* Work force

Indians, American, 11, 13; compared with Aborigines, 12-13

Indigence, 220

Indigenous minorities: Aboriginal, Amerindian, and Negro, 12

Indigenous social controls, and disputes, 101, *see also* Social system

Industrial goods and food, attraction for Aborigines, 122

Infanticide, 60, 203, 327

Infant mortality, 335

Initial conference of Commonwealth and State Aboriginal Authorities (1937), 319-28

Initiation, *see* Religion

Injustice: Brooks killing, 288-90; dispossession, 27; frontier (reaction) 304; Japanese crewmen, 292; jury trial (cross-cultural), 291-2; Tuckiar trial and appeal, 291-2, 295-6, *see also* Frontier conflict, Law and justice, Massacres, Poisoning

Institutionalisation, 52; and assimilation, 339; and social life, 249; apartheid, 256-7; autonomy and political leadership, 241; 'civilising', 89; current problem, 339; depression (impact), 281-2; description of tribal life, 220, 249; exclusions, 241; missionaries, 312-13; paternalism, 257; social and economic effects, 239-41; training, 313

Intelligence, 225; adaptation to civilised environment, 298-9; 'culture free' test of, 298

Integration, 87, 155

'Intelligent parasitism', 8, 217; and labour supply, 208; motives, 115; transitional stage, 210

Inter-governmental co-operation: Central Australian Reserve, 251; large reserves, 251

Iredale, R. R., 380

Islam, 10

INDEX 417

Jay Creek, 315
Japanese: violence against, 290–2
Jones, Rev. John, 274, 276
Jury trial of Aborigines: by settlers, 291–2; tribal matters, 292
Justice: administration, 18, (W.A.) 302; cross-cultural, 291, (tribal matters) 292, (W.A.) 302; punishment, 302; settlers', 18, *see also* Aboriginal Law, Injustice, Law and justice

Kahlin compound, 265–6, 275, 284
Kalumburu Mission, 105
Kelly, J. H., 283, 334
Killalpaninna Mission, 205
Kimberleys, 153–5, 298–9, 301; cattle killing, 195; employment (compared with Qld), 192; reserves, 195
King River, 306
Kinship, *see* Social system
Koonibba Mission, 205
Kopperamanna Mission, 205
Kunmunya Mission, 205

Labour legislation: Qld, 146; W.A., 146, 195–8
Labour relations, 34; sanction of force, 159; White Australia policy, 285, 286; *see also* Work force
Lagassé, Jean H., 7, 9
Laissez-faire, 21; N.S.W. 62–3; Qld, 63
Lake Amadeus Lutheran Mission, 267, 307
Lake Macquarie Mission, 94, 97, 99, 100
Lake Tyers Station, 353–4
Land: alienation, 194; areas and use ('colonial' Australia) 378; claims, 154, 155; conservation, 206–8; for reserves, 231, 250; 'native rights', 24; pressure for (and missions) 95; religion and, 206–8; rightful inheritors, 103; 'settled' Australia, 378; settlers' attitudes, 16, 154; sovereignty, 5–6; 'waste and vacant', 124, *see also* Land revenue, Land rights, etc.
Land Act, 1933–1963 (W.A.) 353n.
Land Acts 1861 (S.A.), 111
Land and Emigration Commissioners (S.A.), 98
Lands Commissioners: Border Police, 114; N.S.W., 75; Reports, 114

Land Fund (S.A.), used for schools, 104
Land grants: missions, 97–9; revenues, 98
Land Regulations (Imperial) (1864), 187
Land revenue: Aboriginal claims, 61; Aboriginal development, 60, 61; Border Police, 61; compensation for real property (S.A.), 83–4; financing protectorate, 58, 61; government control, 173; immigration, 60; prior occupation, 173; public services, 60; reservation for Aborigines (S.A.), 75; S.A., 75, 82–3; sale and lease, 173; use, 98
Land rights, Aboriginal, 12, 14, 16, 310; common law (compared with U.S.A.), 14; depasturing and, 15, 207; entry to (W.A.) 187; mineral rights, 12; 'native' title, 15; nomads, 17; prior occupation, 16, (and land revenue) 173; public opinion, 37, S.A., 75; struggle for life, 208; Vic., 55
Land sales, S.A., 74; Wakefield system, 75
Land settlement, 214; British, 13, (compared with Africa and N.Z.) 13; drought and Aboriginal privations, 288–9; N.T. (waterholes), 206, *see also* Spread of settlement
Land tenure: and missions, 248; mission reserves (reversion), 93, 97
Land use: Aboriginal (S.A.) 75–7, (Swan R.) 67; Aboriginal—white confrontation, 24; agriculture, 29; Bleakley, 267; conflict, 24; free settlers and settler economies, 29, (Tas.), 44; hunting and water rights, 267; impact on way of life, 29; legal relationships (Pt Phillip), 54; pastoralists, 29, (and massacres) 267; patterns, 24; reserve, 247–8; Shoalhaven R., 29
Language groups: Bandjalang, 110; Gumbaingar, 110; Lake Macquarie, 93, 94, 100
La Trobe, C. J., 58, 63
Laurie, Arthur, 170
Law and justice, 46; Aboriginal code, 230; Aboriginal courts on reserves, 312, 314, 322, 329; Aboriginal custom, 86, 204, 294–5, 322, 343, (S.A.) 78, 80, 204; Aboriginal evidence, 35, 80, 127, 128, 131, 158, 160, 165, 174, (admissibility, S.A.) 80, (Qld) 166, 168, (representation, Swan R.) 69;

Aboriginal operations within, 130; Aboriginal matters, 291, (jury trial) 291-2; Aboriginal resistance, 76; Aboriginal subjects, 55; administration, 21, 72-3; application, 35-7, 38, 41, 76, 129, 131, 133, (part-Aborigines) 132, (S.A.) 78-80, (Swan R.) 69, 72; armed police, 310; Arnhem Land, 313; arrests, 114-15, 193-4, (by pastoralists) 115, (and punitive action, W.A.) 194, 200-1; basic problems (Tuckiar case) 305; 200-1; basic problems (Tuckiar case) 305; Bleakley recommendations, 268; British procedures, 310, (and traditional law) 244-5; custom (S.A.), 204; crimes by and against Aborigines, 64, 65; chaining, 81, 115; cross-cultural discussion, 324; 'declaration', 357; efficacy of, 310; enforcement, 123-4, (and social change) 126-8; equality and enforcement, 87; 'folk' systems, 228; frontier problem, 69; Governors' instructions, 65; humanitarian concern, 268; ill treatment, 315; indigenous law, 126; industrial awards, 255; injustices, 160; justice and atrocity (Swan R.), 72; jury trial, 291-2; killings (police and settlers), 288; legal personality, 55, 86, 130; legal procedures (N.T.) 237, (S.A.) 80; legal system, 101; legislation, special, 227, 342, (N.T.) 237; murder, 158; Native Police, 41, 160-2; N.S.W., 128, 134; non-Aborigines, 69; neck chains, 115; offences, 166; pastoral industry, 216; place of (S.A.) 220; pre-literate societies, 228; principle and justice, 228; policy (failure) 81; protective legislation, 136; 'public enemies', 54; rule of, 71; punitive expeditions (S.A.) 79, (W.A.) 200; protection, 173; punishment and confinement, 174; Qld, 128; race relations, 150; reciprocity, 314; recognition, 55; rule of law (Swan R.) 71, 72; S.A., 128; settler actions, 69; settler attitudes, 73, 291-2; special court (W.A.), 303; tribal matters, 268, 292, (and arrests) 285; traditional systems, 228; Tuckiar case, 305; uncontrolled spread of settlement, 80-1; W.A., 128, 131, see also Administration, cross-cultural,

Legal status, Police, Native Police, Punitive expeditions

Law and order: civil police, 150; frontier traditions, 153, 306; institution and maintenance, 150-1; instruments, 151-2; legal protection for all, 150; native custom, 150; police and patrol officers, 305, 306

Law of Evidence Further Amendment Act 1854 (Vic.), 128n.

Legal status, Aboriginal, 20-1, 130-4, alcohol, and social services (W.A.), 359-60; British subjects, 19, 74; Certificate of Citizenship (W.A.), 359; civil rights, 129-30, (S.A.) 357, (W.A.), 359-60; confusion, 351, 352; debasement, 132; 'declared', 351-2; education, 132; exclusion from law-making, 132; exemptions (Qld), 358-9; Gipps and Grey, 133-4; law, equality before, 136; (N.T.), 238; legislation (control, N.T.) 238, (restriction by) 33, 136, (special, W.A.), 360; location (S.A.) 356, 357; N.S.W., 54; Qld, 183, 351-2; racial origin (N.T.), 238; racial categories (S.A.), 357; reversal or procedures, (Qld) 358; S.A., 221; trend to equality, 362; 'under the Act' (Qld), 358, (exemptions) 358; wage, unemployment, and social services, 349; W.A., 54, 194-5, see also Definition, Special Legislation

Legislation, and racial origin, 183

Legislative Council of N.S.W., 62, 127

Leprosy, 314

Le Soeuf, William, 57

'limits of location', 6, 122

Linnean Society, 224

Liquor Ordinance (A.C.T.), 348

Living conditions: Bleakley recommendations, 264; camp, 335; immorality, 264; stations, 210, 335; town, 242

Local government and shire: colour prejudice and discrimination, 363-4

Loddon, 56

Lombardina Catholic Mission, 254

London Missionary Society, 89, 93-4

Long, J. P. M., 212, 242, 367, 368

Lumumba, Patrice, 359

Lutherans and Lutheran Church, 105, 205, 206

Lutheran Mission: Brisbane, 158; desert country, 105

Macarthur River, 217

McCall, Constable, 291, 296-7

McEwen, John: objectives and methods, 328-30, (compared with TPNG) 329, (social change) 330; policy, 328, (long-term) 330

MacGregor, Sir William, 223, 288

McIlwraith, Sir Thomas, 174

Mackay: petition, 171-2; Report, 171-4

McLean, M. T., 322, 327

Macquarie, Governor Lachlan, 28, 29, 90; assimilation, 87; 'civilising' the Aborigines, 93; Native Institution, 89, 92; planned society, 86; stabilising the Aborigines, 93

Maintenance money (W.A.), 193

Makin, C., 379

Malnutrition, 327, (and cash wages) 258, see also Health

Managed settlements, 241

Mandate system and Aboriginal policy, 148

Maningrida, 317

Maoris, compared with Aborigines, 15, 23; race relations, 204

Mapoon Presbyterian Mission, 177, 247, 313

Margaret River, 195

Marndoc, 252

Marriage, 1, 31, 104, 231-2, 236, 281-2, 303, 321, 326, see also Miscegenation

Martial law, 34; N.S.W., 29, 152; Tas., 44

Massacres, 36-8, 42, 112, 115-16, 118, 151, 157-8, 179, 267, 288; as reprisals, 113-14; Border Police, 114; by Aborigines, 78; guilt by association, 42; Kimberley, 257; legal situation, 127; poisoning, 157-8; Risdon, 45, 47, see also Battle of Pinjarra, Battle of Myall Creek

Melville Island Catholic Mission, 267

Meriam Report, 3, 268, (compared with Bleakley) 269

Meston, Archibald, 177-9, 224, 247; Report on Government Scientific Expedition to Bellenden Ker Range (1889), 177-82, 313

Meston Report (1889), 177; and Aborigines, 178-9; basic for Qld legislation, 179; Bellenden Ker, 178; (workers) 179; Cape York, 179-80; employment, 182; exclusion from towns, 182;

massacres, 179; liquor, 181; missions and mission settlements, 182; Native Police, 179-81; opium, 181; paternalism, 180; police, 181; populations, mixed, 181; Protectors, 182; race relations, 180; ration stations, 181; relations with Aborigines, 179; reserves, 182

Methodist Missionary Society, 270, 272

Metis (Canada), 4, 9

Migration, 61

Military force: N.S.W. 86; W.A., 87

Millingimbi Mission, 252

Mineral rights, 12; and discoveries, 340

Miners and mining: Aborigines as, 214-15; Aboriginal social organisation, 215; and environment, 215; and water, 205, 215; Asian, 214-15; copper, 205, 215; deep, 215; fringe camps, 205, 215; frontier, 175; gold, 215; labour, 146; N.T., 214-15; needs, 316; on reserves, 328; Qld, 169-70; race relations, 214; S.A., 214-5; tribal life, 205

Minorities, indigenous: Aboriginal, 2, 5-7, 12; Amerindian and Negro, 12

Miscegenation, 3, 139, 206, 280, 320; S.A., 206; Vic., 354; W.A., 197-8, 303, 312

Missionary Cotton Company, 167

Missions, 58; achievements, 308, 324-5; adaptation, 325; and Aboriginal administration, 220; and Aboriginal Law and beliefs, 102, 247; and culture, 247, 308, (continuity) 246; and reserves, 307, (large) 246, 252; assimilation (agents for) 325; attack on Crocodile Is., 290; attitudes (Aboriginal) 96-7, 100-1; Bleakley Report, 265-6, 271-2; call to, 177; ceremony and ritual, 226; control, 308; conversion, 97, 307, 312-13; cost analyses, 266; desert country, 105; dying race, 103; economic aid (source of), 308; education, 246, (orphans) 91, (settlers) 90, (standards) 323; emphases, 95; employment, 95; functions (frontier) 146, 177, (social) 246; funds, 94; government (aid from) 99, 100, 105, 107, 177, 247-8, 323, (agents for), 106, 186, 253, 266, 270, 323, 325, (policy), 146, 236, 247-8, 250-1, 307-8, 313, 324-5, (reserves) 248, (S.A.) 246, 247; health and hygiene, 323; impetus, 94; independence, 107; institutionalism, 308; institutional paupers, 106; justice (Tuckiar), 295; labour conditions (compared with pastoralist) 308; land for, 95, (pressure for) 95, 97-8, (reversion to Crown) 93; location, 98-9, (quality of land, Qld) 177; Moseley Report, 300-2; need for, 97; N.T., 247, 252-4, 267, 307-8, 312-13; objectives ('civilise and Christianise') 88, 95, 325; Pacific, 95-7; part-Aborigines (responsibilities), 236; paternalism, 275, 290, 308; policy, 100-1, 252-3, 307-8; protectors, 146, 184, 220; Qld, 177, 247-9, 250; recommendations, 265-6; reserves, 329, (large) 250, 252; responses, 246; role, 257, 307; S.A., 204-5; schools, 104-6; segregation, 182, 247; settlers' attitudes, 98; social change, 246-7, 290, 324-5; Social Service payments, 349; supervision (protective), 269; theocratic powers, 106; trading point, 307; tribal people, 267; wages (cash), 274; welfare, 177, 264; W.A., 200-1, 254, 302, 326; workhouse and, 96, *see also* Institutionalisation

Mitchell River Church of England Mission, 247, 248

'Mixed-bloods', *see* Part-Aborigines

Mogumber Aboriginal Settlement, 202

Moodie, Peter, 391

Moola Bulla, 195, 252, 301

Moore, George, 67

Moore River, 298

Moorhouse, Matthew, 79, 83, 104, 205

Moravian Mission: Brethren, 205; Moreton Bay, 99, 100, 105; Wimmera, 164

Moreton Bay: settlement (and Clarence R.) 157; transportation, 109

Moreton Bay Mission, 99

Morley, 273

Moseley, H. D., 194, 300

Moseley Report, 300-4; administration, 302; chaining, 300-1; cruelty, 300; economy, 300-1; health, 300, 301; justice, 302; missions, 302; part-Aborigines, 302; standard of judgment, 300-1; wages, 300

Mt Franklyn, 56

Mt Hann, 252

Mounted Police, 151, 152

Mount Margaret Mission, 254, 307

Multi-purpose institutions: cultural issues, 52; economic prospects, 52; expenditure, 174; health, 53; prototype, 52; responsibility for, 53; segregation, 265, *see also* Institutionalisation, Missions, Reserves

Multi-racial society, 398

Mulvaney, D. J., 88

Munja Station, 252, 253

Murray, Constable, 288

Murray, J. H. P., 150-1, 223-4, 294; native regulations, 294

Murrell, Jack Congo, 133

Myall Creek, 35-7, 39, 43, 112, 133-4, 149; application of law, 35-7; massacre, 35, 39, 43

Myalls, 260, 329

Narre Warren, 56

National Council of Women, 270

National Missionary Council of Australia, 202, 274; conference (1933), 294-5

'Native', 321; categories (W.A.), 352-3; definition, 322, 343, (W.A.) 352-3; protection, 343; status, 343

'Native administration' (Aust.), 146-7

'Native Affairs', *see* Aboriginal Welfare

Native (Citizenship Rights) Act 1944-1951 (W.A.), 359, 360

Native Courts, 305, 312, 322-3, *see also* Law and justice

Native custom, *see* Custom, Social system

Native Institution, N.S.W.: and guerilla warfare, 89; educational, 89; location, 90; missionary, 89; Shelley, 89

Native Labourers' Protection Bill (Qld), 175

Native Police, 5, 37, 41, 62, 159, 175; abolition (Qld) 180-1, (Vic.) 73; Aboriginal life (destruction) 71, 152, 158; administration, instrument of, 39, 137; and other Aborigines, 41; brutality, 160-1; civil or military force, 168-9; control of, 39-40, 152, 161, (Qld) 42; destructive, 166; detribalised, 152; disbanding, 167; dispersal, 42, 160-3, 165-6, 169-70, 186, (Qld policy) 42; establishment, 62, 73, 153; frontiers, 171 (Qld policy) 158-9;

INDEX

functions and powers, 39-40, 168-9; goldrushes, 169; introduction (Qld), 158; labour, Aboriginal, 159; members, 168; Meston Report, 179-80; military force and martial law, 152; N.S.W., 39, 43; organisation, 39; Papuan tradition, 307; punitive force, 153; Port Phillip, 39, 71, 152; purpose, 39-41; Qld, 39, 124, 137, 158-63, 166-72, 180-1, (Select Committee) 159-63; recruitment, 42; responsibility, 39; rights in law, 71; S.A., 153; Select Committee (N.S.W.), 40n.; settlers' views, 40, 158, 159; strength, 152, 169; W.A., 153

'Native' populations, 13-14

'Native' regulations, 101; N.T., 294

'Native rights', Crown as trustee, 19

Native Welfare Act 1963 (W.A.), 353n.

Neck chain, 115, 193-4, 199-201, 322-3, *see also* Chaining

Negro, 12, 13

Neundettelsau Lutheran Mission, 105

Neville, A. O., 201, 331; Aboriginal cattle station, 253-4; assimilation, 321; begging, 327; corporal punishment, 328; courts, 222; criticisms, 326; financial aid, 327; Missions, 253; neck chains, 222; population, 326-7; priority in training, 253; secular policy, 253; wages, 257

Newcastle Waters, 215

New England, 33

New Guinea: administration (cross-cultural), 151, (Qld role), 175; annexation (British attitude), 19; British Protectorate, 174-5; Bruce, S. M., 260; colonial policy, 147-8; law and order, 151; mandate, 147; social change, 309; wage rates, 262, *see also* Papua, TPNG

New Norcia Mission, 105-6, 254

New Zealand, 10, 15; pattern of settlement, 13-14

Nomads: independence, 28; industrial goods (attraction), 317; land rights, 17; leadership, 125; segregation, 317; technology, 19

Non-literate cultures, education, 89

North Australian Territory, 258; administration, 258; Bleakley Report, 259-60; Chief Protector (Cook) 259; health and welfare, 259

North Australian Workers Union, 269, 277

Northern Territory: administration, 206, 258, (Commonwealth) 230, (S.A.) 211-12; control, 211, (Commonwealth) 212, (S.A.) 206; land sales, 206; law, (applicable) 212, (operative) 278, (Qld) 278; protection, 224, (responsibility) 259; reunited, 278; settlers, 206; Special Commission, 224

Northern Territories Aboriginals Act 1910 (S.A.), 206, 219, 230-3; Regulations, 230-4

Northern Territory Aboriginals Ordinance (1918, 1924, 1927, 1936, 1953), 235-6, 348

Northern Territory Act of South Australia (1863), 212

Northern Territory Pastoral Lessees, 269, 270

Northern Territory Welfare Ordinance (1953-1960), 239n., 347

Oaths Amendment Act 1884 (Qld), 128n., 168; Regulations (1866), 168

Oenpelli, 281; government farm, 235

Oenpelli Mission, 251, 252

Ogilvie, E. D., 116-19, 121, 178

Onslow, 301

Onus, William, 337

Opium, 2, 37, 238, 244; legislation, 181-3

Orphan School, 90, 91

Overlanders, 79; areas occupied, 146; 'militia', 151; 'native' labour, 119-20; N.T., 205, 212; resistance (Clarence R.) 112; reprisals, 112

Oyster Bay, 52

Pagan, J. H., 113

Palm Island, 48, 174

Palmerston (Darwin), 206

Pan-Pacific Science Congress, 226

Papua: control of settlement, 153; frontier, 153; labour administration, 223; native lands, 13; status, 222

Parramatta, 28

Parker, Edward, 56, 59

Parry-Okeden, W. E., 168, 170, 181

Parry-Okeden Report (1897), 181-2

Part-Aborigines, 26, 60, 103, 132, 138-41, 171, 303, 326, 342; absorption, 139,

266-7, 281, 286, 320; administrative emphases, 250; and passing, 1, 138, 344, 346, 396-7; apprenticeships, 278; as pressure group, 273; assimilation, 81, 231, 285, 321, (protective-restrictive legislation) 323-4, (Vic.) 354, (W.A.) 303; attitudes towards, 33, 171; beginnings, 26, 33; birth rates, 281; children, 275, (N.T.) 236, (removal) 247-50, 280, (separation from parents) 302; civil rights (W.A.) 202; classification by strain, 265; 'Colonial Australia', 377; colour (Vic.) 354; control and protection, 183, 238, 247, 267, 269-70, 351, (N.T.) 234, (S.A.) 220, (W.A.) 303; 'declared', 351; definition, 139, 183, 278, (N.T.) 231, 342, (Qld) 351, (Vic.) 352, (W.A.) 195; education, 265-6, 279; employment, 138, 279, (N.T.) 234, (W.A.) 196; exclusion from town society, 319; exemption from Aboriginal Ordinance, 280-1, (N.T.) 357; guardianship (W.A.), 303; housing, 256, 280; increase in population, 138, 267, 281, 311, 338, (N. Aust.) 260, (N.T.) 236, (S.A.) 82, 219-20, (Vic.) 354, (W.A.) 195; integration, 340; in white population, 138; institutions for (N.T.), 236; kinship, 138; legislation, 132, 227; legal control, 238; marriage, 281, 282, (N.T.) 232, 236, (W.A.) 303; miscegenation (S.A.) 206; missions (N.T.), 232, 236, (S.A.) 206; Moseley Report, 302; nomads, 367; N.T., 218-19, 231, 236, 311; origin, 33; pastoralists and, 275, 302; police (N.T.) 234; policy, 238, 250, 266-7, 279, 281; population, 232, 311-12, 366-7, (distribution) 366, 370-5, 377, (enumeration 1961), 367, (increase) 195, 219, (ratio to Aboriginal) 366, (self-identification) 367; prostitution, 211; Protector (N.T.), 234, 236; reserves, 267, 272, (Vic.) 354; resistance, 26; rural, 382-3; search for identity (W.A.) 304; segregation, 275; 'Settled Australia', 377; socialisation (Vic.) 354; social structure, custom and law, 138; special legislation, 268, (W.A.) 304; urban, 369, 379-80, 382-3; Vic., 354; voters excluded from institutions, 241;

wages, 269, 278; W.A., 191, 195, 202, 321; White Australia, 280, 321, *see also* Fringe settlements

Passing, 1, 138, 344, 346, 396-7

Pastoral industry, 17; Aboriginal labour, (conditions) 210, 259, 261-2, 264, 275, 326, 332, (dependants) 261-2, (depredations) 29, (punitive measures) 29-30, (essential) 273, (fulfilment) 285; accommodation, 261-2; attitudes, 262; Bleakley recommendations, 263-4, 269, 273-4; Carrington inquiry, 337; children, 196, 275-6, (education) 326; company, 217; cost, 336; criticisms, 299; dependants, 326, 334, (support of) 259, 262; discipline, 261; employment, 330-4, 337-8, (conditions) 210, 326; equal wages, 210; foods, 262, 334; hours worked (compared with armed forces) 333, 335-7; housing, 210, 261, 334-5, 383; hunting rights, 178, 193; incentives, 262; indenture system, 134; inefficiency, 210, inspection, 334; integrated into, 178; labour, 146, 217, (demands) 255, (pool) 221, 256, (station) 269; law, 274; leasehold (consolidation), 283; legislation, 277-8; licensing, 274-6; malnutrition, 326; N.T., 259, 262; northern development, 283; pastoralist, threats, 273; population decline, 326-7; prostitution, 334-5; protectors, 276; rationing agents, 270; settler economics, 273-4; small holders, 283; spread, 29, 30, 175 (impact) 30, 33; station employment, 209; wage employment, 233; wages, 18, 192-3, 259, 334-5, 337, 338, (and expulsion) 277, (cash) 261, 273; wage rates, 273-4; welfare, 335; women, 196, 326, *see also* Wages, Work force

Pastoral leases: conflict of interests, 62; consolidation, 283; N.T., 62; pastoralists' views, 62; prior occupation, 62; rights granted, 61; W.A., 62, *see also* Land, Land use, etc., Wages, Work force

Pastoral industry (N.T.), 209-17, 233, 253-64, 269-70, 273-4, 277-8, 283, 285, 310, 330-2, 337-8; administration, 215-16; contact, 242; conditions, 326, 330; development, 215-16; large company, 212; leases, 280; licences, 278-9; maintenance of employees and dependants, 262, 263, 277; overlanders, 212; political power, 216; Protector's authority, 218; wages (Aboriginal), 216, (part-Aboriginal) 278, (rates) 278, *see also* Wages, Work force

Pastoral industry (Qld): conditions, 326; dependants, 326; employment, 255-7; Provident Fund, 256; wages and rates, 256, 261

Pastoral industry, (W.A.), 67; conditions, 326, (Kimberleys), 299; employment, 191-2, 196, 198; wage rates, 257

Pastoralism (S.A./N.T.): adjustment, 217-18; 'battlers', 217; reprisals, 217; station employment, 217, *see also* Mining, Pastoral industry, Spread of settlement

Pastoral Lessees Association, 269, 278-9

Paterson, T., 313

Patterns of White settlement, eastern Australia, 17

Payne, W. L., 282, 286, *see also* Payne-Fletcher Report

Payne-Fletcher Report (1937), 282-6

Pearling, 180; employment (child) 193, (legislation) 285, (Protectors) 276, (on ships) 175, 180; indenture system, 134; labour, 146; legislation (Qld, W.A.) 146; N.T., 276; recruitment, 276; social change, 290; W.A., 188; wages, 276

Pearling Act 1870 (W.A.), 188

Pearl Shell Fishery Regulation Act 1873 (W.A.), 188

Pensions: entitlement by category, 348-9, (and pastoralists) 349, (on settlements) 349; payment, (direct) 349, (and definition, by States) 349, (institutions) 349, *see also* Social Services

Permanent Mandates Commission, 147-8, 242, 269

Petermann Ranges, 316

Petrie, Tom, 157-9, 164, 166, 167

Phillip, Governor Arthur, 19

Paddington, R., 299

Pine Creek, 215

Plunkett, 35-6

Plomley, N. J. B., 45

Poisoning, 112, 157-8

Point Macleay Mission, 204, 205-220, 322, 356

Point Pearce Mission, 105, 204-5, 220, 322, 350

Police, 18, 33, 181; Aboriginal relations with, 114-15, 149-56, 199-200, (Qld) 169, 181; administrative freedom, 315; agents for government departments, 76; and pastoral industry, 216; and protectorate, 76, 215-16, (N.T.) 259, (W.A.) 196, 201; and settlers, 153, 155; armed, 310; arrests, 37, 71, 114-15, 193, 195, 200-1; as protectors, 176, 184, 194, 205, 216, 259, 302; black trackers, 153, 194-5, (armed) 200-1, 216-17; cattle killing (W.A.), 193; chaining, 71, 115, 193-4, 199-201, 300-1, 322-3; 'good' officials, 216; killings, 161-3; labour, 216; maintenance money, 193; mounted, 65, 69; N.T., 205, 213, 215-17, 234, 237, 259, 315; Port Phillip, 151-2; Qld, 76, 217; reserves, 312; Roth Report, 193-4; S.A., 216-17; trackers, armed, 194-5, 200-1, 211, (rations) 194-5; W.A., 193-5, 200-1, 217, 302, *see also* Chaining, Law and justice, Native Police, Punitive expeditions

Political organisation, 5, 25, 241; Aboriginal crimes, 69, 70; and existence, 207; appointment of native chiefs (W.A.), 68; breakdown, 32; 'King Billy', 25, 68; labour, 209; leadership, 68, 229, 241, (multi-purpose) 207; tribal system, 5, 15; weakness, 5, 14, 15, 23, 31, 32, 229, *see also* Social organisation, Society

Poonindie, 104, 105, 106, 204

Population, 284; and part-Aborigines, 85; basis, 369; 1961 census and departmental, 368-9, (Aust.), 368, 385-6, (A.C.T.), 368, 385-6, (excluded) 369, 376, (N.S.W.), 368, 385-6, (N.T.), 367, 368, 385-6, (S.A.) 367, 368, 385-6, (Tas.) 367-8, 379-80, 385-6, (Vic.) 367, 368, 385-6, (W.A.) 368, 385-6, (and surveys) 347; birth rate, 335; 'Colonial Australia', 376-7; control, 305, (infanticide) 60; death rates, 59; decline, 59, 384, 386, (N.T.) 242, (S.A.) 203, 219-20, (W.A.) 326-7; definition, 366; distribution, 366, 376-7, 379, (N.S.W.) 370, (N.T.), 375-7, (Qld) 372, 377, (rural) 382-3, (S.A.) 377, (Tas.) 378, (urban) 369, 379-83, (Vic.) 371, (W.A.) 373, 374, 376, 377, (total: departmental 1964)

370-5, 377, 383-5; employed, 260; estimates, 367, 368, 376; health (N.T.), 242; increase, 139, 241, 338, 386, 398; minimum (1961) 366, 367; movement (N.T.), 242-4; myalls, 260; nomadic tribes (N. Aust.), 260; numbers (1788-1966), 385-6; protection and control, 220; race and population at risk, 346; rural, 369; 'Settled Australia', 377, 378; social conflict, 59; statistics, 369-99; tribal people, 267; Torres Strait Islanders, 367, 369; urban, 178, 369, 379-84, *see also* Depopulation

Population trends, 384-6; age-sex structure, 338-9, 390-3 (urban and rural) 392; census (1961), 347; children, 388, 390, 392; comparisons (Aust.) 393, (Indians) 385, 392, (Maori) 392; decline (1788-1921), 384, 386; definition of categories, 344; estimates, 346, 385; growth rate, 386, 395; increase, 386, 398 (projected, 1961-81) 396-8

Port Jackson, 28

Port Keats Mission, 246, 307

Port Lincoln Mission, 104

Port Phillip Mission, 99

Port Phillip Protectorate, 34, 36, 53, 97, 99, 135, 229; attitudes (Aboriginal) 57, (settler) 55, 58; Chief Protector, 55-6; costs, 55, 61, (and migration) 61; districts, 56-7; duties, 56; establishment, 55; failure, 87; functions, 57-8; health, Aboriginal, 57; inter-tribal relations, 55, 57-8; land (areas) 56-7, (demarcation) 56, (use) 56; numbers, 56-7; objectives, 56; powers, 56; purpose, 55; race relations, 57; role, 56-8; settlements, compared with missions, 58; status, Aboriginal, 56; welfare, government policy, 56

Porteus, S. D., 298-9

Portus, C. C., 338

Prohibited areas (N.T.), 234

Property rights, 12-13

Prospecting, 215, 271, 328

Prostitution, 180, 196, 264; for alcohol, 30, 33; for food, 262-3, 326, 334; for clothing, 334-5

Protectors and protectorates, 20, 31, 130-1, 138, 239, 309; N.S.W., 227; N.T., 211-13, 216, 218-20, 231-2, 234, 235, 237-41, 259, 276, 313; Port Phillip, 55-8, 62; Qld, 75, 166, 173-4, 182-4, 247; S.A., 75-7, 81, 83-4, 203-5, 211-13, 216, 218, 220; W.A., 66, 68, 195-7, 302, *see also* Missions, Reserves, Police

Provident Fund (Qld), 256

Pseudo-Darwinism, 11, 25, 68, 198

Public health, 224, 228

Publicans' Act 1843 (W.A.), 131

Punitive expeditions, 7, 168, 170, 257; Cape Hawke, 291; New England, 151; 'Pigeon', 191-2; Port Phillip, 151; Woodah Is., 291; N.S.W., 29-30; N.T., 213; S.A., 78, 79, 204; S.A./N.T., 204, 213, 216-17; W.A., 7, 191, 200, *see also* Battle of Pinjarra, Law and justice, Native Police, Police

Race relations, 2, 7-9, 25, 34, 53, 79, 116-17, 186; children, separation, 232; clashes, 77, 162; conciliation, 170; confrontation, 34-5; dependency, 76; equality, 3; extermination (Qld) 182; fringe-dwellers, 112; frontier contacts, 39, 54, 156, 158, (compared with Papua) 153; government (and economic and mission interests,) 259; institutional relief, 62-3; ill-treatment, 7-8; justice, 204; labour force, 187, 212; law and order, 150; mining and prospecting, 214; morality, 30; Native Institution, 89; Qld, 158, 159, 178-80; N.T., 235; pastoral, 210, 212; prejudice, 5; resistance, 79, 89, 113, 169, (Cape York) 169, 170, (compared with Maori) 204; S.A., 74, 76-8; reciprocity, 77, 78; regulation, 38-9; S.A., 84-5, (compared with Vic., W.A.) 85; S.A./N.T., 211, 218; Tas., 46, 48-50; special laws, 342-3; spread of settlements, 33; Swan River, 64; tensions, 339; Tuckiar case, 291; 'war of races', 169, 170; white attitudes, 6-7, 67-8, *see also* Assimilation, Fringe settlements, Segregation

Racism, 225, 343-4

Radcliffe-Brown, A. R., 226, 384, 385

Rationing, 82, 204

Reddall, Rev. Thomas, 91

Referendum (1967), 376

Register of Aborigines (S.A.), 356, 361

Register of Wards (N.T.), 241, 347

Religion, 20, 24, 31, 102; and authority, 309; and economics, 34, 207; Aranda, 206-7; cannibalism, 164; dislocation, 117; disregard, European, 31; environment, 117, 207; initiation, 31, 203, 209; land, 206-8, 318; missions, 102, 253; Murinbata, 164; ritual, 209, 225-6, (mission views) 226; socialisation, 164; spirituality, and social change, 318; symbolism, 164, 225; tensions, 318, *see also* Social system, Society

Report . . . into the Employment and Protection of the Aboriginals in . . . Mackay . . ., 171-4

Report of the Royal Commission . . . upon matters in relation to the condition and treatment of Aborigines (Moseley Report), 300-4

Report on the North Queensland Aborigines and the Native Police (1897), 168

Reprisals, 33, 165; and resistance, 25-6, 33, 79, 113, (stock killing) 67, 201; settler, 33, 38, 66, 114, 116; theft, 113

Reserves, 98, 184; Aboriginal role, 256; administration, 183; attitudes, 57; cash economy, 256; concept, 228; 'colonial Australia', 377, 378; conflict of needs, 316; control, 183; delinquent children, 250; development, 328; economy, 256-7; encroachments, 58; establishment, 46-7, 61-2, 174; exploitation, 329; financing, 60, 234; for full-bloods, 321; inviolable, 228, 316; isolated, 249, 310; joint, 228; labour pool, 221, 255, 256, (role) 221, 256, (wages) 221, 256-7; land (alienation) 194, (tenure) 248, (use) 247-8; large, 248-54, (advantages) 248, 252, (autonomy) 249, (confinement) 248, 250, (costs) 252, (Crown land) 250, (economic value) 250, (education) 252, (entry) 250, (government and) 248, 250-2, (land rights) 93, 250, 285, (missions) 93, 250, 252, (security) 250, (theocracies) 250, 251; mining and prospecting, 328; missions, 246-53, 329; movements of inhabitants, 304, 310; myalls, 329; N.T., 218, 224, 228, 231, 234, 244, 246, 252, 305, 308, 316-17; pastoral leases, 61, 247-8, (extent) 218; Port Phillip, 57-62, 63;

policy, 44, 228, 247-51, (Tas.) 44; Protectors, 182; Qld, 171, 173, 174, 181-4, 247-8, 250, 256, (courts, gaols, police) 312; reasons for, 61-2; role, 257; Roth Report ('W.A.), 190-4; S.A., 75, 83, 84, 203, 204, 218, 251; segregation, 173, 182, 218; small, 60, 62, 63; W.A., 66, 197; unauthorised entry (vessels), 285; V.D.L., 44, 46, *see also* Missions

Resettlement, 249, 316

Richmond River, 34

Ridley, Rev. W., 165

Rights, demand for, 202

Robinson, G. A., 45, 47, 129; administration problem, attacks on Aboriginal camps, 112; Bruny Island, 45; Chief Protector, 55-6, (role) 58; 'civilising' institutions, 89; culture clash, 45, 47; Mission of Conciliation, 47-51; reserves, 61; segregation, 47-50; tuition, 50-1

Roebourne, 301

Roper River, 217

Roper River Church of England Mission, 246, 252

Rosewood Station, 334

Roth Report (W.A.), 157, 190-4, 224; arrests, 193-4; child labour, 193; contract of service, 190; controls, 192; employment, 190-3, 195; hunting rights, 193; neck chains, 193-4; police, 193-4; reserves, 194; wages, 192

Rottnest Island, 48

Royal Commission . . . in relation to the Condition and Treatment of Aborigines, 1935 (W.A.), *see* Moseley Report

Royal Commission into alleged Killing and Burning of Bodies in East Kimberley and into Police methods when Effecting Arrests (1927), 200-2

Royal Commission on the Condition of the Natives (W.A.), *see* Roth Report

Russell, Lord John, 58, 61, 131, 133

Sadlier, Richard, 94

Sale of Waste Lands Act (1842), 60-1

Schools, 91, 103-4

Scott, Archdeacon T. H., 91, 93-4

Segregation, 31, 47-50, 84, 87, 97, 135, 220; missions, 182, 218, 247; nomads, 317; reserves, 218; Swan River, 66

Select Committee on Aborigines (British Settlements) (1837) Report, 20, 23, 35, 51, 53–4, 75, 86
Select Committee on the conditions of Aborigines (N.S.W.), 28n.
Select Committee of House of Commons (1841), 23, 119, 126
Select Committee of the Legislative Assembly of N.S.W. (1856) Report, 39, 41-3
Select Committee of the Legislative Assembly of Queensland (1861) Report, 159–63, 173
Select Committee of the Legislative Council of South Australia (1860) Report, 203–4, 206
Select Committee on the Native Police Force (1856-7), 112
Select Committee on the Native Police Force and the Condition of the Aborigines Generally (1861), 157–69
Settlements, 58, 173–4, 239–40, 316, 331-2, 339; definition of residents, 347-8; employment, 335 (wages) 335-6; eviction (Vic.) 353–4; government prototypes, 52; N.S.W., 316; N.T., 239–41, 313–17; post-war, 336; Qld, 177, 182-3, 256; S.A., 322; Tas., 44, 48-53; Vic., 54-5, *see also* Spread of Settlement
'Settled' Australia, 377-8
Settler democracy, 132, 137, 175
Shelley, William, 89, 90
Shepherds, 30
Sievewright, C. W., 57
Slave Emancipation Act (1834), 53
Slavery, 16
Smith, H. M., 380
Social change, 3-5, 9, 30–4, 51, 64, 140-1, 185, 324; adaptation, 249, 318; adjustment, 30-1, 308, 309; authoritarianism, 240; authorities, colonial, 101; autonomy, 30-3, 210, 308-9, (group) 126; bureaucracy, 327-8; by tuition, 51, 86-7, 101-2; Canada, 9; 'civilisation', 125; colonial administration (TPNG model), 309; colonial legal system, 101; compared with village communities, 318; cross-cultural misunderstanding, 125; de-tribalisation, 240; development, 121; disruption, 249, 318; economy (emphases) 101, (encroachment) 308-9;

education, 125; factors promoting, 30-2, 70, 167, 318; fallacy, 125-6; identity, loss of, 249; institutionalisation, 239–40, 249; land, 101; leadership, 308-9, 318; McEwen policy, 330; mineral discoveries, 340; missions, 100, 246-7, 308, 324-5, 330; 'native regulations', 229-30, 240; nomadic society, 318; Pacific, 96; part-Aborigines, 281; political system and, 4-5, 14, 15, 23, 25-6, 30-2; process of, 68; resettlement, 249-50; reserves, small, 84; resistance, 34; socialisation, 32; theory, 125-6; traditional values, 309; World War II, 332, 339, *see also* Assimilation, Political organisation, Social organisation
'Social engineering', 3
Social organisation, 4-5, 133, 140, 214, 225; and Amerindians, 15; and colonial governments, 102; authority, 129, 130; attempts to break, 70, 129-30; attitudes to whites, 159; breakdown, 181, 225; British justice, 21-5; cash economy, 121; civilisation, 92; complexity, 225; conflict, 59; cultural bases, 69-70, (destruction) 22, 223, (imperatives) 126-7, 133; dispersal, 169; education, 92; elders (W.A.), 69; European views, 87, 225; guerilla warfare, 5; kinship, part-Aborigines, 138; marriage, 104; miners, 215; native custom, 69, 77-8, 101; Native Police, disruption, 42, 169; organisation, 5; opium, 181; population, 59; purposes, 102; ritual, human relationships, 225; significance, 70; S.A., 80; socialisation, 32, 102; spread of settlement, 22-3; structure, 25, 27, 226; W.A., 69-70, *see also* Society
Social planning, 86
Social Services: eligibility (by category) 348-9, (by definition) 349; entitlement (and colour), 355; payment (direct), 349, (to institutions) 349; wage policy (Commonwealth and States) 349
Social status, 86, 87
Social Welfare Ordinance, 1964 (N.T.), 347
Society, Aboriginal, 13; adjustment to changes, 30-1, 55, 133, 209–10, 308, 309; administration of justice, 228, (conflict) 229, 230, (function) 228;

INDEX

alcohol, 30-1; and British justice, 130; assimilation, 340; authority, indigenous, 31, 309-10; autonomy (N.T.), 230, 241; cash economy and disintegration, 212, 307; class, 25; controls, social, 31, 229; culture (change) 133, (contact) 31, (destruction) 223; customary authority, 129; demoralisation (W.A.), 193; destruction (assimilation) 340, (end of overt) 288, 337; disintegration, 129-30, 235, (social) 229; economics, 24, (homogeneity) 12-13; exploitation, economic, 309; family as basis, 33; groups (extended family), 54; institutionalisation, 239-41; kinship, 24; killings, 288; land, relation to, 14, 152; law, 126, 229, (legitimacy) 229-30; leadership, 14, 125, 130; missions, 290; moral code, 229; nomadic, 125; pastoralism and (Qld) 185; pearling, 290; political authority and system, 24, 31, 32, 54-5, 116, 241; practices, 24; religion, 24, 31, 203, 209; shattered, 170; social controls, 101; socialisation, 32, 102, 354; tensions, 290; traditional obligations, 31, 121; trepanning, 290; urbanisation, 178, *see also* Religion, Social system

Soliciting, 280

South, W. G., 220

Sovereignty, Aboriginal, 134

Special courts: TPNG (adjudication) 305, (indigenous custom) 305; W.A., (constitution and responsibilities) 303, (establishment) 303

Special legislation, 343-4; basis, 342-3; legal restrictions, 348-9

Spencer, Baldwin, 224, 226, 234, 248, 265

Spread of Settlement, 17-18, 176; areas occupied, 146; Bathurst, 29-33; Clarence R., 33-4, 53, 108-26; coastal, 24; compared with N.Z., 24; contact, 124, (Palmer and Mitchell R.) 176; Crown land, 24; development needs, 123-4; disintegration (social) 23; dry regions, 205; economic factors, 24; expert, 137; frontiers, 68, 145-6, 175, (compared with N. America) 146, (extension) 146; Goulburn, 29; government control, 123; Hawkesbury R., 28-9; Hunter R., 29; labour

force, (aboriginal) 137, (assigned) 108-9; law and order, 123-4; native rights to land, 24; N.S.W., 17, 29-35; N.T., 205, 207, 210, 212, 242; overlanding, 146; psychological effects, 23; S.A., 77, 78, 80, 203, 205, (beyond control) 81; stock, 108; Tas., 43-4; W.A., 67-8

Stabilisation, 19

Stanner, W. E. H., 243-4, 255-6

Squatters, 112

Starke, Mr Justice, 297

State Children Act 1911 (Qld), 248

Station employment: adjustment, 209; ceremonies, 209; 'station blacks', 122

Stations, pastoral, 108-23, 159, 165, 170, 178, 187-9, 191-2, 195, 208-10, 242, 253-4, 301, 303, 327, 333

Status, 166, 214; access to common services, 356; before self-government, 73; British subject, 134; cash economy, 134; citizenship, 330, (full) 350-1, (rights of) 328-9; confusing, 250; derogation, 194, 227; economic, 134, 332; electoral rights, 345; equality, 3, 136-7, 338, (legal) 227, (and restriction) 136, (mission doctrine) 290, (trend) 350; fringe-dwellers, 331-2; frontier tradition, 338; legal, 31, 136, 227, (subjects of the Crown) 73; N.T., 238, 304; part-Aborigines (legal control) 238, (search for identity) 304; protective legislation, 136; Qld, 166; W.A., 304; social, 24, *see also* Status, legal

Status, legal, 342-65; 'Aboriginal', 183, 191, 231, 236, 348-50, 351, 355-7; assisted Aboriginal, 351-2, 358; classification, 342-64, (by descent) 1, 139, 322, 353-5, (effects) 348-50; compared with *evolué* or *assimilé*, 358-60; definition, 82, 138, 195, 239, (Bureau of Census & Statistics) 344-7, (by group identity) 365, (for administrative and social purposes) 344, 364-5, ('native') 132, 352, 354, 359-60, ('half-caste') 183, 195, 231, 238, 348, 354, (part-Aboriginal) 351-2, ('person of Aboriginal blood') 356-7, (quadroon) 322, (Ward) 239, 241, 347, 357; derogation, 130-2, 183, 194, 221, 227, 304; exemptions, 280, 358-62; military service, 350; social services, 348-9;

wages (award), 349, *see also* Part-Aborigines, Wards

Stirling, James, 19n., 64, 65, 87, 89

Stock, 33, 61-2, 67, 76, 109; killing, 161-2, 193, 195

Strehlow, T. G. H., 206-7, 295, 305, 310-11, 317, 318, 331; recommendations, 315-16

Sturkey, R. D., 187

Subsistence economy; and cash economy, 82, 121; cultural needs, 82; industrial society, 308

Sugar planters, 175

Sunday Island Mission, 254, 301

Survival, 116

Supply of Liquor to Aborigines Prevention Act 1963 (N.S.W.), 358

Systematic colonisation (S.A.), 74

Taplin, Rev. George, 105, 205

Technological change, 10, 11

Tennant Creek, 215; mining, 316

Territory of Papua and New Guinea: area administration, 305; 'restricted areas' policy, 305

Theocracies, 106, 250, 251

Thomas, William, 56

Thomson, Donald, 295, 305, 313-17, 325, 329-30

Threlkeld, Rev. L. E., 93, 94, 100

Tindal, F. C., 114

Tindale, N. B., 385

Tozer, H., 177, 184, 185

Torres Strait Islands, 146, 367, 369, 380

Trade, Aboriginal: clash, 268; employment, 268; foreign contacts, 267; goods, 268; partners, 268

Trade unions, 3, 255, 269, 277, 284

Transportation, 109

Treaty of Waitangi 1840 (N.Z.), 15; Maori land rights, 15

Trepanning, 290

Tribal people and areas, 180, 267

Trust accounts, 260-1; N.T., 232, 279

Trust Territories of Papua and New Guinea, 305, 399

Tuckiar case, 312; basic problems of justice, 305; C.M.S. intervention, 291; trial and sentence, 292, (appeal) 293-7 *passim*

Turnbull, C., 50

United Aborigines Mission, 272; Mt Margaret, 254; Ooldea, 307

Urbanisation, 170, 237, 242, 362, 369, 379-80, 382-3; Cooktown, 178; exclusion from towns, 173, 180, 182, 231, 234, 265

Urbanisation Index, 380-2

Van Diemen's Land, 43

Village social units, 22; and colonisation, 22

Victoria River, 217

Violence: against Aborigines, 213-14; by Aborigines, 290-2, *see also* Law and justice, Native Police

Violet Valley, 252

Wages, Aboriginal, 232, 237; adjustment (industry), 276; award, 276, 337, 338; bush, 260-1; cash, 233, 256, 257, 258, 260-3, 269, 274-7, 299, (incentive) 260, (or kind) 263-4, 274-5, (malnutrition) 258; control (reserves) 256; dependants, 262, 274, 278, 280; disease, 258; economic security, 256, (compared with W.A. and N.T.) 257; equality, 276; fixed minimum, 236; in 1851, compared with free labour, 118-19; living, 33; malnutrition, 258; minimum, 233, 255-6; N.T., 233, 260-2, 278, 301; pastoral, 184-5, 216, 255, 261-2, (and dependants) 261, 273; part-Aboriginal, 278; pearling, 276; Qld, 233, 255-6, 273; rate, 185; restricted, 255; single man's, 256; town, 192, 260-2; trust accounts (N.T. and Qld), 232; W.A., 189, 190, 192, 257, *see also* Missions, Pastoralism, Reserves

Wages: convict, 108; free labour, 109, 118

Wage rates: Barkly Tableland, 270; Bleakley's proposals, 273, 274; Clarence R., 109, 118; dependants, 273; fixed minimum, 263, 264; incentive, 277; mining, 118; minimum and range, 276-7; N. Aust. 260; part-Aboriginal, 278; Qld, 255, 256, (margin for skill) 256, 261, 272; special, 255; trade unions, 255, 269, 277; W.A., 257; Wards, 349

INDEX

Wailbri, 316
Wakefield system, 81
Walker, F., 158
Ward, Barbara, 22
Ward, Russel, 140
Wards (N.T.): alcohol and exemption, 358; control, 339; 'declaration', appeal and onus of proof, 357; definition, 238-9; education, 239; exemptions, 357; exclusion, 241; institutions, 339; isolation, 339; management, 239; marriage, 239; restrictions, legal, 348; wage and unemployment benefit, 349
Wards Employment Ordinance 1953 (N.T.), 192, 238, 338, 347
Warfare: Aborigines and settlers, 114; guerilla, 158
Warrabri, 316
Warramunga, 316
Waste Lands Act 1842 (S.A.), 75
Waterhouse Island, 49
Wave Hill, 218
Weipa Presbyterian Mission, 247
Welfare: and employment (W.A.), 301; children, 263; clothing, 263; costs, 60, 63; death rate (W.A.) 302; definition (non-racial) 347; employment aid, 232-3; government policy, 56, 76; health, 263, 264, (N.T.) 259, (W.A.) 300, 301; health fund (W.A.) 303; hospitals, 301, ('native', W.A.) 303; legislation, 227; leprosarium (W.A.), 303; medicine, tropical (W.A.) 303; missions, 177 (Commonwealth provision) 264, (responsibility and government subsidy) 323; pastoral, 335; protection, 227; rationing, 63, 263; relief, 264; safeguard (Qld), 256; S.A., 219
Welfare Ordinance 1918 (N.T.), 235-8; 1953 (N.T.), 236, 238, 240, 241, 304, 339, 347; 1953-1960 (N.T.), 357n.; 1961 (N.T.), 357n.
Wellington C.M.S. Mission, 97, 98, 99; beginnings, 96; closure, 100; economic effects, 96; funds, 94; inhabitants, 100; land grant, 98
Wells, Mr Justice, 292-7 passim
Wesleyan Missions, 93, 94; Buntingdale, 97; Pt Phillip, 97
Wheeler, F., 167
White Australia Policy, 1, 232, 285-6, 340, 346; and Aboriginal labour, 286;

assimilation of part-Aborigines, 321: colonial administration, 321; international comment, 242, 285-6, 295, 327, 399; TPNG, 399
Willshire, W., 217
Wittfogel, K. A., 22
Wood, G. T., 200
Wool and wool-growing: Aboriginal land rights, 15; work force, 16
Work force, Aboriginal, 16, 17, 28, 34, 66; adaptation (intelligent parasitism), 8, 208-10, 215, 217; adequacy, 82-3; aptitudes, 34; assessment, 255; asset (pastoral) 283; attitudes, 17-18; cattle, 109, 271; cheap supply, 184; children, 334, 335; Clarence River, 109; 'colonial Australia', 16; conditions, 82, 262; contracts, 119; crisis, 118, 120; decimation, 210; demand (sugar industry), 66; depression, 282; discipline, 109; diversity, 83; dying, 258; eastern Australia, 17; economic asset, 18; effective, 166, 283-4; efficiency, 334; employed, 134-5, 284; equal pay, 255; incentives, 135; increase, 398, (implications) 399; industrial awards, 255; farmers, 34; frontiers, 82, 146; goldrushes, 118; land rights, 398; legislation, 146; malnutrition, 262-3; management, 17, 18, 146; migration, 120, 134-5, 399; mining, 215; Native Police, 41; oarsmen, 118-19; overlanding, 119; pastoral skills, 117, 217; prostitution, 262-3; Qld, 159; recruiting, 119-20; responsibility, 83; rewards, 209; scrub clearing, 111; seasonal, 111; settled areas, 135; shepherds, 118-19; shortage, 166, 333; socialising, 209; State responsibilities, 146; station, 178, 217-18; stereotype, 121; stock, 109, 119; sugar industry, 171; supply, 208-9, 211; supervision, 118-19; training, 120-1, 134-5; women, 333-4; wool, 16; W.A., 17, 68, see also Employment, Pastoral Industry, Wages
Work force: Asian, 120, 146, 215; assigned, 108-9; convict, 17, 28; and ticket of leave, (W.A.) 68, 187; crises, 118, 120; European, 120; geographical spread, 147; goldrushes, 118; increase in, 121; indenture system, 16, 171, 172; master and convict servant, 30;

migrant, 16, 120-1, 134-5, 399, (contracts of employment) 120, (employer co-operation) 120; mining, 215; preference, 120; S.A., 82, 221; social spread, 146; Tas., 44; Wakefield system, 75; white, 215
Workhouse, compared with missions, 96

Wyatt, William, 77
Wyndham, 301

Yalata Lutheran Mission, 32n.
Yarra Mission (V.D.L.), 55, 58
Yulgilbar Station, 117-18, 121